Ultimate Terraform for Cloud Security

Master Terraform to Build Secure, Compliant, and Automated Cloud Infrastructures Across AWS, Azure, and GCP

Anish Kumar

www.orangeava.com

First Published: November 2025

Published By: Orange Education Pvt Ltd, AVA®

Address: 9, Daryaganj, Delhi, 110002, India

275 New North Road Islington Suite 1314 London,
N1 7AA, United Kingdom

ISBN (PBK): 978-93-49888-27-2

ISBN (E-BOOK): 978-93-49888-17-3

Scan the QR code to explore our entire catalogue

www.orangeava.com

Dedicated To

All the builders, dreamers, and problem-solvers who believe in automating the mundane to create the extraordinary.

To those who strive to turn ideas into infrastructure, one line of code at a time.

To the curious minds who ask, "What if?" And the persistent hands that answer with "Let us build it."

This book is for you—the architects of the future, shaping the cloud, one stack at a time.

About the Author

Anish Kumar is an accomplished Cloud and DevOps professional with over seven years of experience in designing, architecting, and securing cloud environments. He holds 13 AWS certifications across associate, professional, and specialty levels, along with Kubernetes certifications (CKA, CKAD, and CKS), reflecting his deep expertise in infrastructure automation, container orchestration, and cloud security.

Anish graduated with distinction in Information Technology (IT) from the University of Pune, India, and has contributed to leading organizations such as Dare International, Ohme, and Amazon Web Services. He has successfully led numerous large-scale projects, spanning cloud migrations, secure infrastructure design, and advanced CI/CD implementations, consistently delivering scalable and resilient solutions.

As the author of *Mastering Terraform for the Associate Certification Exam*, AWS CDK *for Infrastructure Automation*, and *Ultimate Terraform for Cloud Security*, Anish is dedicated to helping professionals bridge the gap between theory and real-world cloud practices. His work focuses on empowering engineers to automate security, enforce compliance, and optimize multi-cloud environments, using Terraform, AWS CDK, and modern DevOps methodologies.

Driven by a passion for innovation, Anish continues to share actionable insights and best practices, inspiring cloud engineers and DevOps professionals to build secure, automated, and future-ready infrastructure solutions.

About the Technical Reviewer

Vinodha Kumara is a DevOps and Cloud Engineering specialist with deep expertise in Kubernetes, Infrastructure as Code, and Cloud Security. With a strong foundation in systems engineering and automation, he has contributed extensively to building scalable, secure, and resilient cloud-native platforms, particularly on AWS, GCP, and Oracle Cloud (OCI). His core interest lies in designing systems that not only meet performance and scalability needs but also adhere to strict security and compliance standards from the ground up.

Vinodha has worked across diverse industries including fintech, payments, and microblogging, where he has been instrumental in driving DevSecOps transformations and embedding security practices into CI/CD pipelines. He has implemented cost-effective solutions for high-traffic production environments, including containerized deployments using Docker, Kubernetes, Helm, and Observability stacks. His experience also includes securing workloads using HashiCorp Vault, GCP Secrets Manager, as well as integrating Terraform-based infrastructure with centralized policy enforcement mechanisms.

He currently works as a Senior DevOps Engineer where he leads initiatives around security automation, cloud governance, and Kubernetes optimization. Vinodha is passionate about simplifying complex cloud-native challenges using automation, open-source tooling, and continuous learning. His approach is hands-on, and he is known for bringing both engineering depth and clarity into collaborative cross-functional teams.

Outside of work, Vinodha actively shares technical tips and learnings on platforms such as LinkedIn to help the DevOps community stay ahead in the rapidly evolving cloud ecosystem.

Acknowledgments

I would like to express my heartfelt gratitude to everyone who supported and encouraged me throughout the journey of writing this book, *Ultimate Terraform for Cloud Security.*

First and foremost, I am deeply thankful to my fiancée, Vanshita Kushwaha, whose love, patience, and understanding kept me motivated, even during countless hours spent writing this book. Her unwavering support made this journey possible.

I am also grateful to my brother, Manish Kumar, and my friends, Nikhil Anand, Priyanka Yadav, Bhavin Kumar, and Juhi Patil for their constant motivation and encouragement, inspiring me to turn this vision into reality.

A special thanks to the platforms, courses, and organizations that helped shape my understanding of Terraform and Cloud Security. I appreciate the practical experiences at Amazon Web Services and Dare International which allowed me to apply these skills in real-world environments.

Finally, I sincerely thank the publishing team at Orange Education Pvt. Ltd. for their guidance, patience, and expertise which were invaluable in bringing this book to life.

Thank you all for being an integral part of this memorable journey!

Preface

In today's digital era, cloud computing has become the backbone of modern enterprises, and securing cloud environments is more critical than ever. *Ultimate Terraform for Cloud Security* serves as a comprehensive guide for cloud engineers, DevOps professionals, and security specialists who want to master Terraform for automating, securing, and managing cloud infrastructure across multiple providers.

This book delves into the principles and practices of Infrastructure as Code (IaC) with a strong focus on security automation. By combining Terraform's robust capabilities with modern DevOps practices, it demonstrates how infrastructure automation enhances agility, enforces compliance, mitigates risks, and ensures consistency across cloud environments. Readers will gain a practical understanding of how Terraform can be leveraged to build secure, scalable, and resilient multi-cloud architectures.

Structured to cater to both beginners and seasoned professionals, the book balances theoretical knowledge with hands-on, real-world examples. It covers everything from setting up secure Terraform environments, managing IAM and secrets, automating compliance, and implementing network security, to advanced design patterns and incident response. Detailed case studies illustrate how these concepts are applied in real-world scenarios, helping professionals translate learning into actionable skills.

The book is organized into 16 chapters to provide a progressive and comprehensive learning experience:

Chapter 1. Introduction to Cloud Security and IaC: Understand cloud security evolution, challenges, and the benefits of automating security with Terraform.

Chapter 2. Setting Up and Securing Your Terraform Environment: Learn secure installation, state management, access control, and GitOps practices.

Chapter 3. Advanced Terraform Core Concepts: Explore modules, variables, outputs, workspaces, and debugging techniques for robust automation.

Chapter 4. Multi-Cloud Security Integration: Configure providers, standardize IAM, and write cloud-agnostic Terraform code.

Chapter 5. Policy-as-Code and Governance with Terraform: Implement Sentinel, OPA, and policies to prevent misconfigurations, and enforce governance.

Chapter 6. Terraform Code Scanning and Validation: Use Checkov, TFSec, Terrascan, and custom rules to validate and secure Terraform code.

Chapter 7. Identity and Access Management (IAM) with Terraform: Automate the least privilege, manage cross-account access, and secure credentials.

Chapter 8. Compliance-as-Code for Multi-Cloud Environments: Automate audits, generate compliance reports, and integrate dashboards across clouds.

Chapter 9. Secrets Management and Data Protection: Manage and rotate secrets, encrypt sensitive data, and secure API keys.

Chapter 10. Securing Cloud Network Architectures: Automate firewall rules, VPNs, multi-region networking, and serverless security.

Chapter 11. Secure CI/CD Pipelines with Terraform: Integrate security in pipelines, prevent secret leakage, and automate safe deployments.

Chapter 12. Monitoring and Incident Response in Multi-Cloud Environments: Set up dashboards, alerts, and automate incident response workflows.

Chapter 13. Disaster Recovery and Resilience with Terraform: Automate backups, configure failovers, and build resilient architectures.

Chapter 14. Advanced Design Patterns in Terraform: Optimize modules, manage dependencies, and scale Terraform across projects.

Chapter 15. Real-World Case Studies: Gain insights from secure SaaS architectures, CI/CD security integrations, and compliance automation examples.

Chapter 16. Best Practices and Future Trends: Learn continuous security practices, emerging trends, and enterprise-scale automation strategies.

Thus, this book provides a clear roadmap for securing and automating cloud infrastructure with Terraform. Whether you are beginning your IaC journey or looking to advance your expertise, *Ultimate Terraform for Cloud Security* equips you with the skills, best practices, and real-world insights needed to build secure, compliant, and scalable cloud environments.

Get a Free eBook

We hope you are enjoying your recently purchased book! Your feedback is incredibly valuable to us, and to all other readers looking for great books.

If you found this book helpful or enjoyable, we would truly appreciate it, if you could take a moment to leave a short review with a 5 star rating on Amazon. It helps us grow, and lets other readers discover our books.

As a thank you, we would love to send you a free digital copy of this book, and a **30%** discount code on your next cart value on our official websites:

www.orangeava.com

www.orangeava.in (For Indian Subcontinent)

☑ **Here's how:**

Leave a review for the book on Amazon.

Take a screenshot of your review, and send an email to **info@orangeava.com** (it can be just the confirmation screen).

Once, we receive your screenshot, we will send you the digital file, within 24 hours.

Thank you so much for your support – it means a lot to us!

Downloading the code bundles and colored images

Please follow the links or scan the QR codes to download the
Code Bundles and Images of the book:

https://github.com/ava-orange-education/Ultimate-Terraform-for-Cloud-Security

The code bundles and images of the book are also hosted on
https://rebrand.ly/2c7dc2

In case there's an update to the code, it will be updated on the existing GitHub repository.

Errata

We take immense pride in our work at **Orange Education Pvt Ltd,** and follow best practices to ensure the accuracy of our content to provide an indulging reading experience to our subscribers. Our readers are our mirrors, and we use their inputs to reflect and improve upon human errors, if any, that may have occurred during the publishing processes involved. To let us maintain the quality and help us reach out to any readers who might be having difficulties due to any unforeseen errors, please write to us at :

errata@orangeava.com

Your support, suggestions, and feedback are highly appreciated.

DID YOU KNOW

Did you know that Orange Education Pvt Ltd offers eBook versions of every book published, with PDF and ePub files available? You can upgrade to the eBook version at **www.orangeava.com** and as a print book customer, you are entitled to a discount on the eBook copy. Get in touch with us at: **info@orangeava.com** for more details.

At **www.orangeava.com**, you can also read a collection of free technical articles, sign up for a range of free newsletters, and receive exclusive discounts and offers on Print Books and eBooks.

PIRACY

If you come across any illegal copies of our works in any form on the internet, we would be grateful if you would provide us with the location address or website name. Please contact us at **info@orangeava.com** with a link to the material.

ARE YOU INTERESTED IN AUTHORING WITH US?

If there is a topic that you have expertise in, and you are interested in either writing or contributing to a book, please write to us at **business@orangeava.com**. We are on a journey to help developers and tech professionals to gain insights on the present technological advancements and innovations happening across the globe and build a community that believes Knowledge is best acquired by sharing and learning with others. Please reach out to us to learn what our audience demands and how you can be part of this educational reform. We also welcome ideas from tech experts and help them build learning and development content for their domains.

REVIEWS

Please leave a review. Once you have read and used this book, why not leave a review on the site that you purchased it from? Potential readers can then see and use your unbiased opinion to make purchase decisions. We at Orange Education would love to know what you think about our products, and our authors can learn from your feedback. Thank you!

For more information about Orange Education, please visit **www.orangeava.com**.

Table of Contents

CHAPTER 1
Introduction to Cloud Security and IaC

Introduction

Cloud security has undergone a significant transformation, driven by the widespread adoption of cloud-first strategies across organizations. Initially, security practices mirrored traditional on-premises approaches, relying heavily on perimeter defences and manual processes. However, as cloud environments expanded, major providers such as AWS, GCP, and Azure introduced advanced security frameworks tailored to dynamic, distributed architectures. The shared responsibility model became central, clarifying that while cloud providers manage infrastructure security, customers are responsible for securing their data and workloads. This shift paved the way for automation and Security-as-Code practices, enabling more consistent, scalable, and proactive defences against emerging threats.

Despite advancements, traditional infrastructure security approaches continue to pose challenges, particularly in multi-cloud environments where inconsistencies and configuration drift are common. Manual processes often lead to vulnerabilities, while scalability introduces complexity. Infrastructure as Code (IaC) addresses these issues by promoting repeatable, version-controlled configurations, ensuring security policies are applied uniformly across cloud platforms. Terraform, with its declarative approach, simplifies the automation of security controls and compliance, allowing organizations to manage infrastructure and security at scale. By embedding security directly into provisioning workflows, Terraform reduces the risk of misconfigurations, and enhances the overall cloud security posture.

Structure

In this chapter, we will cover the following topics:

- Evolution of Cloud Security Practices across Cloud Providers
  - Early Cloud Security and Key Concerns
  - Modern Security Frameworks in Cloud Platforms
  - Innovations in Cloud-Native Security
  - Standardizing Security across Providers
- Challenges in Traditional Infrastructure Security Approaches
  - Risks of Manual Processes
  - Limitations in Adapting to Cloud Dynamics
  - Gaps in Monitoring and Visibility
  - High Costs and Complexity

- Infrastructure as Code: Principles and Benefits in Cloud Environments
  - Defining Infrastructure as Code (IaC)
  - Advantages of IaC in Security
  - Principles of Secure IaC
  - Role of IaC in Multi-Cloud Security
- Automating Security with Terraform
  - Benefits of Automation in Cloud Security
  - Terraform Features for Security Automation
  - Leveraging Terraform's Open Source Ecosystem
- Key Components of Terraform for Securing Cloud Workloads
  - Multi-Cloud Integration with Terraform
  - Simplified Security with Terraform Resources
  - Protecting Terraform Operations
  - Writing Secure Terraform Configurations
  - Enhancing Audits with Terraform

Evolution of Cloud Security Practices across Cloud Providers

As cloud computing evolved, so did the need for robust security practices. This section explores how security models have transitioned from the challenges of early cloud adoption to modern, cloud-native frameworks. It also discusses innovations in identity and access management and the critical role of Terraform in achieving standardized, multi-cloud security solutions.

Early Cloud Security and Key Concerns

The evolution of cloud security began with the early adoption of cloud computing. Initially, the cloud was primarily viewed as a cost-effective solution that enabled businesses to scale infrastructure and improve operational efficiencies. However, as organizations began migrating workloads to cloud environments, the security implications quickly became apparent. This shift introduced a host of new challenges that demanded focused attention and innovative solutions.

A major turning point in the cloud security landscape came with the **Capital One data breach in 2019**. In this high-profile incident, a former engineer exploited a misconfigured Web Application Firewall (WAF) hosted on AWS. The attacker used a Server-Side Request Forgery (SSRF) vulnerability to access the EC2 instance metadata service, obtaining temporary credentials that granted access to Amazon S3 buckets containing sensitive customer data. This led to the exfiltration of over 100 million customer records, including Social Security numbers and credit scores.

The breach exposed several critical weaknesses in cloud infrastructure configuration and access management. At the core was the SSRF vulnerability, which allowed unauthorized access to the EC2 metadata service. The temporary credentials retrieved were overly permissive, providing broad access to sensitive data stored in S3. The major issue was a lack of real-time monitoring and alerting; despite the presence of tools such as AWS CloudTrail and VPC Flow Logs, they were not actively leveraged for proactive threat detection. Additionally, the misconfigured WAF failed to prevent malicious requests from reaching the vulnerable endpoint. The combination of insufficient Identity and Access Management (IAM) practices, insecure infrastructure configurations, and limited observability created a perfect opportunity for exploitation.

This incident served as a pivotal wake-up call for both cloud users and providers. In response, AWS introduced Instance Metadata Service Version 2 (IMDSv2), which mandates the use of session-based tokens, significantly reducing the risk posed by SSRF attacks. The breach also spurred a broader industry shift toward least privilege IAM practices, promoting tighter access controls and more granular policy definitions.

Organizations increasingly embraced security by design principles, integrating security controls directly into cloud infrastructure using Infrastructure as Code (IaC) tools such as Terraform. Terraform is an Infrastructure as Code (IaC) tool developed by HashiCorp, which is licensed under the Business Source License (BSL). HashiCorp was later acquired by IBM, further enhancing its capabilities and integration within IBM's cloud ecosystem. Real-time threat detection services such as Amazon GuardDuty, along with automated configuration auditing tools such as AWS Config, became integral to modern cloud security strategies. The breach also catalyzed the widespread adoption of Policy-as-Code frameworks, such as HashiCorp Sentinel and Open Policy Agent (OPA), which enforce compliance and prevent insecure resources from being provisioned.

Overall, the Capital One breach significantly accelerated the maturity of cloud security practices. It underscored the necessity of proactive, automated security measures and reshaped how enterprises approach compliance, threat detection, and infrastructure management in the cloud.

Adapting Security to Early Cloud Adoption

In the early days of cloud adoption, most organizations were primarily concerned with basic security measures such as data protection, identity management, and access control. However, security was often an afterthought, as cloud providers themselves were still developing their own security frameworks. Cloud service providers typically offered basic encryption for data storage and transit but did not offer the same level of security services or infrastructure protection that users were accustomed to with on-premise systems.

Security concerns revolved around unauthorized access, the multi-tenancy nature of cloud platforms, and limited visibility into the cloud infrastructure. At the time, enterprises were more focused on transitioning from traditional data centers to cloud environments, leaving many fundamental aspects of cloud security, such as monitoring, auditing, and incident response.

Shared Environments and Compliance

One of the significant security challenges of the early cloud was dealing with the risks posed by breaches and vulnerabilities within shared environments. Cloud providers, offering multi-tenant solutions, made it difficult to ensure that one tenant's data would not be exposed or compromised by another. This "shared environment" concern prompted providers to implement new isolation mechanisms, while customers themselves started developing their own internal security practices to mitigate such risks.

Another major concern was compliance. As cloud computing evolved, so did the regulatory landscape. Different countries and industries imposed their own security standards, making it difficult for organizations to navigate the requirements in a cloud environment. Cloud service providers needed to offer compliance frameworks for their customers to meet various standards, such as GDPR in Europe, HIPAA in the United States, and PCI-DSS for payment processors.

Modern Security Frameworks in Cloud Platforms

The evolution of cloud security has reached a stage where cloud service providers offer robust, built-in security frameworks that allow users to secure their environments with ease. These frameworks have transformed cloud security, allowing companies to focus on their applications and business needs, while cloud providers handle much of the heavy lifting around infrastructure security.

Each of the major cloud providers, including Amazon Web Services (AWS), Google Cloud Platform (GCP), and Microsoft Azure, follows a similar approach to security models and offers a variety of tools that help organizations manage security risks.

AWS, GCP, and Azure follow the *Shared Responsibility Model*, where the cloud provider manages security of the cloud infrastructure, including the physical security of data centers, network infrastructure, and hypervisor security. Meanwhile, customers are responsible for security in the cloud, which includes managing access to resources, configuring network security, and ensuring that their applications are secure.

This model highlights the shift in responsibility, emphasizing that while cloud providers take care of foundational infrastructure security, users need to adopt best practices to secure their cloud workloads, applications, and data.

Shared Responsibility Model for Cloud Users

The Shared Responsibility Model is a security framework in which cloud service providers are responsible for the **security of the cloud**, while customers are responsible for **security in the cloud**. This model clearly outlines who is responsible for managing specific components based on the cloud service model, whether it is Infrastructure as a Service (IaaS), Platform as a Service (PaaS), or Software as a Service (SaaS).

The Shared Responsibility Model is crucial for understanding cloud security, as it defines the division of responsibilities between cloud service providers and customers. This model offers transparency, ensuring that customers understand what is covered by the provider and what they are expected to manage themselves. Cloud users must implement security policies, configure resources, monitor their environment, and manage their own identity and access management.

For example, in **AWS**, the responsibility for configuring IAM roles, securing Amazon S3 buckets, and setting up Virtual Private Cloud (VPC) security is on the customer, while AWS secures the physical hardware, networking, and AWS-owned services. In **Azure**, while Microsoft ensures that the underlying infrastructure is secure, users must configure Virtual Networks, Role-Based Access Control (RBAC), and enforce identity policies using Azure Active Directory. In **GCP**, the user is responsible for securing Google Compute Engine instances, configuring firewall rules, and protecting data using encryption, while Google secures the data centers and physical hardware.

Innovations in Cloud-Native Security

As cloud adoption accelerated, so did innovations in cloud-native security solutions, designed to provide deeper insights and automated protections for cloud environments. Today, cloud-native security tools are highly sophisticated and integrated with platform services, offering security capabilities that were once not possible in on-premise infrastructures. The following are some tools for AWS, GCP, and Azure clouds:

- **AWS GuardDuty** is a continuous security monitoring service that detects malicious activity and unauthorized behavior within AWS environments. GuardDuty uses machine learning, anomaly detection, and integrated threat intelligence to monitor AWS accounts and workloads. For instance, it can detect unusual API calls or potentially unauthorized access to sensitive data. GuardDuty is effective at identifying threats such as account compromise, data exfiltration, and anomalous network traffic.
- **Google Cloud Security Command Center (SCC)** is an integrated security management and data risk platform for GCP. SCC allows organizations to gain visibility into their security

posture and provides recommendations for improving it. SCC integrates various security tools to help detect and mitigate risks across GCP resources. For example, it provides insights into misconfigured cloud resources, policy violations, and threats against Google Cloud services.

- **Azure Defender** (formerly Azure Security Center) is a unified security management system in Azure that provides advanced threat protection for hybrid cloud workloads. It integrates with other Microsoft security services and offers continuous assessment of cloud resources. Azure Defender is equipped to detect threats and vulnerabilities across Azure services, including virtual machines, databases, containers, and IoT devices.

These cloud-native security services are powerful enablers on their own, but they become even more impactful when managed through Infrastructure as Code. With Terraform, services such as AWS GuardDuty, Google Cloud SCC, and Azure Defender can be provisioned and configured consistently across environments. This approach allows teams to embed security directly into their infrastructure deployments, maintain compliance at scale, and ensure that protections are applied automatically as part of their cloud automation workflows.

Advancements in Identity and Access Management

Over the years, IAM has become central to cloud security. Cloud providers have made significant advancements in IAM capabilities, enabling users to manage access more granularly and securely. These improvements are aimed at preventing unauthorized access, ensuring that only the right users can access specific resources.

AWS IAM enables customers to control access to resources in AWS using policies that define permissions. This includes Multi-Factor Authentication (MFA), Role-Based Access Control (RBAC), and permissions based on the principle of least privilege. **Azure Active Directory (AD)** provides identity management and access control for cloud resources. Azure AD integrates with other Microsoft services, offering Single Sign-On (SSO), MFA, and conditional access policies. **Google Cloud Identity and Access Management (IAM)** allows users to control who can access which resources in GCP. It supports RBAC, audit logging, and integration with Google's identity services to strengthen the security of user accounts and permissions.

Terraform enables organizations to automate the provisioning of cloud-native security tools such as AWS GuardDuty, Azure Defender, and GCP SCC across environments. Security configurations such as IAM policies, encryption, and logging can be codified to ensure consistency and compliance. By integrating Policy-as-Code with tools such as Sentinel and OPA, Terraform helps block misconfigured resources before deployment. This approach embeds security directly into the infrastructure lifecycle, at scale.

Standardizing Security across Providers

In today's multi-cloud and hybrid-cloud environments, organizations need to manage security across different cloud platforms. While each provider offers its own security tools, the complexity of managing security in multi-cloud environments can become overwhelming. To mitigate these challenges, organizations are looking for ways to standardize and automate their cloud security practices.

Overcoming Multi-Cloud Security Challenges

Managing security across multiple cloud providers introduces several challenges, including inconsistent security controls, a lack of integration between platforms, and difficulties in monitoring and enforcing security policies. Each cloud provider has its own security framework, which can lead to inconsistencies in securing resources across platforms. Configuring these security frameworks can be challenging, requiring the use of different tools and technologies.

- **Inconsistent Security Controls:** AWS uses **Security Groups**, GCP relies on **Firewall Rules**, and Azure employs **Network Security Groups (NSGs)**. Although they achieve similar goals, their configurations differ. **IAM Management** varies for AWS IAM, GCP IAM, and Azure RBAC, following distinct syntaxes and policies.
- **Lack of Integration:** Cloud-native security tools are designed to work within their own ecosystems but lack seamless cross-cloud integration. This can make centralized monitoring and incident response cumbersome.
- **Compliance Monitoring Difficulties:** Different compliance frameworks (CIS, PCI DSS, NIST) may have varying implementations per cloud, increasing the risk of misalignment.

To address this, organizations need to establish unified security policies that work across AWS, GCP, and Azure. This requires adopting cloud-agnostic solutions and technologies that can be configured consistently across cloud platforms. Additionally, centralizing monitoring and compliance efforts can help ensure that security policies are applied uniformly across all cloud providers.

Cloud-Agnostic Solutions with Terraform

Terraform, a popular Infrastructure as Code (IaC) tool, is ideal for managing security across multi-cloud environments. By using Terraform, organizations can create and manage security policies and configurations across multiple cloud providers using a single configuration language. Terraform's modular nature allows users to define reusable security modules for IAM, network security, and resource access, enabling them to maintain consistency and compliance across platforms.

Terraform's ability to manage infrastructure across AWS, GCP, and Azure through multi-cloud providers makes it an ideal tool for standardizing security configurations.

- **Declarative Configuration**: Terraform allows security configurations to be expressed as code. This ensures repeatability and reduces manual errors.
- **Reusable Modules**: Security modules can be written once and applied across multiple environments, ensuring consistent configurations.

For example, organizations can use Terraform to define secure networking environments, identity management configurations, and access controls for both AWS and Azure. This eliminates the complexity of managing separate security tools for each cloud provider and ensures consistent application of security measures.

This foundation of understanding cloud security evolution sets the stage for exploring how Infrastructure as Code (IaC) and Terraform can be leveraged to automate and enforce security policies across modern cloud environments.

Challenges in Traditional Infrastructure Security Approaches

Traditional security methods struggle to keep pace with the agility and scale of modern cloud environments. This section delves into the risks of manual processes, limitations in adapting to dynamic cloud workloads, gaps in monitoring and visibility, and the high costs and complexity of legacy security solutions.

Risks of Manual Processes

Manual processes have been a staple in traditional infrastructure security approaches, but these processes introduce significant risks. Security teams have often relied on manual configurations and interventions to secure and manage their infrastructure. However, as infrastructure complexity grows and cloud environments evolve, these manual methods have proven inadequate, leading to a range of challenges.

One of the primary risks of relying on manual processes is the potential for inconsistencies in configurations. When security configurations are handled manually, human error becomes a significant factor. Administrators might accidentally apply incorrect settings, overlook critical security measures, or forget to update configurations, leading to vulnerabilities in the infrastructure.

For example, consider a scenario where an administrator manually configures access control policies for an AWS S3 bucket, forgetting to apply the necessary permissions or leaving the bucket open to public access. This oversight could lead to the exposure of sensitive data. In traditional infrastructure, manual configuration of network access controls could also result in misconfigured firewalls, allowing unauthorized access to critical systems.

Manual processes are also prone to drift over time. As teams deploy changes, patch systems, or modify configurations, the system state can deviate from the desired configuration. This drift makes it difficult to maintain a consistent and secure environment, increasing the likelihood of security issues and breaches.

Limitations in Adapting to Cloud Dynamics

Traditional infrastructure security approaches were designed for static, on-premise environments. Cloud environments, however, are dynamic, scalable, and elastic, requiring a different approach to security. The rapid pace of change in cloud environments presents several challenges for traditional security models, making them ill-suited for modern cloud workloads.

Challenges with Scalability and Elasticity

One of the most significant challenges with traditional security approaches is their inability to scale effectively in cloud environments. In cloud computing, workloads can scale up or down rapidly, and resources are provisioned dynamically. For instance, an organization using AWS Auto Scaling for its EC2 instances might see the number of instances increase or decrease based on traffic demands. Traditional security measures that rely on static configurations often fail to keep pace with this elasticity.

In AWS, security groups are often used to control access to EC2 instances, but manually updating security groups or firewall rules to reflect dynamic scaling can be cumbersome and error-prone. This is especially problematic when the cloud infrastructure is rapidly changing, leading to gaps in security coverage and potential vulnerabilities.

Similarly, in GCP, where services such as Google Kubernetes Engine are commonly used, traditional security models struggle with the dynamic nature of container orchestration. Manual configuration of network policies or identity and access management roles becomes increasingly difficult as the number of containers and services grows.

Also, in Azure, managing security for dynamically scaling resources such as Virtual Machine Scale Sets (VMSS) or Azure Kubernetes Service (AKS) can pose challenges. For instance, keeping Network Security Groups (NSGs) updated with the appropriate rules for scaling workloads requires careful automation. Without automated updates, scaling events may leave resources exposed or improperly restricted, creating vulnerabilities in the security perimeter.

Gaps in Monitoring and Visibility

Traditional security tools often struggle to provide adequate visibility into cloud environments, particularly as they grow in complexity. Monitoring and visibility are crucial for detecting threats, identifying vulnerabilities, and ensuring compliance. In on-premise infrastructure, IT teams could rely on network monitoring tools and Intrusion Detection Systems (IDS) to keep an eye on potential security issues. However, cloud environments present unique challenges that require new approaches to monitoring and visibility.

Limited Tools for Auditing and Real-Time Monitoring

Cloud providers offer various native tools for monitoring and auditing, but traditional monitoring solutions may not be designed to handle the dynamic nature of the cloud.

- For example, **AWS CloudTrail** and **Amazon CloudWatch** provide auditing and monitoring capabilities for AWS resources, but without proper integration with cloud-native tools, traditional monitoring systems may struggle to detect unauthorized access or anomalous behavior.
- Similarly, **Azure Monitor** and **Google Cloud Operations** provide monitoring and logging solutions for Azure and GCP, respectively. However, organizations using multiple cloud providers often face difficulties consolidating monitoring data across different platforms, which can lead to gaps in visibility and delayed responses to security threats.

Real-time monitoring is another area where traditional security approaches fall short. In a dynamic cloud environment, traditional security tools might not be able to detect issues quickly enough. Without real-time alerting, security incidents could go unnoticed until significant damage has been done.

High Costs and Complexity

Maintaining traditional infrastructure security measures can be costly and complex. As organizations migrate to the cloud, they often face the challenge of adapting legacy security measures to a new, dynamic environment. The result is increased operational costs and the complexity of integrating disparate security tools with cloud-native solutions.

Expensive Legacy Security Measures

Many organizations still rely on legacy security tools and approaches, such as on-premise firewalls, intrusion detection systems, and physical security appliances. These tools were designed for static environments and are not well-suited for the cloud's dynamic nature. Furthermore, maintaining these legacy systems often requires significant resources, including dedicated staff, ongoing training, and frequent updates.

By using Terraform, organizations can codify and migrate legacy firewall rules to cloud-native solutions, eliminating the overhead of maintaining physical firewalls.

For example, the cost of maintaining a legacy firewall in a data center can be substantial, particularly when organizations need to manage the complexity of different firewall rules and configurations across multiple locations. In contrast, cloud-native security tools, such as AWS WAF, Google Cloud Armor, or Azure Firewall, are scalable, automated, and integrated into the cloud ecosystem, making them more cost-effective for managing security in a cloud environment. For example, one recent Forrester TEI study found that moving to Palo Alto's Cloud NGFW resulted in **25% savings in firewall deployment costs**, along with a **163% return on investment** over three years, compared to more traditional firewall solutions. Another independent GigaOm study comparing Azure Firewall with hybrid/on-premise models found that unified management and integrated cloud security could reduce operational costs by ≈ 30% and infrastructure costs by ≈ 20%. Incorporating such metrics helps set realistic expectations when evaluating cost-effectiveness of cloud-native firewall tools.

Integration Challenges with Cloud-Native Tools

Legacy security tools are often difficult to integrate with cloud-native solutions. For instance, integrating on-premise network monitoring tools with GCP's Security Command Center, AWS Security Hub, or Azure Defender can be time-consuming and error-prone. Cloud-native tools are designed to work seamlessly within their respective ecosystems, while legacy tools require complex configurations and often fail to take full advantage of cloud scalability.

Organizations must balance the need for achieving strong, comprehensive security coverage and managing the complexity, cost, and operational overhead. Without a unified approach, the costs and challenges of integrating legacy tools with cloud-native security solutions can escalate quickly.

Traditional infrastructure security approaches face significant limitations when applied to cloud environments. The risks of manual processes, difficulties in adapting to the dynamic nature of the cloud, gaps in monitoring and visibility, and the high costs and complexity of legacy security measures make it clear that these approaches are inadequate for securing modern cloud workloads. To effectively manage security in the cloud, organizations need to move beyond traditional security models and embrace automation, scalability, and cloud-native tools. Solutions such as Terraform offer a path to streamline cloud security practices, enabling organizations to deploy and manage security configurations efficiently and consistently across dynamic environments. As the cloud landscape continues to evolve, adopting modern, automated approaches to security will be critical in safeguarding the sensitive data and ensuring compliance.

Infrastructure as Code: Principles and Benefits in Cloud Environments

Infrastructure as Code (IaC) revolutionizes cloud infrastructure management by treating infrastructure configurations as code. This section explores the foundational concepts of IaC, its security advantages, and principles for secure deployment. It also highlights how IaC, particularly with Terraform, simplifies multi-cloud security management through consistency, modularity, and unified practices.

Defining Infrastructure as Code (IaC)

Infrastructure as Code (IaC) refers to the practice of managing and provisioning computing infrastructure through machine-readable script or code, rather than through manual processes. This approach has transformed how organizations deploy and manage infrastructure in cloud environments, especially in the context of security.

Managing Infrastructure through Code-Based Practices

Traditionally, managing infrastructure involved manual configuration of physical or virtual servers, networks, and other resources. This process was often time-consuming, error-prone, and hard to scale. With IaC, infrastructure is treated in the same way as application code, using software development practices such as version control, testing, and automation to manage infrastructure resources.

In cloud environments such as AWS, GCP, and Azure, IaC allows teams to define and deploy resources such as compute instances, storage, networking, and security configurations using code. This code can be version-controlled, shared, and reused across teams, ensuring that the infrastructure is managed efficiently and consistently.

For example, using **Terraform**, a BSL-licensed tool, infrastructure is defined in declarative configuration files (often written in HCL–HashiCorp Configuration Language) that specify the desired state of the infrastructure. Terraform automatically handles the orchestration of cloud resources, ensuring that the infrastructure is deployed as defined.

In **AWS**, IaC can be achieved using **AWS CloudFormation**, which defines resources using JSON or YAML templates. In **GCP**, tools such as **Google Cloud Deployment Manager** allow users to define resources in YAML or Jinja templates. **Azure** supports IaC using **Azure Resource Manager (ARM) templates.** Additionally, Terraform can be used to deploy and manage resources across all major cloud providers, including AWS, GCP, and Azure, in a consistent and repeatable manner.

IaC can be classified into two main approaches: **declarative** and **imperative**.

- **Declarative IaC**: This approach focuses on defining the desired end state of the infrastructure without specifying the steps required to reach that state. The IaC tool manages the underlying process to ensure that the desired state is achieved. This is the more common approach in modern cloud environments, as it abstracts away the details of how infrastructure is deployed. For example, when using **Terraform**, you describe the resources you want, and Terraform handles the steps to make that happen.
- **Imperative IaC**: In this approach, the steps to achieve the desired infrastructure state are explicitly defined in the code. It is more procedural, where each action (such as creating a resource or modifying configurations) is specified.

The declarative model, as employed by tools such as Terraform, is widely adopted for its simplicity and focus on the end result, as it abstracts the management of the infrastructure lifecycle.

Advantages of IaC in Security

IaC provides numerous benefits for improving security in cloud environments, ranging from reducing human error to enabling better auditability and consistency. These advantages play a pivotal role in creating secure, compliant, and automated infrastructure deployments consistently.

Ensuring Consistency and Auditability

One of the key challenges in infrastructure management, even with Infrastructure as Code (IaC), is configuration drift. While IaC helps define and maintain the desired state of infrastructure, drift can still occur due to other automation processes or manual changes that alter various attributes of managed components. This drift can lead to inconsistencies between the defined state and the actual state of the infrastructure, potentially creating security vulnerabilities, if critical configurations are missed or changed unintentionally. It is important to note that while IaC significantly reduces the chances of drift, it does not eliminate the problem entirely.

With IaC, the infrastructure is defined in code, and any changes to the infrastructure are managed through version-controlled files. This ensures that the infrastructure is always in the desired state, with no unexpected modifications. When using **Terraform**, for example, the tool compares the current state of the infrastructure with the desired state as defined in the code, and makes necessary adjustments automatically. If drift occurs, Terraform will detect it and reconcile the environment to the defined configuration.

Infrastructure code, like any other software code, can be stored in version control systems such as **Git**, which makes it possible to track changes to infrastructure over time. This version control introduces several benefits for security:

- **Auditability**: All changes to infrastructure are tracked and logged, making it easier to see who made a change, when it was made, and what changes were implemented. This is crucial for auditing and ensuring that only authorized personnel make security-related adjustments to the infrastructure.

- **Reproducibility**: By using version control, organizations can recreate past infrastructure setups in a consistent manner. This helps in situations where infrastructure needs to be restored or duplicated in a different region or account for disaster recovery or scaling purposes.
- **Rollback**: In the event that a change introduces a security issue, it is possible to revert to a previous version of the infrastructure code, reducing the impact of security vulnerabilities.

Principles of Secure IaC

To ensure that infrastructure as code itself is secure and compliant, certain principles must be followed when designing and implementing IaC. These principles help mitigate risks associated with insecure configurations and ensure that infrastructure deployments adhere to security best practices. The following are some principles of securing IaC:

- **Least Privilege Access Control:** To ensure that resources and users only have the permissions necessary to perform their tasks, Terraform can be used to configure role-based access control (RBAC) policies with fine-grained permissions. For example, in AWS, you can use `aws_iam_role` in combination with `aws_iam_policy_document` to define specific permissions, in GCP, you can configure IAM roles using `google_project_iam_member`, and in Azure, `azurerm_role_assignment` can be used to enforce restricted access.
- **Secrets Management:** Store sensitive data such as API keys, passwords, and database credentials securely. Avoid hardcoding secrets in `.tf` files (Terraform `.tf` files are configuration files that define the infrastructure resources and their settings using HashiCorp Configuration Language (HCL), allowing users to manage and provision cloud resources consistently and repeatably) or Terraform state files. Use external secret management systems to inject secrets securely during runtime. For example, utilize AWS Secrets Manager, GCP Secret Manager, or Azure Key Vault with Terraform resources such as `aws_secretsmanager_secret, google_secret_manager_secret` and `azurerm_key_vault_secret`.
- **Code Versioning and Review:** Maintain IaC code in version control systems (for example, Git) with enforced branch policies and code reviews. This helps track changes, identify misconfigurations early, and roll back to previous states if necessary. For example, use Git workflows for pull requests and enforce pre-merge code scanning tools such as **tfsec**, **Checkov, Terrascan**, or **Sentinel**.
- **Automated Security Scanning:** Automate static code analysis to identify potential misconfigurations and security risks in Terraform code. Integrate these tools into CI/CD pipelines for consistent enforcement. For example, use tools such as **tfsec Checkov, Terrascan,** or **Sentinel** for Terraform security analysis, **AWS Config Rules** for compliance checks, **GCP Policy Intelligence**, or **Azure Policy** to enforce standards during deployments.
- **State File Protection:** Terraform state files contain sensitive information about your infrastructure, such as resource names, IDs, and possibly secrets. Encrypt and restrict access to these files to prevent unauthorized access, data leakage, and potential security breaches. Use remote backends such as AWS S3, Azure Blob Storage, or GCP Cloud Storage with encryption enabled to store these files securely.
- **Immutable Infrastructure:** Favour creating new resources instead of modifying existing ones to ensure deployments are predictable and secure. This eliminates configuration drift and simplifies rollback procedures. For example, use Terraform modules to implement immutable deployment strategies, such as replacing EC2 instances in AWS, Compute Engine instances in GCP, or Azure Virtual Machines.
- **Compliance as Code:** Define and enforce organizational compliance requirements in Terraform code using reusable modules and policy files. This ensures all deployed infrastructure adheres to required standards. For example, use tools such as **AWS Config**, **Google Security Command**

Center, or **Azure Blueprint** to define compliance baselines and enforce them during infrastructure provisioning.

- **Logging and Monitoring Integration:** Integrate Terraform-deployed infrastructure with centralized logging and monitoring tools for real-time insights into security events and system behavior.
- **Environment Segmentation:** Separate environments (for example, dev, test, prod) to limit the blast radius of misconfigurations or security breaches. Use distinct Terraform workspaces or configurations for each environment. For example, use workspaces in Terraform (terraform workspace) or create isolated VPCs in AWS, GCP, and Azure to segregate environments.
- **Regular Updates and Patch Management:** Keep Terraform providers, modules, and cloud services up to date to benefit from the latest security patches and features. For example, periodically update Terraform providers (aws, google, azurerm) and use cloud-native patching mechanisms such as **AWS Systems Manager**, **GCP OS Patch Management**, or **Azure Update Management**.

These principles ensure that Terraform deployments are secure, scalable, and compliant with best practices across cloud environments.

Role of IaC in Multi-Cloud Security

In today's world, organizations often use multiple cloud providers, creating a multi-cloud environment. Managing security in a multi-cloud setup introduces unique challenges due to differences in security models, tools, and practices across providers. IaC plays a crucial role in simplifying the management of security across multiple cloud platforms.

Addressing Unique Security Demands Across Clouds

Each cloud provider has its own set of security features and configurations. For instance, **AWS** has **IAM** for access management, **GCP** uses **Identity and Access Management (IAM)** with policies, and **Azure** offers **Active Directory** integration. The way these tools work can differ significantly, and ensuring consistent security across all these platforms requires a unified approach.

Using Terraform, organizations can define their infrastructure security policies in a consistent way, regardless of the underlying cloud platform. Terraform is cloud-agnostic that allows users to write policies that apply the same principles and practices across AWS, Azure, and GCP, making it easier to maintain security across diverse environments.

For example, an organization might use **Terraform** to define a multi-cloud network across AWS, GCP, and Azure, ensuring that network security groups, access controls, and firewall settings are consistently applied across both environments. This reduces the complexity of managing separate security models in each cloud provider's native tooling.

With IaC, Terraform provides a unified language and tooling for managing infrastructure security across cloud platforms. While you may not need to learn the details of each cloud provider's security services, it is important to note that the modules differ between providers. Instead of mastering the configurations for each provider's security tools, teams can leverage Terraform's provider-specific modules to standardize security practices, ensuring consistent application of security controls across diverse cloud environments.

Infrastructure as Code (IaC) offers a transformative approach to managing cloud infrastructure, especially in terms of improving security, consistency, and automation. Through declarative and imperative approaches, IaC allows organizations to ensure that infrastructure deployments are predictable and auditable. The advantages of IaC in security, such as avoiding drift, enabling version control, and ensuring idempotent deployments, make it an essential tool for cloud security. Additionally,

IaC principles such as modularity, reusability, and the ability to manage multi-cloud environments provide further value. Ultimately, IaC plays a pivotal role in building secure, scalable, and compliant cloud infrastructures, while simplifying security management across multiple platforms.

Automating Security with Terraform

Automation is key to managing security in dynamic cloud environments, and Terraform provides powerful tools for this purpose. This section discusses the benefits of security automation, Terraform's features for managing consistent and multi-cloud security policies, practical use cases for secure deployments, and the value of leveraging Terraform's open-source ecosystem to simplify and enhance security practices.

Benefits of Automation in Cloud Security

Cloud environments are inherently dynamic, requiring robust mechanisms to maintain security at scale. Automation with tools such as Terraform simplifies the management of security policies and minimizes risks. Security threats in the cloud can propagate quickly, and manual intervention is often too slow. Automated deployment and configuration of security services ensure rapid response to potential threats, reducing the attack surface across distributed environments.

With Terraform, security tools such as **AWS GuardDuty, GCP Security Command Center,** and **Azure Defender** can be provisioned and managed programmatically.

The following are some benefits of Automation in Cloud Security:

- **Consistency and standardization**: Automation ensures that security policies, configurations, and controls are applied uniformly across all environments, reducing the risk of human error and configuration drift.
- **Faster response to threats**: Automated security processes, such as real-time monitoring and incident response, enable rapid detection and mitigation of threats, significantly reducing response times.
- **Scalability**: Automation allows security practices to scale effortlessly as the cloud environment grows, without the need for manual intervention, ensuring continuous protection even in large, dynamic infrastructures.
- **Cost efficiency**: By reducing manual labour, automation cuts down on operational costs and minimizes the potential financial impact of security breaches or compliance violations.
- **Improved compliance**: Automated security controls can continuously enforce compliance with regulatory requirements, reducing the risk of non-compliance and ensuring adherence to industry standards.
- **Increased visibility**: Automation enhances the ability to monitor and track security events, providing better visibility into potential vulnerabilities, configuration issues, and compliance status across the infrastructure.
- **Reduced complexity**: Automated security workflows simplify the management of security controls, allowing teams to focus on higher-level tasks and strategy, while ensuring consistent enforcement of security practices.
- **Reducing human errors in cloud environments:** Terraform's declarative syntax reduces human errors by codifying security policies, ensuring consistent and error-free configurations across cloud environments. This automation accelerates threat detection, minimizes misconfigurations, and strengthens security across AWS, GCP, and Azure.

Terraform Features for Security Automation

Terraform is a BSL-licensed Infrastructure as Code (IaC) tool that allows users to define, provision, and manage infrastructure resources using declarative configuration files. By writing configurations in HashiCorp Configuration Language (HCL), users specify the desired state of their infrastructure, such as virtual machines, networks, and storage, across multiple cloud providers or on-premises environments. Terraform then translates these configurations into API calls to the respective cloud services, provisioning the infrastructure accordingly. It uses a state file to track the current infrastructure setup and ensures consistency between the declared configuration and the actual environment. Terraform enables automation, repeatability, and scalability in infrastructure management, supporting version control and collaboration across teams, while promoting cloud-agnostic deployments.

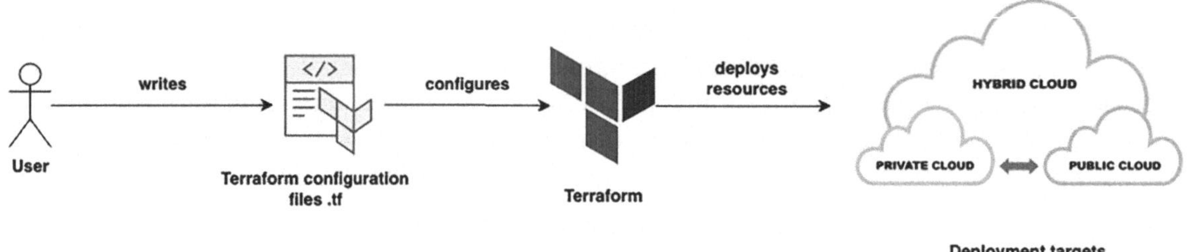

Figure 1.1: *Terraform workflow*

Terraform's distinct features make it an ideal tool for automating and implementing cloud security across diverse environments. Its multi-cloud capabilities are particularly valuable for security teams managing resources across multiple cloud providers, ensuring a consistent and unified security approach. For instance, in AWS, Terraform can be used to deploy IAM roles and policies across various regions and accounts. In GCP, it facilitates managing firewall rules across multiple projects, while in Azure, it allows for automating security group rules across subscriptions.

This cross-cloud functionality not only enhances security management but also helps avoid vendor lock-in, offering greater flexibility in applying security measures across different cloud platforms. Terraform's ability to work seamlessly with AWS, GCP, and Azure allows organizations to implement security policies consistently and efficiently, regardless of the cloud provider they use.

Declarative Syntax for Consistent Security Policies

Terraform's HCL syntax is designed to be both human-readable and machine-executable, making the definition of security policies intuitive and repeatable. HCL's declarative nature allows security teams to describe the desired state of resources, such as firewalls, IAM roles, and encryption settings, without having to worry about the underlying implementation details. This ensures that security configurations can be version-controlled, reused across different environments, and consistently applied, reducing the risk of misconfigurations and enhancing overall security posture. The following are examples of resource configurations across clouds with corresponding security settings:

- Use Terraform to enforce the encryption of EBS volumes in AWS:

```
resource "aws_ebs_volume" "example" {
  size              = 40
  availability_zone = "us-west-2a"
  encrypted         = true
}
```

- Configure GCP's Cloud Storage buckets with uniform security policies:

```
resource "google_storage_bucket" "example" {
  name     = "example-bucket"
  location = "US"
  uniform_bucket_level_access = true
}
```

- Apply network security rules in Azure using Network Security Groups:

```
resource "azurerm_network_security_rule" "example" {
  name                        = "allow_ssh"
  priority                    = 100
  direction                   = "Inbound"
  access                      = "Allow"
  protocol                    = "Tcp"
  source_port_range           = "*"
  destination_port_range      = "22"
  source_address_prefix      = "*"
  destination_address_prefix  = "*"
}
```

Leveraging Terraform's Open Source Ecosystem

The open-source community plays a pivotal role in expanding Terraform's capabilities, offering a wealth of pre-built modules that simplify complex infrastructure configurations while promoting best practices. These community-contributed modules help reduce the effort needed to configure and manage cloud resources securely, ensuring that security measures are consistently implemented across environments. By leveraging these modules, users can streamline their workflows, reduce configuration errors, and implement industry standards with ease.

Notable examples of such modules include the **AWS Security Hub module**, which facilitates centralized security management by aggregating findings from various AWS services for a comprehensive security overview. The **GCP Organization Policy module** ensures that restrictions and governance rules are enforced across all projects, helping maintain compliance. Additionally, the **Azure Sentinel module** enables scalable threat detection, allowing security teams to automate the detection of potential security incidents across large-scale environments. These modules not only save time but also ensure that security configurations align with best practices across different cloud platforms.

The Terraform Registry offers a wide range of security modules. The following are a few examples:

- **AWS**: *terraform-aws-secure-baseline* for foundational security controls.
- **GCP**: *terraform-google-secure-org* for setting up a secure GCP organization.
- **Azure**: *terraform-azurerm-security-center* for automating security recommendations.

Automating security with Terraform not only improves efficiency but also establishes a reliable foundation for managing complex, multi-cloud environments. Its declarative syntax, robust community ecosystem, and practical use cases make it indispensable for modern cloud security practices. By leveraging Terraform's capabilities, organizations can proactively secure their infrastructure while reducing operational overhead and human errors.

Key Components of Terraform for Securing Cloud Workloads

Terraform simplifies cloud security by codifying infrastructure and automating security practices across cloud providers. This section breaks down essential components for securing cloud workloads, focusing on multi-cloud integration, security abstraction, operational safeguards, secure configurations, and audit enhancements.

Multi-Cloud Integration with Terraform

Managing infrastructure across multiple cloud platforms introduces inconsistencies in security practices. Each provider (AWS, GCP, Azure) implements unique identity management, encryption, and network security measures. Terraform mitigates this by standardizing configurations, enabling users to manage security uniformly across providers.

- **AWS**: Security Groups, IAM, and KMS.
- **GCP**: Firewall Rules, IAM policies, and Cloud KMS.
- **Azure**: Network Security Groups (NSGs), RBAC, and Key Vault.

By defining these resources as Terraform code, teams avoid manual intervention, ensuring consistent firewall rules, access controls, and encryption policies.

The following is an example of a multi-cloud security group/firewall definition:

```
provider "aws" {
  region = "us-east-1"
}

provider "google" {
  project = "my-project"
}

provider "azurerm" {
  features {}
}

resource "aws_security_group" "web" {
  name_prefix = "web-sg"
  ingress {
    from_port   = 80
    to_port     = 80
    protocol    = "tcp"
    cidr_blocks = ["0.0.0.0/0"]
  }
}

resource "google_compute_firewall" "http_firewall" {
  name    = "allow-http"
  network = "default"
  allow {
    protocol = "tcp"
    ports    = ["80"]
  }
  source_ranges = ["0.0.0.0/0"]
}

resource "azurerm_network_security_rule" "http_rule" {
  name                        = "allow_http"
  resource_group_name         = "web-rg"
  direction                   = "Inbound"
  access                      = "Allow"
  protocol                    = "Tcp"
```

```
    source_address_prefix        = "*"
    destination_port_range        = "80"
  }
```

Terraform enables the management of security groups, firewalls, and network configurations across multiple cloud providers by using distinct provider blocks for each platform. In the provided example, the **`aws_security_group`**, **`google_compute_firewall`**, and **`azurerm_network_security_rule`** resources define security rules for AWS, Google Cloud, and Azure. The **`aws_security_group`** block allows inbound HTTP traffic on port 80 from any IP address, while the **`google_compute_firewall`** block similarly permits TCP traffic on port 80 from any source range to the specified network in Google Cloud. In Azure, the **`azurerm_network_security_rule`** block allows inbound TCP traffic on port **`80`** from any source IP address to the specified resource group. By leveraging Terraform, organizations can automate and standardize security configurations across AWS, GCP, and Azure, ensuring consistent security practices in multi-cloud environments.

Managing Diverse Cloud Security Standards

In multi-cloud environments, enterprises face the challenge of managing diverse security standards to meet their organizational compliance requirements across cloud providers such as **AWS, GCP, and Azure** with distinct compliance frameworks. These frameworks may include **PCI DSS (Payment Card Industry Data Security Standard), GDPR (General Data Protection Regulation), HIPAA (Health Insurance Portability and Accountability Act), and SOC 2 (System and Organization Controls).**

Ensuring consistent enforcement of these standards across cloud platforms can be complex, as security configurations, data governance, and encryption practices differ between providers. Terraform addresses this challenge by embedding **Policy as Code (PaC)**, enabling automated enforcement of compliance policies across infrastructure deployments.

Policy as Code allows organizations to define and enforce compliance rules directly in Terraform's workflows. PaC ensures that infrastructure deployments adhere to security baselines and compliance requirements by embedding checks within the deployment process.

Tools such as HashiCorp Sentinel, Open Policy Agent (OPA), and Terraform Cloud integrate seamlessly with Terraform, allowing for proactive security enforcement.

Following is an example of Policy as Code (Sentinel) to enforce encryption across clouds:

```
policy "enforce_encryption" {
  source = "./policies/encryption.sentinel"
}
```

Managing diverse cloud security standards is a critical aspect of cloud governance. Terraform simplifies this process by embedding **Policy as Code**, ensuring consistent, automated enforcement of security and compliance rules across AWS, GCP, and Azure. This not only reduces complexity but also enhances the overall security posture of cloud environments.

Simplified Security with Terraform Resources

Terraform abstracts complex cloud-native security settings into reusable modules. These modules encapsulate best practices, reducing configuration drift. For example, encryption, security groups, and storage protection can be templatized and reused across environments.

Following is an example of Encryption and Access Control for AWS s3 bucket:

```
module "s3_bucket" {
  source            = "terraform-aws-modules/s3-bucket/aws"
  bucket            = "secure-data"
```

```
  versioning_enabled = true
  sse_algorithm      = "AES256
}
```

This module provisions an S3 bucket named **"secure-data"** using the Terraform AWS S3 Bucket module, with versioning enabled and server-side encryption (**AES256**) configured for enhanced data security.

Encryption and access control are foundational pillars of cloud security, ensuring that sensitive data is protected from unauthorized access and breaches. In cloud environments, encryption safeguards data at rest (stored data) and in transit (data being transferred), while access control manages who can view, modify, or delete resources.

Terraform simplifies the enforcement of encryption and access control by enabling declarative, infrastructure-as-code configurations that ensure security policies are consistently applied across cloud environments such as AWS, GCP, and Azure. This prevents misconfigurations, reduces manual effort, and aligns cloud resources with compliance standards (PCI DSS, HIPAA, GDPR).

Protecting Terraform Operations

Protecting Terraform operations is essential because Terraform manages sensitive infrastructure components such as state files, secrets, and configuration details. If these details are altered or compromised, then this can have significant security and operational impacts. Rather than simply integrating with identity services, Terraform leverages these IAM capabilities and RBAC policies to strictly control who can execute deployments and make changes. By assigning specific roles and enforcing least privilege access, organizations ensure that only authorized personnel or automation pipelines can trigger Terraform operations, thereby reducing the risk of unauthorized or accidental changes.

In AWS, Terraform uses the provider's **assume_role** configuration to delegate its operations to a dedicated IAM role (for example, **TerraformRole**), which has only the permissions necessary for managing the infrastructure. This minimizes the potential damage from compromised credentials by restricting actions to a defined scope.

AssumeRole for Terraform in AWS:

```
provider "aws" {
  assume_role {
    role_arn = "arn:aws:iam::123456789012:role/TerraformRole"
  }
}
```

In GCP, Terraform provisions a dedicated service account with specific IAM permissions for Terraform deployments, ensuring that only the required operations are executed.

IAM for Terraform Service Account in GCP:

```
resource "google_service_account" "terraform" {
  account_id   = "terraform-admin"
  display_name = "Terraform Admin"
}
```

In Azure, Terraform employs **azurerm_role_assignment** to grant a service principal the necessary permissions, such as the Contributor role within a specified resource group, limiting its access to only the relevant resources.

RBAC for Terraform in Azure:

```
resource "azurerm_role_assignment" "terraform_role" {
  scope                = azurerm_resource_group.example.id
  role_definition_name = "Contributor"
  principal_id         = azuread_service_principal.example.id
}
```

These practices collectively ensure that Terraform deployments are secured through a robust RBAC framework, which not only minimizes unauthorized access but also provides a clear audit trail of all changes, thereby enhancing the overall security posture of the infrastructure.

Fundamentals of Securing Terraform State

Terraform state files store sensitive infrastructure data (such as IAM roles, passwords). Unsecured state files are a critical security risk. Encrypting and locking state files prevents unauthorized access and configuration drift.

- **AWS**: S3 bucket with encryption and DynamoDB for locking.
- **GCP**: GCS bucket with encryption and object versioning.
- **Azure**: Blob storage with SSE and storage account locks.

Writing Secure Terraform Configurations

When deploying cloud infrastructure with Terraform, security must be integrated into the configuration process to prevent accidental exposure, misconfigurations, and vulnerabilities. Secure configurations ensure infrastructure adheres to best practices, reduces the attack surface, and enforces organizational policies.

Terraform configurations often handle sensitive data such as passwords, API keys, and tokens. If not properly secured, these credentials can be unintentionally exposed in CLI outputs, Terraform state files, and log files. To prevent this, Terraform provides the **sensitive** argument in variable definitions. This flag ensures that sensitive data is masked from logs, CLI outputs, and error messages.

Using Input Validation for Robust Setups

Terraform enables input validation to enforce constraints on variable values, ensuring that configurations adhere to best practices and security standards. By rejecting invalid inputs during the *terraform plan* phase, it helps prevent misconfigurations early in the deployment process. Input validation enhances error prevention, enforces policies, and promotes consistency across infrastructure deployments. The following example combines sensitive marking and validation to ensure passwords are long enough while protecting their visibility:

```
variable "admin_password" {
  description = "Admin user password"
  type        = string
  sensitive   = true
  validation {
    condition     = length(var.admin_password) >= 12
    error_message = "Password must be at least 12 characters long."
  }
}
```

Enhancing Audits with Terraform

Terraform enables Infrastructure as Code (IaC), which offers a repeatable, transparent, and auditable method for provisioning cloud environments. Security audits, compliance checks, and infrastructure validation are crucial for maintaining cloud governance and preventing misconfigurations. By leveraging Terraform for audits, organizations can automate compliance enforcement, detect drift, and ensure consistent application of security policies across AWS, GCP, and Azure.

Terraform's Infrastructure as Code (IaC) model enables continuous and repeatable compliance checks by embedding security policies directly into infrastructure definitions. It seamlessly integrates with security scanning tools that validate configurations against established best practices and compliance frameworks, helping to prevent misconfigurations and security risks before deployment. Notable tools for this purpose include **Checkov**, **tfsec**, **Terrascan**, **Open Policy Agent (OPA)**, and **Terraform Sentinel**, all of which enhance the security and reliability of Terraform-managed infrastructure.

By leveraging Terraform for repeatable compliance checks and integrating security scanning tools, organizations can automate infrastructure validation, enforce security best practices, and detect misconfigurations early in the development lifecycle. This proactive approach not only streamlines cloud deployments but also reduces the risk of vulnerabilities and misconfigurations that could lead to security breaches. By embedding compliance and security into the infrastructure as code (IaC) process, organizations ensure consistent governance, maintain regulatory adherence, and enhance the overall security posture across AWS, GCP, and Azure environments. Ultimately, this automation-driven methodology helps to secure cloud infrastructure at scale, fostering resilience and operational efficiency in increasingly complex multi-cloud ecosystems.

Conclusion

The introduction of Infrastructure as Code (IaC) and tools such as Terraform has revolutionized cloud security by addressing many of the limitations associated with traditional infrastructure security. By automating deployments and enforcing consistent configurations, Terraform helps organizations mitigate risks related to manual processes, misconfigurations, and operational drift. The evolution of cloud security, from early concerns about breaches and shared environments to the adoption of advanced cloud-native tools such as AWS GuardDuty, GCP Security Command Center, and Azure Defender, highlights the need for scalable and standardized solutions. Terraform's cloud-agnostic approach allows organizations to unify security management across AWS, GCP, and Azure, providing a consistent framework for managing identity, encryption, and network security, regardless of cloud provider differences.

As organizations continue to navigate the complexities of multi-cloud environments, Terraform plays a critical role in simplifying and automating security at scale. By embedding security policies directly into the infrastructure provisioning process, Terraform reduces human error, accelerates incident response, and ensures compliance with regulatory frameworks. Features such as role-based access control, encrypted state files, and policy-as-code tools such as Sentinel and OPA allow for robust governance and secure operations. Furthermore, by leveraging Terraform's open-source ecosystem and reusable modules, organizations can rapidly implement and adapt security best practices. This chapter establishes Terraform as a cornerstone of modern cloud security strategies, demonstrating how automation and IaC can fortify cloud workloads, enhance visibility, and drive long-term operational efficiency across diverse cloud platforms.

In the next chapter, we will cover the setup and configuration of Terraform for multi-cloud and on-premises environments, emphasizing the importance of securing state files with remote backends and encryption. It also discusses managing multiple environments securely and leveraging GitOps and version control for infrastructure automation.

Questions and Answers

1. **How has cloud security evolved across cloud providers, and what are the key differences between early and modern approaches?**

   Early cloud security focused on adapting traditional security practices to virtualized environments, leading to challenges in managing shared environments and meeting compliance requirements. For example, multi-tenancy in early cloud adoption raised concerns about data isolation. Over time, modern security frameworks introduced the **Shared Responsibility Model**, clarifying that while providers secure the underlying infrastructure, users are responsible for securing their workloads, data, and applications. Innovations such as Identity and Access Management (IAM) advancements and cloud-native tools such as AWS Identity Center, GCP IAM, and Azure Active Directory now enable granular access control and dynamic security policies.

2. **What are the main challenges associated with traditional infrastructure security, and how do they differ from cloud-native approaches?**

   Traditional infrastructure security often relies on manual processes that are error-prone and lack scalability. Key challenges include:

   - **Scalability and Elasticity:** Legacy systems struggle to handle the dynamic scaling capabilities of the cloud.
   - **Monitoring and Visibility:** Limited tools make real-time auditing and anomaly detection difficult.
   - **High Costs and Complexity:** Maintaining and integrating legacy security measures into cloud environments is both expensive and operationally challenging.

   Cloud-native approaches, such as Infrastructure as Code (IaC), address these issues by enabling automation, real-time monitoring, and seamless scalability. Tools such as Terraform simplify security management by codifying security policies, automating provisioning, and providing consistent configurations across multi-cloud setups.

3. **What is Infrastructure as Code (IaC), and how does it benefit cloud security?**

   IaC is a practice where infrastructure resources, such as servers, networks, and security configurations, are defined and managed using code. Benefits of IaC for cloud security include:

   - **Consistency and Auditability:** Codified configurations reduce the risk of human error and ensure uniformity across environments.
   - **Automation:** Security policies and infrastructure can be deployed and updated programmatically, reducing operational overhead.
   - **Multi-Cloud Security:** IaC enables organizations to define and enforce consistent security practices across AWS, GCP, and Azure, addressing unique cloud-specific requirements.

4. **How does Terraform enhance cloud security automation, and what are its key features for securing workloads?**

   Terraform streamlines cloud security automation through features such as:

   - **Declarative Syntax:** Security policies are defined in code, ensuring consistency during deployment.
   - **Open Source Ecosystem:** Terraform's registry provides reusable modules for secure configurations, such as encrypting S3 buckets or creating private subnets.
   - **Multi-Cloud Integration:** Terraform's providers support AWS, GCP, Azure, and more, allowing centralized security management across diverse platforms.

By automating infrastructure provisioning and policy enforcement, Terraform reduces human errors and ensures compliance with security standards.

5. **What are the best practices for writing secure Terraform configurations, and how do they enhance cloud security?**

   Best practices for writing secure Terraform configurations include:

   - **Input Validation:** Use variable blocks with constraints to ensure only valid values are accepted. For instance, enforce minimum password lengths or IP whitelisting in security groups.
   - **Resource Protection:** Implement resource locks and state file encryption to prevent unauthorized access or accidental modifications.
   - **Audit Enhancements:** Use Terraform's state files and logging features to track changes, enabling comprehensive audits and compliance validation.

   These practices improve cloud security by ensuring predictable, controlled deployments and reducing vulnerabilities in configurations.

CHAPTER 2
Setting Up and Securing Your Terraform Environment

Introduction

A secure and well-configured Terraform environment serves as the cornerstone for managing cloud infrastructure at scale. As organizations increasingly adopt multi-cloud and hybrid environments, the need for a streamlined, consistent, and secure Terraform setup becomes essential. This chapter delves into the practical aspects of installing, configuring, and managing Terraform across AWS, Azure, GCP, and on-premises environments. From selecting the right Terraform version to configuring providers and leveraging automation, the goal is to establish a foundation that not only simplifies deployment but also enhances operational efficiency and security.

Beyond initial setup, safeguarding Terraform state files and enforcing strict access controls are critical to protecting sensitive infrastructure data. This chapter explores the importance of securing state files through remote backends, encryption, and state locking mechanisms. Additionally, we will discuss implementing Role-Based Access Control (RBAC) and IAM policies to regulate state file access, ensuring compliance and minimizing the risk of misconfigurations. As environments become more complex, securely managing multiple environments through CI/CD pipelines becomes essential. Finally, by integrating GitOps and version control practices, teams can automate deployments, detect drift, and foster collaboration, resulting in a resilient, scalable, and secure infrastructure ecosystem. By the end of this chapter, you will have the knowledge and practical skills to set up a robust Terraform environment that is secure, scalable, and optimized for multi-cloud and on-premises deployments. You will be equipped to protect sensitive state files, enforce granular access controls, and implement best practices for managing infrastructure configurations using GitOps and automation, ensuring a resilient and compliant cloud infrastructure.

Structure

In this chapter, we will cover the following topics:

- Installing and Configuring Terraform for Multi-Cloud and On-Premises Use
    - Choosing the Right Terraform Version
    - Installing Terraform on Various Platforms
    - Configuring Terraform Providers
    - Leveraging Provider-Specific Features

- Securing State Files with Remote Backends and Encryption
  - Understanding Terraform State Files
  - Choosing Remote Backends
  - Encrypting State Files
  - Implementing State File Locking
  - Backing Up State Files
- Implementing Access Controls for State Management
  - Role-Based Access Control (RBAC) and IAM Integration for State Management
  - Auditing Access Logs
  - Securing multi-Team Access
- Managing Multiple Environments (Development, Staging, Production) Securely
  - Environment-Specific Configuration Management
  - Securing Shared Resources Across Environments
  - Handling Environment-Specific Dependencies
- Leveraging GitOps and Version Control for Infrastructure Automation
  - Setting Up a GitOps Workflow for Terraform
  - Versioning Terraform Modules
  - Addressing Terraform Drift with GitOps
  - Collaborating with Teams Using Version Control

Installing and Configuring Terraform for Multi-Cloud and On-Premises Use

Terraform serves as the backbone of modern Infrastructure as Code (IaC), providing a consistent way to manage cloud resources across AWS, Azure, GCP, and on-premises data centers. One of Terraform's strengths lies in its ability to unify provisioning across multiple environments, ensuring predictable deployments and version control. This section will walk through the process of selecting the right Terraform version, installing Terraform across various platforms, and configuring providers to interact seamlessly with multi-cloud and hybrid infrastructures.

Choosing the Right Terraform Version

Terraform versions evolve rapidly, with new features, bug fixes, and improvements released regularly. Each version brings enhanced compatibility with cloud providers, but not all versions are suitable for every environment, especially in multi-cloud setups. Selecting the right Terraform version ensures compatibility across multi-cloud and on-premises infrastructure.

Terraform follows semantic versioning (for example, `1.5.3`), where minor versions introduce backward-compatible features, while major versions may contain breaking changes. Enterprises often lock their Terraform code to a specific version to avoid unintended updates.

The following are some best practices for Terraform versioning:

- **Version selection:** Cloud providers such as AWS, Azure, and GCP regularly update their APIs and resources. Terraform versions align with these updates, meaning that using an outdated version may lead to deprecated resources or provider incompatibility.
- **LTS (Long-Term Support) versus Latest Release:** For production environments, it is often

best to use LTS releases, ensuring long-term stability. In contrast, development environments may benefit from the latest Terraform versions, leveraging cutting-edge features.

- **Version pinning:** Use **required_version** in Terraform configurations to specify the desired version, ensuring consistency across environments.
- **Compatibility testing:** Test new versions in isolated environments before rolling them into production.
- **Provider compatibility:** Match Terraform versions with supported provider versions (for example, AWS, Azure, GCP).

```
terraform {
  required_version = "~> 1.5.0"
}
```

This configuration ensures Terraform 1.5.x versions are used but restricts automatic upgrades to 1.6.x.

Installing Terraform on Various Platforms

Terraform's installation process is straightforward and versatile, supporting platforms such as Windows, macOS, Linux, and CI/CD pipelines. It involves downloading a single lightweight binary and configuring it within the system's PATH, enabling immediate usability. To further streamline this process, package managers such as Homebrew, Chocolatey, and APT offer a convenient way to install and update Terraform, reducing manual effort and ensuring consistency across environments.

To enhance the efficiency of Terraform deployment, several best practices can be adopted. Automated installation through package managers ensures consistency across multiple systems, making it easier to manage infrastructure at scale. Embedding Terraform installation within CI/CD pipelines simplifies automated infrastructure deployments, ensuring every pipeline execution has the correct Terraform version. For environments requiring multiple Terraform versions, tools such as **tfenv** allow seamless management of version dependencies, avoiding potential compatibility issues. By adhering to these practices, organizations can optimize the use of Terraform in diverse operational contexts.

The following are the steps to install Terraform on various platforms:

- **Linux system**
  - Use the **wget** or **curl** command to download the binary:

    ```
    wget https://releases.hashicorp.com/terraform/<version>/terraform_
    <version>_linux_amd64.zip
    ```
  - Extract the downloaded **.zip** file:

    ```
    unzip terraform_<version>_linux_amd64.zip
    ```
  - Move the Terraform binary to a directory in your system's PATH:

    ```
    sudo mv terraform /usr/local/bin/
    ```
  - Verify Terraform installation

    ```
    terraform --version
    ```
  - Expected output

    ```
    Terraform v<version>
    ```
- **MacOS**
  - Install Terraform via Homebrew:

    ```
    brew tap hashicorp/tap
    brew install hashicorp/tap/terraform
    ```
  - Verify Terraform installation

    ```
    terraform --version
    ```

- Expected output

  ```
  Terraform v<version>
  ```

- **Windows**
  - Install Terraform via Chocolatey:

    ```
    choco install terraform
    ```

  - Verify Terraform installation

    ```
    terraform --version
    ```

  - Expected output

    ```
    Terraform v<version>
    ```

- **CI/CD (GitHub Actions)**

```
steps:
  - name: Install Terraform
    run: |
      wget    https://releases.hashicorp.com/terraform/<version>/
terraform_<version>_linux_amd64.zip
      unzip terraform_1.5.3_linux_amd64.zip
      sudo mv terraform /usr/local/bin/
```

Configuring Terraform Providers

Providers are integral to Terraform's functionality, acting as plugins that bridge the gap between Terraform and cloud platforms such as AWS, Azure, and GCP. Each provider offers a set of resources and data sources specific to the platform, enabling users to manage various aspects of their infrastructure, such as compute instances, storage, and networking, in a declarative way. For instance, the AWS provider allows you to define resources such as EC2 instances, S3 buckets, and IAM policies. Similarly, the Azure provider facilitates the management of virtual networks, resource groups, and Azure AD roles. In GCP, the provider enables managing resources such as Compute Engine instances, Cloud Storage buckets, and IAM policies, making it possible to automate and scale infrastructure deployments across Google Cloud projects. These providers are critical for ensuring Terraform's ability to interact seamlessly with diverse cloud environments.

When initializing a Terraform configuration, providers are automatically downloaded from the Terraform Registry, ensuring you have the correct plugin version for your deployment. Provider configurations typically include parameters such as authentication credentials (for example, access keys for AWS, service principals for Azure, or service accounts for GCP), region settings, and project-specific details. These configurations can be declared directly in Terraform files or securely managed through environment variables. This approach streamlines authentication, ensures scalability, and facilitates efficient resource management across multiple accounts, projects, or subscriptions. By leveraging providers effectively, Terraform users can achieve a consistent and automated approach to managing their cloud infrastructure.

The following are examples for configuring providers across AWS, GCP, and Azure:

```
terraform {
  required_providers {
    aws = {
      source  = "hashicorp/aws"
      version = "~> 5.0"
    }
    google = {
      source  = "hashicorp/google"
      version = "~> 4.0"
    }
```

```
    azurerm = {
      source  = "hashicorp/azurerm"
      version = "~>3.0.0"
    }
  }
}

provider "aws" {
  region  = "us-east-1"
  profile = "default"
}

provider "azurerm" {
  features {}
}

provider "google" {
  credentials = file("account.json")
  project     = "my-gcp-project"
  region      = "us-central1"
}
```

Leveraging Provider-Specific Features

Each cloud provider, such as AWS, Azure, and GCP, offers unique capabilities that can be leveraged to optimize and tailor infrastructure for specific needs. Terraform facilitates access to these provider-specific features by using custom resource blocks within its configurations. These resources allow users to define cloud-specific infrastructure elements, such as EC2 instances in AWS, virtual machines in Azure, or compute instances in GCP, with configuration options specific to each provider's functionality. For instance, AWS provides capabilities for spot instances, while GCP offers preemptible VMs, which can be used to reduce costs while maintaining scalability and performance.

Following best practices when working with these custom resource blocks is essential for efficient and secure infrastructure management. It is recommended to use provider-specific enhancements, such as spot or preemptible instances, to reduce operational costs, while optimizing resource usage. However, before deploying these cost-saving features, it is important to ensure they are thoroughly tested in isolated environments to mitigate the risk of misconfigurations or unexpected behavior in production. This allows teams to safely validate the impact of cloud-native features and ensures that the infrastructure remains robust and secure across various environments.

The following are some provider-specific examples:

- **AWS-Specific Feature (EC2 Spot Instances):**

  ```
  resource "aws_instance" "spot" {
    ami           = "ami-xxxxx"          # Define the AMI id for the instance
    instance_type = "t3.medium"
    spot_price    = "0.040"
  }
  ```

- **Azure-Specific Feature (Resource Groups):**

  ```
  resource "azurerm_resource_group" "rg" {
    name     = "example-resources"
    location = "East US"
  }
  ```

- **GCP-Specific Feature (Preemptible VMs):**

```
resource "google_compute_instance" "vm" {
  name         = "preemptible-vm"
  machine_type = "n1-standard-1"
  zone         = "us-central1-a"
  scheduling {
    preemptible       = true
    automatic_restart = false
  }
}
```

Installing and configuring Terraform for multi-cloud and hybrid environments is a critical step in automating infrastructure. By selecting the right Terraform version, automating installations, and configuring providers correctly, teams can build scalable and secure cloud architectures across AWS, Azure, and GCP. The ability to leverage provider-specific features ensures that organizations can optimize their resources, while maintaining consistency through Infrastructure as Code.

Securing State Files with Remote Backends and Encryption

State files are the foundation of Terraform's infrastructure management, holding the mapping between cloud resources and Terraform configurations. As the single source of truth for deployments, state files are highly sensitive, often containing resource IDs, IP addresses, and even secrets. Properly securing these files is critical to prevent unauthorized access, data corruption, and deployment issues.

This section explores Terraform state files, how to manage them securely using remote backends, and how to implement encryption and locking to ensure data integrity and confidentiality.

Understanding Terraform State Files

Terraform state files (typically named **`terraform.tfstate`**) play a critical role in tracking and managing the current state of the infrastructure that Terraform is responsible for. These files store essential information about the resources Terraform manages, including their properties and relationships. The state file acts as a reference point that allows Terraform to map its configuration to the actual infrastructure deployed in the cloud, making it possible to apply changes incrementally without duplicating resources. Without state files, Terraform would not be able to determine the status of resources, potentially leading to resource duplication, misconfigurations, or inefficient deployments.

When you run the Terraform apply command, Terraform uses the state file to determine the current status of the resources that it manages. It compares the existing infrastructure to the configuration you have defined, calculating the necessary changes. Based on this comparison, Terraform applies the changes to the infrastructure. Once the changes are successfully deployed, the state file is updated with the latest information, ensuring it reflects the current state of your infrastructure. This system allows Terraform to manage changes in a controlled and incremental manner, minimizing the risk of disruptions or errors during deployments.

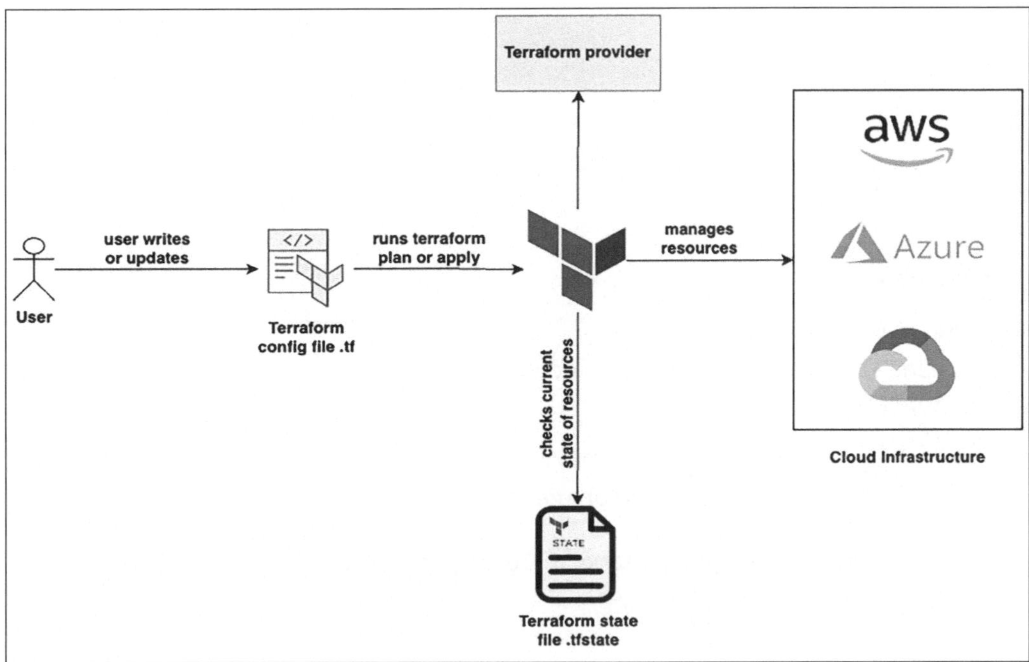

Figure 2.1: *Terraform state*

The following are examples of Terraform state for different resources in AWS, GCP, and Azure for storage resources:

- **AWS**

```
{
  "resources": [
    {
      "type": "aws_s3_bucket",
      "name": "example_bucket",
      "instances": [
        {
          "attributes": {
            "bucket": "example-terraform-state",
            "region": "us-east-1"
          }
        }
      ]
    }
  ]
}
```

- **GCP**

```
{
  "resources": [
    {
      "type": "google_storage_bucket",
      "name": "example_bucket",
      "instances": [
        {
          "attributes": {
            "name": "example-terraform-state",
            "location": "US",
            "storage_class": "STANDARD"
          }
```

```
          }
        ]
      }
    ]
  }
```

- **Azure**

```
{
  "resources": [
    {
      "type": "azurerm_storage_account",
      "name": "example_storage_account",
      "instances": [
        {
          "attributes": {
            "name": "examplestorageacct",
            "location": "East US",
            "resource_group_name": "example-rg",
            "sku": "Standard_LRS",
            "kind": "StorageV2"
          }
        }
      ]
    }
  ]
}
```

The following are some important roles of state files:

- **Tracking Infrastructure Changes**: State files serve as the record of the infrastructure, keeping track of all resources that have been deployed and their current configurations. This allows Terraform to identify and manage existing resources effectively, ensuring that subsequent changes are applied as needed.
- **Facilitating Collaboration**: In team environments, shared state files enable everyone to work from a consistent view of the infrastructure. This eliminates discrepancies between different team members' local environments and ensures a unified approach to infrastructure management.
- **Performance Optimization**: By storing resource mappings locally, state files help Terraform reduce the number of API calls it needs to make to cloud providers. This makes Terraform operations more efficient and speeds up the process of applying changes to the infrastructure.

The following are some security risks associated with unsecured state files:

- **Sensitive Data Exposure**: State files can contain sensitive information, such as cloud credentials, private keys, and secrets, stored in plaintext. Without proper security measures, these files could expose the critical data to unauthorized users.
- **Configuration Drift**: If the state file is modified by unauthorized individuals, it could lead to configuration drift, where the actual infrastructure deviates from the desired state. This can create inconsistencies, making it harder to manage infrastructure accurately.
- **Loss or Corruption**: If a state file is lost or corrupted, it can disrupt the workflow of infrastructure management, potentially resulting in the need to rebuild resources or reconfigure deployments from scratch.

The following are some best practices for managing state files:

- **Avoid Local State**: Local state files are vulnerable to accidental deletion, loss, or lack of collaboration support. Always use remote state management to ensure that the state file is securely stored and accessible to the right users.

- **Limit Access**: Restrict access to state files using Role-Based Access Control (RBAC) to ensure that only authorized users can modify or view the state file.
- **Version Control State Files**: Regularly back up state files and consider implementing version control to prevent data loss. Remote backends such as Amazon S3, Azure Blob Storage, or Google Cloud Storage offer options to version and manage state files securely.

Choosing Remote Backends

Remote backends play a crucial role in Terraform by storing state files in centralized cloud-native storage services such as AWS S3, Azure Blob Storage, or GCP Buckets. This approach significantly improves collaboration in team environments and provides greater resilience to failures compared to local state file management. By storing state files remotely, Terraform ensures that all team members work with the same, up-to-date state, preventing issues caused by out-of-sync configurations or local machine failures.

The following are some benefits of remote backends:

- **State File Storage:** When you run Terraform commands such as terraform apply or terraform plan, Terraform reads from and writes to the remote backend to retrieve and update the state file. This allows for consistent and reliable tracking of infrastructure resources across multiple users and teams.
- **State Locking:** One of the key features of remote backends is state file locking. When multiple users or processes attempt to modify the same state file simultaneously, the backend ensures that only one operation can proceed at a time by using a locking mechanism.
- **Encryption and Security:** Remote backends also enhance the security of state files. Most cloud-based storage services, including AWS S3, Azure Blob Storage, and GCP Buckets, provide encryption both at rest and in transit, ensuring that sensitive data in state files such as credentials and private keys are securely protected.
- **Versioning:** Remote backends support versioning of state files, allowing you to maintain a history of state file changes. This is essential for recovery purposes, as you can roll back to a previous version of the state file, if a deployment goes wrong.

The following are the remote backend configurations for Terraform across AWS, Azure, and GCP:

- **AWS S3**

  ```
  terraform {
    backend "s3" {
      bucket         = "my-terraform-state"
      key            = "infra/terraform.tfstate"
      region         = "us-east-1"
      dynamodb_table = "terraform-lock"  # DynamoDB table for state locking
      encrypt        = true  # Enable encryption at rest
    }
  }
  ```

- **Azure Blob Storage**

  ```
  terraform {
    backend "azurerm" {
      resource_group_name   = "terraform-backend"
      storage_account_name  = "tfstateaccount"
      container_name        = "tfstate"
      key                   = "terraform.tfstate"
  ```

```
    cosmosdb_lock_name    = "terraform-lock"  # Cosmos DB for state locking
  }
}
```

- **GCP Bucket**

```
terraform {
  backend "gcs" {
    bucket  = "my-terraform-state"
    prefix  = "infra/state"
    project = "my-gcp-project"
    lock_table = "terraform-lock"  # Firestore for state locking
  }
}
```

Encrypting State Files

Encryption plays a crucial role in safeguarding Terraform state files by ensuring that sensitive data within the files, such as passwords, API keys, private certificates, or other secrets, remain protected both when stored and during transit. State files inherently contain configuration details and metadata about your infrastructure, which could pose significant security risks if exposed. Encrypting state files mitigates these risks by ensuring that only authorized parties can access the sensitive contents.

Encryption at Rest refers to the protection of state files when they are stored on the backend, such as AWS S3, Azure Blob Storage, or Google Cloud Storage. Encryption at rest ensures that even if an attacker gains access to the storage medium, the state files remain unreadable without the decryption key. Cloud platforms offer native encryption services, such as Amazon S3's SSE-S3, Azure Blob Storage's server-side encryption, and GCP Bucket's object encryption. These features automatically encrypt data before storing it and decrypt it only when accessed with appropriate permissions.

Encryption in Transit is used when Terraform communicates with the backend (for example, during the **`terraform apply`** or **`terraform plan`** phases), and the data is transferred over the network. To prevent any interception or unauthorized access during transit, Terraform uses TLS (Transport Layer Security) encryption. This encrypts the communication channel between your local machine and the remote backend, ensuring that sensitive data, such as access credentials or configuration changes, remains secure while being transferred over potentially insecure networks.

The following attributes can be defined in the Terraform backend block to allow encryption:

- AWS S3 with KMS Integration

```
encrypt = true
kms_key_id = "alias/my-key"
```

- Azure Blob Storage with Customer Managed Keys

```
"encryption": {
  "keySource": "Microsoft.Keyvault"
}
```

- GCP Buckets with Default Encryption

```
"encryption": {
  "defaultKmsKeyName": "projects/my-project/locations/global/keyRings/my-key-ring/cryptoKeys/my-key"
}
```

Implementing State File Locking

State file locking is a critical feature in Terraform that prevents concurrent modifications to state files. In multi-user or team environments, it is common to run multiple **`terraform apply`** or **`terraform`** `plan` commands simultaneously. Without proper state file locking, this can lead to race conditions, where two operations attempt to modify the same resources at the same time, potentially corrupting the state file and leading to inconsistent infrastructure.

State file locking ensures that only one operation can modify the state file at any given time, safeguarding against these conflicts. The lock acts as a mechanism to synchronize Terraform operations, ensuring that only one process is making changes to the state at a time. Once the process completes successfully, the lock is released, allowing other operations to proceed.

The following is a detailed explanation of how Terraform state locking works:

- **When terraform apply runs, a lock is acquired**: When you run `terraform apply,` Terraform automatically attempts to acquire a lock on the state file. This lock is managed by the remote backend (for example, AWS S3 with DynamoDB, Azure Blob with Cosmos DB, or GCP Cloud Storage with Firestore). The purpose of this lock is to prevent any other Terraform process from accessing and modifying the state file while the current operation is in progress.
- **The lock prevents other operations until the first completes or fails**: Once the lock is acquired, Terraform will prevent other operations from accessing the state file. This ensures that only one process is allowed to change the infrastructure at a time, reducing the risk of concurrent operations causing inconsistencies or corruption. If the Terraform apply process completes successfully or is interrupted, the lock is released, and other processes are free to acquire the lock and proceed. In case of failure, the lock is released automatically, but the infrastructure might require manual intervention to resolve any partial changes.

This feature is especially useful in collaborative environments where multiple team members or CI/CD pipelines might interact with the same infrastructure resources, as it ensures a consistent and reliable infrastructure management process. Without state file locking, the risk of data corruption, misconfigurations, or unintentional overrides increases significantly.

Terraform state locking mechanisms for AWS, GCP, and Azure:

- **AWS using DynamoDb:** AWS uses **DynamoDB** as the backend for state file locking. When using DynamoDB for state locking, you need to create a table that will store the lock information. This ensures that Terraform can safely lock the state file during operations, preventing race conditions.

```
resource "aws_dynamodb_table" "terraform_lock" {
  name         = "terraform-lock"
  billing_mode = "PAY_PER_REQUEST"
  hash_key     = "LockID"

  attribute {
    name = "LockID"
    type = "S"
  }
}
```

- **Azure uses Cosmo DB:** Azure uses Cosmos DB to manage state file locks. The Cosmos DB table will act as a lock store to prevent simultaneous changes to the state file, ensuring that only one operation occurs at a time.

```
resource "azurerm_cosmosdb_sql_container" "terraform_lock" {
  name                = "terraform-lock"
  resource_group_name = "my-resource-group"
  cosmosdb_account_name = "my-cosmosdb-account"
  database_name       = "terraform-state"
  partition_key_path = "/LockID"
  throughput          = 400
}
```

- **GCP with Firestore:** In GCP, Firestore is used to implement state locking. Firestore's document-based storage is utilized to handle Terraform's locking mechanism.

```
resource "google_firestore_collection" "terraform_lock" {
  collection_id = "terraform-lock"
  project       = "my-gcp-project"
}
```

Each of these locking mechanisms ensures that Terraform operations are executed one at a time, preventing concurrent writes to the state file, which could otherwise lead to inconsistent infrastructure or data corruption.

Backing Up State Files

In Terraform, state file backups are essential for ensuring disaster recovery and preventing data loss. As Terraform manages infrastructure, it constantly updates the state file to reflect changes in the resources it controls. By maintaining historical versions of state files, Terraform allows you to easily rollback to a previous state in case of errors or unintended changes. This process is crucial in dynamic environments where frequent updates to infrastructure occur, as it ensures you can restore the system to a known working state without significant downtime or loss of configurations.

Terraform relies on cloud storage services such as AWS S3, Azure Blob Storage, and Google Cloud Storage to store state files. These platforms natively support versioning, which means each time a change is made to the state file, a new version is automatically created. In the event of an issue, you can revert to older versions of the state file to recover lost configurations or mitigate configuration drift. This functionality is invaluable for managing complex infrastructure, as it offers a safety net for accidental deletions, misconfigurations, or failures in infrastructure deployments. With versioning enabled, users can manually restore previous versions of the state file whenever necessary, ensuring that the infrastructure is maintained in a consistent and secure state.

The following are the configurations for enabling versioning in storage for AWS, GCP, and Azure to store Terraform state:

- AWS S3 bucket versioning

```
resource "aws_s3_bucket_versioning" "tf_state_versioning" {
  bucket = aws_s3_bucket.tf_state.id

  versioning_configuration {
    status = "Enabled"
  }
}
```

- Azure Blob Storage versioning

```
resource "azurerm_storage_account" "tf_state" {
  name                     = "tfstorageacct"
  resource_group_name      = "tf-backend-rg"
  location                 = "East US"
  account_tier             = "Standard"
  account_replication_type = "LRS"

  blob_properties {
    versioning_enabled = true
  }
}
```

- GCP Bucket versioning

```
resource "google_storage_bucket" "tf_state" {
  name     = "my-tf-state-bucket"
  location = "US"

  versioning {
    enabled = true
  }
}
```

Securing Terraform state files is paramount to ensuring infrastructure integrity and safeguarding sensitive data. By implementing remote backends, encrypting state files, and utilizing state locking, teams can mitigate risks associated with unauthorized access or race conditions. Proper state file management not only enhances security but also supports scalable, collaborative infrastructure automation across cloud environments such as AWS, Azure, and GCP.

Implementing Access Controls for State Management

Terraform state files hold the blueprint of your infrastructure. Unrestricted access can lead to accidental deletions, unauthorized modifications, or security breaches. Implementing proper access controls is essential to securing Terraform state files and ensuring that only authorized users can modify or read sensitive infrastructure data.

This section delves into Role-Based Access Control (RBAC), integration with cloud Identity and Access Management (IAM) systems, access auditing, and multi-team collaboration strategies.

Role-Based Access Control (RBAC) and IAM Integration for State Management

Role-Based Access Control (RBAC) and Identity and Access Management (IAM) are essential for securing Terraform state files. RBAC limits access by assigning permissions to roles rather than individual users, helping enforce the principle of least privilege. IAM services, such as AWS IAM, Azure AD, and GCP IAM, allow you to define specific permissions for users, roles, or services interacting with your infrastructure. By integrating these systems with Terraform's state files, you can enforce secure, scalable access control. When setting up state management, both RBAC and IAM ensure that only authorized users or services can interact with Terraform state files, reducing the risk of unauthorized access or changes.

RBAC works by creating roles for different tasks, such as "**`Admin`**," "**`Developer`**," and "**`Auditor`**," and then assigning permissions to those roles based on the required level of access. Users are then mapped to these roles, controlling their access to the state files. For IAM, policies define what actions users or roles can perform, and these policies are linked to specific Terraform backend configurations. Authentication is enforced through IAM, ensuring that only authorized entities are able to access or modify state files. The use of IAM tools allows for more granular control and flexibility in managing Terraform's state file access across cloud environments.

The following are some benefits of using RBAC and IAM:

- **Granular Access Control:** RBAC allows fine-grained control over who can access and modify Terraform state files by assigning specific roles with tailored permissions, reducing the risk of unauthorized state changes.

- **Centralized Identity Management:** IAM services offer centralized control over identities, enabling administrators to define, enforce, and audit permissions across their entire infrastructure, rather than managing access individually.
- **Scalability:** Both RBAC and IAM scale effectively, as changes to permissions or roles can be made easily without needing to update individual user accounts.
- **Integration with MFA and Temporary Credentials:** Both RBAC and IAM services support Multi-Factor Authentication (MFA) and temporary credentials (for example, AWS STS, Azure Managed Identities, GCP Workload Identity), enhancing security by limiting access duration and reducing exposure to risk.

```
{
  "Version": "2012-10-17",
  "Statement": [
    {
      "Effect": "Allow",
      "Action": [
        "s3:GetObject"
      ],
      "Resource": "arn:aws:s3:::my-terraform-state/*",
      "Principal": {
        "AWS": "arn:aws:iam::123456789012:role/TerraformReadOnlyRole"
      }
    }
  ]
}
```

This example shows an IAM policy that grants read-only access to an AWS S3 bucket string Terraform state files to an IAM role.

```
{
  "bindings": [
    {
      "role": "Storage Blob Data Reader",
      "members": [
        "user:example@domain.com"
      ]
    }
  ]
}
```

The aforementioned example assigns the **Storage Blob Data Reader** role to a user for read-only access to an Azure Blob Storage container where Terraform state files are stored.

```
{
  "bindings": [
    {
      "role": "roles/storage.objectViewer",
      "members": [
        "user:example@domain.com"
      ]
    }
  ]
}
```

The aforementioned IAM policy grants **roles/storage.objectViewer** to a user, allowing them to read the Terraform state files stored in a GCS bucket.

Auditing Access Logs

Auditing access logs for resources managed using Terraform is essential for ensuring transparency, security, and compliance across cloud environments such as AWS, GCP, and Azure. By tracking interactions with Terraform state files, teams can identify who accessed the files, what actions were performed, and when changes occurred. Access logs are generated by cloud-native logging services such as AWS CloudTrail, Azure Monitor, and GCP Logging. These logs provide detailed insights, including user activity, resource modifications, and access timestamps. Immutable logs safeguard data integrity, while integrations with SIEM tools enable real-time monitoring and streamlined security investigations.

To maximize the value of access auditing, organizations should enable comprehensive logging for all Terraform state file interactions and implement anomaly detection to flag unauthorized activities. Logs can be filtered by criteria such as user, action, or resource for granular analysis. Best practices include retaining logs for a minimum of 90 days to support compliance and forensic investigations and automating alerts for unusual patterns. With proper auditing and monitoring, teams can strengthen their security posture and maintain robust oversight of Terraform-managed infrastructure.

Securing Multi-Team Access

Effective multi-team access management is critical in large organizations where multiple teams collaboratively manage infrastructure using shared Terraform state files. Without proper segmentation and access controls, there is a heightened risk of accidental overwrites, unauthorized modifications, and security breaches. To mitigate these challenges, organizations can leverage strategies such as separating state files by environment (for example, development, staging, production) and using Terraform workspaces to isolate state files for different teams or projects. These approaches help maintain order and ensure that changes in one environment do not inadvertently affect others.

Best practices for multi-team state management include creating environment-specific IAM roles to enforce granular access controls, using path-based segregation for state files, and implementing team-based prefixes in remote backends for easier identification and access restriction. These measures ensure that each team operates within its designated scope, reducing conflicts and enhancing security. By combining these techniques, organizations can foster secure, efficient, and collaborative state management workflows across teams.

```
bucket = "my-terraform-state"
key    = "dev/team-a/terraform.tfstate"
```

The preceding example demonstrates path-based segregation of state files by environment in AWS. Similar configurations can be implemented in GCP and Azure to achieve the same level of organization and environment-specific state management.

Implementing access controls for Terraform state management is vital to safeguarding infrastructure from unauthorized modifications. By integrating RBAC and IAM, organizations can ensure their state files remain secure and auditable. This layered approach not only prevents accidental overwrites but also ensures compliance across cloud environments such as AWS, Azure, and GCP.

Managing Multiple Environments (Development, Staging, Production) Securely

Managing cloud infrastructure across development, staging, and production environments can quickly become complex. A misconfiguration in one environment can affect deployments in others, leading to downtime or security vulnerabilities. Securely managing multiple environments in

Terraform ensures consistency, minimizes risk, and allows teams to isolate infrastructure changes during testing and development.

In this section, we explore the use of Terraform workspaces, environment-specific configurations, secure shared resources, automated deployments, and handling dependencies. These practices not only streamline deployment pipelines but also bolster security across different environments.

Environment-Specific Configuration Management

Environment-specific configuration in Terraform enables tailored infrastructure management for development, staging, and production environments while minimizing code duplication. By leveraging distinct variable files (**.tfvars**), you can define unique settings such as instance sizes, regions, and credentials for each environment. This approach simplifies managing multiple environments while ensuring configurations remain modular and reusable. For example, when deploying resources, developers can pass the appropriate environment-specific file using commands such as terraform **apply -var-file="env/dev.tfvars"**. Additionally, Terraform's conditional logic (for example, **count** or **for_each**) can dynamically deploy resources based on the specified environment, further enhancing customization and automation.

By isolating environment-specific details, teams can achieve a clear separation of configurations, making it easier to scale infrastructure as the organization grows. This practice avoids redundancy by centralizing shared components into reusable modules, which can then be parameterized for each environment. Such a structure not only reduces errors but also promotes collaboration by offering a clean, logical way to organize infrastructure as code.

To optimize environment-specific configuration management, sensitive data such as API keys and credentials should be securely stored in secret managers such as AWS Secrets Manager, Azure Key Vault, or GCP Secret Manager. This ensures sensitive information is not exposed in plain text. Furthermore, it is crucial to use **.gitignore** to exclude environment-specific files from being accidentally committed to version control repositories, protecting sensitive information from exposure. Version control should still be implemented for non-sensitive **.tfvars** files, enabling tracking of changes and rollback when needed. By following these practices, teams can maintain secure, efficient, and scalable infrastructure across multiple environments.

```
# dev.tfvars
environment = "dev"
instance_size = "Standard_B2s"

# prod.tfvars
environment = "prod"
instance_size = "Standard_D4s_v3"
```

The preceding example demonstrates the declaration of distinct instance sizes for different environments, organized within separate **.tfvars** files for the Azure cloud environment.

Securing Shared Resources across Environments

Shared resources, such as networks, databases, or IAM policies, are infrastructure components that span multiple environments (for example, development, staging, and production). Managing these shared resources effectively is crucial for maintaining security and operational efficiency across all environments. Misconfigurations or weak security controls in shared resources can introduce vulnerabilities, making them a critical aspect of environment-specific configuration management.

To manage shared resources, Terraform leverages reusable modules. For example, a module for VPC/VNet creation can be designed to provide consistent networking configurations across all environments. Access to these resources is controlled using environment-specific IAM policies that restrict who can perform actions such as read, write, or administrative operations. Additionally, sensitive shared resources, such as databases, are secured using encryption mechanisms both at rest and in transit. Tags or labels are often applied to distinguish resources by environment, facilitating granular access control and resource tracking.

Terraform simplifies the management of shared resources by ensuring consistency across environments, reducing operational overhead through reusability, and enabling centralized enforcement of security policies. To maximize these benefits, follow best practices such as encrypting shared resources with tools such as AWS KMS, Azure Key Vault, or GCP KMS to protect sensitive data. Create Terraform modules for common shared resources to avoid code duplication and enforce uniformity. Implement strict IAM role separation to ensure that read, write, and administrative access are restricted based on user roles and environmental needs. This layered approach helps maintain both security and efficiency in managing shared infrastructure.

```
resource "google_storage_bucket" "shared" {
  name     = "shared-state"
  location = "US"

  uniform_bucket_level_access = true

  lifecycle_rule {
    action {
      type = "Delete"
    }
    condition {
      age = 30
    }
  }
}

resource "google_storage_bucket_iam_binding" "binding" {
  bucket = google_storage_bucket.shared.name
  role   = "roles/storage.objectViewer"

  members = [
    "serviceAccount:dev-access@my-project.iam.gserviceaccount.com",
    "serviceAccount:prod-access@my-project.iam.gserviceaccount.com"
  ]
}
```

The aforementioned snippet demonstrates configuring environment-specific IAM policies for a GCP bucket, which ensures controlled and isolated access for **dev** and **prod** environments.

```
resource "aws_s3_bucket" "shared" {
  bucket = "shared-state"
  force_destroy = true
  tags = {
    Environment = "shared"
  }
}

resource "aws_s3_bucket_policy" "shared_policy" {
  bucket = aws_s3_bucket.shared.id

  policy = jsonencode({
    Version = "2012-10-17"
    Statement = [
```

```
      {
        Effect    = "Allow"
        Principal = {
          AWS = [
            "arn:aws:iam::123456789012:role/dev-access",
            "arn:aws:iam::123456789012:role/prod-access"
          ]
        }
        Action   = ["s3:GetObject", "s3:ListBucket"]
        Resource = [
          "${aws_s3_bucket.shared.arn}",
          "${aws_s3_bucket.shared.arn}/*"
        ]
      }
    ]
  })
}
```

This example provisions an S3 bucket with a bucket policy and assigns IAM role-based access for both **dev** and **prod** environments.

```
resource "azurerm_storage_account" "shared" {
  name                     = "sharedstateacct"
  resource_group_name      = azurerm_resource_group.rg.name
  location                 = azurerm_resource_group.rg.location
  account_tier             = "Standard"
  account_replication_type = "LRS"

  blob_properties {
    delete_retention_policy {
      days = 30
    }
  }

  tags = {
    Environment = "shared"
  }
}

resource "azurerm_storage_container" "shared" {
  name                  = "shared-state"
  storage_account_name  = azurerm_storage_account.shared.name
  container_access_type = "private"
}

resource "azurerm_role_assignment" "dev_blob_reader" {
  scope                = azurerm_storage_account.shared.id
  role_definition_name = "Storage Blob Data Reader"
  principal_id         = azuread_service_principal.dev.id
}

resource "azurerm_role_assignment" "prod_blob_reader" {
  scope                = azurerm_storage_account.shared.id
  role_definition_name = "Storage Blob Data Reader"
  principal_id         = azuread_service_principal.prod.id
}
```

This example Terraform snippet provisions a Blob Storage container with a retention policy and assigns reader roles to **dev** and **prod** service principals.

Handling Environment-Specific Dependencies

In Terraform, managing dependencies between environments is critical to ensure resources are allocated optimally and securely. Different environments, such as development, staging, and production, often have unique requirements for resources such as databases, virtual machines, or networking components. By enabling conditional deployment, Terraform ensures that only the necessary resources are provisioned for each environment, reducing costs and preventing unnecessary complexity. For example, a development environment may use a smaller database size, while production requires high-performance configurations. Conditional deployment ensures that these needs are met without duplicating infrastructure code.

Terraform achieves environment-specific dependency management through parameterized modules and conditional logic. External dependencies such as DNS entries or SSL certificates are defined separately for each environment, often using variables or **.tfvars** files. Modules allow reusability, and parameters can be passed to customize behavior for each environment. Terraform's **count** and **for_each** constructs enable conditional provisioning, ensuring that resources are deployed only when required. This flexibility not only simplifies infrastructure management but also provides dynamic provisioning to meet environment-specific scaling needs.

To optimize dependency management, several best practices can be followed. Using **count** or **for_each** ensures efficient conditional deployment, while dependency locking prevents drift by freezing versions of modules and providers. Regular updates of dependencies, such as external libraries or APIs, help mitigate vulnerabilities and ensure compatibility with the latest features. Additionally, environment-specific configurations can be stored in dedicated files, promoting clarity and maintainability. Adhering to these practices ensures seamless management of environment-specific dependencies, reducing operational overhead and enhancing security.

```
resource "aws_db_instance" "db" {
  count = terraform.workspace == "prod" || terraform.workspace == "dev" ? 1 : 0

  allocated_storage = terraform.workspace == "prod" ? 100 : 20
  engine            = "mysql"
  instance_class    = terraform.workspace == "prod" ? "db.t3.medium" : "db.
t3.micro"
}
```

The provided example creates an AWS DB instance with allocated storage configured based on the environment type.

Managing multiple environments in Terraform not only promotes infrastructure consistency but also enhances security. By leveraging workspaces, automating deployments, and securing shared resources, teams can confidently deploy infrastructure across development, staging, and production environments. This structured approach minimizes risks, simplifies operations, and enforces robust security postures across cloud platforms such as AWS, Azure, and GCP.

Leveraging GitOps and Version Control for Infrastructure Automation

In modern cloud environments, Infrastructure-as-Code (IaC) is the foundation of scalable and reliable deployments. However, managing infrastructure at scale introduces challenges around consistency, drift, and collaboration. GitOps, a methodology that uses Git repositories as the single source of truth for infrastructure automation, offers a robust solution by combining Git workflows with Terraform.

This section explores how to implement GitOps workflows, manage Terraform module versions, address drift, and enhance collaboration across distributed teams.

Setting Up a GitOps Workflow for Terraform

GitOps is a modern DevOps practice that leverages Git repositories as the single source of truth for managing infrastructure and application deployments. This approach ensures all configuration changes are version-controlled, traceable, and auditable. Instead of applying changes directly to infrastructure, developers and operators make updates through Git commits, fostering a collaborative and transparent workflow.

In a GitOps setup for Terraform, the infrastructure code resides in a Git repository. Any updates are made via Pull Requests (PRs), which are reviewed and approved before merging. These changes trigger automated workflows through CI/CD pipelines powered by tools such as GitHub Actions, GitLab CI, or Jenkins. Once approved, Terraform commands (`init`, `plan`, and `apply`) are executed, applying the changes to the target environment. This process not only automates deployments but also maintains consistency across environments, as Git acts as the authoritative source for the infrastructure state.

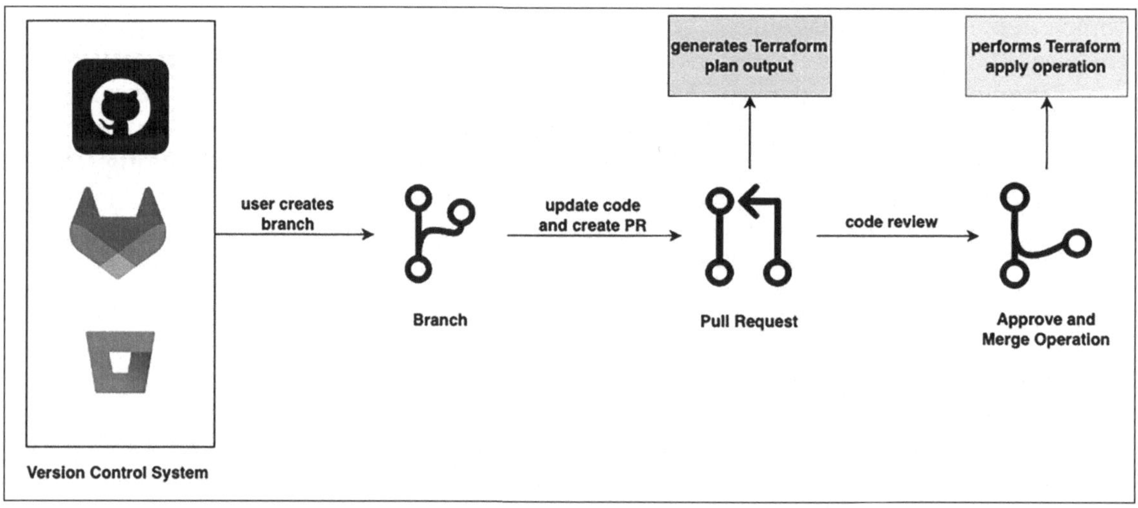

Figure 2.2: *Gitflow*

The following are some features and best practices of GitOps for Terraform:

- **Version-Controlled Infrastructure**: Every change to Terraform configurations is logged, providing a clear history and enabling easy rollbacks if needed.
- **Automated Deployments**: CI/CD pipelines ensure consistent application of changes across environments, reducing manual intervention.
- **Immutable Records**: Deployment history and state are permanently stored in Git, creating an auditable trail.
- **Environment-Specific Repositories**: Organize code by environment (for example, dev, staging, prod) to ensure isolated and manageable deployments.
- **Protected Branches**: Safeguard critical branches (such as main or master) to prevent unauthorized modifications.
- **Automated Workflows**: Integrate Terraform's lifecycle commands (`init`, `plan`, `apply`) into CI/CD pipelines to enforce automation.

- **Security and Access Control**: Use Git repository permissions to control who can propose, review, and approve changes.
- **Regular Audits**: Periodically review repository structures and workflows to ensure alignment with organizational policies.

The following is an example of a GitLab CI pipeline for a Terraform GitOps workflow:

```
stages:
  - plan
  - apply

plan:
  script:
    - terraform init
    - terraform plan -out=tfplan
  artifacts:
    paths:
      - tfplan

apply:
  script:
    - terraform apply tfplan
  when: manual
```

Versioning Terraform Modules

Versioning Terraform modules is crucial for ensuring consistency, stability, and predictability when managing reusable infrastructure components. Modules encapsulate common patterns, but without strict version control, updates can introduce breaking changes across environments. By adopting semantic versioning (for example, **`v1.0.0`**), teams can establish clear expectations for updates, whether they involve minor improvements, new features, or significant changes.

Modules are typically hosted in private or public registries such as Terraform Cloud or GitHub. Projects integrate these modules by referencing specific version constraints, such as **`>=1.0`**, **`<2.0`**. This ensures that updates adhere to predefined compatibility rules. Changes to modules, including version bumps, are managed through Pull Requests (PRs), enabling peer review and testing before deployment. This controlled process mitigates risks and ensures smooth updates across all environments.

The following are some features and best practices of versioning Terraform modules:

- **Predictable Infrastructure Updates**: Semantic versioning ensures updates are transparent and predictable, minimizing disruptions.
- **Reusable and Standardized Components**: Versioning facilitates the reuse of well-tested modules, improving consistency across projects.
- **Rollback Support**: Previous module versions can be easily restored in case of errors or compatibility issues.
- **Adopt Semantic Versioning**: Follow the **`MAJOR.MINOR.PATCH`** convention to communicate the nature of changes clearly.
- **Lock Module Versions**: Use version constraints in your Terraform configurations (for example, **`required_version`**) to prevent unintended updates.
- **Automate Testing**: Implement automated tests for new module versions in staging environments before applying changes to production.
- **Document Module Changes**: Maintain clear release notes or change logs for each version to streamline adoption.

- **Review and Approve Updates**: Use PRs to control and audit module version upgrades, ensuring proper oversight.

Following is an example of AWS S3 Module Versioning:

```
module "s3_bucket" {
  source  = "terraform-aws-modules/s3-bucket/aws"
  version = "~> 3.0"
}
```

Addressing Terraform Drift with GitOps

Terraform drift occurs when the actual infrastructure in a cloud environment deviates from the state declared in Terraform configurations, leading to potential inconsistencies, performance issues, or security risks. GitOps provides a robust solution to address this challenge by treating Git as the single source of truth for infrastructure configurations. The GitOps approach involves continuously reconciling infrastructure with the desired state stored in Git repositories, ensuring that discrepancies are promptly identified and resolved. Terraform workflows are often integrated into GitOps pipelines, leveraging automation to maintain alignment between configurations and live infrastructure.

Drift detection typically involves running periodic Terraform commands, such as `terraform plan`, through cron jobs or scheduled CI/CD pipelines. These runs compare the current infrastructure state with the desired state defined in the Terraform configuration files. Any discrepancies are flagged as drift, triggering alerts to notify teams or initiating automated remediation workflows. By incorporating drift management into GitOps workflows, organizations can ensure infrastructure stability and consistency across all environments, from development to production.

Adopting GitOps for drift management comes with several advantages. Continuous reconciliation prevents configuration drift by ensuring infrastructure changes align with the declared state. Automated remediation can quickly resolve discrepancies, particularly in non-production environments, without manual intervention. To maximize the benefits, best practices include regularly running Terraform plan to monitor drift, automating drift correction in lower environments to streamline workflows, and locking sensitive resources with the **`prevent_destroy`** flag to safeguard critical infrastructure. Together, these practices enhance operational efficiency while reducing the risks associated with drift.

The following is the pipeline configuration snippet for scheduled Terraform drift detection using the **`terraform plan`** command:

```
name: Drift Detection
on:
  schedule:
    - cron: "0 3 * * *"
jobs:
  drift:
    runs-on: ubuntu-latest
    steps:
      - uses: hashicorp/setup-terraform@v1
      - run: terraform plan
```

Collaborating with Teams Using Version Control

Version control systems (VCS) such as Git play a vital role in enabling teams to collaborate effectively on Infrastructure as Code (IaC) projects, particularly with Terraform. By maintaining all Terraform configurations in a Git repository, version control ensures transparency, traceability, and reversibility of changes. Distributed teams can work simultaneously on different features or environments without conflicts, thanks to structured workflows facilitated by version control. Each engineer works on feature branches, contributing incremental updates to infrastructure configurations. Merging these changes into the main branch occurs only after thorough peer reviews through pull requests (PRs), promoting accountability and reducing errors.

Version tags (for example, **`v1.0.0`**) are employed to mark stable releases of infrastructure configurations, ensuring a predictable deployment process across environments. This practice aligns with GitOps principles, where Git serves as the single source of truth. Automated CI/CD pipelines triggered by PRs streamline the testing and deployment of changes, further enhancing collaboration and efficiency. Through version control, teams achieve seamless parallel development, transparent auditing of modifications, and a robust mechanism to revert to previous states if necessary, fostering a secure and scalable infrastructure management process.

Following is an example of a branching strategy for collaboration in a version control system:

```
git checkout -b feature/add-networking
git commit -am "Add VPC for staging"
git push origin feature/add-networking
```

Leveraging GitOps and version control for Terraform automation enhances the scalability, security, and reliability of infrastructure deployments. By integrating Git workflows, versioning modules, conducting code reviews, and automating drift detection, organizations can enforce best practices while maintaining infrastructure as a single source of truth. This collaborative and automated approach not only reduces human error but also accelerates the delivery of secure cloud environments.

Conclusion

In this chapter, we established a comprehensive approach to setting up and securing Terraform environments, laying the groundwork for scalable and secure infrastructure management. By focusing on the installation and configuration of Terraform across multi-cloud and on-premises environments, readers gained insights into selecting the appropriate Terraform versions, configuring cloud providers, and leveraging provider-specific features. Automation of Terraform installation and updates ensures consistency across teams, streamlining the deployment process and reducing manual overhead. This foundational setup not only enhances operational efficiency but also prepares organizations to scale infrastructure securely across AWS, Azure, and GCP.

This chapter also discussed the detailed strategies for safeguarding Terraform state files using remote backends, encryption, and state file locking. By implementing Role-Based Access Control (RBAC) and IAM policies, access to critical infrastructure data is tightly controlled, reducing the risk of unauthorized changes or breaches. Managing multiple environments with environment-specific configurations and CI/CD pipelines ensures the separation of concerns while enabling safe collaboration across teams. Finally, integrating GitOps and version control practices reinforces infrastructure security, mitigates drift, and promotes transparency across distributed teams. This holistic approach empowers organizations to harness the full potential of Terraform, while maintaining robust security postures across their cloud environments.

In the next chapter, we will explore advanced Terraform concepts, including designing reusable modules, handling sensitive data securely, and managing workspaces for multi-environment deployments. It also covers configuring remote execution and debugging Terraform configurations effectively.

Questions and Answers

1. **How to choose the right Terraform version for cloud security needs?**

   Choosing the right Terraform version depends on compatibility, stability, and security updates. Terraform releases frequently introduced new features, deprecate older functionality, and fix security vulnerabilities. The following are some best practices:

   - **Using the latest stable version:** Ensures access to security patches and new features.
   - **Matching provider requirements:** Some Terraform providers (AWS, GCP, Azure) may require specific versions.
   - **Version pinning in code:** Use `terraform.required_version` in terraform blocks to enforce consistency across teams.
   - **Managing upgrades:** Test updates in non-production environments before rolling them out.

   For enterprises, Terraform Cloud and Terraform Enterprise provide version control features, making it easier to enforce consistency across teams.

2. **Why is securing Terraform state files crucial, and what best practices should be followed?**

   Terraform state files contain sensitive information, such as IAM credentials, database passwords, and network configurations. If compromised, they can expose critical infrastructure secrets. The following are some best practices for securing state files:

   - **Using remote backends:** Store state files securely in services such as AWS S3 with DynamoDB locking, GCP Cloud Storage, or Azure Blob Storage.
   - **Encrypting state files:** Use encryption mechanisms (for example, AWS KMS, GCP CMEK, and Azure SSE) to protect the stored data.
   - **State file locking:** Prevent conflicts by enabling state locking with DynamoDB, Cloud Storage locks, or Azure Blob Locks.
   - **Backup and versioning:** Maintain snapshots of state files for recovery in case of corruption or accidental deletions.

   By implementing these security controls, organizations can mitigate the risk of state file leaks and unauthorized modifications.

3. **How does Role-Based Access Control (RBAC) improve Terraform state management security?**

   RBAC ensures that only authorized users and services can access, modify, or manage Terraform state files. Integrating RBAC with IAM policies improves security in the following ways:

   - **Granular access control:** Assign least privilege access, ensuring that users can only perform permitted actions (for example, read-only for auditors, full access for admins).
   - **IAM role integration:** Use AWS IAM policies, GCP IAM bindings, or Azure RBAC to enforce access controls for Terraform backends.
   - **Auditing and logging:** Enable access logging to track who accessed or modified state files, enhancing visibility.
   - **Securing multi-team access:** Use workspaces and permissions to separate environments (development, staging, production) while maintaining strict controls.

   Implementing RBAC ensures that Terraform state files remain secure, minimizing the risk of unauthorized access or accidental modifications.

4. **What are the best practices for managing multiple environments securely in Terraform?**

   Managing multiple environments (development, staging, production) in Terraform requires proper configuration management to prevent security misconfigurations. The following are some best practices:

   - **Using environment-specific configuration files:** Store environment variables separately using Terraform workspaces, backend configurations, or `.tfvars` files.
   - **Securing shared resources:** Apply IAM roles and network policies to control access to shared infrastructure across environments.
   - **Handling dependencies cautiously:** Ensure that resource dependencies are clearly defined using `depends_on` to prevent unintended changes.
   - **Automating environment provisioning:** Use CI/CD pipelines to deploy Terraform configurations with environment-specific parameters.

   By structuring Terraform configurations properly, organizations can avoid misconfigurations and accidental cross-environment access.

5. **How does GitOps enhance Terraform infrastructure security and automation?**

   GitOps integrates Terraform with version control systems (for example, GitHub, GitLab, Bitbucket) to ensure infrastructure security and automation. The following are some key benefits:

   - **Immutable infrastructure:** All changes are reviewed, approved, and stored in Git repositories before deployment.
   - **Versioning for traceability:** Changes in Terraform code are tracked using commits and pull requests, reducing the risk of unauthorized modifications.
   - **Addressing terraform drift:** By comparing live infrastructure state with the desired state in Git, teams can detect and remediate drift automatically.
   - **Collaborative workflows:** Teams can collaborate using branching strategies, pull requests, and peer reviews to enforce security policies.

   GitOps enhances Terraform security by enforcing structured, version-controlled deployments while minimizing misconfigurations and human errors.

CHAPTER 3

Advanced Terraform Core Concepts

Introduction

As organizations scale their infrastructure, Terraform's true power lies in its ability to promote reusability, standardization, and efficiency across complex cloud environments. This chapter delves into advanced Terraform core concepts that form the backbone of scalable and secure Infrastructure as Code (IaC) practices. From designing reusable modules to managing multi-environment deployments with workspaces, these techniques ensure consistency, enhance collaboration, and reduce operational overhead. The sections ahead offer a structured approach to mastering modular architecture, handling sensitive data, and automating environment provisioning critical skills for deploying resilient cloud infrastructures.

Building on foundational Terraform knowledge, this chapter explores the nuances of remote execution, variable precedence, and state isolation, enabling teams to secure and optimize their cloud environments effectively. Readers will gain practical insights into implementing Terraform Cloud, automating CI/CD pipelines, and troubleshooting infrastructure issues with precision. By mastering these advanced concepts, practitioners can confidently tackle large-scale cloud deployments, while adhering to the best practices for security, maintainability, and scalability.

Structure

In this chapter, we will cover the following topics:

- Designing and Structuring Reusable Modules
  - Fundamentals of Terraform Modules
  - Structuring Module Repositories
  - Parameterizing Modules with Variables
  - Composing Infrastructure with Nested Modules
  - Module Versioning and Lifecycle Management
  - Publishing and Sharing Modules
- Using Variables, Outputs, and Handling Sensitive Data Securely
  - Defining and Using Input Variables
  - Setting Up Default Values and Type Constraints
  - Leveraging Output Variables
  - Securely Handling Sensitive Data
  - Variable Precedence and Overrides

- Managing Workspaces for Multi-Environment Deployments
  - Understanding Terraform Workspaces
  - Managing Terraform Workspaces
  - Mapping Workspaces to Environments
  - Isolating State Files by Workspace
  - Workspace Limitations and Alternatives
  - Automating Workspace Management
- Configuring Remote Execution with Terraform Cloud and Alternatives
  - Introduction to Remote Execution
  - Setting Up Terraform Cloud
  - Remote Execution with CI/CD Tools
  - Managing Access Control in Remote Execution
- Debugging and Troubleshooting Terraform Configurations
  - Understanding Terraform Debug Logs
  - Resolving Resource Drift and State Issues
  - Using Terraform Console for Testing
  - Analyzing Dependency Graphs
  - Validating and Formatting Configurations

Designing and Structuring Reusable Modules

Terraform modules are the backbone of scalable and maintainable Infrastructure as Code (IaC). They allow cloud engineers to abstract, encapsulate, and reuse infrastructure configurations, enabling consistency across multiple environments and projects. In this section, we explore the vital aspects of designing Terraform modules that are robust, adaptable, and efficient for long-term cloud infrastructure management.

Fundamentals of Terraform Modules

Terraform modules are essential building blocks that encapsulate multiple resources into a single, reusable unit. These modules can range from simple configurations containing a single resource to intricate setups with multiple interconnected resources, such as virtual networks, compute instances, and databases. By consolidating related resources, modules enable teams to standardize their infrastructure configurations, promote reusability, and reduce redundancy. They also enhance collaboration by providing a clear structure, and separating different parts of the infrastructure into manageable units, making it easier to scale and maintain as environments grow in complexity.

Terraform modules operate on a hierarchical structure. At the top level, the root module serves as the primary entry point for running Terraform commands such as **`terraform plan`** or **`terraform apply`**. This root module typically contains the core configuration files (**`main.tf`**, **`variables.tf`**, **`outputs.tf`**) and calls child modules to manage specific aspects of the infrastructure. Child modules are modular components that can be defined locally in directories or sourced externally from registries such as the Terraform Registry or repositories such as GitHub. This modular design allows teams to integrate proven configurations from trusted sources or share custom-built modules across projects, ensuring consistency and efficiency in managing cloud infrastructure.

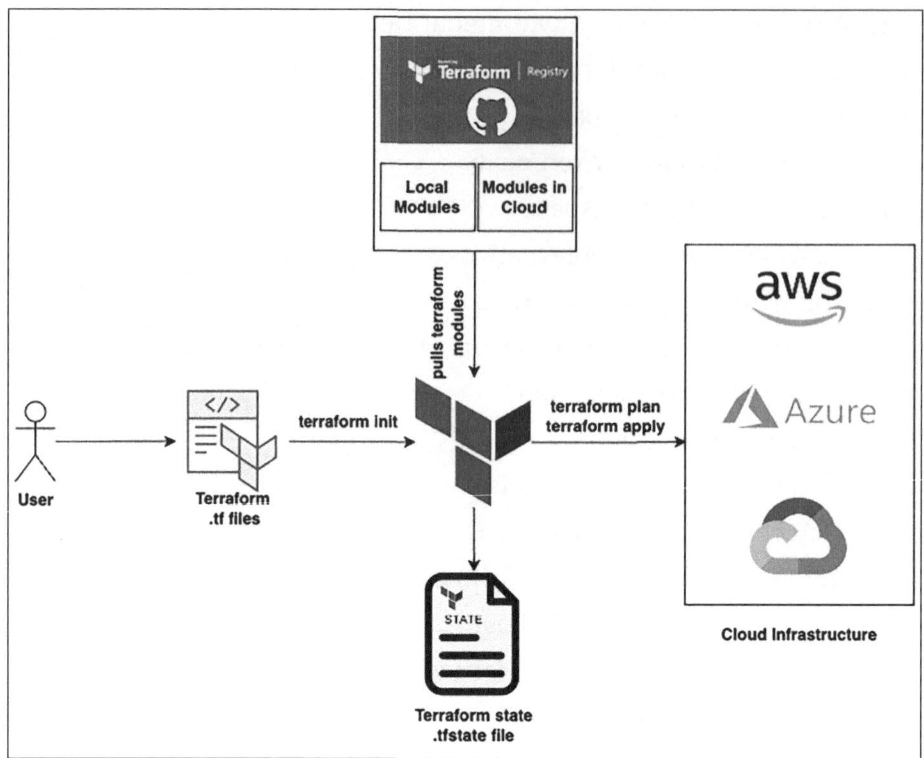

Figure 3.1: *Terraform modules*

```
Module "network" {
  source = "./modules/network"
  vpc_cidr = "10.0.0.0/16"
}
```

This example shows a root module calling a network child module by specifying a source path.

The following are some features and benefits of Terraform modules:

- **Reusability:** Terraform modules streamline workflows by enabling the reuse of standardized configurations across various projects, minimizing redundancy.
- **Consistency:** They enforce uniform patterns for infrastructure provisioning, helping prevent configuration drift, and ensuring reliable deployments.
- **Abstraction:** Modules simplify complex setups by encapsulating intricate configurations behind intuitive and manageable interfaces.
- **Scalability:** By leveraging parameterized inputs, modules efficiently scale to accommodate diverse environments and infrastructure needs.

Structuring Module Repositories

Effectively organizing Terraform modules ensures that infrastructure remains scalable, comprehensible, and easy to manage, even as projects grow in complexity. Proper structure and separation of concerns foster collaboration among team members, reduce the risk of misconfigurations, and facilitate the reuse of code across different environments and teams. By adhering to a standardized approach, teams can ensure a seamless development and deployment process.

A well-structured module repository typically follows a hierarchical layout. For example:

```
/modules
   |-> /network
       |-> main.tf
       |-> variables.tf
       |-> outputs.tf
   |-> /compute
       |-> main.tf
       |-> variables.tf
       |-> outputs.tf
```

- **main.tf**: Houses the core resource definitions, such as VPCs, compute instances, or load balancers, specific to the module.
- **variables.tf**: Declares input variables to customize the module's behavior for various use cases. These inputs allow flexibility without modifying the module's core logic.
- **outputs.tf**: Defines outputs that export essential attributes, such as resource IDs or IP addresses, enabling other modules or resources to reference them.

Each cloud provider's modules should be tailored to address its specific resource offerings:

- **AWS**: Individual modules can handle distinct components such as VPC, EC2 instances, S3 buckets, and RDS databases.
- **GCP**: Common modules include those for VPC, Google Kubernetes Engine (GKE) clusters, and Cloud Storage buckets.
- **Azure**: Modules may focus on resources such as Virtual Networks, Azure Kubernetes Service (AKS) clusters, and Blob Storage accounts.

By separating resources into distinct modules, teams can maintain modularity, simplify troubleshooting, and enable focused updates. This approach not only improves the organization but also enhances the reusability and scalability of Terraform configurations.

Parameterizing Modules with Variables

In Terraform, variables are essential for creating adaptable and versatile modules, enabling dynamic customization and reuse across diverse environments and configurations. By defining inputs in a **variables.tf** file, modules can support varied use cases, such as instance sizes, network ranges, or environment-specific tags, without hard-coded values. This flexibility ensures a single module can function seamlessly across development, staging, and production environments. Customizable deployments are a key benefit, allowing modules to adapt to specific requirements, such as networking CIDR ranges or compute scaling configurations, while avoiding code duplication.

Variables also enhance scalability, enabling horizontal scaling by dynamically passing instance counts or resource allocations. Outputs, defined in an **outputs.tf** file, complement variables by exporting critical resource attributes, such as IDs or IP addresses, for integration with other modules or external systems. Together, variables and outputs reduce operational overhead, improve maintainability, and support modular, environment-agnostic infrastructure, ensuring teams can efficiently manage infrastructure as it evolves alongside application demands.

Following is an example of defining a Terraform module for a VPC in GCP, parameterizing it with a variable (**vpc_cidr**), and then invoking the module with a specific value:

```
# modules/network/main.tf
resource "google_compute_network" "vpc" {
  name                    = "custom-vpc"
  auto_create_subnetworks = false
  routing_mode                         = "REGIONAL"
```

```
}

resource "google_compute_subnetwork" "subnet" {
  name                = "custom-subnet"
  network             = google_compute_network.vpc.id
  ip_cidr_range       = var.vpc_cidr
  region              = "us-central1"
}

# modules/network/variables.tf
variable "vpc_cidr" {
  description         = "CIDR block for the VPC"
  type                = string
}

# modules/network/outputs.tf
output "vpc_id" {
  value = google_compute_network.vpc.id
}

output "subnet_id" {
  value = google_compute_subnetwork.subnet.id
}

# main.tf Calling the module in the root configuration
module "network" {
  source     = "./modules/network"
  vpc_cidr   = "10.1.0.0/16"
}

output "vpc_id" {
  value = module.network.vpc_id
}

output "subnet_id" {
  value = module.network.subnet_id
}
```

The **`vpc_cidr`** variable is declared in the **`variables.tf`** file within the module, enabling dynamic configuration of the CIDR block for flexibility across environments. This variable is then utilized in the module's resource definitions, such as configuring a GCP subnetwork. The module is invoked in the root configuration by specifying its path using the **`source`** attribute and passing the desired value (**`10.1.0.0/16`**) to the **`vpc_cidr`** variable. Additionally, the module defines outputs, such as the VPC and Subnet IDs, which can be accessed in the root configuration for further integration or use in other Terraform modules.

Composing Infrastructure with Nested Modules

Nested modules in Terraform are an advanced technique that enables you to compose smaller, focused modules into larger, higher-level abstractions. By nesting modules, complex infrastructure deployments can be organized into manageable and logical layers, promoting clarity and reusability. For instance, a top-level module can invoke separate nested modules for networking, compute resources, and database configurations, each designed to handle its specific responsibilities. This approach reduces redundancy and allows teams to address individual components independently while maintaining a coherent infrastructure design.

Adopting a layered approach with nested modules ensures a clear separation of concerns, making the codebase easier to manage and scale. To maintain proper resource dependencies, the `depends_on` attribute can enforce the correct order of resource creation, avoiding conflicts during deployment. While nested modules simplify large deployments and foster modular design, they can also introduce challenges, such as debugging and updating interdependent modules. Understanding and managing these dependencies is crucial to avoid introducing unnecessary complexity, ensuring that the benefits of nested modules outweigh potential drawbacks.

```
module "network" {
  source = "./modules/network"
}

module "application" {
  source     = "./modules/app"
  vpc_id     = module.network.vpc_id
  subnet_id = module.network.subnet_id
}

module "database" {
  source     = "./modules/db"
  vpc_id     = module.network.vpc_id
  depends_on = [module.application]
}
```

In this example, nested modules are used to structure infrastructure components into distinct layers. The **`network`** module provisions the foundational network resources, such as VPC and subnets, whose outputs (**`vpc_id`** and **`subnet_id`**) are passed as inputs to the **`application`** and **`database`** modules. This ensures that both application and database resources are correctly attached to the network. The **`database`** module includes a **`depends_on`** attribute to ensure that the application module is deployed first, reflecting a dependency hierarchy.

Module Versioning and Lifecycle Management

Module versioning and lifecycle management are essential practices in Terraform for maintaining stable and predictable infrastructure. Versioning allows teams to manage updates to Terraform modules without unintentionally introducing changes that could disrupt existing environments, especially in production. By applying a versioning strategy, teams can confidently update or roll back modules as needed while preserving the reliability of the infrastructure. This approach ensures that development and production environments remain consistent, reducing the risk of unexpected issues caused by untested module updates. A well-versioned module also facilitates collaboration across teams by clearly defining which iteration of a module is being used in specific deployments.

The use of semantic versioning, following the **`major.minor.patch`** format, is a widely adopted best practice for tracking module changes. Major versions increment signal-breaking changes, minor updates introduce backward-compatible features, and patch versions address bug fixes. Tagging stable releases and maintaining detailed documentation about updates, particularly breaking changes, helps teams transition smoothly between module versions. These practices not only enhance stability but also improve the maintainability of Terraform codebases by enabling a structured approach to the lifecycle management of modules. This is especially beneficial in multi-environment or multi-team setups, where clear version control is crucial for seamless operations.

```
module "network" {
  source  = "git::https://github.com/example/network.git//vpc?ref=v1.2.0"
}
```

In this example, the `network` module is version-pinned by referencing a specific tag (`v1.2.0`) in the Git repository, ensuring that only the defined version is used, thereby preventing unintended changes from future updates.

Publishing and Sharing Modules

Terraform modules facilitate seamless sharing of infrastructure configurations, enabling teams or organizations to promote consistency and reuse. Modules can be shared privately within teams or publicly via platforms such as the Terraform Registry. Private sharing often involves Git repositories or object storage solutions such as S3 or GCS, allowing teams to collaborate securely on customized modules tailored to their specific needs. Public sharing, on the other hand, makes modules widely available, allowing developers worldwide to leverage standardized infrastructure practices. Sharing modules ensures that teams can adopt consistent patterns, reduces duplication of effort, and promotes adherence to security baselines across environments, enhancing operational efficiency.

The following are the steps to publish a module on the Terraform registry:

- **Create a Repository**: Set up a GitHub repository following the Terraform naming conventions: `terraform-<provider>-<module>`.
- **Documentation**: Include a `README.md` file that explains the module's purpose, usage, and example configurations to help users understand its application.
- **Tagging for Versions**: Use Git tags (for example, `v1.0.0`) to indicate stable module versions, making it easier for users to adopt specific iterations.
- **Enable Public Visibility**: Ensure the repository is public and linked to a verified GitHub account for publishing on the Registry.

Publishing modules fosters standardization, making it easier for teams to reuse validated configurations, while also enforcing security and compliance requirements across multiple deployments. Public modules in the Terraform Registry can also benefit the broader Terraform community, promoting innovation and collaboration.

Designing reusable Terraform modules is key to creating scalable, consistent, and manageable infrastructure. By structuring repositories properly, parameterizing with variables, and leveraging nested modules, cloud engineers can significantly reduce complexity and improve efficiency. Version control and sharing further enhance module reusability and team collaboration. As cloud environments grow, well-architected Terraform modules become vital in maintaining order and reducing configuration drift, ultimately contributing to more secure and predictable infrastructure deployments.

Using Variables, Outputs, and Handling Sensitive Data Securely

Variables and outputs form the foundation for creating dynamic, flexible, and secure Terraform configurations. When managing cloud environments, infrastructure must be parameterized to adapt to different environments (development, staging, production) and handle sensitive data such as API keys, credentials, and secrets. This section delves into best practices for defining, securing, and structuring input and output variables to ensure infrastructure remains manageable, scalable, and secure.

Defining and Using Input Variables

Input variables in Terraform serve as a critical mechanism for parameterizing infrastructure configurations, enabling users to tailor deployments without altering the core codebase. By acting as dynamic placeholders, input variables allow developers to reuse the same configuration for different environments or requirements, such as varying instance sizes, CIDR ranges, or region settings. This modular approach not only simplifies infrastructure management but also minimizes the risk of errors that might arise from manually editing resource definitions. With input variables, a single module can cater to diverse scenarios, such as development, staging, and production, by simply adjusting variable values.

The workflow for using input variables is straightforward. Variables are declared in **`.tf`** files using the **`variable`** block, where attributes such as **`type`**, **`default`**, and **`description`** can be specified for clarity and control. These variables are then referenced within resources or modules using interpolation syntax. During execution, values for these variables can be provided in several ways: through environment variables, CLI flags, or variable definition files such as **`terraform.tfvars`**. This flexibility allows Terraform configurations to be adapted seamlessly to different contexts, enhancing both the scalability and maintainability of infrastructure as code.

```
#variables.tf
variable "vnet_address_space" {
  description = "Address space for the Virtual Network"
  type        = string
}

#main.tf
resource "azurerm_virtual_network" "main" {
  name                = "example-vnet"
  location            = "East US"
  resource_group_name = "example-rg"
  address_space       = [var.vnet_address_space]
}

#terraform.tfvars
vnet_address_space = "10.0.0.0/16"
```

In this example, the variable **`vnet_address_space`** is defined in the **`variables.tf`** file, allowing users to customize the address space of the Virtual Network (VNet). Within the **`azurerm_virtual_network`** resource in **`main.tf`**, this variable is referenced in the **`address_space`** attribute, enabling dynamic configuration of the VNet's CIDR block. The specific value **`10.0.0.0/16`** is assigned in the **`terraform.tfvars`** file, which Terraform automatically loads during execution.

Setting Up Default Values and Type Constraints

Terraform variables support default values and type constraints, providing a robust mechanism for enforcing configuration validation and minimizing the risk of errors. Default values serve as pre-defined inputs that are used when no specific value is provided, enabling seamless automation in scenarios where user input might be unnecessary. This feature is particularly useful for simplifying infrastructure deployments, as it allows modules to operate with minimal input while still maintaining flexibility for customization. Type constraints, on the other hand, validate input values to ensure they adhere to the expected data types, such as strings, numbers, or lists. Together, these capabilities create a framework for predictable and reliable infrastructure management.

The use of default values and type constraints offers significant benefits. Reliability is enhanced as configurations are guaranteed to conform to expected patterns, reducing the likelihood of deployment failures caused by invalid inputs. Automation is streamlined, as default values allow for unattended deployments, reducing the need for manual intervention during the provisioning process. Additionally, these safeguards improve security by mitigating the risk of misconfigurations that could lead to vulnerabilities or operational disruptions. By combining these features, Terraform empowers teams to build resilient and secure infrastructure with reduced complexity and increased efficiency.

The following is an example of defining a type and a default value for a variable:

```
variable "instance_type" {
  description = "Type of EC2 instance"
  type        = string
  default     = "t3.micro"
}
```

Following is an example of defining a constraint on a variable of type number, restricting its value to be between 1 and 10:

```
variable "instance_count" {
  description = "Number of instances"
  type        = number
  validation {
    condition     = var.instance_count > 0 && var.instance_count <= 10
    error_message = "Instance count must be between 1 and 10."
  }
}
```

Leveraging Output Variables

Output variables in Terraform serve as a mechanism to expose critical information about the resources created during infrastructure deployment. They provide an easy way to access key resource attributes such as IP addresses, DNS names, or resource IDs, making it convenient to integrate this data into other parts of the infrastructure. For example, the output of a networking module might include the VPC ID and subnet details, which can then be used as inputs for other modules. This capability is particularly useful in large projects where multiple modules need to communicate and share resource information without direct coupling.

In the following example, the output variable is defined to export the VPC ID in a module: `output "vpc_id" {`

```
  description = "ID of the created VPC"
  value       = aws_vpc.main.id
}
```

In this example, an output variable is defined to reference the variable defined in the module while invoking the root module:

```
module "network" {
  source = "./modules/network"
}

output "network_vpc_id" {
  value = module.network.vpc_id
}
```

In addition to improving visibility, output variables promote modularity and reusability by reducing hardcoded dependencies. By passing outputs between modules, Terraform enables a streamlined workflow for chaining infrastructure components and ensures consistency across deployments. Best practices for using outputs include defining only essential information as outputs to avoid exposing sensitive details unnecessarily, and properly documenting these outputs in the module's **README**. This approach enhances collaboration, simplifies debugging, and ensures a cleaner, more maintainable infrastructure codebase.

Securely Handling Sensitive Data

Managing sensitive data in Terraform is a critical aspect of securing infrastructure as code. Sensitive information such as API keys, passwords, and database credentials, if mishandled, can lead to severe security breaches. Terraform addresses this by offering features to securely manage sensitive data, reducing the risk of accidental exposure. For example, variables marked as sensitive ensure that their values are not displayed in logs or outputs. This built-in functionality helps safeguard secrets during execution and prevents them from being inadvertently exposed to team members or included in version control.

To enhance security further, certain best practices should be followed. Avoid hardcoding sensitive information directly in `.tf` files, as this makes credentials vulnerable if the files are shared or pushed to a repository. Instead, use external secret management tools such as HashiCorp Vault or cloud-native services such as AWS Secrets Manager, Azure Key Vault, or Google Secret Manager to securely store and reference credentials. Additionally, automate the rotation of secrets to minimize risks associated with credential leaks. By combining Terraform's sensitive data handling features with these best practices, teams can significantly strengthen the security of their infrastructure.

The following are some methods for securing sensitive data:

- **Sensitive variable flag**

  ```
  variable "db_password" {
    description = "Database password"
    type        = string
    sensitive   = true
  }
  ```

- **Environment variables**

  ```
  export TF_VAR_db_password="MySecretPass123"
  ```

- **Hashicorp Vault:** Vault enables dynamic secrets management, integrating directly with Terraform to retrieve credentials on the fly.

  ```
  data "vault_generic_secret" "db_creds" {
    path = "secret/db"
  }
  ```

- **AWS Secret Manager**

  ```
  data "aws_secretsmanager_secret" "db_creds" {
    name = "db-credentials"
  }
  ```

- **Azure Vault Key**

  ```
  data "azurerm_key_vault_secret" "db_creds" {
    name         = "db-credentials"
    key_vault_id = azurerm_key_vault.example.id
  }
  ```

- **Google Secrets Manager**

  ```
  data "google_secret_manager_secret" "db_creds" {
    secret_id = "db-credentials"
  }
  ```

Variable Precedence and Overrides

Terraform follows a strict order of precedence to determine which value should be applied to a variable. This order helps ensure that the most specific and relevant configuration is used in the infrastructure deployment, while still allowing for flexibility in how variable values are provided.

- **Environment Variables**: When environment variables are set, they take the highest precedence. Terraform looks for environment variables prefixed with **`TF_VAR_`**, followed by the variable name. For example, if you have a variable named **`vpc_cidr`**, you can set it through an environment variable such as **`TF_VAR_vpc_cidr=10.0.0.0/16`**. This approach allows for sensitive data (such as API keys or passwords) to be passed securely without hardcoding them in the configuration files.
- **CLI Flags (`-var`)**: The next level of precedence is the use of CLI flags with the `-var` option when running Terraform commands such as `terraform plan` or `terraform apply`. For example, using **`terraform apply -var="vpc_cidr=10.1.0.0/16"`** will override any previous value provided via environment variables or **`.tfvars`** files. This method is commonly used for quick overrides during a one-time execution.
- **Terraform Files (`terraform.tfvars`)**: If a **`terraform.tfvars`** file is provided, it is read next in the precedence order. Variables defined within this file can supply values to variables in the Terraform configuration. If there are multiple **`.tfvars`** files (for example, **`terraform.dev.tfvars`** and **`terraform.prod.tfvars`**), the file specified with the **`-var-file`** flag takes precedence over the default **`terraform.tfvars`**. This approach is useful for maintaining environment-specific configurations and keeping them separate from the main **`.tf`** files.
- **Default Values in `.tf` Files:** Finally, Terraform checks for default values set directly within the variable definition inside **`.tf`** files. If a variable is not overridden by any other method (environment variables, CLI flags, or **`.tfvars`** files), the default value defined in the configuration will be used. This provides a fallback value but ensures that the variable is always initialized with a sensible default if no other values are supplied.

This prioritization helps Terraform to ensure that users have the flexibility to override default behavior while still providing a clear and structured order of precedence for variable resolution.

Effective management of variables, outputs, and sensitive data is crucial for scalable and secure Terraform deployments. By defining structured variables, enforcing constraints, and implementing secure secrets management, teams can enhance the flexibility and security of their infrastructure. Outputs streamline resource sharing between modules, while variable precedence ensures predictable behavior across environments. These practices not only simplify infrastructure management but also minimize risk, reinforcing the core principles of cloud security in Terraform-based workflows.

Managing Workspaces for Multi-Environment Deployments

Managing infrastructure across multiple environments such as development, staging, and production can be challenging without proper separation. Terraform workspaces provide a simple yet effective way to manage distinct environments within the same configuration. By isolating state files per workspace, Terraform allows users to deploy resources to different environments without duplicating code. This section explores the role of workspaces in multi-environment deployments, their benefits, limitations, and best practices for automation across AWS, GCP, and Azure.

Understanding Terraform Workspaces

Terraform workspaces are a feature designed to manage multiple instances of the same infrastructure configuration by isolating state files. Each workspace maintains an independent state file while sharing the same configuration codebase, enabling logical separation of deployments. This separation streamlines infrastructure management, especially in multi-environment setups, where consistent configurations are applied across development, staging, and production environments.

The following are some key use cases of Terraform workspaces:

- **Multi-Environment Deployments**: Workspaces allow you to deploy and manage distinct environments, such as **dev**, **staging**, and **production**, using a unified codebase while maintaining isolated states.
- **Feature Branch Testing**: They enable the creation of temporary, isolated environments for testing changes made in feature branches, facilitating development without affecting shared resources.
- **Resource Segmentation**: Workspaces can be used to maintain state files for different projects, teams, or regions under a single repository for better organization and reduced duplication.

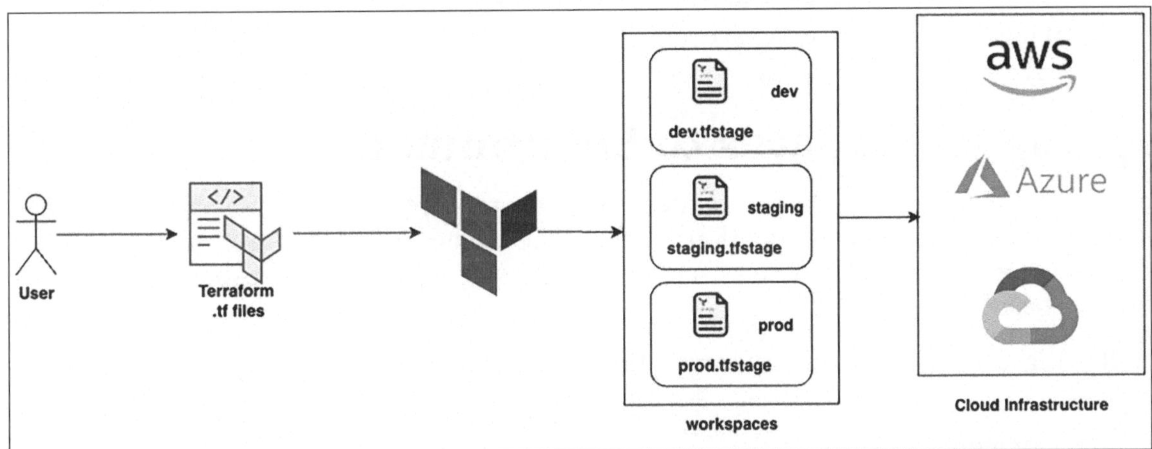

Figure 3.2: *Terraform workspaces*

Terraform initializes with a default workspace named **default**. You can create additional workspaces to represent other environments or use cases. Each workspace has its own state file stored separately, ensuring that changes in one workspace do not impact others. This isolation is particularly useful for environments that share the same infrastructure structure but require separate management and updates.

The following are some features of Terraform workspaces:

- **State isolation**: Workspaces ensure that states are isolated, reducing the risk of cross-environment conflicts or resource overwrites.
- **Code consistency**: Reuse the same configuration for all environments, minimizing duplication and promoting maintainability.
- **Dynamic resource scaling**: Terraform workspaces facilitate scaling resources dynamically based on the needs of each environment. For instance, the **dev** workspace might allocate small EC2 instances, while the **prod** workspace provisions a highly available auto-scaling group with larger instances and optimized storage.
- **Seamless CI/CD integration**: Workspaces integrate easily into CI/CD pipelines, allowing automated, environment-specific deployments based on the selected workspace, ensuring faster and safer infrastructure changes.

Thus, by understanding and effectively using Terraform workspaces, you can achieve better resource segmentation, simplified environment management, and enhanced consistency across deployments.

Managing Terraform Workspaces

The following are some commands that are used to manage workspaces:

- **Create a new workspace**

  ```
  terraform workspace new <workspace-name>
  ```
- **List available workspaces**
  ```
  terraform workspace list
  ```
- **Switch to a workspace**

  ```
  terraform workspace select <workspace-name>
  ```
- **Destroy a workspace**

  ```
  terraform workspace delete <workspace-name>
  ```
- **Showing the current workspace**
  ```
  terraform workspace show
  ```

Mapping Workspaces to Environments

Terraform workspaces provide a practical way to represent logical environments, such as development, staging, and production, within the same infrastructure configuration. Each workspace is tied to an isolated state file, enabling clean separation of resources while allowing shared codebases.

The following are standard environment tiers that are used in the application development lifecycle:

- **Development (dev)**
  - Typically, a lightweight environment with minimal resources for testing and experimentation.
  - Suitable for early-stage development where infrastructure changes are frequent and experimental.
- **Staging (`staging`)**
  - A pre-production environment that closely mirrors the production setup.
  - Used for integration testing, performance tuning, and final validation of changes before deployment to production.
- **Production (prod)**
  - The live environment, fully scaled to meet user demand.
  - Requires stringent controls for resource stability, security, and compliance.

    ```
    locals {
      vm_size = terraform.workspace == "prod" ? "Standard_D4s_v3" :
                terraform.workspace == "staging" ? "Standard_D2s_v3" :
                "Standard_B1s"
    }

    resource "azurerm_linux_virtual_machine" "example" {
      name                = "example-vm-${terraform.workspace}"
      resource_group_name = azurerm_resource_group.example.name
      location            = azurerm_resource_group.example.location
      size                = local.vm_size
      admin_username      = "azureuser"
      admin_ssh_key {
    ```

```
      username    = "azureuser"
      public_key = file("~/.ssh/id_rsa.pub")
    }
    network_interface_ids = [azurerm_network_interface.example.id]
    os_disk {
      caching              = "ReadWrite"
      storage_account_type = "Standard_LRS"
    }
  }
```

The aforementioned Terraform snippet demonstrates mapping workspaces to environments by dynamically setting the VM size (**vm_size**) based on the current workspace (**prod**, **staging**, or others). Each workspace isolates environment-specific resources, while reusing the same configuration, ensuring consistency and logical separation across development tiers.

Isolating State Files by Workspace

In Terraform, state files are crucial for tracking and managing the current state of infrastructure. By isolating state files through the use of workspaces, Terraform ensures that different environments (for example, development, staging, and production) do not interfere with one another. Each workspace has its own separate state file, preventing the risk of conflicting resource changes when multiple teams or environments are using the same Terraform configuration. This isolation is necessary for managing infrastructure at scale, while minimizing the chances of resource overlap or accidental modification of critical environments, such as production, by development or staging environments.

The following are some best practices for isolating state files in workspaces:

- **Use Remote State Backends**: To enhance collaboration and prevent issues such as race conditions or state corruption, it is best to store state files remotely in backends such as AWS S3, Google Cloud Storage (GCS), or Azure Blob Storage. Remote state backends provide features such as state locking, ensuring that only one operation modifies the state at a time, thus preventing conflicts. Additionally, remote backends allow teams to collaborate more effectively by making the state accessible from anywhere.
- **Naming Convention**: When managing state files in workspaces, adopting a consistent naming convention for workspace names within the state file path is critical for clarity. For example, using a path such as **my-project/dev/terraform.tfstate** for the development environment and **my-project/prod/terraform.tfstate** for the production environment can help clearly distinguish between the environments. This helps prevent mistakes where an operation intended for one environment accidentally affects another and keeps the project organized, especially when managing multiple workspaces or teams.

```
terraform {
  backend "s3" {
    bucket = "terraform-state-bucket"
    key    = "project/${terraform.workspace}/terraform.tfstate"
    region = "us-east-1"
  }
}
```

This snippet configures a remote backend for storing Terraform state files in an S3 bucket. The key parameter dynamically creates a unique path for each workspace (**${terraform.workspace}**), ensuring that state files for different environments (for example, **dev**, **staging**, **prod**) are isolated within the same S3 bucket but under separate paths.

Workspace Limitations and Alternatives

Terraform workspaces provide an effective way to manage state isolation across environments, but they come with certain limitations. It is essential to be aware of these drawbacks, and explore alternative strategies to address them.

The following are some limitations of Terraform workspaces:

- **State Deletion Risks**: Deleting a workspace removes its associated state file, which can be a significant risk, especially for production environments. If not carefully managed, this can lead to accidental loss of infrastructure information.
- **Limited Isolation**: While workspaces isolate state files, they do not isolate configurations. This lack of true separation can create dependencies across environments, leading to potential issues if the configurations are not managed properly.
- **Complexity**: In large-scale projects with numerous environments, managing multiple workspaces can become unwieldy, making the process harder to track, maintain, and troubleshoot.

You can consider the following alternatives to address the aforementioned limitation of Terraform workspaces:

- **Directory Structures**: Using separate directories for each environment (for example, **`/dev`**, **`/staging`**, **`/prod`**) helps achieve better isolation of configurations and states. Each directory can have its own set of Terraform files, improving clarity and preventing accidental cross-environment changes.
- **Terraform Cloud/Enterprise**: These platforms provide enhanced workspace-level isolation with features such as Role-Based Access Control (RBAC) and centralized governance, making it easier to manage multiple environments while ensuring secure, controlled access.
- **CI/CD Environment Variables**: By using environment variables within CI/CD pipelines, you can dynamically provision different environments based on pipeline-specific variables. This eliminates the need for multiple workspaces while maintaining separation between environments through automated infrastructure provisioning.

Automating Workspace Management

Automating workspace management in CI/CD pipelines streamlines the process of creating and switching between different Terraform workspaces as part of the deployment workflow. This practice ensures that environments (for example, **`dev`**, **`staging`**, **`prod`**) are consistently created, managed, and destroyed based on pipeline configuration, thus reducing manual errors, and ensuring repeatable deployments.

The provided GitHub Actions example automates the selection and use process within a CI/CD pipeline:

```
jobs:
  terraform:
    steps:
      - name: Create Workspace
        run: terraform workspace select ${{ env.TF_WORKSPACE }}
      - name: Apply Terraform
        run: terraform apply -auto-approve
```

In this example, the pipeline selects a Terraform workspace dynamically based on the value of the environment variable **`TF_WORKSPACE`** (which can be set **`dev`**, **`staging`**, or **`prod`**). Next, Terraform applies the infrastructure changes for the specified workspace without requiring manual intervention. This automation ensures seamless environment-specific deployments with minimal effort.

Terraform workspaces simplify the management of multi-environment deployments by isolating state files, reducing the complexity of managing infrastructure across dev, staging, and production environments. While workspaces offer flexibility and ease of use, they are best suited for lower-tier environments or ephemeral infrastructure. For production workloads, combining workspaces with directory structures or leveraging Terraform Cloud provides enhanced isolation and governance. By automating workspace provisioning and state management, organizations can ensure consistent, scalable, and secure deployments across AWS, GCP, and Azure.

Configuring Remote Execution with Terraform Cloud and Alternatives

Remote execution in Terraform enables infrastructure provisioning and state management from centralized environments, enhancing security, scalability, and collaboration. By offloading execution to cloud services or CI/CD pipelines, teams reduce local dependencies, minimize risks of state corruption, and enable seamless multi-developer workflows. This section delves into Terraform Cloud and other remote execution tools such as AWS CodeBuild, Azure DevOps Services, Google Cloud Build, GitHub Actions, and Jenkins, providing practical insights and cloud-specific examples across AWS, GCP, and Azure.

Introduction to Remote Execution

Remote execution in Terraform allows infrastructure provisioning processes such as running terraform plan and terraform apply to take place on centralized servers or managed platforms instead of individual developer machines. This shift enhances security, collaboration, and scalability, making it especially valuable for managing production environments and complex infrastructures. The following explains the working of remote execution:

- **Execution environment**: Terraform plans and applies are executed on remote platforms such as **Terraform Cloud**, **Terraform Enterprise**, or CI/CD tools such as **GitHub Actions**, **AWS CodeBuild**, **Azure Pipelines**, or **Google Cloud Build**. These environments provide consistent configurations, eliminating discrepancies caused by varying local setups.
- **State management**: The Terraform state file, which tracks the infrastructure's current state, is stored in a **remote backend** (for example, Amazon S3, Google Cloud Storage, or Azure Blob Storage). This ensures centralized state management, improving collaboration and enabling locking mechanisms to prevent conflicts.
- **Collaboration**: Multiple team members can work on the same infrastructure codebase while relying on state locking to prevent simultaneous updates that might corrupt the state.

The following are some features of remote execution:

- **Scalability**: Centralized execution environments handle the resource demands of large-scale Terraform configurations, avoiding bottlenecks on developer machines.
- **State locking**: Remote execution platforms implement locking mechanisms, ensuring that only one user or process can modify the state file at a time. This prevents conflicts and potential state corruption.
- **Audit trails**: Centralized execution environments provide comprehensive logs that detail every infrastructure change, enhancing traceability and governance.

- **Enhanced security**: Sensitive data (such as credentials or access tokens) remains within the controlled remote environment, minimizing exposure risks.

Remote execution is a cornerstone for teams aiming to streamline Terraform workflows, ensure robust security practices, and achieve seamless collaboration in dynamic environments.

Setting Up Terraform Cloud

Terraform Cloud is a managed service provided by HashiCorp that facilitates remote execution, centralized state management, and enhanced collaboration for infrastructure-as-code workflows. By using Terraform Cloud, teams can offload Terraform operations to a secure, centralized platform, integrate with Version Control Systems (VCS), and enforce governance policies with Sentinel—a policy-as-code framework. This enables streamlined workflows, reduced operational overhead, and improved compliance.

The following are the steps to set up Terraform Cloud:

- **Create an account**: Visit Terraform Cloud and sign up using your email or a supported single sign-on provider (for example, Google or GitHub). After signing in, you will access the Terraform Cloud dashboard.
- **Create an organization**: Organizations act as containers for managing multiple workspaces. Navigate to the `"Organizations"` section, create a new organization, and link it to your version control system (for example, GitHub, GitLab, or Bitbucket).
- **Define workspaces**: Within the organization, create workspaces for different environments (for example, `dev`, `staging`, `prod`). Each workspace corresponds to a specific Terraform state file and links directly to a VCS repository or branch.
- **Configure remote backend**: Update your Terraform configuration to point to Terraform Cloud as the remote backend. Add the following to your Terraform `.tf` file:

```
terraform {
  cloud {
    organization = "MyOrg"
    workspaces {
      name = "production"
    }
  }
}
```

Setting up Terraform Cloud centralizes infrastructure operations, enhances collaboration across teams, and provides advanced features such as state locking, audit logging, and Sentinel-based governance, making it an essential tool for modern infrastructure-as-code workflows.

Remote Execution with CI/CD Tools

Integrating Terraform with CI/CD tools, such as GitHub Actions, GitLab CI/CD, Azure DevOps, or Jenkins, brings infrastructure provisioning into the software delivery lifecycle. This combination extends Terraform's remote execution capabilities beyond its native Cloud platform, ensuring consistent and automated deployments while maintaining governance and control.

The following are some best practices for remote execution with CI/CD tools:

- **Automate Drift Detection and Rollback:**
  - Configure the pipeline to run a Terraform plan periodically or upon changes to detect infrastructure drift.

 - Implement rollback mechanisms to revert to a known good state if drifts or failures occur during deployment.
- **Enforce Approval Workflows for Production**:
  - For critical environments such as production, include manual approval steps in the pipeline.
  - Require senior team members to review and approve Terraform plans before execution.

The following are examples of Terraform remote execution across different CI/CD tools:

- **AWS CodeBuild**

```
version: 0.2
phases:
  build:
    commands:
      - terraform init
      - terraform apply -auto-approve
```

- **GitHub Actions**

```
name: Terraform
on: push
jobs:
  terraform:
    steps:
      - name: Init
        run: terraform init
      - name: Apply
        run: terraform apply -auto-approve
```

- **Jenkins Pipeline**

```
pipeline {
    agent any
    stages {
        stage('Terraform Apply') {
            steps {
                sh 'terraform init'
                sh 'terraform apply -auto-approve'
            }
        }
    }
}
```

- **Azure Pipeline**

```
trigger:
- main
- script: terraform init
  displayName: 'Terraform Init'
- script: terraform apply -auto-approve
  displayName: 'Terraform Apply'
```

- **Google Cloud Build**

```
steps:
- name: 'hashicorp/terraform:1.10.3'
  args: ['init']
- name: 'hashicorp/terraform:1.10.3'
  args: ['apply', '-auto-approve']
```

Managing Access Control in Remote Execution

Access control is a critical aspect of secure Terraform remote execution. It ensures that only authorized users can access sensitive resources, execute infrastructure changes, and interact with the Terraform state. This not only prevents unauthorized access but also promotes compliance with organizational policies and industry standards. The following outlines the access control features available across platforms:

- **Terraform Cloud**: Provides built-in Role-Based Access Control (RBAC) for managing permissions at a granular level.
- **AWS, GCP, Azure**: Use their respective Identity and Access Management (IAM) systems to secure resources and limit operations during remote execution.
- **Third-party CI/CD Tools**: Often integrate with IAM or offer custom user management systems.

The following are some best practices for access control:

- **Enable Multi-Factor Authentication (MFA):**
  - Require MFA for all sensitive operations to enhance security and reduce unauthorized access risks.
- **Restrict permissions:**
  - Assign workspace-specific roles to ensure users can only access and modify resources relevant to their responsibilities.
  - Follow the principle of least privilege by granting only the necessary permissions.
- **Log and audit Terraform operations:**
  - Use audit logs to track changes made to the infrastructure.
  - Ensure all Terraform apply actions are logged and reviewed periodically to identify anomalies or unauthorized activities.
- **Integrate with IAM systems:**
  - For platforms such as AWS, Azure, and GCP, integrate Terraform remote execution with native IAM to manage access seamlessly.
  - Use policies to define actions allowed per user or group.
- **Use API tokens securely:**
  - Rotate tokens regularly and store them securely using tools such as AWS Secrets Manager, Azure Key Vault, or HashiCorp Vault.

In Terraform Cloud, roles define the actions a user or team can perform. These include:

- **Admins:**
  - Full access to perform any action, including creating, planning, applying, and modifying Terraform configurations.
  - Ideal for infrastructure leads or DevOps managers.
  - Can manage workspaces, policies, and integrations.
- **Operators:**
  - Permissions to run terraform plan and terraform apply but cannot modify configurations or state.
  - Typically assigned to engineers deploying resources.

- **Auditors:**
  - View-only access to plans, applies, and state files.
  - Suitable for compliance teams needing insights without operational privileges.

```
resource "tfe_team" "dev_team" {
  name         = "Development Team"
  organization = "example-org"
}

resource "tfe_team_access" "workspace_access" {
  workspace_id = tfe_workspace.example.id
  team_id      = tfe_team.dev_team.id
  access       = "plan"
}
```

This policy ensures that only the **`"Development Team"`** has **`plan`** access to a specific workspace.

Configuring remote execution elevates Terraform workflows by centralizing infrastructure management, enforcing security controls, and promoting collaboration. Terraform Cloud offers a seamless path for remote execution, while alternatives such as AWS CodeBuild, Azure Pipeline, Google Cloud Build, GitHub Actions, and Jenkins provide customizable, cost-effective solutions. By automating Terraform runs, integrating remote state, and securing execution pipelines, organizations can achieve robust, scalable, and secure cloud deployments across AWS, GCP, and Azure.

Debugging and Troubleshooting Terraform Configurations

Debugging is a critical skill for Terraform practitioners, ensuring infrastructure is deployed reliably and consistently. Terraform configurations, while powerful, can encounter issues due to syntax errors, resource drift, misconfigurations, or state corruption. This section provides a comprehensive guide to diagnosing and resolving common Terraform issues, enhancing the overall reliability of Infrastructure as Code (IaC).

Understanding Terraform Debug Logs

Terraform debug logs offer a granular view of Terraform's internal operations, enabling users to troubleshoot issues during plan, apply, or destroy commands. These logs provide detailed information on configuration parsing, resource interactions, and API communications, making them essential for diagnosing complex problems or identifying misconfigurations.

Debug logs in Terraform are controlled by the **`TF_LOG`** environment variable, which defines the level of verbosity. Each verbosity level captures a specific depth of information:

- **`TRACE`**: The most detailed level of logging, capturing every internal function call and execution detail. Useful for deep dives into Terraform's operation, but generates extensive logs.
- **`DEBUG`**: Offers a high level of detail, including configuration files, module paths, and state operations. Typically used for troubleshooting issues related to resource creation or configuration.
- **`INFO`**: Provides general information about Terraform operations, such as which resources are being planned or applied. Suitable for monitoring standard workflows.
- **`WARN`**: Highlights potential issues or warnings that might not immediately break the execution but could lead to problems in the future.
- **`ERROR`**: Logs only errors that halt Terraform execution, making it the most concise level.

Logs can be saved to a file for later analysis by setting the **TF_LOG_PATH** environment variable. For example:

```
export TF_LOG=DEBUG
export TF_LOG_PATH=terraform.log
terraform plan
```

The following are some best practices for Terraform debug logs:

- **Limit Verbosity**: Use high verbosity levels (**DEBUG**, **TRACE**) only when necessary. Prolonged use can degrade performance and clutter output.
- **Organize Logs by Environment**: Create separate logs for each workspace or environment for better traceability. For example, **TF_LOG_PATH=dev.log**, **TF_LOG_PATH=prod.log**.
- **Incremental Analysis**: Start troubleshooting with **ERROR** or **WARN** to identify major issues. Increase verbosity (**INFO**, **DEBUG**, **TRACE**) only if further details are required.
- **Secure Logs**: Ensure sensitive data, such as secrets or keys, is masked or stored securely when enabling verbose logging.
- **Monitor Performance**: Verbose logging (for example, **TRACE**) can impact execution speed. Enable it only on non-production systems or for isolated troubleshooting.

Hence, by leveraging Terraform debug logs effectively, users can quickly identify the root causes of issues, optimize configurations, and enhance the reliability of their IaC workflows.

Resolving Resource Drift and State Issues

Resource drift happens when live infrastructure diverges from the configuration defined in Terraform. This can occur due to the following reasons:

- **Manual Changes**: Updates made directly in the cloud console or CLI.
- **External Factors**: Automatic scaling, service updates, or external scripts modifying resources.
- **Configuration Overlap**: Multiple tools or teams managing the same resources.

Drift can result in inconsistencies between the desired state (defined in Terraform configuration) and the actual state, potentially causing operational disruptions or security risks.

Terraform's workflow inherently includes mechanisms to detect and resolve drift:

- **Detection during `terraform plan`**: When you run the **`terraform plan`**, Terraform compares the current state stored in the state file with the live infrastructure. Drift in Terraform is identified as changes or discrepancies between these states.
- **Resolution during `terraform apply`**: Running **`terraform apply`** reconciles the drift by enforcing the desired configuration and aligning the live infrastructure with the state file.
- **Manual drift detection with `terraform refresh`**: **`terraform refresh`** updates the state file to match the live infrastructure without making changes, helping identify drift for review.

The following are some best practices for managing resource drift:

- **Avoid manual changes**: Ensure all infrastructure updates are made through Terraform configurations and pipelines to maintain consistency and avoid human errors. Enforce RBAC to restrict direct access to resources, reducing the risk of unauthorized changes.
- **Enable automated drift detection**: Incorporate **`terraform plan`** into CI/CD pipelines to continuously detect and report drift. Immediate notifications allow teams to address discrepancies promptly, minimizing operational disruptions.

- **Use Terraform Cloud drift detection**: Leverage Terraform Cloud's built-in drift detection and alerting capabilities for automated monitoring. This ensures timely identification of changes, particularly in production environments, and simplifies tracking.
- **Log and monitor changes**: Keep comprehensive logs of all Terraform operations (for example, **`plan`**, **`apply`**, **`destroy`**) for audit and compliance purposes. Use cloud-native tools such as AWS CloudTrail, GCP Audit Logs, or Azure Monitor to identify and analyze manual changes.
- **Plan for state management**: Securely store state files in remote backends (for example, S3, GCS, Azure Blob) with versioning and locking mechanisms to prevent conflicts. Regularly back up state files and validate their integrity to ensure data is recoverable and consistent.

State file inconsistencies can compound drift problems. The following are some useful ways to address them effectively:

- **Rebuild state file using `terraform import`**: For resources missing from the state file, use **`terraform import`** to reintroduce them without recreating the infrastructure.
- **State reconciliation**: Use **`terraform state`** commands to remove orphaned resources or modify state attributes when drift cannot be resolved automatically.
- **Collaborate across teams**: Use Terraform workspaces or segregated state files to prevent conflicts between environments or teams.

Using Terraform Console for Testing

Terraform Console is an interactive command-line environment designed to evaluate Terraform expressions, query outputs, and test configurations in real-time. It provides a safe space to experiment with Terraform syntax and logic without making changes to the actual infrastructure. The functionality of Terraform Console is as follows:

- The console allows users to inspect variables, outputs, and resource attributes dynamically during the development process.
- It helps validate expressions, conditionals, and interpolations, offering immediate feedback on syntax or logic.
- By querying the state file directly, it enables users to retrieve resource attributes or verify configurations without running a Terraform apply.

```
terraform console
> aws_instance.example.private_ip
"10.0.1.12"
```

This queries the private IP of a specific AWS instance from the state file, providing quick insight into resource attributes without needing a full plan or apply.

The following are some best practices of the Terraform Console:

- **Test Complex Expressions**: When working with intricate conditionals, loops, or interpolations, use **`terraform console`** to validate and debug them in isolation, ensuring correctness before incorporating them into the configuration.
- **Query State**: Use the console to directly extract resource attributes from the state file, saving time and avoiding the risk of unnecessary infrastructure changes during debugging or validation processes.

Therefore, by integrating Terraform Console into your workflow, you can improve efficiency and reduce errors during the development and troubleshooting phases.

Analyzing Dependency Graphs

A dependency graph in Terraform is a visual representation of the relationships and dependencies between various resources in your infrastructure. It helps ensure that Terraform provisions resources in the correct order, following all dependencies. This visualization is useful for identifying misconfigurations, ensuring that resources are correctly linked, and preventing errors caused by circular dependencies. The following is the working principle of the Terraform dependency graph:

- **Graph generation:** Terraform generates a dependency graph by analyzing the resources in your configuration files and the relationships between them. You can generate the graph using the following command:

  ```
  terraform graph | dot -Tpng > graph.png
  ```

  This command outputs the graph in PNG format, which can then be reviewed to understand the resource dependencies.

- **Upstream and downstream dependencies:** The graph highlights upstream (dependent) and downstream (dependent on) relationships between resources. Explicit dependencies are defined by user input, while implicit dependencies are automatically inferred based on resource references.

The following are some best practices for the Terraform dependency graph:

- **Review for cycles:** Circular dependencies can prevent Terraform from determining the correct order of operations. Identifying and breaking these cycles is crucial for successful provisioning. This can often be done by decoupling resources into smaller, more independent modules.
- **Optimize for parallel execution:** By minimizing explicit dependencies, you can allow Terraform to provision resources in parallel, which improves efficiency, and reduces the overall execution time. Ensure that only necessary dependencies are defined, allowing for better concurrency during the apply phase.

Validating and Formatting Configurations

Validation and formatting are necessary practices in Terraform to ensure that your infrastructure code is error-free and consistently styled. Validation helps catch configuration issues before execution, reducing the risk of failed deployments or misconfigurations. Formatting ensures that the code adheres to a standardized style, improving readability and consistency, especially in collaborative environments where multiple teams may work on the same infrastructure codebase.

- **`terraform validate`** command checks the syntax and structure of your Terraform configuration files. It validates the configuration's logic and ensures it adheres to Terraform's syntax rules. However, it does not communicate with any cloud provider APIs. It is purely a local check to detect issues such as missing or incorrect resource configurations, invalid argument values, or improper module use.
- **`terraform fmt`** command automatically reformats your Terraform configuration files to follow Terraform's canonical style. It ensures that the HCL (HashiCorp Configuration Language) code adheres to the best practices for readability and consistency, such as proper indentation, spacing, and alignment of parameters.

The following are some benefits of Terraform formatting and validation:

- **Error prevention:** Running **`terraform validate`** ensures that configuration files are logically sound before applying them, reducing the chances of runtime errors.
- **Consistency across teams:** **`terraform fmt`** standardizes the formatting of Terraform files, making it easier for team members to read and understand each other's code.

- **Code quality:** Both validation and formatting help maintain high code quality by preventing mistakes early, and ensuring uniformity, which is especially important in large infrastructure projects.

Debugging and troubleshooting Terraform configurations ensure smooth infrastructure deployment, and minimize errors. By leveraging debug logs, drift detection, and dependency graphs, teams can proactively address potential issues. Terraform Console and validation tools enhance confidence in deployments, fostering consistent infrastructure practices across AWS, GCP, and Azure.

Conclusion

In this chapter, we explored the essential advanced features of Terraform that form the backbone of secure, scalable, and maintainable Infrastructure as Code (IaC) practices. From designing reusable modules to managing complex multi-environment deployments, each section builds on foundational knowledge to equip cloud practitioners with the skills needed to create efficient and production-ready infrastructure. The integration of variables, outputs, and sensitive data handling ensures flexibility and security, while the introduction to Terraform workspaces and remote execution workflows highlights the importance of environment isolation and collaborative execution.

By mastering these advanced concepts, engineers can streamline infrastructure workflows, enforce consistency across deployments, and reduce operational risks. As Terraform projects grow in complexity, debugging and troubleshooting skills become increasingly critical for maintaining resilience and performance. This chapter bridges the gap between fundamental Terraform knowledge and expert-level implementation, setting the stage for more sophisticated automation, compliance, and security practices covered in the following chapters.

In the next chapter, we will focus on integrating security across multi-cloud environments, including configuring providers and leveraging provider-specific security features. It also covers writing cloud-agnostic Terraform code, standardizing IAM and security policies, and addressing multi-cloud security challenges as well as the best practices.

Questions and Answers

1. **How do reusable Terraform modules improve infrastructure scalability and maintainability?**

   Reusable Terraform modules enhance infrastructure scalability and maintainability by promoting code reusability, reducing duplication, and enforcing consistency across deployments. Instead of defining resources repeatedly, modules allow infrastructure components such as networking, databases, or compute instances to be encapsulated into reusable templates. This modular approach simplifies maintenance and accelerates infrastructure provisioning.

   For instance, a VPC module can be created to provision a standardized VPC with subnets, security groups, and route tables. By using input variables, the module remains flexible for different environments (dev, staging, and production). Additionally, nested modules allow teams to compose complex architectures efficiently, while maintaining clear separation between components. Using Terraform Registry or private module repositories, organizations can version and share modules, ensuring controlled updates and standardized deployments across multi-cloud environments.

2. **How can sensitive data, such as API keys and passwords, be securely managed in Terraform configurations?**

   Sensitive data in Terraform configurations should be handled carefully to prevent accidental exposure. Terraform provides **several mechanisms** to securely manage secrets:

   - **Using sensitive variables**: Marking variables as sensitive ensures that their values are not printed in logs or outputs, reducing the risk of exposure.

     ```
     variable "db_password" {
     type      = string
     sensitive = true
     }
     ```

   - **Storing secrets in secure storage**: Instead of hardcoding secrets, use external secret management tools such as AWS Secrets Manager, HashiCorp Vault, or SSM Parameter Store to fetch sensitive values dynamically.
   - **Leveraging environment variables**: Terraform allows passing sensitive values via environment variables (**`TF_VAR_db_password`**), which helps avoid storing them in **`.tf`** files or state files.
   - **Encrypting the Terraform state** - When using remote backends (for example, S3, Terraform Cloud), enabling encryption-at-rest ensures that sensitive values stored in the state file remain secure.

By following these best practices, teams can prevent unauthorized access to sensitive information, while maintaining security compliance.

3. **How do Terraform Workspaces facilitate multi-environment deployments, and what are their limitations?**

   Terraform Workspaces provide a built-in mechanism for managing multiple environments (such as dev, staging, and prod) using a single configuration, while maintaining separate state files. This is particularly useful for organizations that need to isolate infrastructure resources per environment.

Working of workspaces:

- The default workspace is used when no workspace is specified.
- New workspaces can be created using terraform workspace new **`<env_name>`**.
- Workspaces can be switched with terraform workspace select **`<env_name>`**.
- Each workspace maintains its **own state file**, preventing resource conflicts across environments.

Limitations of workspaces:

- Workspaces do not support advanced isolation, such as separate AWS accounts or VPCs per environment, making them less suitable for enterprise-scale multi-environment setups.
- They cannot be easily integrated with CI/CD pipelines that require explicit environment separation.
- Managing different provider configurations (for example, separate AWS credentials per environment) requires additional workarounds.

Alternatives: Many teams prefer managing environments **using** separate state backends per environment (for example, S3 buckets with different prefixes) or Terraform Cloud workspaces, which provide enhanced automation and access control.

4. **What are the key benefits of using Terraform Cloud for remote execution, and how does it compare to the alternatives?**

   Terraform Cloud enables remote execution, where Terraform runs on HashiCorp's managed infrastructure, rather than locally. This improves security, scalability, and collaboration for teams managing complex infrastructure.

Key benefits of Terraform Cloud remote execution:

- **Centralized state management**: Stores state remotely, reducing the risk of local state file corruption.
- **Role-Based Access Control (RBAC)**: Allows fine-grained access control for different team members.
- **Run queuing and policy enforcement**: Ensures controlled deployments using Sentinel policies and run approvals.
- **Built-in CI/CD integrations**: Supports GitHub, GitLab, Bitbucket, and other VCS integrations for automated Terraform runs.

For organizations requiring full governance, auditability, and state management, Terraform Cloud is a strong choice. However, if teams prefer self-hosted or cloud-native CI/CD options, solutions such as Jenkins, GitHub Actions, or AWS CodeBuild may be more flexible.

5. **How can Terraform users effectively debug and troubleshoot issues such as resource drift and dependency conflicts?**

   Debugging Terraform configurations requires a systematic approach to diagnose resource drift, state inconsistencies, and dependency conflicts. Here are the key techniques:

   - **Enable debug logs**: Running Terraform with debug logs (`TF_LOG=DEBUG` terraform apply) provides detailed insights into execution steps and errors.
   - **Use Terraform plan to detect drift**: Running Terraform plan regularly helps detect drift cases where the actual infrastructure state deviates from Terraform's expected state.
   - **Leverage Terraform console for testing expressions**: The Terraform console allows evaluating variables and interpolations before applying changes.
   - **Analyze the dependency graph**: Running terraform graph | `dot -Tpng > graph.png` visualizes resource dependencies, helping identify cyclical dependencies or misconfigurations.
   - **Format and validate code**: Using terraform fmt and terraform validate ensures that configurations are syntactically correct and follow best practices.

Thus, by following these debugging techniques, teams can proactively prevent failures and ensure smooth Terraform deployments in production environments.

Chapter 4
Multi-Cloud Security Integration

Introduction

The shift towards multi-cloud architectures has introduced unprecedented levels of flexibility, scalability, and resilience for organizations. However, this increased complexity also amplifies the challenges of managing security across diverse platforms such as AWS, Azure, and GCP. This chapter focuses on streamlining cloud security operations through Terraform, enabling unified policy enforcement, consistent identity management, and provider-specific security enhancements. By leveraging Terraform's Infrastructure as Code (IaC) capabilities, security teams can simplify governance, automate compliance, and minimize vulnerabilities in multi-cloud environments without sacrificing the distinct advantages offered by each provider.

This chapter delves into the critical aspects of configuring Terraform providers for multi-cloud deployments, highlighting techniques for managing authentication, provider versions, and scoping. It also explores how to harness provider-specific security features within a unified framework to fortify infrastructure across clouds. Readers will learn how to abstract cloud-specific configurations for portability, standardize IAM and security policies, and tackle key multi-cloud security challenges such as identity federation, inter-cloud communication, and Zero Trust implementation. By the end of this chapter, readers will be equipped to implement secure, scalable, and consistent multi-cloud architectures using Terraform, aligning with the modern security best practices and compliance requirements.

Structure

In this chapter, we will cover the following topics:

- Configuring Providers for Multi-Cloud Environments
  - Understanding Multi-Provider Configurations
  - Authenticating across Cloud Platforms
  - Managing Provider Versions and Compatibility
  - Defining Region and Account Scoping
- Leveraging Provider-Specific Security Features in a Unified Framework
  - Implementing AWS-Specific Security Features
  - Using Azure Security Features
  - Enabling GCP Security Tools
  - Centralizing Security Policies with Terraform
- Writing Cloud-Agnostic Terraform Code for Portability
  - Abstracting Cloud-Specific Configurations

   - Validating Configurations across Clouds
- Standardizing IAM and Security Policies across Providers
   - Designing Cross-Cloud IAM Structures
   - Writing Shared Security Policies in Terraform
   - Implementing Attribute-Based Access Control (ABAC)
- Addressing Multi-Cloud Security Challenges and Best Practices
   - Cross-Cloud Identity Federation
   - Securing Inter-Cloud Communication
   - Enforcing Data Sovereignty across Clouds
   - Implementing Zero Trust Networking in Multi-Cloud

Configuring Providers for Multi-Cloud Environments

Terraform's ability to manage infrastructure across multiple cloud platforms is one of its core strengths, making it an essential tool for organizations adopting multi-cloud strategies. By configuring providers for AWS, Azure, and GCP within a single Terraform project, teams can deploy and manage resources across clouds seamlessly. This section delves into the intricacies of configuring and managing multiple providers to ensure security, scalability, and consistency across cloud environments.

Understanding Multi-Provider Configurations

Multi-provider configurations in Terraform allow users to deploy and manage resources across multiple cloud platforms, such as AWS, Azure, and Google Cloud, within a single project. This capability extends the flexibility of Infrastructure as Code (IaC) by enabling seamless multi-cloud deployments, which are becoming increasingly common in modern IT environments. By defining and managing resources in one consolidated configuration file, organizations can implement hybrid or multi-cloud strategies more efficiently while maintaining a centralized approach to infrastructure provisioning.

Terraform achieves multi-provider functionality through the use of **`provider blocks`**. Each provider block is responsible for defining the configuration and authentication details required to connect to a specific cloud platform. For example, a project can have separate provider blocks for AWS, Azure, and GCP, each configured with its respective credentials, region, and other necessary parameters. To handle multiple providers within the same project, Terraform employs **`aliases`** to distinguish between them. These aliases enable users to define multiple instances of the same provider or differentiate between providers for multi-region or multi-cloud deployments. By referencing these aliases within resource blocks, Terraform ensures that resources are correctly associated with the intended provider.

```
terraform {
  required_providers {
    aws = {
      source  = "hashicorp/aws"
      version = "~> 5.0"
    }
    azurerm = {
      source  = "hashicorp/azurerm"
      version = "~> 3.0"
    }
```

```
    google = {
      source  = "hashicorp/google"
      version = "~> 5.0"
    }
  }
}

provider "aws" {
  alias  = "use1"
  region = "us-east-1"
}

provider "aws" {
  alias  = "usw2"
  region = "us-west-2"
}

provider "azurerm" {
  alias   = "eastus
  features {}
  location = "East US"
}

provider "azurerm" {
  alias   = "westeurope"
  features {}
  location = "West Europe"
}

provider "google" {
  alias  = "uscentral1"
  region = "us-central1"
}

provider "google" {
  alias  = "euwest1"
  region = "europe-west1"
}
```

This Terraform configuration defines three providers: AWS, Azure, and Google Cloud. Each provider is specified with its source and version requirements in the **`required_providers`** block, ensuring compatibility with specific versions. The AWS provider is configured for the **`us-east-1`** region, while the Azure provider includes a features block, which is mandatory even if left empty. The Google Cloud provider is set up to deploy resources in the us-central1 region. This setup enables multi-cloud infrastructure management within a single Terraform project.

Authenticating across Cloud Platforms

Authentication in Terraform is crucial for ensuring secure interactions between IaC configurations and cloud providers such as AWS, Azure, and GCP. It verifies that only authorized entities can access and modify cloud resources. Each provider has its own authentication approach: AWS employs IAM roles and policies, Azure leverages Service Principals, and GCP utilizes Service Accounts. Terraform harmonizes these diverse mechanisms, offering a consistent framework for deploying infrastructure across various cloud platforms.

Terraform uses authentication credentials to connect to cloud APIs, and these credentials can be provided through environment variables, configuration files, or directly within provider blocks in

Terraform code. Its authentication system supports both static credentials and dynamic, token-based methods. For instance, AWS users can authenticate using temporary credentials generated by AssumeRole, Azure can take advantage of Managed Identities for automated and secure access, and GCP can utilize Workload Identity Federation to dynamically generate short-lived tokens without relying on persistent service account keys. This adaptability empowers organizations to implement authentication strategies aligned with their security policies and operational workflows.

```
#AWS
provider "aws" {
  region = "us-east-1"
  assume_role {
    role_arn     = "arn:aws:iam::123456789012:role/MyTerraformRole"
    session_name = "terraform-session"
  }
}
```

The **assume_role** block in Terraform defines the IAM role that should be assumed for access. This process generates temporary credentials dynamically, providing secure access to AWS resources.

```
#GCP
provider "google" {
  region = "us-central1"
  credentials = jsonencode({
    "type": "external_account",
    "audience": "//iam.googleapis.com/projects/PROJECT_NUMBER/locations/
global/workloadIdentityPools/POOL_ID/providers/PROVIDER_ID",
    "subject_token_type": "urn:ietf:params:oauth:token-type:jwt",
    "token_url": "https://sts.googleapis.com/v1/token",
    "credential_source": {
      "file": "/path/to/oidc-token-file"
    }
  })
}
```

The credentials block in Terraform uses a JSON configuration to authenticate with GCP via Workload Identity Federation. This configuration includes the **audience** and **token_url** fields, which specify the identity provider and token exchange endpoint. Terraform then retrieves a temporary token by using an OIDC token file, eliminating the need for static credentials.

```
#Azure
provider "azurerm" {
  features {}
  use_msi = true
  subscription_id = "00000000-0000-0000-0000-000000000000"
}
```

The **use_msi** attribute allows Terraform to authenticate securely using the Managed Identity assigned to an Azure VM, App Service, or other resources.

Managing Provider Versions and Compatibility

Terraform providers act as plugins that enable Terraform to interact with various cloud platforms and services such as AWS, Azure, GCP, and others. Providers are constantly evolving, with updates introducing new features, security enhancements, bug fixes, and occasionally, deprecations of older functionality. Keeping provider versions aligned, particularly in multi-cloud or hybrid environments, is vital to maintaining stability and avoiding compatibility issues that could disrupt infrastructure deployments. Without careful version management, users risk encountering breaking changes that may lead to errors or misconfigurations in their IaC workflows.

Terraform allows users to specify provider versions within the **required_providers** block of a configuration file. This feature ensures consistent behaviour by enabling users to **"pin"** specific versions of providers that are known to work with their infrastructure code.

- **Version pinning**: By explicitly setting the version constraints (for example: **~> 3.0** or **>= 2.5.0, < 3.0**), users can control which provider versions Terraform uses during operations. This helps prevent unintentional upgrades to newer, potentially incompatible versions that might introduce breaking changes.
- **Version resolution**: When Terraform initializes, it downloads the required provider versions specified in the configuration. If the specified version is not available or conflicts with other dependencies, Terraform will flag the issue before proceeding.
- **Multi-Cloud scenarios**: For organizations managing infrastructure across multiple providers, aligning the provider versions across different configurations is crucial. Inconsistent versions can lead to discrepancies in supported features, syntax, or behaviour, causing challenges in maintaining uniformity and reliability.
- **Managing updates**: Regularly reviewing provider changelogs and testing updates in isolated environments ensures that new versions can be adopted safely without disrupting production systems. Tools such as terraform state replace-provider can assist in transitioning between provider versions if required.

```
terraform {
  required_providers {
    aws = {
      source  = "hashicorp/aws"
      version = "~> 5.0"
    }
    azurerm = {
      source  = "hashicorp/azurerm"
      version = "~> 3.0"
    }
    google = {
      source  = "hashicorp/google"
      version = "~> 5.0"
    }
  }
}
```

By adopting a structured approach to managing provider versions and compatibility, Terraform users can ensure stable and predictable infrastructure operations while minimizing risks associated with changes in provider functionality.

Defining Region and Account Scoping

Region and account scoping in Terraform ensures that resources are deployed to the intended cloud environments. This is especially critical for multi-cloud or multi-account projects, where infrastructure may span various regions or accounts within AWS, Azure, GCP, or other platforms. Proper scoping prevents unintentional deployments in incorrect locations, which could lead to compliance issues, resource mismanagement, or increased operational overhead. It enables users to maintain a clear separation of resources across diverse environments while supporting the unique requirements of different regions or accounts.

Terraform achieves scoping by defining account and region details within the provider blocks of configuration files. These blocks can include attributes such as account IDs, region names, and custom profiles to precisely control where and how resources are provisioned. Users can create multiple provider configurations to handle deployments across different accounts or regions, and these can be dynamically selected using aliases or variables. This flexibility allows Terraform users to efficiently manage infrastructure across complex, distributed setups while ensuring that resources are deployed in their intended locations.

```
provider "aws" {
  alias  = "dev"
  region = "us-east-1"
  profile = "dev-account"
}

provider "aws" {
  alias  = "prod"
  region = "us-west-2"
  profile = "prod-account"
}
```

The snippet defines two AWS provider configurations in Terraform with distinct scopes for region and account. The first provider, aliased as **"dev,"** targets the **"us-east-1"** region and uses the **"dev-account"** profile, while the second, aliased as **"prod,"** operates in the **"us-west-2"** region with the **"prod-account"** profile. This setup enables seamless management of resources across multiple AWS accounts and regions within the same configuration.

Configuring providers for multi-cloud environments lays the groundwork for scalable, secure, and consistent infrastructure deployments. By understanding how to authenticate, manage versions, and scope providers correctly, organizations can mitigate risks and ensure smooth cross-cloud operations. This section not only enables seamless infrastructure deployment but also highlights the importance of security and compatibility in multi-cloud environments.

Leveraging Provider-Specific Security Features in a Unified Framework

Multi-cloud environments provide flexibility and prevent vendor lock-in, but they introduce complexity in securing resources across different platforms. Each cloud provider offers unique security services and tools, yet managing them in silos can lead to inconsistencies and gaps. This section focuses on harnessing provider specific security features such as AWS GuardDuty, Azure Defender for Cloud, and GCP Security Command Center, while unifying and automating policies through Terraform to achieve a cohesive security posture across cloud environments.

Implementing AWS-Specific Security Features

AWS offers a suite of powerful security tools to safeguard cloud resources, emphasizing identity management, encryption, and threat detection. Key services such as **Identity and Access Management (IAM)**, **Key Management Service (KMS)**, and **GuardDuty** provide essential mechanisms to enforce access control, protect sensitive data, and identify potential threats. Terraform simplifies the implementation of these features, enabling consistent, automated deployment across multiple environments. The following are some AWS services that can be helpful in building a secure environment in the AWS cloud:

- **IAM**: Terraform can manage IAM roles, policies, and users, allowing fine-grained access control to AWS resources. You can define the least-privilege access policies to ensure that users and applications have only the permissions they need.

- **KMS**: Terraform supports creating and managing KMS keys to encrypt the sensitive data. These keys can be used with other AWS services, such as S3 or RDS, to secure data at rest.
- **GuardDuty**: Terraform enables the activation of GuardDuty across accounts and regions. GuardDuty continuously monitors AWS accounts and infrastructure for malicious activity, such as unauthorized API calls or compromised instances, and sends alerts for quick remediation.

```
#IAM
resource "aws_iam_policy" "s3_read_only_policy" {
  name        = "S3ReadOnlyPolicy"
  description = "Provides read-only access to objects in the specified S3 buck-
et"

  policy = jsonencode({
    Version = "2012-10-17"
    Statement = [
      {
        Effect    = "Allow"
        Action    = ["s3:ListBucket"]
        Resource  = "arn:aws:s3:::example-bucket"
      },
      {
        Effect    = "Allow"
        Action    = ["s3:GetObject"]
        Resource  = "arn:aws:s3:::example-bucket/*"
      }
    ]
  })
}
```

The policy allows **s3:GetObject** action, enabling read-only access to all objects within the bucket named **example-bucket**.

```
#KMS
resource "aws_kms_key" "s3_encryption_key" {
  description             = "KMS key for S3 bucket encryption"
  deletion_window_in_days = 30
  enable_key_rotation     = true
}

resource "aws_kms_key_policy" "s3_encryption_policy" {
  key_id = aws_kms_key.s3_encryption_key.key_id

  policy = jsonencode({
    Version = "2012-10-17"
    Id      = "s3-kms-policy"
    Statement = [
      {
        Sid       = "AllowRootAccess"
        Effect    = "Allow"
        Principal = {
          AWS = "arn:aws:iam::123456789012:root"
        }
        Action    = "kms:*"
        Resource  = "arn:aws:kms:REGION:ACCOUNT_ID:key/KEY_ID"  #Specify the
KMS key ARN
      },
      {
```

```
          Sid       = "AllowS3BucketEncryption"
          Effect    = "Allow"
          Principal = {
            AWS = "arn:aws:iam::123456789012:role/kms-role"
          }
          Action    = [
            "kms:Encrypt",
            "kms:Decrypt",
            "kms:ReEncrypt*",
            "kms:GenerateDataKey*",
            "kms:DescribeKey"
          ]
          Resource  = "*"
        }
      ]
    })
  }
```

The KMS key (**s3_encryption_key**) is configured with key rotation enabled to enhance security by periodically generating new cryptographic material. The associated policy grants full administrative control to the root account, while also authorizing an IAM role (**kms-role**) to perform encryption and decryption operations, ensuring secure and controlled access to the key's functionalities.

```
#GuardDuty
resource "aws_guardduty_detector" "audit_account" {
  enable = true
}

resource "aws_guardduty_organization_admin_account" "org_admin" {
  admin_account_id = "123456789012" # Audit account ID
}

resource "aws_guardduty_member" "member_account" {
  account_id                 = "987654321098" # Member account ID
  detector_id                = aws_guardduty_detector.audit_account.id
  email                      = "security@example.com"
  invite                     = true
  disable_email_notification = false
}

resource "aws_guardduty_organization_configuration" "org_config" {
  detector_id     = aws_guardduty_detector.audit_account.id
  auto_enable     = true
}
```

The configuration of GuardDuty involves enabling it in the audit account using the **aws_guardduty_detector** resource. The audit account is designated as the administrator for managing GuardDuty across the organization through the **aws_guardduty_organization_admin_account** resource. For centralized monitoring, the **aws_guardduty_member** resource is used to add and invite member accounts. Additionally, the **aws_guardduty_organization_configuration** ensures that **GuardDuty** is automatically enabled in all member accounts, enforcing organization-wide security monitoring.

By automating AWS security features with Terraform, you can achieve consistent and scalable protection for your cloud infrastructure, ensuring alignment with the best practices and compliance requirements. Additionally, there are numerous other AWS services available to help configure a secure and robust infrastructure in the AWS cloud. For further details on other AWS security services, refer to the AWS documentation.

Using Azure Security Features

Using Azure security features within Terraform provides an integrated and scalable approach to securing cloud resources. Azure offers a robust set of tools to protect infrastructure, applications, and data, allowing organizations to maintain control over their security posture. With Azure Security Center, Network Security Groups (NSGs), and Azure Key Vault, you can implement a multi-layered defence strategy. These tools ensure proactive protection, continuous monitoring, and quick response to potential vulnerabilities or threats. The following are some Azure services that can be helpful in building a secure environment in the Azure cloud:

- **Azure Security Center (Microsoft Defender for Cloud):** This tool helps to continuously monitor and assess your Azure resources for security vulnerabilities, providing hardening recommendations and compliance tracking. It ensures that all security configurations align with best practices and regulatory standards.
- **Network Security Groups (NSGs):** NSGs act as a firewall that controls both inbound and outbound network traffic to and from Azure resources. By defining rules within NSGs, you can control access to critical resources and prevent unauthorized communication, ensuring that only legitimate traffic flows through the network.
- **Azure Key Vault:** Azure Key Vault is a cloud service that securely stores and manages sensitive information such as secrets, encryption keys, and certificates. It is commonly used to safeguard credentials, API keys, and other sensitive data, ensuring that only authorized applications and users have access to them.

```
#Security center
resource "azurerm_security_center_subscription_pricing" "example" {
  tier = "Standard"
}

resource "azurerm_security_center_workspace" "example" {
  name                = "example-security-center"
  location            = "East US"
  resource_group_name = "example-resource-group"
}
```

The **azurerm_security_center_subscription_pricing** resource activates Microsoft Defender for Cloud at the subscription level, with the "Standard" tier offering advanced security capabilities such as vulnerability assessments and threat protection. Additionally, the **azurerm_security_center_workspace** resource sets up the security center workspace, which serves as the location for storing and analyzing security data.

```
# NSG
resource "azurerm_network_security_group" "example" {
  name                = "example-nsg"
  location            = "East US"
  resource_group_name = "example-resource-group"

  security_rule {
    name                        = "Allow-SSH"
    priority                   = 100
    direction                  = "Inbound"
    access                     = "Allow"
    protocol                   = "Tcp"
    source_port_range          = "*"
    destination_port_range     = "22"
```

```
        source_address_prefix      = "*"
        destination_address_prefix = "*"
      }
    }
```

The **azurerm_network_security_group** resource is used to create a Network Security Group (NSG) in the specified location and resource group. It defines security rules to manage traffic flow. For instance, the **Allow-SSH** rule permits inbound SSH traffic on port **22** from any source. The priority of the rules is crucial, as Azure processes NSG rules based on their priority order, with lower numbers indicating higher precedence.

```
#Key vault
resource "azurerm_key_vault" "example" {
  name                = "example-keyvault"
  location            = "East US"
  resource_group_name = azurerm_resource_group.example.name
  sku_name            = "standard"

  access_policy {
    tenant_id = "<tenant_id>"
    object_id = "<object_id>"

    key_permissions = [
      "get",
      "list",
      "create",
      "delete"
    ]

    secret_permissions = [
      "get",
      "list"
    ]
  }
}
```

This **azurerm_key_vault** resource creates an Azure Key Vault, with an access policy allowing a specific user (identified by **object_id**) to perform key and secret management operations such as **get**, **list**, **create**, and **delete**. It ensures that only authorized entities can access the sensitive data stored within the Key Vault.

Incorporating these services with Terraform allows for automated security management, which ensures compliance, reduces human error, and supports continuous monitoring, ultimately contributing to a more secure and resilient Azure environment. Additionally, there are numerous other Azure services available to help configure a secure and robust infrastructure in the Azure cloud. For further details on other Azure security services, refer to the Azure documentation.

Enabling GCP Security Tools

Google Cloud Platform (GCP) offers a suite of powerful security tools to safeguard cloud environments, including Security Command Center (SCC), Identity and Access Management (IAM), and Key Management Service (KMS). These tools are essential for managing permissions, encrypting data, and detecting threats, ensuring that cloud resources remain secure, compliant, and protected against vulnerabilities. Using Terraform to implement these services allows for automated, repeatable security configurations, enabling a secure foundation for workloads on

GCP. The following are some GCP services that can be helpful in building a secure environment in the GCP cloud:

- **Identity and Access Management (IAM)**: IAM controls access to GCP resources by assigning permissions and roles to users, groups, or service accounts.
- **Key Management Service (KMS)**: KMS allows you to create, manage, and use cryptographic keys for data encryption in GCP at rest.
- **Security Command Center (SCC)**: SCC provides centralized visibility into your GCP environment, detecting misconfigurations, vulnerabilities, and threats across all your resources.

```
#IAM
resource "google_project_iam_binding" "example" {
  project = "<project_id>"
  role    = "roles/storage.admin"

  members = [
    "user:example-user@example.com"
  ]
}
```

This example configuration binds the **storage.admin IAM** role to a user, granting them permissions to manage Google Cloud Storage resources in the specified project.

```
#KMS
resource "google_kms_key_ring" "example" {
  name     = "example-key-ring"
  location = "global"
  project  = "<project_id>"
}

resource "google_kms_crypto_key" "example" {
  name     = "example-key"
  key_ring = google_kms_key_ring.example.id
  project  = "<project_id>"

  rotation_period = "100000s"
  next_rotation_time = "2025-01-01T00:00:00Z"
}
```

This configuration creates a KMS key ring and a cryptographic key, enabling the encryption of sensitive data in GCP. The key is set to rotate every 100,000 seconds to enhance security.

```
#Security command center
resource "google_security_center_organization_settings" "example" {
  organization = "<organization_id>"
  enable_asset_discovery = true
}
```

This Terraform configuration enables Security Command Center for an entire GCP organization, allowing SCC to monitor the resources and detect vulnerabilities or threats.

By leveraging these tools with Terraform, organizations can ensure a consistent security posture across their GCP environments, while simplifying the management and deployment of security configurations. Additionally, there are numerous other GCP services available to help configure a secure and robust infrastructure in the GCP cloud. For further details on other GCP security services, refer to the GCP documentation.

Centralizing Security Policies with Terraform

In a multi-cloud environment, organizations often use multiple cloud providers such as AWS, Azure, and GCP. Centralizing security policies across these platforms can be a challenging task due to the unique security models and compliance requirements of each provider. Terraform enables organizations to create reusable, centralized security modules that enforce consistent policies across AWS, Azure, and GCP, while respecting the specific security controls and configurations of each cloud provider. By leveraging Terraform's declarative nature, security policies can be centrally managed, automated, and applied across various environments, reducing the risk of misconfigurations and ensuring adherence to security best practices.

```
module "multi_cloud_security" {
  source = "./security_module"

  aws_vpc_id          = "vpc-12345678"
  azure_subnet_id      = "/subscriptions/abc/resourceGroups/rg1/providers/
Microsoft.Network/virtualNetworks/vnet1/subnets/subnet1"
  gcp_network_id       = "projects/my-project/global/networks/default"

  # Add other configuration parameters specific to each cloud provider as needed
}
```

This Terraform module (**`multi_cloud_security`**) configures security policies for a multi-cloud environment. It takes parameters such as **`aws_vpc_id`**, **`azure_subnet_id`**, and **`gcp_network_id`** to define the relevant resources for each cloud provider. The module ensures that the correct security configurations—whether they are AWS Security Groups, Azure Network Security Groups (NSGs), or GCP Firewall Rules—are applied according to the cloud provider's native infrastructure.

Writing Cloud-Agnostic Terraform Code for Portability

As organizations adopt multi-cloud strategies, the ability to write Terraform configurations that are portable across AWS, Azure, and GCP becomes crucial. Cloud-agnostic Terraform code minimizes rework, reduces management overhead, and enables consistent infrastructure provisioning regardless of the cloud provider. This section explores techniques to abstract cloud-specific details, create reusable modules, and validate configurations for portability across multiple platforms.

Abstracting Cloud-Specific Configurations

Cloud abstraction in Terraform refers to the practice of creating Infrastructure as Code (IaC) configurations that deploy similar resources across multiple cloud providers (AWS, Azure, GCP, and so on) while accounting for the specific nuances, configurations, and requirements of each provider. This enables you to use a single Terraform configuration to manage resources across various cloud environments, minimizing the effort needed to rework or replicate infrastructure definitions for different clouds. The key to achieving this abstraction lies in Terraform's support for conditionals, dynamic blocks, and reusable modules, which allow the infrastructure code to dynamically adjust based on the cloud provider in use.

- **Conditionals:** In Terraform, you can use `if` or `count` functions to define conditional logic that switches between cloud-specific configurations at runtime. This allows the same block of code to adapt based on the provider being used, making it possible to write one configuration that works across AWS, Azure, and GCP.

- **Dynamic Blocks:** Dynamic blocks in Terraform allow you to generate code based on input variables or resources. This is particularly useful when working with cloud-specific resource properties that vary across providers. By using dynamic blocks, you can create modular configurations that adapt their structure according to the cloud provider or environment at hand.
- **Modules:** Terraform modules encapsulate specific configurations into reusable components. By defining separate modules for each cloud provider, you can abstract cloud-specific resource definitions, making it easier to deploy consistent infrastructure while allowing each module to expose a standardized interface. This modular approach ensures that Terraform code can be reused across different cloud environments without duplicating effort or manually adjusting configurations for each provider.

```
variable "cloud_provider" {
  type = string
}

resource "aws_instance" "example" {
  count = var.cloud_provider == "aws" ? 1 : 0
  ami           = "ami-123456"
  instance_type = "t2.micro"
}

resource "azurerm_virtual_machine" "example" {
  count = var.cloud_provider == "azure" ? 1 : 0
  name                = "examplevm"
  location            = "East US"
  resource_group_name = "example-rg"
  size                = "Standard_B1s"
}

resource "google_compute_instance" "example" {
  count = var.cloud_provider == "gcp" ? 1 : 0
  name         = "example-instance"
  machine_type = "e2-micro"
  zone         = "us-central1-a"
}
```

This Terraform snippet defines a variable **`cloud_provider`** to dynamically choose which cloud provider's resources to deploy. Based on the value of **`cloud_provider`**, it conditionally creates an AWS EC2 instance, an Azure Virtual Machine, or a GCP Compute instance using the count parameter. If the provider matches the respective condition (for example, **`"aws"`**, **`"azure"`**, or **`"gcp"`**), the resource is created; otherwise, the count is set to 0, and the resource is not created. This allows for cross-cloud abstraction in a single Terraform configuration.

Validating Configurations across Clouds

Validation in Terraform ensures that infrastructure code works as intended across multiple cloud environments (for example, AWS, Azure, GCP). It involves testing configurations for consistency, syntax errors, and cloud-specific issues, making it easier to maintain cloud-agnostic Infrastructure-as-Code (IaC). Validation improves the reliability of deployments and reduces risks when managing infrastructure in multi-cloud environments. The following are some methods that can be leveraged to validate Terraform configurations:

- **Terraform validate**: This built-in command checks for syntax errors and logical issues within Terraform configuration files. It ensures that the configuration is syntactically correct and can be planned and applied without issues. For example, it will catch missing variables or incorrect resource definitions, helping prevent deployment failures across clouds.

```
terraform validate
```

- **Linting**: Tools such as **tflint** are used to analyze Terraform files for cloud-specific best practices and common mistakes. These tools can detect improper configurations, resource limits, and security flaws specific to a cloud provider (for example, using deprecated resource attributes or incorrect IAM roles in AWS).

```
tflint --config .tflint.hcl
```

- **Testing**: To ensure cross-cloud compatibility, deploy configurations in sandbox or test environments. This can be achieved by using tools such as Terraform plan in multiple provider configurations or using automated testing frameworks to validate that the resources are correctly provisioned across AWS, Azure, and GCP without any errors.

```
terraform plan -var cloud_provider=aws
terraform plan -var cloud_provider=azure
terraform plan -var cloud_provider=gcp
```

By validating configurations early in the development lifecycle, you can ensure that your Terraform code is robust, portable, and ready for deployment across different cloud providers.

Writing cloud-agnostic Terraform code ensures infrastructure remains portable, scalable, and maintainable across AWS, Azure, and GCP. Abstracting cloud-specific configurations can streamline multi-cloud deployments while minimizing code duplication. Validating configurations across environments further strengthens security and reduces the risk of deployment errors. This approach enables teams to manage multi-cloud infrastructures consistently, driving operational efficiency and enhancing cloud security.

Standardizing IAM and Security Policies across Providers

Security in multi-cloud environments hinges on maintaining consistent Identity and Access Management (IAM) policies across providers. AWS, Azure, and GCP each have distinct IAM frameworks, which can create complexity when designing cross-cloud architectures. Standardizing IAM roles, permissions, and security policies across providers not only simplifies management but also reduces the risk of misconfigurations and potential breaches.

In this section, we explore how to design cross-cloud IAM structures, map provider-specific IAM implementations to common patterns, and write shared security policies using Terraform. We will also discuss Attribute-Based Access Control (ABAC) and secure management of service accounts.

Designing Cross-Cloud IAM Structures

Designing cross-cloud IAM structures in Terraform involves creating and managing IAM configurations that provide consistent, secure, and scalable permission models across multiple cloud environments, including AWS, Azure, and GCP. This ensures that users, services, and applications can be controlled with uniform access policies, regardless of the cloud provider. A cross-cloud IAM strategy simplifies identity management, reduces security risks, and improves operational efficiency by standardizing role and access control policies across all cloud platforms.

Each cloud provider has its own mechanisms for managing identities and permissions. While they may differ in implementation, the overall approach can be standardized with Terraform to maintain consistency across platforms.

- **AWS IAM**: AWS uses IAM to control access to resources within the AWS environment. IAM roles and policies are created and attached to users or services to define permissions. IAM roles are also used for cross-account access and identity federation, allowing users from external sources (such as corporate directories or other cloud providers) to access AWS resources.
- **Azure RBAC (Role-Based Access Control)**: Azure uses RBAC to manage permissions for resources. Azure RBAC defines roles such as Owner, Contributor, and Reader, which can be assigned to users, groups, or service principals. Roles control who can access resources and what actions they can perform. These roles are assigned at different levels: subscription, resource group, or resource level.
- **GCP IAM**: Google Cloud IAM defines roles and permissions at the project or organization level. Service accounts in GCP are used to manage permissions for applications or services that interact with Google Cloud resources. Roles can be predefined or custom, with each role granting specific permissions to interact with services or resources.

```
module "cross_cloud_iam" {
  source = "./iam_module"
  aws_role_name = "aws-example-role"
  azure_role_name = "azure-example-role"
  gcp_role_name = "gcp-example-role"
}
```

This module defines IAM roles and permissions for AWS, Azure, and GCP based on common parameters, ensuring that the same access model is applied consistently across cloud platforms. This approach simplifies security governance, improves compliance, and reduces the complexity of managing access control across multi-cloud infrastructures.

By designing a cross-cloud IAM structure in Terraform, organizations can ensure that their access control policies are consistent, secure, and scalable, enabling smooth operations across multiple cloud environments.

Writing Shared Security Policies in Terraform

Writing shared security policies in Terraform enables organizations to enforce consistent security practices across various cloud providers, including AWS, Azure, and GCP. By defining shared security policies, organizations can ensure that critical configurations, such as restricting public access to storage buckets, enforcing encryption, or limiting administrative access, are applied uniformly. This helps maintain a secure and compliant cloud environment regardless of the provider and reduces the likelihood of human error or misconfigurations that can lead to security vulnerabilities.

Terraform allows organizations to define shared security policies in a reusable manner using modules, conditional logic, and provider-specific configurations. This ensures that security policies can be consistently applied across all cloud environments (AWS, Azure, and GCP), and the policies can be tailored to meet the specific needs of each provider.

- **Reusable policy templates**: Terraform modules can be used to create security policies that work across multiple cloud platforms. These modules can define common security configurations, such as ensuring that storage buckets are not publicly accessible, that encryption is enforced, and that administrative access is limited to specific users or services.
- **CIS Benchmarks and custom policies**: Terraform allows you to integrate industry security standards, such as CIS benchmarks, to ensure that your cloud resources adhere to recognized best practices. You can also define custom policies specific to your organization's security requirements, such as limiting the permissions granted to administrative users or ensuring the use of secure authentication methods.

```
module "shared_security_policies" {
  source = "./security_module"

  aws_s3_bucket = {
    bucket_name = "example-bucket"
    public_access_block = true
    encryption = "AES256"
  }

  azure_storage_account = {
    account_name = "examplestorage"
    public_access = false
    encryption = "AES256"
  }

  gcp_storage_bucket = {
    bucket_name = "example-bucket-gcp"
    uniform_bucket_level_access = true
    encryption = "AES256"
  }
}
```

This Terraform module defines shared security policies for cloud storage resources across AWS, Azure, and GCP. For AWS, it ensures the S3 bucket is not publicly accessible and uses **AES256** encryption. In Azure, it disables public access to the storage account and enforces **AES256** encryption. For GCP, it enables uniform bucket-level access to the storage bucket and applies **AES256** encryption, ensuring consistent security practices across all cloud providers.

Implementing Attribute-Based Access Control (ABAC)

Attribute-Based Access Control (ABAC) is a model where access permissions are determined based on the attributes of the resources and the users requesting access. Unlike Role-Based Access Control (RBAC), which assigns permissions based on fixed roles, ABAC offers more dynamic flexibility by evaluating resource tags, user attributes, or metadata. This approach allows for finer-grained access control, making it ideal for complex, dynamic environments.

In Terraform, ABAC can be implemented by defining policies that leverage attributes such as tags, environment variables, or metadata. These policies can be set to grant or deny access based on resource attributes, such as the department or environment, and the user attributes, such as the role or team affiliation.

- **AWS ABAC**: AWS allows ABAC through IAM policies, where permissions are dynamically assigned based on the tags attached to resources. You can create policies that allow or deny actions based on specific resource tags, such as **"Environment: Production"** or **"Department: Finance."**
- **Azure ABAC**: Azure supports ABAC via Azure RBAC with tag-based policies that can govern access to resources depending on tags such as **"Project: X"** or **"Region: US-East."** By using these attributes, Azure enforces access rules that adapt to the environment's specifics.
- **GCP ABAC**: GCP leverages IAM policies with conditions, where access is granted or denied based on metadata attributes such as labels on resources or service account attributes.

```
resource "azuread_service_principal" "example" {
  display_name = "example-service-principal"
  tags         = ["Environment=Production", "Project=X"]
}
```

This example creates an Azure Active Directory (AAD) service principal named **"example-service-principal"** with tags to identify its environment (**"Production"**) and associated project (**"X"**).

Standardizing IAM and security policies across AWS, Azure, and GCP helps streamline operations, reduce complexity, and enhance security posture. By designing cross-cloud IAM structures and implementing ABAC, organizations can create a unified security framework. Writing shared Terraform policies ensures consistent enforcement of security standards, while careful management of service accounts mitigates risks associated with automation. This approach simplifies security governance, reduces cloud sprawl, and minimizes misconfigurations in multi-cloud environments.

Addressing Multi-Cloud Security Challenges and Best Practices

As organizations adopt multi-cloud strategies, they encounter unique security challenges, including identity sprawl, inconsistent security controls, and complex data governance. To mitigate these risks, robust security architectures must integrate identity federation, secure inter-cloud communication, data sovereignty enforcement, and Zero Trust principles across AWS, Azure, and GCP environments.

This section explores practical methods to address multi-cloud security risks while highlighting best practices to create a resilient and compliant cloud ecosystem.

Cross-Cloud Identity Federation

Cross-cloud identity federation enables users to authenticate once using a central identity provider and access resources across multiple cloud platforms without needing separate identities for each. This reduces the administrative overhead of managing multiple credentials, improves security by centralizing authentication, and streamlines access management across AWS, Azure, and GCP. Cross-cloud identity federation is essential for organizations using multi-cloud environments, as it ensures a consistent and secure access control model across cloud providers.

In Terraform, cross-cloud identity federation can be configured by integrating identity management services from each cloud provider or using third-party identity providers. Here is how each cloud provider supports identity federation:

- **AWS**: AWS IAM Identity Center (formerly AWS SSO) allows organizations to federate access to AWS resources by integrating with identity providers such as Active Directory, Okta, or other SAML 2.0 providers. IAM Identity Center manages the authentication process and assigns roles across AWS accounts, ensuring users have the appropriate permissions without needing separate AWS credentials.
- **Azure**: Azure uses Azure Active Directory (AAD) for identity federation, allowing seamless Single Sign-On (SSO) across Azure services. By integrating with AAD, users can authenticate once and access Azure resources while maintaining Role-Based Access Control (RBAC) through Azure AD, which assigns roles and permissions across multiple Azure subscriptions.
- **GCP**: Google Cloud Platform relies on IAM to provide federated access through third-party identity providers such as Okta, AAD, or Google Identity. By setting up identity federation, users can authenticate via an external identity provider and access GCP resources with the necessary IAM roles assigned.

```
resource "google_project_iam_binding" "example" {
  project = "my-gcp-project"
  role    = "roles/viewer"
```

```
    members = [
      "user:example-user@example.com",
      "group:group@example.com"
    ]
  }

  resource "google_iam_policy" "external_identity_policy" {
    bindings = [
      {
        role    = "roles/storage.objectViewer"
        members = [
          "principal://okta.com/identity/your-id-provider"
        ]
      }
    ]
  }
```

In this example, GCP IAM binding is configured to allow federated users from external identity providers (for example, Okta) to access GCP resources such as storage with the **`roles/storage.objectViewer`** role.

Securing Inter-Cloud Communication

Securing inter-cloud communication enables safe and efficient data exchange between services deployed across AWS, Azure, and GCP. This minimizes exposure to external threats while maintaining high performance and reliability. Solutions such as VPNs, VPC/VNet peering, and shared encryption keys ensure data confidentiality and integrity across cloud environments.

Terraform can orchestrate secure communication between clouds by provisioning and managing resources such as VPN gateways, encrypted tunnels, and cross-cloud network peering configurations. These setups ensure that sensitive data remains within secure, private networks while enabling seamless integration between services hosted on different platforms.

- **AWS**: Create a Site-to-Site VPN using AWS VPN Gateway to securely connect to Azure VNet or GCP VPC.
- **Azure**: Use Azure VPN Gateway to establish connections to GCP VPC or AWS VPC.
- **GCP**: Configure Cloud VPN to set up secure tunnels linking to AWS or Azure.

```
resource "aws_vpn_gateway" "example" {
  vpc_id = "vpc-12345678"
  amazon_side_asn = "65000"
}

resource "aws_vpn_connection" "to_azure" {
  customer_gateway_id = "cgw-12345678"
  type = "ipsec.1"
  static_routes_only = false

  tunnel1_preshared_key = "example-key-123"
  tunnel1_inside_cidr = "169.254.10.0/30"
  tunnel2_preshared_key = "example-key-456"
  tunnel2_inside_cidr = "169.254.11.0/30"
}
```

This example configures a VPN Gateway and establishes a Site-to-Site VPN connection with Azure using IPsec tunnels and pre-shared keys.

Enforcing Data Sovereignty across Clouds

Data sovereignty refers to the practice of ensuring that sensitive data remains within specific geographic boundaries to comply with local regulations and industry standards. This is vital for industries such as healthcare, finance, and government, which operate under strict data residency laws, such as GDPR or HIPAA.

Terraform enables the enforcement of data sovereignty by defining infrastructure configurations that restrict data storage and processing to specific regions across AWS, Azure, and GCP. By leveraging Terraform's multi-cloud capabilities, organizations can automate compliance and manage region-locked resources uniformly.

- **AWS**: Use S3 bucket policies and region-specific bucket creation to ensure data is stored within approved locations. For example: Store healthcare data in the us-east-1 region to meet HIPAA requirements.
- **Azure**: Configure region-locked storage accounts to restrict data residency. For example: Deploy storage accounts in the UK South region to adhere to UK data protection laws.
- **GCP**: Specify regional or multi-regional storage buckets to control where data is stored. For example: Use a bucket in the europe-west1 region to comply with GDPR.

```
resource "azurerm_storage_account" "sovereign_storage" {
  name                     = "sovereignstorage"
  resource_group_name      = "sovereign-rg"
  location                 = "UK South"
  account_tier             = "Standard"
  account_replication_type = "LRS"

  tags = {
    environment = "production"
    compliance  = "UK-GDPR"
  }
}
```

The **`azurerm_storage_account`** resource provisions a storage account locked to the **`UK South`** region to comply with GDPR and other UK data laws.

Implementing Zero Trust Networking in Multi-Cloud

Zero Trust Networking is a security model that assumes no entity, whether internal or external to the network, should be inherently trusted. Access to resources is continuously verified based on identity, device health, and context, ensuring granular control over resource interactions. This approach mitigates the risks of lateral movement, unauthorized access, and insider threats.

Terraform simplifies the implementation of Zero Trust Networking across AWS, Azure, and GCP by automating the deployment of security controls and integrating access mechanisms into Infrastructure as Code (IaC). Each cloud provider offers tools and services to support Zero Trust principles:

- **AWS:**
  - **AWS Network Firewall**: Protects VPC traffic with customizable rules for stateful and stateless filtering.
  - **IAM Policies**: Granular identity and access control for users, applications, and services.
  - **AWS PrivateLink**: Secures communication between VPCs or services using private connectivity.

- **Azure:**
  - **Azure Firewall**: Centralized, scalable firewall for inspecting and controlling traffic.
  - **Just-In-Time (JIT) VM Access**: Limits VM access to authorized users and short time windows.
  - **Azure AD Conditional Access**: Enforces user-based policies with context-aware conditions.
- **GCP:**
  - **BeyondCorp Framework**: Implements context-aware access for securing resources based on Google's Zero Trust principles.
  - **Identity-Aware Proxy (IAP)**: Secures application access by verifying identity and context for each request.

```
resource "google_project_iam_binding" "iap_binding" {
  project = "example-project"
  role    = "roles/iap.tunnelResourceAccessor"

  members = [
    "user:example@example.com"
  ]
}

resource "google_compute_firewall" "zero_trust_firewall" {
  name    = "zero-trust-firewall"
  network = "default"

  allow {
    protocol = "tcp"
    ports    = ["22", "443"]
  }

  target_tags = ["secure-access"]
}
```

This example creates IAM bindings and Identity-Aware Proxy to enforce context-aware access, while firewall rules allow only authorized traffic to specific resources.

Addressing multi-cloud security challenges requires proactive strategies to federate identities, secure inter-cloud communication, enforce data sovereignty, and adopt Zero Trust principles. By integrating these practices across AWS, Azure, and GCP, organizations can establish a consistent and resilient security posture, reducing risks and aligning with global compliance standards. This unified approach not only mitigates vulnerabilities but also strengthens overall cloud security operations.

Conclusion

This chapter explored the complexities and strategies necessary for securing cloud environments across AWS, Azure, and GCP using Terraform. We began by configuring multi-provider setups, addressing how to authenticate across platforms and manage version compatibility to prevent drift and misconfigurations. By defining scoped provider blocks for different regions and accounts, we established resource isolation and minimized exposure risks. Leveraging provider-specific security tools such as AWS GuardDuty, Azure Security Center, and GCP's Security Command Center, we maintained a consistent security framework, while utilizing each platform's strengths.

In addition to provider-specific tools, the chapter emphasized writing cloud-agnostic Terraform code to enhance portability and reduce cloud lock-in. Through abstraction techniques, shared IAM structures, and Attribute-Based Access Control (ABAC), we created reusable policies that aligned with security benchmarks across platforms. We also addressed challenges such as identity federation, cross-cloud communication, and data sovereignty, ensuring that security practices extend seamlessly across environments. By enforcing Zero Trust principles and implementing secure communication channels, the chapter provided a holistic approach to mitigating risks in multi-cloud environments, ultimately strengthening the overall security posture of distributed cloud architectures.

In the next chapter, we will cover the integration of policy-as-code and governance using Terraform, including an overview of Sentinel and Open Policy Agent (OPA). It focuses on writing, testing, and enforcing security policies across environments, preventing misconfigurations, and providing practical examples of advanced security policies.

Questions and Answers

1. **How do multi-provider configurations and proper authentication enhance security in multi-cloud environments?**

   Understanding multi-provider configurations allows teams to orchestrate resources across AWS, Azure, and GCP using Terraform. By establishing secure authentication methods such as leveraging IAM roles, service principals, and service accounts, organizations can enforce consistent access controls and minimize risks of unauthorized access. This approach not only ensures that each provider's security features are utilized effectively but also simplifies managing cross-cloud credentials and reduces complexity in hybrid environments.

2. **Why is managing provider versions and defining region/account scoping important for multi-cloud security integration?**

   Managing provider versions and defining region/account scoping are critical to maintaining compatibility and consistency across different cloud environments. Using Terraform to pin provider versions helps prevent unexpected behavior during upgrades and ensures that security configurations remain intact. Additionally, clearly defining regions and account scopes allows organizations to tailor resource deployments to specific compliance and latency requirements, thereby reducing the risk of misconfigurations and ensuring robust, secure, and regionally compliant deployments.

3. **What strategies can be used to leverage provider-specific security features while maintaining a unified security framework?**

   Terraform enables organizations to take advantage of provider-specific security features—such as AWS IAM policies and GuardDuty, Azure Security Center, and GCP Security Command Center—while centralizing security policies across clouds. By using Terraform modules, teams can encapsulate these features into reusable components and enforce a unified security framework that applies consistent policies regardless of the underlying provider. This strategy simplifies multi-cloud security management and ensures that each provider's unique capabilities are effectively utilized within a consolidated governance model.

4. **How can writing cloud-agnostic Terraform code improve portability and consistency across AWS, GCP, and Azure?**

   Cloud-agnostic Terraform code abstracts away provider-specific configurations, making it easier to deploy and manage infrastructure consistently across multiple cloud platforms. By using variables, dynamic blocks, and reusable modules, teams can create flexible configurations that adapt to different environments. This abstraction not only simplifies code maintenance and reduces duplication but also improves portability, allowing organizations to switch or integrate additional cloud providers with minimal rework while maintaining strong security practices.

5. **What are the key challenges in multi-cloud security integration, and how does implementing Zero Trust and cross-cloud identity federation address these issues?**

   Multi-cloud security integration involves addressing challenges such as disparate identity management systems, inconsistent network security controls, and varying data sovereignty regulations. Implementing Zero Trust principles ensures that every access request is continuously verified, regardless of its origin, thereby reducing the risk of lateral movement in the event of a breach. Additionally, cross-cloud identity federation streamlines access control by enabling unified authentication and authorization across multiple cloud platforms. Together, these approaches help create a cohesive security posture that minimizes vulnerabilities, ensures compliance with data residency laws, and enhances overall operational resilience in multi-cloud environments.

CHAPTER 5
Policy-as-Code and Governance with Terraform

Introduction

As cloud environments grow increasingly complex, ensuring security, compliance, and governance at scale becomes a critical challenge. Manual enforcement of security policies is prone to human error, inconsistent implementations, and compliance gaps, making automation a necessity. Policy-as-Code (PaC) offers a scalable solution by embedding security and compliance requirements directly into Terraform workflows, ensuring that cloud infrastructure adheres to organizational and regulatory standards before deployment. In this chapter, we explore the key Policy-as-Code tools that integrate with Terraform Sentinel, Terraform's native policy engine designed for HashiCorp Terraform Enterprise, **and** Open Policy Agent (OPA), a flexible, open-source policy framework that extends beyond Terraform to multi-cloud and Kubernetes environments. By comparing their capabilities, we will identify the best use cases for enforcing governance across AWS, Azure, and GCP.

Beyond selecting a policy engine, implementing Policy-as-Code effectively requires structured policy creation, testing, and enforcement within Terraform workflows. This chapter provides step-by-step guidance on writing reusable security policies using Sentinel and OPA, embedding them within Terraform modules, and automating their application across cloud environments. We will explore strategies for preventing misconfigurations and drift, including automated remediation, drift detection, and real-time enforcement using cloud-native tools such as AWS Config, Azure Policy, and GCP Security Command Center. Finally, through practical examples, we will demonstrate how to enforce critical security policies—such as restricting public S3 access, enforcing network security rules, and ensuring compliance with data protection regulations—across AWS, Azure, and GCP. By the end of this chapter, you will have a comprehensive understanding of how to integrate Policy-as-Code with Terraform to achieve scalable, automated, and auditable cloud governance.

Structure

In this chapter, we will cover the following topics:

- Overview of Sentinel and Open Policy Agent (OPA)
  - Sentinel: Terraform's Native Policy Engine
  - Open Policy Agent (OPA): Cloud-Agnostic Governance
  - Comparing Sentinel and OPA for Policy Enforcement
- Writing and Testing Security Policies for Any Cloud Provider
  - Defining Policy-as-Code Standards
  - Writing Sentinel Policies: Syntax and Logic

    - Developing OPA Policies with Rego
    - Testing and Validating Policies
- Enforcing Governance across Environments with Terraform Modules
    - Modularizing Governance for Multi-Cloud
    - Embedding Policies in Shared Modules
    - Automating Policy Attachments to Projects and Teams
    - Versioning and Managing Policy Changes
- Preventing Misconfigurations and Drift Using Policies
    - Drift Detection with Terraform and OPA
    - Policy-Based Resource Tagging and Classification
    - Misconfiguration Prevention: Guardrails for Cloud Resources
    - Auto-Remediation with Terraform and Sentinel
    - Continuous Monitoring and Real-Time Enforcement
- Practical Examples of Advanced Security Policies
    - AWS Security Policies
    - Azure Security Policies
    - GCP Security Policies
    - Cross-Cloud Data Protection Policies
    - Custom Policy Repositories and Catalogs

Overview of Sentinel and Open Policy Agent (OPA)

As cloud environments grow in complexity, the need for automated governance and security becomes critical. Policy-as-Code (PaC) is an essential practice for defining, codifying, and enforcing policies across cloud resources. This section explores two leading policy as code tools, Sentinel and Open Policy Agent (OPA), that integrate seamlessly with Terraform to provide governance, compliance, and security controls in multi cloud environments.

Both tools allow cloud engineers to enforce security rules at the infrastructure provisioning stage, preventing misconfigurations and ensuring continuous compliance. This section highlights how these tools function, their advantages, and how they can be incorporated into the existing workflows for AWS, Azure, and GCP environments.

Sentinel: Terraform's Native Policy Engine

Sentinel is HashiCorp's **Policy-as-Code (PaC) framework** designed to enforce governance, security, and compliance policies within Terraform Cloud and Terraform Enterprise. By integrating policy enforcement at the **infrastructure provisioning stage**, Sentinel ensures that all Terraform configurations adhere to predefined **security, operational, and compliance standards** before they are deployed.

Sentinel policies act as **guardrails** by evaluating Terraform plans and applying rules that determine whether infrastructure changes are permitted. These policies can prevent misconfigurations, enforce cost controls, and ensure compliance with industry standards such as **CIS, HIPAA, and GDPR**.

Sentinel is particularly useful in large-scale infrastructure environments where enforcing consistent security policies across multiple teams is critical. It allows organizations to implement **fine-grained**

access controls over infrastructure changes, reducing the risk of security vulnerabilities and misconfigurations.

Sentinel operates as an embedded policy engine within Terraform Enterprise and Terraform Cloud, where it intercepts Terraform workflows during the **`terraform plan`** and **`terraform apply`** phases. It evaluates the Terraform execution plan against a set of defined policies and determines whether the changes comply with security and governance rules.

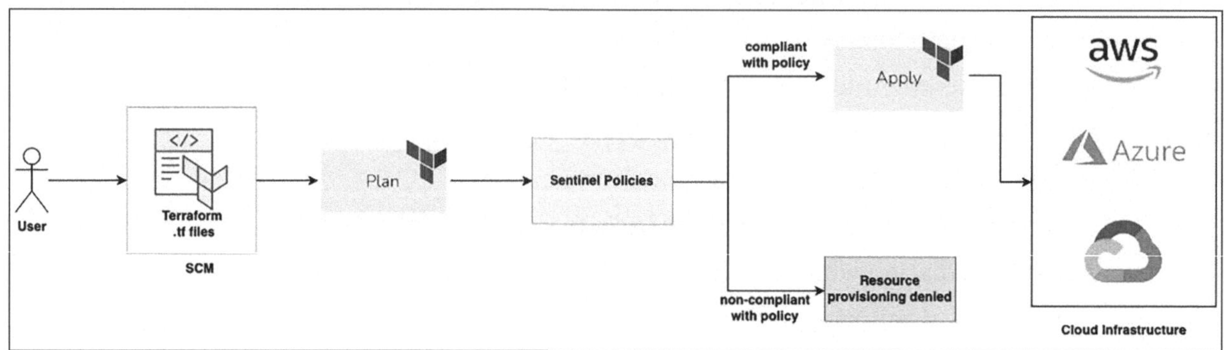

Figure 5.1: *Terraform Sentinel workflow*

Sentinel provides three enforcement levels to control how strictly policies are applied:

- **Advisory mode:** In advisory mode, Sentinel policies generate warnings when non-compliant infrastructure configurations are detected but do not block the deployment process. This mode is primarily used for monitoring purposes, allowing organizations to assess policy violations without enforcing strict compliance. It serves as a guidance mechanism, helping teams adopt best practices by providing recommendations while still permitting infrastructure changes to proceed.
- **Soft mandatory mode:** In this mode, Sentinel policies block non-compliant infrastructure deployments but allow manual overrides with appropriate approval. This mode is useful for enforcing governance while maintaining flexibility, as it ensures critical policies are followed while permitting exceptions when necessary. Typically, it is applied to policies that require human review, such as enforcing cost constraints or ensuring proper resource tagging, allowing teams to balance compliance with operational needs.
- **Hard mandatory mode:** In hard mandatory mode, Sentinel policies strictly enforce compliance by completely blocking non-compliant infrastructure deployments without any option for override. This mode is used for enforcing critical security and compliance requirements that must not be violated under any circumstances. It is commonly applied to high-risk policies, such as prohibiting public S3 buckets or enforcing encryption standards, ensuring that essential security measures are always upheld.

Sentinel pulls data from multiple sources to perform policy validation, which include:

- **Terraform configuration files**: Reads **`.tf`** and **`.tfvars`** files to evaluate declared resource configurations.
- **Terraform state file**: Extracts real-time infrastructure data to ensure compliance with deployed resources.
- **Provider APIs & external sources**: Fetches additional data (for example, AWS IAM policies, cloud cost estimates, or security vulnerability feeds) for **dynamic** policy checks.

```
import "tfplan/v2" as tfplan
policy "s3_bucket_encryption" {
  main = rule {
    all tfplan.resource_changes.aws_s3_bucket as bucket {
```

```
      bucket.change.after.server_side_encryption_configuration[0].rule.apply_
server_side_encryption_by_default
    }
  }
}
```

This Sentinel policy ensures that all AWS S3 buckets in the Terraform plan have server-side encryption enabled by enforcing the presence of an encryption configuration.

Features and Best Practices

The following are some features and best practices of Sentinel:

- **Seamless integration with Terraform Cloud/Enterprise:** Sentinel is seamlessly integrated into Terraform Cloud and Terraform Enterprise, allowing organizations to enforce policies with minimal setup. Since policies are evaluated automatically during Terraform runs, there is no need for separate security or compliance tools, ensuring governance is maintained as part of the existing infrastructure provisioning workflow.
- **Hierarchical policy management:** Terraform Sentinel supports hierarchical policy management, allowing organizations to enforce policies at different levels based on their governance needs. Policies can be applied globally across all Terraform projects or restricted to specific workspaces, ensuring tailored enforcement for different teams or environments. This flexibility enables stricter compliance requirements for production environments while allowing greater leniency for development and staging, balancing security with operational efficiency.
- **Writing effective Sentinel policies:** Writing effective Sentinel policies requires leveraging its lightweight Domain-Specific Language (DSL), which is designed for rule-based logic and infrastructure validation. To ensure consistency and scalability, policies should be modular and reusable, allowing organizations to enforce standardized security and compliance frameworks across multiple projects. Best practices include implementing CIS benchmarks for cloud security, enforcing HIPAA and GDPR compliance for data protection, and defining custom policies to prevent misconfigurations such as ensuring all EC2 instances are launched within a private subnet. By following these principles, organizations can maintain strong governance while streamlining infrastructure management.
- **Automating compliance with Sentinel:** Automating compliance with Sentinel allows organizations to enforce security and compliance checks seamlessly, minimizing the need for manual audits and reducing the risk of human error. By defining policies within Sentinel, teams can ensure that infrastructure adheres to best practices while maintaining deployment speed. This approach enables developers and engineers to focus on innovation without compromising security or regulatory requirements.

Open Policy Agent (OPA): Cloud-Agnostic Governance

Open Policy Agent (OPA) is an open-source, general-purpose policy engine that enables policy enforcement across various environments, including Terraform, Kubernetes, API gateways, and CI/CD pipelines. Unlike Terraform Sentinel, which is tightly integrated with Terraform Cloud and Enterprise, OPA is cloud-agnostic and can be used across multiple cloud providers and platforms. This flexibility makes OPA a powerful choice for organizations seeking a unified policy enforcement framework across their infrastructure and application layers.

OPA uses the **Rego policy language** to define rules that evaluate infrastructure configurations and determine whether they comply with specified policies. These policies are executed against input data, and OPA returns a decision, such as **allow** or **deny**, based on the rule definitions. Additionally, OPA can dynamically fetch data from external APIs or Terraform provider state, enabling more dynamic and context-aware policy enforcement. By integrating OPA with Terraform, organizations can ensure infrastructure adheres to security, compliance, and operational best practices before deployment.

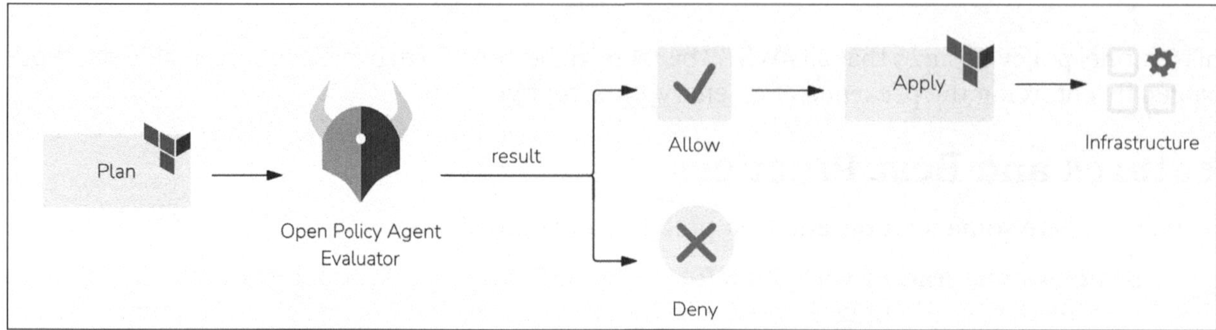

***Figure 5.2:** Workflow of OPA for Terraform (source)*

The Open Policy Agent offers the following two deployment models:

- **Local OPA agent**: The Local OPA Agent runs alongside Terraform, enforcing policy rules during the provisioning phase. When a Terraform plan is executed, the OPA agent evaluates the configuration against predefined policies and determines whether the infrastructure changes comply with security and governance standards. This model ensures real-time validation, preventing non-compliant resources from being deployed while keeping policy enforcement close to the execution environment.
- **OPA as a Service**: In this model, OPA operates as an independent service and integrates with Terraform via APIs. Terraform sends infrastructure configuration data to the remote OPA service, which evaluates it against the defined policies and returns an allow or deny decision. This centralized approach enables policy management across multiple teams and environments, ensuring consistency and simplifying compliance enforcement at scale.

```
package azure_security
default allow = false
allow {
  input.resource.type == "azurerm_network_security_group"
  input.resource.properties.security_rules[_].access == "Deny"
}
```

This OPA policy ensures that all Azure Network Security Groups (NSGs) have at least one security rule explicitly set to **Deny**, enforcing traffic restrictions for improved security.

```
package aws_security

default allow = false

allow {
  input.resource.type == "aws_s3_bucket_public_access_block"
  input.resource.properties.block_public_acls == true
  input.resource.properties.block_public_policy == true
  input.resource.properties.ignore_public_acls == true
  input.resource.properties.restrict_public_buckets == true
}
```

This example allows only AWS S3 buckets that have all public access block settings enabled for secure access control.

```
package gcp_security

default allow = false
```

```
allow {
  input.resource.type == "google_storage_bucket"
  input.resource.properties.uniform_bucket_level_access.enabled == true
}
```

The aforementioned example allows only Google Cloud Storage buckets with uniform bucket-level access enabled for centralized IAM control.

Features and Best Practices

Following are some features and best practices of Open Policy Agent:

- **Cloud-agnostic**: OPA is designed to work across AWS, Azure, GCP, Kubernetes, and on-premises environments, making it a versatile choice for organizations managing multi-cloud and hybrid infrastructure. Unlike Sentinel, which is tightly coupled with Terraform Cloud, OPA provides flexibility to enforce policies beyond Terraform, such as within Kubernetes workloads or API gateways. This broad compatibility allows organizations to standardize policy enforcement across their entire IT ecosystem.
- **Extensibility**: Beyond Terraform, OPA can be integrated into microservices security, API access control, and CI/CD pipelines, making it a highly adaptable policy engine. It can retrieve data dynamically from Terraform state files, cloud provider metadata, or external APIs, enabling dynamic and context-aware policy decisions. This flexibility ensures that policies can be tailored to meet diverse security and compliance requirements across different platforms.
- **Best practice**: A recommended best practice is to store OPA policies in version control systems such as Git and integrate them with Terraform workflows. This approach allows teams to track policy changes, enforce version control, and automate compliance checks as part of their Infrastructure-as-Code (IaC) pipelines. By embedding policy enforcement into Terraform execution, organizations can reduce human errors, improve security posture, and maintain consistent governance across all deployments.

Comparing Sentinel and OPA for Policy Enforcement

The following Comparison of Sentinel and OPA for policy enforcement highlights their differences in integration, scope, complexity, and best use cases, helping you to choose the right tool for infrastructure and security governance for your organization.

- **Integration:** Sentinel is natively integrated with Terraform Cloud and Enterprise, requiring minimal setup and offering seamless policy enforcement within Terraform workflows. In contrast, Open Policy Agent (OPA) integrates externally with Terraform CLI, requiring additional configuration to validate infrastructure changes.
- **Scope:** Sentinel is designed exclusively for Terraform, making it a specialized solution for enforcing policies within Terraform-based infrastructure provisioning. OPA, on the other hand, is cloud-agnostic and can be used across AWS, Azure, GCP, Kubernetes, API gateways, and CI/CD pipelines, allowing broader policy enforcement beyond Terraform.
- **Policy language:** Sentinel uses its own Sentinel DSL (Domain-Specific Language), which is optimized for infrastructure governance within Terraform. OPA utilizes Rego, a more flexible and expressive policy language designed for diverse policy enforcement scenarios beyond infrastructure.
- **Complexity:** Sentinel is simpler to implement, especially for organizations already using Terraform Cloud or Enterprise, as it requires minimal configuration. OPA provides greater flexibility but comes with higher complexity, requiring additional setup and deeper knowledge of the Rego language for advanced policy enforcement.

- **Enforcement modes:** Sentinel offers three predefined enforcement modes–Advisory, Soft Mandatory, and Hard Mandatory, to control how policies impact Terraform deployments. OPA, in contrast, provides fully customizable enforcement, allowing users to define their own decision-making logic and response actions based on specific use cases.

Following are the best use cases for Sentinel and Open Policy Agent:

- Sentinel is ideal for organizations that exclusively use Terraform Enterprise, as it provides a built-in, Terraform-native policy enforcement mechanism with minimal overhead.
- OPA is best suited for organizations managing multi-cloud environments, Kubernetes clusters, and non-Terraform workloads, offering broader enforcement capabilities beyond infrastructure provisioning.

Policy-as-Code tools such as Sentinel and OPA provide essential governance mechanisms for modern cloud infrastructure. Sentinel offers tight Terraform integration, ideal for organizations deeply embedded in HashiCorp's ecosystem. Meanwhile, OPA provides flexibility for multi-cloud and Kubernetes deployments. Integrating these tools into CI/CD pipelines fortifies security, minimizes drift, and ensures consistent compliance, forming a cornerstone of secure cloud automation.

Writing and Testing Security Policies for Any Cloud Provider

Policy-as-Code (PaC) transforms cloud governance by embedding security policies directly into the infrastructure provisioning lifecycle. By codifying compliance rules and best practices, organizations can automate enforcement, ensuring cloud environments align with frameworks such as CIS Benchmarks, NIST, and ISO 27001. This section delves into the creation and testing of security policies that are reusable across AWS, Azure, and GCP, enabling consistent governance in multi-cloud environments.

Crafting PaC involves defining standards, implementing policies with tools such as Sentinel and Open Policy Agent (OPA), and validating these policies to minimize errors. This ensures infrastructure deployments are secure, compliant, and resilient to misconfigurations.

Defining Policy-as-Code Standards

Policy-as-Code (PaC) standards define a structured approach to cloud security by enforcing predefined rules and best practices during infrastructure provisioning. These standards ensure that cloud resources are consistently configured to align with organizational policies and industry compliance frameworks such as CIS, NIST, and ISO 27001. By codifying security and governance policies within Terraform workflows, organizations can automate compliance, reduce human errors, and maintain a secure infrastructure at scale.

PaC standards are derived from well-established security frameworks that provide benchmarks for cloud security best practices. For example, the Center for Internet Security (CIS) offers hardened security guidelines for cloud providers, while the National Institute of Standards and Technology (NIST) provides a comprehensive security framework widely adopted by enterprises and government agencies. ISO 27001, a globally recognized standard, outlines best practices for information security management. Organizations translate these frameworks into Terraform-compatible policies using tools such as Sentinel (Terraform Enterprise) or Open Policy Agent (OPA) to enforce compliance checks before infrastructure changes are applied. These policies run during the `terraform plan` and `terraform apply` phases, ensuring that non-compliant resources are either flagged or blocked based on predefined enforcement rules.

Features and Best Practices

Following are some features and best practices for defining Policy-as-Code standards:

- **Baseline templates**: Organizations should develop reusable policy templates for frequently used cloud services, such as AWS S3, Azure Network Security Groups (NSG), and GCP IAM. These templates provide a foundation for security and compliance, reducing the need to write policies from scratch for each project. By standardizing these templates, teams can enforce security at scale while ensuring consistency across environments.
- **Versioning and modularity**: Policies should be stored in version-controlled repositories such as Git to track changes, facilitate collaboration, and allow iterative improvements over time. Using modular policy structures enables organizations to define policies in smaller, reusable components that can be applied to different projects, making policy enforcement more manageable and scalable.
- **Policy layers**: Organizations should implement multi-layered policy enforcement by applying policies at different levels, such as the organization, project, and environment. For example, global security policies can be enforced across an entire organization, while specific policies tailored to production, staging, and development environments ensure that different compliance requirements are met without restricting flexibility where needed.

By implementing Policy-as-Code standards within Terraform, organizations can proactively enforce security, compliance, and governance, ensuring that infrastructure is secure, scalable, and audit-ready from the moment it is provisioned.

Writing Sentinel Policies: Syntax and Logic

Sentinel is HashiCorp's Policy-as-Code (PaC) language designed for enforcing security, compliance, and operational best practices within Terraform Enterprise and Terraform Cloud. It allows organizations to define custom policies that validate Terraform infrastructure plans before changes are applied. Written in a lightweight Domain-Specific Language (DSL), Sentinel enables fine-grained control over infrastructure provisioning by evaluating Terraform plans (`tfplan`) and ensuring they comply with predefined security and governance rules.

Sentinel follows a structured approach to policy enforcement in Terraform:

- **Policy definition**: Users write Sentinel policies that define constraints for infrastructure resources, such as requiring encryption on storage buckets or restricting the use of public IP addresses.
- **Plan evaluation**: When Terraform executes a terraform plan, it generates a detailed summary of proposed infrastructure changes, which Sentinel uses as input for policy validation.
- **Enforcement**: Sentinel evaluates the Terraform plan against defined policies. Depending on the policy enforcement mode (Advisory, Soft Mandatory, or Hard Mandatory), Terraform will either allow, warn, or block non-compliant infrastructure changes.

Sentinel Policy Structure

Sentinel policies are structured into key components that define how rules are applied and enforced:

- **Imports**: Sentinel loads Terraform state (`tfplan`) and other external data sources, allowing policies to evaluate resource attributes, configuration changes, and existing state.
- **Rules**: Policies define specific conditions that must be met. Rules can check for security settings (for example, encryption enabled), compliance requirements (for example, IAM role restrictions), or operational constraints (for example, instance type restrictions).

- **Policy blocks**: Rules are grouped within policy blocks, providing structured enforcement logic. Policy blocks define the conditions for compliance and specify whether violations should trigger warnings or block deployment.

```
import "tfplan/v2" as tfplan
policy "gcp_instance_type" {
  main = rule {
    all tfplan.resource_changes.google_compute_instance as instance {
      instance.change.after.machine_type in ["e2-micro", "e2-small"]
    }
  }
}
```

This Sentinel policy ensures that Google Cloud VM instances are only provisioned with specific machine types, such as e2-micro or e2-small.

Developing OPA Policies with Rego

Open Policy Agent (OPA) is an open-source policy enforcement engine that allows organizations to enforce security, compliance, and governance policies across cloud infrastructure, Kubernetes, API gateways, and microservices. Unlike Terraform Sentinel, which is tightly integrated with Terraform Cloud/Enterprise, OPA is cloud-agnostic and works across AWS, Azure, GCP, and on-premises environments.

Rego is OPA's policy language, designed to define rule-based policies that evaluate configurations and determine whether they meet compliance and security requirements. Rego policies specify what configurations are allowed or denied, enabling fine-grained control over infrastructure provisioning.

Following is the working of Open Policy Agent:

- **Policy definition**: Administrators write Rego policies that define constraints for Terraform resources, such as restricting specific instance types, enforcing encryption on storage buckets, or ensuring IAM roles follow least privilege principles.
- **Data evaluation**: OPA evaluates Terraform plans (**`tfplan`**), provider state, or Kubernetes configurations against the defined Rego policies. It dynamically fetches relevant data to perform policy checks.
- **Enforcement**: Based on the evaluation, OPA returns an allow or deny decision. If a Terraform plan violates a policy, OPA can block deployment, ensuring non-compliant infrastructure is not provisioned.

```
package aws.s3
default allow = false
allow {
  input.resource.type == "aws_s3_bucket"
  input.resource.encryption == "AES256"
}
```

This OPA policy ensures that all AWS S3 buckets must have **`AES256`** encryption enabled; otherwise, the resource creation will be denied.

Testing and Validating Policies

Testing policies is crucial to prevent false positives and ensure accuracy, avoiding scenarios where valid infrastructure changes are mistakenly blocked. By validating policies before applying them in production, organizations can confirm that security and compliance rules function as intended without disrupting legitimate deployments. Effective testing helps fine-tune policies, ensuring they align with business requirements while maintaining governance.

Testing Sentinel Policies

Following the steps involved in testing and validating Sentinel policies:

- **Sentinel CLI**: Sentinel provides a Command-Line Interface (sentinel apply) that allows developers to test policies locally using mock data. This enables policy validation without executing actual Terraform plans.
- **Mocking plans**: Terraform plans can be **simulated with mock data** to test different infrastructure scenarios. This approach helps evaluate how policies behave under various conditions before enforcing them in real environments.

Following is an example of testing and validating Terraform Sentinel policy:

- This Sentinel policy ensures that all Azure Storage Accounts have encryption enabled.

```
import "tfplan/v2" as tfplan
policy "azure_storage_encryption" {
  main = rule {
    all tfplan.resource_changes.azurerm_storage_account as storage {
      storage.change.after.enable_blob_encryption == true
    }
  }
}
```

- To test this policy, create a mock Terraform plan as shown:

```
{
  "tfplan": {
    "resource_changes": {
      "azurerm_storage_account.test": {
        "change": {
          "after": {
            "enable_blob_encryption": true
          }
        }
      }
    }
  }
}
```

- Run the test with Sentinel CLI using sentinel apply

```
sentinel apply azure_storage_encryption.sentinel
```

If encryption is enabled, the policy will pass; else, the policy will fail.

Testing OPA Policies

The following are the steps involved in testing and validating OPA policies:

- **OPA CLI**: OPA provides a CLI (opa eval) that executes Rego policies against sample data. This allows users to test policies in isolation, ensuring they produce the correct allow/deny decisions based on input configurations.
- **Unit tests**: OPA supports writing unit tests for policies, allowing teams to define multiple test cases that validate expected policy behavior. By automating policy testing, organizations can ensure consistent enforcement across different Terraform deployments.

Following is an example of testing and validating OPA policy:

- This OPA policy ensures that all Azure Network Security Groups (NSGs) have at least one security rule denying traffic.

```
package azure.nsg
default allow = false
allow {
  input.resource.type == "azurerm_network_security_group"
  some rule
  input.resource.properties.security_rules[rule].access == "Deny"
}
```

- To test the policy, create a sample input file (**nsg.json**) with **an** NSG configuration:

```
{
  "resource": {
    "type": "azurerm_network_security_group",
    "properties": {
      "security_rules": [
        {
          "name": "deny_all",
          "access": "Deny"
        }
      ]
    }
  }
}
```

- Run the test with OPA CLI using opa eval

```
opa eval -i nsg.json -d azure_nsg.rego "data.azure.nsg.allow"
```

If an NSG rule with access: Deny exists, the policy will return true; else, it will be denied.

Writing and testing security policies across cloud environments ensures consistent governance and security. By leveraging Sentinel for Terraform-native environments and OPA for cloud-agnostic enforcement, organizations can achieve robust compliance across AWS, Azure, and GCP. This standardization mitigates risks, accelerates cloud adoption, and fortifies cloud security postures.

Enforcing Governance across Environments with Terraform Modules

As organizations scale their cloud environments, enforcing consistent governance across AWS, Azure, and GCP becomes increasingly complex. Terraform modules provide a scalable approach to standardize infrastructure provisioning while embedding security and compliance checks directly into the deployment process. By modularizing governance policies, teams can achieve uniformity, reduce drift, and ensure adherence to best practices across multi-cloud environments.

This section explores how Terraform modules can be leveraged to enforce governance, covering design patterns for multi-cloud deployments, embedding policies, automating policy attachments, and managing policy versions.

Modularizing Governance for Multi-Cloud

Modular governance in Terraform refers to structuring governance policies into reusable modules, ensuring consistent security and compliance enforcement across multi-cloud environments. Instead of duplicating policy logic for AWS, Azure, and GCP, governance modules are designed to be cloud-agnostic and adaptable, allowing organizations to scale Infrastructure as Code (IaC) efficiently. By abstracting policy enforcement, Terraform enables organizations to apply standardized security configurations, such as IAM roles, encryption, and logging, regardless of the underlying cloud provider. The following explains the working of modular governance:

- **Policy abstraction**: Governance policies, including IAM role assignments, encryption standards, logging configurations, and network security, are written as Terraform modules. These modules act as predefined compliance blueprints, ensuring every resource provisioned adheres to security best practices.
- **Provider blocks**: Terraform abstracts cloud-specific settings within provider blocks, enabling seamless integration across AWS, Azure, and GCP. This allows the same governance logic to be reused across different cloud providers while adapting to platform-specific implementations.
- **Resource provisioning**: When infrastructure is provisioned using these governance modules, security policies are automatically enforced. Terraform ensures that all resources (VMs, storage, databases, and networking) comply with predefined security and compliance standards, reducing misconfigurations and security risks.

```
module "secure_gcs_bucket" {
  source             = "./modules/gcs_bucket"
  encryption_enabled = true
  versioning_enabled = true
}
```

This Terraform module ensures that Google Cloud Storage buckets are created with encryption and versioning enabled for enhanced security and data protection.

Following are some best practices of modular governance:

- **Abstraction layers**: Separate core governance logic from cloud-specific configurations, allowing Terraform modules to remain adaptable across different providers. This separation ensures that compliance policies remain uniform while accommodating provider-specific differences.
- **Parameterization**: Use input variables to dynamically configure modules based on the cloud environment. For example, an encryption setting for AWS S3, Azure Blob Storage, and GCP Cloud Storage can be parameterized within a single module, avoiding redundant policy definitions.
- **Minimal duplication**: Maintain a centralized module repository with conditional logic (**`count`**, **`for_each, or depends_on`**) to switch between AWS, Azure, and GCP dynamically. This reduces code duplication and simplifies maintenance by ensuring governance policies are managed in a single location.

By modularizing governance in Terraform, organizations can enforce compliance at scale, maintain consistent security policies, and streamline multi-cloud infrastructure provisioning without duplicating effort across different cloud platforms.

Embedding Policies in Shared Modules

Embedding Sentinel or Open Policy Agent (OPA) policies directly within Terraform modules ensures that security, compliance, and governance checks are enforced at the source of resource provisioning. By integrating policies into modules, organizations prevent misconfigurations before deployment, reducing security risks and operational overhead. This approach guarantees policy adherence from development to production, ensuring that every infrastructure resource meets predefined compliance requirements without requiring separate policy enforcement tools. The following steps show how policies work with modules:

- **Policy definition**: Organizations write Sentinel or OPA policies and store them inside the module directory alongside Terraform configuration files. These policies define security and governance rules, such as enforcing encryption, restricting public access, or mandating IAM role constraints.
- **Module invocation**: When Terraform calls a shared module, it automatically evaluates and enforces the embedded policies. This ensures that all infrastructure created via the module complies with security best practices before deployment.
- **Shared module approach**: Instead of enforcing policies separately for each project, organizations use centralized governance modules that are reused across multiple cloud environments (AWS, Azure, GCP). This ensures consistent security enforcement, reducing duplication and maintaining a single source of truth for compliance.

```
policy "storage_encryption" {
  main = rule {
    all tfplan.resource_changes as resource {
      resource.type in ["aws_s3_bucket", "azurerm_storage_account", "google_
storage_bucket"] and
      resource.change.after.server_side_encryption_configuration != null
    }
  }
}
```

This Sentinel policy enforces server-side encryption for all storage resources within a shared storage module, ensuring compliance across AWS S3, Azure Blob Storage, and GCP Cloud Storage.

By embedding policies within Terraform modules, organizations streamline security governance, eliminate post-deployment compliance fixes, and create a scalable, policy-driven infrastructure that automatically enforces best practices across all cloud environments.

Automating Policy Attachments to Projects and Teams

Manually enforcing policies across multiple cloud projects and teams can lead to configuration drift, inconsistent governance, and security gaps. Automating policy attachment ensures that governance rules, security controls, and compliance policies are consistently applied across all cloud environments without human intervention. By integrating policy automation into Terraform workflows, organizations can eliminate manual errors, **improve security posture**, and maintain a uniform policy framework across AWS, Azure, and GCP projects.

- **Dynamic attachments**: Terraform enables the automated assignment of policies to cloud projects, accounts, and teams by dynamically referencing cloud identity management systems (for example, AWS IAM, Azure RBAC, GCP IAM). Policies are provisioned at scale, ensuring they are applied immediately whenever new projects or accounts are created.
- **Team-based access**: Policies are mapped to specific teams, departments, or business units based on IAM roles, service accounts, or group memberships. This ensures Role-Based Access Control (RBAC) is enforced, granting appropriate permissions and applying security rules per team.
- **Project scoping**: Terraform automates policy assignments based on environment type (development, staging, production). This allows different levels of security enforcement, such as relaxed access controls in dev environments while ensuring strict compliance in production.

```
variable "team_policies" {
  type = map(string)
  default = {
```

```
    devops_team   = "arn:aws:iam::aws:policy/AdministratorAccess"
    security_team = "arn:aws:iam::aws:policy/SecurityAudit"
    finance_team  = "arn:aws:iam::aws:policy/Billing"
  }
}

resource "aws_iam_group" "teams" {
  for_each = var.team_policies
  name     = each.key
}

resource "aws_iam_policy_attachment" "attach" {
  for_each   = var.team_policies
  name       = "${each.key}_policy_attachment"
  groups     = [aws_iam_group.teams[each.key].name]
  policy_arn = each.value
}

resource "aws_iam_policy" "tag_based_policy" {
  name        = "tagged_policy"
  description = "IAM policy applied based on tags"

  policy = jsonencode({
    Version = "2012-10-17"
    Statement = [
      {
        Effect   = "Allow"
        Action   = ["s3:ListBucket", "ec2:DescribeInstances"]
        Resource = "*"
        Condition = {
          StringEquals = {
            "aws:ResourceTag/Environment" = "production"
          }
        }
      }
    ]
  })
}

resource "aws_iam_policy_attachment" "tag_enforced" {
  name       = "tag_enforced_policy"
  groups     = ["devops_team"]
  policy_arn = aws_iam_policy.tag_based_policy.arn
}
```

This Terraform script dynamically attaches IAM policies to multiple teams based on a mapping variable and applies policies conditionally using resource tags, ensuring automated and scalable IAM policy enforcement.

The following are some best practices for automating policy attachments:

- **Dynamic mapping**: Use **for_each** loops and dynamic blocks in Terraform to dynamically attach policies to multiple teams, projects, or environments, reducing code duplication and ensuring efficient policy deployment.
- **Tag-based enforcement**: Leverage resource tags to determine which policies should be attached to specific cloud projects. This enables flexible policy enforcement, where policies are assigned dynamically based on predefined tagging strategies.

- **CI/CD integration**: Automate policy attachment using Terraform within CI/CD pipelines, ensuring that security and governance policies are enforced as part of the infrastructure provisioning process. This approach prevents non-compliant resources from being deployed by embedding policy checks into the DevOps workflow.

By automating policy attachments with Terraform, organizations can enforce security at scale, improve compliance, and reduce operational overhead, ensuring that policies are applied consistently and dynamically across multi-cloud environments.

Versioning and Managing Policy Changes

Versioning policies in Terraform is critical for tracking changes, ensuring stability, and enabling rollback mechanisms when enforcing security and compliance rules. By maintaining versioned policies, organizations can audit modifications, enforce specific versions across environments, and avoid unintended disruptions caused by misconfigured policies. Versioning also ensures that Terraform deployments consistently apply approved and tested policy rules, reducing security risks and operational overhead.

- **Semantic versioning**: Policies are tagged with versions such as v1.0, v1.1, or v2.0, allowing teams to track iterations over time. This ensures that each update is documented and enables organizations to enforce specific policy versions across Terraform deployments for consistency.
- **Module versioning**: Terraform references specific policy versions within modules, preventing breaking changes from affecting infrastructure. This means a Terraform module will always use the correct, tested policy version, avoiding unintended compliance violations.
- **Rollback mechanisms**: If a newly deployed policy version causes unintended issues or misconfigurations, Terraform can rollback to a stable policy version, ensuring that infrastructure governance remains intact. This approach minimizes downtime and prevents policy misconfigurations from impacting production environments.

```
module "rbac_policy" {
  source  = "git::https://github.com/org/terraform-modules.git//azure-rbac"
  version = "v1.2.0"
}
```

This Terraform script references a specific version (v1.2.0) of an Azure RBAC policy module from a Git repository, ensuring controlled and versioned policy enforcement across environments.

The following are some best practices for versioning and managing policy changes:

- **Changelogs**: Maintain a detailed changelog documenting every policy update, including the changes made, reasons for modifications, and any potential impact. This helps in troubleshooting and provides an audit trail for governance.
- **Testing**: New policies should be validated in a staging environment before rolling them out to production. This ensures that policy changes do not disrupt Terraform workflows or introduce compliance risks.
- **Granular control**: Different Terraform environments (for example, development, staging, production) may require different policy versions. Implementing granular control allows teams to apply stricter policies in production while maintaining flexibility in lower environments.

By implementing versioned policies in Terraform, organizations can ensure stability, enforce compliance across environments, and minimize disruptions caused by policy changes, resulting in a more secure and controlled infrastructure provisioning process.

Terraform modules serve as the backbone for enforcing governance across multi-cloud environments. By embedding policies directly within modules, automating attachments, and versioning governance frameworks, organizations can achieve scalable, consistent, and compliant infrastructure deployments. This modular approach minimizes drift, accelerates policy adoption, and ensures cloud environments remain secure as they scale.

Preventing Misconfigurations and Drift Using Policies

In rapidly evolving cloud environments, misconfigurations and infrastructure drift are among the primary causes of security vulnerabilities and compliance failures. Drift occurs when changes are made directly to cloud resources without updating the underlying Terraform code, resulting in discrepancies between the desired and actual state of infrastructure. Misconfigurations, on the other hand, stem from human error, lack of standardization, or oversight during provisioning.

By leveraging Policy-as-Code (PaC) frameworks such as Sentinel and Open Policy Agent (OPA), organizations can proactively enforce security guardrails, detect drift early, and even automate remediation. This section explores how policies can be used to maintain infrastructure integrity across AWS, Azure, and GCP.

Drift Detection with Terraform Sentinel and OPA

Drift detection in Terraform identifies discrepancies between Terraform's state file and the actual cloud infrastructure. Terraform maintains a state file that represents the expected configuration of resources. However, when changes are made outside Terraform, such as manual modifications in the cloud provider console or updates from external automation tools, the actual infrastructure no longer matches the state file. Drift detection helps flag these inconsistencies, ensuring that infrastructure remains aligned with the desired state and compliance policies.

- **Terraform plan phase**: When running terraform plan, Terraform compares the current cloud infrastructure state with the state file. Any unexpected changes (drift) are flagged in the plan output, highlighting resources that have been modified outside Terraform.
- **OPA integration**: Terraform Sentinel and Open Policy Agent (OPA) enforce governance policies during the plan or apply phases. These policies validate detected drift and ensure that infrastructure aligns with security and compliance standards. For example, a Sentinel or OPA policy can prevent changes that remove encryption from a storage bucket or weaken IAM permissions.
- **Drift reporting**: When drift is detected, Terraform Sentinel and OPA policies can trigger actions such as:
    - Alerts to notify security or operations teams.
    - Blocking deployments if compliance-critical resources have been modified.
    - Auto-remediation through Terraform automation, reverting changes back to the desired state.

```
policy "azure_iam_role_drift" {
  main = rule {
    all tfplan.resource_changes.azurerm_role_assignment as role {
      role.change.after == role.change.before
    }
  }
}
```

This policy ensures that RBAC role assignments remain unchanged, preventing unauthorized modifications in Azure IAM roles outside Terraform workflows.

The following are some best practices for configuring drift detection:

- **Frequent drift checks**: Integrate drift detection into CI/CD pipelines to continuously monitor infrastructure and identify unauthorized changes before they cause security or operational risks.
- **Immutable infrastructure**: Encourage re-deployment over manual changes, ensuring all modifications are performed through Terraform and not manually via cloud consoles.
- **Tagging and auditing**: Use resource tagging to track changes and establish clear audit trails, helping teams investigate and resolve drift by identifying who modified resources outside Terraform workflows.

By leveraging Terraform Sentinel and OPA for drift detection, organizations can maintain control over infrastructure, prevent compliance violations, and enforce security best practices, ensuring that infrastructure remains consistent, secure, and predictable across cloud environments.

Policy-Based Resource Tagging and Classification

Tagging is essential for resource traceability, cost allocation, security, and governance across cloud environments. By enforcing consistent tagging policies, organizations can categorize resources, track expenses, and ensure compliance with regulatory or operational requirements. Without standardized tagging, cloud environments can become disorganized, making it difficult to monitor usage, enforce policies, or apply security controls effectively. Automated policy-based tagging helps maintain visibility, accountability, and classification across AWS, Azure, and GCP.

- **Tag enforcement**: Policies are defined in Terraform to ensure that specific tag keys and values (for example, Environment, Owner, CostCenter) are attached to all resources at the time of creation. If required tags are missing, Terraform can either warn users or block deployment.
- **OPA/Sentinel rules**: Terraform Sentinel and Open Policy Agent (OPA) validate whether all resources comply with mandatory tagging policies before they are provisioned. Policies can enforce required tags, standardized formats, or conditional tags based on resource type. For example, a Sentinel or OPA policy could require that all production resources have a **`CostCenter`** tag to enable financial tracking.

```
package gcp.tags
deny[msg] {
  input.resource.labels["Environment"] == ""
  msg = "GCP Resource must have an 'Environment' tag"
}
```

This OPA policy ensures that GCP resource groups must have an Environment tag assigned; otherwise, deployment is denied.

The following are some best practices for tagging:

- **Consistent tag taxonomy**: Establish a standardized tagging schema across AWS, Azure, and GCP to ensure consistency. Organizations should define mandatory tags, naming conventions, and usage guidelines to avoid inconsistencies.
- **Tag auditing**: Regularly audit cloud resources using Terraform state files, cloud provider APIs, or policy checks to identify non-compliant or missing tags. Implement automated checks that flag or remediate improperly tagged resources.
- **Tagging as a guardrail**: **Treat tag enforcement as a security and compliance guardrail**, ensuring that critical resources cannot be deployed without proper tags. Sentinel or OPA policies should **block resource creation** if required tags are missing or incorrectly formatted, preventing policy violations before they impact production.

By automating resource tagging through Terraform, organizations can enforce governance policies at scale, improve cost and security management, and maintain organizational standards across multi-cloud environments.

Misconfiguration Prevention: Guardrails for Cloud Resources

Guardrails are policy enforced boundaries that prevent insecure or non compliant cloud configurations from being deployed through Terraform. They act as preventive controls, ensuring that critical misconfigurations such as publicly accessible S3 buckets, overly permissive IAM roles, unencrypted storage, or open security group ports are automatically detected and blocked before deployment. By integrating guardrails into Terraform workflows, organizations can enforce security, compliance, and operational best practices without relying on manual reviews.

- **Sentinel and OPA guardrails**: Guardrails are implemented as Sentinel or Open Policy Agent (OPA) policies. These policies define acceptable configurations, such as requiring encryption on databases, restricting security group rules, or enforcing tagging requirements. Any Terraform resource that violates these guardrails is flagged or blocked.
- **Terraform plan stage**: Terraform evaluates guardrails during the terraform plan phase. If policy violations are detected, such as an S3 bucket without encryption or a virtual machine deployed in an unapproved region, Terraform will fail the plan, preventing misconfigurations before resources are provisioned.
- **Enforced compliance**: Terraform only allows resource creation if all guardrail checks pass. Depending on the policy enforcement mode, Terraform may warn, require approval, or strictly block non-compliant infrastructure. This ensures that every deployed resource adheres to security, governance, and compliance standards.

```
policy "s3_no_public" {
  main = rule {
    all tfplan.resource_changes.aws_s3_bucket as bucket {
      bucket.change.after.acl != "public-read"
    }
  }
}
```

This Sentinel policy ensures that AWS S3 buckets are not publicly accessible by preventing the public-read ACL from being set.

By integrating Terraform guardrails with Sentinel and OPA, organizations can prevent misconfigurations at scale, enforce security policies consistently, and maintain a strong cloud governance framework across AWS, Azure, and GCP environments.

Auto-Remediation with Terraform Sentinel and OPA

Auto-remediation is the process of automatically correcting non-compliant infrastructure configurations identified through drift detection or policy violations in Terraform. Instead of relying on manual intervention, auto-remediation reduces operational overhead, ensures continuous compliance, and minimizes security exposure time by restoring misconfigured resources to a compliant state. This approach helps enforce governance policies at scale, ensuring that all cloud resources remain secure and aligned with best practices.

- **Policy trigger**: Terraform Sentinel or Open Policy Agent (OPA) enforces policies during the terraform plan or terraform apply phases. When a resource violates security or compliance policies, such as an unencrypted database, an overly permissive IAM role, or an exposed S3 bucket, Terraform detects the issue and flags it for remediation.

- **Rollback mechanism**: If Terraform detects an infrastructure drift (manual changes made outside of Terraform), it can automatically revert the resource to its last compliant state using Terraform's state management. This ensures that infrastructure always aligns with the desired configuration, eliminating unintended deviations.
- **Remediation scripts**: When a policy violation is detected, Terraform can trigger corrective scripts to modify or delete non-compliant resources. For example, an auto-remediation policy might:
    - Disable public access to an S3 bucket.
    - Enforce encryption on an unprotected database.
    - Restrict security group rules that allow unrestricted access.
    - Revert IAM role changes that grant excessive permissions.

```
package example.nsg
deny[msg] {
  input.network_security_group.rules[_].destination_port_range == "0-65535"
  msg = "Open port detected - NSG must restrict access"
}
```

This OPA policy ensures that Azure Network Security Groups (NSGs) do not allow unrestricted access to all ports (`0-65535`) by enforcing port restrictions.

By integrating auto-remediation with Terraform Sentinel and OPA, organizations can enforce compliance at scale, prevent security risks in real-time, and maintain cloud governance efficiently across AWS, Azure, and GCP.

Continuous Monitoring and Real-Time Enforcement

Continuous monitoring in Terraform ensures that security, compliance, and governance policies are enforced beyond the initial provisioning stage, addressing infrastructure drift, compliance violations, and evolving security threats dynamically. Without real-time enforcement, resources that were initially compliant may become misconfigured over time due to manual changes, infrastructure drift, or policy updates. By continuously evaluating cloud environments, Terraform ensures that deviations from best practices are detected and remediated in real time, maintaining a secure and compliant infrastructure.

- **Cloud-native tools**: Terraform integrates with AWS Config, Azure Policy, and GCP Security Command Center, which continuously monitor infrastructure changes and detect misconfigurations. These tools provide a real-time view of compliance status and trigger alerts when policies are violated.
- **Terraform integration**: Terraform syncs with these cloud-native monitoring tools to enforce compliance at every stage of the infrastructure lifecycle. When terraform apply is executed, Terraform validates resources against compliance rules, preventing misconfigured deployments.
- **Policy evaluation**: Sentinel and Open Policy Agent (OPA) periodically re-evaluate deployed cloud environments for policy violations. If drift is detected, Terraform can trigger auto-remediation or block further modifications until compliance is restored.

The following are some best practices for continuous monitoring and real-time enforcement:

- **Holistic coverage**: Ensure all critical resources (for example, databases, IAM roles, networking rules, encryption settings) across AWS, Azure, and GCP are continuously monitored for security and compliance violations.

- **Granular policies**: Apply detailed, fine-grained policies tailored to specific services and environments, ensuring different compliance requirements for development, staging, and production environments.
- **Alerting and reporting**: Integrate Terraform's monitoring tools with Slack, email, or SIEM solutions to receive real-time alerts whenever a compliance violation or drift is detected. This enables teams to respond quickly to misconfigurations before they become security risks.

By leveraging Terraform with cloud-native monitoring tools and real-time enforcement policies, organizations can ensure continuous security, proactive compliance, and governance automation across multi-cloud environments.

Preventing misconfigurations and drift is essential for maintaining secure and compliant cloud environments. By embedding policies into Terraform workflows, automating drift detection, enforcing tagging standards, and deploying auto-remediation mechanisms, organizations can minimize risk and ensure consistent governance across AWS, Azure, and GCP. Continuous monitoring further strengthens this approach by offering real-time enforcement and remediation capabilities.

Practical Examples of Advanced Security Policies

In cloud environments, advanced security policies are crucial for mitigating risks, ensuring compliance, and protecting sensitive workloads. By leveraging Policy-as-Code (PaC) frameworks such as Sentinel and Open Policy Agent (OPA), organizations can create scalable, automated guardrails that enforce strict security measures across AWS, Azure, and GCP environments.

This section delves into real-world implementations of complex security policies, providing hands-on examples that address common vulnerabilities in cloud configurations. Each example illustrates how to enforce policy-driven security controls at the infrastructure level, ensuring consistent governance across multi-cloud architectures.

AWS Security Policies

AWS offers powerful tools to manage and secure cloud infrastructure, but misconfigurations can lead to significant vulnerabilities. The following examples highlight common security gaps and demonstrate how to enforce preventive controls using Policy-as-Code:

Example 1: Prevent public access to AWS S3 buckets

This Sentinel policy ensures that AWS S3 buckets are not publicly accessible by enforcing that the block public access settings are enabled for every bucket.

```
import "tfplan/v2" as tfplan

policy "s3_no_public_access" {
  main = rule {
    all tfplan.resource_changes.aws_s3_bucket as bucket {
      bucket.change.after.block_public_acls and
      bucket.change.after.block_public_policy and
      bucket.change.after.ignore_public_acls and
      bucket.change.after.restrict_public_buckets
    }
  }
}
```

This policy blocks any Terraform deployment where **public access settings are not explicitly disabled**, ensuring **strong security and compliance** for AWS S3 buckets.

Example 2: Restrict EC2 Instances to Specific AMIs

This OPA policy restricts the creation of EC2 instances to a list of pre-approved Amazon Machine Images (AMIs).

```
package example.ec2
deny[msg] {
  input.resource_changes[_].type == "aws_instance"
  input.resource_changes[_].change.after.ami_id != "ami-12345678"
  msg = "Only approved AMIs are allowed"
}
```

This OPA policy ensures that **only an approved Amazon Machine Image (AMI) (ami-12345678) can be used for AWS EC2 instances**, blocking unauthorized AMIs.

Azure Security Policies

Azure environments face similar misconfiguration risks, particularly in network security and data storage. The following examples address common issues that can expose Azure environments to potential threats:

Example 1: Ensure NSGs Restrict Traffic to Known IP Ranges

This OPA policy blocks overly permissive NSG (Network Security Group) rules, ensuring that only traffic from specific IP ranges is allowed.

```
package example.nsg
deny[msg] {
  input.network_security_group.rules[_].source_address_prefix == "0.0.0.0/0"
  msg = "Inbound rules must restrict traffic to known IP ranges"
}
```

The policy evaluates NSG rules during Terraform apply, blocking configurations with **`0.0.0.0/0`** in inbound rules.

Example 2: Enforcing Security for Azure Virtual Machines

This Sentinel policy ensures that Azure Virtual Machines (VMs) have encryption enabled, use approved VM sizes, and are deployed within a secure network.

```
import "tfplan/v2" as tfplan

policy "secure_azure_vm" {
  main = rule {
    all tfplan.resource_changes.azurerm_virtual_machine as vm {
      vm.change.after.os_disk[0].encryption_settings.enabled and
      vm.change.after.size in ["Standard_D2s_v3", "Standard_D4s_v3"] and
      vm.change.after.network_interface_ids != []
    }
  }
}
```

This policy enforces disk encryption, restricts VM sizes to approved types, and ensures VMs are attached to a network interface, enhancing security for Azure Virtual Machines.

GCP Security Policies

Google Cloud environments require policies that enforce IAM and network configurations to prevent privilege escalation and external exposure.

Example 1: Enforcing Security for GCP Compute Engine

This Sentinel policy ensures that Google Cloud Compute Engine instances have disk encryption enabled, use approved machine types, and are not exposed to the public internet.

```
import "tfplan/v2" as tfplan

policy "secure_gcp_compute_engine" {
  main = rule {
    all tfplan.resource_changes.google_compute_instance as instance {
      instance.change.after.boot_disk[0].disk_encryption_key != null and
      instance.change.after.machine_type in ["e2-standard-2", "n2-standard-4"]
and
      not any instance.change.after.network_interface as ni {
        ni.access_config != null
      }
    }
  }
}
```

This policy enforces disk encryption, restricts machine types to approved configurations, and blocks public IP exposure, ensuring Google Cloud Compute Engine instances remain secure.

Example 2: Prevent External IPs on Sensitive GCE Instances

This OPA policy ensures that sensitive GCE instances are not assigned external IP addresses.

```
package example.gce
deny[msg] {
  input.gce_instance.network_interface.access_config != null
  msg = "GCE instances must not have external IP addresses"
}
```

Cross-Cloud Data Protection Policies

In multi-cloud environments, ensuring consistent data security and compliance across AWS, Azure, and GCP is critical. Cross-cloud data protection policies enforce uniform encryption, data residency requirements, and access controls, preventing misconfigurations that could lead to data breaches, compliance violations, or regulatory penalties. Without a standardized approach, organizations risk inconsistent security settings, making data vulnerable in one cloud while secure in another. Terraform Sentinel and Open Policy Agent (OPA) provide automated policy enforcement to ensure that all cloud storage, databases, and data transfer mechanisms meet security and compliance standards.

Cross-cloud data protection policies can be enforced using Sentinel and OPA to validate infrastructure configurations before provisioning. These policies prevent the creation of non-compliant resources, ensuring that:

- Encryption is enabled by default for all cloud storage services, including AWS S3, Azure Blob Storage, and Google Cloud Storage (GCS).
- Data residency restrictions are enforced by blocking storage creation in unauthorized regions.
- Access control policies ensure that sensitive data is not publicly exposed and follows least privilege principles.

```
package cross_cloud.data_protection

deny[msg] {
  input.resource.type == "aws_s3_bucket"
  input.resource.region != "us-east-1"
```

```
    msg = "AWS S3 buckets must be created in us-east-1"
  }

  deny[msg] {
    input.resource.type == "azurerm_storage_account"
    input.resource.location != "eastus"
    msg = "Azure Storage accounts must be created in eastus"
  }

  deny[msg] {
    input.resource.type == "google_storage_bucket"
    input.resource.location != "us-central1"
    msg = "GCP Storage buckets must be created in us-central1"
  }
```

This OPA policy restricts cloud storage creation to approved regions, ensuring data residency compliance.

Custom Policy Repositories and Catalogs

Custom policy repositories serve as centralized storage for Policy-as-Code (PaC) rules, enabling organizations to standardize, reuse, and enforce governance policies across multiple cloud environments. By maintaining a dedicated repository for Terraform Sentinel or Open Policy Agent (OPA) policies, organizations can:

- Improve collaboration among teams by ensuring all policies are accessible and version-controlled.
- Reduce duplication by defining reusable security and compliance policies instead of maintaining scattered or redundant configurations.
- Ensure consistent governance by applying standardized security rules across AWS, Azure, GCP, and hybrid environments.

By treating policies as reusable components, organizations increase efficiency, minimize compliance risks, and streamline multi-cloud security enforcement.

Implementing advanced security policies across AWS, Azure, and GCP is critical for safeguarding cloud environments. These practical examples highlight how Policy-as-Code can enforce stringent controls, prevent misconfigurations, and promote secure, compliant infrastructure deployments. As cloud environments evolve, continuous refinement of these policies ensures long-term governance and resilience.

Conclusion

As cloud environments continue to evolve, Policy-as-Code (PaC) has become an essential strategy for enforcing security, compliance, and governance in infrastructure automation. This chapter explored the key policy engines, Sentinel and Open Policy Agent (OPA), providing a comparative analysis of their capabilities, integrations, and best use cases for AWS, Azure, and GCP. By leveraging Terraform's ability to enforce security policies at scale, organizations can standardize governance, reduce misconfigurations, and ensure adherence to industry frameworks such as CIS, NIST, and SOC2. Writing and testing policies using Sentinel and OPA, implementing them within Terraform modules, and automating policy enforcement across teams and projects allow enterprises to build scalable, audit-ready cloud environments.

Beyond policy enforcement, the ability to detect and remediate misconfigurations proactively is crucial to maintaining a secure cloud posture. Through drift detection, policy-based tagging, and continuous monitoring, organizations can identify security violations in real time and take automated remediation actions using Terraform. Practical examples in this chapter demonstrated real-world security policies across AWS, Azure, and GCP, addressing critical risks such as publicly exposed storage, misconfigured network rules, and improper identity access management. As Terraform continues to evolve, integrating Policy-as-Code with infrastructure automation will remain a cornerstone of cloud security, enabling teams to maintain compliance, reduce risk, and accelerate cloud adoption with confidence.

In the next chapter, we will explore the Terraform code scanning and validation tools, including Checkov, TFSec, and Terrascan, for ensuring secure deployments. It covers comparing scanning tools, writing custom validation rules, and best practices for maintaining code quality and security across environments.

Questions and Answers

1. **What is Policy-as-Code (PaC), and why is it essential for cloud security?**

   Policy-as-Code (PaC) is a methodology that enables organizations to define, enforce, and automate security and compliance policies using code. Instead of relying on manual audits or documentation, PaC ensures that security policies are codified, version-controlled, and enforced consistently across infrastructure deployments. This approach is crucial for cloud security because it eliminates human errors, reduces misconfigurations, and maintains compliance with industry standards such as CIS, NIST, and SOC 2. Terraform integrates with Sentinel and Open Policy Agent (OPA) to enforce policies during infrastructure provisioning, preventing security violations before resources are deployed.

2. **How do Sentinel and Open Policy Agent (OPA) differ in enforcing cloud security policies?**

   Sentinel is Terraform's native policy engine, designed to enforce policies within Terraform Enterprise and Cloud. It provides deep integration with Terraform workflows, enabling fine-grained control over infrastructure deployments. However, Sentinel is limited to Terraform and requires a Terraform Enterprise license.

   Open Policy Agent (OPA) is a cloud-agnostic policy engine that supports Terraform, Kubernetes, API gateways, and other platforms. OPA uses Rego, a declarative policy language, to define rules that can enforce governance across multiple cloud providers. Unlike Sentinel, OPA is open-source and can be used independently of Terraform, making it a more flexible choice for multi-cloud environments. The decision between Sentinel and OPA depends on the organization's infrastructure strategy and governance needs.

3. **How can Terraform be used to prevent infrastructure misconfigurations and enforce security best practices?**

   Terraform can prevent misconfigurations and enforce security best practices by integrating PaC frameworks such as Sentinel and OPA into its workflow. Organizations can define guardrails that automatically check configurations before resources are provisioned. Some examples include:

   - Drift detection to identify configuration changes outside of Terraform.
   - Automated security checks to prevent publicly accessible S3 buckets, open security groups, or unencrypted databases.
   - Policy-based tagging to ensure that resources have proper ownership, cost allocation, and compliance labels.
   - Auto-remediation policies that revert or correct non-compliant infrastructure changes.

   By embedding security policies directly within Terraform modules, organizations can proactively mitigate risks, enforce governance, and ensure compliance across multi-cloud environments.

4. **How does GitOps improve Terraform-based infrastructure governance?**

   GitOps is a declarative approach to infrastructure automation that leverages Git as the single source of truth for configuration and policy enforcement. When combined with Terraform and PaC tools such as Sentinel and OPA, GitOps enables:

   - Version-controlled policies, ensuring that infrastructure adheres to security baselines.
   - Automated compliance checks before merging infrastructure changes into production.
   - Policy-driven rollbacks that automatically revert non-compliant changes.
   - Collaborative governance, where teams can review and approve policies before they are enforced.

   By integrating Terraform with GitOps workflows, organizations can enforce strong governance practices, minimize manual intervention, and maintain an auditable history of infrastructure and security policies.

5. **What are some real-world examples of security policies that can be implemented using Terraform?**

   Several real-world security policies can be codified and enforced using Terraform with Sentinel or OPA:

   - **AWS:** Prevent public access to S3 buckets and restrict EC2 instances to approved AMIs.
   - **Azure:** Ensure Network Security Groups (NSGs) block unauthorized traffic and enforce security best practices for Azure Virtual Machines.
   - **GCP:** Prevent external IP addresses on sensitive Compute Engine instances and enforce encryption for Cloud Storage buckets.
   - **Cross-Cloud Policies:** Implement data residency policies, ensuring that sensitive data remains within specific geographical regions.

   These policies proactively mitigate security risks, enforce compliance, and automate governance, ensuring cloud infrastructure remains secure and audit-ready.

CHAPTER 6
Terraform Code Scanning and Validation

Introduction

In this chapter, we delve into the critical practice of Terraform code scanning and validation, a cornerstone for securing Infrastructure as Code (IaC) deployments in today's cloud environments. Readers will explore the significance of automated code scanning, which helps mitigate common vulnerabilities by integrating tools directly into CI/CD pipelines and shifting security left into the development lifecycle. We begin with an overview of Terraform code scanning, examining its role in identifying potential misconfigurations and security gaps early in the process. The chapter then provides a deep dive into three prominent scanning tools: Checkov, TFSec, and Terrascan, detailing their capabilities, how they work, and how they can be integrated into development workflows. In addition, we compare these tools across features, performance, and use cases, ensuring you understand which tool fits best for your team's needs and multi-cloud scenarios.

Building on these fundamentals, the chapter further explores the creation of custom security policies using policy-as-code approaches, with practical guidance on writing rules in Sentinel and OPA's Rego language. We also discuss best practices for ensuring code quality, such as managing policy exceptions, enforcing version control, and scaling code scanning in large teams to maintain robust security standards. By the end of this chapter, readers will be equipped to implement a comprehensive, automated security validation process for Terraform configurations, enabling them to detect and remediate vulnerabilities effectively across AWS, Azure, and GCP environments.

Structure

In this chapter, we will cover the following topics:

- Introduction to Terraform Code Scanning for Secure Deployments
  - Significance of Code Scanning in Terraform
  - Role of Code Validation in CI/CD Pipelines
  - Shifting Security Left with Terraform Scanning
- Deep Dive into Checkov for Comprehensive Security Scans
  - Introduction to Checkov
  - Working of Checkov
  - Running Checkov in CI/CD Pipelines
  - Analyzing and Remediating Checkov Findings
- TFSec: Lightweight and Effective Scanning Tool
  - Introduction to TFSec
  - Working of TFSec

  - Integrating TFSec into Development Pipelines
- Terrascan: Policy-as-Code for Multi-Cloud Environments
  - Overview of Terrascan
  - Working of Terrascan
  - Automating Terrascan in CI/CD Pipelines
- Comparing Popular Code Scanning Tools for Terraform
  - Feature Comparison (Checkov versus TFSec versus Terrascan)
- Writing Custom Rules for Terraform Code Validation
  - The Need for Custom Rules
  - Writing Custom Checkov Policies (YAML)
  - Crafting Custom TFSec Rules (Go Language)
  - Defining Custom Terrascan Policies (OPA Rego)
- Best Practices for Ensuring Code Quality and Security
  - Managing Policy Exceptions and Overrides
  - Version Control for Security Policies
  - Scaling Code Scanning in Large Teams

Introduction to Terraform Code Scanning for Secure Deployments

As organizations increasingly adopt Infrastructure as Code (IaC) to automate cloud deployments, security must evolve to match the speed and scale of infrastructure provisioning. Terraform, one of the most popular IaC tools, enables teams to define, version, and deploy infrastructure in a declarative manner. However, Terraform's flexibility also introduces potential misconfigurations, security vulnerabilities, and compliance gaps. This is where Terraform code scanning becomes essential.

Terraform code scanning involves analyzing HCL (HashiCorp Configuration Language) files to detect insecure configurations, policy violations, and non-compliant resources before deployment. By integrating code scanning into development workflows, teams can enforce security best practices, ensure compliance with standards such as CIS (Center for Internet Security) benchmarks, and reduce the likelihood of deploying vulnerable infrastructure.

This section explores the significance of code scanning, its role in CI/CD pipelines, and how shifting security left can enhance the overall security posture of cloud environments.

Significance of Code Scanning in Terraform

Terraform code scanning is a critical practice in Infrastructure as Code (IaC) that involves the static analysis of Terraform configuration files to detect potential security vulnerabilities, misconfigurations, and compliance violations before deploying infrastructure. By identifying these issues early in the development cycle, organizations can prevent security breaches, ensure adherence to best practices, and maintain robust cloud environments. The following are some common vulnerabilities addressed by Terraform scanning:

- **Open security groups:** Overly permissive ingress or egress rules in AWS Security Groups, Azure Network Security Groups (NSGs), or GCP Firewalls can expose services to unauthorized access.

- **Unencrypted data storage:** Failing to enable encryption for data at rest in services such as AWS S3, Azure Blob Storage, or GCP Cloud Storage can lead to data breaches.
- **Excessive IAM permissions:** Assigning broad permissions to IAM roles or service accounts can result in privilege escalation or unauthorized resource access.
- **Unrestricted public access:** Publicly exposing resources such as databases, virtual machines, or storage buckets can make them vulnerable to attacks.

Terraform code scanning tools analyze configuration files (for example, `.tf` or `.tf.json`) by applying predefined or custom rulesets. These tools simulate the execution of Terraform code without deploying resources, identifying risks that violate security benchmarks. The following are some best practices of Terraform scanning:

- **Regular updates:** Keep scanning tools up-to-date to cover the latest cloud vulnerabilities.
- **Continuous integration:** Integrate code scanning into CI/CD pipelines to ensure consistent security checks.
- **Policy refinement:** Continuously refine policies to match evolving security requirements.

By implementing Terraform code scanning, organizations can proactively manage security risks, maintain compliance, and ensure the integrity of their cloud infrastructure deployments.

Role of Code Validation in CI/CD Pipelines

Integrating Terraform code validation into Continuous Integration/Continuous Deployment (CI/CD) pipelines is essential for ensuring that infrastructure as code (IaC) configurations are secure, compliant, and free from errors before deployment. This automated validation process acts as a gatekeeper, preventing non-compliant infrastructure changes from reaching production environments. The following is the working of Terraform validation in CI/CD pipelines:

- **Terraform plan stage:** The CI/CD pipeline generates a Terraform plan that simulates the proposed infrastructure changes. This plan outlines the actions Terraform will take when applying the configuration.
- **Security scan:** Automated tools such as TFSec, Terrascan, or Checkov scan the generated plan or the Terraform configuration files for security violations, misconfigurations, and policy breaches.
- **Blocking deployment:** If vulnerabilities or compliance issues are detected during the scan, the pipeline is configured to fail, preventing the deployment. Developers are then prompted to address and rectify the identified issues before reattempting deployment.

The following is an example of a GitHub Actions workflow that triggers Checkov scans for Terraform code on each pull request:

```
name: Terraform Security Scan
on: pull_request
jobs:
  security:
    runs-on: ubuntu-latest
    steps:
      - name: Checkout Code
        uses: actions/checkout@v2
      - name: Run Checkov Scan
        run: checkov -d .
```

The following are some benefits of Terraform code validation in CI/CD pipelines:

- **Define severity levels:** Establish pipeline breakpoints for critical vulnerabilities, causing the pipeline to fail and block deployment. For non-critical issues, allow the pipeline to pass with warnings, ensuring that minor issues are acknowledged without hindering development progress.

- **Regular updates:** Keep validation and scanning tools up-to-date to ensure the latest security vulnerabilities and compliance standards are checked.
- **Custom policies:** Develop custom policies that reflect your organization's specific security and compliance requirements, in addition to standard checks.
- **Continuous monitoring:** Implement continuous monitoring and periodic reviews of the CI/CD pipeline to adapt to evolving security landscapes and infrastructure changes.

By embedding Terraform code validation into CI/CD pipelines, organizations can proactively manage infrastructure security and compliance, ensuring that only vetted and secure configurations are deployed across all environments.

Shifting Security Left with Terraform Scanning

Shifting security left is a proactive approach that integrates security measures into the earliest phases of the software development lifecycle. Instead of waiting for the deployment or production phase to identify security issues, this strategy embeds security directly into the coding, planning, and review stages. In the context of Terraform, which is widely used for managing cloud infrastructure as code, shifting security left means running code scans and validations during development to catch misconfigurations and vulnerabilities before they become part of live infrastructure.

Shifting security left means that security is not treated as an afterthought or a final checkpoint but as an integral component of the development process. For Terraform, this involves running scanning tools and validations on configuration files during code creation and review.

To effectively shift security left in Terraform workflows, consider integrating several practices into your development process:

- **IDE Integration:** Integrate scanning tools directly into your Integrated Development Environment (IDE). Plugins and extensions (for example, the Checkov plugin for VSCode) can automatically analyze Terraform code as you write it. This integration offers real-time feedback, helping developers spot issues immediately without needing to run separate commands or wait for a build. For example, a developer editing a Terraform file in VSCode might see an inline warning if a resource is missing encryption or if an overly permissive IAM policy is defined.
- **Pre-Commit Hooks:** Pre-commit hooks ensure that code is scanned locally before it is even committed to version control. This automated step acts as a final check to catch common security issues before they make their way into the shared repository. Tools such as TFSec or Terrascan can be integrated into a pre-commit hook. When a developer attempts to commit changes, the hook runs a scan of the Terraform configuration.

  ```
  pre-commit install
  pre-commit run -a
  ```

  This command sequence installs pre-commit hooks and then runs them on all files. If a vulnerability is detected, the commit is blocked until the issue is resolved.

- **Pull Request reviews:** Automating scans as part of the Pull Request (PR) review process provides an additional layer of security. When a PR is submitted, the CI/CD pipeline can trigger a scan of the changed Terraform files. This ensures that any potential issues are identified during code review rather than after the code has been merged. For example, developers might run terraform validate alongside Checkov or TFSec as part of the PR checks. Any issues found are reported directly in the PR, prompting the developer to fix the code before merging.

The following are some of the best practices for shift-left security with Terraform:

- **Integrate policy-as-code frameworks:** Use tools such as Sentinel (available in Terraform Cloud) to enforce organization-wide security and compliance rules early in the development process. These frameworks allow you to codify policies that are automatically applied to Terraform configurations.
- **Maintain and update scanning tools:** Security tools and policies need to evolve with emerging threats. Regularly update your scanning tools (such as Checkov, TFSec, and Terrascan) to ensure they include the latest vulnerability definitions and best practices.
- **Customize scanning rules:** In addition to using pre-built policies, develop custom rules that reflect your organization's unique security requirements. This ensures that your specific risk factors and compliance mandates are thoroughly checked.
- **Automate as much as possible:** Incorporate these scans into your CI/CD pipelines so that every code commit, pull request, and build automatically undergoes rigorous security checks. This automation not only reduces human error but also ensures consistency across all stages of development.

Terraform code scanning is a cornerstone of secure cloud deployments. By identifying misconfigurations early and embedding security into CI/CD pipelines, teams can prevent vulnerabilities from propagating into production environments. Shifting security left ensures that Terraform configurations adhere to security best practices, reducing drift and enhancing governance across AWS, Azure, and GCP environments. As organizations scale their IaC initiatives, continuous scanning will remain integral to achieving secure, compliant, and resilient cloud infrastructure.

Deep Dive into Checkov for Comprehensive Security Scans

As Infrastructure as Code (IaC) becomes the backbone of cloud provisioning, ensuring the security and compliance of Terraform configurations is paramount. *Checkov*, developed by Bridgecrew (now part of Prisma Cloud by Palo Alto Networks), is one of the most comprehensive and widely adopted open-source static analysis tools designed to secure IaC frameworks, such as Terraform, CloudFormation, Kubernetes, and Docker.

Checkov scans Terraform files to detect misconfigurations, policy violations, and non-compliance with security benchmarks such as CIS (Center for Internet Security), NIST (National Institute of Standards and Technology), and cloud-provider best practices. Its lightweight design, ease of integration, and extensive support for AWS, Azure, and GCP make it an essential tool for DevOps, cloud engineers, and security teams.

This section explores how Checkov operates, key policies it enforces, and practical steps to incorporate it into CI/CD pipelines for continuous security validation.

Introduction to Checkov

Checkov is a powerful static code analysis tool specifically designed for Infrastructure as Code (IaC), with a strong focus on Terraform configurations. It analyzes Terraform files written in HashiCorp Configuration Language (HCL), as well as Terraform plans exported in JSON format, to identify potential security vulnerabilities and misconfigurations before any cloud resources are provisioned. By enforcing policies as code, Checkov enables organizations to embed security checks directly into the development lifecycle, ensuring that security best practices are adhered to from the outset. The following are some capabilities of Checkov:

- **Extensive built-in policies**: Checkov comes with over 1,500 built-in policies that cover a wide range of security benchmarks and cloud best practices. These policies are designed to align with industry standards such as the CIS (Center for Internet Security) benchmarks, ensuring that your Terraform configurations follow proven security guidelines.

- **Custom policy support**: Organizations often have unique security requirements that go beyond standard benchmarks. Checkov supports custom policy definitions using formats such as YAML, Python, and Rego.
- **Integration with CI/CD platforms**: Checkov is built to integrate seamlessly into modern DevSecOps pipelines. It can be incorporated into various CI/CD platforms such as Terraform Cloud, GitHub Actions, GitLab CI/CD, and Jenkins. By integrating Checkov into these workflows, every code commit or pull request is automatically scanned, ensuring that only secure and compliant code is merged and deployed.

The following are some benefits of Checkov:

- **Consistency across multi-cloud environments**: Checkov offers uniform security checks regardless of whether your Terraform configurations target AWS, GCP, Azure, or other cloud providers. This consistency is crucial in multi-cloud environments, where ensuring that security standards are applied uniformly can be challenging.
- **Automation and early vulnerability detection**: By automating the scanning process, Checkov helps catch vulnerabilities early in the development lifecycle–long before they make it into production. This proactive approach reduces the risk of costly fixes and minimizes potential exposure to security breaches.
- **Scalability for large projects**: As infrastructure grows, manually reviewing Terraform configurations becomes impractical. Checkov scales effortlessly, validating large-scale projects with minimal manual overhead. This scalability ensures that as your environment expands, your security posture remains robust and compliant.

Working of Checkov

Checkov is a static analysis tool designed specifically for scanning Infrastructure as Code (IaC) configurations, especially Terraform files for security vulnerabilities, misconfigurations, and deviations from best practices. Unlike dynamic testing methods that require resource deployment, Checkov performs a thorough static analysis, which means it inspects code without actually creating or altering any cloud resources. This approach helps reduce risks and catch issues early in the development lifecycle. The following is a detailed explanation of how Checkov works, broken down into its key components:

- **Parsing terraform code**: Checkov begins by scanning the provided directory for Terraform configuration files (typically files with a `.tf` extension). This includes not only the primary configuration files but also any referenced modules and dependencies. By doing so, Checkov builds a complete picture of the infrastructure setup, even when configurations are spread across multiple files or modules.
- **Applying security policies**: Once the Terraform files are parsed, Checkov applies a library of predefined security policies against the configuration. These policies cover a wide range of best practices and compliance standards, including guidelines from CIS benchmarks, NIST, and other industry standards. Each policy is associated with a unique identifier (for example, **`CKV_AWS_18`**) and specifies a particular security control or configuration requirement. In addition to its extensive built-in policies, Checkov supports custom policies defined using YAML, Rego (OPA), or Python. This flexibility allows organizations to tailor the tool's checks to meet their unique security and compliance requirements.
- **Generating detailed reports**: After applying the policies, Checkov compiles a detailed report that lists each policy check, along with the outcome of that check. The report clearly indicates

which checks passed and which failed, including details about the resource, file location, and the severity of the issue. For example, when running the following command:

```
checkov -d ./terraform_code
```

Checkov scans the Terraform files within the `./terraform_code` directory. A typical output entry might look like as follows:

```
Check: CKV_AWS_18 - Ensure S3 buckets have server-side encryption
File: main.tf
Result: FAILED
```

This entry indicates that the S3 bucket configuration in **`main.tf`** did not meet the expected security standard that is it lacks server-side encryption.

Running Checkov in CI/CD Pipelines

Integrating Checkov into your CI/CD pipeline is a powerful way to ensure that every change to your Terraform code is automatically scanned for security vulnerabilities and misconfigurations before deployment. This integration not only helps catch issues early in the development lifecycle but also promotes a culture of DevSecOps where security is a continuous concern. The following is an example of configuring Checkov in a CI/CD pipeline for Terraform, using GitHub Actions as an example:

```
name: Terraform Checkov Scan

on: [pull_request]

jobs:
  security:
    runs-on: ubuntu-latest
    steps:
      - name: Checkout code
        uses: actions/checkout@v2

      - name: Install Checkov
        run: pip install checkov

      - name: Run Checkov
        run: checkov -d . --soft-fail
```

Refer to the following explanation of the aforementioned Workflow:

- **Trigger (on: `[pull_request]`):** The workflow is set to run on every pull request. This ensures that any changes proposed to the Terraform codebase are automatically scanned before they are merged.
- **Job environment (runs-on: ubuntu-latest):** The job runs on the latest Ubuntu runner, providing a consistent environment for running Checkov.
- **Checkout step:** The workflow uses the **`actions/checkout@v2`** action to clone the repository. This step is crucial because it provides the pipeline with the latest Terraform files that need to be scanned.
- **Installation of Checkov:** Using **`pip install checkov`**, the pipeline installs Checkov. This command ensures that the latest version of Checkov is available for scanning.
- **Execution of Checkov:** The command **`checkov -d . --soft-fail`** instructs Checkov to perform the following:
  - Scan the current directory (`-d .`), which contains the Terraform code.

- Use the **--soft-fail** flag so that even if non-critical issues are detected, the pipeline continues to run, logging warnings instead of failing immediately.

Analyzing and Remediating Checkov Findings

Checkov is a static analysis tool that, when integrated with Terraform workflows, performs security scans on your IaC code and produces detailed reports. These reports highlight failed checks by listing policy IDs, affected resources, severity levels, and actionable remediation steps. The findings help teams quickly identify misconfigurations and vulnerabilities before cloud infrastructure is provisioned, enabling faster and more secure deployments.

After running Checkov against your Terraform code, you receive a comprehensive report that can be exported in multiple formats, such as CLI output, JSON, or JUnit XML. The report typically includes:

- **Check ID and description:** Each finding is associated with a unique identifier (for example, **CKV_AZURE_41**) and a short description that explains the security concern or misconfiguration.
- **Resource details:** The report specifies the resource type and name (for instance, an Azure Network Security Group), along with the exact file and line number where the issue was detected. This precision makes it easier for developers to locate and inspect the problematic code.
- **Severity levels:** Findings are often tagged with severity ratings (such as low, medium, or high), allowing teams to prioritize fixes based on the potential impact of the vulnerability.
- **Remediation Guidance:** For each failed check, Checkov provides clear remediation steps. This might include modifying specific configuration blocks or applying best practice settings, thereby guiding developers toward a secure configuration.

The following is an example output from Checkov for an Azure resource, along with remediation instructions. In this case, the report identifies that an Azure Network Security Group (NSG) rule allows unrestricted inbound access for RDP (port 3389), which can pose a significant security risk.

```
Check: CKV_AZURE_41 - Ensure NSG does not allow unrestricted RDP access
Resource: azurerm_network_security_group.my_nsg
File: /example.tf:1-17
Remediation: Modify the Terraform configuration to restrict access:
```

The following is the remediation snippet to fix the findings generated by Checkov:

```
resource "azurerm_network_security_group" "my_nsg" {
  name                = "myNSG"
  location            = var.location
  resource_group_name = azurerm_resource_group.my_rg.name

  security_rule {
    name                       = "Allow_RDP"
    priority                   = 100
    direction                  = "Inbound"
    access                     = "Allow"
    protocol                   = "Tcp"
    source_port_range          = "*"
    destination_port_range     = "3389"
    source_address_prefixes    = ["192.168.1.0/24"]  # Restrict access to a
trusted IP range
    destination_address_prefix = "*"
  }
}
```

Checkov provides a powerful, scalable solution for securing Terraform configurations across AWS, Azure, and GCP environments. By embedding Checkov into CI/CD pipelines and automating policy enforcement, organizations can **shift security left**, reduce vulnerabilities, and ensure **consistent cloud governance**. As IaC adoption grows, tools such as Checkov will play a pivotal role in **preventing misconfigurations** and enabling secure, compliant infrastructure at scale.

TFSec: Lightweight and Effective Scanning Tool

In the landscape of Terraform code scanning tools, TFSec stands out for its simplicity, speed, and effectiveness. Designed as a lightweight security scanner, TFSec focuses on analyzing Terraform configurations for misconfigurations and vulnerabilities without requiring extensive setup or dependencies. Its appeal lies in its ability to provide instant feedback during development, making it an ideal choice for developers looking to secure their Infrastructure-as-Code (IaC) with minimal effort.

Unlike more comprehensive tools such as Checkov, TFSec prioritizes ease of use and fast scans, ensuring developers can quickly validate configurations as part of their local development workflow or integrate it seamlessly into CI/CD pipelines. This section explores TFSec's core functionality, common use cases, and how it fits into the broader Terraform security landscape.

Introduction to TFSec

TFSec performs static analysis on Terraform code, without actually provisioning any cloud resources, to detect security vulnerabilities and misconfigurations. It inspects `.tf` files as well as Terraform plan JSON outputs, comparing the code against a set of predefined rules. These rules are based on best practices and common misconfigurations observed in cloud environments. TFSec is designed to be fast and easy to use. It requires minimal setup and integrates smoothly into developers' workflows, providing immediate feedback during the development phase. By analyzing code statically (that is, without executing it), TFSec ensures that potential issues are caught early, thereby reducing the risk of deploying insecure infrastructure.

TFSec provides a robust set of features that help developers and security teams maintain secure Terraform configurations:

- **Vulnerability detection:** TFSec comes with a comprehensive set of rules that cover a wide range of security issues. These rules are based on best practices and industry standards, which means you can trust that your configurations are being checked against recognized security benchmarks.
- **Terraform plan compatibility:** TFSec is not limited to scanning raw `.tf` files; it can also analyze Terraform plan outputs in JSON format. This allows for a more comprehensive security assessment by evaluating the planned changes before they are applied.
- **Customizable rule definitions:** For organizations with specific security requirements, TFSec supports YAML-based rule definitions. This enables teams to create custom checks that align with their internal policies and compliance standards.

Running TFSec against a Terraform codebase is straightforward. Consider a scenario where you have a directory containing your Terraform files. You can invoke TFSec using the following command, and it returns findings:

```
tfsec ./terraform_code

[AWS012] AWS S3 bucket should not have public access
  - resource: aws_s3_bucket.my_bucket
  - file: main.tf
  - line: 14
```

The **`tfsec`** output warns that the S3 `bucket` **`aws_s3_bucket.my_bucket`** defined in **`main.tf`** at line 14 has public access enabled, which poses a security risk. Publicly accessible S3 buckets can expose sensitive data and should be restricted to private access unless explicitly required.

Working of TFSec

TFSec works by performing a static analysis of your Terraform code, scanning the configuration files without actually provisioning any resources, to detect potential security vulnerabilities and misconfigurations. The following is the detailed working of TFSec:

- **Parsing Terraform Configuration**
  - **File discovery:** TFSec begins by scanning the specified directory for Terraform configuration files (files with the `.tf` extension). It identifies all relevant files, including those in nested modules or subdirectories, to form a complete picture of your infrastructure code.
  - **Parsing the code:** Using an HCL (HashiCorp Configuration Language) parser, TFSec reads and interprets the structure of the Terraform code. This process converts the code into an internal representation (such as an abstract syntax tree) that includes all resources, variables, and modules defined in your configuration to resolve references between resources, making it easier for the tool to analyze each component.
- **Static Analysis and Rule Application**
  - **Security policies:** TFSec comes with a comprehensive set of built-in security policies based on industry best practices and standards. These policies cover a wide range of potential issues. Additionally, TFSec supports custom policy definitions. Users can define their own rules using simple YAML configurations, allowing organizations to enforce their unique security and compliance requirements.
  - **Policy evaluation:** For each resource defined in your Terraform files, TFSec applies the relevant security policies. The tool checks if the resource configurations comply with the expected best practices. If a configuration violates any policy, TFSec flags it as an issue. The analysis is entirely static; that is, TFSec does not execute or deploy the infrastructure but rather inspects the code itself.
- **Processing Terraform Plan Outputs**
  - **Plan file scanning:** Besides scanning raw Terraform configuration files, TFSec can also process Terraform plan outputs in JSON format. TFSec can parse this JSON output to evaluate what changes are about to be made and ensure that no security policies are being violated in the planned state. By analyzing both the configuration and the execution plan, TFSec provides a more comprehensive assessment of your infrastructure. This dual approach helps catch issues that might not be evident by looking at the code alone.
- **Generating Reports and Output**
  - **Result aggregation:** Once all checks have been applied, TFSec aggregates the results. For each failed check, it generates the following:
    - The specific policy or rule that was violated (often identified by a unique check ID)
    - The resource and file location where the issue was detected (including line numbers)
    - A brief description of the problem and recommended remediation steps
  - **Output formats:** TFSec supports multiple output formats to integrate seamlessly into various workflows, such as CLI output, JSON, and JUnit XML.
  - **Soft-fail mode:** When run with the **`--soft-fail`** flag, TFSec will report issues as warnings rather than causing the entire process or pipeline to fail. This mode is particularly useful during early development or in environments where you want to track issues without blocking deployments.

Integrating TFSec into Development Pipelines

Integrating TFSec into your development pipelines for Terraform ensures that any misconfigurations or security vulnerabilities are identified and addressed at the earliest stages of the development process. By embedding TFSec as part of your CI/CD workflow, you can automate the validation of Terraform code, preventing insecure configurations from being merged or deployed into production. This proactive approach to security helps teams maintain a high level of security hygiene throughout the development lifecycle. The following is an example using GitHub Actions that demonstrates how to integrate TFSec into your pipeline:

```
name: TFSec Scan

on: [pull_request]

jobs:
  security:
    runs-on: ubuntu-latest
    steps:
      - name: Checkout code
        uses: actions/checkout@v2
      - name: Run TFSec
        uses: aquasecurity/tfsec-action@v1
        with:
          working-directory: .
```

The following is the explanation of the aforementioned pipeline script:

- **Triggering on pull requests:** The workflow is set to trigger on every pull request. This ensures that whenever code changes are proposed, TFSec scans the Terraform configuration before the code is merged, thereby catching security issues early in the process.
- **Checkout code:** The first step uses the **`actions/checkout@v2`** action to pull the latest version of your code repository. This makes sure that TFSec has access to all the Terraform configuration files that need to be analyzed.
- **Running TFSec:** The pipeline then executes the TFSec scan using the **`aquasecurity/tfsec-action@v1 action`**. The **`working-directory: .`** parameter indicates that TFSec should run in the repository's root directory where the Terraform files are located. This action automatically scans the code, evaluates it against a comprehensive set of built-in security policies, and outputs a report detailing any detected vulnerabilities.

TFSec provides a fast, easy-to-use Terraform scanning solution that complements the broader landscape of IaC security tools. Its lightweight nature makes it ideal for developers looking to catch misconfigurations **early in the development cycle**, promoting secure infrastructure from the start. While it may not have the depth of Checkov, its speed and simplicity ensure **quick adoption and seamless integration**, reinforcing Terraform code security across AWS, Azure, and GCP environments.

Terrascan: Policy-as-Code for Multi-Cloud Environments

In the evolving landscape of Infrastructure as Code (IaC), multi-cloud environments are becoming the norm for organizations striving for resilience and flexibility. However, managing security across diverse cloud platforms presents significant challenges. Terrascan, an open-source static code analyzer, addresses this by enabling policy-as-code enforcement across cloud-native infrastructure.

Terrascan's ability to perform multi-cloud scanning–covering AWS, Azure, GCP, and Kubernetes–makes it a versatile tool in proactively detecting misconfigurations, enforcing compliance standards, and reducing cloud security risks. This section explores Terrascan's core features, provider support, and how to leverage its OPA (Open Policy Agent) Rego-based policies for custom governance.

Overview of Terrascan

Terrascan is an open-source Infrastructure as Code (IaC) security scanner developed by Tenable, designed to help teams detect compliance violations and misconfigurations within Terraform codebases. It performs static analysis on Terraform files, checking them against a comprehensive library of predefined security policies as well as any custom rules defined by the user. This proactive scanning helps organizations ensure that their Terraform configurations meet security and compliance standards before resources are provisioned.

Terrascan reads Terraform configuration files and Terraform plans (if provided), comparing them against a set of security policies. These policies are defined using the Open Policy Agent (OPA) Rego language, allowing for both out-of-the-box checks and user-customizable rules. This dual approach ensures that Terrascan can enforce standard security practices while also adapting to an organization's unique compliance requirements. The following are some features of Terrascan:

- **Multi-cloud support:** Terrascan is designed to work across various cloud platforms, including AWS, Azure, GCP, as well as container orchestration platforms such as Kubernetes. This multi-cloud capability ensures that security is uniformly enforced, regardless of where your infrastructure is deployed.
- **Policy-as-code:** Utilizing OPA Rego for policy definition, Terrascan treats security policies as code. This means policies are version-controlled, customizable, and can be integrated directly into your development workflows. It empowers teams to define, enforce, and update security standards programmatically.
- **Extensibility:** Beyond the default policies provided, Terrascan supports the creation of custom rules. This extensibility allows organizations to tailor the scanner to meet their specific security baselines and compliance requirements, ensuring that even niche or proprietary standards are enforced.
- **CI/CD integration:** Terrascan can be easily embedded into CI/CD pipelines. This automation enables continuous security validation on every code commit or pull request, preventing misconfigurations from progressing further down the deployment pipeline.
- **Resource-level analysis:** Terrascan does not just perform a high-level scan; it drills down to the resource level. Whether scanning raw Terraform files or analyzing Terraform plan outputs, it applies granular security checks to each resource defined in your configuration. This detailed analysis helps pinpoint exactly where a policy violation occurs.

Suppose you want to scan a Terraform file (`main.tf`) that defines a Google storage bucket. You can run Terrascan with a command like this:

```
terrascan scan -t gcp -f main.tf
# -t specifies the target cloud provider (for example, gcp, aws, azure)
# -f specifies the file to scan (in this case, main.tf)
```

sample output:

```
Policy Violation: GCP Storage bucket should have uniform bucket-level access
enabled
  - Resource: google_storage_bucket.my_bucket
  - File: main.tf
  - Line: 3
```

The following is the explanation for the aforementioned output:

- **Policy violation:** The output indicates that the Terraform configuration violates a policy requiring that a GCP Storage bucket must have uniform bucket-level access enabled.
- **Resource:** The issue is detected on the resource **`google_storage_bucket.my_bucket`**.
- **Location:** The output pinpoints the problem to the file **`main.tf`** at line 3, helping developers quickly locate and address the misconfiguration.

Working of Terrascan

Terrascan is an open-source security scanner developed by Tenable that focuses on Infrastructure as Code (IaC) security, specifically for Terraform. It works by performing a static analysis of your Terraform configuration files, identifying misconfigurations and compliance violations before the code is applied to provision any cloud resources. The following is the detailed working of Terrascan:

- **File discovery and parsing**
  - **Scanning the files:** Terrascan begins by scanning the specified directory for Terraform configuration files and Terraform plan outputs. This step ensures that all relevant files, including those within nested modules or subdirectories, are identified.
  - **Parsing the configuration:** Using a parser for HashiCorp Configuration Language (HCL), Terrascan reads the Terraform files and converts the code into an internal data structure often similar to an Abstract Syntax Tree (AST). This parsed representation captures the defined resources, variables, modules, and their interdependencies, forming the basis for subsequent analysis.
- **Static analysis and policy evaluation**
  - **Built-in and custom policies:** Terrascan leverages a library of predefined security policies. These policies are formulated using Open Policy Agent's (OPA) Rego language, enabling policy-as-code. They cover common security best practices and compliance benchmarks for various cloud providers (AWS, Azure, GCP, Kubernetes, and so on). Terrascan allows organizations to write custom policies in Rego. This extensibility ensures that specific security or compliance requirements unique to an organization can be integrated into the scanning process.
  - **Rule matching:** For each resource defined in the Terraform configuration, Terrascan applies these rules. It examines the resource attributes and settings, such as access controls, encryption configurations, and network policies, to determine whether they meet the prescribed security standards.
  - **Resource-level analysis:** Terrascan performs granular checks at the resource level. Whether the target is a virtual machine, storage bucket, or network security group, each component is individually scrutinized for misconfigurations or policy violations.
- **Output generation and reporting**
  - **Aggregating results:** Once the analysis is complete, Terrascan aggregates the findings. It generates detailed reports that list every policy violation, including:
    - A unique check ID (for example, **`CKV_AWS_41`** for an AWS-related check)
    - A description of the violation (for example, **`"AWS S3 bucket must have versioning enabled"`**)
    - The specific resource that triggered the violation (for example, **`aws_s3_bucket.my_bucket`**)
    - The file name and line number where the issue was detected

- **Output formats:** The tool supports multiple output formats such as YAML, JSON, and even JUnit XML, making it easy to integrate into various workflows and CI/CD pipelines. These formats allow both human-readable reports and machine-parsed outputs for further automated processing.

Automating Terrascan in CI/CD Pipelines

Automating Terrascan in CI/CD pipelines for Terraform embeds continuous security validation into your development lifecycle. This integration ensures that every code change is automatically scanned for compliance violations and misconfigurations before being deployed, reducing the risk of introducing insecure code into production.

The following is an example GitHub Actions workflow that demonstrates how to automate Terrascan scans for Terraform configurations. This workflow triggers on both push and pull request events, ensuring that every code update is thoroughly checked.

```
name: Terrascan Scan

on: [pull_request]

jobs:
  scan:
    runs-on: ubuntu-latest
    steps:
      - name: Checkout code
        uses: actions/checkout@v2

      - name: Run Terrascan
        uses: tenable/terrascan-action@v1
        with:
          iac_type: terraform
          iac_version: v14
```

The following is the explanation of the preceding pipeline snippet:

- **Trigger event:** The workflow is configured to run on pull_request events, ensuring that any changes to the codebase trigger a scan. This means every pull request will be validated for security compliance.
- **Checkout step:** The **`actions/checkout@v2`** step clones your repository so that the latest Terraform files are available for scanning. This step is essential for providing Terrascan with the necessary context to analyze your IaC code.
- **Run terrascan step:** The workflow uses the **`tenable/terrascan-action@v1`** action to run the Terrascan scan. The parameters **`iac_type: terraform`** and **`iac_version: v14`** specify that the scan is for Terraform code and that it targets Terraform version 14 configurations. This step automates the analysis of your Terraform files against Terrascan's library of security policies.

Terrascan delivers a powerful multi-cloud policy-as-code solution for Terraform security, enhancing cloud governance by automating security checks across AWS, Azure, GCP, and Kubernetes. Its Rego-based custom policies and extensive provider support make it indispensable for teams operating in complex, multi-cloud environments. By integrating Terrascan into CI/CD pipelines, organizations can detect and remediate vulnerabilities early, ensuring their infrastructure is secure by design.

Comparing Popular Code Scanning Tools for Terraform

As Terraform continues to dominate Infrastructure as Code (IaC) deployments, the need for robust code scanning tools has become essential for ensuring secure cloud environments. This section provides a comprehensive comparison of Checkov, TFSec, and Terrascan, three of the most popular Terraform security tools. Each tool offers unique strengths, catering to different needs across small, medium, and large-scale deployments. By understanding their capabilities, performance, and best-fit scenarios, teams can make informed decisions about integrating them into their cloud security workflows.

Feature Comparison (Checkov versus TFSec versus Terrascan)

When selecting a Terraform IaC security scanner, it is important to understand the unique strengths and trade-offs of each tool. The following is a detailed feature comparison between Checkov, TFSec, and Terrascan, covering key aspects such as cloud support, policy frameworks, integration options, performance, and more:

- **Cloud support**
  - **Checkov:** Checkov supports a wide range of cloud providers, including AWS, Azure, GCP, and extends its reach to Kubernetes environments. This broad support makes it well-suited for organizations that manage diverse, multi-cloud infrastructures.
  - **TFSec:** TFSec primarily focuses on AWS, Azure, and GCP. While it covers the most commonly used cloud providers, its scope is slightly narrower, which can be ideal for teams whose deployments are limited to these environments.
  - **Terrascan:** Like Checkov, Terrascan offers extensive multi-cloud support (AWS, Azure, GCP) along with Kubernetes. This capability is especially useful for organizations that require uniform security checks across various types of infrastructure.
- **Policy framework**
  - **Checkov:** It uses a flexible approach with a library of predefined policies (often expressed in YAML or HCL) that can be extended through custom configurations. This dual approach allows for granular control over security rules.
  - **TFSec:** TFSec offers a set of predefined, simple rules designed for quick scanning. Its policy framework is straightforward, which contributes to its speed and ease of use but might limit deeper customization compared to other tools.
  - **Terrascan:** Terrascan leverages OPA's Rego language for policy definition. This "policy-as-code" approach provides high customization potential, enabling organizations to write complex, tailored rules that meet specific compliance requirements.
- **CI/CD integration**
  - **Checkov:** Checkov is highly integrable with popular CI/CD platforms such as GitHub, GitLab, Jenkins, and CircleCI. This makes it easy to embed into various development workflows for continuous security validation.
  - **TFSec:** While TFSec supports integrations with Terraform Cloud and common platforms such as GitHub and GitLab, its focus is on being a lightweight CLI tool that can be easily run in a pipeline.

- **Terrascan:** Terrascan supports integrations with GitHub Actions, CircleCI, and Terraform Cloud, among others. Its ability to operate as part of an automated CI/CD process ensures that every code change is validated against security policies before deployment.

- **Performance**
  - **Checkov:** Checkov performs deep scans that are moderately fast. The comprehensive nature of its checks might mean slightly longer runtimes, which is acceptable for environments that prioritize thoroughness over speed.
  - **TFSec:** TFSec is known for its high performance. It is lightweight and designed to perform quick scans, making it an excellent choice when rapid feedback is essential during development cycles.
  - **Terrascan:** Terrascan offers a balance, delivering moderate to high performance. Its performance may vary based on the complexity of custom OPA Rego policies, but it generally scales well in both small and large deployments.
- **Customization**
  - **Checkov:** With support for both predefined and custom policies written in YAML or JSON, Checkov offers high levels of customization. This flexibility is beneficial for organizations that need to enforce very specific security requirements.
  - **TFSec:** TFSec provides a simpler set of rules with limited customization options. Its design prioritizes ease of use and speed, which is advantageous for quick scans but may not satisfy all advanced compliance needs.
  - **Terrascan:** Using OPA Rego for policy definitions, Terrascan delivers high customization potential. Organizations can write sophisticated, custom policies that integrate seamlessly with their internal security frameworks.
- **Ease of use**
  - **Checkov:** While powerful, Checkov can be moderately complex to set up and configure due to the extensive options available. It requires a bit more initial configuration but pays off with its rich feature set.
  - **TFSec:** TFSec is very user-friendly, featuring a simple CLI that requires minimal setup. Its straightforward design makes it easy for developers to start scanning code quickly without a steep learning curve.
  - **Terrascan:** Terrascan strikes a balance; it is moderately easy to use, though configuring custom policies with Rego may require additional effort. Once set up, it provides detailed insights and robust customization.
- **Reporting**
  - **Checkov:** Checkov offers detailed reporting with various output formats such as JSON and CLI output. This makes it easier to integrate with automated pipelines and to conduct further analysis.
  - **TFSec:** TFSec provides basic CLI reporting. While its reports are clear and quick to generate, they might not include as much depth or detail as Checkov or Terrascan.
  - **Terrascan:** Terrascan provides detailed reports available in JSON, YAML, and CLI formats. These comprehensive reports help pinpoint issues with precision, making remediation more straightforward.
- **Policy library**
  - **Checkov:** Checkov's policy library is extensive and includes checks based on industry standards such as CIS, NIST, and PCI-DSS. This makes it well-suited for organizations with rigorous compliance requirements.

    - **TFSec:** TFSec focuses on detecting common misconfigurations, providing a straightforward set of rules that cover the most frequent security issues in Terraform configurations.
    - **Terrascan:** Terrascan offers a rich policy library that includes CIS benchmarks and allows for custom Rego policies. This dual approach helps organizations maintain both standard and customized security controls.
- **Scalability**
    - Checkov and Terrascan are designed to handle large-scale, complex infrastructure deployments. Their deep scanning capabilities and detailed reports make them suitable for enterprise environments with diverse cloud resources.
    - TFSec is extremely scalable as well, particularly for teams that need fast scans and immediate feedback, though its focus on simplicity might limit some advanced features.
- **Use cases**
    - Checkov is best suited for organizations requiring robust, customizable security checks that adhere to multiple compliance frameworks.
    - TFSec fits teams looking for a fast, lightweight tool that integrates seamlessly into their development pipelines with minimal setup.
    - Terrascan is ideal for enterprises that need detailed, granular security analysis with high customization via OPA Rego policies, especially when operating across multiple clouds.

Choosing the right Terraform scanning tool depends heavily on the team size, cloud strategy, and security requirements. TFSec offers unmatched speed and ease of use, making it ideal for early-stage development. Checkov delivers comprehensive security for enterprise environments, while Terrascan excels in policy enforcement across multi-cloud platforms. For robust cloud security, organizations often benefit from combining these tools in a layered scanning approach, reinforcing security throughout the Terraform lifecycle.

Writing Custom Rules for Terraform Code Validation

While predefined rules in tools such as Checkov, TFSec, and Terrascan cover a broad spectrum of common misconfigurations, organizations often face unique security requirements that standard benchmarks (such as CIS, NIST) may not address. Writing custom policies bridges this gap, enabling cloud teams to enforce internal governance standards, regulatory requirements, and best practices that align with their cloud architecture.

This section explores the rationale for custom rule creation and provides a hands-on approach to crafting policies for each major scanning tool, ensuring AWS, Azure, and GCP environments are compliant with internal security mandates.

The Need for Custom Rules

Organizations today operate in complex, diverse environments where compliance requirements and internal security standards can vary widely. Generic policies may not capture every nuance of an organization's cloud architecture, business processes, or industry-specific regulations. Custom policies enable teams to tailor security checks to:

- **Address specific compliance gaps:** Predefined policies might not cover every regulatory requirement an organization faces. For example, while CIS benchmarks provide a solid foundation, they may not fully account for additional internal security controls or industry-specific mandates.

- **Enforce niche cloud configurations:** Businesses often deploy services with unique configurations that are not addressed by standard policies. Custom policies allow organizations to enforce these niche configurations, such as specialized network segmentation, data handling rules, or access control measures across all deployments.
- **Establish internal governance standards:** Organizations may have internal guardrails or governance standards that go beyond external compliance frameworks. Writing custom policies allows companies to codify these internal rules, ensuring consistency across development teams and cloud environments.
- **Automate security for new services:** As organizations innovate and adopt new cloud services, these services may lack predefined security checks within existing policy libraries. Custom rules enable teams to quickly implement security controls for these emerging technologies, ensuring that new services are secured from the outset.

Consider a financial institution using Azure Key Vault for managing sensitive encryption keys. Standard security policies might mandate basic encryption and access controls. However, the institution might have a higher standard requiring double encryption (encrypting keys at rest with an additional layer) due to the critical nature of financial data and regulatory mandates. By writing a custom policy, the organization can enforce this extra layer of security across all deployments, ensuring that every Azure Key Vault instance complies with its stringent internal guidelines—even though this requirement exceeds standard CIS benchmarks.

Writing Custom Checkov Policies (YAML)

Checkov enables organizations to extend their built-in security checks by writing custom policies in YAML format. These custom policies allow you to define specific conditions that your Terraform resources must meet, conditions that may not be covered by the default rules. This flexibility is especially useful when your environment has unique compliance requirements or when you need to enforce niche configurations that reflect your internal governance standards. The following is a detailed explanation of how Checkov custom policies work:

- **Terraform parsing and conversion:** When Checkov runs, it scans your Terraform configuration files (written in HashiCorp Configuration Language, HCL). Internally, Checkov converts these files into a JSON representation. This standardized format simplifies the process of applying policies uniformly across different resource types.
- **YAML policy structure:** The policy file begins with metadata that includes a unique ID, a name, a category, and a severity level (for example, **`HIGH`**, **`MEDIUM`**, **`LOW`**). This metadata helps in organizing and prioritizing the rules. This definition section of the policy outlines the condition that the resource must meet. You specify the type of check (for example, attribute existence, value equality), the resource types to which the rule applies, the specific attribute to check, and the operator to compare values (for example, equals, exists). Optionally, you can specify the expected value.
- **Execution:** When Checkov scans your Terraform code, it evaluates each resource against the custom policy. If a resource does not meet the defined conditions, Checkov flags it as a violation. These findings are then aggregated into detailed reports that pinpoint the file and line number of the issue.

Let us create a custom policy to ensure that every Azure Storage Account has secure transfer enabled. This is a common security best practice that ensures data is transmitted over secure HTTPS connections.

- **Define rule metadata**

  Create a YAML file (for example, **`azure_storage_secure_transfer.yaml`**) in your custom policies directory. Start by defining the metadata for your policy:

```
metadata:
  id: "CKV_CUSTOM_AZURE_001"
  name: "Ensure Azure Storage Accounts have secure transfer enabled"
  category: "security"
  severity: "HIGH"
```

  - **id:** A unique identifier for the policy.
  - **name:** A descriptive name that conveys what the policy enforces.
  - **category:** The classification of the policy (for example, security, compliance).
  - **severity:** The risk level if the policy is violated.

- **Define the conditions**

  Next, define the conditions that must be met. In this case, the policy will check that the **`enable_https_traffic_only`** attribute for **`azurerm_storage_account`** is set to `true`.

```
definition:
  cond_type: attribute
  resource_types:
    - azurerm_storage_account
  attribute: enable_https_traffic_only
  operator: equals
  expected_value: true
```

  - **`cond_type`**: Specifies that the check is based on an attribute of the resource.
  - **`resource_types`**: Lists the Terraform resource types this rule applies to. In this example, it is **`azurerm_storage_account`** for Azure Storage Accounts.
  - **`attribute`**: The specific attribute to check **`enable_https_traffic_only`** in this case.
  - **`operator`**: The comparison operator. Using equals ensures the attribute's value must exactly match the expected value.
  - **`expected_value`**: The value that the attribute must have (in this case, true).

- **Deploy and Scan**

  After defining the custom policy, save your YAML file in a directory (for example, **`./custom_policies`**). To run Checkov with your custom policies, execute the following command:

```
checkov -d . --external-checks-dir ./custom_policies/
```

  - **-d .**: Specifies that Checkov should scan the current directory.
  - **--external-checks-dir:** Points Checkov to the directory containing your custom policies.

  When you run this command, Checkov will parse your Terraform files, convert them into JSON, and then apply both its built-in and your custom policies. If any Azure Storage Account does not have **`enable_https_traffic_only`** set to `true`, Checkov will report a violation with details about the resource, file, and line number.

Crafting Custom TFSec Rules (Go Language)

Customizing TFSec using the Go programming language allows you to write highly flexible, programmatic policies tailored to your organization's unique security requirements. Instead of relying solely on predefined checks, you can extend TFSec's functionality by crafting your own rules. These custom rules are written in Go and work by evaluating Terraform's HCL (or JSON) representation using condition checks implemented as Go functions and structs. The following is a detailed explanation of how custom TFSec rules work:

1. **Parsing and evaluation:** TFSec processes Terraform files by first parsing them from HCL into an intermediary JSON format. This transformation standardizes the resource representation

so that rules can uniformly evaluate different aspects of your infrastructure. Custom rules are written as Go functions that operate on the parsed data. They use Go's type system, specifically structs and functions, to inspect resource attributes, compare values, and determine whether a resource meets a particular security criterion.

2. **Rule registration:** Each custom rule is defined as a Go struct containing metadata such as a unique rule ID, service name, summary, impact description, resolution advice, and severity level. This metadata helps in categorizing and prioritizing policy violations. The custom rule is registered with TFSec using a registration function (typically in an **`init()`** function). Once registered, TFSec includes your rule in its scan cycle and applies it to all relevant Terraform resources.

Let us walk through an example of writing a custom rule in Go for AWS. In our example, we will create a rule that checks whether AWS S3 buckets have encryption enabled.

- **Create a rule file**

  Create a Go file (for example, **`custom_rule.go`**) within your custom rules package (for example, package custom). The file will contain the rule's definition and the registration logic.

```
package custom

import (
    "github.com/aquasecurity/tfsec/pkg/rule"
)

// init registers the custom rule when the package is imported.
func init() {
    rule.Register(rule.Rule{
        ID:            "CUSTOM_001",
        Service:       "AWS",
        ShortCode:     "s3-encryption",
        Summary:       "Ensure S3 Buckets have encryption enabled",
        Impact:        "Sensitive data stored in S3 could be exposed if not en-
crypted",
        Resolution:    "Enable server-side encryption on S3 buckets",
        Provider:      "aws",
        Severity:      rule.SeverityHigh,
        // Additional fields such as documentation URL or explanation can be
added as needed.
    })
}
```

  - **Package declaration:** The file starts with `package custom`, grouping your custom rules in a dedicated package.
  - **Import statement:** The custom rule uses TFSec's rule package, which provides the necessary structs and functions for defining rules.
  - **Rule registration:** Inside the **`init()`** function, the rule is registered using **`rule.Register()`.** This ensures that whenever TFSec runs and imports your package, it automatically includes your custom rule.
  - **Rule Metadata:**
    - **ID:** A unique identifier (**`"CUSTOM_001"`**) to differentiate this rule.
    - **Service:** Indicates the cloud service targeted (here, **`"AWS"`**).
    - **ShortCode:** A brief code (**`s3-encryption`**) that summarizes the rule's intent.
    - **Summary:** A concise description of what the rule checks.

    - **Impact and resolution:** Explain the potential impact if the rule is not followed and how to resolve the issue.
    - **Provider and Severity:** Define the target provider and the severity level. **`rule.SeverityHigh`** is defined for this example.

  In a real-world implementation, you would also include the logic that examines the Terraform JSON representation to verify that the **`server_side_encryption_configuration`** attribute exists and is properly configured. For simplicity, this example focuses on rule registration and metadata.

- **Compile and Run TFSec**

  After writing your custom rule, ensure your custom rules are compiled along with TFSec. Depending on your setup, this might involve adding your custom package to TFSec's source tree or compiling a custom binary that includes your rules. Run **`tfsec`** using the following command:

```
tfsec .
```

  This command instructs TFSec to scan the current directory. During the scan, TFSec will process your custom rules along with its built-in ones. If any S3 bucket does not have encryption enabled, your custom rule (**`CUSTOM_001`**) will trigger and report a violation.

```
[CUSTOM_001] Custom check: S3 bucket should have encryption enabled
  - Resource: aws_s3_bucket.my_unencrypted_bucket
  - File: main.tf
  - Line: 10
  - Description: S3 buckets should have encryption enabled to protect data at
rest.
```

Defining Custom Terrascan Policies (OPA Rego)

Terrascan leverages Open Policy Agent (OPA) and its declarative language, Rego, to enable a robust policy-as-code approach for Terraform security. With Terrascan, you can write custom policies in Rego that define the conditions under which your Terraform resources are considered compliant. This flexibility is particularly useful when default policies do not fully capture the unique security and compliance needs of your organization. The following is a detailed explanation of how custom Terrascan policies work:

- **Rego policies:** Terrascan uses Rego, a high-level declarative language, to define policies that Terraform resources must satisfy. These policies express conditions that inspect the JSON representation of Terraform configurations (converted from HCL). The use of Rego allows for expressive, flexible, and modular policy definitions.
- **Evaluation process:**
    - **Input data:** Terrascan converts your Terraform configurations (or plans) into a JSON format. This JSON is provided as input to the Rego policy.
    - **Rule logic:** The Rego policy defines conditions under which a resource is considered compliant. For example, a policy might check if a certain attribute exists, has a specific value, or meets a complex condition.
    - **Default behavior:** Typically, a policy will set a default value (for example, **`default allow = false`**), meaning that unless a resource explicitly meets the defined conditions, it is flagged as non-compliant.
- **Enforcement:** When Terrascan runs, it applies your custom Rego policies to every resource in your Terraform configuration. Any resource that fails to meet the policy conditions is reported as a violation, providing details such as the resource type, file location, and line number.

For this example, consider a common security best practice for Google Cloud: ensuring that every Google Cloud Storage bucket (represented by the Terraform resource **google_storage_bucket**) has Uniform Bucket-Level Access (UBLA) enabled.

- **Define the Policy in Rego**

  Create a file (for example, **gcp_storage_ubla.rego**) in your custom policies directory. The following Rego code defines a policy that enforces the UBLA requirement:

```
package terrascan.gcp.storage

# Default is to deny if conditions are not met.
default allow = false

# Allow if the resource is a Google Storage Bucket with UBLA enabled.
allow {
    input.resource_type == "google_storage_bucket"
    # Check that the attribute for uniform bucket-level access exists and is
enabled.
    input.parsed_body.uniform_bucket_level_access.enabled == true
    # parsed_body refers to the JSON decoded representation of the Terraform
resource configuration.
}
```

  - **Package declaration**: The policy starts with the package declaration `package terrascan.gcp.storage`, which organizes the policy under a logical namespace for GCP storage-related rules.
  - **Default behavior**: `default allow = false` indicates that by default, a resource is not compliant unless it explicitly meets the conditions defined.
  - **Condition check**: The allow rule is only true if:
    - The `input.resource_type` is `google_storage_bucket`, it means the policy applies only to Google Cloud Storage buckets.
    - The attribute `uniform_bucket_level_access.enabled` exists in the resource's configuration and is set to `true`. This condition verifies that the bucket has uniform bucket-level access enabled.

- **Deploy and Scan**

  After defining your custom Rego policy, save it to a directory (for example, **./custom_policies/**).

```
custom_policies/
└── gcp/
└── storage/
└── gcp_storage_ubla.rego
```

  To run Terrascan using your custom policy, execute the following command in your terminal:

```
terrascan scan -p . --policy-path ./custom_policies/
```

  - **`terrascan scan -p .`**: This command tells Terrascan to scan the current directory that contains your Terraform configurations.
  - **`--policy-path ./custom_policies/`**: This flag points Terrascan to your directory containing custom policies. Terrascan will load the Rego policy files from this location and apply them during the scan.

Writing custom Terraform code validation rules empowers organizations to enforce security standards tailored to their cloud environments. By leveraging tools such as Checkov (YAML), TFSec

(Go), and Terrascan (Rego), teams can address compliance gaps, secure cloud deployments, and build confidence in their IaC workflows.

Best Practices for Ensuring Code Quality and Security

Ensuring that Terraform code adheres to high-security standards is essential to protecting cloud environments from vulnerabilities and misconfigurations. While tools such as Checkov, TFSec, and Terrascan provide automated scans, maintaining secure infrastructure requires adopting best practices throughout the Terraform development lifecycle.

This section outlines practical strategies to enforce security, manage exceptions, and scale security policies across large cloud environments. By embedding these practices into Infrastructure as Code (IaC) workflows, organizations can enhance resilience and reduce the risk of breaches.

Managing Policy Exceptions and Overrides

Terraform static scanning tools such as Terrascan, Checkov, and TFSec automatically evaluate your Infrastructure-as-Code (IaC) for compliance with security policies. However, certain Terraform configurations may need to deviate from these strict policies for short-term operational reasons (for example, testing new features or handling legacy systems). To ensure that these deviations (exceptions) are not inadvertently left in place indefinitely, a well-defined process for managing policy exceptions and overrides is essential.

The following are some methods that can be leveraged, such as controlled overrides, tagging strategies, and regular reviews; organizations can ensure that policy exceptions remain temporary and are actively monitored until they are resolved:

- **Controlled overrides:** Allow exceptions only when they are explicitly approved, with clear documentation and defined expiration dates. Controlled overrides ensure that any deviation from the standard policy is deliberate and time-bound. When writing custom Terrascan policies using OPA Rego, you can embed logic that permits an exception if the resource is marked appropriately. For instance, for an AWS S3 bucket, you might allow a policy override if a specific tag indicates an approved exception:

  ```
  package terrascan.exception

  default allow = false

  allow {
    input.resource_type == "aws_s3_bucket"
    input.tags["exception_approved"] == "true"
  }
  ```

- **Tagging exceptions:** Use tags within your Terraform resources to mark policy exceptions. Tags should include not only a flag for exception approval but also metadata such as an expiration date. This allows for easy tracking and automated monitoring of exceptions.

  ```
  resource "google_storage_bucket" "example" {
    name     = "example-bucket"
    location = "US"

    labels = {
      exception_approved = "true"
      expiry_date        = "2024-03-01"
  ```

```
    }
  }
```

- **Exception reviews:** Implement a regular review process for all exceptions to ensure they remain justified over time. Automated notifications and periodic audits can help identify exceptions that are nearing or have exceeded their expiration dates.

Version Control for Security Policies

Version controlling security policies for Terraform static scanning tools is essential to maintain a secure, agile, and auditable infrastructure. As threats evolve and cloud services introduce new features, your policy-as-code must be updated accordingly. Version control helps manage these changes, ensuring that your policies remain aligned with your infrastructure while offering audit trails and rollback capabilities.

The following is a detailed explanation of how to implement effective version control strategies for security policies:

- **Store policies in Git:** Keep all your custom policies for tools such as Checkov, TFSec, and Terrascan in a centralized Git repository serving as the single source of truth for your security policies, with each subdirectory (for example, `checkov/`, `tfsec/`, `terrascan/`) containing the policies specific to that tool.

```
/policies
├── checkov/
│   └── custom_policy.yaml
├── tfsec/
│   └── custom_rule.go
└── terrascan/
    └── custom_policy.rego
```

- **Tagging and branching:** Use Git tags to mark stable releases of your security policies (for example, **`v1.0.0`**) for production tracking and rollback, while creating separate feature branches to develop and test new policies without affecting the main baseline, merging validated changes back into the main branch, and tagging them appropriately.
- **Automate policy updates:** Integrate your version-controlled policies into your CI/CD pipelines to automate testing and validation of new policy changes, ensuring they behave as expected before deployment, while using automated tools to alert relevant teams when updates are merged or new tags are created, so everyone can prepare for any necessary adjustments in their infrastructure code.

Scaling Code Scanning in Large Teams

In large organizations, managing and enforcing security policies across a sprawling, multi-cloud infrastructure presents significant challenges. When teams operate across multiple cloud accounts, regions, and environments, scaling code scanning for Terraform becomes a complex task. Ensuring that security policies are consistently applied requires both robust strategies and efficient tools. To overcome these challenges, organizations can implement several strategies:

- **Multi-account policies:** Utilize tools such as AWS Organizations Service Control Policies (SCPs), Azure Blueprints, or GCP Organization Policies to enforce security standards across all cloud accounts. This centralized approach ensures that all teams adhere to the same security framework, regardless of where their infrastructure is deployed.
- **Centralized policy repositories:** Store all security policies in a central repository. This repository acts as the single source of truth and allows teams to distribute standardized policies across their environments.

```
terraform:
  extra_args:
    - "policy_set=my_policy_set"
```

- **Distributed scanning agents**: Deploy scanning tools such as Terrascan or TFSec across various CI/CD environments with distributed scanning agents that independently validate infrastructure changes, while integrating them into pipelines across multiple teams to ensure continuous security validation, rapid feedback, and remediation of issues before reaching production.

Adopting best practices for Terraform code quality and security ensures resilient, scalable, and compliant cloud environments. By enforcing least privilege, integrating continuous scanning, managing exceptions, and scaling across large environments, organizations can significantly reduce their risk posture. Security becomes an integral part of the development lifecycle, aligning with the broader goals of Infrastructure as Code and cloud governance.

Conclusion

In this chapter, we explored the crucial role of Terraform code scanning and validation in securing Infrastructure as Code (IaC) deployments. We began by emphasizing the importance of early detection of vulnerabilities through automated scanning, discussing how shifting security left in CI/CD pipelines can drastically reduce risk. The deep dive into tools such as Checkov, TFSec, and Terrascan provided a detailed understanding of their scanning processes, integration methods, and the nuances of each tool in different cloud environments. Furthermore, we examined how custom rules crafted using Sentinel, OPA, and specialized scripting languages can tailor security policies to meet specific organizational needs, ensuring that governance remains both robust and flexible. The comparison of popular scanning tools, along with best practices for code quality and policy management, equips teams with the insights needed to choose the right tools and strategies for their unique environments.

Overall, this chapter has demonstrated that embedding security into Terraform code is not merely a best practice but a necessity for resilient cloud infrastructures. By automating code scanning, enforcing governance through policy-as-code, and integrating these processes within CI/CD pipelines, organizations can achieve continuous compliance and rapidly remediate vulnerabilities. The lessons and examples provided across AWS, Azure, and GCP offer a comprehensive guide for adopting these strategies at scale, ensuring that as your infrastructure evolves, your security posture remains both proactive and adaptive.

In the next chapter, we will explore how to design secure and scalable IAM architectures using Terraform across multiple cloud providers. It covers automating least privilege policies, managing cross-account or multi-project access, centralizing IAM for multi-cloud environments, and resolving common IAM misconfigurations.

Questions and Answers

1. **Why is code scanning essential in Terraform, and how does it contribute to the overall cloud security?**

   Terraform code scanning is critical because it identifies **misconfigurations**, **vulnerabilities**, and **compliance** gaps in infrastructure-as-code before resources are provisioned. By scanning code for common issues such as **unsecured access policies, unencrypted storage**, or **improper resource dependencies,** teams can mitigate risks early in the development lifecycle. This proactive approach helps enforce a secure baseline and reduces the likelihood of costly security breaches. For instance, scanning a Terraform configuration that provisions an AWS S3 bucket can reveal if public access is enabled unintentionally, allowing remediation before deployment.

Furthermore, code scanning fits seamlessly into CI/CD pipelines, enhancing security by **shifting testing lef**t, catching issues during the development and code review stages rather than after deployment. Tools such as **Checkov, TFSec,** and **Terrascan** automatically analyze Terraform configurations against security benchmarks, ensuring that security policies (such as those defined by CIS or NIST) are adhered to across AWS, Azure, and GCP. This continuous validation not only improves security posture but also reinforces compliance and governance standards throughout the infrastructure lifecycle.

2. **How do Checkov, TFSec, and Terrascan differ in their approach to scanning Terraform code, and what are the unique strengths of each tool?**

   Checkov, TFSec, and **Terrascan** are all designed to detect vulnerabilities and misconfigurations in Terraform code, but they differ in focus and methodology. Checkov excels in **comprehensive static analysis** by scanning YAML, JSON, and HCL configurations. It comes with a wide array of built-in policies aligned with industry standards and offers detailed remediation guidance. Checkov is well-suited for teams looking for extensive coverage across various cloud platforms, including AWS, Azure, and GCP, and its integration into CI/CD pipelines (for example, GitLab, GitHub Actions, Jenkins) makes it a robust choice for enterprise environments.

   TFSec, on the other hand, is known for its **lightweight and fast scanning capabilities**. It focuses on quickly identifying critical misconfigurations with minimal overhead, which makes it ideal for smaller teams or for early-stage development pipelines where speed is essential. TFSec is especially valued for its ease of integration with Terraform Cloud and its ability to provide rapid feedback during code commits.

   Terrascan distinguishes itself by adopting a **policy-as-code approach, leveraging Open Policy Agent (OPA)** for defining custom, extensible policies that enforce complex security and compliance standards across multi-cloud environments. Its strength lies in its ability to offer granular, customizable policy enforcement that can be integrated with CI/CD workflows through tools such as CircleCI and GitHub Actions. Each tool has its pros and cons, and the choice often depends on the organization's scale, the complexity of its environments, and specific security requirements.

3. **What are the benefits of embedding security scanning into CI/CD pipelines, and how does this practice "shift security left" in Terraform deployments?**

   Embedding security scanning into CI/CD pipelines offers significant benefits by integrating **security into every stage** of the software delivery process. This approach, often referred to as `"shift-left security"`, ensures that vulnerabilities and misconfigurations are detected early, reducing the risk of insecure code making it into production. For example, by integrating Checkov or TFSec into a GitHub Actions workflow, any detected issues are flagged during the build phase, allowing developers to address them immediately before deployment.

   Additionally, automating security validation within CI/CD pipelines enforces consistency across deployments. It creates a feedback loop where every commit, pull request, or merge triggers a security scan, ensuring that changes adhere to defined security policies. This continuous validation not only improves the overall security posture but also streamlines compliance reporting and audit readiness. In multi-cloud environments, whether on AWS, GCP, or Azure, this practice guarantees that all deployed infrastructure meets the organization's security benchmarks, significantly reducing the likelihood of post-deployment vulnerabilities.

4. **How can organizations extend Terraform's scanning capabilities through custom rules, and what are the best practices for developing these rules?**

   Organizations often have unique security requirements that go beyond the standard policies offered by tools such as Checkov, TFSec, and Terrascan. Custom rules allow teams to **tailor policy enforcement to their specific needs**, ensuring that even unique configurations adhere to security best practices. For example, a company might need to enforce a custom rule that ensures specific resource tags are applied to every AWS resource for cost allocation and compliance. Custom Checkov policies can be written in YAML, TFSec rules in Go, and Terrascan policies using OPA's Rego language to achieve this.

   Best practices for developing custom rules include thoroughly documenting the policy rationale, rigorously testing rules in non-production environments, and integrating them into your CI/CD pipeline to catch violations early. It is also important to version control these custom policies so that any changes are tracked and can be rolled back if needed. By creating a robust library of custom policies, organizations not only enhance their security posture but also foster consistency across their Terraform configurations, regardless of whether the environment is AWS, GCP, or Azure.

5. **What best practices should be followed to ensure high code quality and security in Terraform projects, especially in multi-cloud environments?**

   Ensuring high code quality and security in Terraform projects requires a disciplined approach that encompasses version control, automated scanning, and continuous monitoring. Key best practices include using linters and formatters (for example, **`terraform fmt`** and **`tflint`**) to enforce consistent code style, implementing pre-commit hooks to prevent insecure code from entering the repository, and integrating comprehensive code scanning tools into CI/CD workflows.

   In multi-cloud environments, it is also critical to modularize code to promote **reusability and standardization** across AWS, GCP, and Azure. Best practices such as managing policy exceptions carefully, maintaining a version-controlled policy repository, and scaling code scanning processes for large teams ensure that security remains consistent even as infrastructure complexity increases. These measures help to reduce manual errors, enforce governance, and maintain a resilient, secure cloud infrastructure.

CHAPTER 7
Identity and Access Management (IAM) with Terraform

Introduction

Securing access to cloud resources is a cornerstone of cloud security, and Identity and Access Management (IAM) plays a pivotal role in enforcing access controls across AWS, GCP, and Azure. This chapter delves into designing robust IAM architectures using Terraform, ensuring that permissions are both secure and scalable. Readers will explore core IAM concepts such as roles, policies, service accounts, and Role-Based Access Control (RBAC) for each cloud provider. Detailed sections cover structuring AWS IAM roles and policies, managing GCP service accounts and role bindings, and implementing Azure RBAC with custom role definitions, ensuring consistent, secure access to cloud resources.

The chapter also addresses the complexities of managing IAM in multi-account and multi-project environments, showcasing strategies for configuring cross-account roles in AWS Organizations, hierarchical policies in GCP, and management groups in Azure. Emphasizing the principle of least privilege, readers will learn to automate minimal-permission IAM policies using Terraform's dynamic blocks and validate their effectiveness with tools such as AWS IAM Access Analyzer and Azure Policy. Centralized IAM management for multi-cloud environments is explored using Terraform workspaces and reusable modules, while securing temporary credentials through AWS STS, GCP impersonation, and Azure Managed Identities ensures controlled short-term access. Finally, the chapter concludes with techniques for identifying and resolving IAM misconfigurations through Terraform state analysis and automated remediation, equipping readers to maintain secure and compliant cloud environments at scale.

Structure

In this chapter, we will cover the following topics:

- Designing Secure IAM Architectures across Providers
  - Understanding IAM Core Concepts
  - AWS IAM: Structuring Roles, Policies, and Groups
  - GCP IAM: Managing Service Accounts and Role Bindings
  - Azure IAM: Role Assignments and RBAC with Terraform
- Managing Cross-Account or Multi-Project Access Securely
  - Multi-Account IAM Strategies for AWS Organizations
  - GCP Multi-Project Access Management

  - Azure Management Groups for Cross-Subscription IAM
- Automating Least Privilege Policies with Terraform
  - Writing Minimal Permission IAM Policies
  - Terraform Dynamic Blocks for Least Privilege Automation
  - Policy Simulation and Testing in AWS and Azure
- Centralized IAM Management for Multi-Cloud Environments
  - Using Terraform Workspaces for Multi-Cloud IAM Management
  - Cross-Cloud Role Management with Terraform Modules
- Securing Temporary Credentials and Access Tokens
  - AWS STS and AssumeRole Automation
  - GCP Impersonation and Token Management
  - Azure Managed Identities and Temporary Credentials
- Identifying and Resolving IAM Misconfigurations
  - Terraform State Analysis for IAM Configuration Audits
  - Automated Remediation of IAM Misconfigurations

Designing Secure IAM Architectures Across Providers

Identity and Access Management (IAM) is a cornerstone of cloud security, providing mechanisms to control who can access cloud resources and what actions they can perform. Designing secure IAM architectures across AWS, GCP, and Azure requires an understanding of each platform's IAM model, how policies are structured, and how access is enforced. This section explores IAM fundamentals and practical Terraform implementations to create robust and scalable IAM architectures across multi-cloud environments.

Understanding IAM Core Concepts

Identity and Access Management (IAM) frameworks form the cornerstone of cloud security by controlling how identities such as users, groups, services, and applications interact with cloud resources. These frameworks enable organizations to enforce security policies, ensure least privilege, and manage access across diverse cloud environments. The following provides a brief explanation of how IAM works:

IAM enforces the principle of least privilege, meaning that each principal receives only the permissions necessary to perform its tasks. Access control is applied at various hierarchical levels, such as accounts, projects, subscriptions, or individual resources. For example, in a cloud environment, you might restrict access to sensitive resources by defining a policy at the account level while allowing broader access at the project level.

Terraform further enhances IAM by enabling organizations to codify their IAM configurations. This means that security policies, role assignments, and access controls can be defined in code and version-controlled. As a result, Terraform ensures consistent, repeatable, and auditable deployments of IAM configurations across multiple cloud environments.

The following are some key differences across providers for IAM:

- **AWS:** AWS utilizes both resource-based policies (attached directly to resources) and identity-based policies (attached to users, groups, or roles). This dual approach allows for flexible, granular control of access, enabling policies to be directly enforced at the resource level as well as across identities.

- **GCP:** Google Cloud adopts a hierarchical model where policies can be applied at the project, folder, or organization level. This structure allows for centralized management of permissions, making it easier to propagate consistent security controls across an entire organization.
- **Azure:** Azure implements IAM through Role-Based Access Control (RBAC). Permissions are granted through role assignments that can be applied at various scopes, including subscriptions, resource groups, or individual resources. This granular approach ensures that access is tightly controlled based on the specific requirements of each environment.

AWS IAM: Structuring Roles, Policies, and Groups

AWS Identity and Access Management (IAM) provides a robust framework for controlling access to AWS resources, and Terraform is a powerful tool to codify and automate these configurations. By structuring roles, policies, and groups with Terraform, organizations can implement fine-grained access controls consistently and at scale. The following are the key components of AWS IAM resources:

- **IAM roles:** Roles are designed to delegate permissions to AWS services or applications. They allow services such as EC2 or Lambda to assume a role and perform actions on your behalf. Roles can be defined with a minimal set of permissions and later expanded as necessary, ensuring that only the required permissions are granted.
- **IAM policies:** Policies are JSON documents that explicitly define which actions are allowed or denied on specific AWS resources. They are attached to roles, users, or groups to enforce permissions. Policies can be AWS managed, customer managed, or inline, providing flexibility in how permissions are structured.
- **Groups:** Groups are logical collections of IAM users. They simplify management by allowing administrators to assign policies to a group rather than managing permissions on an individual basis. All users within the group inherit the group's policies, ensuring consistent permission settings across multiple users.

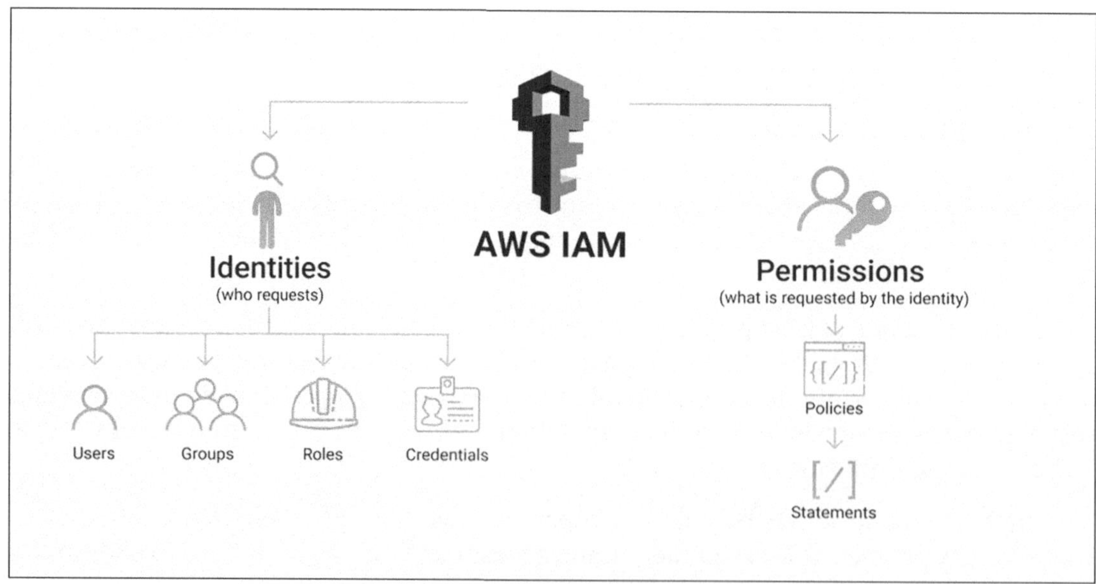

Figure 7.1: AWS IAM

```
resource "aws_iam_role" "example" {
  name = "example-role"

  assume_role_policy = jsonencode({
```

```
    Version = "2012-10-17",
    Statement = [{
      Action    = "sts:AssumeRole",
      Effect    = "Allow",
      Principal = {
        Service = "ec2.amazonaws.com"
      }
    }]
  })
}

resource "aws_iam_policy_attachment" "example-attach" {
  name       = "example-attach"
  roles      = [aws_iam_role.example.name]
  policy_arn = "arn:aws:iam::aws:policy/AmazonS3ReadOnlyAccess"
}
```

This snippet creates an IAM role named **`"example-role"`** that can be assumed by EC2 instances and attaches the AWS-managed AmazonS3ReadOnlyAccess policy to it.

The following are some best practices for IAM in AWS:

- **Use managed policies:** Leverage AWS managed policies where possible to reduce complexity. AWS-managed policies are maintained by AWS and are kept up-to-date with the latest best practices, reducing the administrative overhead on your side.
- **Implement Service Control Policies (SCPs):** At the organizational level, use SCPs to set permission guardrails across your AWS accounts. SCPs work in conjunction with IAM policies to ensure that even if a role or user is granted broad permissions, the SCP will restrict actions at the organizational level.
- **Enforce Multi-Factor Authentication (MFA):** For roles that provide access to sensitive resources, enforce MFA. Adding MFA ensures an additional layer of security, helping prevent unauthorized access even if credentials are compromised.

GCP IAM: Managing Service Accounts and Role Bindings

GCP IAM is designed around a resource hierarchy that allows you to manage permissions at various levels (**`Organization`** -> **`Folder`** -> **`Project`** -> **`Resource`**). IAM policies can be set at any of these levels and inherited downwards. When managing service accounts and role bindings with Terraform, you can codify your IAM configurations to ensure consistency and enforce the best practices. The following are the key components in GCP IAM:

- **Service accounts:** Service accounts in GCP act as non-human identities used by applications, services, or virtual machines to authenticate and interact with Google Cloud APIs. They are essential for automating tasks and securely accessing resources without relying on personal credentials.
- **Role bindings:** Role bindings attach roles to service accounts (or other principals) to grant them the necessary permissions. In GCP, roles are a collection of permissions that determine what actions a service account can perform. Role bindings can be applied at various levels of the resource hierarchy, ensuring that permissions are managed in a scalable and organized manner.
- **Custom roles:** When predefined roles do not meet your specific needs, custom roles allow you to define granular permissions. This ensures that service accounts or users have exactly the access required, nothing more and nothing less, helping to adhere to the principle of least privilege.

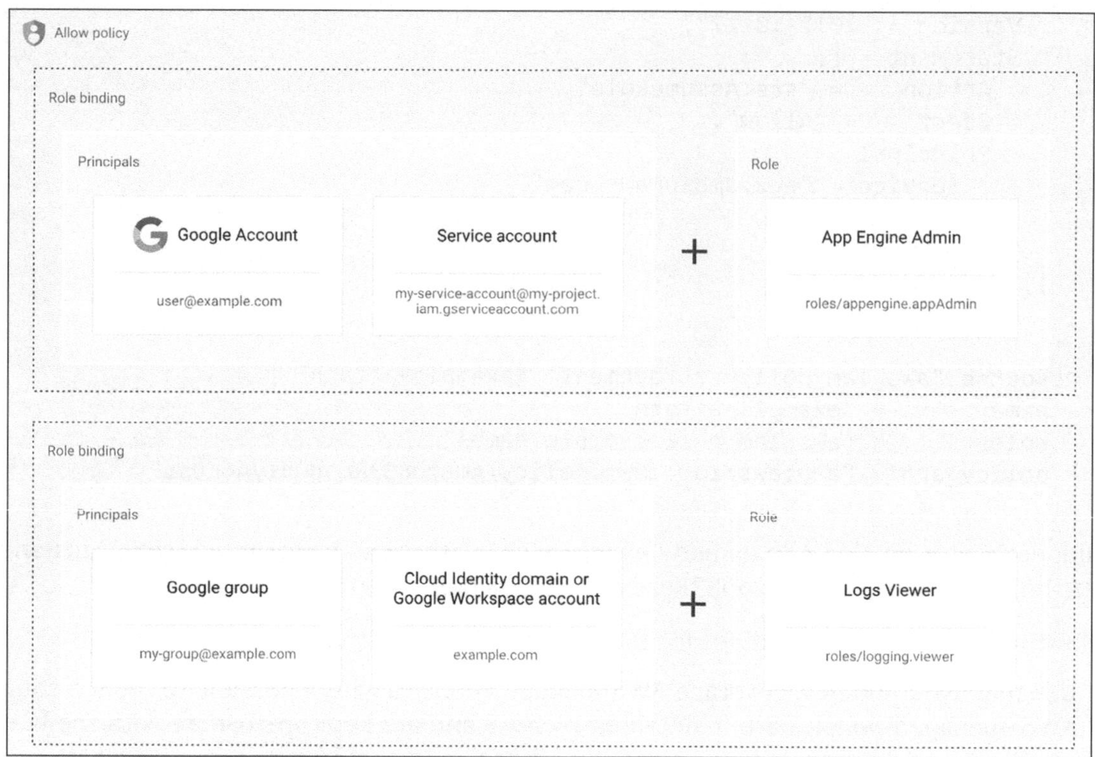

***Figure* 7.2:** GCP IAM

```
variable "project_id" {
  description = "The GCP project ID"
  type        = string
}

resource "google_service_account" "example" {
  account_id   = "example-sa"
  display_name = "Example Service Account"
  project      = var.project_id
}

resource "google_project_iam_binding" "example" {
  project = "my-project"
  role    = "roles/storage.admin"

  members = [
    "serviceAccount:${google_service_account.example.email}"
  ]
}
```

This snippet creates a Google Cloud service account named **`"example-sa"`** and assigns it the **`"roles/storage.admin"`** role in project **`"my-project"`** via an IAM binding.

The following are some best practices for IAM in GCP:

- **Use minimal roles:** Always assign the smallest set of permissions necessary for a service account to perform its intended function. This minimizes potential security risks by limiting access to only what is essential.
- **Organizational policies:** To streamline management, apply IAM policies at higher levels of the resource hierarchy, such as the folder or organization level. This approach ensures consistency across all projects and reduces the administrative overhead associated with managing individual project-level permissions.

- **Avoid wildcards:** Overly broad permissions (for example, using the **`roles/editor`** role) can expose your environment to unnecessary risk. Instead, use specific roles or custom roles that provide fine-grained access control.

Azure IAM: Role Assignments and RBAC with Terraform

Azure's IAM model is built on Role-Based Access Control (RBAC), which enables fine-grained access management by assigning roles to users, groups, or applications at various scopes, and Terraform helps codify these configurations for consistency and scalability. The following are the core components of Azure IAM:

- **Role assignments:** These are the links between an identity (a user, group, or service principal) and a role that defines what actions that identity can perform. In Azure, you can apply these assignments at different levels: management group, subscription, resource group, or individual resource, ensuring that access is granted exactly where it is needed.
- **Custom roles:** When the built-in roles (such as **`Reader`** or **`Contributor`**) do not meet specific security or operational requirements, custom roles allow you to define granular permission sets tailored to your organization's needs. Custom roles enable precise control over what actions an identity can perform on resources.
- **Scope levels:** RBAC in Azure can be enforced at multiple levels of the resource hierarchy. This means that you can assign roles at a high level (such as the subscription or management group) for broad control, or at a more granular level (such as a resource group or individual resource) for targeted access. This hierarchical structure ensures that access controls are both flexible and scalable.

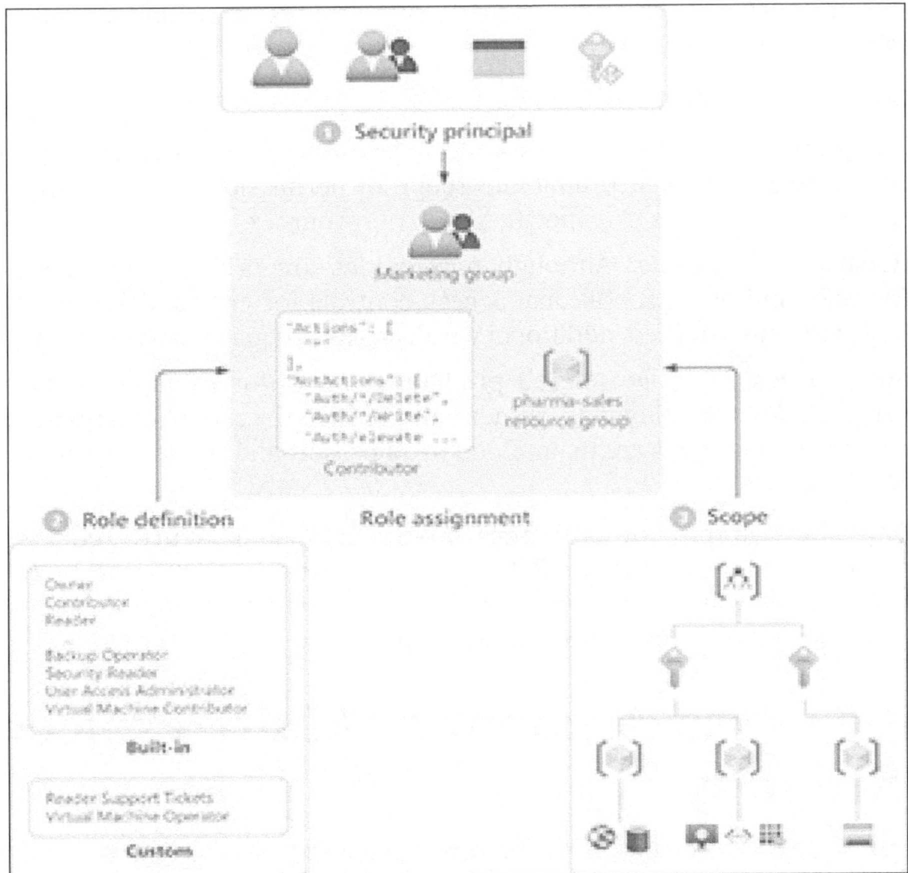

Figure 7.3: Azure IAM

```
# Defines a custom Azure role with specific permissions (for example, read
access to storage accounts,
# start access to virtual machines) scoped to a specific resource group.
resource "azurerm_role_definition" "example" {
  name        = "example-custom-role"
  scope       = azurerm_resource_group.example.id
  description = "Custom role for example purposes"

  permissions {
    actions = [
      "Microsoft.Storage/storageAccounts/read",
      "Microsoft.Compute/virtualMachines/start/action",
    ]
    not_actions = []
  }

  assignable_scopes = [
    azurerm_resource_group.example.id
  ]
}

# Assigns the above custom role to a specific Azure AD user at the resource
group level.
resource "azurerm_role_assignment" "example" {
  scope              = azurerm_resource_group.example.id
  role_definition_id = azurerm_role_definition.example.id
  principal_id       = azuread_user.example.id
}
```

This snippet creates a custom Azure role definition in a resource group and assigns it to a specified Azure AD user via a role assignment.

The following are some of the best practices for IAM in Azure:

- **Resource group isolation:** Isolate resources into different resource groups and apply RBAC at the resource group level to limit the scope of permissions. This practice helps contain potential security breaches to a specific group of resources.
- **Conditional access policies:** Although permissions are primarily managed via Azure AD, enforcing MFA and other conditional access controls for critical roles ensures that even if credentials are compromised, additional verification is required before access is granted.
- **Use built-in roles:** Leverage Azure's predefined roles (for example, Reader, Contributor) wherever possible to simplify management and reduce the risk of creating overly permissive custom roles. Built-in roles are maintained by Microsoft and reflect best practices for access control.

Designing secure IAM architectures across AWS, GCP, and Azure requires a thorough understanding of each platform's IAM models and capabilities. By leveraging Terraform to codify IAM configurations, organizations can enforce the least privilege, automate access control, and maintain consistent security across multi-cloud environments.

Managing Cross-Account or Multi-Project Access Securely

As organizations scale their cloud infrastructure, managing access across multiple accounts, projects, or subscriptions becomes increasingly complex. Multi-cloud environments and multi-account architectures introduce challenges in maintaining consistent security policies, enforcing least privilege, and avoiding identity sprawl. This section focuses on designing secure cross-account access strategies using Terraform for AWS, GCP, and Azure to ensure streamlined access control, while minimizing security risks.

Multi-Account IAM Strategies for AWS Organizations

AWS Organizations allows you to centrally manage and govern multiple AWS accounts. This multi-account strategy not only supports security isolation and compliance but also enables flexible management of access controls across accounts. With cross-account IAM strategies, you can securely grant access between accounts, ensuring that only authorized users or services assume roles in different accounts without the need to recreate identical IAM configurations in each one. The following are the detailed steps for configuring a cross-account IAM role:

- **Account A (Trusting Account):** This is the account that owns the AWS resources (for example, S3 bucket) and wants to allow access to IAM roles in another account.
- **Account B (Trusted Account):** This account will assume the IAM role in Account A to access its resources.
- **IAM role in Account A:** This role will have permissions to access specific AWS resources.
- **IAM role in Account B:** This role will assume the role in Account A.

```
# IAM Role in Account A which allows Account B's role to assume it
(Cross-account trust setup)
resource "aws_iam_role" "account_a_role" {
  name = "AccountA-CrossAccountRole"

  assume_role_policy = jsonencode({
    Version = "2012-10-17",
    Statement = [{
      Effect = "Allow",
      Principal = {
        AWS = "arn:aws:iam::222222222222:role/AccountB-Role"
      },
      Action = "sts:AssumeRole"
    }]
  })
}

# IAM Policy in Account A granting read access to S3 bucket and objects
resource "aws_iam_policy" "account_a_policy" {
  name   = "AccountA-S3ReadPolicy"
  policy = jsonencode({
    Version = "2012-10-17",
    Statement = [{
      Effect   = "Allow",
      Action   = ["s3:ListBucket", "s3:GetObject"],
      Resource = [
        "arn:aws:s3:::example-bucket",
        "arn:aws:s3:::example-bucket/*"
      ]
    }]
  })
}

# Attach the S3 read policy to the IAM Role in Account A
```

```
resource "aws_iam_role_policy_attachment" "account_a_attach" {
  policy_arn = aws_iam_policy.account_a_policy.arn
  role       = aws_iam_role.account_a_role.name
}

# IAM Role in Account B which assumes the role in Account A (trusted principal
setup)
resource "aws_iam_role" "account_b_role" {
  provider = aws.account_b

  name = "AccountB-Role"

  assume_role_policy = jsonencode({
    Version = "2012-10-17",
    Statement = [{
      Effect = "Allow",
      Principal = {
        AWS = "arn:aws:iam::111111111111:root"
      },
      Action = "sts:AssumeRole"
    }]
  })
}
```

This Terraform snippet creates a cross-account IAM role in **Account A** that can be assumed by an IAM role in **Account B**, allowing secure access to S3 resources without sharing credentials.

- IAM Role AccountB-Role in Account B assumes AccountA-CrossAccountRole in Account A.
- The trust relationship is established via **`assume_role_policy`** in Account A.
- Permissions are granted through the policy attached to the role in Account A.

GCP Multi-Project Access Management

Multi-Project IAM in GCP leverages its hierarchical structure spanning organizations, folders, projects, and individual resources to centralize and simplify access control. This approach allows security policies defined at higher levels (such as the organization or folder) to automatically propagate to all child projects and resources, ensuring consistent permission management across a multi-project environment. The following are the detailed steps for managing multi-project IAM in GCP using Terraform:

- **Organization:** The top-level container that represents your company. Policies applied here affect all resources within the organization.
- **Folders:** Used to group related projects (for example, by department or function). Policies set at the folder level cascade to all projects within that folder.
- **Projects:** The basic unit where GCP resources are created. Each project inherits policies from its parent folder (if applicable) and the organization.
- **Resources:** Individual services (such as Compute Engine instances, Cloud Storage buckets, and so on) can also have specific IAM policies attached.

```
# Assign Viewer role at the folder level for the engineering team
resource "google_folder_iam_member" "engineering_viewer" {
  folder_id = "1234567890"  # Replace with your Folder ID
  role      = "roles/viewer"
  member    = "group:engineering-team@example.com"
}
```

```
# Assign Storage Admin role at the project level for the CI/CD service account
resource "google_project_iam_member" "storage_admin" {
  project = "my-project-123456"  # Replace with your Project ID
  role    = "roles/storage.admin"
  member  = "serviceAccount:ci-cd-service@my-project-123456.iam.gserviceac-
count.com"
}
```

This Terraform configuration assigns a viewer role to an engineering team at the folder level and a storage admin role to a CI/CD service account at the project level, demonstrating GCP multi-project access management.

Azure Management Groups for Cross-Subscription IAM

Azure's cross-subscription IAM leverages its hierarchical RBAC model by using Management Groups to centrally manage and enforce access control policies across multiple subscriptions. This approach allows organizations to define and apply consistent IAM policies, such as role assignments and access restrictions, at higher levels (for example, **`management group`** or **`folder`**), which then automatically propagate to all child subscriptions and resources. The following are the detailed steps to implement Azure Management Groups for cross-subscription IAM:

- **Management groups:** At the top of the Azure hierarchy, Management Groups are containers that organize subscriptions. They allow centralized governance, enabling policies and role assignments to be applied uniformly across all associated subscriptions.
- **Subscriptions:** Subscriptions are grouped under management groups. Policies set at the management group level cascade to all subscriptions within that group.
- **Resource groups and resources:** Within subscriptions, resources are organized into resource groups. IAM can also be applied at this level for even finer control.

```
 # Create an Azure Management Group named "example-mg" to organize
subscriptions under a common hierarchy
resource "azurerm_management_group" "example" {
  name         = "example-mg"
  display_name = "Example Management Group"
}

# Associate an existing Azure subscription to the above management group
resource "azurerm_management_group_subscription_association" "example" {
  management_group_id = azurerm_management_group.example.name
  subscription_id     = var.subscription_id
}
# Assign the built-in "Contributor" role to a specified principal (user, group,
or service principal)
# at the scope of the management group created above, granting contributor
permissions within that group
resource "azurerm_role_assignment" "example" {
  scope                = "/providers/Microsoft.Management/management-
Groups/${azurerm_management_group.example.name}"
  role_definition_name = "Contributor"
  principal_id         = var.principal_id
}
```

This Terraform snippet creates an Azure Management Group, associates a subscription with it, and assigns the Contributor role at the management group level for cross-subscription IAM.

Managing IAM across multiple AWS accounts, GCP projects, and Azure subscriptions requires leveraging each platform's hierarchical IAM model. Terraform simplifies this process by codifying IAM policies, enabling organizations to manage access consistently and securely at scale. By enforcing least privilege, centralizing policy management, and regularly auditing permissions, organizations can mitigate the risks associated with sprawling multi-cloud environments.

Automating Least Privilege Policies with Terraform

Enforcing the Principle of Least Privilege (PoLP) is critical to cloud security. Least privilege ensures that identities, whether users, services, or applications, receive the minimum level of permissions required to perform their tasks. This minimizes the risk of accidental or malicious misuse of excessive permissions.

Terraform simplifies the automation and deployment of least privilege policies across AWS, GCP, and Azure, ensuring consistency and scalability. In this section, we explore how to craft minimal IAM policies, leverage Terraform dynamic blocks for scalable automation, and validate policy effectiveness through simulation tools.

Writing Minimal Permission IAM Policies

Writing minimal permission IAM policies means granting only the specific, necessary permissions for a user, service, or application to perform its tasks, without any broad or wildcard access. This practice limits the potential attack surface by ensuring that each entity has the least privilege required to function, reducing the risk of misuse or accidental exposure of resources. A minimal IAM policy:

- **Explicitly grants necessary permissions:** It defines only the actions that are required for a task, avoiding broad permissions such as wildcards (for example, `"Action": "*"`).
- **Improves security:** By adhering to the principle of least privilege, it limits access and minimizes risk.
- **Is tailored to specific use cases:** It is based on a thorough understanding of the resource requirements and operational needs, ensuring that no extra privileges are granted.

The following are the examples for a minimal IAM policy for AWS, GCP, and Azure:

In AWS, IAM policies are written in JSON format and specify the allowed or denied actions on resources. Terraform is used to codify these policies for scalable, repeatable deployments.

```
resource "aws_iam_policy" "minimal_s3_read_only" {
  name        = "MinimalS3ReadOnlyPolicy"
  description = "Grants read-only access to a specific S3 bucket"
  policy      = jsonencode({
    "Version": "2012-10-17",
    "Statement": [
      {
        "Effect": "Allow",
        "Action": [
          "s3:ListBucket",
          "s3:GetObject"
        ],
        "Resource": [
          "arn:aws:s3:::example-bucket",
          "arn:aws:s3:::example-bucket/*"
```

```
            ]
          }
        ]
      })
    }
```

This policy grants only the **s3:ListBucket** and **s3:GetObject** permissions on the specific bucket **"example-bucket"** and its objects, ensuring minimal required access for read-only operations.

GCP IAM policies can be defined using custom roles, which specify a list of permissions required for a particular function. Terraform can manage these custom roles to enforce minimal privilege.

```
resource "google_project_iam_custom_role" "minimal_storage_viewer" {
  role_id     = "minimalStorageViewer"
  title       = "Minimal Storage Viewer"
  description = "Custom role with minimal permissions for viewing storage
buckets"
  project     = "my-project-id"

  permissions = [
    "storage.buckets.get",
    "storage.objects.get",
    "storage.objects.list"
  ]
}
```

This custom role grants only the specific permissions needed to view storage buckets and objects (**storage.buckets.get**, **storage.objects.get**, and **storage.objects.list**), ensuring that entities with this role can only perform read operations on storage resources.

In Azure, IAM is implemented using Role-Based Access Control (RBAC). Custom roles can be defined in JSON or HCL-like syntax via Terraform, which details the allowed actions on resources. This enables you to create minimal policies tailored to your specific security requirements.

```
resource "azurerm_role_definition" "minimal_storage_viewer" {
  name        = "MinimalStorageViewer"
  scope       = azurerm_resource_group.example.id
  description = "Custom role with minimal permissions for viewing storage
accounts"

  permissions {
    actions = [
      "Microsoft.Storage/storageAccounts/read"
    ]
    not_actions = []
  }

  assignable_scopes = [
    azurerm_resource_group.example.id
  ]
}
```

This custom role is defined for a specific resource group and grants only the permission to read storage account information (**Microsoft.Storage/storageAccounts/read**), ensuring that the role provides the minimal access necessary for monitoring or auditing storage accounts.

Terraform Dynamic Blocks for Least Privilege Automation

Dynamic blocks in Terraform allow you to generate repeated configuration blocks programmatically, making it easier to create and manage complex IAM policies with the principle of least privilege. Instead of hardcoding multiple similar blocks, dynamic blocks use variables or input lists to iterate and create the necessary blocks automatically, ensuring that only the required permissions are granted.

In the context of least privilege automation, dynamic blocks can be leveraged to create fine-grained IAM policies that adjust based on input parameters, thereby minimizing human error and maintaining a consistent security posture. The following explains the working of dynamic blocks:

- **Iterative generation:** Dynamic blocks iterate over a list or map, generating multiple configuration blocks based on each element in the collection. This is particularly useful when you need to apply similar policies or conditions to different resources or roles.
- **Parameterization:** By using dynamic blocks, you can define IAM policies where the permissions or conditions vary according to input variables. This approach aligns with the principle of least privilege by ensuring that policies are precisely tailored to the resource requirements.
- **Reduced duplication:** Instead of copying and pasting similar IAM statements, dynamic blocks consolidate repetitive code, making your Terraform configuration more maintainable and less error-prone.

```
# Variable to specify the GCP project ID where IAM binding will be applied
variable "project_id" {
  description = "The ID of the GCP project."
  type        = string
}


# Variable defining the list of members (users, groups, or service accounts) to
bind the IAM role to
variable "members" {
  description = "List of members to bind the role to."
  type        = list(string)
}

# Variable defining optional conditions for the IAM binding using a list of
objects,
# each containing title, description, and expression for conditional IAM
bindings
variable "conditions" {
  description = "List of conditions for the IAM binding."
  type = list(object({
    title       = string
    description = string
    expression  = string
  }))
  default = []
}

# Resource to bind the "roles/storage.objectViewer" IAM role to specified
members
```

```
# in the given GCP project. Supports optional conditional bindings through
'condition' blocks.
resource "google_project_iam_binding" "project_binding" {
  project = var.project_id
  role    = "roles/storage.objectViewer"
  members = var.members

  # Dynamically create one or more 'condition' blocks if any conditions are
provided
  dynamic "condition" {
    for_each = var.conditions
    content {
      title       = condition.value.title
      description = condition.value.description
      expression  = condition.value.expression
    }
  }
}
```

This Terraform snippet uses a dynamic block to generate condition blocks within a GCP IAM binding, enabling fine-grained, least privilege access control based on variable conditions.

Policy Simulation and Testing in AWS, Azure, and GCP

Policy simulation involves running scenarios where IAM policies are evaluated to determine if they grant (or deny) access as intended. These tools simulate real-world access requests and analyze the resulting permissions, providing insights into any gaps, redundancies, or overly permissive rules in your IAM policies. This proactive testing helps ensure that your policies adhere to the principle of least privilege while avoiding potential security risks.

AWS – IAM Access Analyzer

AWS IAM Access Analyzer simulates the behavior of your IAM policies to identify unused permissions and validate that only the intended entities can access your resources.

```
resource "aws_accessanalyzer_analyzer" "example" {
  analyzer_name = "example-analyzer"
  type          = "ACCOUNT"
}
```

This Terraform resource creates an IAM Access Analyzer in your AWS account. The analyzer inspects IAM policies and resource-based policies, simulating access scenarios to identify any unintended access permissions or unused privileges.

GCP – Policy Troubleshooter

GCP's Policy Troubleshooter tool simulates IAM policy enforcement by processing access requests against your defined policies. It helps identify whether a given access request will be allowed or denied based on the current policy configuration.

```
resource "google_iam_policy" "audit" {
  project     = "example-project"
  policy_data = jsonencode({
    auditConfigs = [{
      service = "allServices"
    }]
  })
}
```

This Terraform resource sets up an IAM policy in GCP with audit configurations. Although primarily for auditing, such configurations enable you to simulate policy enforcement, allowing you to analyze how your IAM policies behave in response to various access scenarios.

Azure – Policy Insights and Azure Policy

Azure Policy, in conjunction with Policy Insights, validates RBAC and custom policies by simulating access and highlighting misconfigurations. It ensures that your role assignments and access controls meet your governance standards.

```
resource "azurerm_policy_definition" "deny_wildcards" {
  name         = "deny-wildcards"
  policy_type  = "Custom"
  mode         = "All"
  policy_rule  = file("deny-wildcards.json")
}
```

This Terraform resource defines a custom Azure Policy that, for instance, denies the assignment of overly broad roles (such as **`roles/editor`**). The policy_rule is loaded from an external JSON file (**`deny-wildcards.json`**), which contains the specific rules that simulate and enforce the intended restrictions. Azure Policy Insights can then be used to monitor and review the compliance status of this policy across your resources.

Automating least privilege policies with Terraform enhances security posture by minimizing excessive permissions across AWS, GCP, and Azure environments. Writing minimal IAM policies, leveraging dynamic blocks, and continuously simulating and testing policies ensures that organizations can maintain secure and compliant cloud environments at scale. By adopting these practices, teams can systematically enforce least privilege, reducing the risk of privilege escalation and unauthorized access.

Centralized IAM Management for Multi-Cloud Environments

Managing IAM across multiple cloud providers is one of the most challenging aspects of cloud security. Each cloud provider, AWS, Azure, and GCP, uses unique IAM structures, APIs, and policy definitions. Organizations operating in multi-cloud environments must maintain consistent access controls while adhering to the unique requirements of each platform.

Terraform enables centralized IAM management by allowing Infrastructure as Code (IaC) to provision and maintain IAM roles, policies, and permissions across cloud providers. This section explores how to leverage Terraform workspaces and reusable modules to standardize IAM policies in multi-cloud environments.

Using Terraform Workspaces for Multi-Cloud IAM Management

Terraform Workspaces allow you to isolate state and configuration within a single Terraform codebase, making it an ideal tool for managing multi-cloud IAM resources in AWS, GCP, and Azure from one repository. In this context, workspaces enable you to conditionally deploy cloud-specific IAM resources based on the active workspace, ensuring that each cloud's IAM policies are managed in a consistent, scalable manner without duplicating code.

Following is an example Terraform configuration that uses the built-in variable `terraform.workspace` to deploy different IAM resources based on whether the active workspace is set to **"aws"**, **"gcp"**, or **"azure"**:

```
locals {
  current_workspace = terraform.workspace
}

# AWS Provider
provider "aws" {
  alias  = "aws"
  region = "us-west-2"
}

# GCP Provider
provider "google" {
  alias   = "gcp"
  project = "my-gcp-project"
  region  = "us-central1"
}

# Azure Provider
provider "azurerm" {
  alias           = "azure"
  features        = {}
  subscription_id = "00000000-0000-0000-0000-000000000000"
}

############################
# AWS IAM Resource (if workspace is "aws")
############################
resource "aws_iam_role" "example" {
  count = local.current_workspace == "aws" ? 1 : 0

  name = "example-role-aws"

  assume_role_policy = jsonencode({
    Version = "2012-10-17",
    Statement = [{
      Effect    = "Allow",
      Principal = {
        Service = "ec2.amazonaws.com"
      },
      Action = "sts:AssumeRole"
    }]
  })
}

############################
# GCP IAM Resource (if workspace is "gcp")
############################
resource "google_service_account" "example" {
  count = local.current_workspace == "gcp" ? 1 : 0

  account_id   = "example-sa-gcp"
  display_name = "Example Service Account"
```

```
}

##############################
# Azure IAM Resource (if workspace is "azure")
##############################
resource "azurerm_resource_group" "example" {
  count    = local.current_workspace == "azure" ? 1 : 0
  name     = "example-rg"
  location = "East US"
}

resource "azurerm_role_assignment" "example" {
  count = local.current_workspace == "azure" ? 1 : 0

  scope                = azurerm_resource_group.example[0].id
  role_definition_name = "Contributor"
  principal_id         = "00000000-0000-0000-0000-000000000000"  # Replace
with the actual principal ID
}
```

The following is the detailed explanation of the aforementioned Terraform snippet:

- **Local variable for workspace:**
  - The local variable **current_workspace** captures the active Terraform workspace using the built-in variable **terraform.workspace**. This variable is used to conditionally create resources based on the target cloud provider.
- **Provider configuration:**
  - Three provider blocks are defined for AWS, GCP, and Azure, each with an alias. This allows the configuration to support multiple cloud providers simultaneously.
- **Conditional resource creation:**
  - **AWS:** The **aws_iam_role** resource is created only if the active workspace is **aws**. It defines an IAM role that allows EC2 instances to assume it via the specified assume role policy.
  - **GCP:** The **google_service_account** resource is created only when the active workspace is **gcp**. It sets up a service account that can be used to access GCP resources.
  - **Azure:** Two resources are conditionally created if the active workspace is `azure`:
    - An **azurerm_resource_group** is created to provide a scope.
    - An **azurerm_role_assignment** assigns the Contributor role to a specified principal within that resource group.
- **Count parameter:**
  - The **count** meta-argument is used in each resource to ensure that only the relevant resources for the active workspace are created. If the condition evaluates to **false**, **count** is set to **0**, and the resource is not instantiated.

Cross-Cloud Role Management with Terraform Modules

Terraform modules enable cross-cloud role management by encapsulating IAM configurations into reusable, parameterized components. This approach allows you to manage AWS, GCP, and Azure IAM roles in a consistent way while abstracting provider-specific details. The following module demonstrates how to conditionally create an IAM role (or equivalent) based on an input variable for the target provider. The following is an example of cross-cloud role management Terraform modules:

```
/modules/iam_role
  ├── main.tf
  ├── variables.tf
  └── outputs.tf

#main.tf
variable "cloud" {}

resource "aws_iam_role" "iam_role" {
  count = var.cloud == "aws" ? 1 : 0
  name  = "multi-cloud-role"
  assume_role_policy = file("aws_trust.json")
}

resource "google_project_iam_member" "iam_binding" {
  count   = var.cloud == "gcp" ? 1 : 0
  project = "example-project"
  role    = "roles/viewer"
  member  = "user:jane@example.com"
}

resource "azurerm_role_assignment" "iam_assignment" {
  count                = var.cloud == "azure" ? 1 : 0
  scope                = azurerm_resource_group.rg.id
  role_definition_id  = data.azurerm_role_definition.reader.id
  principal_id         = azurerm_user_assigned_identity.identity.id
}
```

The following is the detailed explanation of the aforementioned Terraform code snippet:

- **Parameterization with variable `"cloud"`:** The module accepts a variable cloud that indicates the target cloud provider (for example, **`aws`**, **`gcp`**, or **`azure`**). This allows the same module to be reused in different cloud environments by simply changing the input value.
- **Conditional resource creation using count:** Each IAM resource block uses the count meta-argument to determine whether it should be created.
  - For AWS, if **`var.cloud`** equals **`aws`**, the module creates an **`aws_iam_role`** with a trust policy loaded from an external file (**`aws_trust.json`**).
  - For GCP, if **`var.cloud`** equals **`gcp`**, the module creates a **`google_project_iam_member`** resource that assigns the **`roles/viewer`** role to a specific user in a project.
  - For Azure, if **`var.cloud`** equals `azure`, the module creates an **`azurerm_role_assignment`** resource that assigns a reader role to a user-assigned identity within a specified resource group.
- **Modular and reusable design:** By encapsulating these cross-cloud IAM configurations into a single module, you can maintain a centralized repository of IAM policies that is both version-controlled and easily updated. This approach ensures consistency and scalability when managing access across multiple cloud platforms.

Centralized IAM management across AWS, GCP, and Azure with Terraform improves operational efficiency and enhances security. By utilizing Terraform workspaces and reusable modules organizations can enforce IAM consistency and minimize misconfigurations. These practices lead to stronger access controls, streamlined IAM processes, and improved cloud security across multi-cloud environments.

Securing Temporary Credentials and Access Tokens

In cloud environments, temporary credentials and access tokens play a crucial role in minimizing the risks associated with long-lived static credentials. Short-lived credentials provide a mechanism to enforce the principle of least privilege dynamically and limit the exposure window in the event of compromise.

Terraform can automate the creation, distribution, and lifecycle management of temporary credentials across AWS, GCP, and Azure. This section delves into the strategies to leverage AWS STS (Security Token Service), GCP impersonation, and Azure Managed Identities, ensuring temporary credentials are managed securely at scale.

AWS STS and AssumeRole Automation

AWS Security Token Service (STS) is a core security service that issues temporary, limited-privilege credentials for IAM users or roles, enabling secure, short-term access to AWS resources. This mechanism is fundamental to the AssumeRole workflow, which minimizes the risks associated with long-term credentials by providing ephemeral tokens that expire after a configurable period (from 15 minutes up to 12 hours). The following steps show the working of AWS STS and AssumeRole:

- **Role Creation:** In AWS, you start by defining an IAM role with a trust policy that specifies which entities (users, groups, or AWS services) are allowed to assume that role. The role is granted only the specific permissions necessary for its tasks, following the principle of least privilege.
- **AssumeRole Operation:** When an IAM user or service assumes a role using the AWS STS AssumeRole API, AWS issues temporary security credentials (access key, secret key, and session token). These credentials are valid only for a limited time, reducing the risk of long-term exposure if compromised. The temporary credentials can then be used to access AWS resources as defined by the role's permissions.
- **Policy Enforcement:** The permissions associated with the assumed role are enforced strictly. Even if the calling entity has broader permissions, the temporary credentials only allow actions permitted by the role's policy. This ensures that access is always aligned with the minimum required privileges for the task at hand.

```
resource "aws_iam_role" "app_role" {
  name = "app-access-role"

  assume_role_policy = jsonencode({
    Version = "2012-10-17",
    Statement = [{
      Action = "sts:AssumeRole",
      Effect = "Allow",
      Principal = {
        Service = "ec2.amazonaws.com"
      }
    }]
  })
}

resource "aws_iam_policy" "app_policy" {
  name        = "app-access-policy"
  description = "Policy for temporary access"
  policy      = file("policies/app_policy.json")
```

```
}

resource "aws_iam_role_policy_attachment" "app_policy_attachment" {
  role       = aws_iam_role.app_role.name
  policy_arn = aws_iam_policy.app_policy.arn
}
```

The following is the detailed explanation of the aforementioned Terraform code snippet:

- The **aws_iam_role** resource creates an IAM role named **app-access-role** that is configured to be assumed by EC2 instances (as indicated by the Principal in the trust policy).
- The **aws_iam_policy** resource defines a custom policy **app-access-policy** loaded from an external JSON file. This policy outlines the precise permissions (for example, **S3 read-only access**) that the role should grant.
- The **aws_iam_role_policy_attachment** resource attaches the defined policy to the IAM role, ensuring that the temporary credentials issued via STS have the necessary permissions to perform specific tasks.

After deploying the above Terraform configuration, an IAM user or service can assume the role using the AWS CLI:

```
aws sts assume-role --role-arn arn:aws:iam::123456789012:role/app-access-role
--role-session-name "AppSession"
```

This command requests temporary credentials for the **app-access-role** from AWS STS, with the **--role-session-name** parameter designating a session name that aids in auditing and tracking. Once the role is successfully assumed, the temporary credentials enable access to AWS resources in accordance with the permissions defined in the role's attached policy.

GCP Impersonation and Token Management

In Google Cloud Platform (GCP), service account impersonation allows users or services to temporarily act on behalf of a service account without requiring static credentials such as long-lived keys. This enhances security by reducing the risk of key exposure while still allowing access to required resources. Instead of distributing private keys, users or applications are granted the **iam.serviceAccountTokenCreator** role, allowing them to generate short-lived OAuth 2.0 tokens or assume service account identities. The following explains the working of GCP impersonation and token management:

- **Service account creation:** A service account is created with the necessary permissions to perform specific actions within GCP.
- **Impersonation policy:** The **iam.serviceAccountTokenCreator** role is assigned to specific users or services, granting them the ability to generate temporary OAuth tokens.
- **Token generation:** Terraform or the Google Cloud CLI (**gcloud**) can trigger API calls to impersonate the service account, generating OAuth tokens valid for up to one hour. These tokens are then used for authentication when accessing GCP resources.

```
resource "google_service_account" "app_service_account" {
  account_id   = "app-service-account"
  display_name = "App Service Account"
}

resource "google_service_account_iam_binding" "binding" {
  service_account_id = google_service_account.app_service_account.name
  role               = "roles/iam.serviceAccountTokenCreator"
  members            = ["user:admin@example.com"]
}
```

The following is the detailed explanation of the aforementioned Terraform code snippet:

- **Service account creation:** The **google_service_account** resource creates a new service account with:
  - **account_id:** The unique identifier for the service account (app-service-account).
  - **display_name:** A human-readable name (App Service Account).
- **Impersonation policy:**
  - The **google_service_account_iam_binding** assigns the role **roles/iam.serviceAccountTokenCreator** to the specified user (admin@example.com).
  - This grants the user permission to generate and use temporary OAuth tokens via impersonation.

```
# Authenticate using a service account key file (if required)
gcloud auth activate-service-account --key-file key.json

# Generate an access token for impersonation
gcloud auth print-access-token
```

The following is the detailed explanation of the aforementioned CLI Commands:

- **gcloud auth activate-service-account --key-file key.json**: Authenticates the user using a service account key file, allowing access to GCP resources.
- **gcloud auth print-access-token**: Generates a short-lived OAuth 2.0 access token for authenticating API requests on behalf of the service account.

Azure Managed Identities and Temporary Credentials

Managed Identities in Azure are available in two forms: System-Assigned and User-Assigned. A System-Assigned Identity is directly tied to a specific resource, such as a virtual machine, and is created, managed, and automatically removed by Azure when the resource is deleted. In contrast, a User-Assigned Identity is created as an independent Azure resource that can be attached to multiple services, allowing for shared, reusable identities. This approach eliminates the need for static credentials by providing temporary, automatically rotated tokens for secure access to Azure services. The following explains the working of managed identities in Azure:

- **Creation of a managed identity:** A service (for example, an Azure VM) is provisioned with a managed identity, either system-assigned or user-assigned. This identity is registered in Azure AD and is granted permissions to access specific resources.
- **Impersonation and token retrieval:** When the resource needs to access another Azure service (for example, Azure Management), it does not use stored credentials. Instead, it queries the Azure Instance Metadata Service (IMDS) via a special endpoint (**http://169.254.169.254/metadata/identity/oauth2/token**). IMDS validates the request and issues a temporary OAuth token, which the resource then uses to authenticate its API calls.
- **Temporary credentials:** The tokens are short-lived (typically valid for up to one hour) and are automatically refreshed as needed, reducing the risks associated with long-term credential exposure.

```
resource "azurerm_user_assigned_identity" "app_identity" {
  name                = "appIdentity"
  resource_group_name = azurerm_resource_group.rg.name
  location            = azurerm_resource_group.rg.location
}

resource "azurerm_virtual_machine" "app_vm" {
  name                = "appVM"
```

```
  resource_group_name = azurerm_resource_group.rg.name
  location            = azurerm_resource_group.rg.location
  vm_size             = "Standard_DS1_v2"

  identity {
    type         = "UserAssigned"
    identity_ids = [azurerm_user_assigned_identity.app_identity.id]
  }
}
```

The following is the explanation of the aforementioned Terraform snippet:

- **User-Assigned identity (`azurerm_user_assigned_identity`):** This resource creates a user-assigned managed identity named **`appIdentity`** within a specified resource group. The identity is independent, meaning it can later be attached to multiple resources if needed.
- **Virtual machine with managed identity (`azurerm_virtual_machine`):** The VM resource named `appVM` is provisioned in the same resource group and location as the managed identity. The identity block specifies that the VM will use a **`UserAssigned`** identity. The **`identity_ids`** attribute links the VM to the previously created managed identity (**`azurerm_user_assigned_identity.app_identity.id`**).

When the VM is running, it can automatically request a token from IMDS using a command such as:

```
curl http://169.254.169.254/metadata/identity/oauth2/token?resource=https://
management.azure.com/ -H Metadata:true
```

This command triggers a call to IMDS, which responds with a temporary OAuth token for the resource, allowing the VM to securely access Azure Management services without the need for stored credentials.

Temporary credentials and access tokens form the backbone of secure, dynamic access management in the cloud. AWS STS, GCP impersonation, and Azure Managed Identities provide robust mechanisms to minimize credential exposure and enforce least privilege dynamically. By automating these processes with Terraform, organizations enhance security, reduce operational overhead, and create scalable, policy-driven identity solutions across multi-cloud environments.

Identifying and Resolving IAM Misconfigurations

IAM misconfigurations are one of the most common security vulnerabilities in cloud environments. Overly permissive roles, misapplied policies, and privilege escalation paths can lead to severe breaches. Terraform provides an Infrastructure-as-Code (IaC) approach to managing IAM, but mistakes in code or policy drift can still result in vulnerabilities.

In this section, we explore leveraging Terraform state files for auditing and automating remediation to enforce least privilege and secure identity practices across AWS, GCP, and Azure.

Terraform State Analysis for IAM Configuration Audits

Terraform state analysis plays a critical role in auditing and validating IAM configurations across your cloud infrastructure. The Terraform state file is a comprehensive snapshot of all resources managed by Terraform, including detailed information about IAM policies, roles, and bindings. By analyzing this state, security teams can verify that the intended access controls are in place and remain compliant with organizational best practices, such as the principle of least privilege. This approach not only helps detect configuration drift but also ensures that any changes in IAM settings are intentional and properly documented.

In the context of GCP, IAM resources such as **google_project_iam_binding** and **google_project_iam_member** resources are defined within your Terraform configuration and recorded in the state file upon deployment. For example, consider the following Terraform snippet for GCP IAM:

```
resource "google_project_iam_binding" "example" {
  project = "my-gcp-project"
  role    = "roles/storage.objectViewer"
  members = [
    "user:jane@example.com",
    "serviceAccount:my-service-account@my-gcp-project.iam.gserviceaccount.com"
  ]
}
```

This resource assigns the **roles/storage.objectViewer** role to both a user and a service account within a specific project. When this configuration is applied, Terraform records the details of the binding, including the specific role, project, and members, in its state file. Auditing this state file can reveal if only the intended identities have access, or if there are any unintended, overly permissive assignments. Tools and scripts can parse the state file (or use commands such as **terraform state show**) to automatically check that all IAM configurations meet defined security standards and that no unauthorized changes have been introduced.

Ultimately, using Terraform state analysis for IAM configuration audits enables organizations to maintain a secure, compliant cloud environment by continuously verifying that IAM policies are correctly implemented and remain in line with evolving security requirements.

Automated Remediation of IAM Misconfigurations

Automated Remediation of IAM Misconfigurations for Terraform involves using Terraform lifecycle hooks and conditional logic to detect, correct, and reapply secure IAM configurations automatically, ensuring that any misconfigurations or drift are remediated in real-time without manual intervention. The following explains how auto-remediations can be set up for IAM misconfiguration:

- **Pre-apply hooks:** Validate IAM configurations before applying changes to catch misconfigurations early and ensure that only secure, intended configurations are deployed.
- **Post-apply validation:** Re-run policy checks after deployment to detect configuration drift or unintended changes, identifying any misconfigured roles or permissions.
- **Self-healing configurations:** Automatically trigger updates or rollbacks by reapplying correct IAM policies using Terraform's lifecycle and provisioners to maintain the desired secure state.

```
resource "azurerm_role_definition" "restricted_role" {
  name        = "restricted-role"
  scope       = data.azurerm_subscription.primary.id
  permissions {
    actions = ["Microsoft.Compute/virtualMachines/read"]
  }
}

resource "null_resource" "fix_iam" {
  triggers = {
    drift_detection = timestamp()
  }

  provisioner "local-exec" {
    command = <<EOT
```

```
      terraform import azurerm_role_definition.restricted_role /subscrip-
tions/${data.azurerm_subscription.primary.id}/providers/Microsoft.Authoriza-
tion/roleDefinitions/${azurerm_role_definition.restricted_role.id}
    EOT
  }
}
```

The following is the explanation of the below Terraform snippet:

- **`azurerm_role_definition.restricted_role`:** Creates an Azure role named **`restricted-role`** with minimal read permissions for virtual machines and scopes it to a specific subscription, enforcing least privilege.
- **`null_resource.fix_iam`:** Uses a timestamp trigger to detect configuration drift and automatically remediates by re-importing the role definition into Terraform's state via a local-exec provisioner.

Identifying and resolving IAM misconfigurations is critical to maintaining a secure cloud environment. Terraform state analysis audits existing deployments for drift. Automated remediation ensures self-healing IAM configurations, protecting cloud environments from privilege escalation and unauthorized access.

By integrating these practices into Terraform workflows, organizations establish a proactive defense mechanism against IAM vulnerabilities, reinforcing cloud security at every stage of the development lifecycle.

Conclusion

Effective Identity and Access Management (IAM) is essential for securing cloud infrastructure, and Terraform provides a powerful, scalable approach to implementing IAM across AWS, GCP, and Azure. This chapter explored key IAM concepts, including roles, policies, service accounts, and role-based access control, with practical examples for each cloud platform. Readers learned how to design secure IAM architectures, manage multi-account and multi-project access, and automate least privilege policies using Terraform's dynamic blocks. By leveraging Terraform workspaces and reusable modules, organizations can maintain consistent IAM configurations across multi-cloud environments, ensuring both scalability and compliance.

Additionally, securing temporary credentials with AWS STS, GCP impersonation, and Azure Managed Identities helps minimize long-term access risks. The chapter also highlighted the importance of proactive security through IAM configuration audits and automated remediation using Terraform state analysis and lifecycle hooks. By applying these principles and best practices, organizations can reduce their attack surface, enforce least privilege access, and maintain robust IAM governance across diverse cloud ecosystems. With Terraform as the foundation for IAM automation, teams can achieve enhanced security, operational efficiency, and compliance at scale.

In the next chapter, we will focus on implementing compliance-as-code across multi-cloud environments using Terraform. It covers automating compliance audits, creating custom rules for regulatory standards, integrating with security dashboards, and generating compliance reports with real-world examples.

Questions and Answers

1. **How can Terraform help maintain secure and scalable IAM architectures across AWS, GCP, and Azure?**

   Terraform enables organizations to define and provision IAM resources consistently across cloud providers using Infrastructure as Code (IaC). By codifying IAM roles, policies, service accounts, and role bindings, teams can implement scalable, secure access control, while ensuring compliance. Terraform's modular approach allows reusable definitions, and dynamic blocks simplify the creation of least privilege policies, reducing manual errors and enhancing security.

2. **What is the advantage of using Terraform to manage cross-account IAM access in AWS Organizations?**

   Using Terraform, teams can configure cross-account roles and Service Control Policies (SCPs) within AWS Organizations, ensuring consistent access control across accounts. Terraform automates role creation, trust relationships, and SCP enforcement, reducing manual effort and minimizing misconfigurations. By codifying these settings, organizations maintain secure, scalable, and auditable access control, essential for managing complex multi-account environments.

3. **How do Terraform dynamic blocks simplify the creation of least privilege IAM policies?**

   Terraform dynamic blocks allow users to automate the generation of repetitive policy elements, reducing code duplication and simplifying policy definitions. For example, when defining AWS IAM permissions, dynamic blocks enable the iterative creation of resource-level permissions with minimal code, ensuring only the necessary permissions are granted. This approach aligns with the principle of least privilege, enhancing security, while streamlining IAM management.

4. **Why is it important to secure temporary credentials, and how does Terraform help automate this process?**

   Temporary credentials, such as AWS STS tokens, GCP impersonation tokens, and Azure Managed Identities, limit access duration, reducing the risk of credential compromise. Terraform automates the provisioning of these short-lived credentials, ensuring secure access without manual intervention. By codifying AssumeRole configurations, service account impersonation, and Managed Identities, Terraform enhances both security and operational efficiency.

5. **How can Terraform help identify and remediate IAM misconfigurations across cloud environments?**

   Terraform enables proactive identification of IAM misconfigurations by analyzing state files, ensuring policies and permissions align with security best practices. Automated audits can detect excessive permissions, missing role bindings, and misconfigured trust relationships. Additionally, Terraform's lifecycle hooks and conditional logic allow automated remediation, ensuring misconfigurations are quickly corrected, reducing the risk of unauthorized access.

CHAPTER 8
Compliance-as-Code for Multi-Cloud Environments

Introduction

As organizations continue adopting multi-cloud strategies, ensuring regulatory compliance and security across AWS, Azure, and GCP has become increasingly complex. Traditional compliance audits and security checks are often manual, time-consuming, and prone to human error, making it difficult to maintain continuous adherence to standards such as CIS Benchmarks, NIST, GDPR, HIPAA, and PCI DSS. Compliance-as-Code (CaC) offers a solution by embedding compliance policies directly into Infrastructure-as-Code (IaC) workflows using Terraform. This approach enables organizations to automate compliance audits, enforce encryption and network security standards, as well as remediate misconfigurations proactively. By leveraging cloud-native tools such as AWS Config, Azure Policy, and GCP Policy Intelligence, enterprises can maintain real-time visibility into compliance posture, while reducing operational overhead.

This chapter explores how Terraform can be used to automate compliance across multi-cloud environments, integrate with security dashboards, and generate compliance reports for audits. We will discuss writing custom rules to meet regulatory standards, implementing compliance automation workflows, and enforcing encryption and access controls through Terraform configurations. Additionally, we will examine real-world case studies where organizations have successfully deployed Compliance-as-Code to meet SOC 2, FedRAMP, and GDPR requirements. By the end of this chapter, readers will have a deep understanding of how to implement Compliance-as-Code effectively, ensuring that their cloud environments remain secure, auditable, and compliant at scale.

Structure

In this chapter, we will cover the following topics:

- Automating Compliance Audits with Terraform and Cloud-Native Tools
  - Defining Compliance-as-Code in Multi-Cloud Environments
  - Leveraging AWS Config, Azure Policy, and GCP Policy Intelligence
  - Deploying CIS Benchmarks and NIST Frameworks with Terraform
  - Enforcing Encryption and Network Security Standards
  - Remediating Non-Compliance Automatically with Terraform
- Writing Custom Rules to Address Regulatory Standards
  - Mapping Terraform Configurations to GDPR Requirements
  - Automating HIPAA Compliance for Cloud Resources

    - Defining PCI DSS Controls with Terraform Policies
- Integrating with Security and Compliance Dashboards across Providers
    - Connecting Terraform with AWS Security Hub
    - Integrating Terraform with Azure Security Center
    - Enabling GCP Security Command Center with Terraform
    - Multi-Cloud Dashboard Integration via HashiCorp Consul
- Generating Compliance Reports Using Terraform Modules
    - Building Reusable Terraform Modules for Compliance Reports
    - Exporting Compliance Data to CSV, JSON, and PDF
    - Archiving and Versioning Compliance Reports
- Real-World Examples of Compliance-as-Code in Action
    - Enforcing SOC 2 Compliance in AWS with Terraform
    - Implementing FedRAMP Controls in Azure
    - Managing GDPR Compliance for GCP Workloads
    - Multi-Cloud Compliance-as-Code for Financial Services
    - Lessons Learned from Compliance-as-Code Deployments

Automating Compliance Audits with Terraform and Cloud-Native Tools

In the evolving landscape of cloud security, maintaining compliance across multi-cloud environments are critical to preventing vulnerabilities, mitigating risks, and meeting industry regulations. Automating compliance checks with Terraform and native cloud tools streamlines audits, enforces best practices, and ensures that configurations adhere to organizational and regulatory requirements. This section delves into how Terraform can seamlessly integrate with AWS, Azure, and GCP to automate compliance at scale, providing robust, repeatable processes to uphold security postures across environments.

Defining Compliance-as-Code in Multi-Cloud Environments

Compliance-as-Code (CaC) is an approach that integrates regulatory and security standards directly into Terraform's Infrastructure-as-Code (IaC), automating the validation of cloud configurations against established compliance frameworks such as GDPR, HIPAA, CIS, and NIST. This proactive strategy ensures that every change to your infrastructure is immediately checked for adherence to compliance requirements, thereby minimizing the risk of misconfigurations, reducing manual audits, and promoting a secure, standardized deployment process across multiple cloud environments. The following explains the working of Compliance as Code:

- **Automated security checks:** By embedding compliance rules within Terraform code, organizations can automate the enforcement of security policies during the provisioning and updating of cloud resources. Terraform applies these rules as part of the deployment process, ensuring that the cloud infrastructure consistently meets compliance standards.
- **Provider-specific configurations:** Compliance rules can be tailored to each cloud provider. For example, AWS might use Config Rules and Service Control Policies (SCPs) defined in Terraform, while Azure could leverage Azure Policy definitions, and GCP might employ

Organization Policies. This ensures that the same core compliance principles are enforced, even though the underlying mechanisms differ by the provider.

- **Continuous validation:** Integrated into CI/CD pipelines, these automated checks allow for "shift-left" security, meaning that potential compliance issues are identified and remediated early in the development cycle. This helps prevent drift and ensures rapid response to any deviation from required standards.

The following are some key features and best practices of Compliance as Code:

- **Version control for compliance rules:** Store your compliance rules in a version-controlled repository such as Git to track changes, maintain audit trails, and ensure traceability. This practice not only documents the evolution of your policies but also enables collaboration and rollback, if necessary.
- **Modular design:** Use Terraform modules to encapsulate reusable compliance configurations such as those for encryption, IAM policies, and logging. A modular design helps standardize deployments across various environments and reduces duplication of code.
- **Shift-left security:** Embed compliance checks early in your CI/CD pipelines to catch misconfigurations before they reach production. This proactive stance ensures that every commit and pull request is automatically validated against your compliance benchmarks.
- **Multi-cloud support:** Design your compliance rules to be as cloud-agnostic as possible while still allowing for provider-specific adjustments. This approach ensures consistent enforcement across AWS, Azure, and GCP, enabling centralized management even in diverse cloud environments.

Compliance-as-Code using Terraform in multi-cloud environments automates the process of validating and enforcing security and compliance standards across AWS, Azure, and GCP. This approach leverages version-controlled, modular code and integrated CI/CD pipelines to ensure that every infrastructure change complies with the necessary regulatory frameworks, thus standardizing security practices and reducing the risk of human error.

Leveraging AWS Config, Azure Policy, and GCP Policy Intelligence

Leveraging AWS Config, Azure Policy, and GCP Policy Intelligence for Terraform allows organizations to automate compliance audits using native cloud services, ensuring that resource configurations continuously adhere to regulatory and security standards without manual intervention. These tools provide real-time monitoring, assessment, and remediation capabilities across different cloud providers, and Terraform enables you to provision and manage them as code for consistency and scalability. The following are some services across AWS, Azure, and GCP to configure compliance:

- **AWS Config:** AWS Config continuously tracks and records AWS resource configurations, then evaluates them against predefined rules to identify non-compliant resources. For example, a rule such as `"ENCRYPTED_VOLUMES"` checks if EBS volumes are encrypted. This automated monitoring helps ensure that any deviation from security best practices is quickly detected, and can trigger remediation actions.

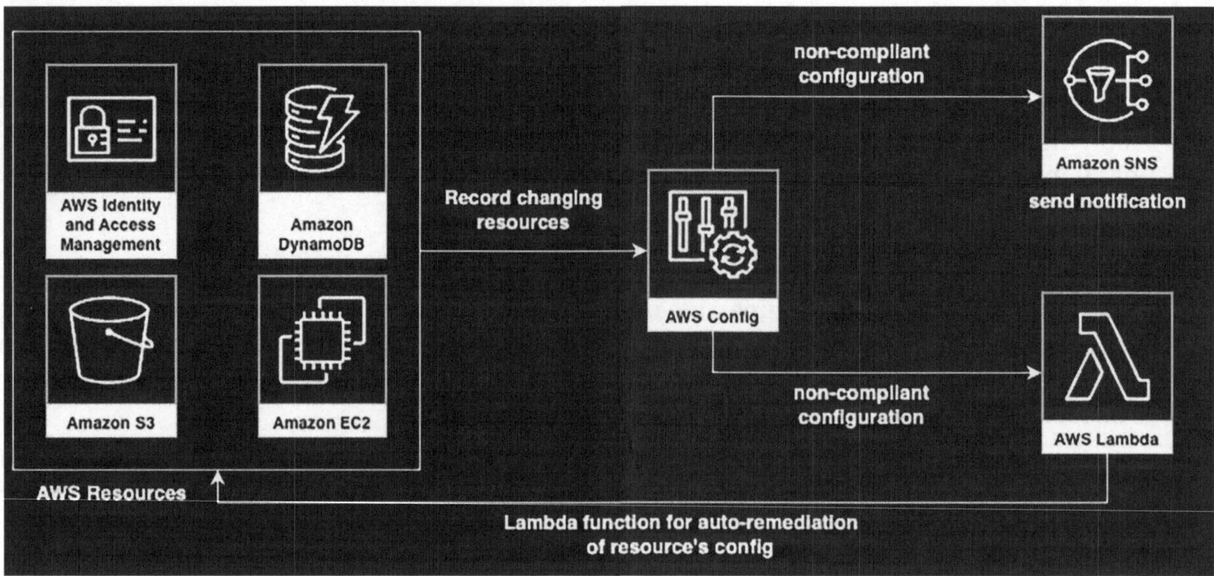

Figure 8.1: *AWS Config*

```
resource "aws_config_config_rule" "encrypted_volumes" {
  name = "encrypted-volumes"
  source {
    owner             = "AWS"
    source_identifier = "ENCRYPTED_VOLUMES"
  }
}
```

This Terraform snippet creates an AWS Config rule named "**`encrypted-volumes`**" that uses the AWS-managed **`ENCRYPTED_VOLUMES`** rule to ensure EBS volumes are encrypted.

- **Azure policy:** Azure policy enforces governance across Azure environments by applying policy definitions that evaluate resources against organizational standards. It can automatically remediate non-compliant resources and prevent the deployment of resources that do not meet the criteria. For example, with Azure Policy, you can enforce that all resources must use TLS for secure communication, therefore maintaining a strong security posture across all subscriptions.

```
resource "azurerm_policy_assignment" "require_tls" {
  name                 = "require-tls"
  policy_definition_id = azurerm_policy_definition.enforce_tls.id
  scope                = azurerm_subscription.example.id
}
```

This Terraform snippet assigns the **`"enforce_tls"`** policy to the specified Azure subscription, ensuring that all resources within it comply with the TLS requirements.

- **GCP policy intelligence:** It provides insights into policy violations by analyzing IAM configurations, and recommending adjustments to enforce the principle of least privilege. It helps identify gaps in access controls and suggests improvements, ensuring that resources are not overexposed and that access rights are tightly managed.

```
resource "google_project_iam_policy" "policy_enforcement" {
  project     = "example-project"
  policy_data = file("policy.json")
}
```

This Terraform snippet applies an IAM policy defined in **`"policy.json"`** to the **`"example-project"`** in GCP, enforcing the specified access controls.

To implement these compliance audits with Terraform, best practices include using managed policies for common compliance checks, such as encryption or secure transport, and automating alerts for non-compliance using serverless functions such as AWS Lambda, Azure Functions, or GCP Cloud Functions.

By automating compliance audits through these native cloud services and managing them with Terraform, organizations can achieve continuous, consistent, and scalable governance across multi-cloud environments, significantly reducing manual overhead and enhancing overall security posture.

Deploying CIS Benchmarks and NIST Frameworks with Terraform

Deploying CIS Benchmarks and NIST Frameworks with Terraform involves leveraging Infrastructure-as-Code to enforce standardized security and compliance guidelines across your cloud environments. Both CIS benchmarks and NIST frameworks offer best practices and recommendations to protect cloud resources against evolving threats. Terraform modules enable you to codify these guidelines into repeatable, version-controlled configurations that automatically apply to your cloud infrastructure, ensuring consistency and reducing the risk of human error.

CIS benchmarks: CIS benchmarks are a set of best practices provided by the Center for Internet Security that focus on securing operating systems, network devices, cloud services, and applications. By deploying Terraform modules based on these benchmarks, you can automatically enforce recommended configurations—such as secure network settings, strict access controls, and robust logging for services across your AWS, Azure, and GCP environments. For example, you might deploy a Terraform module that configures AWS Config rules based on CIS recommendations for encryption and access control, ensuring that all resources adhere to the latest security standards.

NIST frameworks: The National Institute of Standards and Technology (NIST) provides comprehensive frameworks, such as NIST SP 800-53 and the NIST Cybersecurity Framework, which outline security controls and best practices for protecting information systems. Deploying these frameworks with Terraform involves creating modules that enforce specific security controls (for example, access controls, auditing, incident response) as defined by NIST. This can include automating the deployment of role-based access policies, logging mechanisms, and configuration baselines that meet NIST standards. By integrating NIST-based configurations into your Terraform workflows, you ensure that your cloud environments are not only secure but also compliant with widely recognized federal and industry regulations.

The following are some examples of compliant resources in AWS, GCP, and Azure:

```
resource "aws_instance" "compliant_ec2" {
  ami           = "ami-0c55b159cbfafe1f0"  # Replace with an appropriate AMI
  instance_type = "t2.micro"
  associate_public_ip_address = false
  tags = {
    Name       = "CompliantEC2"
    Compliance = "CIS_NIST"
  }
}

resource "aws_config_config_rule" "ec2_no_public_ip" {
  name = "ec2-instance-no-public-ip"
  source {
    owner             = "AWS"
    source_identifier = "EC2_INSTANCE_NO_PUBLIC_IP"
  }
}
```

This Terraform snippet provisions an EC2 instance without a public IP and tags it for CIS/NIST compliance, while also deploying an AWS Config rule to ensure that no EC2 instances are assigned public IPs, thereby enforcing secure configurations.

```
resource "azurerm_resource_group" "example" {
  name     = "example-rg"
  location = "East US"
}

resource "azurerm_virtual_machine" "compliant_vm" {
  name                  = "example-vm"
  resource_group_name   = azurerm_resource_group.example.name
  location              = azurerm_resource_group.example.location
  vm_size               = "Standard_DS1_v2"
  network_interface_ids = [azurerm_network_interface.example.id]
  # Image and OS configuration details omitted for brevity

  tags = {
    Compliance = "CIS_NIST"
  }
}

resource "azurerm_policy_assignment" "deny_public_ip" {
  name                 = "deny-public-ip-vms"
  policy_definition_id = azurerm_policy_definition.deny_public_ip.id  # Assume
this definition enforces no public IPs on VMs
  scope                = azurerm_resource_group.example.id
}
```

This Terraform snippet provisions an Azure VM without a public IP and tags it for CIS/NIST compliance, while also applying a policy at the resource group level that denies public IP assignments to VMs, ensuring secure configurations.

```
resource "google_compute_instance" "compliant_instance" {
  name         = "compliant-instance"
  machine_type = "n1-standard-1"
  zone         = "us-central1-a"

  boot_disk {
    initialize_params {
      image = "debian-cloud/debian-9"  # Replace with an appropriate image
    }
  }

  network_interface {
    network = "default"
    # By omitting the access_config block, no public IP is assigned.
  }

  labels = {
    compliance = "CIS_NIST"
  }
}
```

This Terraform snippet provisions a GCP Compute Engine instance without a public IP by omitting the **access_config** block, ensuring compliance with CIS and NIST security standards.

By adopting these practices, you create a dynamic and resilient security framework that not only enforces CIS benchmarks and NIST standards across your multi-cloud environments but also adapts to evolving threats and regulatory requirements. This integration of Compliance-as-Code with Terraform ensures that your infrastructure remains secure, auditable, and aligned with the highest standards of cybersecurity and governance.

Enforcing Encryption and Network Security Standards

Encryption and network security are fundamental components of regulatory compliance frameworks such as CIS, NIST, PCI-DSS, and HIPAA. Terraform can be used to enforce encryption at rest and in transit, as well as implement **firewall policies** that restrict unauthorized access to cloud resources. This ensures that the data remains protected against threats, while meeting security best practices. The following are some key aspects of enforcing encryption and network security:

- **Encryption at rest**: Utilize Cloud-native Key Management Services (KMS) (for example, AWS KMS, Azure Key Vault, and Google Cloud KMS) to encrypt storage volumes, databases, as well as object storage. Enforce encryption policies to ensure that all the stored data is encrypted by default.
- **Encryption in transit**: Enforce TLS/SSL certificates for secure communication between services. Use Terraform to configure load balancers and API gateways to enforce TLS policies.
- **Network security and firewalls**: Implement strict firewall rules to deny open inbound access (especially SSH, RDP, and HTTP). Use Terraform to configure security groups, Firewalls, network ACLs, and private subnets to restrict access.

```
resource "aws_kms_key" "s3_encryption_key" {
  description             = "KMS key for S3 encryption"
  enable_key_rotation     = true
}

resource "aws_s3_bucket" "secure_bucket" {
  bucket = "secure-data-storage"
  server_side_encryption_configuration {
    rule {
      apply_server_side_encryption_by_default {
        sse_algorithm     = "aws:kms"
        kms_master_key_id = aws_kms_key.s3_encryption_key.id
      }
    }
  }
}
```

This Terraform code snippet creates an S3 bucket and a KMS key, and uses the KMS key to encrypt the S3 bucket.

```
resource "azurerm_network_security_group" "restricted_nsg" {
  name                = "restricted-nsg"
  resource_group_name = "security-group"
  location            = "East US"

  security_rule {
    name                       = "Allow-HTTPS"
    priority                   = 100
    direction                  = "Inbound"
    access                     = "Allow"
    protocol                   = "Tcp"
    source_port_range          = "*"
    destination_port_range     = "443"
    source_address_prefix     = "*"
```

```
    destination_address_prefix = "*"
  }

  security_rule {
    name                       = "Deny-All-Inbound"
    priority                   = 200
    direction                  = "Inbound"
    access                     = "Deny"
    protocol                   = "*"
    source_port_range          = "*"
    destination_port_range     = "*"
    source_address_prefix      = "*"
    destination_address_prefix = "*"
  }
}
```

This example creates a security group that restricts inbound traffic to **only HTTPS (443)** and blocks all other access.

```
resource "google_kms_key_ring" "my_keyring" {
  name     = "secure-keyring"
  location = "us-central1"
}

resource "google_kms_crypto_key" "my_crypto_key" {
  name     = "secure-key"
  key_ring = google_kms_key_ring.my_keyring.id
  purpose  = "ENCRYPT_DECRYPT"
}

resource "google_compute_disk" "encrypted_disk" {
  name  = "encrypted-disk"
  type  = "pd-ssd"
  zone  = "us-central1-a"
  size  = 100

  disk_encryption_key {
    kms_key_self_link = google_kms_crypto_key.my_crypto_key.id
  }
}
```

In this example, the GCP Compute Engine disk is encrypted using Google Cloud KMS.

Terraform enables organizations to enforce encryption and network security as part of their infrastructure deployment. By configuring encryption at rest, encryption in transit, and network access controls, teams can meet compliance requirements, while reducing security risks.

Remediating Non-Compliance Automatically with Terraform

Automated remediation of IAM misconfigurations with Terraform involves detecting non-compliant resources and automatically triggering corrective actions to restore compliance. This process leverages cloud-native automation services such as AWS Lambda, Azure Automation/Functions, and GCP Cloud Functions to run predefined remediation workflows, thereby reducing manual intervention and minimizing security risks. The following explains the working of auto-remediation for IAM misconfiguration:

- **Detection and triggering:**
  - **Pre-deployment checks:** Terraform and cloud-native compliance tools (such as AWS Config, Azure Policy, or GCP Policy Intelligence) identify misconfigurations before or after deployment.
  - **Event triggers:** When a non-compliance event is detected, cloud event sources (for example, CloudWatch Events, Azure Event Grid, or GCP Pub/Sub) can trigger remediation functions.
- **Automated remediation:**
  - **Corrective actions:** The triggered function executes corrective commands (such as updating IAM policies or reconfiguring resources) to remediate the non-compliance.
  - **Lifecycle integration:** Terraform's lifecycle hooks and conditional logic can be used to integrate these remediation steps directly into the infrastructure deployment process, ensuring that any deviations are automatically corrected.
- **Self-Healing configurations:**
  - **Automated rollbacks/updates:** In case of drift, Terraform can automatically reapply the correct configuration by triggering the remediation function.
  - **Continuous monitoring:** Regular post-deployment validation ensures that resources remain compliant over time.

```
resource "azurerm_resource_group" "example" {
  name     = "example-rg"
  location = "East US"
}

resource "azurerm_storage_account" "function_storage" {
  name                     = "functionstorageacct"
  resource_group_name      = azurerm_resource_group.example.name
  location                 = azurerm_resource_group.example.location
  account_tier             = "Standard"
  account_replication_type = "LRS"
}

resource "azurerm_app_service_plan" "example" {
  name                = "example-plan"
  location            = azurerm_resource_group.example.location
  resource_group_name = azurerm_resource_group.example.name
  sku {
    tier = "Dynamic"
    size = "Y1"
  }
}

resource "azurerm_function_app" "remediation" {
  name                       = "remediation-func"
  location                   = azurerm_resource_group.example.location
  resource_group_name        = azurerm_resource_group.example.name
  app_service_plan_id        = azurerm_app_service_plan.example.id
  storage_account_name       = azurerm_storage_account.function_storage.
name
  storage_account_access_key = azurerm_storage_account.function_storage.
primary_access_key
```

```
    app_settings = {
      "FUNCTIONS_WORKER_RUNTIME" = "python"
    }
  }
```

The following is the explanation of the aforementioned Terraform code snippet:

- Deploys a GCP Cloud Function (remediation-function) that executes remediation logic from the code archive remediation.zip.
- The function can be triggered via HTTP (or integrated with Pub/Sub) to automatically correct non-compliant IAM configurations in response to policy violation events.

Automating compliance audits with Terraform not only strengthens cloud security but also ensures regulatory alignment at scale. By integrating native tools such as AWS Config, Azure Policy, and GCP Policy Intelligence, organizations can achieve seamless, continuous compliance monitoring. This proactive approach reduces the risk of misconfigurations, enhances visibility, and fosters resilience in multi-cloud environments.

Writing Custom Rules to Address Regulatory Standards

Cloud compliance often extends beyond the out-of-the-box capabilities provided by cloud-native tools. While platforms such as AWS Config, Azure Policy, and GCP Policy Intelligence offer robust compliance checks, organizations frequently face unique regulatory requirements that demand custom policies. Writing custom rules allows organizations to address specific mandates under GDPR, HIPAA, PCI DSS, and other frameworks, ensuring comprehensive protection of the sensitive data and cloud resources. This section explores how to craft tailored policies, map cloud resources to regulatory standards, and automate enforcement to mitigate compliance risks.

Mapping Terraform Configurations to GDPR Requirements

Mapping Terraform Configurations to GDPR requirements involves embedding compliance controls into your cloud infrastructure to ensure that the personal data is processed, stored, and transferred in accordance with GDPR mandates. This approach leverages Terraform to enforce stringent security measures such as encryption, data minimization, strict access controls, and robust logging, reducing the risk of non-compliance and associated fines.

General Data Protection Regulation (GDPR) requires organizations to implement strict controls over personal data, mandating encryption both at rest and in transit, limiting data collection to what is necessary, and ensuring that access to sensitive information is tightly controlled. In the cloud, this means configuring resources so that data is automatically encrypted, public access is minimized or eliminated, and all access is logged and monitored to detect any unauthorized activity.

Terraform enables organizations to codify these compliance controls directly into the provisioning process. By defining infrastructure as code, Terraform ensures that every resource is deployed with the necessary security settings. For instance, you can enforce encryption by configuring Key Management Service (KMS) settings, restrict public access by enabling uniform access policies, and set up logging mechanisms for audit trails. This automation not only reduces manual errors but also ensures that security standards are consistently applied across all environments.

```
# Create a Key Ring for GDPR-compliant encryption
resource "google_kms_key_ring" "gdpr_keyring" {
  name     = "gdpr-keyring"
  location = "us-central1"
}

# Create a Crypto Key for encrypting bucket data
resource "google_kms_crypto_key" "gdpr_key" {
  name     = "gdpr-key"
  key_ring = google_kms_key_ring.gdpr_keyring.id
  purpose  = "ENCRYPT_DECRYPT"
}

# Create a logging bucket to store access logs
resource "google_storage_bucket" "log_bucket" {
  name                          = "gdpr-log-bucket"
  location                      = "US"
  force_destroy                 = true       # Delete bucket even if not empty
not recommended for prod
  uniform_bucket_level_access   = true       # Use only IAM for access control
  public_access_prevention      = "enforced"  # Block all public access
}

# Explicitly denies public access by setting a condition that always evaluates
to false
resource "google_storage_bucket_iam_binding" "deny_public" {
  bucket = google_storage_bucket.gdpr_bucket.name
  role   = "roles/storage.objectViewer"
  members = ["allUsers"]

  condition {
    title       = "DenyPublicAccess"
    description = "Block allUsers access for GDPR compliance"
    expression  = "false"
  }
}

# Create the GDPR-compliant storage bucket
resource "google_storage_bucket" "gdpr_bucket" {
  name                          = "gdpr-compliant-bucket"
  location                      = "US"
  force_destroy                 = false
  uniform_bucket_level_access   = true

  # Enforce encryption at rest with a customer-managed key
  encryption {
    default_kms_key_name = google_kms_crypto_key.gdpr_key.id
  }

  # Enable logging for auditing access to the bucket
  logging {
    log_bucket        = google_storage_bucket.log_bucket.name
    log_object_prefix = "access-logs/"
  }
```

```
    labels = {
      compliance = "GDPR"
    }
  }
```

This is an example Terraform configuration for a GCP Storage Bucket that enforces encryption at rest using a Customer-Managed Encryption Key (CMEK), restricts public access through uniform bucket-level access, and enables logging for monitoring access. Tools such as Open Policy Agent (OPA) or Terraform Sentinel can be used to automate compliance validation and enforce GDPR-related policies during infrastructure provisioning.

Automating HIPAA Compliance for Cloud Resources

Automating HIPAA compliance for cloud resources with Terraform involves embedding the necessary security controls into your infrastructure code to ensure that electronic Protected Health Information (ePHI) is handled in accordance with HIPAA regulations. HIPAA mandates strict requirements for encryption, access controls, logging, and monitoring to protect sensitive health data. By using Terraform, organizations can deploy cloud resources with built-in compliance measures, ensuring that encryption is enforced both at rest and in transit, public access is restricted, and auditing is continuously performed, all while reducing the manual overhead of compliance checks. The following explains how HIPAA compliance can be configured for cloud resources:

- **Policy enforcement at provisioning:** Terraform modules are written to include security controls such as encryption configurations, network security rules, and logging settings directly in the resource definitions. This ensures that every resource is deployed in a compliant state, with no additional manual configuration required after provisioning.
- **Automated remediation and drift detection:** By integrating compliance checks into CI/CD pipelines and using native monitoring tools (for example, AWS Config, Azure Policy, or GCP Policy Intelligence), Terraform can detect and automatically remediate deviations from the defined secure state, ensuring ongoing compliance with HIPAA requirements.
- **Standardized and repeatable deployments:** With Infrastructure-as-Code, organizations can version-control their compliance settings and deploy them uniformly across multiple environments. This consistent, automated approach minimizes the risk of human error and ensures that all deployments adhere to HIPAA standards from the start.

```
# Retrieve the current client configuration
data "azurerm_client_config" "current" {}

# Create a resource group
resource "azurerm_resource_group" "example" {
  name     = "hipaa-rg"
  location = "East US"
}

# Create a Log Analytics Workspace for diagnostics
resource "azurerm_log_analytics_workspace" "example" {
  name                = "hipaa-law"
  location            = azurerm_resource_group.example.location
  resource_group_name = azurerm_resource_group.example.name
  sku                 = "PerGB2018"
  retention_in_days   = 30
}

# Create a Key Vault for managing encryption keys
resource "azurerm_key_vault" "example" {
  name                = "hipaa-kv"
```

```
  resource_group_name = azurerm_resource_group.example.name
  location            = azurerm_resource_group.example.location
  tenant_id           = data.azurerm_client_config.current.tenant_id
  sku_name            = "standard"
}

# Create a Key Vault Key for encryption
resource "azurerm_key_vault_key" "example" {
  name         = "hipaa-key"
  key_vault_id = azurerm_key_vault.example.id
  key_type     = "RSA"
  key_size     = 2048
}

# Create a HIPAA-compliant Storage Account with enforced encryption and secure
transfer
resource "azurerm_storage_account" "example" {
  name                     = "hipaastorageacct"
  resource_group_name      = azurerm_resource_group.example.name
  location                 = azurerm_resource_group.example.location
  account_tier             = "Standard"
  account_replication_type = "LRS"
  enable_https_traffic_only = true

  encryption {
    services {
      blob {
        enabled = true
      }
      file {
        enabled = true
      }
    }
    key_source = "Microsoft.Keyvault"
    key_vault_properties {
      key_name     = azurerm_key_vault_key.example.name
      key_version  = azurerm_key_vault_key.example.version
      key_vault_id = azurerm_key_vault.example.id
    }
  }
}

# Restrict access by applying network rules that deny public access and allow
only internal IP ranges
resource "azurerm_storage_account_network_rules" "example" {
  resource_group_name  = azurerm_resource_group.example.name
  storage_account_name = azurerm_storage_account.example.name

  default_action             = "Deny"
  bypass                     = ["AzureServices"]
  ip_rules                   = ["10.0.0.0/16"]
}

# Enable diagnostic settings for logging and monitoring
resource "azurerm_monitor_diagnostic_setting" "example" {
  name                       = "hipaa-diagnostics"
```

```
    target_resource_id         = azurerm_storage_account.example.id
    log_analytics_workspace_id = azurerm_log_analytics_workspace.example.id

    log {
      category = "StorageRead"
      enabled  = true
      retention_policy {
        enabled = true
        days    = 30
      }
    }

    metric {
      category = "AllMetrics"
      enabled  = true
      retention_policy {
        enabled = true
        days    = 30
      }
    }
  }
```

This Terraform configuration provisions a HIPAA-compliant Azure Storage Account with enforced encryption, secure transfer, restricted network access, and robust logging, ensuring continuous compliance with HIPAA requirements.

Defining PCI DSS Controls with Terraform Policies

PCI DSS is a set of security standards designed to protect cardholder data during storage, processing, and transmission. It requires organizations that handle credit card information to implement robust controls, such as:

- **Encryption:** All sensitive data must be encrypted both at rest and in transit to prevent unauthorized access.
- **Firewall configurations:** Network perimeters must be secured with firewalls to isolate and protect cardholder data environments.
- **Strict access controls:** Only authorized personnel should have access to cardholder data, and access should be restricted using Role-Based Access Control and Multi-Factor Authentication.

These controls aim to minimize the risks of data breaches, financial fraud, and non-compliance that can lead to substantial fines and reputational damage.

Terraform enables organizations to automate the deployment and management of PCI DSS controls by codifying compliance requirements into reusable modules and policies. The key ways Terraform supports PCI compliance include:

- **Secure VPC configuration:** Terraform can be used to create Virtual Private Clouds (VPCs) with proper network segmentation and isolation, ensuring that the sensitive data resides within controlled environments.
- **Security groups and firewall rules:** Terraform allows you to define security groups and firewall configurations that enforce strict inbound and outbound traffic rules. This ensures that only necessary ports and protocols are open, reducing the attack surface.
- **Access control management:** Terraform facilitates the implementation of Role-Based Access Control (RBAC) and other IAM configurations across cloud providers, ensuring that only authorized users have access to sensitive systems and data.

- **Consistent, automated deployments:** By treating compliance controls as code, Terraform provides version-controlled, and repeatable deployments that help maintain compliance across diverse environments (AWS, Azure, and GCP).

This approach not only reduces the risk of human error but also makes it easier to audit and update compliance controls as regulatory requirements evolve.

```
# Define a secure VPC for PCI DSS compliance
resource "google_compute_network" "secure_vpc" {
  name                    = "pci-secure-vpc"
  auto_create_subnetworks = false
}

# Create a subnet within the secure VPC
resource "google_compute_subnetwork" "pci_subnet" {
  name          = "pci-subnet"
  region        = "us-central1"
  network       = google_compute_network.secure_vpc.id
  ip_cidr_range = "10.0.0.0/24"
}

# Define a firewall rule that only allows HTTP, HTTPS, and SSH traffic from a
trusted IP range
resource "google_compute_firewall" "pci_firewall" {
  name    = "pci-firewall"
  network = google_compute_network.secure_vpc.id

  allow {
    protocol = "tcp"
    ports    = ["80", "443", "22"]
  }

  source_ranges = ["203.0.113.0/24"]  # Replace with your trusted IP range
  target_tags   = ["pci-compliant"]
}

# Create a KMS Key Ring to organize related encryption keys
resource "google_kms_key_ring" "pci_keyring" {
  name     = "pci-keyring"                # Name of the key ring
  location = "us-central1"                # Location/region where the key ring
is stored
}

# Create a Crypto Key for encryption and decryption tasks within the key ring
resource "google_kms_crypto_key" "pci_key" {
  name     = "pci-vm-key"                  # Name of the KMS key
  key_ring = google_kms_key_ring.pci_keyring.id  # Reference to the previously
created key ring
  purpose  = "ENCRYPT_DECRYPT"            # Purpose of the key (encrypting and
decrypting data)
}

# Create a Compute Engine instance with encrypted boot disk
resource "google_compute_instance" "pci_instance" {
  name         = "pci-compliant-instance"
  machine_type = "n1-standard-1"
  zone         = "us-central1-a"
```

```
# Use a secure boot disk with customer-managed encryption key (CMEK)
  boot_disk {
    initialize_params {
      image = "debian-cloud/debian-11"
    }

    # Apply CMEK for encryption (recommended for PCI compliance)
    kms_key_self_link = "projects/YOUR_PROJECT_ID/locations/global/keyRings/
YOUR_KEYRING/cryptoKeys/YOUR_KEY"
  }

  shielded_instance_config {
    enable_secure_boot          = true    # Ensures only signed and verified OS
images are used
    enable_vtpm                 = true    # Enables virtual TPM for integrity
verification
    enable_integrity_monitoring = true    # Monitors boot integrity of the VM
  }

  metadata = {
    enable-oslogin             = "TRUE"   # Use IAM roles for SSH access
instead of static keys
    block-project-ssh-keys     = "TRUE"   # Disable project-wide SSH keys for
tighter control
  }

  network_interface {
    network    = google_compute_network.secure_vpc.id
    subnetwork = google_compute_subnetwork.pci_subnet.id
    # Omitting the access_config block ensures that no public IP is assigned.
  }

  tags = ["pci-compliant"]

  labels = {
    compliance = "PCI_DSS"
  }
}

# (Optional) Configure logging via Cloud Logging for continuous monitoring and
audit
resource "google_logging_project_sink" "pci_sink" {
  name        = "pci-compliance-logs"
  destination = "bigquery.googleapis.com/projects/${var.project_id}/datasets/
pci_logs"
  filter      = "resource.type=\"gce_instance\" AND labels.compliance=\"PCI_
DSS\""
  project     = "example-project-id"
}
```

This Terraform configuration deploys a PCI DSS-compliant GCP environment by provisioning a secure VPC, restricted firewall rules, an encrypted Compute Engine instance without a public IP, and integrated logging for continuous monitoring.

Integrating with Security and Compliance Dashboards across Providers

As organizations expand their cloud presence across AWS, Azure, and GCP, managing compliance at scale becomes increasingly complex. Each cloud provider offers security dashboards such as AWS Security Hub, Azure Security Center, and GCP Security Command Center that centralize threat detection, compliance insights, and resource monitoring. However, unifying these dashboards into a single pane of glass remains a challenge for multi-cloud environments.

By integrating Terraform with these dashboards, organizations can automate compliance data ingestion, enforce security baselines, and receive continuous insights across cloud platforms. This section explores how Terraform facilitates seamless integration with native security dashboards, aggregates compliance reports, and streamlines governance through tools such as HashiCorp Consul.

Connecting Terraform with AWS Security Hub

Connecting Terraform with AWS Security Hub provides a powerful, automated way to monitor and manage the security posture of your AWS environment. AWS Security Hub aggregates security findings from various AWS services, such as GuardDuty, Config, and Inspector, offering a centralized dashboard that highlights misconfigurations, vulnerabilities, and compliance issues based on industry standards such as the CIS benchmarks, as well as custom rules. By integrating Security Hub with Terraform, you can provision and configure AWS resources with built-in security settings that automatically report their status to Security Hub, enabling continuous compliance checks and streamlined remediation workflows. The following explains how Terraform integrates with AWS Security Hub:

- **Provisioning Security Hub:** Terraform can create and manage AWS Security Hub resources, ensuring that your account is registered and active within Security Hub. This provides the foundation for aggregating security findings from across your environment.
- **Enabling security standards:** Terraform allows you to subscribe to predefined security standards, such as the AWS Foundational Security Best Practices, which automatically check your resources against established CIS benchmarks and best practices. This helps ensure that your infrastructure complies with critical security requirements from the moment it is deployed.
- **Continuous compliance and monitoring:** By using Terraform to provision AWS Config rules, you can track real-time drift in configurations related to IAM, networking, storage, and other security-critical areas. These configurations continuously feed security findings into Security Hub, providing an up-to-date picture of your security posture.
- **Automated remediation:** Terraform can also be integrated with AWS Lambda functions through lifecycle hooks to trigger remediation actions when non-compliant configurations are detected. This **`"self-healing"`** approach ensures that any deviations from your security baselines are promptly corrected, maintaining a secure environment at all times.

```
resource "aws_securityhub_account" "example" {}

resource "aws_securityhub_standards_subscription" "cis" {
  standards_arn = " arn:aws:securityhub:::ruleset/cis-aws-foundations-bench-
mark/v/1.2.0"
}
```

This Terraform configuration enables AWS Security Hub and subscribes your account to the AWS Foundational Security Best Practices standard, automating continuous compliance monitoring against CIS benchmarks.

Integrating Terraform with Azure Security Center

Azure Security Center, now part of Microsoft Defender for Cloud, is a comprehensive security management system that provides advanced threat protection for Azure and hybrid environments. It continuously assesses your cloud environment against regulatory frameworks such as PCI DSS, ISO 27001, and SOC 2, helping you identify vulnerabilities, misconfigurations, and potential threats. This service not only offers real-time security monitoring and recommendations but also facilitates proactive remediation to improve your overall security posture.

Terraform enables you to automate the deployment and management of Azure resources in a way that aligns with the security best practices recommended by Azure Security Center. By codifying compliance baselines and security configurations into your Terraform modules, you ensure that all critical services, such as virtual machines, databases, and storage accounts, are provisioned securely from the outset. This integration provides several key benefits:

- **Consistent security baselines:** Every resource deployed via Terraform can adhere to a predefined security standard, reducing the risk of manual misconfiguration.
- **Continuous monitoring and compliance:** Once deployed, Azure Security Center continuously monitors your resources, ensuring that any deviations from the secure configuration are detected and reported.
- **Automated remediation:** By integrating with Terraform, you can automate responses to security alerts, streamlining the process of bringing non-compliant resources back into alignment.

```
resource "azurerm_security_center_subscription_pricing" "example" {
  tier          = "Standard"
  resource_type = "VirtualMachines"
}
```

This Terraform snippet enables Azure Security Center for Virtual Machines by setting the subscription pricing tier to **`"Standard"`**, ensuring enhanced threat protection and continuous compliance monitoring.

Enabling GCP Security Command Center with Terraform

GCP Security Command Center (SCC) is a centralized security management and data risk platform that aggregates security findings, inventory assets, and monitors compliance across all your GCP projects. It continuously scans services such as Google Compute Engine (GCE), Google Cloud Storage (GCS), and IAM configurations to detect misconfigurations, vulnerabilities, and potential threats, providing real-time insights and helping teams stay on top of security risks.

Terraform can integrate with SCC to ensure that every GCP resource is automatically registered and monitored according to your security policies. This automation enables immediate flagging of security violations, such as misconfigured IAM roles or network vulnerabilities, and can trigger remediation workflows. By defining SCC configurations in Terraform, you not only standardize and automate security checks across your projects but also maintain an auditable, version-controlled infrastructure that complies with industry regulations.

The following Terraform snippet enables SCC notifications by creating a notification configuration. This configuration instructs SCC to publish security alerts (referred to as **`"FINDING"`** events) to a specified Pub/Sub topic. This integration ensures that any security finding detected by SCC is immediately communicated to your operations team, enabling rapid remediation.

```
resource "google_security_center_notification_config" "example" {
  config_id    = "example-notification"
  description = "Notification for security alerts"
  pubsub_topic = "projects/my-project/topics/security-notifications"
  event_types = ["FINDING"]
}
```

By leveraging Terraform to provision and manage SCC configurations, organizations can automate compliance monitoring and secure their cloud environments effectively, ensuring that all security findings are promptly identified and addressed.

Multi-Cloud Dashboard Integration via HashiCorp Consul

HashiCorp Consul is a powerful, multi-cloud service mesh solution that provides a unified platform for service discovery, configuration management, and network segmentation. In the context of compliance and governance, Consul plays a crucial role by aggregating compliance and configuration data from services deployed across multiple cloud providers such as AWS, Azure, and GCP. This centralization enables organizations to maintain a consistent view of their multi-cloud environment, monitor adherence to security standards, and quickly identify non-compliant configurations, all from a single dashboard.

Terraform integrates with Consul via dedicated providers, enabling users to register and manage cloud services within Consul as part of their Infrastructure-as-Code workflows. By leveraging Terraform to automate the registration of services into Consul, organizations can ensure that the compliance status, configuration settings, and network endpoints of resources are consistently reported and updated. This unified approach facilitates seamless multi-cloud governance by allowing data from different cloud environments to be aggregated into a single, easily accessible dashboard. Additionally, integrating Terraform with Consul enables dynamic configuration management and service discovery, both of which are critical for maintaining secure and compliant cloud architectures.

The following is an example Terraform snippet that demonstrates how to register a service with Consul to reflect a multi-cloud compliance status:

```
resource "consul_service" "example" {
  name = "multi-cloud-compliance"
  tags = ["aws", "azure", "gcp"]
  address = "10.0.0.1"
}
```

By integrating Terraform with HashiCorp Consul, organizations can automate the registration and continuous monitoring of multi-cloud resources, ensuring that compliance data is centrally aggregated and easily accessible through a unified dashboard. This approach streamlines multi-cloud governance, enhances visibility into security and compliance status across AWS, Azure, and GCP, and supports dynamic configuration management to meet evolving regulatory requirements.

Integrating Terraform with security and compliance dashboards empowers organizations to centralize governance across AWS, Azure, and GCP. This integration not only streamlines compliance reporting but also automates remediation, enhancing overall cloud security posture. By leveraging tools such as AWS Security Hub, Azure Security Center, and GCP SCC, organizations gain unparalleled visibility and control, reducing operational overhead and fostering a proactive approach to compliance.

Generating Compliance Reports Using Terraform Modules

Compliance reporting is a cornerstone of cloud governance, providing a clear view of an organization's adherence to security frameworks, regulatory mandates, and internal policies. As infrastructure scales across AWS, Azure, and GCP, the need for automated, consistent, and reproducible compliance reporting grows. Terraform, as a declarative Infrastructure as Code (IaC) tool, not only provisions infrastructure but can also generate detailed compliance reports by leveraging its state files, outputs, and custom modules.

In this section, we explore how Terraform modules can be structured to produce compliance documentation, track configuration drift, and automate the creation of audit-ready reports in various formats. By integrating Terraform with cloud-native logging and monitoring services, organizations can maintain a centralized, version-controlled repository of compliance data, reducing the effort required for audits and fostering a proactive security posture.

Building Reusable Terraform Modules for Compliance Reports

Compliance modules in Terraform are reusable, pre-defined blocks of code designed to standardize the process of generating compliance reports across various cloud environments. These modules encapsulate all the necessary logic to query infrastructure, validate configurations, and output summaries that indicate adherence to specific regulatory standards such as GDPR, HIPAA, and PCI DSS. By abstracting the compliance logic into dedicated modules, organizations can ensure that compliance checks are consistent and easily maintainable across multiple environments.

Terraform's modular architecture allows teams to build compliance checks into separate, reusable modules. For example, you might create modules that verify critical security settings such as encryption at rest, secure IAM policies, or proper network configurations. Once defined, these modules can be invoked in different environments simply by passing in the necessary parameters (such as cloud region, account IDs, or specific policy names). This approach not only reduces code duplication but also ensures uniformity in how compliance is enforced throughout your infrastructure.

```
module "iam_compliance" {
  source         = "./modules/iam_compliance"
  aws_account_id = var.account_id
}

output "iam_report" {
  value = module.iam_compliance.report
}
```

This snippet invokes a reusable Terraform module for AWS IAM compliance by passing in the AWS account ID and outputs the generated compliance report, streamlining automated compliance monitoring and reporting.

The following are some best practices for reusable modules for compliance reporting:

- **Modularize checks by service:** Create separate modules for different services (for example, S3, EC2, and VPC) to maintain clarity and ensure that each module has a focused responsibility. This separation of concerns makes the modules easier to manage, update, and test.
- **Parameterize inputs:** Design your modules to accept dynamic inputs such as cloud regions, account IDs, and policy names. This flexibility allows the same module to be deployed across different environments and cloud providers without modification.

- **Use outputs for reporting:** Ensure that each module outputs key compliance data (for example, a JSON report) that can be used for audit purposes or integrated into a centralized compliance dashboard. This makes it easier to track compliance status over time and across multiple environments.

Exporting Compliance Data to CSV, JSON, and PDF

Exporting the compliance data in various formats such as CSV, JSON, and PDF provides a standardized, easily shareable, and audit-friendly way to capture the state of your infrastructure's security posture. This practice is crucial for organizations that need to maintain traceable compliance records, perform regular audits, and distribute compliance reports to diverse stakeholders such as auditors, management, or regulatory bodies. Exporting compliance data serves several key purposes:

- **Easy sharing and reporting:** Converting the compliance data into formats such as CSV, JSON, or PDF makes it simple to share with different teams and external auditors.
- **Auditability:** Standardized report formats provide a clear, consistent record of compliance status that can be stored, reviewed, and audited over time.
- **Automated documentation:** By automating the export of compliance data, organizations can ensure that their documentation is always up-to-date with the latest security configurations, reducing manual effort and the risk of errors.

Terraform inherently outputs data in JSON format, which is both machine-readable and structured. To extend this capability, additional tools such as custom Python scripts can be used to convert JSON outputs into CSV or PDF formats. This conversion can be automated using Terraform's **`local-exec`** provisioner or integrated into CI/CD pipelines via AWS Lambda, Azure Functions, or GCP Cloud Functions. The process typically involves:

- **Generating Terraform outputs:** Capturing the compliance data as JSON using Terraform output blocks.
- **Processing outputs:** Using a **`local-exec`** provisioner to run external scripts or commands that transform the JSON output into other formats, such as CSV or PDF.
- **Embedding metadata:** Including relevant metadata such as timestamps, resource tags, or version information in the exported files for traceability and audit purposes.

```
output "gcp_compliance_report" {
  value = jsonencode(google_project_iam_policy.my_policy)
}

provisioner "local-exec" {
  command = "echo '${self.value}' > compliance_report.json"
}
```

This Terraform configuration exports GCP compliance data as a JSON file using a **`local-exec`** provisioner, enabling automated, audit-ready reports that can be converted to CSV or PDF for multi-format compliance documentation.

The following are some best practices for exporting the compliance data:

- **Automate formatting:** Integrate Terraform outputs with automation pipelines (using tools such as AWS Lambda, Azure Functions, or GCP Cloud Functions) to ensure that compliance reports are automatically generated and converted into the desired formats as part of your deployment process.
- **Embed metadata:** Enhance your exported compliance data by including additional metadata such as timestamps, resource identifiers, and version numbers. This practice improves traceability, and helps auditors understand the context of the compliance data.

- **Support multiple formats:** Provide options to export data in both machine-readable (JSON) and human-readable formats (CSV, PDF). JSON is ideal for automated processing and integration with dashboards, while CSV and PDF are more accessible for manual reviews and formal reporting.

Archiving and Versioning Compliance Reports

Archiving and versioning compliance reports in Terraform is essential for maintaining a detailed historical record of your security and compliance posture. By systematically storing and versioning these reports, organizations can demonstrate continuous improvement, provide traceability for audits, and meet regulatory requirements. Over time, archived compliance reports become invaluable when analyzing trends, identifying recurring issues, or providing evidence during regulatory audits.

Terraform outputs can be stored locally or in cloud storage services such as AWS S3, Azure Blob Storage, or Google Cloud Storage (GCS). These outputs capture the compliance status and configuration snapshots of your infrastructure. Versioning tools such as Git or built-in storage versioning (for example, S3 bucket versioning) preserve historical snapshots of these outputs, allowing you to maintain a timeline of compliance data. This process can be automated using scheduled Terraform runs or CI/CD pipelines, ensuring that compliance reports are archived at regular intervals without manual intervention.

```
resource "azurerm_resource_group" "example" {
  name     = "example-rg"
  location = "East US"
}

resource "azurerm_storage_account" "example" {
  name                     = "examplestorageacct"
  resource_group_name      = azurerm_resource_group.example.name
  location                 = azurerm_resource_group.example.location
  account_tier             = "Standard"
  account_replication_type = "LRS"

  # Enable blob versioning to preserve historical snapshots of stored data
  enable_blob_versioning   = true
}

resource "azurerm_storage_container" "compliance" {
  name                  = "compliance-reports"
  storage_account_name  = azurerm_storage_account.example.name
  container_access_type = "private"
}

resource "azurerm_storage_blob" "compliance_report" {
  # Use a timestamp to generate a unique filename for each report version
  name                   = "compliance_report_${timestamp()}.json"
  storage_account_name   = azurerm_storage_account.example.name
  storage_container_name = azurerm_storage_container.compliance.name
  type                   = "Block"
  # Path to the local compliance report file that will be uploaded
  source                 = "path/to/report.json"
}
```

This Terraform configuration provisions an Azure Storage Account with blob versioning enabled, creates a container for compliance reports, and uploads a versioned compliance report file, ensuring that historical snapshots are preserved for audit and traceability purposes.

Generating compliance reports using Terraform modules streamlines governance and audit readiness across multi-cloud environments. By automating report generation, organizations reduce the manual effort required for compliance, ensure consistency across accounts, and maintain long-term archives for regulatory scrutiny. This approach not only fosters a culture of continuous compliance but also positions Terraform as a critical tool for cloud security and governance at scale.

Real-World Examples of Compliance-as-Code in Action

In this section, we explore practical implementations of Compliance-as-Code (CaC) across AWS, Azure, and GCP environments. Real-world examples demonstrate how organizations have automated compliance with regulatory standards such as SOC 2, FedRAMP, and GDPR. By applying Terraform configurations to enforce policies, generate compliance reports, and automate remediation, these examples provide insights into the scalability and flexibility of Compliance-as-Code.

Enforcing SOC 2 Compliance in AWS with Terraform

SOC 2 is an auditing procedure that ensures service providers securely manage data to protect the privacy of their clients. It focuses on five trust service principles: security, availability, processing integrity, confidentiality, and privacy. For AWS-based environments, this means that your cloud resources must be configured to provide strong encryption, both at rest and in transit, maintain comprehensive audit logging, and enforce strict access controls based on the principle of least privilege. Non-compliance can result in significant financial penalties and damage to your organization's reputation, making it critical to automate compliance enforcement.

Terraform configurations can enforce SOC 2 compliance by automating several key components:

- **AWS Config rules:** These rules continuously monitor your AWS resources and configurations for compliance with SOC 2 requirements. Terraform can be used to provision and manage these rules, ensuring that non-compliant resources are flagged for remediation.
- **AWS CloudTrail:** CloudTrail is used to capture detailed logs of API calls and user activities across your AWS account. By deploying CloudTrail through Terraform, you ensure that all actions are logged, providing an audit trail necessary for SOC 2 compliance.
- **S3 Bucket encryption:** Enforcing server-side encryption on S3 buckets using AWS Key Management Service (KMS) ensures that sensitive data is protected at rest. Terraform can configure these settings automatically, preventing accidental exposure of the data.
- **IAM roles with least privilege:** Terraform helps define and enforce IAM roles that only grant the minimal permissions required for each task. This minimizes the risk of unauthorized access and data breaches.

```
# AWS Config Rule to check that all S3 buckets have server-side encryption
enabled
resource "aws_config_config_rule" "s3_encryption_check" {
  name = "s3-bucket-server-side-encryption-enabled"
  source {
    owner             = "AWS"
    source_identifier = "S3_BUCKET_SERVER_SIDE_ENCRYPTION_ENABLED"
  }
}
```

This AWS Config Rule enables continuous monitoring and automatic drift detection by alerting when S3 buckets do not have server-side encryption enabled, which is a key SOC 2 compliance expectation.

```
# KMS key for encrypting the SOC2 CloudTrail S3 bucket
resource "aws_kms_key" "soc2_bucket_key" {
  description             = "KMS key for encrypting SOC2 CloudTrail S3 bucket"
  deletion_window_in_days = 10
  enable_key_rotation     = true
}

# S3 bucket to store SOC2 CloudTrail logs with encryption enabled using the
KMS key
resource "aws_s3_bucket" "soc2_data" {
  bucket = "soc2-cloudtrail-data"

  server_side_encryption_configuration {
    rule {
      apply_server_side_encryption_by_default {
        kms_master_key_id = aws_kms_key.soc2_bucket_key.arn
        sse_algorithm     = "aws:kms"
      }
    }
  }
}

# CloudTrail to capture and log AWS API events, storing them in the encrypted
S3 bucket
resource "aws_cloudtrail" "soc2_trail" {
  name                          = "soc2-cloudtrail"
  s3_bucket_name                = aws_s3_bucket.soc2_data.id
  include_global_service_events = true
  kms_key_id                    = "alias/soc2-cloudtrail-key"
}
```

This Terraform configuration enforces SOC 2 compliance in AWS by provisioning an encrypted S3 bucket for sensitive data, and deploying CloudTrail to log API activity, ensuring continuous monitoring and adherence to strict security standards.

By leveraging Terraform to deploy these configurations, organizations can automate the enforcement of SOC2 controls within their AWS environment. The example demonstrates how to secure sensitive data with encryption in an S3 bucket and how to capture the detailed audit logs with CloudTrail, both of which are essential for maintaining SOC2 compliance. This automated, code-driven approach minimizes manual intervention, ensures consistent security practices, and facilitates rapid remediation of any deviations from compliance standards.

Implementing FedRAMP Controls in Azure

FedRAMP (Federal Risk and Authorization Management Program) sets the security baseline for cloud products and services used by U.S. government agencies. In Azure, achieving FedRAMP compliance means:

- **Data protection:** Ensuring that the sensitive data, particularly ePHI or government data, is encrypted both at rest and in transit.
- **Access control:** Enforcing strict access controls and least privilege principles through Azure Policy and IAM.
- **Network security:** Configuring Network Security Groups (NSGs) to restrict inbound and outbound traffic to only authorized sources.
- **Continuous monitoring:** Utilizing tools such as Microsoft Defender for Cloud and Azure Monitor to provide ongoing security assessments and alerts.

Terraform enables the deployment of secure Azure resources by automating the configuration of compliance controls. This is achieved through:

- **Azure policy:** Terraform can provision custom policy definitions that enforce specific configurations, such as ensuring encryption settings are enabled on storage accounts.
- **NSG configuration:** By managing NSGs with Terraform, you can enforce network restrictions to prevent unauthorized access, meeting the network security standards required by FedRAMP.
- **Automated monitoring:** Terraform can be integrated with Azure Monitor and Microsoft Defender for Cloud to continuously track compliance status and trigger remediation when deviations occur.

```
resource "azurerm_policy_definition" "fedramp_policy" {
  name         = "fedramp-encryption-policy"
  policy_type  = "Custom"
  mode         = "All"

  policy_rule = jsonencode({
    if = {
      field = "Microsoft.Storage/storageAccounts/encryption.requireInfrastruc-
tureEncryption"
      equals = "false"
    }
    then = {
      effect = "Deny"
    }
  })
}
```

This Terraform snippet defines a custom Azure Policy that denies the creation of storage accounts without infrastructure encryption, ensuring compliance with FedRAMP controls for data protection.

By integrating Terraform with Azure's compliance tools, such as Azure Policy, organizations can automate the enforcement of FedRAMP controls across their cloud infrastructure. This not only ensures that all resources such as storage accounts, meet critical security requirements like encryption, but also provides a scalable, auditable solution that continuously monitors compliance. Leveraging Terraform for these tasks minimizes manual effort, reduces human error, and ensures that your cloud environment is secure and compliant with the government standards.

Managing GDPR Compliance for GCP Workloads

GDPR mandates strict controls over the processing, storage, and transfer of personal data. This includes requirements for data residency, encryption, and obtaining user consent. In the cloud, meeting GDPR means ensuring that sensitive data is securely stored and accessed only by authorized parties, with full audit trails in place. Terraform helps enforce these requirements by automating the provisioning of GCP resources with built-in encryption, access controls, and audit logging, thereby reducing the risk of non-compliance.

Terraform enables the deployment of secure GCP resources by automating the configuration of compliance controls. This is achieved through:

- **Deploy Google Cloud KMS for encryption:** Terraform is used to deploy Google Cloud Key Management Service (KMS) resources, which encrypt sensitive data at rest. By specifying a Customer-Managed Encryption Key (CMEK) in resource configurations, you ensure that all data stored in services such as Cloud Storage is encrypted according to GDPR requirements.
- **Implement IAM roles to restrict data access:** Terraform can also be used to configure IAM roles and policies that limit data access to only those users or services with a legitimate need,

adhering to the principle of least privilege. This prevents unauthorized access to personal data.

- **Enable audit logging:** Enabling audit logs is critical for GDPR compliance, as it provides a detailed record of who accessed data and when. Terraform can automate the setup of logging for sensitive GCP projects, ensuring that all operations are tracked for auditing and monitoring purposes.

```
 # KMS Key Ring for GDPR encryption (in EU region)
resource "google_kms_key_ring" "gdpr_ring" {
  name     = "gdpr-keyring"
  location = "europe-west1"  # EU-compliant location
}

# KMS Crypto Key used to encrypt sensitive GDPR data
resource "google_kms_crypto_key" "gdpr_key" {
  name     = "gdpr-encryption-key"
  key_ring = google_kms_key_ring.gdpr_ring.id
  purpose  = "ENCRYPT_DECRYPT"
}

# Grant encryption/decryption access to specific service account
resource "google_kms_crypto_key_iam_binding" "gdpr_key_access" {
  crypto_key_id = google_kms_crypto_key.gdpr_key.id
  role          = "roles/cloudkms.cryptoKeyEncrypterDecrypter"

  members = [
    "serviceAccount:gdpr-access-sa@your-project-id.iam.gserviceaccount.com"
  ]
}

# Storage bucket to hold GDPR-sensitive data with CMEK and audit logs
resource "google_storage_bucket" "gdpr_bucket" {
  name     = "gdpr-sensitive-data"
  location = "EU"

  # Enable CMEK encryption
  encryption {
    default_kms_key_name = google_kms_crypto_key.gdpr_key.id
  }

  # Enable object-level and admin activity audit logs
  logging {
    log_bucket        = "gdpr-audit-logs-bucket"  # This bucket must exist
    log_object_prefix = "access-logs/"
  }
}

# Grant minimal access to read/write data for the specific service account
resource "google_storage_bucket_iam_binding" "gdpr_bucket_access" {
  bucket = google_storage_bucket.gdpr_bucket.name
  role   = "roles/storage.objectAdmin"

  members = [
    "serviceAccount:gdpr-access-sa@your-project-id.iam.gserviceaccount.com"
  ]
}
```

This Terraform configuration deploys a GDPR-compliant GCP storage bucket in the EU, encrypting data at rest using a customer-managed KMS key, ensuring that sensitive information is securely stored in accordance with GDPR requirements.

By using Terraform to define and deploy resources in GCP, organizations can automate the enforcement of GDPR compliance requirements. This configuration ensures that the sensitive data is stored within the EU, encrypted with a customer-managed key, and access is strictly controlled. Automating these controls reduces manual overhead, minimizes the risk of human error, and provides an auditable, consistent approach to data protection that aligns with the GDPR mandates.

Multi-Cloud Compliance-as-Code for Financial Services

Financial institutions that operate across multiple cloud environments must adhere to rigorous compliance standards such as PCI DSS and ISO 27001 to safeguard sensitive financial data and ensure secure operations. Terraform provides a unified, code-driven platform to enforce these security policies across major cloud providers such as AWS, Azure, and GCP. By leveraging Terraform, organizations can codify compliance controls into Infrastructure-as-Code, ensuring that security configurations are consistently applied, easily auditable, and continuously enforced across all cloud environments. The following explains the working of multi-cloud compliance as code for financial services:

- **Deploy PCI-compliant storage:** Terraform can provision secure storage solutions on AWS, Azure, and GCP that meet PCI DSS requirements. For example, on AWS, encrypted S3 buckets using customer-managed keys ensure that data at rest is protected. Similarly, on Azure, you can configure Azure Blob Storage with encryption enabled, and on GCP, you can enforce encryption on Cloud Storage buckets using Google Cloud KMS. This multi-cloud approach ensures that regardless of the provider, the sensitive data is encrypted and secure.
- **Automate VPC flow logs and firewall rules:** To meet compliance and security standards, it is crucial to monitor network traffic and restrict unauthorized access. Terraform can automate the configuration of VPC flow logs and firewall rules across all cloud providers. This includes enabling AWS VPC flow logs, configuring Azure Network Security Groups (NSGs) with specific inbound/outbound rules, and setting up GCP firewall rules to restrict access. These measures provide critical visibility into network activity and help prevent data breaches by enforcing strict access controls.
- **Centralize compliance reporting through HashiCorp Consul:** In a multi-cloud environment, centralizing compliance reporting is essential for monitoring, auditing, and ensuring consistency. HashiCorp Consul can be integrated with Terraform to aggregate compliance data from various cloud providers into a single, unified dashboard. This centralized reporting enables compliance teams to quickly identify and remediate issues, track compliance trends over time, and maintain a clear audit trail that is essential for regulatory reviews.

By utilizing Terraform for multi-cloud compliance-as-code, financial institutions can enforce security policies consistently across AWS, Azure, and GCP, ensuring that all storage, networking, and access controls are aligned with PCI DSS and ISO 27001 standards. This approach not only simplifies the deployment and management of compliance controls but also centralizes reporting and monitoring, ultimately reducing risks, and supporting the stringent regulatory requirements of the financial services industry.

Lessons Learned from Compliance-as-Code Deployments

Real-world deployments of Compliance-as-Code using Terraform have highlighted the critical importance of staying agile in a constantly evolving regulatory landscape. Organizations quickly learned that maintaining up-to-date compliance policies is essential, as regulations and security threats continually change. Regular policy updates ensure that Terraform configurations remain aligned with the latest standards and help prevent vulnerabilities from creeping into production.

Continuous testing is another key lesson. By validating Terraform plans against compliance frameworks before deployment, organizations can catch misconfigurations early. Integrating these validations into CI/CD pipelines automates the review process, ensuring that every change is scrutinized for compliance before it is applied, which dramatically reduces the risk of non-compliant infrastructure updates.

Regular audits also play a vital role in long-term compliance. Automated and manual audits provide a clear, historical record of compliance posture, enabling teams to identify drift and make necessary adjustments. These audits, combined with automated policy reviews, create a robust feedback loop that helps organizations maintain consistent, secure, and compliant cloud environments over time. The following are some best practices:

- **Validate Terraform plans:** Always check Terraform plans against compliance frameworks to catch any misconfigurations early.
- **Automate policy reviews:** Integrate automated compliance checks into your CI/CD pipelines to ensure continuous monitoring.
- **Conduct regular audits:** Perform frequent audits to verify that your infrastructure remains compliant over the long term.

These real-world examples demonstrate the transformative potential of Compliance-as-Code in simplifying regulatory adherence across AWS, Azure, and GCP. By embedding compliance checks directly into Terraform configurations, organizations not only enhance their security posture but also achieve greater operational efficiency. Moving forward, integrating Policy-as-Code frameworks will be pivotal in ensuring that cloud environments remain secure, resilient, and compliant with evolving industry standards.

Conclusion

Compliance-as-Code is transforming cloud security by embedding regulatory and organizational requirements directly into infrastructure provisioning. This chapter explored how Terraform, combined with cloud-native security tools such as AWS Config, Azure Policy, and GCP Policy Intelligence, enables automated compliance audits and enforcement. By defining compliance frameworks such as CIS Benchmarks and NIST standards in Terraform configurations, organizations can ensure continuous monitoring and remediation of misconfigurations. Additionally, we discussed how to write custom compliance rules tailored to industry-specific regulations such as GDPR, HIPAA, and PCI DSS, ensuring that cloud workloads align with critical security and privacy mandates.

Beyond automation, Terraform facilitates centralized compliance reporting and dashboard integration across AWS, Azure, and GCP, providing security teams with real-time visibility into cloud environments. By leveraging Terraform modules, organizations can generate audit-ready compliance reports in various formats, ensuring transparency and regulatory adherence. Through real-world case studies, we highlighted successful implementations of Compliance-as-Code in sectors such as finance, healthcare, and government, showcasing both best practices and common pitfalls. As enterprises continue adopting multi-cloud strategies, integrating compliance into Terraform workflows will be essential for maintaining security, governance, and regulatory compliance at scale.

In the next chapter, we will delve into secure secrets management and data protection strategies using Terraform. It covers native solutions for secret storage, encryption with key management services, automated secret rotation, and safeguarding sensitive data such as API keys and credentials.

Questions and Answers

1. **How can Compliance-as-Code help organizations maintain security across Multi-Cloud Environments?**

   Compliance-as-Code (CaC) automates compliance enforcement by embedding security policies directly into Terraform configurations, ensuring continuous adherence to regulatory requirements across AWS, Azure, and GCP. By leveraging cloud-native tools such as AWS Config, Azure Policy, and GCP Policy Intelligence, organizations can detect misconfigurations in real time, enforce encryption and network security policies, and trigger automated remediation workflows. This approach reduces manual efforts, minimizes human error, and ensures consistent security postures across multi-cloud environments.

2. **What are the key differences between AWS Config, Azure Policy, and GCP Policy Intelligence in compliance automation?**

   AWS Config, Azure Policy, and GCP Policy Intelligence provide cloud-native compliance monitoring, but they operate differently. AWS Config tracks configuration changes and evaluates compliance against predefined rules, Azure Policy enforces compliance through policy assignments and initiatives, and GCP Policy Intelligence uses AI-driven insights to recommend security improvements. By integrating these tools with Terraform, organizations can automate compliance audits, enforce security best practices, and maintain continuous visibility into their cloud environments.

3. **How can Terraform help enforce regulatory compliance standards such as GDPR, HIPAA, and PCI DSS?**

   Terraform enables organizations to define Infrastructure-as-Code (IaC) policies that align with regulatory standards such as GDPR, HIPAA, and PCI DSS. For instance, Terraform can enforce GDPR compliance by ensuring encryption for data at rest and in transit, HIPAA compliance by restricting access to sensitive healthcare data, and PCI DSS compliance by securing cloud-based payment environments. By writing custom Terraform policies and leveraging compliance modules, organizations can automate regulatory enforcement and ensure audit readiness.

4. **How can organizations integrate Terraform with cloud security dashboards for centralized compliance monitoring?**

   Terraform can be integrated with cloud security dashboards such as AWS Security Hub, Azure Security Center, and GCP Security Command Center to centralize compliance insights. This allows organizations to aggregate security findings, automate policy enforcement, and visualize compliance status across cloud environments. Additionally, tools such as HashiCorp Consul can unify compliance metrics from multiple cloud providers, providing a single-pane-of-glass view for security teams to track and manage compliance posture.

5. **What are some real-world use cases of Compliance-as-Code, and what lessons can be learned from them?**

   Real-world use cases of Compliance-as-Code include enforcing SOC 2 controls in AWS, implementing FedRAMP compliance in Azure, and managing GDPR compliance in GCP. Organizations in financial services have also used Compliance-as-Code to automate security controls across multi-cloud environments. Therefore, the key lessons learned from these deployments include the importance of modular Terraform code for scalability, proactive compliance monitoring to prevent drift, and integrating remediation workflows to address violations in real time.

CHAPTER 9
Secrets Management and Data Protection

Introduction

In today's cloud environments, protecting sensitive information is paramount. This chapter focuses on Secrets Management and Data Protection in Terraform, demonstrating how to securely store, encrypt, and rotate credentials, API keys, and other crucial data across AWS, Azure, and GCP. Readers will explore how cloud-native secret management tools such as AWS Secrets Manager, Azure Key Vault, and Google Secret Manager can be integrated with Terraform to automate the creation, retrieval, and auditing of secrets. The chapter also covers encryption of the best practices using provider-native Key Management Services (KMS) to secure data both at rest and in transit, ensuring that sensitive information remains protected across diverse infrastructures.

Building on this foundation, the chapter delves into automating secret rotation to mitigate the risk of credential leaks with least privilege access. Additionally, it examines methods to secure API keys and tokens in Terraform code by externalizing variables, referencing secret managers, and masking sensitive outputs. Finally, the chapter outlines strategies for implementing end-to-end encryption from provisioning encrypted storage buckets to automating TLS certificate management, ensuring comprehensive protection for sensitive data throughout its lifecycle. By the end of this chapter, readers will have a robust set of best practices to safeguard their cloud infrastructures using Terraform.

Structure

In this chapter, we will cover the following topics:

- Managing Secrets with Native Solutions
  - Overview of Secrets Management in AWS, Azure, and GCP
  - Storing and Retrieving Secrets with Terraform
  - Implementing IAM Policies for Secret Access
  - Auditing and Logging Secret Access
- Encrypting Secrets Using Provider-Native Key Management Services
  - Terraform Integration with KMS for Secret Encryption
  - Configuring Automatic Key Rotation
  - Managing Cross-Region and Multi-Cloud Key Replication
- Automating Secret Rotation across Cloud Providers
  - Automate Secret Rotation
  - Configuring AWS Secrets Manager for Automatic Rotation
  - Implementing Secret Rotation in Azure Key Vault
  - Rotating GCP Secrets with Cloud Functions

    - Cross-Cloud Secret Synchronization
- Securing API Keys, Tokens, and Credentials in Terraform Code
    - Externalizing Sensitive Variables in Terraform
    - Referencing Secrets from Secret Managers
    - Securing Terraform Plan and Apply Pipelines
    - Masking Sensitive Outputs in Terraform State
- Implementing End-to-End Encryption for the Sensitive Data
    - End-to-End Encryption Fundamentals
    - Provisioning Encrypted Storage Buckets
    - Encrypting Traffic with TLS and Certificates

Managing Secrets with Native Solutions

Secrets management is a critical component of cloud security. As organizations scale their cloud environments, managing sensitive credentials such as API keys, database passwords, and encryption keys becomes complex. Terraform, coupled with cloud-native secret management tools such as AWS Secrets Manager, Azure Key Vault, and Google Secret Manager, provides a scalable solution to securely manage and distribute secrets. This section explores how to integrate Terraform with these native tools to enforce secure, automated, and auditable secrets management across multi-cloud environments.

Overview of Secrets Management in AWS, Azure, and GCP

Secrets management is the process of securely storing, managing, and retrieving the sensitive information such as API keys, passwords, certificates, and encryption keys. In cloud environments, this practice is crucial to minimizing credential exposure and ensuring that sensitive data is protected from unauthorized access. Cloud providers offer dedicated tools for secrets management that integrate with their security and identity frameworks, providing robust mechanisms to enforce access controls and automate key rotation. The following are secret management services in different cloud providers:

- **AWS Secrets Manager:** AWS Secrets Manager provides a secure solution for storing, rotating, and managing secrets such as database credentials and API keys. It seamlessly integrates with AWS Identity and Access Management (IAM) to allow fine-grained access control, ensuring that only authorized users and services can retrieve sensitive information. This service also supports automated secret rotation, reducing the risk of credential leaks over time.
- **Azure Key Vault:** Azure Key Vault offers a centralized repository for managing secrets, certificates, and encryption keys. With robust Role-Based Access Control (RBAC) and integration with Azure Active Directory, it ensures that access to sensitive data is strictly controlled. Additionally, Key Vault simplifies the management of cryptographic keys used for encryption, helping organizations meet compliance and security standards.
- **Google Secret Manager:** Google Secret Manager is a centralized service that securely stores API keys, passwords, certificates, and other sensitive data. Integrated with GCP's IAM and Cloud Audit Logs, it enables precise control over who can access secrets and provides audit trails for compliance purposes. Its design ensures that secrets can be dynamically retrieved by applications at runtime, maintaining a secure environment without the need for hardcoded credentials.

The following explains the working of secret management in the cloud:

- **Encryption:** Secrets stored in these cloud services are encrypted using the respective provider's key management systems, AWS KMS for AWS Secrets Manager, Azure Key Vault for Azure, and GCP KMS for Google Secret Manager. This encryption ensures that sensitive data is protected both at rest and in transit.
- **Access control:** Access to secrets is strictly governed by IAM policies, RBAC, or secret-specific permissions. This means that only authenticated and authorized users or services can retrieve the secrets, which enforces the principle of least privilege. For example, a developer might have permission to retrieve an API key for a service but not to view database credentials.
- **Dynamic retrieval:** Applications and workloads can dynamically retrieve secrets at runtime, ensuring that sensitive information is never hardcoded in source code or configuration files. This dynamic retrieval helps maintain security and compliance, as credentials can be rotated regularly without requiring code changes.

The following are some best practices for secret management in the cloud:

- **Centralize secrets:** Store all sensitive credentials in a centralized secrets management system rather than embedding them in code. This reduces the risk of accidental exposure and simplifies management.
- **Rotate secrets regularly:** Automate the rotation of secrets to ensure that even if credentials are compromised, the window of exposure is minimized. Regular rotation also aligns with compliance requirements and reduces the risks associated with long-lived credentials.
- **Enforce least privilege:** Restrict access to secrets based on roles and responsibilities. Use the principle of least privilege to ensure that only those who absolutely need access to sensitive data have it, thereby limiting the potential impact of any breaches.

Storing and Retrieving Secrets with Terraform

Storing and retrieving secrets with Terraform involves automating the provisioning and management of secret resources by interfacing directly with cloud-native secrets management services. This automation ensures that sensitive information, such as API keys, passwords, and certificates, is securely stored, centrally managed, and dynamically injected into your cloud environments without hard-coding credentials in your infrastructure code. The following explains the working of secret management in the cloud:

- **Provisioning secrets resources:** Terraform resources are used to create and manage secret storage within each cloud provider's native solution. This setup involves defining secrets, setting their values, and configuring policies to control access.
- **Secure storage:** Secrets are encrypted using the provider's key management service (for example, AWS KMS, Azure Key Vault, GCP KMS), ensuring that sensitive data is protected both at rest and in transit.
- **Dynamic retrieval:** When applications or services require these secrets, they can be dynamically retrieved at runtime through secure APIs. This dynamic injection eliminates the need to embed secrets directly in your code or configuration files, reducing the risk of exposure.
- **Consistent management:** Using Terraform to manage secrets allows you to apply version control, automated updates, and consistent policies across multiple environments, making the overall security posture easier to maintain and audit.

```
# Create a Secrets Manager secret to securely store sensitive credentials
resource "aws_secretsmanager_secret" "example" {
  name        = "example-secret"
  description = "This secret contains example credentials"
```

```
}

# Configure automatic rotation for the Secrets Manager secret using a Lambda
function
resource "aws_secretsmanager_secret_rotation" "example_rotation" {
  secret_id           = aws_secretsmanager_secret.example.id
  rotation_lambda_arn = aws_lambda_function.secret_rotation.arn
  rotation_rules {
    automatically_after_days = 30
  }
}

resource "aws_secretsmanager_secret_version" "example" {
  secret_id     = aws_secretsmanager_secret.example.id
  secret_string = jsonencode({
    username = "admin"
    password = "supersecretpassword"
  })
}

aws secretsmanager get-secret-value --secret-id example-secret   # Retrieve the
current value of the secret named "example-secret" from AWS Secrets Manager
```

This configuration creates a secret in AWS Secrets Manager named **"example-secret"** and stores a JSON-encoded credential (username and password) as its value. The secret version resource manages the secret's current value, allowing you to update and rotate credentials automatically.

```
resource "azurerm_resource_group" "example" {
  name     = "example-rg"
  location = "East US"
}

resource "azurerm_key_vault" "example" {
  name                = "examplekv"
  resource_group_name = azurerm_resource_group.example.name
  location            = azurerm_resource_group.example.location
  tenant_id           = data.azurerm_client_config.current.tenant_id
  sku_name            = "standard"
}

resource "azurerm_key_vault_secret" "example" {
  name         = "example-secret"
  value        = "supersecretvalue"
  key_vault_id = azurerm_key_vault.example.id
}
```

This snippet provisions an Azure Resource Group and a Key Vault within it, then creates a secret named **"example-secret"** in the Key Vault with the value **"supersecretvalue"**. The secret is securely stored and managed by Azure Key Vault.

```
resource "google_secret_manager_secret" "example" {
  secret_id = "example-secret"
  replication {
    automatic = true
  }
}

resource "google_secret_manager_secret_version" "example" {
  secret      = google_secret_manager_secret.example.id
```

```
  secret_data = base64encode("supersecretvalue")
}

gcloud secrets versions access latest --secret="example-secret"  # Retrieve the
current value of the secret named "example-secret" from GCP Secrets Manager
```

This configuration creates a secret in GCP Secret Manager with the identifier **`"example-secret"`** using automatic replication. A new version of the secret is then created, where the secret data (**`"supersecretvalue"`**) is base64 encoded. This ensures that sensitive data is securely stored and versioned in GCP Secret Manager.

Implementing IAM Policies for Secret Access

Implementing IAM policies for secret access with Terraform means defining granular permissions that control who can view or manage sensitive information, such as API keys, passwords, and certificates. These policies enforce the principle of least privilege, ensuring that only authorized identities, whether users, groups, or service accounts, can access the secrets. This approach not only protects critical data but also supports compliance with security standards by limiting potential exposure. The following are the access control models:

- **Resource-level access control:** IAM policies are applied directly to resources, ensuring that access controls are enforced at the point where the secret is stored. This minimizes the risk of unauthorized access.
- **ABAC and RBAC models:** Cloud providers offer both Attribute-Based Access Control (ABAC) and Role-Based Access Control (RBAC).
  - RBAC allows you to assign roles with a predefined set of permissions (for example, a **`"secretAccessor"`** role).
  - ABAC provides additional granularity by allowing permissions to be granted based on attributes, such as tags or labels.

  These models enable you to create precise, flexible policies that only allow the necessary actions on the secrets.

```
resource "google_secret_manager_secret" "example" {
  secret_id = "example-secret"
  replication {
    automatic = true
  }
}

# RBAC: Grant specific users and service accounts access to the secret
resource "google_secret_manager_secret_iam_binding" "example_binding" {
  secret_id = google_secret_manager_secret.example.id
  role      = "roles/secretmanager.secretAccessor"
  members   = [
    "user:example@example.com",
    "serviceAccount:my-service-account@my-project.iam.gserviceaccount.com",
  ]
}

# ABAC: Conditional access based on user email domain (example.com)
resource "google_secret_manager_secret_iam_member" "example_abac" {
  secret_id = google_secret_manager_secret.example.id
  role      = "roles/secretmanager.secretAccessor"
  member    = "user:conditional-user@example.com"
```

```
    condition {
      title       = "emailDomainCondition"
      description = "Allow access only if user's email domain is example.com"
      expression  = "request.auth != null && endsWith(request.auth.claims.email,
'@example.com')"
    }
  }
```

This configuration creates a secret in Google Secret Manager and applies both RBAC and ABAC controls. RBAC is enforced by granting fixed IAM roles to specified users and service accounts, while ABAC restricts access dynamically based on user attributes such as email domain.

The following are some best practices for Secret access management:

- **Enforce the principle of least privilege:** Grant only the minimum necessary permissions to users, groups, or service accounts to access secrets, reducing the attack surface.
- **Apply resource-level access control:** Attach IAM policies directly to secrets or secret resources to ensure fine-grained control and limit unauthorized access.
- **Use RBAC for role assignments:** Leverage predefined roles such as **`secretAccessor`** to simplify management and enforce consistent permission sets across users or services.
- **Incorporate ABAC for fine-grained access:** Utilize attribute-based conditions (for example, tags, labels, user attributes) to tailor access dynamically based on context, enhancing security flexibility.
- **Regularly review and audit IAM policies:** Continuously monitor and update access policies to adapt to changing organizational needs and to detect potential misconfigurations.
- **Integrate with automation and compliance tools:** Use tools such as OPA or Terraform Sentinel to enforce policy compliance automatically, ensuring secrets access follows organizational and regulatory standards.
- **Limit secret exposure:** Avoid embedding secrets directly in code or environment variables; always control access through IAM and secret management systems.
- **Use service accounts with scoped permissions:** Assign secrets access to service accounts with narrowly scoped permissions rather than broad user access for better control and auditability.

Auditing and Logging Secret Access

Auditing secret access is crucial for maintaining accountability, detecting unauthorized actions, and ensuring the overall security of sensitive information. In the context of Terraform, automating the configuration of auditing and logging for secret access ensures that every interaction with your secret management systems is recorded and monitored. Cloud providers offer built-in auditing tools, such as Azure Monitor for Azure, AWS CloudTrail for AWS, and Cloud Audit Logs for GCP, to track and monitor activities across their platforms. For example, Azure Key Vault can be monitored using Azure Monitor and Log Analytics, which collect detailed logs and metrics about every access event. This logging helps organizations maintain compliance with regulatory standards, investigate security incidents, and continuously improve their security posture.

```
data "azurerm_client_config" "current" {}

# Create a Resource Group
resource "azurerm_resource_group" "example" {
  name     = "example-rg"
  location = "East US"
}

# Create an Azure Key Vault
```

```
resource "azurerm_key_vault" "example" {
  name                = "example-vault"
  location            = azurerm_resource_group.example.location
  resource_group_name = azurerm_resource_group.example.name
  tenant_id           = data.azurerm_client_config.current.tenant_id
  sku_name            = "standard"
}

# Create a Log Analytics Workspace to store diagnostics logs
resource "azurerm_log_analytics_workspace" "example" {
  name                = "example-law"
  location            = azurerm_resource_group.example.location
  resource_group_name = azurerm_resource_group.example.name
  sku                 = "PerGB2018"
  retention_in_days   = 30
}

# Enable diagnostic settings for the Key Vault to capture audit logs and
metrics
resource "azurerm_monitor_diagnostic_setting" "example" {
  name                       = "keyvault-diagnostics"
  target_resource_id         = azurerm_key_vault.example.id
  log_analytics_workspace_id = azurerm_log_analytics_workspace.example.id

  log {
    category = "AuditEvent"
    enabled  = true
    retention_policy {
      enabled = true
      days    = 30
    }
    # Collects and retains key vault audit logs for security and compliance
monitoring
  }

  metric {
    category = "AllMetrics"
    enabled  = true
    retention_policy {
      enabled = true
      days    = 30
    }
    # Collects and retains performance and usage metrics for monitoring key
vault health
  }
}
```

This Terraform snippet configures diagnostic settings for an Azure Key Vault, exporting audit logs and metrics to an Azure Log Analytics Workspace for continuous monitoring and compliance auditing of secret access.

Managing secrets through cloud-native solutions and Terraform is a cornerstone of secure cloud infrastructure. By leveraging AWS Secrets Manager, Azure Key Vault, and Google Secret Manager, organizations can centralize sensitive data, automate rotation, enforce fine-grained IAM controls, and ensure comprehensive auditing. This proactive approach to secrets management strengthens the overall security posture, minimizing the risk of credential leaks and enhancing compliance across multi-cloud environments.

Encrypting Secrets Using Provider-Native Key Management Services

Encryption is a fundamental aspect of securing secrets across cloud environments. By encrypting secrets at rest and in transit, organizations reduce the risk of unauthorized access and data breaches. Provider-native Key Management Services (KMS) offer scalable, centralized encryption solutions that integrate with other cloud services. In this section, we explore how AWS KMS, Azure Key Vault, and Google Cloud KMS (GCP KMS) work, and how Terraform can automate and enforce encryption practices across multi-cloud environments.

Terraform Integration with KMS for Secret Encryption

Key Management involves handling all aspects of encryption keys used to secure sensitive information. This includes:

- **Creation:** Generating cryptographic keys used to encrypt data.
- **Rotation:** Regularly updating keys to reduce the risk of compromise.
- **Usage:** Controlling which applications and services can access the keys to encrypt or decrypt data.
- **Deletion:** Securely retiring keys that are no longer needed.

KMS tools provided by cloud vendors, such as AWS KMS, Azure Key Vault, and Google Cloud KMS, automate these processes, ensuring that data remains secure without the need for manual intervention.

Terraform simplifies the provisioning and management of KMS resources, automating encryption workflows and applying keys to sensitive data. The following is the working of KMS management with Terraform:

- **Automated provisioning:** Terraform scripts define the resources required for KMS (such as keys, key rings, or vaults) and deploy them consistently across your cloud environment. This allows for repeatable and auditable key management practices.
- **Integration with secrets management:** When storing secrets (for example, in AWS Secrets Manager, Azure Key Vault, or Google Secret Manager), Terraform links these secrets to the corresponding KMS resources, ensuring that the secrets are encrypted with Customer-Managed Keys (CMKs).
- **Dynamic application of encryption:** The encryption settings are applied at resource creation. For example, an S3 bucket or a storage account is automatically configured to use a specified KMS key, ensuring that data is encrypted both at rest and in transit.
- **Centralized control and auditing:** Using Terraform to manage KMS resources centralizes control over encryption keys. This not only improves security by applying the principle of least privilege but also facilitates comprehensive logging and auditing of key usage.

```
resource "aws_kms_key" "example" {
  description             = "KMS key for secret encryption"
  deletion_window_in_days = 10 # Key will be scheduled for deletion 10 days
after being marked for removal (soft delete window)
}

resource "aws_secretsmanager_secret" "secret" {
  name                    = "db-password"
  kms_key_id              = aws_kms_key.example.id
```

```
  recovery_window_in_days = 7
}
```

This snippet creates an AWS KMS key for secret encryption and links it to a Secrets Manager secret to securely store a database password.

```
resource "azurerm_key_vault" "example" {
  name                = "vault-example"
  location            = "East US"
  resource_group_name = "resource-group"
}

resource "azurerm_key_vault_key" "example" {
  name         = "key-example"
  key_vault_id = azurerm_key_vault.example.id
  key_type     = "RSA"
  key_size     = 2048
}
```

This snippet provisions an Azure Key Vault and a key within it for encrypting sensitive data, enabling secure key management.

```
resource "google_kms_key_ring" "example" {
  name     = "example-key-ring"
  location = "us-central1"
}

resource "google_kms_crypto_key" "example" {
  name     = "example-key"
  key_ring = google_kms_key_ring.example.id
  purpose  = "ENCRYPT_DECRYPT"
}
```

This snippet creates a GCP KMS key ring and a crypto key, facilitating encryption and decryption of sensitive data across GCP services.

The following are some best practices for encrypting secrets with KMS:

- **Use Customer-Managed Keys (CMKs):** Customer-Managed Keys offer greater control over encryption processes, including key rotation policies and access management.

```
resource "aws_kms_key" "s3_key" {
  # Customer-managed KMS key with key rotation for S3 bucket encryption
  description             = "Customer-managed key for S3 bucket encryption"
  enable_key_rotation     = true
  deletion_window_in_days = 7
}

resource "aws_s3_bucket" "secure_data" {
  # S3 bucket encrypted using the customer-managed KMS key
  bucket = "my-secure-bucket"

  server_side_encryption_configuration {
    rule {
      apply_server_side_encryption_by_default {
        sse_algorithm     = "aws:kms"
        kms_master_key_id = aws_kms_key.s3_key.arn
      }
    }
  }
}
```

- **Apply least privilege access:** Restrict permissions on KMS resources to only those users or services that require them, reducing the potential for unauthorized access.
- **Enable logging for key usage:** Enable audit logging for KMS resources to monitor key usage, helping to detect anomalies and support compliance audits.
- **Automate key rotation:** Configure automated key rotation policies where supported, ensuring that keys are regularly updated to mitigate the risk of compromise.

Configuring Automatic Key Rotation

Key rotation is the process of periodically replacing encryption keys to minimize the risk and impact of key compromise. By regularly rotating keys, organizations reduce the window during which an attacker could exploit a compromised key, thereby enhancing data protection. Cloud providers offer automated key rotation features to achieve this without manual intervention, ensuring continuous security without downtime. However, if not managed properly, key rotation can introduce operational complexity, especially when keys are used across multiple services or environments.

```
resource "aws_kms_key" "example" {
  enable_key_rotation = true
}
```

This snippet enables automatic rotation for an AWS KMS key, ensuring that the key is replaced on a predefined schedule to minimize exposure.

```
resource "azurerm_key_vault_key" "example" {
  key_vault_id = azurerm_key_vault.example.id
  key_type     = "RSA"
  key_size     = 2048
  rotation_policy {
    automatic = true
  }
}
```

The aforementioned example creates an Azure Key Vault key with automatic rotation enabled, regularly updating the key to maintain secure encryption.

```
resource "google_kms_crypto_key" "example" {
  rotation_period = "7776000s"  // 90 days
}
```

This code sets up a GCP KMS crypto key with a 90-day rotation period, ensuring periodic key renewal for enhanced data security.

By integrating automated key rotation into Terraform configurations, organizations can ensure that encryption keys are regularly refreshed without disrupting services. This proactive measure not only enhances overall security by limiting the lifespan of any compromised keys but also simplifies compliance with regulatory requirements for data protection.

Managing Cross-Region and Multi-Cloud Key Replication

In today's global and multi-cloud environments, ensuring the availability and durability of encryption keys is paramount for disaster recovery and compliance. Cross-region replication enhances fault tolerance by ensuring that encryption keys remain accessible even if an entire region experiences an outage. When combined with Terraform, this approach enables consistent, automated deployment of key replication strategies across AWS and GCP, thereby supporting multi-cloud resilience and compliance requirements. Note that Azure currently does not support KMS key cross-region replication, which should be considered when designing your encryption key management strategy. The following are some benefits of multi-region keys:

- **Enhanced fault tolerance:** Replicating keys across regions ensures that even during a regional outage, your encrypted data remains accessible because the keys are available in another geographic location.
- **Disaster recovery:** Replica keys serve as a backup for primary keys, reducing downtime and facilitating swift recovery in case of failures.
- **Compliance and data residency:** Multi-region replication helps organizations comply with regulatory requirements by ensuring that data encryption and key management meet geographical and security standards.

```
provider "aws" {
  alias  = "primary"
  region = "us-east-1"
}

provider "aws" {
  region = "us-west-2"
}

resource "aws_kms_key" "primary" {
  provider = aws.primary

  description             = "Multi-Region primary key"
  deletion_window_in_days = 30
  multi_region            = true

  tags = {
    environment = "prod"
    compliance  = "PCI-DSS"
    replicated  = "true"
  }
}

resource "aws_kms_replica_key" "replica" {
  description             = "Multi-Region replica key"
  deletion_window_in_days = 7
  primary_key_arn         = aws_kms_key.primary.arn

  tags = {
    environment = "prod"
    compliance  = "PCI-DSS"
    replicated  = "true"
  }
}
```

This Terraform configuration provisions a multi-region AWS KMS primary key in us-east-1 with a 30-day deletion window and a corresponding replica key in us-west-2 with a 7-day deletion window, ensuring robust key replication for fault tolerance and disaster recovery.

```
resource "google_kms_key_ring" "multi_region" {
  name     = "example-key-ring"
  location = "us"  # Multi-region location; 'us' represents a multi-region in GCP

  labels = {
    environment = "prod"
```

```
    compliance  = "GDPR"  # Optional compliance labeling
  }
}

resource "google_kms_crypto_key" "example" {
  name            = "example-key"
  key_ring        = google_kms_key_ring.multi_region.id
  purpose         = "ENCRYPT_DECRYPT"
  rotation_period = "7776000s"  # Rotate every 90 days

  labels = {
    environment = "prod"
    compliance  = "GDPR"  # Optional compliance labeling
  }
}
```

This snippet provisions a multi-region key ring in GCP and a crypto key with a 90-day rotation period, ensuring secure encryption and periodic key renewal.

Encrypting secrets using provider-native Key Management Services strengthens cloud security by safeguarding sensitive data at every stage. Terraform simplifies the provisioning and automation of KMS across AWS, Azure, and GCP, ensuring secrets are encrypted by design. Thus, by enforcing the best practices such as automatic key rotation and cross-region replication, organizations can build resilient, secure, and compliant multi-cloud environments.

Automating Secret Rotation across Cloud Providers

Secrets such as database passwords, API keys, and access tokens are critical to cloud infrastructure. However, secrets can become compromised over time, creating potential vulnerabilities. Automating secret rotation ensures that secrets are updated regularly without manual intervention, significantly reducing the risk of credential leaks and unauthorized access. In this section, we explore secret rotation mechanisms across AWS, Azure, and GCP, focusing on automation through Terraform.

Automate Secret Rotation

Secret rotation is the practice of periodically updating sensitive credentials such as API keys, passwords, certificates, and encryption keys to minimize the window of opportunity for attackers in the event of a compromise. By replacing old secrets with new ones and invalidating previous versions, organizations can significantly mitigate risk and maintain a strong security posture.

Automating secret rotation is critical for reducing the potential impact of credential leaks. Regularly updating secrets ensures that even if an attacker gains access to a compromised key, the useful window for exploitation is minimal. Additionally, automating this process minimizes human error, as manual rotations are prone to oversight and delays. Compliance frameworks such as PCI-DSS and SOC 2 mandate periodic secret rotation as part of their security controls, so automation not only improves security but also helps organizations maintain regulatory compliance.

The following explains the process of automatic secret rotation:

- **Secret storage:** Cloud providers securely store secrets using dedicated services such as AWS Secrets Manager, Azure Key Vault, or Google Secret Manager. These services encrypt the secrets using customer-managed or provider-managed keys.
- **Automated triggers:** Rotation is initiated automatically based on predefined schedules or triggers, which update the secret at regular intervals without manual intervention.

- **Dynamic retrieval:** Applications and services are configured to dynamically retrieve the latest version of the secret at runtime, ensuring that they always use up-to-date credentials without the need to hardcode or manually update values.

Terraform plays a pivotal role in automating secret rotation by allowing you to provision and manage these cloud-native secret management resources as code. This means you can define your secret rotation policies and schedules in Terraform configurations, version-control them, and deploy them consistently across environments. Terraform ensures that every secret is automatically updated and that its lifecycle is managed according to your security policies. The following are some best practices for automating secret rotation:

- **Automate with cloud-native tools:** Leverage the built-in secret rotation capabilities of services such as AWS Secrets Manager, Azure Key Vault, or GCP Secret Manager, and manage these settings through Terraform.
- **Implement monitoring:** Integrate monitoring tools to track the success of rotation jobs and alert teams to any failures, ensuring that secrets are always rotated as expected.
- **Enforce least privilege:** Restrict access to the secret rotation configuration and the secrets themselves to only the essential services and personnel, reducing the risk of unauthorized access.

Hence, by integrating these practices into your Terraform workflows, you can achieve an automated, robust, and compliant secret rotation strategy that minimizes risks, and enhances the security of your cloud environments.

Configuring AWS Secrets Manager for Automatic Rotation

AWS Secrets Manager provides built-in capabilities for automatically rotating secrets, ensuring that sensitive credentials such as database passwords are periodically updated without manual intervention. This native feature is particularly useful for compliance and security best practices, as it minimizes the risk of long-lived secrets being compromised. By integrating with AWS Lambda, Secrets Manager can trigger a rotation function on a predefined schedule, update the secret, and archive old versions for traceability. Terraform enables you to provision these resources as code, ensuring consistent, auditable, and automated secret management across your AWS infrastructure. The following explains the steps for AWS Secrets Manager secret automatic rotation:

- **Automated trigger via AWS Lambda:** A Lambda function is set up to act as the rotation trigger. On a scheduled basis (for example, every 30 days), the Lambda function executes the rotation process. This function is responsible for generating a new secret value, updating the target resource (such as an Amazon RDS database), and archiving the old secret version for historical records.
- **Secrets Manager updates:** AWS Secrets Manager integrates with the rotation Lambda function by updating the secret when the function completes its process. The new secret is then applied to the target service, ensuring that only the latest credentials are in use. This process minimizes downtime and ensures continuous security without manual updates.
- **Archiving and traceability:** Old versions of the secret are retained within Secrets Manager, which allows you to audit changes over time. This traceability is crucial for compliance purposes and for troubleshooting any issues that may arise from secret rotations.

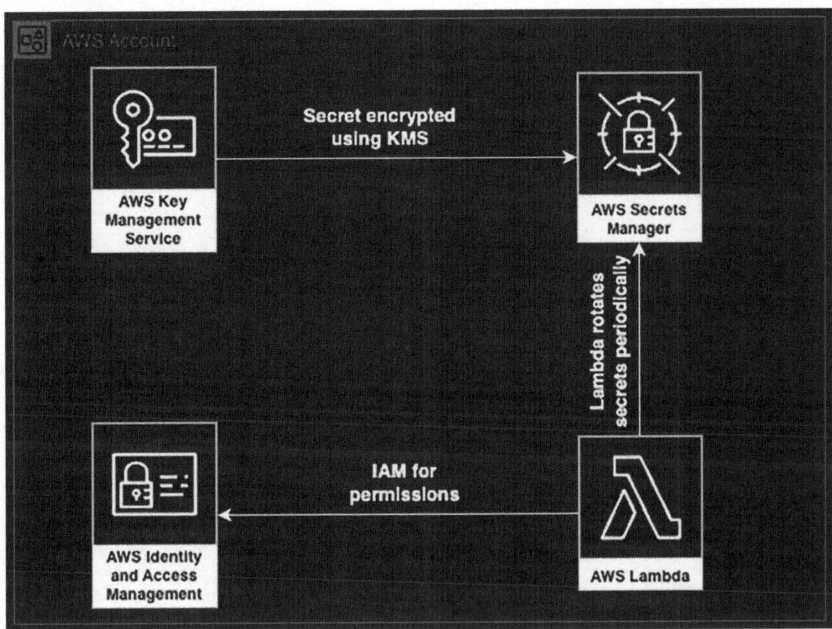

Figure 9.1: *Secrets management*

```
resource "aws_secretsmanager_secret" "db_secret" {
  name        = "rds-rotation-secret"
  description = "RDS DB password secret"
}

resource "aws_secretsmanager_secret_rotation" "rotation" {
  secret_id           = aws_secretsmanager_secret.db_secret.id    # The ID of
the secret to rotate
  rotation_lambda_arn = aws_lambda_function.secret_rotation.arn  # Lambda
function ARN that performs the rotation
  rotation_rules {
    automatically_after_days = 30                                # Rotate
secret automatically every 30 days
  }
}
```

This Terraform snippet configures AWS Secrets Manager to automatically rotate an RDS database password every 30 days using a Lambda function, ensuring continuous secret security and compliance.

Implementing Secret Rotation in Azure Key Vault

Azure Key Vault is a centralized service for storing and managing sensitive information such as passwords, certificates, and encryption keys. One of its key features is the ability to automate secret rotation, which is critical for maintaining security and compliance, especially in regulated environments. With Terraform, you can automate the provisioning of Azure Key Vault and configure policies or schedules that integrate with Azure Functions to manage secret rotation. The following explains the steps for secret rotation in Azure Key Vault:

- **Secrets storage:** Secrets are securely stored in Azure Key Vault, where they are encrypted at rest and managed centrally.
- **Scheduled rotation:** An Azure Function can be configured to trigger on a schedule (for example, every 30 days) using Azure Automation schedules. This function will generate a new secret, update the Key Vault, and propagate the updated value to all linked resources.

- **Dynamic propagation:** Once a secret is rotated, the updated credentials are automatically available to any Azure resources that retrieve them from the Key Vault, ensuring seamless operations and minimal disruption.

```
# Creates an Azure Key Vault to securely store keys, secrets, and certificates
resource "azurerm_key_vault" "example" {
  name                = "keyvault-example"
  location            = "East US"
  resource_group_name = "example-rg"
}

# Stores a secret (e.g., application password) inside the specified Key Vault
resource "azurerm_key_vault_secret" "example" {
  name         = "app-password"
  value        = "SuperSecret123"
  key_vault_id = azurerm_key_vault.example.id
}

# Defines an automation schedule to trigger tasks periodically (e.g., secret
rotation every 30 days)
resource "azurerm_automation_schedule" "example" {
  name                = "rotation-schedule"
  resource_group_name = "example-rg"
  frequency           = "Day"
  interval            = 30
}
```

This Terraform configuration provisions an Azure Key Vault with a secret and sets up an automation schedule to trigger secret rotation every 30 days, enabling secure, automated management of sensitive credentials.

Rotating GCP Secrets with Cloud Functions

Google Cloud Secret Manager, when integrated with Cloud Functions, Cloud Scheduler, and Pub/Sub, provides an automated solution for rotating secrets. This integration ensures that secrets are updated regularly without manual intervention, reducing the risk of compromised credentials. With Terraform, you can provision all the necessary resources to automate secret rotation, ensuring that sensitive information remains secure and compliant with the organizational policies. The following explains the steps to rotate secrets in GCP:

- **Secrets storage:** Secrets are securely stored in GCP Secret Manager, which encrypts data at rest and maintains version history for auditability.
- **Automated trigger:** A Cloud Scheduler job publishes a message to a Pub/Sub topic at predefined intervals (for example, every 30 days), triggering the rotation process.
- **Cloud function execution:** A Cloud Function listens for Pub/Sub events, and when triggered, it executes custom logic to generate a new secret version. This function updates the secret in Secret Manager and archives the previous version.
- **Dynamic updates:** Applications retrieving the secret dynamically receive the new version, ensuring uninterrupted service while maintaining robust security.

```
# Create a secret in GCP Secret Manager
resource "google_secret_manager_secret" "example" {
  secret_id   = "example-secret"
  replication {
    automatic = true
  }
```

```
}

# Create an initial version of the secret
resource "google_secret_manager_secret_version" "example_version" {
  secret      = google_secret_manager_secret.example.id
  secret_data = base64encode("initial-secret-data")
}

# Create a Pub/Sub topic to trigger the rotation
resource "google_pubsub_topic" "rotate_topic" {
  name = "secret-rotation-topic"
}

# Create a storage bucket to hold the Cloud Function source code
resource "google_storage_bucket" "function_bucket" {
  name          = "function-source-bucket-${random_id.bucket_suffix.hex}"
  location      = "us-central1"
  force_destroy = true
}

# Generate a random suffix for the bucket name
resource "random_id" "bucket_suffix" {
  byte_length = 4
}

# Upload the Cloud Function source code to the bucket
resource "google_storage_bucket_object" "function_zip" {
  name   = "rotate_secret_function.zip"
  bucket = google_storage_bucket.function_bucket.name
  source = "path/to/rotate_secret_function.zip"  # Path to your function zip
file and it should not contain secrets or credentials
}

# Create a Cloud Function to handle secret rotation
resource "google_cloudfunctions_function" "rotate_secret" {
  name                  = "rotateSecretFunction"
  description           = "Rotates the secret in Secret Manager"
  runtime               = "python39"
  available_memory_mb   = 256
  source_archive_bucket = google_storage_bucket.function_bucket.name
  source_archive_object = google_storage_bucket_object.function_zip.name
  entry_point           = "rotate_secret"  # Python function name in your code

  event_trigger {
    event_type = "google.pubsub.topic.publish"
    resource   = google_pubsub_topic.rotate_topic.id
  }
}

# Schedule the Cloud Function to run every 30 days via Cloud Scheduler
resource "google_cloud_scheduler_job" "rotate_job" {
  name        = "secret-rotation-job"
  description = "Triggers secret rotation every 30 days"
    schedule = "0 0 1 * *"  # On the 1st of every month
  time_zone   = "UTC"

  pubsub_target {
```

```
    topic_name = google_pubsub_topic.rotate_topic.name
    data       = base64encode("trigger rotation")
  }
}
```

This Terraform configuration automates secret rotation in GCP by provisioning a Secret Manager secret, a Cloud Function triggered via Pub/Sub and Cloud Scheduler to update the secret every 30 days, ensuring continuous security of the sensitive credentials.

Cross-Cloud Secret Synchronization

In multi-cloud environments, maintaining consistent and secure secret management across AWS, Azure, and GCP is critical. Cross-cloud secret synchronization ensures that when a secret is rotated or updated in one environment, the changes are automatically and securely propagated to other cloud platforms. This approach minimizes manual intervention, reduces configuration drift, and maintains a unified security posture across all providers. The following explains the working of cross-cloud secret synchronization management:

- **Centralized rotation trigger:** A central secret rotation job, typically orchestrated by a service such as HashiCorp Vault or a dedicated automation script, initiates the rotation process. When a secret is updated or rotated, this central job generates the new secret values, and prepares them for distribution.
- **Secure transmission:** Once the new secret values are generated, they must be securely transmitted to each cloud provider. This is typically achieved through encrypted communication channels and APIs provided by AWS Secrets Manager, Azure Key Vault, and GCP Secret Manager. Ensuring secure transmission protects the secrets during transit and prevents unauthorized interception.
- **Terraform orchestration:** Terraform plays a pivotal role by orchestrating the distribution of these secrets across cloud providers using provider-specific modules. By encapsulating the secret synchronization logic within dedicated Terraform modules (for example, one for AWS, one for Azure, and one for GCP), organizations can standardize the process, ensure consistency, and maintain an auditable, version-controlled approach to secret management.

  ```
  module "aws_secret" {
    source = "./aws-secret"
  }

  module "azure_secret" {
    source = "./azure-secret"
  }

  module "gcp_secret" {
    source = "./gcp-secret"
  }
  ```

This Terraform configuration uses provider-specific modules to orchestrate the secure synchronization of rotated secrets across AWS, Azure, and GCP, ensuring consistent secret management in a multi-cloud environment.

Automating secret rotation across cloud providers strengthens infrastructure security by minimizing the risk of stale or compromised credentials. AWS, Azure, and GCP provide robust tools for automating secret rotation, and Terraform enhances this process by codifying workflows across environments. By embracing automation and cross-cloud synchronization, organizations achieve greater resilience, compliance, and security, ensuring that secrets remain protected at all times.

Securing API Keys, Tokens, and Credentials in Terraform Code

API keys, tokens, and credentials are fundamental to interacting with cloud services and third-party APIs. However, storing sensitive information directly within Terraform code introduces significant risks, including accidental exposure through code repositories or Terraform state files. This section covers strategies to secure sensitive data in Terraform configurations using external secret management solutions and best practices for CI/CD pipelines for AWS, Azure, and GCP environments.

Externalizing Sensitive Variables in Terraform

Externalizing sensitive variables is the practice of managing critical information such as API keys, passwords, or tokens outside of your Terraform configuration files. Instead of hardcoding these secrets directly into your code, which can lead to unintentional exposure through version control systems, they are stored externally using environment variables, `.tfvars` files, or encrypted external files. This approach significantly minimizes the risk of sensitive data leakage and enhances your overall security posture. The following explains the ways to manage sensitive variables:

- **Environment variables:** Sensitive values are set as environment variables on your system. Terraform automatically reads these variables at runtime, mapping them to your defined Terraform variables. This avoids hardcoding secrets in your code and keeps them out of your source repository.
- **`.tfvars` files:** You can store sensitive variables in separate .tfvars files, which Terraform uses to override default variable values. These files should be excluded from version control (using `.gitignore`) to prevent unauthorized access.
- **External secrets files:** Credentials can be stored in encrypted files managed by tools such as SOPS (Secrets OPerationS). During execution, these files are decrypted to supply the necessary secrets to Terraform, ensuring sensitive data remains secure both at rest and in transit.

```
variable "aws_access_key" {
  description = "AWS Access Key"
  type        = string
  sensitive   = true
}

variable "aws_secret_key" {
  description = "AWS Secret Key"
  type        = string
  sensitive   = true
}

provider "aws" {
  access_key = var.aws_access_key
  secret_key = var.aws_secret_key
}
export TF_VAR_aws_access_key="AKIA..."
export TF_VAR_aws_secret_key="wJalrXUtn..."
```

By setting the corresponding environment variables (**`TF_VAR_aws_access_key`** and **`TF_VAR_aws_secret_key`**), Terraform automatically picks up these values during runtime, keeping sensitive credentials out of the codebase.

This Terraform configuration uses environment variables to securely manage AWS credentials, keeping sensitive data out of the codebase and ensuring dynamic, secure secret retrieval at runtime.

Referencing Secrets from Secret Managers

Secret referencing in Terraform enables you to dynamically retrieve sensitive data such as API keys, passwords, and certificates from dedicated secret management services (such as AWS Secrets Manager, Azure Key Vault, or GCP Secret Manager) at runtime. This method ensures that plaintext credentials are never hardcoded in your Terraform configurations or stored in version control, thereby reducing the risk of credential exposure.

- **Dynamic retrieval:** Terraform providers query the secret management service (for example, Azure Key Vault, AWS Secrets Manager, or GCP Secret Manager) to retrieve the current value of a secret.
- **Injection at runtime:** The retrieved secret is injected into your Terraform workflow during execution, allowing resources to be provisioned using up-to-date credentials.
- **State management:** By default, these secrets are not persisted in plaintext within Terraform state files, preserving their confidentiality.

```
data "azurerm_key_vault_secret" "example" {
  name         = "db-password"
  key_vault_id = azurerm_key_vault.example.id
}

output "db_password" {
  value     = data.azurerm_key_vault_secret.example.value
  sensitive = true
}
```

This Terraform configuration retrieves a secret from Azure Key Vault and outputs its value as a sensitive variable, ensuring secure, dynamic access to credentials without exposing plaintext data.

By referencing secrets from Azure Key Vault using Terraform, you ensure that sensitive credentials are securely managed and dynamically injected during infrastructure provisioning. This approach minimizes the risk of exposure while maintaining compliance with best security practices.

Securing Terraform Plan and Apply Pipelines

Securing Terraform pipelines is critical because CI/CD processes that execute **`terraform plan`** and **`terraform apply`** require sensitive credentials, such as API keys or service account credentials. Pipeline security focuses on protecting these secrets during execution to prevent accidental exposure, which could lead to unauthorized access or data breaches. Ensuring that credentials remain secure throughout the pipeline execution process is essential for maintaining the integrity of your infrastructure deployments. The following are different ways to manage secrets for pipelines:

- **Storing secrets in pipeline tools:** Sensitive credentials are stored in secure pipeline secret stores, such as GitHub Secrets, GitLab CI variables, or AWS CodePipeline's secret management system. This prevents sensitive data from being hardcoded in your Terraform configuration or exposed in code repositories.
- **Injecting secrets at runtime:** During the execution of Terraform commands, the pipeline injects these secrets into the runtime environment as environment variables. This dynamic injection ensures that the credentials are available only during execution and not stored in the Terraform state or logs in plaintext.
- **Masking credentials:** Environment variables are used to mask credentials in the output, ensuring that even if logs are reviewed, the sensitive values remain hidden. This adds an additional layer of security to the CI/CD pipeline.

```
name: Terraform Plan

on: [push]

jobs:
  plan:
    runs-on: ubuntu-latest
    steps:
      - name: Checkout code
        uses: actions/checkout@v2

      - name: Set up Terraform
        uses: hashicorp/setup-terraform@v1

      - name: Terraform Init
        run: terraform init
        env:
          GOOGLE_CREDENTIALS: ${{ secrets.GOOGLE_CREDENTIALS }}

      - name: Terraform Plan
        run: terraform plan
        env:
          GOOGLE_CREDENTIALS: ${{ secrets.GOOGLE_CREDENTIALS }}
```

This GitHub Actions workflow securely executes Terraform commands for GCP by injecting sensitive credentials via environment variables, protecting secrets during plan and apply phases in the CI/CD pipeline.

The following are some best practices for managing secrets for pipelines:

- **Use secret scanning tools:** Employ tools that automatically scan your pipeline configuration for exposed keys or credentials to ensure no sensitive data is inadvertently leaked.
- **Rotate CI/CD secrets frequently:** Regularly update and rotate credentials stored in pipeline secret stores to minimize the risk of compromise over time.
- **Encrypt sensitive pipeline artifacts:** Ensure that any logs or artifacts produced by the pipeline that might contain sensitive data are encrypted and securely stored, protecting them from unauthorized access.

By implementing these practices and integrating secure secret handling into your Terraform CI/CD pipelines, you can ensure that your infrastructure deployments remain both secure and compliant with industry standards.

Masking Sensitive Outputs in Terraform State

Terraform state files can contain sensitive information such as API keys, passwords, and other credentials that, if exposed, could pose a significant security risk. Masking these outputs is a critical security practice that prevents sensitive data from appearing in Terraform outputs, logs, or state files. This ensures that sensitive values remain confidential and are not inadvertently leaked during operations or when sharing state information. The following explains how to mask sensitive outputs in Terraform state:

- **Sensitive flag:** Terraform allows you to mark outputs as sensitive using the **`sensitive = true`** flag. When an output is marked sensitive, its actual value will not be displayed in the CLI output or logs.

- **State file protection:** Although sensitive outputs are still stored in the state file, Terraform masks them in outputs and ensures that they are not inadvertently printed during command executions, thereby reducing the risk of exposure.

```
resource "google_secret_manager_secret" "example" {
  secret_id = "db-password"
  replication {
    automatic = true
  }
}

resource "google_secret_manager_secret_version" "example_version" {
  secret      = google_secret_manager_secret.example.id
  secret_data = base64encode("supersecretpassword")
}

output "db_password" {
  value     = google_secret_manager_secret_version.example_version.secret_data
  sensitive = true
}
```

This Terraform configuration retrieves a secret from GCP Secret Manager, outputs it as a sensitive value, and ensures that sensitive data remains masked in the Terraform state and logs.

Masking sensitive outputs in Terraform state is a vital security measure that prevents the exposure of confidential data. By marking outputs as sensitive, you ensure that even though secrets are stored in state files for operational purposes, they are not displayed in plain text during routine Terraform operations. This approach is essential for protecting sensitive information and maintaining a robust security posture in your cloud infrastructure.

Securing API keys, tokens, and credentials in Terraform is crucial for safeguarding cloud infrastructure. By externalizing sensitive variables, leveraging secret managers, and masking outputs, organizations can significantly reduce the risk of credential leaks. Integrating secure practices into pipelines ensures a holistic approach to secrets management, enhancing the overall security posture of multi-cloud environments.

Implementing End-to-End Encryption for Sensitive Data

Encryption is a cornerstone of data protection, ensuring sensitive information remains secure throughout its lifecycle, whether at rest, in transit, or in use. End-to-end Encryption (E2EE) applies encryption consistently, from data creation to consumption, preventing unauthorized access even if the infrastructure is compromised. This section explores how to provision encrypted storage, secure traffic with TLS, encrypt databases, and implement data masking and tokenization using Terraform across AWS, Azure, and GCP.

End-to-End Encryption Fundamentals

End-to-End Encryption (E2EE) is a security model where data is encrypted at its source and remains encrypted throughout its journey during transit, storage, and even while being processed until it reaches the authorized recipient who possesses the decryption key. This means that, unlike traditional encryption methods, which may decrypt data at intermediary stages for processing, E2EE maintains encryption continuously, ensuring that sensitive information is protected against unauthorized access at every step of its lifecycle. Terraform can be used to automate and enforce these encryption policies across your infrastructure, making it easier to manage E2EE in cloud environments. The following are the different types of encryption:

- **Data at rest:** Data stored in databases, storage buckets, or filesystems is encrypted using cloud-native Key Management Services (KMS) or Hardware Security Modules (HSM). Terraform can automate the provisioning of these encryption resources, ensuring that every storage resource is automatically encrypted using customer-managed or provider-managed keys. For example, you can configure AWS S3, Azure Storage, or GCP Cloud Storage to always use encryption keys during provisioning, which guarantees that data remains secure even when stored.

```
# Create a customer-managed KMS key for encryption
resource "aws_kms_key" "s3_key" {
  description         = "Customer-managed key for S3 bucket encryption"
  enable_key_rotation = true
}

# Create an S3 bucket with default encryption using the KMS key
resource "aws_s3_bucket" "secure_bucket" {
  bucket = "my-secure-bucket"

  server_side_encryption_configuration {
    rule {
      apply_server_side_encryption_by_default {
        sse_algorithm     = "aws:kms"
        kms_master_key_id = aws_kms_key.s3_key.arn
      }
    }
  }
}
```

- **Data in transit:** When data moves between services or from users to applications, it is encrypted using TLS (Transport Layer Security) protocols. Terraform can help configure load balancers, API gateways, and network settings to enforce TLS for all communications, ensuring that data is protected from interception or tampering as it travels across networks.

```
# Request an ACM Certificate for your domain (example.com)
resource "aws_acm_certificate" "example_cert" {
  domain_name       = "example.com"
  validation_method = "DNS"
  lifecycle {
    create_before_destroy = true
  }
}

# (Optional) DNS validation record for ACM certificate
resource "aws_route53_record" "cert_validation" {
  name    = aws_acm_certificate.example_cert.domain_validation_options[0].
resource_record_name
  type    = aws_acm_certificate.example_cert.domain_validation_options[0].
resource_record_type
  zone_id = "Z1234567890ABCDEFG"  # Your Route53 Hosted Zone ID
  records = [aws_acm_certificate.example_cert.domain_validation_options[0].
resource_record_value]
  ttl     = 60
}
```

```
# Validate the ACM certificate using DNS
resource "aws_acm_certificate_validation" "example_cert_validation" {
  certificate_arn         = aws_acm_certificate.example_cert.arn
  validation_record_fqdns = [aws_route53_record.cert_validation.fqdn]
}

# Create a security group allowing HTTPS traffic
resource "aws_security_group" "alb_sg" {
  name        = "alb-sg"
  description = "Allow HTTPS inbound traffic"
  vpc_id      = "vpc-xxxxxxxx"

  ingress {
    protocol    = "tcp"
    from_port   = 443
    to_port     = 443
    cidr_blocks = ["0.0.0.0/0"]
  }

  egress {
    protocol    = "-1"
    from_port   = 0
    to_port     = 0
    cidr_blocks = ["0.0.0.0/0"]
  }
}

# Create an Application Load Balancer (ALB)
resource "aws_lb" "example" {
  name               = "example-alb"
  internal           = false
  load_balancer_type = "application"
  security_groups    = [aws_security_group.alb_sg.id]
  subnets            = ["subnet-xxxxxxx1", "subnet-xxxxxxx2"]
}

# Create an HTTPS listener using the validated ACM certificate
resource "aws_lb_listener" "https_listener" {
  load_balancer_arn = aws_lb.example.arn
  port              = 443
  protocol          = "HTTPS"
  ssl_policy        = "ELBSecurityPolicy-2016-08"

  certificate_arn = aws_acm_certificate_validation.example_cert_validation.
certificate_arn

  default_action {
    type = "fixed-response"

    fixed_response {
      content_type = "text/plain"
      message_body = "Secure connection established"
      status_code  = "200"
    }
  }
}
```

- **Data in use:** Data processing and computations are potential points of vulnerability. Advanced E2EE implementations can leverage techniques such as secure enclaves, in-memory encryption, or ephemeral key usage to protect data while it is being used. Although more challenging to implement directly with Terraform, the overall strategy can be integrated by provisioning services that support these advanced features, ensuring that sensitive data is encrypted even during processing.

The following are some salient features and best practices of end-to-end encryption:

- **Zero trust:** In a zero-trust environment, every access request is verified regardless of the network origin. With E2EE, even if an attacker breaches the infrastructure, the encrypted data remains inaccessible without the decryption keys. Terraform can enforce zero-trust principles by configuring strict access controls and ensuring that only authorized identities have access to decryption keys.
- **Granular control:** E2EE allows for detailed, role-based access control to encryption keys. By leveraging Terraform, you can define precise IAM policies and permissions that restrict access to keys on a need-to-know basis, ensuring that only specific services or users can decrypt sensitive data.
- **Compliance:** Many regulatory frameworks, including GDPR, HIPAA, and PCI-DSS, require robust encryption measures. Implementing E2EE with Terraform ensures that your infrastructure meets these compliance standards by enforcing consistent encryption practices across all environments.
- **Use of Hardware Security Modules (HSM):** For enhanced security, storing encryption keys in HSMs provides a higher level of protection against unauthorized access. Terraform supports provisioning HSM-backed keys through cloud providers' managed services, ensuring that keys are stored in a tamper-resistant hardware environment.
- **Automate encryption key rotation:** Regular key rotation is a best practice that minimizes the risk of long-term exposure. Terraform can automate key rotation policies, ensuring that encryption keys are updated periodically without manual intervention. This reduces the impact of any potential key compromise.
- **Adopt multi-cloud KMS strategies:** In a multi-cloud environment, using provider-specific KMS resources in AWS, Azure, and GCP allows you to enforce a unified encryption strategy across all platforms. Terraform can orchestrate these deployments, ensuring redundancy and consistency in key management across your entire infrastructure.

By integrating E2EE with Terraform, organizations can automate the enforcement of robust encryption measures across data at rest, in transit, and in use. This approach not only secures sensitive information through strict access controls and zero-trust principles but also helps meet regulatory compliance requirements. Leveraging Terraform for automating key rotation and provisioning multi-cloud KMS resources further enhances the security and resilience of your cloud infrastructure, providing a scalable solution for end-to-end data protection.

Provisioning Encrypted Storage Buckets

Securing storage buckets with encryption is a critical practice for protecting sensitive data both at rest and in transit. Encrypted storage ensures that any data stored within these buckets is automatically encrypted upon entry and decrypted only for authorized retrieval, thereby reducing the risk of unauthorized data access. Cloud providers offer built-in encryption capabilities through Server-Side Encryption (SSE) and, in some cases, Client-Side Encryption (CSE), which can be managed using their respective Key Management Services (KMS). Terraform automates the provisioning of these encrypted storage resources, ensuring that encryption settings are consistently applied across your infrastructure.

- **Server-Side Encryption (SSE):** In SSE, the cloud provider automatically encrypts data as it is stored using either provider-managed keys or Customer-Managed Keys (CMK). This process happens transparently to the user and ensures that data remains protected even if the storage infrastructure is compromised.
- **Client-Side Encryption (CSE):** In CSE, data is encrypted by the client before it is transmitted to the cloud provider. The encrypted data is then stored in the bucket, and only the client holds the decryption keys. Although this method provides an additional layer of security, it typically requires developers to manage keys and encryption libraries manually, increasing implementation complexity and operational overhead compared to SSE.

```
resource "aws_s3_bucket" "example" {
  bucket = "secure-data-bucket"

  server_side_encryption_configuration {
    rule {
      apply_server_side_encryption_by_default {
        sse_algorithm = "aws:kms"
      }
    }
  }
}
```

This Terraform snippet provisions an AWS S3 bucket with server-side encryption enabled using AWS KMS, ensuring all stored objects are automatically encrypted.

```
resource "azurerm_storage_account" "example" {
  name                     = "securestorage"
  resource_group_name      = "example-group"
  location                 = "West US"
  account_tier             = "Standard"
  account_replication_type = "LRS"
  enable_https_traffic_only = true
}
```

This Terraform snippet creates an Azure Storage Account in West US with HTTPS enforced and Locally Redundant Storage (LRS), providing secure storage with built-in encryption.

```
resource "google_storage_bucket" "example" {
  name          = "secure-data-bucket-gcp"
  location      = "US"
  force_destroy = true

  encryption {
    default_kms_key_name = google_kms_crypto_key.example.id
  }
}
```

This configuration is a Cloud Storage bucket in the US and uses the crypto key for default encryption, ensuring secure, customer-managed encryption of data.

Encrypting Traffic with TLS and Certificates

Transport Layer Security (TLS) encrypts data during transmission, safeguarding sensitive information from eavesdropping and tampering. TLS certificates, issued by trusted Certificate Authorities (CAs), authenticate endpoints and establish secure communication channels, ensuring that data is protected end-to-end, whether at load balancers, API gateways, or directly at application endpoints.

- **Certificate issuance:** Certificates are issued by Certificate Authorities and provide a means of verifying the identity of an endpoint.
- **TLS termination:** TLS terminates at strategic points such as load balancers or API gateways, decrypting incoming traffic before it is passed on to backend services, or directly at the application level, ensuring encrypted communication between clients and servers.

```
resource "aws_acm_certificate" "example" {
  domain_name       = "example.com"
  validation_method = "DNS"
}
```

This Terraform snippet provisions an AWS ACM certificate for **`"example.com"`** using DNS validation, enabling TLS encryption for secure communications.

```
resource "google_compute_managed_ssl_certificate" "example" {
  name    = "example-cert"
  managed {
    domains = ["example.com"]
  }
}
```

This Terraform snippet creates a managed SSL certificate in GCP for **`"example.com"`**, automating TLS encryption for secure load balancer traffic.

```
resource "azurerm_app_service_certificate_order" "example" {
  name                = "example-cert-order"
  resource_group_name = azurerm_resource_group.example.name
  location            = azurerm_resource_group.example.location
  distinguished_name  = "CN=example.com"
  product_type        = "Standard"
}
```

This Terraform snippet creates an Azure App Service Certificate Order for **`"example.com"`** in the **`"example-rg"`** resource group, initiating the DNS-based validation process for SSL certificate issuance.

Implementing end-to-end encryption ensures data remains secure across its lifecycle, significantly enhancing the security posture of cloud environments. By leveraging Terraform to provision encrypted storage and secure traffic with TLS, organizations can achieve comprehensive data protection.

Conclusion

In this chapter, we explored the critical components of securing sensitive information in cloud environments using Terraform. We began by examining native secrets management tools, such as AWS Secrets Manager, Azure Key Vault, and Google Secret Manager, and demonstrated how Terraform can automate the process of storing, retrieving, and auditing secrets. We also delved into integrating cloud-native Key Management Services (KMS) to encrypt data both at rest and in transit, highlighting best practices such as automatic key rotation and cross-region replication to ensure high availability and robust disaster recovery. Furthermore, automating secret rotation across cloud providers and securing sensitive credentials within Terraform code were shown to be essential steps in reducing the risk of credential leaks. Finally, we covered end-to-end encryption, from provisioning encrypted storage buckets to automating TLS certificate management, ensuring comprehensive protection of sensitive data throughout its lifecycle.

Overall, this chapter underscores that a proactive and automated approach to secrets management and data protection is indispensable for maintaining a secure cloud infrastructure. By leveraging Terraform's powerful automation capabilities, organizations can enforce consistent security policies, rapidly remediate vulnerabilities, and ensure compliance with industry standards. The strategies presented not only minimize the risk of data breaches but also enhance operational efficiency and resilience across AWS, Azure, and GCP, paving the way for a more secure and compliant cloud environment.

In the next chapter, we will dive deep into securing cloud network architectures with Terraform by automating firewall rules, security groups, and VPN configurations. It also addresses multi-region networking, securing serverless and edge architectures, and integrating web application firewalls for enhanced application security.

Questions and Answers

1. **How can Terraform be used to securely store and retrieve secrets across AWS, Azure, and GCP?**

   Terraform enables secure storage and retrieval of secrets by integrating with cloud-native secret management solutions such as AWS Secrets Manager, Azure Key Vault, and Google Secret Manager. Using Terraform, users can provision secret stores, define access policies, and retrieve secrets dynamically in their infrastructure code. Terraform's provider-specific resources, such as **`aws_secretsmanager_secret`**, **`azurerm_key_vault_secret`**, and **`google_secret_manager_secret`**, allow for automated secret creation and access control. By following least-privilege IAM policies, users can ensure that only authorized roles and applications can retrieve secrets, minimizing the risk of exposure.

2. **Why is secret rotation important, and how can Terraform automate this process across multiple cloud providers?**

   Secret rotation is critical for reducing the risk of credential leaks and unauthorized access. Regularly rotating secrets ensures that even if a secret is compromised, its validity period is limited. Terraform supports secret rotation by integrating with AWS Secrets Manager, Azure Key Vault, and GCP Secret Manager, which offer automated rotation capabilities. For example, in AWS, Terraform can configure a Lambda function to periodically rotate secrets, while in Azure, Key Vault rotation policies can be managed via Terraform's **`azurerm_key_vault_secret_rotation_policy`**. In GCP, Terraform can trigger Cloud Functions for automated secret rotation. Terraform also enables cross-cloud secret synchronization, ensuring consistency in multi-cloud environments.

3. **What are the best practices for securing API keys, tokens, and credentials in Terraform code?**

   To prevent accidental exposure of sensitive credentials, Terraform users should follow best practices such as externalizing secrets, using secret managers, and securing Terraform state files. Instead of hardcoding API keys in Terraform configurations, users should reference them from environment variables or external secret stores using **`terraform_variable_sensitive`** or data blocks. Terraform also supports injecting secrets dynamically from secret managers at runtime. Additionally, Terraform state files should be secured by enabling encryption for remote state storage (for example, AWS S3 with KMS encryption, Azure Blob with SSE, or GCP Cloud Storage with CMEK). Sensitive outputs should be masked using **`sensitive = true`** in Terraform configurations to prevent accidental logging or exposure in CI/CD pipelines.

4. **How does Terraform integrate with cloud-native Key Management Services (KMS) to encrypt secrets and data?**

   Terraform facilitates encryption of secrets and sensitive data by integrating with cloud-native Key Management Services (KMS) such as AWS KMS, Azure Key Vault, and Google Cloud KMS. Using Terraform, users can create, manage, and apply encryption keys to various resources. For example, Terraform's **`aws_kms_key`**, **`azurerm_key_vault_key`**, and **`google_kms_crypto_`**

key allow users to define encryption keys and enforce key policies. Terraform also supports automatic key rotation, ensuring that encryption keys are periodically replaced for enhanced security. In multi-cloud deployments, Terraform can configure cross-region and cross-cloud key replication to maintain availability and compliance with regulatory requirements.

5. **How can Terraform help implement end-to-end encryption for sensitive data at rest, in transit, and in use?**

   Terraform enables end-to-end encryption by provisioning encrypted storage, enforcing secure communication, and managing cryptographic keys. For data at rest, Terraform can create encrypted S3 buckets, Azure Blob storage accounts, and GCP Cloud Storage buckets with native encryption mechanisms such as AWS KMS, Azure SSE, and Google CMEK. For data in transit, Terraform automates TLS/SSL certificate management using **aws_acm_certificate**, **azurerm_app_service_certificate**, and **google_compute_ssl_certificate**, ensuring encrypted communication between services. Additionally, Terraform helps enforce encryption policies at the application level, ensuring that all sensitive data remains protected throughout its lifecycle.

CHAPTER 10
Securing Cloud Network Architectures

Introduction

In today's cloud-driven landscape, securing network architectures is a fundamental pillar of an organization's security posture. A well-architected cloud network ensures defense-in-depth, minimizes attack surfaces, and enables secure connectivity across hybrid and multi-cloud environments. This chapter explores how Terraform can be leveraged to design and automate secure cloud networks, implementing best practices such as network segmentation, zero trust principles, high availability, and automated firewall policies. Readers will learn how to build multi-tier network architectures using Terraform, enforce least-privilege access controls, and automate security configurations across AWS, Azure, and GCP. Additionally, the chapter delves into securing hybrid cloud networks by automating VPN and private connectivity solutions, ensuring seamless yet protected communication between cloud and on-premises infrastructures.

As cloud networks become increasingly complex and distributed, it is essential to implement automation-driven security measures to maintain compliance and mitigate evolving threats. This chapter covers multi-region networking strategies, including VPC peering, interconnects, global load balancing, and disaster recovery automation to enhance resiliency. It also explores securing serverless and edge architectures by enforcing network controls on API gateways, CDNs, and private links. Finally, readers will learn how to integrate Web Application Firewalls (WAF) using Terraform to protect against web-based attacks and dynamically update security rules with threat intelligence feeds. By the end of this chapter, readers will have a comprehensive understanding of how Terraform can be used to automate, secure, and scale cloud network architectures across multiple cloud providers.

Structure

In this chapter, we will cover the following topics:

- Designing Secure Network Architectures
  - Principles of Secure Cloud Networking
  - Multi-Tier Network Architecture with Terraform
  - Implementing Network Segmentation and Isolation
  - Designing High-Availability Network Architectures
  - Implementing Zero Trust Network Access (ZTNA)
- Automating Firewall Rules, Security Groups, and Network ACLs
  - Managing Security Groups and NACLs with Terraform
  - Automating Azure NSGs and GCP Firewall Rules
  - Conditional Firewall Rules Based on Environment
  - Monitoring and Auditing Firewall Changes

    - Blocking Malicious Traffic with Dynamic IP Lists
- Configuring VPNs and Secure Connectivity for Hybrid Clouds
    - Provisioning AWS Site-to-Site VPN
    - Deploying Azure VPN Gateway and ExpressRoute
    - GCP Cloud VPN and Interconnect Automation
- Setting Up Multi-Region Networking with Terraform
    - Designing Multi-Region VPC Peering and Interconnects
    - Multi-Region DNS and Traffic Routing
    - Configuring Global Load Balancers and Failover
    - Resiliency Testing and Disaster Recovery Setup
- Securing Serverless and Edge Architectures Using Terraform
    - Network Design for Serverless Architectures
    - Deploying Edge Security with AWS CloudFront and Azure CDN
    - Securing API Gateways with Network Controls
    - Implementing Private Link for Serverless Communication
- Integrating Web Application Firewalls (WAF) for Application Security
    - Provisioning AWS WAF, Azure WAF, and GCP Cloud Armor
    - Dynamic WAF Updates Based on Threat Feeds

Designing Secure Network Architectures

In cloud environments, secure network design is the foundation for protecting workloads and data from breaches, misconfigurations, and unauthorized access. By leveraging Terraform, cloud engineers can implement repeatable, scalable, and auditable secure network architectures across AWS, Azure, and GCP. This section delves into core principles, practical Terraform configurations, and best practices for crafting cloud networks that prioritize defense-in-depth, isolation, and high availability.

Principles of Secure Cloud Networking

Secure cloud networking is the practice of designing and implementing network architectures in the cloud to minimize attack surfaces, control traffic flow, and ensure the Confidentiality, Integrity, and Availability (CIA) of resources. This approach is fundamental for protecting sensitive data and applications from unauthorized access and cyberattacks. By applying principles such as segmentation, isolation, and zero trust, organizations can create robust cloud environments that enforce strict security controls, and reduce the risk of lateral movement by attackers.

At its core, secure cloud networking involves configuring network components and policies to ensure that only authorized traffic flows between resources. It incorporates various strategies to compartmentalize and protect the network. For instance, segmentation divides the network into distinct zones such as public, private, and Demilitarized Zones (DMZs) to limit exposure and restrict the potential impact of a breach. Isolation further ensures that critical workloads are confined to private subnets with no direct internet access, reducing the risk of external attacks. Finally, the zero trust model is implemented to continuously verify every access request, regardless of the network's internal or external origin, ensuring that all traffic is authenticated and authorized based on identity and context.

- **Segmentation:** This principle involves dividing the network into isolated zones. For example, a cloud network may have a public zone for web-facing services, a private zone for internal application servers, and a DMZ for intermediary services such as load balancers. By segregating these zones, organizations can control and monitor the flow of traffic between them, ensuring that if one segment is compromised, the breach does not automatically spread to the entire network.

- **Isolation:** Isolation takes segmentation further by ensuring that the most sensitive workloads operate within private subnets that have no direct exposure to the internet. This minimizes the risk of unauthorized access, as external attackers cannot directly reach these critical resources. Isolation is often enforced through strict network Access Control Lists (ACLs) and security groups that tightly regulate inbound and outbound traffic.
- **Zero trust:** The zero trust model assumes that no entity, whether inside or outside the network, is inherently trustworthy. In practice, this means that every access request is verified through multi-factor authentication, identity-based policies, and continuous monitoring. Zero-trust architectures enforce granular access controls and validate every user and device, thereby reducing the risk of unauthorized lateral movement within the network.

The following are some important features and best practices for secure cloud networking:

- **Least privilege:** Apply the principle of least privilege by granting each resource only the minimum access required to perform its function. This minimizes the potential impact if a resource is compromised, as an attacker would have access only to a limited set of functions and data.
- **Layered defense:** Implement a multi-layered security strategy by deploying firewalls, Network Security Groups (NSGs), and routing rules at different levels of the network. Layered defense ensures that even if one security control fails, others remain in place to protect the network. For example, a firewall might block unauthorized external traffic, while an NSG within a virtual network controls internal traffic between subnets.
- **Encryption:** Secure data in transit using TLS to prevent interception and tampering, and ensure that data at rest is encrypted using cloud-native Key Management Services (KMS). Encryption adds an essential layer of security by making data unreadable without the proper decryption keys, even if it is intercepted or accessed by unauthorized parties.

Multi-Tier Network Architecture with Terraform

Multi-tier network architecture separates your application into distinct layers, typically public, private, and data tiers, to enhance security, scalability, and manageability. By isolating the web, application, and database layers into separate subnets, organizations can enforce tighter access controls and reduce the attack surface. Terraform simplifies the provisioning of such architectures by codifying the creation of Virtual Private Clouds (VPCs), subnets, routing tables, and security groups, ensuring that each tier is correctly isolated and secured.

- **Public tier (web layer):** This layer accepts traffic from the internet, often through load balancers. It is typically placed in a public subnet with an Internet Gateway, allowing external access while enforcing controlled entry points via security groups and firewalls.
- **Private tier (app layer):** The application layer resides in a private subnet, isolated from direct internet access. It processes requests from the web layer and communicates with the data tier, often through internal routing and NAT gateways, ensuring that sensitive operations remain shielded.
- **Data tier (DB layer):** The data layer, hosting databases and other critical storage, operates in isolated subnets with no direct public exposure. Access is strictly limited to the application layer to maintain the confidentiality and integrity of data.

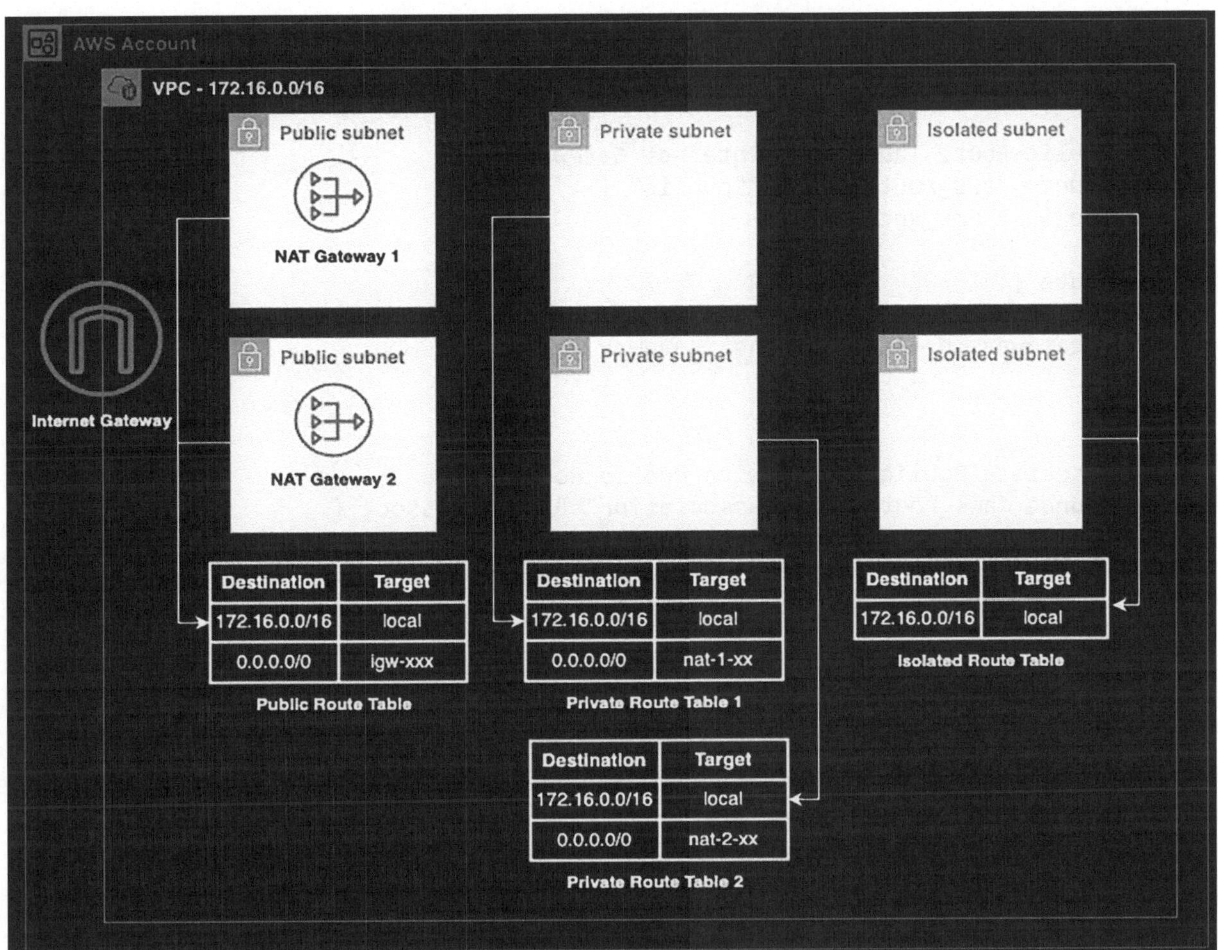

***Figure 10.1:** Network architecture*

```
# Create a VPC
resource "aws_vpc" "main" {
  cidr_block = "10.0.0.0/16"
}

# Public Subnet for Web Layer
resource "aws_subnet" "public" {
  vpc_id                  = aws_vpc.main.id
  cidr_block              = "10.0.1.0/24"
  map_public_ip_on_launch = true
}

# Private Subnet for App Layer
resource "aws_subnet" "private" {
  vpc_id     = aws_vpc.main.id
  cidr_block = "10.0.2.0/24"
}

# Isolated Subnet for Data Tier (DB Layer)
resource "aws_subnet" "data" {
  vpc_id     = aws_vpc.main.id
  cidr_block = "10.0.3.0/24"
}

# Internet Gateway for Public Subnet
```

```
resource "aws_internet_gateway" "gw" {
  vpc_id = aws_vpc.main.id
}

# Public Route Table with Internet Gateway
resource "aws_route_table" "public" {
  vpc_id = aws_vpc.main.id

  route {
    cidr_block = "0.0.0.0/0"
    gateway_id = aws_internet_gateway.gw.id
  }
}

# Associate Public Subnet with Public Route Table
resource "aws_route_table_association" "public_assoc" {
  subnet_id      = aws_subnet.public.id
  route_table_id = aws_route_table.public.id
}

# (Optional) NAT Gateway and Private Route Table would be configured for the
private subnet if outbound internet access is required.
```

This Terraform configuration provisions a multi-tier AWS network architecture with public, private, and data subnets to securely isolate web, application, and database layers, ensuring controlled access and enhanced security.

Implementing Network Segmentation and Isolation

Network segmentation is a critical security measure that divides a cloud network into isolated segments or tiers, such as web, application, and database layers, to restrict lateral movement in the event of a breach. Isolation further ensures that sensitive workloads, especially in production, operate in private subnets with strictly controlled access to the internet. Terraform automates the creation and configuration of these network segments, defining subnets, ACLs, and firewall rules to enforce security boundaries across your infrastructure.

- **Segmentation using subnet ACLs, NSGs, and firewalls:** In a segmented network, different environments (development, staging, production) are placed in separate subnets with their own access control lists. This isolation limits the potential spread of an attack by confining traffic within designated segments.
- **Isolation of critical workloads:** Private subnets are configured without direct internet access. Resources in these subnets use NAT gateways or VPNs for outbound connectivity, ensuring that critical applications and databases remain inaccessible from the public internet.

```
# Allow internal traffic for production resources on specific ports (HTTP and
HTTPS)
resource "google_compute_firewall" "allow_internal" {
  name      = "allow-internal-traffic"
  network   = google_compute_network.main.id
  direction = "INGRESS"
  priority  = 1000

  allow {
    protocol = "tcp"              # Allow TCP protocol
    ports    = ["80", "443"]      # Allow HTTP (80) and HTTPS (443) ports
  }
```

```
  source_ranges = ["10.0.0.0/16"]
  target_tags   = ["prod"]
}

# Deny all external traffic for production resources
resource "google_compute_firewall" "deny_external" {
  name      = "deny-external-traffic"
  network   = google_compute_network.main.id
  direction = "INGRESS"
  priority  = 2000

  deny {
    protocol = "all"             # Deny all protocols (complete block)
  }

  source_ranges = ["0.0.0.0/0"]
  target_tags   = ["prod"]
}
```

This Terraform configuration deploys GCP firewall rules that allow internal traffic and deny external access for production resources, ensuring secure network segmentation and isolation.

Designing High-Availability Network Architectures

High-Availability (HA) network architectures are essential for ensuring continuous service availability, even in the event of failures or outages. In Azure, HA networks are achieved by provisioning redundant infrastructure across multiple availability zones, configuring load balancers for efficient traffic distribution, and setting up failover mechanisms to automatically reroute traffic during disruptions. Terraform plays a pivotal role in automating this process by allowing you to codify the network layers, routing rules, and resource configurations required for a resilient HA architecture.

- **Deployment across multiple availability zones:** Resources are provisioned in different Availability Zones (AZs) within a region to achieve fault tolerance. This means that if one AZ fails, resources in another AZ can continue serving traffic without interruption.
- **Redundant paths and load balancing:** Load balancers, such as the Azure Load Balancer or Application Gateway, distribute incoming traffic across multiple VMs or services deployed in separate AZs. This redundancy ensures that no single point of failure can disrupt service availability.
- **Failover mechanisms for disaster recovery:** Multi-region or multi-AZ deployments allow for automatic failover in the event of an outage. Routing rules and health probes continuously monitor the status of resources and ensure that traffic is directed only to healthy endpoints.

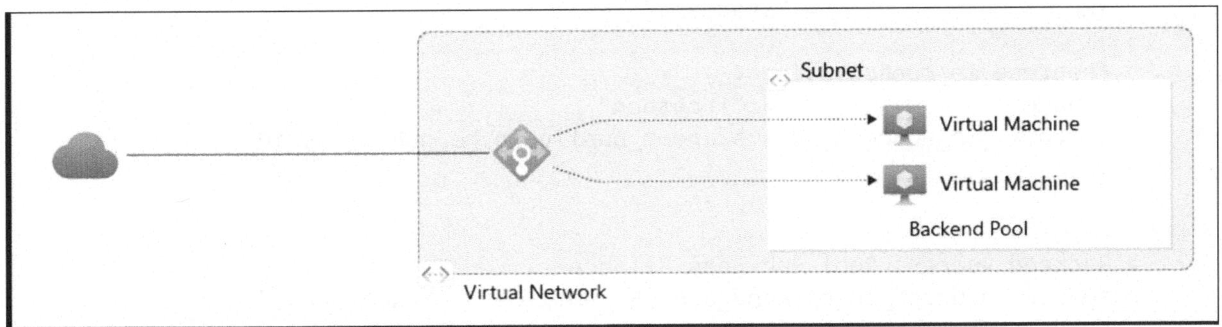

Figure 10.2: *High-Availability network architecture*

```
# Resource Group
resource "azurerm_resource_group" "ha_rg" {
  name     = "ha-rg"
  location = "East US"
}

# Virtual Network
resource "azurerm_virtual_network" "ha_vnet" {
  name                = "ha-vnet"
  address_space       = ["10.0.0.0/16"]
  location            = azurerm_resource_group.ha_rg.location
  resource_group_name = azurerm_resource_group.ha_rg.name
}

# Public Subnet (for Load Balancer)
resource "azurerm_subnet" "public_subnet" {
  name                 = "public-subnet"
  resource_group_name  = azurerm_resource_group.ha_rg.name
  virtual_network_name = azurerm_virtual_network.ha_vnet.name
  address_prefixes     = ["10.0.1.0/24"]
}

# Private Subnet (for VMs)
resource "azurerm_subnet" "private_subnet" {
  name                 = "private-subnet"
  resource_group_name  = azurerm_resource_group.ha_rg.name
  virtual_network_name = azurerm_virtual_network.ha_vnet.name
  address_prefixes     = ["10.0.2.0/24"]
}

# Public IP for Load Balancer
resource "azurerm_public_ip" "ha_public_ip" {
  name                = "ha-public-ip"
  location            = azurerm_resource_group.ha_rg.location
  resource_group_name = azurerm_resource_group.ha_rg.name
  allocation_method   = "Static"
  sku                 = "Standard"
}

# Azure Load Balancer
resource "azurerm_lb" "ha_lb" {
  name                = "ha-lb"
  location            = azurerm_resource_group.ha_rg.location
  resource_group_name = azurerm_resource_group.ha_rg.name
  sku                 = "Standard"

  frontend_ip_configuration {
    name                 = "frontend"
    public_ip_address_id = azurerm_public_ip.ha_public_ip.id
  }
}

# Backend Address Pool for Load Balancer
resource "azurerm_lb_backend_address_pool" "ha_backend_pool" {
  name                = "ha-backend-pool"
  resource_group_name = azurerm_resource_group.ha_rg.name
  loadbalancer_id     = azurerm_lb.ha_lb.id
```

```
}

resource "azurerm_lb_probe" "http_probe" {
  name                = "http-probe"
  resource_group_name = azurerm_resource_group.ha_rg.name
  loadbalancer_id     = azurerm_lb.ha_lb.id
  protocol            = "Http"
  port                = 80
  request_path        = "/"
}

resource "azurerm_lb_rule" "http_rule" {
  name                           = "http-rule"
  resource_group_name            = azurerm_resource_group.ha_rg.name
  loadbalancer_id                = azurerm_lb.ha_lb.id
  protocol                       = "Tcp"
  frontend_port                  = 80
  backend_port                   = 80
  frontend_ip_configuration_name = "frontend"
  backend_address_pool_id        = azurerm_lb_backend_address_pool.ha_back-
end_pool.id
  probe_id                       = azurerm_lb_probe.http_probe.id
}

# Network Interface for VM in Private Subnet (AZ1)
resource "azurerm_network_interface" "vm_nic1" {
  name                = "vm-nic-1"
  location            = azurerm_resource_group.ha_rg.location
  resource_group_name = azurerm_resource_group.ha_rg.name

  ip_configuration {
    name                          = "internal"
    subnet_id                     = azurerm_subnet.private_subnet.id
    private_ip_address_allocation = "Dynamic"
    load_balancer_backend_address_pools_ids = [azurerm_lb_backend_address_
pool.ha_backend_pool.id]
  }
}

# Network Interface for VM in Private Subnet (AZ2)
resource "azurerm_network_interface" "vm_nic2" {
  name                = "vm-nic-2"
  location            = azurerm_resource_group.ha_rg.location
  resource_group_name = azurerm_resource_group.ha_rg.name

  ip_configuration {
    name                          = "internal"
    subnet_id                     = azurerm_subnet.private_subnet.id
    private_ip_address_allocation = "Dynamic"
    load_balancer_backend_address_pools_ids = [azurerm_lb_backend_address_
pool.ha_backend_pool.id]
  }
}

# Linux Virtual Machine in AZ1
resource "azurerm_linux_virtual_machine" "vm1" {
  name                = "ha-vm-1"
```

```
  resource_group_name = azurerm_resource_group.ha_rg.name
  location            = azurerm_resource_group.ha_rg.location
  size                = "Standard_DS1_v2"
  admin_username      = "azureuser"
  network_interface_ids = [azurerm_network_interface.vm_nic1.id]
  admin_password      = "Password1234!"  # Replace with secure credentials in 
production
  zone                = "1"              # Deploy VM1 in Availability Zone 1

  source_image_reference {
    publisher = "Canonical"
    offer     = "UbuntuServer"
    sku       = "18.04-LTS"
    version   = "latest"
  }
}

# Linux Virtual Machine in AZ2
resource "azurerm_linux_virtual_machine" "vm2" {
  name                = "ha-vm-2"
  resource_group_name = azurerm_resource_group.ha_rg.name
  location            = azurerm_resource_group.ha_rg.location
  size                = "Standard_DS1_v2"
  admin_username      = "azureuser"
  network_interface_ids = [azurerm_network_interface.vm_nic2.id]
  admin_password      = "Password1234!"  # Replace with secure credentials in 
production
  zone                = "2"              # Deploy VM2 in Availability Zone 2

  source_image_reference {
    publisher = "Canonical"
    offer     = "UbuntuServer"
    sku       = "18.04-LTS"
    version   = "latest"
  }
}
```

This Terraform configuration provisions a high-availability network architecture in Azure by deploying a Virtual Network with public and private subnets, a load balancer, and redundant VMs, ensuring continuous service availability through fault tolerance and traffic distribution.

Implementing Zero Trust Network Access (ZTNA)

Zero Trust Network Access (ZTNA) is a security model that continuously verifies every device, user, and request, regardless of its location, rather than assuming that internal traffic is inherently trustworthy. This approach enforces strict identity-based policies and network segmentation to minimize the risk of unauthorized access. Terraform helps implement ZTNA by codifying these identity-based controls and firewall rules, ensuring that only explicitly verified and authorized traffic can access resources.

- **Integration with Identity Providers:** ZTNA relies on integrating with IAM policies and external identity providers (such as Okta or Azure AD) to ensure that each request and device is continuously authenticated and authorized.
- **Strict firewall policies:** Terraform can deploy firewall policies and security groups that enforce granular traffic verification. These rules block all traffic by default, allowing only

explicitly permitted flows between verified endpoints, thereby reducing the lateral movement of potential attackers.

```
resource "aws_security_group" "web_sg" {
  name   = "web-sg"
  vpc_id = var.vpc_id

  ingress {
    from_port   = 80
    to_port     = 80
    protocol    = "tcp"
    cidr_blocks = ["0.0.0.0/0"]
  }

  ingress {
    from_port   = 443
    to_port     = 443
    protocol    = "tcp"
    cidr_blocks = ["0.0.0.0/0"]
  }

  egress {
    from_port   = 0
    to_port     = 0
    protocol    = "-1"
    cidr_blocks = ["0.0.0.0/0"]
  }
}
```

This Terraform snippet provisions an AWS Security Group that allows inbound HTTP and HTTPS traffic from anywhere, with unrestricted outbound traffic, securing instances at the network interface level.

Designing secure cloud networks requires adherence to core principles of segmentation, isolation, and zero trust. With Terraform, organizations can codify multi-tier architectures, automate firewall rules, and implement high-availability configurations consistently across AWS, Azure, and GCP. By adopting these best practices, cloud architects minimize the risk of breaches and ensure resilient cloud network designs.

Automating Firewall Rules, Security Groups, and Network ACLs

Automating network protection mechanisms such as firewalls, security groups, and network ACLs forms the backbone of cloud security. Manual configuration is prone to errors, misconfigurations, and drift. By leveraging Terraform, cloud engineers ensure consistent and scalable network policies that dynamically adapt to evolving security requirements. This section explores automating firewall rules across AWS, Azure, and GCP to secure workloads efficiently.

Managing Security Groups and NACLs with Terraform

Security Groups (SGs) and Network ACLs (NACLs) are critical components of cloud network security that control inbound and outbound traffic at different layers. While SGs are applied at the instance or VM level and are stateful (meaning they automatically allow return traffic for permitted inbound requests), NACLs operate at the subnet level and are stateless (evaluating each packet independently according to rule priority). This ensures that traffic control configurations are consistent, repeatable, and version-controlled across your cloud infrastructure, which minimizes configuration drift and reduces the risk of misconfigurations.

- **Security groups:** Security groups define rules to allow or deny traffic at the instance level. This is because SGs are stateful; if an inbound rule permits traffic, the response traffic is automatically allowed. Terraform modules can be used to standardize SG definitions across multiple instances and environments.
- **Network ACLs:** NACLs control traffic at the subnet level, applying rules that are processed in order of rule number. Since NACLs are stateless, both inbound and outbound rules must be defined explicitly. Terraform can automate the creation and updating of NACLs, ensuring that all subnet-level traffic adheres to your security policies.

```
resource "aws_network_acl" "example_nacl" {
  vpc_id = var.vpc_id

  # Allow inbound HTTP traffic from a trusted range
  ingress {
    protocol   = "tcp"
    rule_no    = 100
    action     = "allow"
    cidr_block = "203.0.113.0/24"
    from_port  = 80
    to_port    = 80
  }

  # Allow inbound HTTPS traffic from a trusted range
  ingress {
    protocol   = "tcp"
    rule_no    = 110
    action     = "allow"
    cidr_block = "203.0.113.0/24"
    from_port  = 443
    to_port    = 443
  }

  # Deny all other inbound traffic
  ingress {
    protocol   = "-1"
    rule_no    = 120
    action     = "deny"
    cidr_block = "0.0.0.0/0"
    from_port  = 0
    to_port    = 0
  }

  # Allow all outbound traffic
  egress {
    protocol   = "-1"
    rule_no    = 100
    action     = "allow"
    cidr_block = "0.0.0.0/0"
    from_port  = 0
    to_port    = 0
  }
}
```

This Terraform configuration provisions an AWS Network ACL that permits inbound HTTP/HTTPS traffic from a trusted CIDR block while denying all other inbound traffic, enforcing subnet-level security controls.

Automating Azure NSGs and GCP Firewall Rules

Securing network traffic is a crucial part of any cloud security strategy. Azure Network Security Groups (NSGs) and GCP Firewall Rules are two fundamental components used to control traffic flow within virtual networks. NSGs in Azure are used to filter network traffic to and from resources, such as Virtual Machines (VMs) or entire subnets, by defining inbound and outbound rules. Similarly, GCP Firewall Rules enforce traffic filtering at the instance or subnet level within a Virtual Private Cloud (VPC). By automating the provisioning of these security controls using Terraform, organizations can enforce consistent, organization-wide security policies, minimize manual errors, and ensure that every deployed resource adheres to the defined security posture.

- **Azure NSGs:** Terraform provisions NSGs and attaches rules that define which types of network traffic are allowed or denied to VMs or subnets. These rules are processed at the network interface or subnet level, ensuring that only authorized traffic reaches your applications.

```
resource "azurerm_network_security_group" "example" {
  name                = "example-nsg"
  location            = azurerm_resource_group.example.location
  resource_group_name = azurerm_resource_group.example.name

  security_rule {
    name                       = "allow-ssh"
    priority                   = 100
    direction                  = "Inbound"
    access                     = "Allow"
    protocol                   = "Tcp"
    source_port_range          = "*"
    destination_port_range     = "22"
    source_address_prefix     = "*"
    destination_address_prefix = "*"
  }

  security_rule {
    name                       = "deny-all-other-inbound"
    priority                   = 200
    direction                  = "Inbound"
    access                     = "Deny"
    protocol                   = "*"
    source_port_range          = "*"
    destination_port_range     = "*"
    source_address_prefix     = "*"
    destination_address_prefix = "*"
  }
}
```

  This Terraform snippet provisions an Azure NSG in a specified resource group with rules that allow inbound SSH traffic and deny all other inbound traffic, enforcing VM-level security.

- **GCP firewall rules:** In GCP, firewall rules are applied at the VPC level. They filter traffic based on defined rules that allow or deny connections to instances or entire subnets, thereby protecting your infrastructure from unauthorized access.

```
resource "google_compute_firewall" "example" {
  name    = "example-firewall"
  network = google_compute_network.default.name
```

```
  allow {
    protocol = "tcp"
    ports    = ["80", "443"]
  }

  deny {
    protocol = "all"
    ports    = ["0-65535"]
  }

  source_ranges = ["0.0.0.0/0"]
  target_tags   = ["web"]
}
```

This Terraform snippet creates a GCP firewall rule that allows inbound TCP traffic on ports **80** and **443** for instances tagged **"web"** while denying all other traffic, ensuring robust network security at the VPC level.

Conditional Firewall Rules Based on Environment

Conditional firewall rules in Terraform allow you to tailor your network security policies dynamically based on environment variables such as dev, staging, or production. By using conditional logic (for example, **count** or **for_each** loops) and environment-specific flags, you can enforce stricter rules for production workloads while providing flexibility for development and testing environments. This approach helps maintain both scalability and consistency across different environments without duplicating code.

- **Dynamic resource creation:** Terraform uses conditional constructs such as **count** or **for_each** to create or modify firewall rules based on the value of an environment variable. For example, if the environment is **"prod"**, the configuration might restrict inbound traffic to a specific CIDR block, whereas a **"dev"** environment might allow more permissive access.
- **Environment-specific configurations:** By parameterizing variables such as environment or using Terraform workspaces, you can manage multiple environments with the same code base, ensuring that each environment enforces appropriate security levels.

```
resource "aws_security_group" "example" {
  name        = "example-sg-${var.environment}"
  description = "Security group for ${var.environment} environment"
  vpc_id      = var.vpc_id

  ingress {
    description = "Allow HTTP traffic"
    from_port   = 80
    to_port     = 80
    protocol    = "tcp"
    cidr_blocks = var.environment == "prod" ? ["203.0.113.0/24"] :
["0.0.0.0/0"]
  }

  ingress {
    description = "Allow HTTPS traffic"
    from_port   = 443
    to_port     = 443
    protocol    = "tcp"
    cidr_blocks = var.environment == "prod" ? ["203.0.113.0/24"] :
["0.0.0.0/0"]
```

```
    }

    tags = {
      Environment = var.environment
    }
  }
```

This Terraform configuration creates an AWS Security Group with conditional ingress rules that restrict HTTP/HTTPS traffic to a trusted CIDR block in production while allowing open access in non-production environments, ensuring environment-specific network security.

Monitoring and Auditing Firewall Changes

Monitoring firewall rule changes is essential to ensure that unauthorized modifications do not compromise your network security. By continuously tracking changes to firewall configurations, organizations can quickly detect and remediate misconfigurations, ensuring that environments remain secure and compliant with internal and regulatory standards. Terraform can integrate with cloud-native monitoring and auditing services such as AWS CloudWatch, Azure Monitor, and GCP Audit Logs to track changes in firewall settings, maintain an audit trail, and trigger automated remediation workflows when necessary.

Monitoring firewall changes involves tracking updates to security configurations (such as Security Groups, NSGs, or firewall rules) to detect any unauthorized or accidental modifications. These logs provide accountability and help ensure that only approved changes are made. Terraform facilitates this process by provisioning the necessary monitoring resources and configuring them to capture, log, and alert on firewall rule changes.

- **Integration with cloud monitoring tools:** Terraform provisions resources that send firewall change logs to services such as AWS CloudWatch Logs, Azure Monitor, or GCP Audit Logs.
- **Automated logging and alerts:** Logs are collected continuously and can trigger notifications via Amazon SNS, Azure Event Grid, or GCP Pub/Sub if any unexpected changes are detected.
- **Audit and compliance:** Regular auditing of these logs ensures that all changes are tracked, providing a historical record that can be reviewed during compliance audits and helping to enforce security policies.

```
# Create a Log Analytics Workspace
resource "azurerm_log_analytics_workspace" "example" {
  name                = "example-law"
  location            = azurerm_resource_group.example.location
  resource_group_name = azurerm_resource_group.example.name
  sku                 = "PerGB2018"
  retention_in_days   = 30
}

# Enable diagnostic settings for the NSG to capture firewall events
resource "azurerm_monitor_diagnostic_setting" "firewall_audit" {
  name                       = "nsg-firewall-audit"
  target_resource_id         = azurerm_network_security_group.example.id
  log_analytics_workspace_id = azurerm_log_analytics_workspace.example.id

  log {
    category = "NetworkSecurityGroupEvent"
    enabled  = true

    retention_policy {
      enabled = true
```

```
            days    = 30
          }
        }
      }
```

This Terraform configuration monitors Azure NSG firewall changes by sending diagnostic logs to an Azure Log Analytics Workspace, enabling continuous auditing and alerting of any modifications to firewall rules.

Blocking Malicious Traffic with Dynamic IP Lists

Dynamic IP lists are collections of IP addresses sourced from threat intelligence feeds that identify known malicious actors. These lists are used to automatically update firewall or WAF rules across cloud providers such as AWS, Azure, and GCP, effectively blocking traffic from harmful sources. By automating rule updates, Terraform ensures that your infrastructure is continuously protected against evolving threats without requiring manual intervention.

- **Dynamic data sources:** Terraform can integrate with external APIs or third-party services that provide real-time threat intelligence. These sources supply updated lists of malicious IP addresses.
- **Automated rule updates:** Terraform uses these dynamic IP lists to configure security resources (such as WAFs or firewall rules) to block traffic from the listed IPs. This is achieved using provider-specific resources that support IP set configuration.

```
resource "google_compute_security_policy" "bad_ips" {
  name = "bad-ip-list-policy"

  rule {
    action   = "deny(403)"
    priority = 1000

    match {
      versioned_expr = "SRC_IPS_V1"
      config {
        src_ip_ranges = ["203.0.113.10/32", "203.0.113.20/32"]
      }
    }
  }
}
```

This Terraform configuration provisions a GCP Cloud Armor security policy that denies traffic from specified malicious IP ranges, enabling dynamic, automated blocking of threats across your cloud infrastructure.

Automating firewall rules, security groups, and NACLs with Terraform ensures scalable, consistent, and secure cloud networks. By codifying rules and integrating environment-based conditions, organizations reduce misconfigurations and improve network security posture across AWS, Azure, and GCP. This approach minimizes attack surfaces, streamlines auditing, and simplifies traffic control in multi-cloud deployments.

Configuring VPNs and Secure Connectivity for Hybrid Clouds

In hybrid cloud environments, securely connecting on-premises data centers to cloud networks is critical for workload migration, disaster recovery, and consistent application performance. Virtual Private Networks (VPNs) and dedicated connectivity services provide encrypted, low-latency channels that protect data in transit. Terraform simplifies and automates the deployment of these connectivity solutions, reducing manual errors, improving scalability, and ensuring consistent configurations across AWS, Azure, and GCP environments. This section delves into automating VPN provisioning and hybrid connectivity using Terraform, covering site-to-site VPNs, private interconnects, and cross-cloud secure routing.

Provisioning AWS Site-to-Site VPN and Direct Connect

AWS enables secure hybrid cloud connectivity through two primary solutions: AWS Site-to-Site VPN and AWS Direct Connect. Site-to-Site VPN provides an encrypted connection over the internet, while Direct Connect establishes a dedicated private network link between an on-premises data center and AWS, ensuring low latency and high bandwidth. Terraform automates the provisioning of both solutions, ensuring consistency, reducing deployment time, and facilitating scalability.

AWS Direct Connect

- **Dedicated Network Link**: A physical private fiber connection is provisioned between an AWS Direct Connect location and an on-premises data center.
- **Virtual Interfaces (VIFs)**: Direct Connect supports private VIFs for connecting to VPCs and public VIFs for accessing AWS services (for example, S3, DynamoDB).
- **Direct Connect Gateway (DXGW)**: Enables cross-region access by connecting multiple VPCs across different AWS regions.
- **Hybrid Redundancy**: Can be combined with Site-to-Site VPN as a backup for failover in case of a Direct Connect outage.

AWS Site-to-Site VPN

- **Virtual Private Gateway (VGW)**: AWS terminates the VPN connection at a Virtual Private Gateway, which attaches to the target VPC.
- **Customer Gateway (CGW)**: The on-premises VPN device is represented in AWS as a Customer Gateway, requiring a public IP.
- **IPsec Tunnels**: Two IPsec tunnels are established to provide redundancy and automatic failover.
- **Routing**: Uses BGP (preferred) for dynamic routing or manually configured static routes.
- **Encryption**: Traffic is encrypted using `AES-256` to maintain confidentiality and integrity.

```
# Define the Customer Gateway (CGW)
resource "aws_customer_gateway" "cgw" {
  bgp_asn    = 65000
  ip_address = "203.0.113.12"  # On-premises VPN device public IP
  type       = "ipsec.1"
}

# Create the VPN connection
resource "aws_vpn_connection" "vpn" {
  vpn_gateway_id      = aws_vpn_gateway.vpn_gateway.id
  customer_gateway_id = aws_customer_gateway.cgw.id
  type                = "ipsec.1"

  tunnel1_inside_cidr = "169.254.10.0/30"
  tunnel2_inside_cidr = "169.254.11.0/30"
}
```

This Terraform configuration provisions an AWS Site-to-Site VPN by creating a Customer Gateway and VPN connection with redundant IPsec tunnels.

Deploying Azure VPN Gateway and ExpressRoute

Azure offers two primary hybrid connectivity options that enable secure communication between on-premises networks and Azure Virtual Networks. The VPN Gateway establishes a site-to-site VPN connection using encrypted IPsec/IKE tunnels, while ExpressRoute provides a dedicated, private fiber connection that bypasses the public internet for low-latency, high-bandwidth communication. Together, these solutions form the backbone of a robust hybrid cloud architecture, ensuring continuous service availability and data protection.

ExpressRoute

- **Dedicated Connection:** Provides a private, high-bandwidth fiber link between on-premises networks and Azure, bypassing the internet.
- **Performance:** Offers low latency and high reliability for mission-critical workloads and large data transfers.
- **Integration:** Connects to Azure VNets through a Virtual Network Gateway, ensuring secure, seamless communication.
- **Redundancy:** Supports multiple circuits for redundancy and failover, ensuring continuous connectivity.

VPN Gateway

- **Virtual Network Gateway:** Attaches to an Azure VNet, serving as the endpoint for encrypted VPN connections.
- **Local Network Gateway:** Represents on-premises equipment with a public IP and specifies the on-premises network address range.
- **IPsec/IKE Tunnels:** Establishes one or more encrypted tunnels using IPsec/IKE protocols to secure data in transit.
- **Routing and Redundancy:** Supports static or dynamic (BGP) routing for failover and high availability.
- **Encryption:** Utilizes strong encryption algorithms (for example, `AES-256`) to protect data, ensuring confidentiality and integrity.

```
# Provision an Azure VPN Gateway
resource "azurerm_virtual_network_gateway" "vpn_gateway" {
  name                = "example-vpn-gateway"
  location            = azurerm_resource_group.example.location
  resource_group_name = azurerm_resource_group.example.name
  type                = "Vpn"
  vpn_type            = "RouteBased"
  sku                 = "VpnGw1"

  ip_configurations {
    name                          = "vnetGatewayConfig"
    public_ip_address_id          = azurerm_public_ip.vpn_public_ip.id
    subnet_id                     = azurerm_subnet.gateway_subnet.id
  }
}

# Create a Local Network Gateway representing on-premises device
resource "azurerm_local_network_gateway" "local_gateway" {
```

```
  name                = "example-local-gateway"
  resource_group_name = azurerm_resource_group.example.name
  location            = azurerm_resource_group.example.location
  gateway_address     = "203.0.113.1"  # On-premises public IP
  address_space       = ["192.168.1.0/24"]
}

# Establish the VPN Connection
resource "azurerm_virtual_network_gateway_connection" "vpn_connection" {
  name                       = "example-vpn-connection"
  location                   = azurerm_resource_group.example.location
  resource_group_name        = azurerm_resource_group.example.name
  virtual_network_gateway_id  = azurerm_virtual_network_gateway.vpn_gateway.id
  local_network_gateway_id    = azurerm_local_network_gateway.local_gateway.id
  connection_type            = "IPsec"
  routing_weight             = 10
  shared_key                 = "YourSharedKey123!"  # Pre-shared key for
IPsec connection
}
```

This Terraform configuration provisions an Azure VPN Gateway with associated IP configuration, creates a local network gateway representing an on-premises device, and establishes an IPsec VPN connection between the Azure VNet and the on-premises network using a shared key.

GCP Cloud VPN and Interconnect Automation

Google Cloud Platform (GCP) provides two key hybrid connectivity solutions: Cloud VPN and Cloud Interconnect. Cloud VPN establishes secure, IPsec-based site-to-site VPN tunnels over the public internet, while Cloud Interconnect offers dedicated, high-speed private connectivity between on-premises networks and GCP. Terraform enables the automated provisioning of these connectivity solutions, allowing organizations to create scalable and secure hybrid cloud architectures that seamlessly integrate on-premises and cloud resources.

Cloud VPN

- **Resources:** Terraform provisions VPN gateways, tunnels, and associated routing configurations to create secure, encrypted connections between an on-premises network and a GCP Virtual Private Cloud (VPC).
- **Encryption:** Utilizes IPsec/IKE protocols with strong encryption (for example, **`AES-256`**) to secure data in transit.
- **Redundancy:** Typically deploys multiple tunnels for high availability and automatic failover.

Cloud Interconnect

- **Resources:** Terraform automates the provisioning of Direct Interconnect resources such as dedicated connections and virtual interfaces.
- **Performance:** Offers low-latency, high-bandwidth connectivity with improved reliability compared to VPN over the internet.
- **Integration:** Connects to multiple GCP regions and supports dynamic routing with BGP, enabling efficient traffic distribution and redundancy.

```
# Provision a VPN Gateway in a specific region
resource "google_compute_vpn_gateway" "vpn_gateway" {
  name    = "example-vpn-gateway"
  network = google_compute_network.example_network.name
  region  = "us-central1"
}
```

```
# Create a VPN Tunnel to connect to the on-premises network
resource "google_compute_vpn_tunnel" "vpn_tunnel" {
  name                   = "example-vpn-tunnel"
  vpn_gateway            = google_compute_vpn_gateway.vpn_gateway.id
  peer_ip                = "203.0.113.12"       # On-premises VPN device public
IP
  shared_secret          = "your-shared-secret"
  ike_version            = 2
  local_traffic_selector = ["10.0.0.0/16"]
  remote_traffic_selector = ["192.168.1.0/24"]
}
```

This Terraform configuration provisions a GCP Cloud VPN gateway and tunnel, establishing an encrypted IPsec connection between a GCP VPC and an on-premises network using a shared secret and dynamic traffic selectors.

Automating VPN provisioning and hybrid cloud connectivity with Terraform ensures secure, resilient, and scalable communication channels between on-premises and cloud environments. By standardizing VPN setups across AWS, Azure, and GCP, organizations reduce complexity, enhance security, and minimize downtime in hybrid cloud deployments.

Setting Up Multi-Region Networking with Terraform

As cloud adoption scales globally, businesses increasingly deploy workloads across multiple regions to improve fault tolerance, reduce latency, and ensure application availability. Multi-region network architectures provide resilience by distributing resources geographically, ensuring that failures in one region do not compromise the entire infrastructure.

Terraform enables organizations to automate and standardize the deployment of multi-region networks across AWS, Azure, and GCP, simplifying the creation of VPC peerings, global load balancers, and DNS configurations. This section covers the design and automation of multi-region networks to enhance global availability, scalability, and security.

Designing Multi-Region VPC Peering and Interconnects

Multi-region VPC peering and interconnects enable seamless, secure, and low-latency communication between virtual networks that are deployed across different geographic regions. This design is crucial for global application deployments, as it allows resources in disparate regions to interact as if they were in the same network, while maintaining strict security controls and optimizing network performance.

AWS

- **Inter-region VPC peering:** Establishes a peering connection between VPCs in different AWS regions, enabling private IP communication without traversing the public internet.
- **Key features:** Auto-acceptance, route propagation, and secure connectivity with low latency.

```
resource "aws_vpc_peering_connection" "peer" {
  peer_vpc_id = "vpc-0abcd1234efgh5678"
  vpc_id      = aws_vpc.main.id
  peer_region = "us-west-2"
  auto_accept = true
}
```

This Terraform snippet provisions an AWS VPC peering connection between VPCs in different regions (with the peer in **"us-west-2"**) and auto-accepts the connection for secure inter-region communication.

Azure

- **VNet peering:** Allows peering between Virtual Networks (VNets) in different regions, enabling resources to communicate directly with each other with high throughput and low latency.
- **Key features:** Bidirectional connectivity and minimal latency impact.

```
resource "azurerm_virtual_network_peering" "peer" {
  name                         = "vnet-peer"
  resource_group_name          = azurerm_resource_group.main.name
  virtual_network_name         = azurerm_virtual_network.main.name
  remote_virtual_network_id    = azurerm_virtual_network.remote.id
}
```

This Terraform snippet establishes VNet peering in Azure, connecting a primary virtual network to a remote virtual network for secure, low-latency communication across regions.

GCP

- **VPC peering:** Connects VPC networks within or across regions for private communication between resources.
- **Key features:** Direct connectivity with redundancy and secure private links.

```
resource "google_compute_network_peering" "peer" {
  name         = "peering-connection"
  network      = google_compute_network.main.self_link
  peer_network = google_compute_network.remote.self_link
}
```

This Terraform snippet creates a VPC peering connection in GCP, linking two VPC networks for private and secure inter-region communication.

Multi-Region DNS and Traffic Routing

Multi-region DNS and traffic routing distribute incoming user requests across multiple regions to ensure that traffic is directed to the closest and healthiest endpoints. This not only improves performance by reducing latency but also enhances availability through automatic failover during regional outages. By automating this process with Terraform, organizations can ensure that their global applications maintain high performance, resilience, and security without manual intervention.

- **AWS Route 53:** AWS Route 53 is a highly scalable DNS service that routes traffic based on policies such as geolocation, latency, and failover, ensuring that users are connected to the best-performing endpoint within AWS.
- **Azure Traffic Manager:** Azure Traffic Manager is a DNS-based traffic load balancer that directs user requests to the most responsive endpoints globally, using methods such as performance and geographic routing to optimize user experience and distribute traffic effectively.
- **GCP Cloud DNS:** GCP Cloud DNS provides global DNS resolution with low latency by leveraging Google's highly available infrastructure, ensuring that DNS queries are answered quickly and efficiently across multiple regions.

```
resource "aws_route53_record" "example" {
  zone_id = aws_route53_zone.example.zone_id
  name    = "example.com"
```

```
    type    = "A"
    alias {
      name                   = aws_elb.example.dns_name
      zone_id                = aws_elb.example.zone_id
      evaluate_target_health = true
    }
  }
```

This snippet provisions an AWS Route 53 alias record that routes DNS traffic to a healthy ELB endpoint for **"example.com"**, ensuring efficient and resilient traffic distribution.

The following are some best practices for configuring DNS and traffic routing for a multi-region setup:

- **Health checks:** Configure continuous health checks for endpoints to automatically detect outages and reroute traffic to healthy resources.
- **Latency-based routing:** Use latency-based routing policies to direct users to the region with the lowest latency, enhancing overall application responsiveness.
- **DNS failover:** Implement automated DNS failover to quickly redirect traffic to backup regions in the event of a failure, ensuring uninterrupted service.

Configuring Global Load Balancers and Failover

Global load balancers are essential for distributing traffic across multiple regions to ensure high availability and scalability. They help prevent a single-region failure from impacting application performance by intelligently routing user requests to the most optimal endpoint, regardless of geographic location. This capability is critical for organizations that deploy applications globally and require both performance optimization and disaster recovery resilience.

- **AWS Global Accelerator:** Routes traffic to the optimal endpoint across AWS regions based on factors such as health, latency, and routing policies, thereby enhancing application availability and performance.
- **Azure Front Door:** Distributes HTTP/HTTPS traffic globally while incorporating a built-in Web Application Firewall (WAF) for additional security, ensuring that user requests are directed to the most responsive and secure endpoint.
- **GCP Global Load Balancer:** Manages cross-region traffic by automatically balancing loads and providing failover capabilities. It ensures that if one region experiences issues, traffic is seamlessly redirected to another healthy region, maintaining continuous service availability.

```
resource "google_compute_global_address" "example" {
  name         = "global-lb-address"
  address_type = "EXTERNAL"
  ip_version   = "IPV4"
}
```

This Terraform snippet provisions a globally accessible external IPv4 address in GCP, serving as a foundational element for a Global Load Balancer that enables multi-region traffic routing and automatic failover.

Resiliency Testing and Disaster Recovery Setup

Resiliency testing involves simulating failures such as regional outages to validate that your Disaster Recovery (DR) processes work as intended. The goal is to ensure seamless failover and continuous availability of critical applications, even in the event of unexpected disruptions. By incorporating resiliency testing into your infrastructure management, you can identify weaknesses in your DR plan, improve recovery times, and ensure compliance with Service Level Agreements (SLAs) for uptime. Terraform plays a pivotal role in automating the setup of DR components, making it possible to simulate failures and monitor the effectiveness of your failover strategies consistently across cloud environments.

- **Simulation of failures:** Resiliency testing typically involves intentionally simulating regional or component-level failures to observe how the system responds and to validate that failover mechanisms activate as expected.
- **Monitoring and health checks:** Critical components, such as DNS routing and load balancing, are continuously monitored using health checks. These health checks detect anomalies or outages and trigger automated failover processes.
- **Automated recovery:** Once a failure is detected, the disaster recovery setup automatically reroutes traffic from the affected region to a healthy, redundant region or backup system, ensuring that service disruption is minimized.
- **Feedback loop:** The data collected during these tests informs improvements in the DR strategy, allowing teams to adjust configurations and optimize recovery workflows over time.

```
resource "azurerm_traffic_manager_profile" "dr_profile" {
  name                   = "example-traffic-manager"
  resource_group_name = azurerm_resource_group.example.name
  traffic_routing_method = "Priority"

  dns_config {
    relative_name = "example-tm"
    ttl           = 30
  }

  monitor_config {
    protocol    = "HTTP"
    port        = 80
    path        = "/health"
  }
}

resource "azurerm_traffic_manager_endpoint" "primary" {
  name                  = "primary-endpoint"
  profile_id           = azurerm_traffic_manager_profile.dr_profile.id
  type                  = "AzureEndpoints"
  target_resource_id = azurerm_app_service.primary.id
  priority              = 1
}

resource "azurerm_traffic_manager_endpoint" "backup" {
  name                  = "backup-endpoint"
  profile_id           = azurerm_traffic_manager_profile.dr_profile.id
  type                  = "AzureEndpoints"
  target_resource_id = azurerm_app_service.backup.id
  priority              = 2
}
```

This Terraform configuration provisions an Azure Traffic Manager profile that routes traffic between primary and backup endpoints, ensuring automatic failover in case of an outage.

Automating multi-region network architectures with Terraform enables organizations to build resilient, scalable cloud environments. By leveraging VPC peering, global load balancers, and automated DNS failover, businesses can ensure seamless traffic distribution and maintain availability even during regional failures.

Securing Serverless and Edge Architectures Using Terraform

As serverless computing and edge deployments gain traction, securing these architectures becomes critical to safeguarding sensitive data and ensuring the integrity of distributed applications. Unlike traditional cloud environments, serverless architectures abstract infrastructure management, allowing developers to focus on code rather than servers. However, this abstraction introduces unique challenges in network security, such as managing VPC access, securing API gateways, and protecting serverless functions from DDoS and injection attacks.

Terraform simplifies the deployment of secure serverless and edge architectures by automating the provisioning of VPC endpoints, API gateways, and CDN distributions with integrated security controls. This section explores designing secure serverless networks and implementing edge security with Terraform across AWS, Azure, and GCP.

Network Design for Serverless Architectures

Serverless functions such as AWS Lambda, Azure Functions, and Google Cloud Functions run in isolated execution environments that, by default, do not have direct access to Virtual Private Clouds (VPCs). To securely integrate serverless functions with other cloud resources, it is essential to design network architectures that allow these functions to access VPC-based resources privately. This is typically achieved by deploying VPC endpoints or private access configurations, which ensure that serverless functions communicate securely with internal resources without exposing sensitive data over the public internet.

- **AWS Lambda:** AWS Lambda functions can be configured to access VPC resources by specifying a VPC configuration that attaches the function to specific subnets and security groups, enabling private communication with resources such as databases or internal APIs.
- **Azure Functions:** Azure Functions can access internal services by leveraging private endpoints, which enable secure, private connectivity to resources such as Azure Storage or SQL databases without routing traffic over the public internet.
- **GCP Cloud Functions:** GCP Cloud Functions use Private Google Access to communicate with resources in VPC networks, allowing functions to securely interact with Compute Engine instances or Cloud SQL databases without requiring public IP addresses.

```
resource "aws_lambda_function" "example" {
  function_name = "secure-function"
  handler       = "index.handler"
  runtime       = "nodejs14.x"
  vpc_config {
    subnet_ids         = ["subnet-0abcd1234efgh5678"]
    security_group_ids = ["sg-01234abcd"]
  }
}
```

This Terraform snippet provisions an AWS Lambda function configured with VPC settings to enable secure, private access to internal resources via specific subnets and security groups.

Deploying Edge Security with AWS CloudFront, Azure CDN, and GCP Cloud CDN

Edge security leverages Content Delivery Networks (CDNs) to cache content at geographically distributed edge locations, reducing latency and protecting origin servers from DDoS attacks. By integrating with built-in DDoS protection and WAF solutions, these CDNs help secure global applications while ensuring high performance and availability. Terraform automates the provisioning and configuration of these services, enabling a consistent and scalable approach to edge security across multiple cloud providers.

- **AWS CloudFront:** Distributes content globally from edge locations, and integrates with AWS Shield to protect against DDoS attacks, while also allowing integration with AWS WAF to filter malicious web traffic.
- **Azure CDN:** Delivers content with low latency by caching it at global edge nodes and leverages Azure Front Door (or built-in CDN features) to enforce security policies and provide Web Application Firewall (WAF) capabilities for filtering and protecting traffic.
- **GCP Cloud CDN:** Caches content at Google's globally distributed edge locations, delivering low-latency access to users while encrypting data in transit using TLS, ensuring that both performance and security are maintained.

```
# Provision an Azure Front Door instance
resource "azurerm_frontdoor" "example" {
  name                = "example-frontdoor"
  resource_group_name = azurerm_resource_group.example.name
  location            = azurerm_resource_group.example.location

  backend_pool {
    name = "example-backend-pool"
    backend {
      address    = azurerm_storage_account.example.primary_web_endpoint
      http_port = 80
      https_port = 443
      priority   = 1
      weight     = 50
    }
  }

  frontend_endpoint {
    name      = "example-frontend"
    host_name = "example.azurefd.net"
  }

  routing_rule {
    name                = "example-routing-rule"
    accepted_protocols = ["Https"]
    patterns_to_match  = ["/*"]
    frontend_endpoints = [azurerm_frontdoor.example.frontend_endpoint[0].name]
    route_configuration {
      forwarding_configuration {
        backend_pool_name = azurerm_frontdoor.example.backend_pool[0].name
      }
    }
  }
}
```

```
# Create an Azure WAF Policy
resource "azurerm_web_application_firewall_policy" "example" {
  name                = "example-waf-policy"
  resource_group_name = azurerm_resource_group.example.name
  location            = azurerm_resource_group.example.location

  custom_rules {
    name      = "BlockBadBots"
    priority  = 1
    rule_type = "MatchRule"
    match_conditions {
      match_variables {
        variable_name = "RequestHeader"
        selector      = "User-Agent"
      }
      operator     = "Contains"
      match_values = ["BadBot"]
    }
    action = "Block"
  }
}

# Link the WAF Policy to the Front Door instance
resource "azurerm_frontdoor_firewall_policy_link" "example_link" {
  frontdoor_id                        = azurerm_frontdoor.example.id
  web_application_firewall_policy_id  = azurerm_web_application_firewall_policy.
example.id
}
```

This Terraform configuration provisions an Azure Front Door with an integrated WAF policy that blocks malicious traffic, ensuring secure, low-latency content delivery with robust edge security.

Securing API Gateways with Network Controls

API gateways provide a centralized entry point for your applications, managing API requests, authentication, and rate limiting. Securing these gateways involves implementing network controls such as Web Application Firewalls (WAFs), TLS encryption, and IP whitelisting to ensure that only legitimate traffic reaches your backend services. Terraform enables you to automate the deployment and configuration of these security measures across multiple cloud providers, thereby ensuring consistency and reducing manual errors.

- **AWS API Gateway:** Enforces security policies by integrating with AWS WAF and using IAM-based authorization to control access, while also supporting TLS encryption to secure data in transit.
- **Azure API Management:** Secures APIs by applying custom firewall rules and leveraging private link access, ensuring that only authorized traffic can reach the backend, along with built-in rate limiting and monitoring capabilities.
- **GCP API Gateway:** Implements network security policies including TLS encryption and rate limiting; integrates with services such as Cloud Armor for advanced traffic filtering and protection against DDoS attacks.

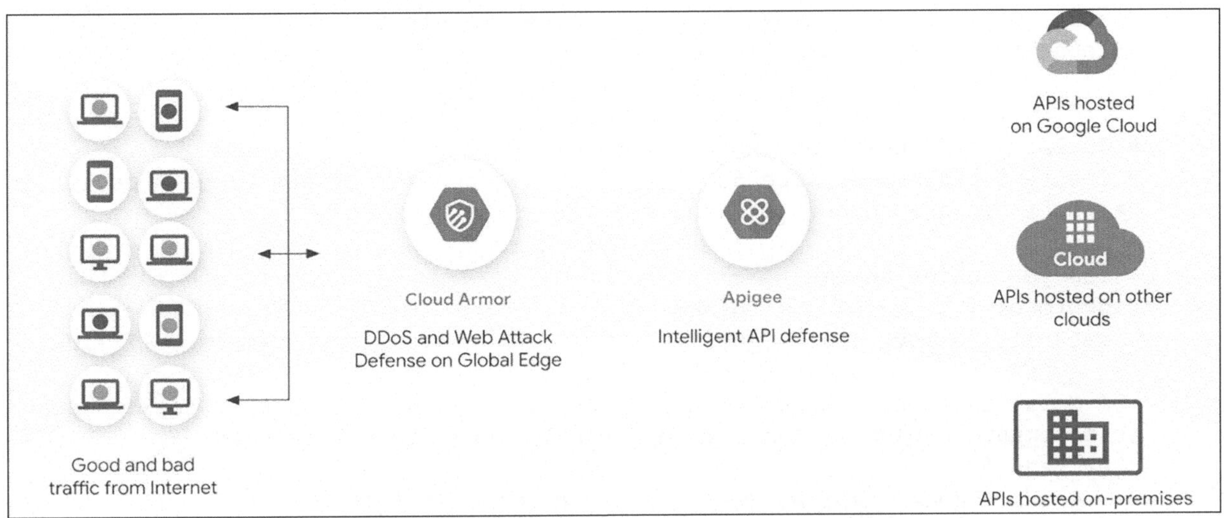

Figure 10.3: *API gateway with Network controls*

```
# 1. Security Policy (Cloud Armor)
# Create a Cloud Armor Security Policy to block malicious IPs
resource "google_compute_security_policy" "example" {
  name        = "example-api-security-policy"
  description = "Security policy to block malicious IPs from accessing the API"

  rule {
    priority = 1000
    action   = "deny(403)"
    match {
      versioned_expr = "SRC_IPS_V1"
      config {
        src_ip_ranges = ["203.0.113.0/24"]
      }
    }
  }
}

# 2. API Gateway Setup
# Create an API Gateway API
resource "google_api_gateway_api" "example" {
  api_id = "example-api"
}

# Create an API Gateway API configuration using an OpenAPI document
resource "google_api_gateway_api_config" "example" {
  api       = google_api_gateway_api.example.id
  config_id = "v1"
  openapi_documents {
    document {
      path     = "openapi.yaml"
      contents = file("openapi.yaml")
    }
  }
}

# Deploy the API Gateway in a specific region
resource "google_api_gateway_gateway" "example" {
  gateway_id = "example-gateway"
```

```
  api_config = google_api_gateway_api_config.example.id
  location   = "us-central1"
}

# 3. Backend (NEG / Cloud Run / Compute)
# Create a backend service for the load balancer and attach Cloud Armor policy
resource "google_compute_backend_service" "api_backend" {
  name                  = "example-api-backend"
  load_balancing_scheme = "EXTERNAL"
  protocol              = "HTTPS"
  security_policy       = google_compute_security_policy.example.self_link

  # Note: In a real-world scenario, you would point to a proper backend such
as a Compute Engine instance group or NEG linked to API Gateway.
  backend {
    group = google_api_gateway_gateway.example.self_link
  }
}

# 4. URL Map for Routing
# Configure a URL map to route requests to the backend service
resource "google_compute_url_map" "api_url_map" {
  name            = "example-api-url-map"
  default_service = google_compute_backend_service.api_backend.self_link
}

# 5. TLS Termination (HTTPS Proxy)
# Create a target HTTPS proxy that uses the URL map
resource "google_compute_target_https_proxy" "api_https_proxy" {
  name             = "example-api-https-proxy"
  url_map          = google_compute_url_map.api_url_map.self_link
  ssl_certificates = ["your-ssl-cert-self_link"]  # Replace with your actual
SSL certificate resource self-link
}

# Create a global forwarding rule to direct HTTPS traffic to the target proxy
resource "google_compute_global_forwarding_rule" "api_forwarding_rule" {
  name                  = "example-api-forwarding-rule"
  ip_address            = google_compute_global_address.lb_ip.address
  target                = google_compute_target_https_proxy.api_https_proxy.
self_link
  port_range            = "443"
  load_balancing_scheme = "EXTERNAL"
  ip_protocol           = "TCP"
}
```

This Terraform code configures a secure API Gateway deployment on GCP by integrating Cloud Armor WAF and a global load balancer. It sets up an API Gateway, enforces security policies to block malicious IPs, and routes traffic through an HTTPS load balancer to enhance API security, scalability, and resiliency.

Implementing Private Link for Serverless Communication

PrivateLink enables secure, private connectivity between serverless functions and VPC resources without sending traffic over the public internet. By using PrivateLink, organizations can isolate internal communications and protect sensitive data from exposure, thereby reducing the attack surface and ensuring that serverless functions such as AWS Lambda, Azure Functions, and GCP Cloud Functions communicate securely with backend services.

- **AWS PrivateLink:** Provides a secure connection by creating VPC endpoints that allow AWS Lambda functions to access VPC resources directly, without traversing the public internet.
- **Azure Private Link:** Establishes private connectivity between Azure Functions and Virtual Networks (VNets), ensuring that communications remain within the trusted network boundaries of Azure.
- **GCP Private Service Connect:** Enables secure communication between VPCs and managed services by creating private connections, allowing serverless functions to interact with these services without exposure to the public internet.

```
resource "aws_vpc_endpoint" "example" {
  vpc_id       = aws_vpc.main.id
  service_name = "com.amazonaws.vpce.us-east-1.lambda"
}
```

This Terraform snippet provisions an AWS VPC Endpoint for Lambda, enabling secure, private connectivity between serverless functions and VPC resources without public internet exposure.

Securing serverless and edge architectures requires a comprehensive approach involving private networking, WAFs, and CDNs. By automating these deployments with Terraform, organizations can build resilient and secure serverless environments that protect against evolving cyber threats.

Integrating Web Application Firewalls (WAF) for Application Security

Web Application Firewalls (WAFs) are critical for protecting cloud-hosted applications from common web exploits, such as SQL injection, Cross-Site Scripting (XSS), and Cross-Site Request Forgery (CSRF). By filtering and monitoring HTTP traffic between clients and applications, WAFs provide an essential layer of defense that complements traditional network security measures.

Integrating WAFs into cloud environments can be complex, especially when managing multiple cloud platforms. Terraform simplifies this by automating the provisioning, customization, and scaling of WAF services across AWS, Azure, and GCP. This section explores automating WAF deployments and implementing dynamic rule sets to secure applications against evolving threats.

Provisioning AWS WAF, Azure WAF, and GCP Cloud Armor

AWS WAF, Azure WAF, and GCP Cloud Armor are managed security services designed to protect web applications by filtering HTTP/S traffic and blocking malicious requests. These services enable organizations to define custom rules that identify and block traffic patterns associated with known attacks such as SQL injection, cross-site scripting, and DDoS attacks, ensuring that only legitimate traffic reaches their applications. By using Terraform, you can automate the provisioning and configuration of these WAF solutions, thereby standardizing your security controls across multiple cloud environments.

- **AWS WAF:** AWS WAF integrates with services such as AWS CloudFront, Application Load Balancer (ALB), and API Gateway to protect web applications by inspecting incoming HTTP/S requests. With AWS WAF, you can define custom rules (or use managed rule groups) to block, allow, or count web requests based on conditions such as IP addresses, HTTP headers, or query strings, thereby mitigating common web exploits and DDoS attacks.

- **Azure WAF:** Azure WAF works in conjunction with Azure Front Door, Application Gateway, and Azure CDN to safeguard web applications. It allows you to configure custom firewall rules that filter malicious traffic, enforce security policies, and provide protection against common vulnerabilities. Azure WAF is integrated with Azure's global delivery network to offer low-latency and high availability, ensuring that only trusted traffic reaches your applications.
- **GCP Cloud Armor:** GCP Cloud Armor provides protection for applications hosted behind Google Cloud HTTP/S Load Balancers. It uses predefined security policies and custom rules to filter incoming traffic based on IP address, geographic origin, and other attributes. Cloud Armor leverages Google's global network to deliver low-latency performance and defend against DDoS attacks, ensuring that web applications remain available and secure.

```
resource "aws_waf_web_acl" "example" {
  name        = "example-waf"
  metric_name = "exampleWAF"
  default_action {
    type = "ALLOW"
  }

  rule {
    name     = "SQLInjectionRule"
    priority = 1

    action {
      type = "BLOCK"
    }

    predicate {
      data_id = aws_waf_sql_injection_match_set.sql.id
      negated = false
      type    = "SQL_INJECTION_MATCH"
    }
  }
}
```

This Terraform snippet provisions an AWS WAF Web ACL that blocks SQL injection attempts by defining a rule with a specific SQL injection match predicate, ensuring that malicious requests are prevented from reaching the application.

Dynamic WAF Updates Based on Threat Feeds

Dynamic WAF rules integrate real-time threat intelligence feeds to automatically update security policies as new attack vectors emerge. This dynamic approach ensures that Web Application Firewalls (WAFs) remain current and effective against evolving threats without requiring manual intervention, thereby reducing the window of vulnerability and enhancing overall security posture.

- **AWS:** AWS WAF supports dynamic IP set updates, allowing third-party threat intelligence sources to feed updated lists of malicious IP addresses directly into WAF configurations. This integration ensures that as new threats are identified, the IP sets are automatically updated to block unwanted traffic.
- **Azure:** In Azure, integration between Azure Sentinel and Azure WAF allows for automatic rule updates. Azure Sentinel ingests threat intelligence data and, when integrated with WAF policies (for example, via Azure Front Door or Application Gateway), can trigger updates to block newly identified malicious IP addresses or patterns, keeping your defenses aligned with the latest security insights.

- **GCP:** GCP Cloud Armor supports dynamic configuration by allowing the import of external IP lists and applying geo-based restrictions. This enables administrators to dynamically update security policies to reflect current threat intelligence, ensuring that traffic from known malicious sources is blocked automatically.

```
resource "google_compute_security_policy" "example" {
  name = "dynamic-policy"

  rule {
    action   = "deny(403)"
    priority = 1000
    match {
      config {
        src_ip_ranges = ["203.0.113.0/24"]
      }
    }
  }
}
```

This Terraform snippet provisions a GCP Cloud Armor security policy that denies HTTP access (`403`) to traffic originating from a specified IP range, enabling dynamic WAF updates based on threat intelligence feeds.

Automating WAF deployment with Terraform ensures that applications are protected from common web vulnerabilities while maintaining scalability and flexibility. By integrating threat feeds, customizing rules, and positioning WAFs at critical points, organizations can significantly reduce the risk of web-based attacks.

Conclusion

Securing cloud network architectures is a critical aspect of maintaining a robust security posture in modern cloud environments. In this chapter, we have explored various strategies to design, automate, and enforce security controls using Terraform, ensuring that cloud networks remain resilient against evolving threats. From implementing secure network segmentation and zero trust principles to automating firewall rules and security groups, organizations can achieve consistency and scalability in their cloud security policies. By leveraging Terraform, engineers can provision secure connectivity for hybrid cloud environments, establish multi-region networking for high availability, and enhance application protection with Web Application Firewalls (WAF). These automated solutions not only reduce manual configurations but also help maintain compliance with security best practices across AWS, Azure, and GCP.

As cloud infrastructures continue to expand, automation-driven security becomes indispensable for managing complexity and mitigating risks. We have discussed securing serverless architectures, edge deployments, and hybrid connectivity using Terraform, ensuring a defense-in-depth approach. Additionally, integrating real-time monitoring, dynamic security updates, and threat intelligence feeds further strengthens an organization's ability to respond to security incidents proactively. By adopting Infrastructure as Code (IaC) for network security, organizations can achieve a balance between agility and protection, fostering a secure, scalable, and resilient cloud environment. The principles and techniques covered in this chapter will enable cloud engineers and security professionals to build and maintain secure cloud networks efficiently, ensuring both performance and security are optimized for modern cloud workloads.

In the next chapter, we delve into building secure CI/CD pipelines with Terraform, focusing on automating security scans, preventing secrets leakage, and integrating with GitOps workflows. It also covers secure rollbacks, deployments, and leveraging security testing tools such as Checkov, TFSec, and Terrascan.

Questions and Answers

1. **How does Terraform help in designing a secure multi-tier cloud network architecture?**

   Terraform enables the automation and enforcement of security best practices when designing a multi-tier cloud network architecture. By using Terraform, organizations can provision Virtual Private Clouds (VPCs) with distinct layers–public, private, and Demilitarized Zone (DMZ)–to enforce network segmentation. Security groups, Network ACLs, and firewall policies can be automatically configured to restrict access between tiers, ensuring that only necessary traffic flows between different parts of the infrastructure. Additionally, Terraform modules can be reused to standardize secure networking practices across multiple environments, reducing manual errors and improving scalability.

2. **What are the key differences between Security Groups, Network ACLs, and Web Application Firewalls (WAF), and how can they be automated using Terraform?**

   Security Groups and Network ACLs (NACLs) are essential for controlling inbound and outbound traffic at different layers of the network, while Web Application Firewalls (WAF) protect applications from web-based threats such as SQL injection and Cross-Site Scripting (XSS). Security Groups function as stateful firewalls at the instance level, whereas NACLs provide stateless rules for subnet-level filtering. WAFs analyze HTTP/S traffic for malicious patterns. Terraform simplifies the automation of these security mechanisms by managing security group rules, subnet NACLs, and WAF policies as code, allowing organizations to maintain consistent security configurations across AWS, Azure, and GCP with minimal manual intervention.

3. **How can Terraform help implement Zero Trust Network Access (ZTNA) in cloud environments?**

   Terraform enables Zero Trust Network Access (ZTNA) by automating network policies that enforce least-privilege access, continuous authentication, and micro-segmentation. It allows organizations to define fine-grained access control rules using AWS Security Groups, Azure Network Security Groups (NSGs), and GCP firewall policies. Terraform can also provision identity-aware proxies, VPN-less access solutions, and PrivateLink connections to restrict communication to authenticated and authorized entities only. By codifying these policies, organizations can enforce ZTNA principles at scale and maintain dynamic security controls that adapt to changing workloads and threats.

4. **How can Terraform enhance hybrid cloud security by automating VPNs and secure connectivity?**

   Terraform facilitates hybrid cloud security by automating the provisioning of VPNs and secure connectivity solutions across AWS, Azure, and GCP. It enables organizations to create AWS Site-to-Site VPNs, Azure VPNs, and GCP Cloud VPNs configurations using declarative Infrastructure-as-Code templates. By automating these network connections, Terraform ensures that data flows securely between on-premises environments and the cloud, with encryption and failover mechanisms built in. Additionally, Terraform can integrate security monitoring tools to track VPN performance, detect anomalies, and enforce compliance with corporate security policies.

5. **Why is multi-region networking crucial for cloud security, and how does Terraform help achieve it?**

   Multi-region networking enhances cloud security by improving fault tolerance, disaster recovery, and latency optimization for global applications. Terraform simplifies the deployment of multi-region VPC peering, cross-region DNS resolution, and global load balancers across

AWS, Azure, and GCP. It automates the setup of AWS Global Accelerator, Azure Front Door, and GCP Global Load Balancer, ensuring high availability and secure traffic routing between geographically distributed workloads. Additionally, Terraform can be used to test disaster recovery plans by simulating regional failovers and validating failback mechanisms, ensuring business continuity even in the face of regional outages or cyber threats.

Chapter 11
Secure CI/CD Pipelines with Terraform

Introduction

In today's fast-paced cloud environments, secure and resilient CI/CD pipelines are critical to deploying infrastructure safely and reliably. This chapter explores how to build robust, multi-cloud CI/CD pipelines using Terraform for AWS, Azure, and GCP. From designing pipelines that meet security and compliance requirements to managing IAM roles and enforcing least-privilege access, we cover key principles that help teams prevent vulnerabilities early in the deployment process. You will learn best practices for securing artifact repositories, integrating policy controls, and automating security across every stage of the pipeline. Whether you are using Jenkins, GitHub Actions, GitLab, or other CI/CD platforms, this chapter focuses on how to keep Terraform workflows locked down and audit-ready.

In addition to pipeline design and access management, this chapter dives deep into automating security scans and continuous validation. We will demonstrate how to integrate tools such as Checkov, TFSec, and Terrascan into CI/CD workflows to catch misconfigurations before they reach production. You will also learn to combine Terraform deployments with GitOps workflows for automated delivery, infrastructure drift prevention, and secure code review practices. Furthermore, this chapter addresses secret management, automated rollbacks, safe deployment strategies such as canary and blue/green patterns, and infrastructure testing using Kitchen-Terraform, Terratest, InSpec, Sentinel, and Conftest. By the end, you will be equipped to build fully automated, secure CI/CD pipelines that align with industry standards and protect cloud environments at scale.

Structure

In this chapter, we will cover the following topics:

- Building Secure CI/CD Pipelines across Providers
    - Designing Secure Multi-Cloud CI/CD Pipelines
    - Identity and Access Management for Pipelines
    - Least Privilege Access for CI/CD
    - Secure Artifact Storage and Registry Integration
- Automating Security Scans in CI/CD Workflows with Checkov, Tfsec, and Terrascan
    - Configuring Checkov for Static Analysis in Pipelines
    - Using TFSec to Detect Terraform Vulnerabilities
    - Implementing Terrascan for Compliance Enforcement
- Integrating Terraform with GitOps for Continuous Delivery
    - GitOps Workflow for Terraform Deployment

   - Role of Git Repositories in Securing Terraform
   - Automating Pull Request Reviews and Approvals
   - Preventing Drift with Automated Reconciliation
- Preventing Secrets Leakage in CI/CD Pipelines
   - Storing Secrets Securely
   - Encrypting Secrets in Environment Variables
   - Detecting and Preventing Secrets in Code Repositories
- Automating Rollbacks and Deployments Securely
   - Implementing Automated Rollbacks with Terraform State
   - Canary Deployments and Incremental Rollouts
   - Safe Infrastructure Updates with Blue/Green Deployments
   - Monitoring Deployment Failures and Triggering Rollbacks
- Security Testing Tools for Terraform Code in CI/CD
   - Security Unit Testing with Kitchen-Terraform
   - Dynamic Analysis with InSpec and Terratest
   - Continuous Validation with Sentinel and Conftest

Building Secure CI/CD Pipelines Across Providers

Continuous Integration and Continuous Deployment (CI/CD) pipelines are the backbone of modern cloud infrastructure deployments, facilitating automation, speed, and consistency in development workflows. However, as pipelines handle sensitive data, credentials, and direct access to cloud environments, securing them is paramount. Terraform plays a crucial role in designing, provisioning, and securing cloud resources across providers (AWS, Azure, GCP) by integrating Infrastructure-as-Code (IaC) with security best practices.

This section explores the design and implementation of secure CI/CD pipelines across multi-cloud environments. The goal is to ensure that infrastructure deployments are resilient, compliant, and secure at every stage from source code to production.

Designing Secure Multi-Cloud CI/CD Pipelines

A secure multi-cloud CI/CD pipeline orchestrates the entire deployment process across AWS, Azure, and GCP while enforcing strict governance, compliance, and security standards. By leveraging Terraform as a unified Infrastructure-as-Code (IaC) tool, organizations can ensure that infrastructure configurations remain consistent across different cloud providers. This approach minimizes errors, enforces best practices, and provides full auditability, allowing teams to confidently manage deployments in diverse cloud environments.

- **Terraform-driven provisioning:** CI/CD pipelines use Terraform to define, provision, and manage cloud resources. This includes the entire lifecycle of infrastructure from validation and testing to final deployment, ensuring that every change is codified and reproducible.
- **Pipeline stages:** The deployment process is divided into multiple stages:
   - **Source:** Terraform configuration files are stored in a Git repository.
   - **Validation:** Terraform configurations are validated against syntax and compliance rules.
   - **Security scanning:** Tools integrated into the pipeline scan the Terraform code for misconfigurations and vulnerabilities.

- **Infrastructure deployment:** Terraform plans are applied to provision resources across AWS, Azure, and GCP.
- **Automated rollbacks:** In case of deployment failures or security issues, pipelines can automatically rollback to the previous stable state.

- **Reproducibility and auditability:** Throughout the deployment, Terraform generates plans that are reviewed and approved, ensuring that every configuration change is traceable and auditable. This end-to-end automation enables a consistent and secure infrastructure deployment process across all targeted cloud environments.

The following are some best practices for configuring a CI/CD pipeline:

- **Pipeline isolation:** Maintain separate CI/CD pipelines for development, staging, and production environments. This segmentation reduces the blast radius in case of issues, ensuring that testing and development activities do not impact production systems.
- **Environment-specific variables:** Use Terraform workspaces or environment variables to manage configuration differences between environments. This prevents misconfigurations and ensures that each environment receives the appropriate settings, credentials, and resource parameters.
- **Immutable infrastructure:** Embrace an immutable infrastructure model by rebuilding resources from scratch with Terraform rather than modifying existing resources. This approach reduces the risk of configuration drift and ensures that deployments are predictable and consistent.
- **Tagging and labeling:** Apply consistent tags (in AWS) or labels (in GCP and Azure) to all resources. This not only improves auditability and facilitates compliance reporting but also aids in cost tracking and resource management across multi-cloud deployments.

Identity and Access Management for Pipelines

IAM controls who can execute Terraform pipelines and access cloud resources, ensuring that only authorized users and services can perform infrastructure deployments. Proper IAM configuration is essential to prevent unauthorized access and privilege escalation, thereby protecting sensitive resources and maintaining a secure cloud environment.

- **Pipeline role assumption:** Terraform pipelines are configured to assume specific IAM roles during execution. This means that instead of using personal credentials, the pipeline uses a dedicated role with the precise permissions needed for deployment.
- **Least privilege access:** By assigning the minimum necessary permissions to the roles used by the pipeline, organizations can ensure that the pipeline can only execute required tasks and nothing more, thereby minimizing the risk of exploitation.
- **Securing pipeline identities:** Different cloud providers use different mechanisms for secure pipeline identities: AWS utilizes IAM roles, Azure uses service principals, and GCP uses IAM service accounts. These identities are managed separately from personal accounts to maintain security and compliance.

```
# Define a dedicated IAM role for Terraform pipeline execution
resource "aws_iam_role" "pipeline_role" {
  name = "terraform-pipeline-role"
  assume_role_policy = jsonencode({
    Version = "2012-10-17",
    Statement = [
      {
        Action = "sts:AssumeRole",
        Effect = "Allow",
```

```
        Principal = {
          Service = "codebuild.amazonaws.com"  # Assuming the pipeline is
running in AWS CodeBuild
        }
      }
    ]
  })
}

# Attach a policy with least privilege required for the deployment
resource "aws_iam_role_policy" "pipeline_policy" {
  name   = "terraform-pipeline-policy"
  role   = aws_iam_role.pipeline_role.id
  policy = jsonencode({
    Version = "2012-10-17",
    Statement = [
      {
        Action = [
          "ec2:DescribeInstances",
          "s3:ListBucket",
          "s3:GetObject",
          "s3:PutObject",
          "kms:Decrypt"    # only if you're using KMS-encrypted state or secrets
        ],
        Effect   = "Allow",
        Resource = "*"
      }
    ]
  })
}

# Example of how the pipeline would assume the role using AWS STS (this is
typically done in your CI/CD script)
# aws sts assume-role --role-arn arn:aws:iam::<account-id>:role/terraform-pipe-
line-role --role-session-name "TerraformSession"
```

This Terraform configuration creates a dedicated AWS IAM role with a least-privilege policy for CI/CD pipeline execution, enabling secure, short-lived credential management via AWS STS for Terraform deployments.

Least Privilege Access for CI/CD

Least privilege access ensures that CI/CD pipelines, developers, and service accounts are granted only the minimum permissions necessary to perform their tasks. This principle is crucial for reducing the attack surface and limiting potential damage in case of a security breach, as it prevents unnecessary or excessive access to cloud resources.

- **Custom IAM policies and roles:** Terraform is used to create custom IAM policies and roles that are specifically tailored to the needs of your CI/CD pipeline. These policies restrict the actions that can be performed, ensuring that only required operations, such as deploying a specific resource group or updating a particular service, are allowed.
- **Granular access at the appropriate scope:** Access can be granted at the project (GCP), subscription (Azure), or account (AWS) level with fine-grained permissions. In Azure, for example, you can scope permissions to a specific resource group, ensuring that the CI/CD pipeline only interacts with resources in that group.

- **Temporary and time-bound access:** Where applicable, access should be granted for a limited duration (using short-lived credentials or temporary elevated access), which helps mitigate the risk if credentials are compromised.

```
# Define a custom Azure role for CI/CD pipelines with least privilege access
resource "azurerm_role_definition" "ci_cd_role" {
  name              = "CI/CD Pipeline Role"
  scope             = azurerm_resource_group.example.id
  description       = "Custom role for CI/CD pipeline with limited permissions
to deploy resources in a specific resource group"
  permissions {
    actions = [
      "Microsoft.Resources/subscriptions/resourceGroups/read",
      "Microsoft.Resources/deployments/*",
      "Microsoft.Compute/virtualMachines/read",
      "Microsoft.Storage/storageAccounts/read"
    ]
    not_actions = []
  }
  assignable_scopes = [
    azurerm_resource_group.example.id
  ]
}

# Assign the custom role to a CI/CD service principal (or managed identity)
resource "azurerm_role_assignment" "ci_cd_role_assignment" {
  principal_id       = data.azurerm_client_config.current.object_id
  role_definition_id = azurerm_role_definition.ci_cd_role.id
  scope              = azurerm_resource_group.example.id
}

data "azurerm_client_config" "current" {}
```

This Terraform configuration creates a custom Azure role with minimal permissions for CI/CD pipelines, scoped to a specific resource group, and assigns it to a service principal to ensure least privilege access during deployments.

Secure Artifact Storage and Registry Integration

Securing artifact storage involves protecting repositories that hold build artifacts, Terraform state files, Docker images, and other binaries, which often contain sensitive information. In multi-cloud environments, using secure storage and registry solutions such as AWS S3, Azure Blob Storage, or GCP Cloud Storage ensures that these artifacts are encrypted, access-controlled, and auditable. With Terraform, you can automate the provisioning of these repositories, enforce encryption at rest and in transit, and implement state locking mechanisms to prevent concurrent modifications that could corrupt infrastructure. This approach minimizes unauthorized access, maintains artifact integrity, and ensures a robust disaster recovery process by keeping versioned, immutable backups.

- **Encrypted storage:** Artifacts are stored in cloud storage buckets configured with server-side encryption using services such as AWS KMS, Azure Key Vault, or GCP CMEK, ensuring data protection at rest.
- **Access controls:** Access to artifact repositories is restricted using IAM policies, bucket policies, or Access Control Lists (ACLs). Audit logs capture every interaction, providing a detailed record of who accessed what and when.

- **State locking:** Terraform state locking mechanisms, such as using DynamoDB for AWS, Blob Locks for Azure, or native GCS bucket locking for GCP, prevent simultaneous modifications that could lead to state corruption.
- **Immutable and versioned artifacts:** Storing versioned artifacts ensures that each update is recorded, enabling safe rollbacks in case of deployment failures or security incidents. This practice also supports compliance requirements by preserving historical data for audits.

```
# Create a Key Ring for artifact encryption
resource "google_kms_key_ring" "artifact_key_ring" {
  name     = "artifact-key-ring"
  location = "us"
}

# Create a Crypto Key for encrypting stored artifacts
resource "google_kms_crypto_key" "artifacts_key" {
  name     = "artifacts-key"
  key_ring = google_kms_key_ring.artifact_key_ring.id
  purpose  = "ENCRYPT_DECRYPT"
}

# Provision a GCP Storage Bucket with encryption, versioning, and lifecycle
rules
resource "google_storage_bucket" "artifact_bucket" {
  name          = "my-artifact-bucket-12345"
  location      = "US"
  force_destroy = true        # This attribute is not recommended for prod

  uniform_bucket_level_access = true

  versioning {
    enabled = true
  }

  encryption {
    default_kms_key_name = google_kms_crypto_key.artifacts_key.id
  }

  lifecycle_rule {
    action {
      type = "Delete"
    }
    condition {
      age = 365
    }
  }
}
```

This Terraform configuration provisions a GCP Cloud Storage bucket for secure artifact storage with server-side encryption using a customer-managed KMS key, versioning enabled for immutable backups, and lifecycle rules for automated retention management.

Building secure CI/CD pipelines with Terraform across AWS, Azure, and GCP environments is essential for protecting cloud infrastructure. By following best practices in identity management, least privilege access, artifact security, and multi-cloud designs, organizations can ensure that their CI/CD pipelines are resilient to attacks and compliant with security policies. Terraform's automation capabilities streamline pipeline provisioning, reducing the risk of human error and enforcing consistent security across environments.

Automating Security Scans in CI/CD Workflows with Checkov, TFSec, and Terrascan

Security misconfigurations in Terraform code can introduce vulnerabilities into cloud environments. By integrating automated scanning tools into CI/CD pipelines, organizations can proactively identify issues before deployment, ensuring infrastructure is compliant with security best practices.

Checkov, TFSec, and Terrascan are three leading open-source tools designed to perform static and dynamic analysis of Terraform code. They detect vulnerabilities, enforce Policy-as-Code (PaC), and provide remediation suggestions, automating the security layer within pipelines across AWS, Azure, and GCP.

This section explores how to integrate these tools into CI/CD pipelines, ensuring that Terraform configurations are continuously assessed for security misconfigurations, compliance violations, and policy drift.

Configuring Checkov for Static Analysis in Pipelines

Checkov is a powerful static code analysis tool developed by Bridgecrew (now part of Palo Alto Networks) that scans Terraform and other IaC files for misconfigurations and security vulnerabilities. It supports multiple cloud environments, including AWS, Azure, GCP, and Kubernetes, and evaluates configurations against established compliance frameworks such as CIS, NIST, and PCI-DSS. This proactive scanning process helps ensure that only secure and compliant infrastructure is deployed.

- **Static analysis:** Checkov examines Terraform files (`.tf`), HCL files (`.tf.json` and `.tfplan`), and even state files (`terraform.tfstate`) to identify security misconfigurations before deployment, catching issues such as overly permissive IAM policies or missing encryption settings.
- **Custom policies:** Users can extend Checkov's capabilities by writing custom policies in Python. This allows organizations to enforce internal security requirements tailored to their specific needs in addition to standard compliance checks.
- **Pipeline integration:** Checkov seamlessly integrates with CI/CD pipelines (for example, Jenkins, GitHub Actions, GitLab CI, Azure DevOps), enabling automated security scans during code commits and pull requests. This ensures that any vulnerabilities or compliance issues are detected and remediated early in the development lifecycle.

```
name: Terraform Security Scan
on: push
jobs:
  terraform-checkov:
    runs-on: ubuntu-latest
    steps:
- name: Install Checkov (alternative)
  run: pip install checkov

      - name: Checkout Code
        uses: actions/checkout@v2

      - name: Run Checkov
        uses: bridgecrewio/checkov-action@v12
        with:
```

```
            directory: ./terraform
            framework: terraform
            soft_fail: false
```

This GitHub Actions workflow integrates Checkov into a Terraform CI/CD pipeline to automatically scan Terraform configurations for security and compliance issues, failing the build if vulnerabilities are found.

Using TFSec to Detect Terraform Vulnerabilities

TFSec is an open-source static analysis tool developed by Aqua Security that scans Terraform configuration files to detect security vulnerabilities and misconfigurations. It is designed to be lightweight and fast, making it an ideal choice for DevOps teams who need to integrate security into their CI/CD pipelines without adding significant overhead. TFSec helps ensure that Terraform code adheres to cloud-native best practices across AWS, Azure, and GCP, reducing the risk of deploying insecure infrastructure.

- **Real-time scanning:** TFSec is executed as part of the build process in CI/CD pipelines. It scans Terraform (`.tf`) files for potential vulnerabilities such as overly permissive security groups, public storage buckets, and incorrect or excessive IAM configurations. This early detection allows teams to address issues before resources are deployed into production.
- **Output formats:** TFSec generates scan results in various formats, including JSON, JUnit, and SARIF. These output formats enable seamless integration with security dashboards and automated tools, providing clear, actionable insights that can be incorporated into broader security monitoring and compliance workflows.
- **Terraform provider support:** TFSec supports multiple cloud providers, including AWS, Azure, and GCP, by leveraging rules that align with each provider's best practices. This ensures that regardless of the cloud platform, Terraform configurations are analyzed for vulnerabilities relevant to that environment, leading to a more robust and secure infrastructure.

```
stages:
  - tfsec

tfsec:
  image: aquasec/tfsec
  script:
    - tfsec ./terraform
  allow_failure: false
```

This GitLab CI configuration runs TFSec within a Docker container to scan Terraform code in real-time for security vulnerabilities, ensuring that any detected issues block the pipeline and prevent insecure deployments.

Implementing Terrascan for Compliance Enforcement

Terrascan is a static analysis tool that enforces security and compliance policies on Terraform configurations. Unlike other tools such as Checkov and TFSec, Terrascan places a strong emphasis on compliance-as-code, ensuring that your infrastructure meets regulatory standards such as GDPR, HIPAA, and SOC 2. By integrating Terrascan into your Terraform workflows, you can automatically validate that your infrastructure definitions adhere to best practices and regulatory requirements before they are deployed.

- **Policy engine:** Terrascan leverages the Open Policy Agent (OPA) to evaluate your Terraform code against over 500 built-in policies. This comprehensive policy engine ensures that any insecure configurations or non-compliant settings are identified early in the deployment process.

- **Multi-cloud support:** Terrascan supports multiple cloud providers, including AWS, Azure, and GCP. This enables you to scan your Terraform configurations for security vulnerabilities and compliance issues across diverse cloud environments, ensuring a unified compliance posture regardless of the underlying provider.
- **Deployment flexibility:** Terrascan is highly flexible in how it can be deployed. It can be run as a standalone CLI tool, containerized service, or integrated directly into CI/CD pipelines. This adaptability makes it easy to incorporate into your existing automation workflows, ensuring continuous compliance enforcement throughout the development lifecycle.

```
pipeline {
    agent any
    stages {
        stage('Terrascan') {
            steps {
                sh 'terrascan scan -i terraform --non-recursive'
            }
        }
    }
}
```

This Jenkins pipeline stage runs Terrascan to scan Terraform configurations for security and compliance issues, ensuring that your infrastructure meets regulatory standards before deployment.

Automating security scans in CI/CD pipelines using Checkov, TFSec, and Terrascan ensures Terraform configurations are secure and compliant before deployment. By catching misconfigurations early, organizations minimize cloud vulnerabilities and strengthen their security posture across AWS, Azure, and GCP environments. Integrating these tools fosters a proactive security culture, aligning with DevSecOps principles.

Integrating Terraform with GitOps for Continuous Delivery

GitOps extends DevOps principles by leveraging Git as the single source of truth for declarative infrastructure and application management. In the context of Terraform, GitOps automates infrastructure deployment by synchronizing Terraform code stored in Git repositories with cloud environments, ensuring consistent and secure infrastructure provisioning.

This section explores how GitOps workflows can be integrated with Terraform to automate deployments, maintain compliance, and prevent drift across AWS, Azure, and GCP. By aligning infrastructure deployments with Git-based workflows, teams achieve improved traceability, auditability, and rollback capabilities.

GitOps Workflow for Terraform Deployment

A GitOps workflow for Terraform deployment leverages Git as the single source of truth for your Infrastructure-as-Code (IaC) and uses automated pipelines to deploy changes reliably across environments. In this approach, all Terraform configurations are stored in a Git repository where every commit and pull request represents a potential change to your infrastructure. These changes trigger CI/CD pipelines that automatically run Terraform commands such as terraform plan and terraform apply to provision or update cloud resources. The Git repository not only serves as a version-controlled record of your desired state but also enables rollback and auditing, ensuring that any change is transparent and reproducible.

- **Code repository as single source of truth:** All Terraform configurations are stored in Git, which acts as the canonical record of your infrastructure state. Every change to the infrastructure is made through code commits and pull requests, ensuring that all modifications are versioned and reviewable.

- **Automated CI/CD pipelines:** When changes are committed to the repository, automation tools (for example, Jenkins, GitHub Actions, GitLab CI, or Azure DevOps) are triggered to execute the Terraform workflow. The pipeline typically performs the following steps:
    - **Validation:** Linting and syntax checks are executed to ensure that the Terraform code adheres to best practices.
    - **Terraform Plan:** The pipeline runs a terraform plan to generate an execution plan that details the proposed changes, which can be reviewed and approved by team members.
    - **Terraform Apply:** Once the changes are approved, terraform apply is executed to implement the changes in the cloud environment.
    - **State Management:** The Terraform state is stored in a secure backend (for example, AWS S3 with DynamoDB state locking, Azure Blob Storage, or GCP Cloud Storage) to ensure consistency and prevent conflicts.
- **Continuous monitoring and auditing:** The GitOps workflow supports continuous monitoring of deployments through automated logging and auditing. Changes to the infrastructure are fully traceable through the Git history, and any deviation from the desired state can be detected and automatically rolled back if necessary.

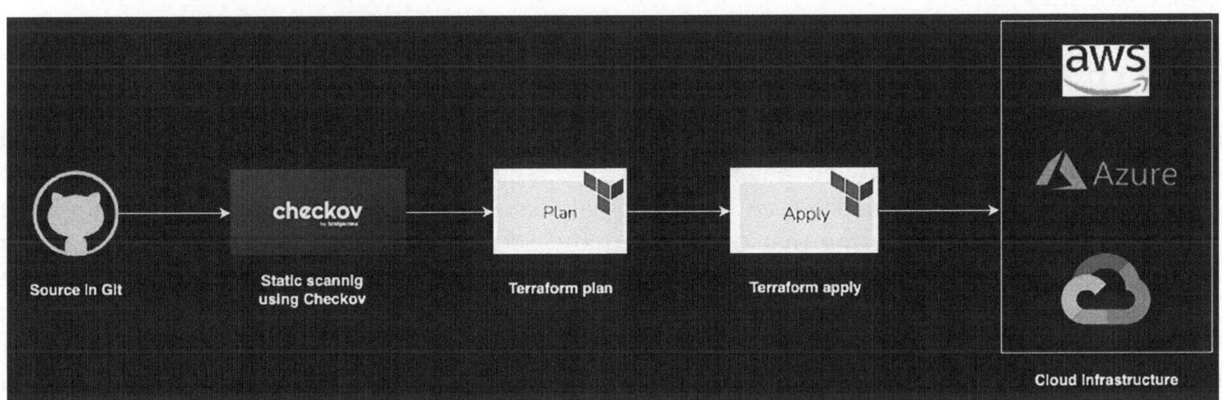

Figure 11.1: *Pipeline for Terraform deployment*

```
jobs:
  terraform:
    runs-on: ubuntu-latest
    environment: production
    permissions:
      id-token: write
      contents: read
    steps:
      - name: Checkout Repository
        uses: actions/checkout@v3

      - name: Configure AWS Credentials
        uses: aws-actions/configure-aws-credentials@v2
        with:
          role-to-assume: arn:aws:iam::<ACCOUNT_ID>:role/<GitHubActionsRole>
          aws-region: us-east-1

      - name: Setup Terraform
        uses: hashicorp/setup-terraform@v2
```

```
      with:
        terraform_version: "1.5.0"

    - name: Terraform Init
      run: terraform init -input=false

    - name: Run Checkov Scan
      uses: bridgecrewio/checkov-action@v12
      with:
        directory: ./terraform
        framework: terraform
        soft_fail: false  # set to true in dev to avoid failing build

    - name: Terraform Plan
      run: terraform plan -input=false -out=tfplan

    - name: Terraform Apply
      if: github.ref == 'refs/heads/main'
      run: terraform apply -input=false -auto-approve tfplan
```

This GitHub Actions pipeline deploys AWS infrastructure using Terraform by assuming an IAM role via GitHub's OIDC integration, eliminating the need for static credentials and ensuring secure, role-based authentication.

Role of Git Repositories in Securing Terraform

Git repositories serve as the backbone for securing Terraform workflows by providing a structured, auditable, and version-controlled environment for managing infrastructure code. By enforcing GitOps practices, every infrastructure change must first be committed, reviewed, and approved through the repository, ensuring that only vetted and secure code is applied to the environment. Access controls, such as branch protection and role-based permissions, further restrict who can modify the code, while mandatory pull request reviews and automated security scans help catch potential vulnerabilities before they are merged. This rigorous process creates a comprehensive audit trail, allowing organizations to track every change, roll back problematic updates, and maintain a high standard of security across all deployments.

- **Commit-based changes:** Infrastructure changes are made via commits to the Git repository, which trigger automated pipelines to validate and deploy the updates. This ensures that every modification is recorded, versioned, and can be reviewed for security and compliance.
- **Access controls:** Repository access is tightly controlled using branch protection rules and role-based permissions, so only authorized users can merge changes into critical branches, reducing the risk of unauthorized modifications.
- **Code review policies:** Mandatory pull request reviews and automated security scans are enforced to ensure that any new code adheres to security best practices before being merged into the main branch.
- **Audit trail:** Every change is fully traceable through Git history, providing an immutable record of all modifications. This audit trail is crucial for compliance, debugging, and continuous improvement of security practices.

Automating Pull Request Reviews and Approvals

Automating Pull Request (PR) reviews in a Terraform workflow ensures that every change to infrastructure code undergoes thorough examination before being merged into the main branch. This process reduces the risk of introducing insecure configurations by integrating mandatory reviews, policy checks, and automated security scans. By embedding these controls into the GitOps workflow, organizations enhance collaboration, enforce security best practices, and maintain a strict audit trail of all infrastructure changes.

- **Automated PR checks:** When a PR is opened, automated tools such as Checkov, TFSec, and Terrascan are triggered to perform static security scans on the Terraform code. These scans check for misconfigurations, vulnerabilities, and deviations from compliance standards, ensuring that potential security issues are identified early.
- **Approval gates:** Before merging, the PR must pass through mandatory approval gates. Multiple reviewers must assess and approve the changes, ensuring that any critical modifications have been vetted for security and operational impact. This peer-review process acts as a safeguard against inadvertent misconfigurations and reinforces the principle of least privilege.
- **CI Pipelines:** CI/CD pipelines are integrated with the PR process so that Terraform commands (such as **`terraform init`** and **`terraform plan`**) are automatically executed as part of the review. This validation step ensures that the proposed changes are not only syntactically correct but also align with the desired state of the infrastructure, thereby catching potential errors before deployment.

```
name: Terraform Plan
on:
  pull_request:
    branches:
      - main
jobs:
  terraform:
    runs-on: ubuntu-latest
    steps:
      - uses: actions/checkout@v2
      - run: terraform init
      - run: terraform plan
```

This GitHub Actions workflow triggers on pull requests to the main branch, checking out the code, initializing Terraform, and running a Terraform plan to validate infrastructure changes before they are merged.

Preventing Drift with Automated Reconciliation

Infrastructure drift occurs when the actual state of cloud resources diverges from the intended configuration stored in Git repositories. This divergence can result from manual changes, configuration errors, or external factors, leading to environments that are no longer compliant with the defined Infrastructure-as-Code (IaC). A GitOps approach prevents drift by continuously enforcing reconciliation loops, which automatically detect and correct deviations, ensuring that the live environment consistently reflects the desired state defined in code.

- **Continuous monitoring:** GitOps agents and monitoring tools constantly observe the live cloud environment, comparing the current state of resources with the desired state as specified in the Git repository. This ongoing surveillance promptly detects any differences, whether intentional or accidental.
- **Auto-healing:** When drift is detected, automated reconciliation processes are triggered. These processes typically invoke Terraform commands (such as **`terraform apply`**) to restore the environment to its desired state. This auto-healing mechanism ensures that any deviation from the prescribed configuration is corrected quickly, reducing downtime and preventing security or compliance issues.
- **Manual overrides:** Despite the benefits of automation, there are scenarios where teams need to intervene manually. For critical incidents or planned maintenance, auto-reconciliation

can be paused or overridden to allow for controlled changes without triggering the automated correction process. This flexibility ensures that while automation maintains consistency, human judgment can be applied when necessary.

Integrating Terraform with GitOps enhances infrastructure security, automation, and compliance by leveraging Git as the single source of truth. By automating pull requests, enforcing Git controls, and continuously reconciling environments, organizations secure infrastructure deployments across AWS, Azure, and GCP. This GitOps-driven approach reduces manual errors, mitigates drift, and accelerates secure infrastructure delivery.

Preventing Secrets Leakage in CI/CD Pipelines

Securing secrets is crucial to protecting sensitive data, including API keys, database passwords, and encryption credentials, in Terraform-based CI/CD pipelines. Mismanaged secrets are a common attack vector, often leading to unauthorized access and compromised environments.

This section explores secret management strategies using tools such as HashiCorp Vault, AWS Secrets Manager, and cloud-native services. We will discuss best practices for encrypting secrets, scanning repositories for accidental leakage, and dynamically generating ephemeral secrets to minimize exposure risk.

Storing Secrets Securely

Storing secrets securely means protecting sensitive information such as API keys, database credentials, and certificates from unauthorized access. Secret management tools such as HashiCorp Vault, AWS Secrets Manager, Azure Key Vault, and GCP Secret Manager provide dedicated, encrypted storage solutions, granular access controls, and audit logging. These tools ensure that sensitive data remains secure throughout its lifecycle, from storage to dynamic retrieval during deployments. Terraform integrates with these services, enabling you to manage secrets as code and retrieve them securely at runtime, thereby minimizing the risk of exposing credentials in source code or version control systems.

- **HashiCorp Vault:** Vault stores secrets securely and can dynamically generate credentials with a limited lifespan, ensuring that even if a credential is compromised, its exposure is minimized. Terraform can be configured to query Vault at runtime, fetching the latest secure values without embedding them directly in the code.
- **AWS Secrets Manager:** AWS Secrets Manager encrypts sensitive data at rest using AWS KMS and supports automatic credential rotation, which ensures that secrets remain up-to-date. Terraform provisions secrets in AWS Secrets Manager and manages secret versions, making them available to pipelines and applications without hardcoding.
- **Azure Key Vault and GCP Secret Manager:** Both services provide similar functionality to AWS Secrets Manager by encrypting secrets using cloud-native key management systems, enforcing access control through IAM (Azure RBAC for Key Vault and GCP IAM for Secret Manager), and enabling secure retrieval of secrets during deployments. Terraform can integrate with these services to automate secret storage and dynamic retrieval securely.

```
resource "aws_secretsmanager_secret" "db_password" {
  name = "db_password"
}

resource "random_password" "db_secret" {
  length  = 16
  special = true
}
```

```
resource "aws_secretsmanager_secret_version" "db_password_value" {
  secret_id     = aws_secretsmanager_secret.db_password.id
  secret_string = jsonencode({
    username = "admin"
    password = random_password.db_secret.result
  })
}
```

This Terraform configuration creates an AWS Secrets Manager secret named **"db_password"** and uses a randomly generated 16-character password for the **"admin"** user, ensuring secure and dynamic credential management.

Encrypting Secrets in Environment Variables

CI/CD pipelines require sensitive data, such as passwords and API keys, to be passed as environment variables during deployment. Encrypting these variables ensures that such secrets are not exposed in plaintext during execution, reducing the risk of unauthorized access or accidental leakage.

- **Key Management Service (KMS):** Cloud providers such as AWS KMS, Azure Key Vault, and GCP KMS are used to encrypt secrets. These services securely encrypt sensitive data before it is injected into environment variables, ensuring that even if intercepted, the data remains protected.
- **Secrets as environment variables:** When the CI/CD pipeline runs, the encrypted secrets are decrypted at runtime and then injected into the environment variables for the application or service. This allows secure use of sensitive data without storing it in plaintext in code or configuration files.
- **Terraform Integration:** Terraform can seamlessly retrieve these encrypted secrets from a secret management service and inject them into deployment environments. By using Terraform data sources and resource configurations, you can automate the secure transfer of sensitive data, ensuring that your applications always receive the correct credentials at runtime.

```
data "azurerm_key_vault_secret" "app_password" {
  name         = "app-password"
  key_vault_id = azurerm_key_vault.example.id
}

resource "azurerm_app_service" "example" {
  name                = "example-app-service"
  location            = azurerm_resource_group.example.location
  resource_group_name = azurerm_resource_group.example.name
  app_settings = {
    "APP_PASSWORD" = data.azurerm_key_vault_secret.app_password.value
  }
}
```

This Terraform configuration retrieves an encrypted secret from Azure Key Vault and securely injects it as an environment variable into an Azure App Service, ensuring that the sensitive data remains protected during deployment.

Detecting and Preventing Secrets in Code Repositories

Detecting secrets in code repositories involves actively scanning your version-controlled code to identify and prevent the accidental exposure of sensitive data, such as API keys, passwords, and tokens. This practice is critical for maintaining security and compliance, as misconfigured pipelines or public repositories may inadvertently reveal secrets. Tools such as GitLeaks and TruffleHog are used to scan repositories for hard-coded secrets and alert teams to potential risks before they lead to breaches.

- **Scanning pipelines:** During the CI/CD process, tools such as GitLeaks and TruffleHog are executed to scan the codebase for sensitive information. This automated check ensures that any hardcoded secrets are detected before the code is merged or deployed.
- **Pre-commit hooks:** These tools can also be configured as pre-commit hooks to prevent commits that contain sensitive data. This proactive measure blocks potential leaks by ensuring that secrets are not even pushed to the repository.
- **Continuous monitoring:** Periodic scans of the repository help maintain security over time, ensuring that even if secrets are accidentally committed later, they are quickly identified and remediated. This continuous vigilance is key to preventing long-term exposure of sensitive data.

```
name: Secret Scan
on: pull_request

jobs:
  secret_scan:
    runs-on: ubuntu-latest
    steps:
      - uses: actions/checkout@v2
      - uses: zricethezav/gitleaks-action@v1
        with:
          config-path: .gitleaks.toml
```

This GitHub Actions workflow triggers a secret scan using Gitleaks on every pull request to detect and prevent the accidental commit of sensitive information in Terraform code repositories.

Preventing secrets leakage in CI/CD pipelines is essential for maintaining cloud security. By leveraging tools such as Vault, AWS Secrets Manager, and GitLeaks, teams can automate secret storage, encrypt sensitive data, and detect accidental exposures. This comprehensive approach reduces the risk of breaches and enhances the overall security posture of Terraform-based CI/CD pipelines.

Automating Rollbacks and Deployments Securely

In modern CI/CD pipelines, ensuring that infrastructure changes can be deployed safely and reverted quickly in case of failure is a cornerstone of cloud security. Automated rollback strategies minimize downtime and mitigate the risks of misconfigurations or accidental deployments. Terraform's robust state management, coupled with deployment patterns such as blue/green and canary releases, ensures secure and predictable infrastructure updates.

This section explores various rollback mechanisms and deployment strategies that leverage Terraform to create resilient, fault-tolerant infrastructure across AWS, GCP, and Azure.

Implementing Automated Rollbacks with Terraform State

Terraform state files record the current configuration of your deployed infrastructure. By leveraging state versioning, you can revert your environment to a previously known good state when errors or misconfigurations occur. This rollback capability is critical for maintaining stability and quickly recovering from unintended changes in production environments.

- **State Snapshots:** Each time you run `terraform apply`, Terraform automatically generates or updates a state file that captures a snapshot of your deployed infrastructure. These snapshots serve as a historical record of your infrastructure configuration, allowing you to see how your environment has evolved over time.

- **Rollback by state restoration:** If a deployment introduces an error or misconfiguration, you can restore your infrastructure to a previous state by pulling an older version of the state file and running terraform apply with that state. This rollback process essentially reverts your infrastructure to match the configuration described in the older state snapshot.
- **Remote state management:** Storing Terraform state files in remote backends (such as AWS S3, Azure Blob Storage, or GCP Cloud Storage) enables secure, centralized storage with built-in versioning and state locking. State locking, for instance, using AWS DynamoDB, prevents concurrent modifications that could lead to state corruption, while version history allows you to track and revert changes when necessary.

```
terraform {
  backend "s3" {
    bucket         = "terraform-state-bucket"
    key            = "prod/terraform.tfstate"
    region         = "us-east-1"
    dynamodb_table = "terraform-lock"
  }
}
```

Rollback process

- Use the **`terraform state pull`** command to retrieve the current state file and save it as a backup, or manually select a previous version from your remote backend.

```
terraform state pull > state-backup.tfstate
```

- Apply the older state file using **`terraform apply`** to restore your infrastructure to its previous state.

```
terraform apply state-backup.tfstate
```

This Terraform configuration sets up an AWS S3 backend with state locking for secure, version-controlled state management, enabling automated rollbacks by restoring previous state snapshots when necessary.

Canary Deployments and Incremental Rollouts

Canary deployments involve gradually introducing infrastructure changes to a small subset of your environment, serving as an early test (the canary) before a full-scale rollout. This approach minimizes the blast radius in case of failures, allowing teams to monitor performance and detect issues early. With Terraform, you can automate and manage these deployments using modularized code, making it easier to isolate canary environments and incrementally scale changes based on feedback and performance metrics.

- **Incremental updates:** Deploy changes to a small, isolated canary environment first, typically by provisioning a minimal number of instances or resources. This controlled deployment helps validate new configurations before applying them across the entire environment.
- **Traffic shifting:** Use techniques such as load balancers or routing rules to direct only a small percentage of traffic to the canary deployment. This gradual traffic shift minimizes the risk of widespread disruption while allowing you to observe the performance of the new infrastructure.
- **Terraform modularization:** Leverage Terraform modules to encapsulate the configuration of the canary environment. By deploying these modules separately from the main production

stack, you can adjust parameters such as **`target_size`** or resource configurations incrementally as you scale up the deployment.

```
resource "google_compute_instance_group" "canary_group" {
  name        = "canary-group"
  zone        = "us-central1-a"
  target_size = 1
}
```

This Terraform snippet provisions a GCP instance group for a canary deployment, initially scaling to one instance to enable incremental rollouts and gradual traffic shifting for safe, controlled infrastructure updates.

Safe Infrastructure Updates with Blue/Green Deployments

Blue/green deployment is a strategy that minimizes downtime and reduces risk by running two identical production environments, one active (blue) and one idle (green). New application versions are deployed to the idle (green) environment, which is then thoroughly tested. Once the green environment is verified as stable, traffic is seamlessly switched over from blue to green, making the green environment the new production. If any issues arise, traffic can be quickly reverted to the blue environment, ensuring minimal disruption.

- **Dual environments:** Two identical environments (blue and green) are maintained, where the blue environment represents the current production setup, and the green environment is used for staging new releases.
- **Deployment and validation:** Terraform provisions the new version of your application in the green environment. Comprehensive testing, either automated or manual, is performed to validate that the new release meets all quality and security requirements.
- **Traffic switching:** Once validated, a traffic manager such as AWS Route 53 with weighted or latency-based routing, GCP Cloud Load Balancing, or Azure Traffic Manager is used to reroute user traffic from the blue environment to the green environment. This ensures that users are seamlessly served by the new environment with minimal downtime, regardless of the cloud provider.
- **Rollback capability:** If any issues are detected post-deployment, the traffic can be quickly redirected back to the blue environment, ensuring a swift rollback to the stable configuration.
- **Terraform modularization:** Terraform modules can be used to create and manage both environments and the associated traffic management configurations, ensuring consistency, repeatability, and ease of rollback across deployments.

```
# Provision an App Service Plan
resource "azurerm_app_service_plan" "example" {
  name                = "example-app-service-plan"
  location            = azurerm_resource_group.example.location
  resource_group_name = azurerm_resource_group.example.name
  sku {
    tier = "Standard"
    size = "S1"
  }
}

# Create the Production App Service (Blue Environment)
resource "azurerm_app_service" "blue" {
```

```
  name                = "example-app-blue"
  location            = azurerm_resource_group.example.location
  resource_group_name = azurerm_resource_group.example.name
  app_service_plan_id = azurerm_app_service_plan.example.id

  app_settings = {
    "WEBSITE_RUN_FROM_PACKAGE" = "https://example.com/blue.zip"
  }
}

# Create a Deployment Slot for the Green Environment
resource "azurerm_app_service_slot" "green" {
  name                = "green"
  app_service_name    = azurerm_app_service.blue.name
  resource_group_name = azurerm_app_service.blue.resource_group_name
  app_service_plan_id = azurerm_app_service_plan.example.id

  app_settings = {
    "WEBSITE_RUN_FROM_PACKAGE" = "https://example.com/green.zip"
  }
}

# Perform slot swap: green becomes production
resource "azurerm_app_service_slot_swap" "swap" {
  app_service_name    = azurerm_app_service.blue.name
  resource_group_name = azurerm_app_service.blue.resource_group_name
  source_slot_name    = "green"
  target_slot_name    = "production"
}
```

This Terraform configuration sets up a blue/green deployment in Azure by provisioning a production App Service (blue) and a deployment slot (green) for testing new application versions, enabling seamless traffic switching and rollback for high-availability deployments.

Monitoring Deployment Failures and Triggering Rollbacks

Monitoring deployment health is critical to ensuring that infrastructure remains stable and performant. In a Terraform-driven workflow, continuous monitoring of deployed resources helps detect failures such as high CPU utilization, misconfigurations, or performance degradations that may require a rollback to a previously known good state. By integrating Terraform with monitoring tools such as AWS CloudWatch, Prometheus, and Azure Monitor, automated alerts can be generated to trigger remediation actions such as rolling back a deployment, thereby minimizing downtime and ensuring system reliability.

- **Health checks:** Terraform allows you to define health checks that continuously validate the status of your resources after deployment. These checks can monitor metrics such as CPU utilization, memory usage, and application response times to determine whether the deployed resources are functioning as expected.
- **Alerting:** When a monitored metric crosses a defined threshold, monitoring tools (for example, AWS CloudWatch) trigger alerts. These alerts can notify teams via various channels or trigger automated remediation actions. For example, if an alarm detects that CPU utilization is unusually high, it may indicate an overloaded or misconfigured resource.
- **Rollback triggers:** Automated rollback mechanisms can be integrated into the pipeline. When an alert is triggered, it can automatically execute actions such as terraform destroy

or reapply a stable version of the infrastructure state, ensuring that the environment is promptly reverted to a known good configuration.

```
resource "aws_cloudwatch_metric_alarm" "rollback_alarm" {
  alarm_name          = "rollback-on-error"
  comparison_operator = "GreaterThanThreshold"
  evaluation_periods  = 1
  metric_name         = "CPUUtilization"
  namespace           = "AWS/EC2"
  period              = 60
  statistic           = "Average"
  threshold           = 90
  alarm_actions       = [aws_autoscaling_policy.rollback.arn]
}
```

This Terraform snippet creates an AWS CloudWatch alarm that monitors EC2 CPU utilization and triggers an Auto Scaling rollback action if the average CPU usage exceeds 90%, ensuring that deployment failures are detected and remedial actions are automatically initiated.

Automating rollbacks and secure deployments is essential for reducing the risk of outages, ensuring resilient infrastructure, and maintaining security. By leveraging Terraform state for rollbacks, implementing canary and blue/green deployment patterns, and integrating real-time monitoring, teams can confidently deploy cloud infrastructure with minimal disruption. These strategies provide robust mechanisms to revert misconfigurations and deliver fault-tolerant environments across AWS, Azure, and GCP.

Security Testing Tools for Terraform Code in CI/CD

Security testing is a critical aspect of deploying Terraform-based infrastructure through CI/CD pipelines. By integrating automated security testing tools directly into the pipeline, organizations can detect vulnerabilities, misconfigurations, and policy violations early in the deployment cycle. This proactive approach ensures that infrastructure adheres to compliance standards and security best practices across cloud providers such as AWS, GCP, and Azure.

This section delves into essential tools that help enforce security through unit testing, policy validation, and dynamic analysis. Each tool serves a distinct purpose in securing Terraform code from development to production.

Security Unit Testing with Kitchen-Terraform

Kitchen-Terraform is an integration testing framework that enables security unit testing of Terraform configurations by spinning up real cloud resources in isolated, temporary environments. It adopts a test-kitchen approach to provision, validate, and then tear down infrastructure, ensuring that the deployed configurations meet security and compliance standards without impacting production.

- **Test workflow:** Kitchen-Terraform provisions cloud resources based on your Terraform code, runs tests using InSpec (or other testing frameworks) to validate security configurations (for example, ensuring encryption, proper IAM roles, secure network settings), and finally tears down the temporary environment once tests complete.
- **Isolated testing:** Tests are run in temporary environments, isolating them from production, which minimizes the risk of unintended modifications or security breaches during the testing process.

- **Repeatable tests:** All tests are defined as code, ensuring that every deployment is consistently validated against a fixed set of security requirements, making it easier to catch regressions or misconfigurations over time.

The following is an example configuration for using Kitchen-Terraform to test an AWS infrastructure module, such as an S3 bucket with security configurations:

```
# .kitchen.yml
driver:
  name: terraform
  state_file: "terraform.tfstate"

provisioner:
  name: terraform
  variable_files:
    - terraform.tfvars

verifier:
  name: inspec

platforms:
  - name: aws

suites:
  - name: default
    verifier:
      inspec_tests:
        - test/integration/default

# test/integration/default/default_test.rb
describe aws_s3_bucket(bucket_name: 'example-bucket') do
  it { should exist }
  its('public_access_block') { should cmp true }
end
```

The following is the explanation of the aforementioned code snippet:

- **`.kitchen.yml` configuration:**
  - **Driver:** Uses the terraform driver to manage the Terraform state file.
  - **Provisioner:** The terraform provisioner deploys infrastructure using variables from `terraform.tfvars`.
  - **Verifier:** Configured to use InSpec to run tests defined in the test/integration/default directory.
  - **Platforms and suites:** The configuration targets AWS and defines a test suite named `"default"` that will verify the deployed infrastructure.
- **InSpec test (`default_test.rb`):** This test checks that an S3 bucket named `"example-bucket"` exists and that its public access block is enabled, ensuring that the bucket is secured against public exposure.

Dynamic Analysis with InSpec and Terratest

Dynamic analysis involves testing the live, provisioned infrastructure to verify that it meets security and compliance benchmarks. Unlike static code analysis, which examines the code for potential issues before deployment, dynamic analysis tools such as InSpec and Terratest execute tests on the actual resources created by Terraform. This ensures that misconfigurations and vulnerabilities that only manifest at runtime are detected, providing actionable feedback to improve overall security.

- **InSpec:**
  - **Human-readable tests:** InSpec is a testing framework that uses readable, Ruby-based controls to verify infrastructure compliance.
  - **Live infrastructure validation:** It runs tests against live resources, checking for configuration settings (for example, ensuring that HTTPS is enabled on Azure Blob Storage, Amazon S3, or Google Cloud Storage).
  - **Actionable feedback:** InSpec produces reports that highlight compliance issues, making it easier for teams to remediate problems in their infrastructure.
- **Terratest:**
  - **Infrastructure deployment and testing:** Terratest is a Golang-based tool that automates the deployment of Terraform infrastructure, runs tests against the deployed resources, and then tears them down.
  - **End-to-end testing:** It verifies that the infrastructure behaves as expected in a live environment, offering an end-to-end validation that includes both functional and security aspects.
  - **Automated rollback:** Terratest helps ensure that any non-compliant or failing infrastructure configurations are quickly identified, allowing for rapid remediation.

```
control "azure-blob-https" do
  title "Ensure HTTPS is enabled for Azure Blob Storage"
  describe azurerm_storage_account(resource_group: 'example-group', name:
'exampleaccount') do
    it { should have_https_traffic_only }
  end
end
```

This InSpec control tests an Azure Storage Account to ensure HTTPS-only access is enabled, exemplifying dynamic analysis of live infrastructure to validate security configurations in Terraform deployments.

Continuous Validation with Sentinel and Conftest

Sentinel (developed by HashiCorp) and Conftest (an Open Policy Agent-based tool) are used to continuously validate Terraform code against predefined security and compliance policies. Sentinel is integrated within Terraform Enterprise and provides a robust, policy-as-code framework for enforcing rules before and after deployments, while Conftest extends these capabilities into CI/CD pipelines, ensuring that every commit adheres to the organization's standards.

- **Policy enforcement:** Sentinel policies run during both pre-deployment and post-deployment phases to enforce strict security controls. These policies automatically evaluate Terraform configurations and block any non-compliant changes.
- **CI/CD integration:** Conftest is integrated into CI/CD pipelines (using tools such as GitHub Actions, GitLab CI, or Jenkins) to run policy checks on Terraform code with every commit, ensuring continuous compliance throughout the development lifecycle.
- **Gatekeeping:** If a policy is violated, the pipeline is halted, preventing non-compliant infrastructure from being deployed. This **`"gatekeeping"`** mechanism ensures that only secure and compliant configurations are promoted to production.

```
package terraform.gcp

deny[msg] {
  input.resource_type == "google_storage_bucket"
  not input.resource.attributes.iamConfiguration.uniformBucketLevelAccess.
enabled
  msg = "GCP storage buckets must have uniform bucket-level access enabled to
prevent public access."
}
```

These policies ensure continuous validation of Terraform configurations, blocking insecure AWS S3 buckets and enforcing secure GCP storage bucket settings, thus integrating robust, automated security controls into the CI/CD pipeline.

Security testing tools play a vital role in ensuring the integrity and compliance of Terraform infrastructure. By incorporating Kitchen-Terraform, InSpec, Terratest, Sentinel, and Conftest into CI/CD workflows, organizations can proactively detect vulnerabilities and enforce policy compliance across AWS, GCP, and Azure. These tools provide layered defense mechanisms, protecting infrastructure from misconfigurations and minimizing deployment risks.

Conclusion

In this chapter, we explored the critical components required to build secure, automated CI/CD pipelines for Terraform deployments across AWS, Azure, and GCP. By following best practices in designing multi-cloud pipelines, implementing robust IAM configurations, enforcing least-privilege access, and securing artifact storage, you can establish a strong foundation for safe infrastructure delivery. We also covered the importance of proactively integrating security scans using tools such as Checkov, TFSec, and Terrascan to catch vulnerabilities and misconfigurations before they become production risks. Additionally, leveraging GitOps workflows and structuring repositories with strict review processes ensures that infrastructure changes are not only automated but also compliant with security and governance standards.

As organizations move towards continuous deployment and rapid delivery, preventing secrets leakage, automating safe rollbacks, and employing controlled rollout strategies become indispensable. Techniques such as canary deployments, blue/green updates, and infrastructure drift detection enhance resilience while reducing operational risks. Finally, incorporating security testing frameworks such as Kitchen-Terraform, InSpec, Terratest, Sentinel, and Conftest into CI/CD workflows guarantees ongoing validation and compliance. With these practices, you can confidently manage Terraform-based deployments in fast-moving cloud environments, knowing that security is built into every stage of your pipeline.

In the next chapter, we will dive deep into monitoring and incident response in multi-cloud environments, focusing on setting up security dashboards, automating alerts, and integrating threat detection tools. It also covers best practices for logging, monitoring, and using Terraform to streamline security automation and response processes.

Questions and Answers

1. **How can I design secure multi-cloud CI/CD pipelines for Terraform deployments across AWS, Azure, and GCP?**

   Designing secure multi-cloud CI/CD pipelines involves enforcing security compliance by isolating deployment environments, using dedicated IAM roles and policies per cloud provider, and implementing secure communication channels between pipeline stages. Additionally, artifact repositories must be locked down, and credentials should be rotated frequently.

Pipeline configurations should also include built-in automated security scans and policy-as-code checks to prevent misconfigurations from reaching production.

2. **What are the best practices for managing IAM and implementing least privilege for Terraform pipelines?**

   IAM best practices include assigning narrowly scoped roles with the minimum required permissions for each pipeline stage. Service accounts or pipeline users must only have access to resources necessary for their tasks. For CI/CD tools such as Jenkins, GitLab, and GitHub Actions, you should integrate role-based access controls, avoid long-lived credentials, and enforce permission boundaries. Periodic audits and automated policy validations further ensure that privilege escalation and overly permissive access are prevented.

3. **How can I automate security scans for Terraform code in CI/CD pipelines using tools such as Checkov, TFSec, and Terrascan?**

   Checkov, TFSec, and Terrascan can be integrated into CI/CD pipelines to automatically analyze Terraform configurations during build or pre-deployment stages. Checkov performs static analysis to catch security misconfigurations; TFSec can perform both static and dynamic checks for vulnerabilities, and Terrascan enforces compliance with industry benchmarks. These tools should be configured to fail builds on critical issues and generate detailed reports to help developers remediate problems before deployment.

4. **How can GitOps workflows enhance Terraform deployment security and ensure infrastructure compliance?**

   GitOps workflows, when implemented with tools such as ArgoCD or Flux, allow Terraform deployments to be triggered automatically from version-controlled Git repositories. This ensures that all infrastructure changes are auditable and peer-reviewed. Git repositories serve as the single source of truth, supporting strict branching strategies, mandatory pull request reviews, automated security checks, and continuous reconciliation to detect drift. This process enforces both versioning and security controls for Terraform infrastructure.

5. **What strategies can be used to prevent secret leakage in Terraform CI/CD pipelines, and how can accidental exposure be detected?**

   Secrets management should rely on tools such as HashiCorp Vault or cloud-native secret managers (AWS Secrets Manager, Azure Key Vault, GCP Secret Manager), with environment variables encrypted and short-lived tokens used where possible. Additionally, scanning tools such as GitLeaks and TruffleHog can be integrated into CI/CD workflows to detect any accidental secrets committed to repositories. Automated alerts and immediate remediation steps ensure that secrets exposure is caught and addressed before reaching production.

CHAPTER 12
Monitoring and Incident Response in Multi-Cloud Environments

Introduction

In today's rapidly evolving cloud landscape, securing multi-cloud environments requires a robust monitoring and incident response strategy. Organizations leveraging AWS, Azure, and GCP must establish centralized security monitoring dashboards, automate alerting mechanisms, and integrate threat detection tools to identify and mitigate security risks effectively. This chapter explores how to deploy unified security dashboards across multiple cloud providers, utilizing tools such as Grafana, AWS CloudWatch, Azure Monitor, and GCP Operations Suite. By leveraging Terraform, we ensure consistent and scalable deployment of monitoring solutions, enabling real-time visualization and correlation of security metrics. Cross-cloud security metric aggregation further enhances visibility, allowing teams to detect anomalies and potential threats before they escalate.

Beyond monitoring, automating incident response is crucial to minimizing security breaches and ensuring quick remediation. This chapter delves into serverless security automation using AWS Lambda, Azure Functions, and Google Cloud Functions to trigger real-time alerts and execute response actions. Additionally, we explore Terraform-based approaches for deploying cloud-native threat detection services such as AWS GuardDuty, Azure Defender, and GCP Security Command Center. By integrating automated response playbooks and AI-driven anomaly detection models, organizations can proactively handle security incidents across multiple cloud environments. Finally, we discuss best practices for log collection, retention policies, and multi-cloud incident response automation, providing a comprehensive framework for securing modern cloud infrastructures.

Structure

In this chapter, we will cover the following topics:

- Setting Up Security Monitoring Dashboards across Providers
  - Designing Unified Multi-Cloud Dashboards
  - Visualizing Security Metrics with Grafana and Cloud-Native Tools
  - Deploying Pre-Built Terraform Modules for Monitoring
  - Cross-Cloud Security Metric Correlation
- Automating Alerts and Incident Response with Serverless Solutions
  - Configuring Lambda, Azure Functions, and Cloud Functions for Alerts
  - Integrating SNS, Pub/Sub, and Event Grid for Notifications
  - Building Response Playbooks in Terraform for Incident Handling

- Integrating Threat Detection and Investigation Tools
  - Deploying AWS GuardDuty, Azure Defender, and GCP Security Command Center
  - Terraform Configuration for Continuous Threat Monitoring
  - Correlating Threat Intelligence Data across Clouds
  - Investigating Security Incidents with CloudTrail, Log Analytics, and GCP Logs
- Best Practices for Logging and Monitoring Across Clouds
  - Standardizing Log Collection and Aggregation
  - Enabling Multi-Cloud Log Retention Policies
  - Real-Time Anomaly Detection in Logs
- Leveraging Terraform for Security Automation and Incident Response
  - Deploying Multi-Region Monitoring with Terraform
  - Automating Policy Enforcement with Sentinel and OPA
  - Scaling Incident Response across Multi-Cloud Environments

Setting Up Security Monitoring Dashboards across Providers

In modern multi-cloud environments, securing infrastructure across AWS, Azure, and GCP requires centralized monitoring to detect threats and anomalies in real-time. Terraform provides a unified approach to deploying monitoring dashboards, automating the provisioning of observability tools, and ensuring consistent security insights across providers. This section explores how to design, deploy, and visualize security dashboards across cloud platforms, leveraging Terraform to simplify the process and ensure scalability.

Designing Unified Multi-Cloud Dashboards

A unified multi-cloud dashboard consolidates security and performance metrics from AWS, Azure, and GCP into a single, centralized view. This enables security and operations teams to monitor infrastructure health, detect threats, and respond to incidents across different cloud platforms without switching between separate consoles. By leveraging Terraform to provision integrations and configure data pipelines, organizations can achieve consistent, real-time monitoring across their entire hybrid environment.

- **Data aggregation:** Logs and metrics from cloud-native monitoring services such as AWS CloudWatch, Azure Monitor, and GCP Operations Suite are collected and ingested into a centralized dashboard tool (for example, Grafana). This consolidation enables comprehensive analysis and visibility into the health and security of your infrastructure.
- **Normalization:** Terraform provisions integrations that transform and normalize data into consistent formats. This ensures that metrics from different clouds (for example, login attempts, VM health, network traffic) are comparable and can be visualized uniformly on the dashboard.
- **Multi-account monitoring:** Dashboards are configured to aggregate data from multiple cloud accounts or subscriptions. This allows teams to monitor hybrid environments seamlessly and enables scalability as your infrastructure grows.
- **Role-based access control (RBAC):** Access to the unified dashboard is controlled through RBAC, ensuring that only authorized users can view or modify sensitive performance and security data.

```
resource "grafana_data_source" "cloudwatch_assumeARN" {
  type = "cloudwatch"
  name = "cw-assumeARN-example"

  json_data_encoded = jsonencode({
    defaultRegion = "us-east-1"
    authType      = "grafana_assume_role"
    assumeRoleArn = "arn:aws:iam:: ${var.aws_account_id}:role/${var.assume_
role}"
  })
}
```

This Terraform configuration sets up a Grafana data source for AWS CloudWatch, enabling centralized ingestion of CloudWatch metrics into Grafana for unified multi-cloud monitoring, with secure authentication via an IAM role.

Visualizing Security Metrics with Grafana and Cloud-Native Tools

Visualization tools such as Grafana transform raw monitoring data into dynamic, interactive dashboards that enable real-time tracking of security metrics and anomalies. By integrating cloud-native monitoring services such as AWS CloudWatch, Azure Monitor, and GCP Operations Suite with Grafana, organizations can consolidate and analyze security logs, API calls, and performance metrics across multi-cloud environments. Terraform automates the provisioning of these integrations, ensuring that dashboards are consistent, scalable, and reproducible, which empowers security teams to make informed decisions quickly.

- **Terraform configuration:** Terraform provisions Grafana instances and configures data sources that connect directly to cloud-native monitoring tools. It also deploys pre-built dashboards tailored to visualize security metrics, streamlining the setup process and ensuring consistency across environments.
- **Plugin integration:** Grafana plugins are used to connect to specific cloud monitoring services. For instance, the Azure Monitor plugin can pull metrics and logs directly from Azure Monitor, enabling dynamic updates on the Grafana dashboard without manual intervention.
- **Custom panels:** Terraform scripts can define custom Grafana panels that display specific security metrics such as login attempts, API call frequency, or VM health statistics. These panels offer detailed, granular views of security data, helping teams identify and respond to potential threats efficiently.

```
 # Configure a Grafana data source for Azure Monitor
resource "grafana_data_source" "azure_monitor" {
  name = "Azure Monitor"         # Display name of the data source in Grafana
  type = "azuremonitor"          # Type of data source (Azure Monitor)

  # JSON configuration for non-sensitive values
  json_data_encoded = <<JSON
{
  "azureCloud": "AzureCloud",                              # Azure
environment (for example, AzureCloud, AzureUSGovernment)
  "subscriptionId": "${var.azure_subscription_id}",        # Azure
Subscription ID
  "tenantId": "${var.azure_tenant_id}",                    # Azure Active
Directory Tenant ID
  "defaultWorkspace": "${var.azure_log_analytics_workspace_id}"# Default Log
Analytics Workspace ID for querying logs
```

```
}
JSON

  # JSON configuration for sensitive values (kept secure in Grafana)
  secure_json_data_encoded = <<JSON
{
  "clientId": "${var.azure_client_id}",        # Azure App Registration Client
ID
  "clientSecret": "${var.azure_client_secret}" # Azure App Registration Client
Secret
}
JSON
}
```

This Terraform snippet configures a Grafana data source for Azure Monitor, securely retrieving and displaying metrics from Azure using an API-based integration, enabling real-time visualization of security and performance data in a unified dashboard.

Deploying Pre-Built Terraform Modules for Monitoring

Pre-built Terraform modules simplify the deployment of monitoring solutions by providing ready-to-use, modular infrastructure configurations that have been tested and shared by the community. These modules, available on the Terraform Registry, allow you to quickly provision and customize dashboards and observability tools across multiple cloud providers such as AWS, Azure, and GCP, ensuring consistency and saving valuable time. By using these modules, organizations can implement monitoring solutions that meet their security and operational requirements with minimal manual configuration.

- **Module repositories:** Pre-built modules for monitoring are hosted on the Terraform Registry. These modules come with standardized configurations for popular monitoring tools and dashboards, such as AWS CloudWatch, Azure Monitor, and GCP's Cloud Monitoring.
- **Infrastructure as Code (IaC):** Terraform modules enable teams to provision entire monitoring setups by simply invoking pre-built modules in their Terraform code. This reduces manual configuration, minimizes errors, and ensures that monitoring infrastructure is deployed consistently across environments.
- **Customization:** Although pre-built, these modules are highly configurable. Users can adjust settings such as dashboard layouts, metric filters, and alert thresholds to tailor the monitoring solution to their specific needs, ensuring that the final implementation meets both operational and security requirements.

```
module "monitoring_dashboard" {
  source  = "terraform-google-modules/monitoring-dashboard/google"
  version = "~> 1.0"

  dashboards = [
    {
      display_name = "Example Dashboard"
      row = [
        {
          panels = [
            {
              title = "CPU Utilization"
              type  = "metric"
              data = [
                {
```

```
                  filter = "resource.type = \"gce_instance\" AND metric.type =
\"compute.googleapis.com/instance/cpu/utilization\""
                  aggregation = {
                    alignment_period   = "60s"
                    per_series_aligner = "ALIGN_MEAN"
                  }
                }
              ]
            }
          ]
        }
      ]
    }
  ]
}
```

This Terraform configuration uses a pre-built module to provision a GCP Cloud Monitor dashboard that visualizes CPU utilization metrics for Compute Engine instances, enabling centralized and customizable monitoring of infrastructure performance.

Cross-Cloud Security Metric Correlation

Cross-cloud security metric correlation is the process of aggregating logs and metrics from multiple cloud platforms, such as AWS, Azure, and GCP, to identify patterns that may indicate security threats. By correlating data across diverse environments, organizations can gain a unified view of their security posture, quickly detect anomalies, and respond to incidents in a coordinated manner.

- **Log aggregation:** Terraform automates the provisioning of log aggregation pipelines that collect logs from various cloud monitoring services, such as AWS CloudWatch, Azure Monitor, and GCP Cloud Logging. This centralized collection of logs ensures that all security-relevant events from multiple clouds are available for analysis in one place.
- **Correlation engines:** Tools such as Grafana, Elastic Stack, or Splunk serve as correlation engines that analyze the aggregated logs to identify anomalies and patterns indicative of potential threats. These engines process data using machine learning or rule-based algorithms to flag suspicious activities that may otherwise go unnoticed in isolated systems.
- **Normalization:** Since logs and metrics can differ in format and structure across cloud providers, normalization is essential. Terraform can provision integrations that standardize this data, making it easier to compare and correlate metrics from AWS, Azure, and GCP. This normalization ensures that security teams receive meaningful insights regardless of the cloud origin.
- **Unified logging:** Ensure that logs from AWS CloudWatch, Azure Monitor, and GCP Cloud Logging are aggregated into a single repository or dashboard. This unification simplifies monitoring and analysis across multi-cloud environments.
- **Threat detection:** Employ advanced correlation engines that leverage machine learning or rule-based approaches to analyze the aggregated data. This enables early detection of patterns that might signify a coordinated attack or misconfiguration across cloud platforms.
- **Visualization:** Visualize the correlated metrics and logs in a unified dashboard using tools such as Grafana. Effective visualization helps security teams quickly interpret complex data, prioritize alerts, and take timely action to mitigate threats.

Setting up monitoring dashboards across AWS, Azure, and GCP ensures visibility into cloud environments and enhances incident response capabilities. By using Terraform to automate deployments and integrate monitoring tools such as Grafana, organizations achieve scalability, reduce manual overhead, and detect cross-cloud anomalies more effectively. The next section will explore automating alerts and incident response through serverless solutions, continuing the journey toward comprehensive cloud security.

Automating Alerts and Incident Response with Serverless Solutions

Automating alerts and incident response is crucial for managing security in multi-cloud environments. Serverless solutions allow cloud providers to trigger automated workflows when security events occur, ensuring rapid response and mitigation. AWS Lambda, Azure Functions, and Google Cloud Functions enable real-time reaction to anomalies, while Terraform facilitates consistent deployment of these serverless solutions. This section explores how serverless architectures can streamline alerting and remediation, ensuring that security incidents are addressed swiftly and uniformly across AWS, Azure, and GCP.

Configuring Lambda, Azure Functions, and Cloud Functions for Alerts

Serverless compute functions such as AWS Lambda, Azure Functions, and GCP Cloud Functions allow you to execute custom code in response to specific events (for example, security breaches, failed logins, or anomalous network activity). These functions enable automated alerting and remediation without the need to manage servers, thereby streamlining the response to security incidents.

- **Event-driven triggers:** Serverless functions are automatically triggered by cloud events. For example, AWS CloudWatch can monitor metrics or log events (such as unauthorized S3 bucket access), and when an event meets defined criteria, it triggers a Lambda function. Similarly, Azure Functions can be triggered by alerts from Azure Monitor, and GCP Cloud Functions can be triggered by Pub/Sub messages generated by Cloud Logging events.
- **Execution:** Once triggered, the serverless function executes custom code (written in languages such as Python, Node.js, Go, and so on) within an isolated environment. This code can perform various tasks, such as sending notifications to security teams, isolating or shutting down compromised resources, or scaling security groups to mitigate an ongoing threat.

```
# Lambda function to alert unauthorized S3 access
resource "aws_lambda_function" "alert_lambda" {
  filename         = "alert_function.zip"          # Zip file containing your
Lambda code
  function_name    = "S3UnauthorizedAccessAlert"
  role             = aws_iam_role.lambda_exec.arn
  handler          = "index.handler"
  runtime          = "python3.8"
  source_code_hash = filebase64sha256("alert_function.zip")
}

# CloudWatch Log Group (assuming S3 access logs are being delivered here)
resource "aws_cloudwatch_log_group" "s3_access_logs" {
  name = "/aws/s3/access-logs"
}

# Metric filter to detect unauthorized access events in S3 logs
resource "aws_cloudwatch_log_metric_filter" "unauthorized_filter" {
```

```
  name           = "UnauthorizedS3AccessFilter"
  log_group_name = aws_cloudwatch_log_group.s3_access_logs.name
  pattern        = "{ $.errorCode = \"AccessDenied\" }"

  metric_transformation {
    name      = "UnauthorizedS3Access"
    namespace = "Custom/S3"
    value     = "1"
  }
}

# CloudWatch Alarm to trigger the Lambda function upon unauthorized access
detection
resource "aws_cloudwatch_metric_alarm" "unauthorized_access_alarm" {
  alarm_name          = "UnauthorizedS3AccessAlarm"
  comparison_operator = "GreaterThanThreshold"
  evaluation_periods  = 1
  metric_name         = aws_cloudwatch_log_metric_filter.unauthorized_filter.
metric_transformation[0].name
  namespace           = aws_cloudwatch_log_metric_filter.unauthorized_filter.
metric_transformation[0].namespace
  period              = 60
  statistic           = "Sum"
  threshold           = 0
  alarm_description   = "Alarm when unauthorized S3 bucket access is detected."
  alarm_actions       = [aws_lambda_function.alert_lambda.arn]
}
```

This Terraform configuration automates the detection and response to unauthorized S3 access by deploying a Lambda function that is triggered via a CloudWatch alarm, which monitors a custom metric generated from CloudWatch log data.

Integrating SNS, Pub/Sub, and Event Grid for Notifications

Cloud-native messaging services AWS Simple Notification Service (SNS), Google Pub/Sub, and Azure Event Grid enable real-time distribution of security alerts and infrastructure notifications. These services facilitate immediate visibility into security incidents by triggering notifications based on specific cloud events, such as non-compliant resources, failed authentication attempts, or anomalous network activity.

- **Publisher-subscriber model:** Security functions, monitoring tools, or cloud policy engines (for example, AWS Config, Azure Policy, GCP Security Command Center) publish alerts to messaging services. Subscribers such as security teams, incident response workflows, or remediation pipelines receive notifications in real time.
- **Multi-channel alerts:** Notifications can be routed to multiple endpoints, including email, SMS, Slack, Microsoft Teams, webhooks, or third-party SIEM tools (for example, Splunk, Datadog, Elastic Stack).

```
# Create an Azure Event Grid Topic
resource "azurerm_eventgrid_topic" "security_alerts" {
  name                = "security-alerts-topic"
  resource_group_name = azurerm_resource_group.example.name
  location            = azurerm_resource_group.example.location
}
```

```
# Create an Azure Event Grid Subscription to trigger on non-compliant resources
resource "azurerm_eventgrid_event_subscription" "policy_alerts" {
  name                  = "policy-noncompliance-sub"
  scope                 = "/providers/Microsoft.PolicyInsights/policyStates/
latest"  # Monitors policy state changes
  event_delivery_schema = "EventGridSchema"

  webhook_endpoint {
    url = "https://example.com/security-alert-webhook"  # Replace with actual
webhook
  }
}

# Example: Azure Policy Definition to Enforce Compliance
resource "azurerm_policy_definition" "restrict_public_ip" {
  name         = "restrict-public-ip"
  policy_type  = "Custom"
  mode         = "All"
  display_name = "Restrict Public IP for VMs"

  policy_rule = jsonencode({
    if = {
      field = "Microsoft.Network/publicIPAddresses"
      exists = "true"
    }
    then = {
      effect = "deny"
    }
  })
}

# Assign the policy to a resource group
resource "azurerm_policy_assignment" "restrict_public_ip_assign" {
  name                 = "restrict-public-ip-assignment"
  policy_definition_id = azurerm_policy_definition.restrict_public_ip.id
  scope                = azurerm_resource_group.example.id
}
```

This Terraform configuration deploys an Azure Event Grid topic and subscription that triggers alerts via webhook when an Azure Policy detects non-compliant resources, enabling continuous and automated security notifications.

Building Response Playbooks in Terraform for Incident Handling

Incident response playbooks are automated, codified procedures designed to manage and mitigate security threats quickly and efficiently. With Terraform, these playbooks are defined as Infrastructure as Code (IaC), enabling organizations to standardize and automate their incident response strategies. By provisioning serverless functions, messaging pipelines, and remediation workflows, Terraform-based playbooks ensure that the necessary actions to contain and resolve incidents are executed promptly and consistently.

- **Terraform orchestration:** Terraform provisions the components required for an incident response playbook. This includes deploying serverless functions (such as AWS Lambda, Azure Functions, or GCP Cloud Functions), messaging systems, and automated workflows that kick in when a security incident is detected. These components work together to execute predefined remediation steps, such as adjusting firewall rules or scaling security groups.

- **Conditional logic:** Terraform can implement conditional branching within its modules or through integration with external tools. This enables different automated actions based on the type and severity of the incident. For example, if a specific anomaly is detected, Terraform might trigger a function to block traffic from a malicious IP range; if a different type of incident occurs, it might instead initiate resource scaling or other corrective actions.
- **Role mapping:** Playbooks also define role mapping by assigning specific tasks to different security teams or service accounts. This structured approach ensures that each aspect of the incident response is handled by the appropriate personnel or automated process, reducing confusion and enabling faster recovery.

The following Terraform snippet demonstrates how to provision a Cloud Armor security policy on GCP that can be used in an incident response playbook. When triggered, this policy will block anomalous traffic by denying requests from a specified IP range. In a complete solution, a Cloud Function or other automation would update this policy dynamically based on threat intelligence.

```
resource "google_compute_security_policy" "incident_response" {
  name        = "incident-response-policy"
  description = "Security policy to block anomalous traffic during incidents"

  rule {
    priority = 1000
    action   = "deny(403)"
    match {
      versioned_expr = "SRC_IPS_V1"
      config {
        src_ip_ranges = ["10.1.2.3/32"]  # Placeholder IP; replace dynamically
during an incident
      }
    }
  }
}
```

Automating incident response with serverless solutions transforms cloud security by reducing response times and enabling scalable, cost-effective operations. By leveraging AWS Lambda, Azure Functions, and GCP Cloud Functions along with Terraform, organizations build robust, repeatable workflows that mitigate threats in real time. The next section explores how to integrate threat detection and investigation tools into these workflows, enhancing overall cloud security resilience.

Integrating Threat Detection and Investigation Tools

Threat detection and investigation tools are essential for maintaining a proactive cloud security posture. By integrating native threat detection services such as AWS GuardDuty, Azure Defender, and Google Cloud Security Command Center, organizations can identify malicious activities and vulnerabilities across their cloud environments. Terraform plays a crucial role in automating the deployment and configuration of these services, ensuring consistency and scalability. This section explores how to deploy, configure, and manage these tools while correlating threat intelligence data across multi-cloud environments to streamline investigations and incident response.

Deploying AWS GuardDuty, Azure Defender, and GCP Security Command Center

Cloud-native threat detection services such as AWS GuardDuty, Azure Defender, and GCP Security Command Center continuously monitor cloud environments for malicious activity, unauthorized access, and misconfigurations. They analyze cloud traffic, logs, and configurations to detect threats in real-time, enabling rapid incident response and enhancing overall security. These services help ensure that your environment complies with security best practices and regulatory standards by proactively identifying potential risks.

- **AWS GuardDuty:** AWS GuardDuty continuously analyzes CloudTrail logs, VPC Flow Logs, and DNS logs to identify threats such as unauthorized API calls, port scanning, and data exfiltration attempts from services such as S3. Once enabled, GuardDuty uses machine learning and threat intelligence to flag suspicious activity without requiring any additional configuration.
- **Azure Defender:** Azure Defender provides comprehensive threat detection by analyzing signals from Azure Security Center, Azure Activity Logs, and external threat intelligence. It monitors and protects Azure resources by automatically identifying vulnerabilities and suspicious behaviors.
- **GCP Security Command Center (SCC):** GCP SCC aggregates data from Cloud Logging, VPC Flow Logs, and other monitoring sources to scan for vulnerabilities, misconfigurations, and active threats. It leverages built-in rules and threat intelligence to provide a unified view of your security posture across GCP resources.

```
# Enable AWS GuardDuty
resource "aws_guardduty_detector" "main" {
  enable = true
}

# Create an SNS Topic for GuardDuty alerts
resource "aws_sns_topic" "guardduty_alerts" {
  name = "GuardDutyAlerts"
}

# Create a CloudWatch Event Rule to detect S3 data exfiltration findings
resource "aws_cloudwatch_event_rule" "guardduty_findings" {
  name        = "GuardDuty-S3DataExfiltration"
  description = "Trigger when GuardDuty detects S3 data exfiltration attempts"
  event_pattern = <<EOF
{
  "source": [
    "aws.guardduty"
  ],
  "detail-type": [
    "GuardDuty Finding"
  ],
  "detail": {
    "type": [
      "UnauthorizedAccess:DataExfiltration.S3"
    ]
  }
}
EOF
}
```

```
# Set the SNS Topic as a target for the CloudWatch Event Rule
resource "aws_cloudwatch_event_target" "guardduty_target" {
  rule      = aws_cloudwatch_event_rule.guardduty_findings.name
  target_id = "GuardDutySNSTarget"
  arn       = aws_sns_topic.guardduty_alerts.arn
}
```

This Terraform configuration enables AWS GuardDuty and sets up a CloudWatch event rule to detect S3 data exfiltration attempts, triggering an SNS notification for real-time alerting and incident response.

Terraform Configuration for Continuous Threat Monitoring

Continuous threat monitoring with Terraform automates the deployment and configuration of cloud-native security services to detect, alert, and respond to threats in real time. By managing these services as code, Terraform ensures that monitoring tools are consistently deployed across environments, reducing misconfigurations and enhancing overall scalability and compliance.

- **Terraform modules:** Pre-built modules are available for AWS GuardDuty, Azure Defender, and GCP Security Command Center. These modules automate the activation and policy enforcement of security monitoring services, ensuring that all necessary checks are in place from the start.
- **Continuous monitoring:** By maintaining up-to-date Terraform state files, Terraform enables continuous monitoring for drift or configuration changes. This ongoing validation ensures that any deviation from the desired state is detected quickly, triggering remediation processes if needed.

```
# Create a Resource Group
resource "azurerm_resource_group" "example" {
  name     = "example-rg"
  location = "East US"
}

# Enable Azure Defender for a resource type (e.g., Virtual Machines)
resource "azurerm_security_center_subscription_pricing" "example" {
  resource_type = "VirtualMachines"
  tier          = "Standard"
}

# Configure a Security Center Contact to receive alerts
resource "azurerm_security_center_contact" "example" {
  resource_group_name = azurerm_resource_group.example.name
  email               = "security@example.com"
  name               = "vm-notifications"
  alert_notifications = true
  alerts_to_admins    = true
}
```

This Terraform configuration enables Azure Defender for Virtual Machines and sets up a Security Center contact to receive alerts, ensuring continuous threat monitoring and prompt notification of security incidents.

Correlating Threat Intelligence Data across Clouds

Cross-cloud threat intelligence correlation aggregates security data from AWS, Azure, and GCP to provide a unified view of potential threats across a multi-cloud environment. This approach enhances incident response and overall security by detecting patterns that may not be apparent when clouds are monitored separately.

- **Data Aggregation:** Terraform provisions log aggregation pipelines that collect logs and threat intelligence feeds from services such as AWS GuardDuty, Azure Defender, and GCP Security Command Center. This unified data collection allows for centralized analysis of security events.
- **Correlation engines:** Tools such as Splunk, the Elastic Stack, or cloud-native solutions such as Azure Sentinel and GCP Chronicle are used to correlate logs across clouds. These engines analyze data to identify anomalies or coordinated attack patterns, providing actionable insights.
- **Normalization:** Data from various sources is normalized and transformed into a common format to ensure consistency in how metrics and logs are compared across different cloud environments, which facilitates accurate cross-cloud threat detection.

```
resource "google_pubsub_topic" "scc_alerts" {
  name = "scc-alerts"
}

resource "google_pubsub_subscription" "scc_alerts_sub" {
  name  = "scc-alerts-sub"
  topic = google_pubsub_topic.scc_alerts.id
  push_config {
    # This push endpoint should be your AWS API Gateway endpoint that triggers
a Lambda function in AWS.
    push_endpoint = "https://<aws-api-gateway-endpoint>/scc-alerts"
  }
}
```

This GCP configuration creates a Pub/Sub topic for SCC alerts and a push subscription that forwards these alerts to an AWS API Gateway endpoint.

```
# Enable AWS Security Hub
resource "aws_securityhub_account" "example" {}

# Create an SNS Topic to receive alerts (optional step)
resource "aws_sns_topic" "scc_alerts" {
  name = "scc-alerts-sns"
}

# Create an API Gateway to receive GCP push notifications
resource "aws_api_gateway_rest_api" "scc_api" {
  name = "scc-alert-api"
}

resource "aws_api_gateway_resource" "scc_resource" {
  rest_api_id = aws_api_gateway_rest_api.scc_api.id
  parent_id   = aws_api_gateway_rest_api.scc_api.root_resource_id
  path_part   = "scc-alerts"
}

resource "aws_api_gateway_method" "scc_post" {
  rest_api_id   = aws_api_gateway_rest_api.scc_api.id
  resource_id   = aws_api_gateway_resource.scc_resource.id
  http_method   = "POST"
  authorization = "NONE"
```

```
}

# Lambda function to process SCC alerts and forward to Security Hub
resource "aws_lambda_function" "scc_to_sh" {
  function_name = "scc-to-securityhub"
  filename      = "lambda.zip"  # Your packaged Lambda code
  handler       = "index.handler"
  runtime       = "python3.8"
  role          = aws_iam_role.lambda_exec.arn
}

# API Gateway integration with Lambda
resource "aws_api_gateway_integration" "scc_integration" {
  rest_api_id             = aws_api_gateway_rest_api.scc_api.id
  resource_id             = aws_api_gateway_resource.scc_resource.id
  http_method             = aws_api_gateway_method.scc_post.http_method
  integration_http_method = "POST"
  type                    = "AWS_PROXY"
  uri                     = aws_lambda_function.scc_to_sh.invoke_arn
}

# Permission for API Gateway to invoke the Lambda function
resource "aws_lambda_permission" "apigw" {
  statement_id  = "AllowAPIGatewayInvoke"
  action        = "lambda:InvokeFunction"
  function_name = aws_lambda_function.scc_to_sh.function_name
  principal     = "apigateway.amazonaws.com"
  source_arn    = "${aws_api_gateway_rest_api.scc_api.execution_arn}/*/*"
}
```

This AWS configuration enables Security Hub, provisions an API Gateway with a POST method integrated with a Lambda function, and grants API Gateway permission to invoke the Lambda, which processes GCP SCC alerts forwarded via Pub/Sub.

Investigating Security Incidents with CloudTrail, Log Analytics, and GCP Logs

Cloud log services such as AWS CloudTrail, Azure Log Analytics, and GCP Logs provide the essential data required for investigating security incidents. These services capture detailed records of all actions performed on your cloud resources, enabling security teams to trace events, identify compromised resources, and conduct forensic investigations. By leveraging Terraform to configure and manage these logging services, organizations can automate the collection and querying of log data, ensuring consistent, long-term retention and facilitating rapid incident response.

- **Log analysis:** Cloud log services aggregate and store detailed logs (for example, AWS CloudTrail logs, Azure Activity Logs, and GCP Audit Logs). Security teams can query these logs for specific patterns such as failed login attempts or unauthorized API calls to identify potential security incidents.
- **Incident workflows:** Automated workflows can be built using Terraform to trigger responses when certain log patterns are detected. For example, a CloudWatch metric filter can be set up to detect IAM policy changes and trigger an alert, which in turn can activate incident response processes such as automated remediation or manual investigation.
- **Forensics:** Logs are retained for extended periods to allow for in-depth forensic analysis after an incident. This long-term storage and historical record enable teams to reconstruct events, understand the attack vectors, and improve future defences.

```
# Create a CloudWatch Log Metric Filter to detect IAM policy changes
resource "aws_cloudwatch_log_metric_filter" "iam_policy_changes" {
  name           = "IAMPolicyChanges"
  log_group_name = "/aws/cloudtrail/your-log-group"  # Replace with your
actual CloudTrail log group name
  pattern        = "{ $.eventSource = \"iam.amazonaws.com\" && $.eventName =~
/^(Put|Delete|Create)/ }"

  metric_transformation {
    name      = "IAMPolicyChangesCount"
    namespace = "SecurityMetrics"
    value     = "1"
  }
}

# Create a CloudWatch Alarm that triggers when an IAM policy change is detected
resource "aws_cloudwatch_metric_alarm" "iam_policy_alarm" {
  alarm_name          = "IAMPolicyChangesAlarm"
  comparison_operator = "GreaterThanThreshold"
  evaluation_periods  = 1
  metric_name         = aws_cloudwatch_log_metric_filter.iam_policy_changes.
metric_transformation[0].name
  namespace           = aws_cloudwatch_log_metric_filter.iam_policy_changes.
metric_transformation[0].namespace
  period              = 300
  statistic           = "Sum"
  threshold           = 1
  alarm_actions       = [var.alarm_action_arn]  # ARN of the SNS topic or
other notification service to trigger alerts
}
```

This Terraform configuration sets up an AWS CloudWatch metric filter and alarm to detect IAM policy changes from CloudTrail logs, enabling automated alerting and incident response for security investigations.

Integrating threat detection and investigation tools across AWS, Azure, and GCP strengthens security postures and reduces the risk of undetected threats. By automating deployments with Terraform and correlating threat data, organizations achieve comprehensive visibility and faster incident response. The next section will explore best practices for logging and monitoring across multi-cloud environments to further enhance security readiness.

Best Practices for Logging and Monitoring Across Clouds

Effective logging and monitoring are essential for securing cloud environments, ensuring compliance, and identifying potential security incidents. In multi-cloud environments, inconsistencies in logging formats, retention policies, and access controls can create blind spots and complicate investigations. This section focuses on establishing standardized logging practices across AWS, Azure, and GCP using Terraform to automate deployments, enforce retention policies, and enable anomaly detection. By following these best practices, organizations can achieve greater visibility, reduce the risk of misconfigurations, and respond more efficiently to threats.

Standardizing Log Collection and Aggregation

Standardizing log collection and aggregation involves consolidating logs and metrics from various cloud sources into a unified, centralized platform. This allows organizations to monitor, analyze, and troubleshoot security and operational events consistently across AWS, Azure, and GCP. By using Terraform to provision log collectors and exporters, you can automate the setup of monitoring pipelines that ensure logs are collected, normalized, and made available for analysis in a single pane of glass.

- **Log sources:** Terraform provisions collectors that pull logs from multiple sources, such as virtual machines, containers, network flows, and cloud-native logging services (for example, Azure Monitor, AWS CloudWatch, GCP Logging).
- **Data normalization:** Logs from different cloud providers often come in different formats. Terraform can configure integrations (for example, with Logstash or other data transformation tools) to normalize this data, ensuring that logs are uniformly formatted and easily correlated in the central dashboard.

```
# Create a Resource Group
resource "azurerm_resource_group" "example" {
  name     = "example-rg"
  location = "East US"
}

# Create a Log Analytics Workspace for storing logs
resource "azurerm_log_analytics_workspace" "example" {
  name                = "example-law"
  location            = azurerm_resource_group.example.location
  resource_group_name = azurerm_resource_group.example.name
  sku                 = "PerGB2018"
  retention_in_days   = 30
}

# Create an Event Hub Namespace for log export (to be ingested by ELK)
resource "azurerm_eventhub_namespace" "example" {
  name                = "example-ehns"
  location            = azurerm_resource_group.example.location
  resource_group_name = azurerm_resource_group.example.name
  sku                 = "Standard"
  capacity            = 2
}

# Create an Event Hub within the Namespace
resource "azurerm_eventhub" "example" {
  name                = "example-eh"
  namespace_name      = azurerm_eventhub_namespace.example.name
  resource_group_name = azurerm_resource_group.example.name
  partition_count     = 4
  message_retention   = 1
}

# Create an Event Hub Authorization Rule for access control
resource "azurerm_eventhub_authorization_rule" "example" {
  name                = "example-auth-rule"
  namespace_name      = azurerm_eventhub_namespace.example.name
  eventhub_name       = azurerm_eventhub.example.name
  resource_group_name = azurerm_resource_group.example.name
```

```
  listen              = true
  send                = true
  manage              = false
}

# Provision an Azure Storage Account as the source of logs
resource "azurerm_storage_account" "example" {
  name                     = "examplestoracc"
  resource_group_name      = azurerm_resource_group.example.name
  location                 = azurerm_resource_group.example.location
  account_tier             = "Standard"
  account_replication_type = "LRS"
}

# Configure Diagnostic Settings to send logs to both Log Analytics and Event
Hub
resource "azurerm_monitor_diagnostic_setting" "example" {
  name                       = "diag-setting"
  target_resource_id         = azurerm_storage_account.example.id
  log_analytics_workspace_id = azurerm_log_analytics_workspace.example.id

  eventhub_authorization_rule_id = azurerm_eventhub_authorization_rule.exam-
ple.id
  eventhub_name                  = azurerm_eventhub.example.name

  log {
    category = "StorageRead"
    enabled  = true
    retention_policy {
      enabled = true
      days    = 30
    }
  }

  log {
    category = "StorageWrite"
    enabled  = true
    retention_policy {
      enabled = true
      days    = 30
    }
  }

  metric {
    category = "AllMetrics"
    enabled  = true
    retention_policy {
      enabled = true
      days    = 30
    }
  }
}
```

This Terraform configuration provisions an Azure Log Analytics Workspace and an Event Hub to centralize and export logs from an Azure Storage Account, standardizing log collection and enabling integration with ELK for cross-cloud monitoring.

Enabling Multi-Cloud Log Retention Policies

Log retention policies define the duration for which logs are stored before they are archived or deleted. In a multi-cloud environment, having consistent retention periods is crucial to meet compliance requirements and prevent data loss. Terraform allows you to automate the enforcement of uniform retention policies across AWS, Azure, and GCP, ensuring that logs are retained for the required duration and managed efficiently.

- **Policy definition:** Terraform scripts define retention policies for cloud logging services such as AWS CloudWatch, Azure Log Analytics, and GCP Logging. These policies specify how long logs should be kept before being purged or archived, ensuring compliance with regulatory standards.
- **Automation:** By codifying these policies as Infrastructure as Code, Terraform ensures that the same log retention settings are consistently applied across environments. This automation minimizes human error and simplifies the management of log retention across multiple clouds.
- **Archival solutions:** In addition to retention, Terraform can also configure long-term archival solutions. For example, logs can be stored in AWS S3 with lifecycle policies, Azure Blob Storage with retention policies, or GCP Cloud Storage buckets configured with a retention policy (for example, Coldline storage) to ensure that critical logs are preserved for forensic analysis and compliance audits.

```
# Create a GCP Storage Bucket with a retention policy (e.g., 30 days)
resource "google_storage_bucket" "logs_bucket" {
  name          = "logs-bucket-unique"  # Ensure this name is globally unique
  location      = "US"
  force_destroy = true

  retention_policy {
    retention_period = 2592000  # Retain logs for 30 days (in seconds)
  }
}

# Create a Cloud Logging Project Sink that exports logs to the storage bucket
resource "google_logging_project_sink" "example" {
  name        = "sink-example"
  destination = "storage.googleapis.com/${google_storage_bucket.logs_bucket.
name}"
}
```

This Terraform configuration provisions a GCP Storage bucket with a 30-day retention policy and creates a logging sink to export logs to this bucket, standardizing log retention and archival across the environment.

Real-Time Anomaly Detection in Logs

Real-time anomaly detection leverages AI/ML-driven analytics to continuously analyze cloud logs and identify suspicious activities such as unauthorized access or data exfiltration across multi-cloud environments. By integrating threat detection services (such as AWS Lookout, Azure Sentinel, and GCP Chronicle) with Terraform, organizations can automate the deployment of monitoring pipelines that analyze logs in real time, detect deviations from normal patterns, and reduce false positives through sophisticated pattern recognition.

- **Log streaming:** Logs from various sources are continuously streamed to an AI/ML service (for example, AWS Lookout for Metrics, Azure Sentinel, or GCP Chronicle) using logging sinks and event streaming tools. This ensures that every security-relevant event is available for real-time analysis.

- **Pattern recognition:** The AI/ML model analyzes the historical log data and identifies patterns that indicate normal behavior. When current log entries deviate from these patterns, such as unexpected spikes in traffic or anomalous API calls, the system flags them as potential security threats.

```
# Create a Pub/Sub Topic to forward logs to Chronicle
resource "google_pubsub_topic" "chronicle_topic" {
  name = "chronicle-topic"
}

# Create a Cloud Logging Sink that exports logs to the Pub/Sub Topic
resource "google_logging_project_sink" "chronicle_sink" {
  name        = "chronicle-sink"
  destination = "pubsub.googleapis.com/projects/${var.project_id}/topics/${-
google_pubsub_topic.chronicle_topic.name}"
  # Optionally, apply a filter to only export relevant logs
  filter      = "severity>=ERROR"
}
```

This Terraform configuration provisions a Cloud Logging sink and Pub/Sub topic in GCP to export high-severity logs to Chronicle for real-time anomaly detection, enabling continuous, automated threat analysis.

By standardizing log collection, enforcing retention policies, deploying anomaly detection, and implementing RBAC, organizations can establish robust multi-cloud logging and monitoring practices. Automating these processes with Terraform ensures consistency, reduces human error, and improves cloud security posture. This section provides the foundational best practices for comprehensive log management across AWS, Azure, and GCP, ensuring scalable and secure cloud operations.

Leveraging Terraform for Security Automation and Incident Response

Security automation and incident response are critical components of cloud security operations, ensuring rapid identification and mitigation of threats across distributed environments. Terraform's Infrastructure as Code (IaC) capabilities enable teams to automate security workflows, enforce policies, and create scalable incident response mechanisms across AWS, Azure, and GCP. By designing reusable Terraform modules, implementing multi-region monitoring, and automating policy enforcement, organizations can build robust and resilient security postures. This section explores how Terraform can be harnessed to build secure incident response workflows, deploy monitoring across regions, and enforce security compliance at scale, providing a cohesive and automated approach to cloud security.

Deploying Multi-Region Monitoring with Terraform

Multi-region monitoring ensures that security observability spans across multiple cloud regions, providing redundancy and failover capabilities. This approach guarantees that if one region experiences an outage or performance degradation, monitoring continues in another region, ensuring continuous visibility into the health and security of your infrastructure. By using Terraform to automate the deployment of monitoring services, organizations can achieve comprehensive, consistent, and resilient observability across all regions.

- **Resource provisioning:** Terraform provisions monitoring resources (for example, AWS CloudWatch, Azure Monitor, GCP Operations) in multiple regions. This allows you to deploy identical monitoring configurations that track the same metrics from different geographic locations.

- **Failover configuration:** When one region becomes unavailable, the monitoring setup automatically shifts to a secondary region. This failover mechanism ensures that alerting and logging remain uninterrupted even during regional outages.
- **Data synchronization:** Terraform can also manage the configuration of log shipping and data replication across regions, ensuring that logs and metrics are synchronized and aggregated into a unified view for centralized analysis.

```
# Default provider configuration for us-east-1
provider "aws" {
  region = "us-east-1"
}

# Additional provider configuration for us-west-2
provider "aws" {
  alias  = "west"
  region = "us-west-2"
}

# CloudWatch alarm in us-east-1
resource "aws_cloudwatch_metric_alarm" "alarm_east" {
  alarm_name          = "example-alarm-east"
  comparison_operator = "GreaterThanThreshold"
  evaluation_periods  = 1
  metric_name         = "CPUUtilization"
  namespace           = "AWS/EC2"
  period              = 300
  statistic           = "Average"
  threshold           = 80
  alarm_description   = "Alarm when CPU utilization exceeds 80% in us-east-1"
  actions_enabled     = true
}

# CloudWatch alarm in us-west-2 using the aliased provider
resource "aws_cloudwatch_metric_alarm" "alarm_west" {
  provider            = aws.west
  alarm_name          = "example-alarm-west"
  comparison_operator = "GreaterThanThreshold"
  evaluation_periods  = 1
  metric_name         = "CPUUtilization"
  namespace           = "AWS/EC2"
  period              = 300
  statistic           = "Average"
  threshold           = 80
  alarm_description   = "Alarm when CPU utilization exceeds 80% in us-west-2"
  actions_enabled     = true
}
```

This Terraform configuration deploys AWS CloudWatch alarms in both us-east-1 and us-west-2 regions, ensuring multi-region monitoring for high availability and continuous observability of infrastructure metrics.

Automating Policy Enforcement with Sentinel and Open Policy Agent

Policy-as-Code (PaC) ensures that cloud infrastructure adheres to predefined security and compliance standards by automatically validating infrastructure configurations during deployment. Tools such as HashiCorp Sentinel and Open Policy Agent (OPA) allow organizations to codify these policies as code, which are then enforced during Terraform deployments. This proactive validation prevents misconfigurations, limits exposure of sensitive resources (such as public IPs), and maintains continuous compliance with regulatory requirements.

- **Policy definition:** Write policies using Sentinel or OPA (Rego) to enforce specific security controls. For example, you might write rules to enforce encryption for storage resources or to restrict the creation of public IP addresses on Azure.
- **Policy enforcement:** When Terraform runs, these policies are evaluated against the planned infrastructure changes. If the Terraform configuration violates any of the rules, the deployment is blocked, ensuring that only compliant resources are provisioned.
- **Continuous compliance:** By integrating policy enforcement into the Terraform workflow, your cloud environment is continuously monitored for compliance. Any drift or deviation from the defined policies is caught early, and corrective measures can be automatically triggered.

```
package terraform.azure

deny[msg] {
  input.resource_type == "azurerm_public_ip"
  msg = "Public IP addresses are not allowed in this configuration."
}
```

This OPA policy, written in Rego, denies the deployment of any Azure resource that creates a public IP address, enforcing secure configurations and preventing non-compliant infrastructure from being provisioned by Terraform.

Scaling Incident Response across Multi-Cloud Environments

A multi-cloud incident response strategy involves deploying **`"quarantine"`** VMs in various cloud environments to isolate and remediate compromised resources. By automating these deployments with Terraform, organizations ensure that incident response mechanisms are consistent and repeatable across AWS, Azure, and GCP. This approach minimizes the blast radius of security incidents, improves recovery times, and enforces uniform security policies.

- **Infrastructure as Code (IaC):** Terraform modules encapsulate the logic for deploying quarantine VMs, ensuring that the same configuration is applied across different cloud providers. This leads to consistent deployments and simplifies maintenance and updates.
- **Multi-provider support:** By configuring provider blocks for AWS, Azure, and GCP within the same Terraform configuration, you can deploy resources concurrently across clouds. This unified approach makes it easier to manage incident response in a multi-cloud environment.
- **Automated deployment:** The Terraform module automatically provisions quarantine VMs along with necessary configuration details (such as instance type, image, network settings, and tags). These VMs can then be used to isolate compromised workloads or run remediation scripts.

```
# AWS provider configuration
provider "aws" {
  region = "us-east-1"
}

# Azure provider configuration
provider "azurerm" {
  features {}
  subscription_id = var.azure_subscription_id
  tenant_id       = var.azure_tenant_id
  client_id       = var.azure_client_id
  client_secret   = var.azure_client_secret
}

# GCP provider configuration
provider "google" {
  project = var.gcp_project
  region  = "us-central1"
}

# Module invocation to deploy quarantine VMs across clouds
module "quarantine_vm" {
  source = "./modules/quarantine_vm"

  instance_name = "quarantine-vm"
  aws_ami       = var.aws_ami
  aws_instance_type = var.aws_instance_type
  azure_resource_group = var.azure_resource_group
  azure_location       = var.azure_location
  azure_vm_size        = var.azure_vm_size
  azure_image_publisher= var.azure_image_publisher
  azure_image_offer    = var.azure_image_offer
  azure_image_sku      = var.azure_image_sku
  azure_admin_username = var.azure_admin_username
  azure_admin_password = var.azure_admin_password
  gcp_zone       = var.gcp_zone
  gcp_machine_type = var.gcp_machine_type
  gcp_image         = var.gcp_image

  providers = {
    aws     = aws
    azurerm = azurerm
    google  = google
  }
}
```

This Terraform module deploys quarantine VMs across AWS, Azure, and GCP by using provider-specific configurations within a unified module, ensuring consistent incident response capabilities across multi-cloud environments.

Leveraging Terraform for security automation streamlines incident response, enforces policies, and ensures continuous compliance across AWS, Azure, and GCP. By developing secure Terraform modules, automating monitoring, and scaling incident response workflows, organizations can fortify their cloud environments against evolving threats.

Conclusion

As cloud adoption grows, organizations must implement a robust and proactive approach to security monitoring and incident response across AWS, Azure, and GCP. This chapter provided a comprehensive guide to setting up multi-cloud security monitoring dashboards, leveraging Terraform for automated deployment, and integrating tools such as Grafana, AWS CloudWatch, Azure Monitor, and GCP Operations Suite. By aggregating security metrics from multiple cloud platforms and correlating threat data, organizations can gain real-time visibility into their cloud security posture. Automating alerts and incident response with serverless solutions such as AWS Lambda, Azure Functions, and Google Cloud Functions ensures that security teams can react swiftly to threats, minimizing the impact of potential breaches.

Furthermore, integrating cloud-native threat detection services such as AWS GuardDuty, Azure Defender, and GCP Security Command Center enhances an organization's ability to identify and investigate security incidents effectively. Terraform plays a critical role in automating security operations, from deploying log aggregation solutions to enforcing security policies with HashiCorp Sentinel and Open Policy Agent. By implementing best practices for multi-cloud log retention, anomaly detection, and incident response automation, organizations can establish a resilient security framework that scales seamlessly across cloud environments. Ultimately, leveraging Terraform for security automation enables businesses to maintain continuous security monitoring, enforce compliance, and respond to evolving threats with agility and precision.

In the next chapter, we will focus on enhancing disaster recovery and resilience using Terraform by automating backups, multi-region failovers, and recovery plans. It also covers building resilient architectures with autoscaling and load balancers, along with conducting disaster recovery drills and tests.

Questions and Answers

1. **How can organizations effectively set up a unified security monitoring dashboard across AWS, Azure, and GCP?**

   Organizations can create a unified security monitoring dashboard by aggregating security metrics from AWS CloudWatch, Azure Monitor, and GCP Operations Suite. This can be achieved using Grafana, which integrates with these cloud-native tools to provide a centralized visualization of security events. Terraform can be used to deploy pre-built modules that configure these dashboards efficiently, ensuring rapid setup and consistency across cloud environments. Additionally, cross-cloud security metric correlation helps detect anomalies by analyzing security logs across multiple platforms.

2. **What are the benefits of using serverless technologies for automated security alerts and incident response?**

   Serverless technologies such as AWS Lambda, Azure Functions, and Google Cloud Functions enable organizations to automate incident detection and response without managing infrastructure. These services can be configured to trigger based on security events, analyze logs in real time, and execute predefined actions, such as isolating compromised resources. By integrating serverless functions with messaging services such as AWS SNS, Google Pub/Sub, and Azure Event Grid, organizations can send instant alerts to security teams, ensuring swift action against threats.

3. **How does Terraform help in integrating and automating cloud-native threat detection services?**

   Terraform provides Infrastructure-as-Code (IaC) capabilities to automate the provisioning of threat detection services such as AWS GuardDuty, Azure Defender, and GCP Security Command Center. Using Terraform modules, security teams can define configurations for continuous threat monitoring, ensuring that all cloud environments have uniform security policies in place. Additionally, Terraform can be used to aggregate threat intelligence feeds from multiple providers, improving the accuracy of threat investigations and enhancing security postures across multi-cloud setups.

4. **What best practices should organizations follow for logging and monitoring in a multi-cloud environment?**

   To ensure consistent logging and monitoring across AWS, Azure, and GCP, organizations should adopt standardized log collection and aggregation practices using tools such as the ELK Stack, Azure Log Analytics, and GCP Logging. Terraform can be leveraged to enforce multi-cloud log retention policies, ensuring compliance with industry standards and regulations. Additionally, implementing AI/ML-driven anomaly detection models helps organizations identify suspicious activities in logs in real-time, reducing the likelihood of undetected security incidents.

5. **How can Terraform be used to scale incident response across multiple cloud environments?**

   Terraform enables organizations to scale incident response by automating the deployment of multi-region monitoring solutions, ensuring high availability and redundancy. Security policies can be enforced programmatically using HashiCorp Sentinel and Open Policy Agent (OPA), allowing teams to define compliance rules as code. Terraform-based automation workflows streamline incident response processes across AWS, Azure, and GCP, reducing manual intervention and improving response times during security events.

CHAPTER 13
Disaster Recovery and Resilience with Terraform

Introduction

In an era of increasing cloud reliance and digital transformation, ensuring uninterrupted service availability and robust Disaster Recovery (DR) mechanisms is no longer optional; it is a strategic necessity. This chapter delves into how Terraform can be harnessed to automate disaster recovery and build highly resilient, multi-cloud architectures. With a focus on Infrastructure-as-Code (IaC) principles, this chapter guides readers through designing and implementing DR plans that span across AWS, Azure, and GCP. From automating cross-cloud backup strategies to enforcing consistent retention policies and orchestrating cross-region replication, you will learn how to create provider-agnostic solutions that ensure data durability and business continuity even during major outages.

Beyond backup automation, the chapter explores how Terraform can be used to configure multi-region failover strategies for both applications and databases. It outlines the use of global load balancers, DNS-based routing, and autoscaling mechanisms to build fault-tolerant architectures that dynamically adapt to traffic spikes and failures. Readers will also discover how to simulate outages, conduct DR drills, and validate backup restorations using Terraform workflows. The chapter concludes by introducing fully automated recovery plans that include instant rollbacks, RTO/RPO compliance, and continuous updates through Terraform versioning, empowering organizations to respond swiftly and confidently during crises.

Structure

In this chapter, we will cover the following topics:

- Automating Backup Strategies with Provider-Agnostic Solutions
    - Implementing Automated Snapshots for Storage and Databases
    - Multi-Cloud Backup with HashiCorp Vault and Terraform
    - Enforcing Backup Retention Policies across Providers
    - Data Replication and Cross-Region Backups
- Configuring Multi-Region Failover for Databases and Applications
    - Automating Database Replication and Failover
    - Deploying Global Load Balancers for Application Failover
    - Multi-Region DNS Failover with Terraform
- Building Resilient Architectures with Autoscaling and Load Balancers
    - Autoscaling Workloads across Regions
    - Stateless Architecture Design for Application Resilience

- Conducting Disaster Recovery Drills and Testing Plans
  - Simulating Outages with Terraform
  - Automated Testing of Backup Restoration
  - Monitoring and Reporting DR Drill Results
- Automating Recovery Plans and Configurations with Terraform
  - Building Infrastructure-as-Code Recovery Workflows
  - Automating RTO (Recovery Time Objective) and RPO (Recovery Point Objective) Policies
  - Instant Rollback and Disaster Recovery with Terraform
  - Continuous DR Plan Updates and Versioning

Automating Backup Strategies with Provider-Agnostic Solutions

Automated backups play a vital role in ensuring business continuity and safeguarding against data loss. With Terraform and provider-specific or agnostic modules, organizations can design consistent, scalable backup strategies across AWS, Azure, and GCP. This section covers how to implement automated backup workflows using Infrastructure as Code (IaC), enabling cross-cloud resilience, reducing operational overhead, and minimizing potential downtime.

Implementing Automated Snapshots for Storage and Databases

Snapshots are point-in-time backups of storage volumes or databases that help recover data in the event of accidental deletion, data corruption, or disaster. Implementing automated snapshots ensures that backups occur consistently and securely, without relying on manual processes.

Terraform leverages cloud provider APIs to define and provision snapshot automation policies as code. Instead of manually triggering backups, Terraform allows users to declaratively define schedules, retention periods, and tagging rules. This not only standardizes backup operations but also makes them repeatable, auditable, and scalable across environments. The following are some features and best practices for automating snapshots for storage and databases:

- **Tagging:** Apply consistent tags (for example, **`backup=true`**) to volumes or databases to automatically include them in snapshot workflows.
- **Immutable Backups:** Use IAM policies or cloud-native settings to prevent modifications or deletions of snapshots once created.
- **Lifecycle Policies:** Set up automatic expiration and cleanup of older snapshots to optimize cost and storage use.

```
# Create an IAM role for AWS DLM to manage snapshots
resource "aws_iam_role" "dlm_role" {
  name = "dlm-lifecycle-role"
  assume_role_policy = jsonencode({
    Version = "2012-10-17",
    Statement = [
      {
        Effect    = "Allow",
        Principal = {
          Service = "dlm.amazonaws.com"
        },
```

```
        Action    = "sts:AssumeRole"
      }
    ]
  })
}

# Attach a policy to the IAM role with the required permissions for DLM
resource "aws_iam_role_policy" "dlm_policy" {
  name = "dlm-policy"
  role = aws_iam_role.dlm_role.id
  policy = jsonencode({
    Version = "2012-10-17",
    Statement = [
      {
        Effect   = "Allow",
        Action   = [
          "ec2:CreateSnapshot",
          "ec2:DeleteSnapshot",
          "ec2:DescribeVolumes",
          "ec2:DescribeSnapshots"
        ],
        Resource = "*"
      }
    ]
  })
}

# Create a Data Lifecycle Manager (DLM) lifecycle policy for EBS snapshots
resource "aws_dlm_lifecycle_policy" "ebs_snapshot_policy" {
  description        = "Automated daily snapshot policy for EBS volumes with
Backup=true tag"
  execution_role_arn  = aws_iam_role.dlm_role.arn
  state              = "ENABLED"

  policy_details {
    resource_types = ["VOLUME"]
    target_tags = {
      backup = "true"
    }

    schedules {
      name      = "daily-snapshot"
      copy_tags = true

      create_rule {
        interval      = 24
        interval_unit = "HOURS"
      }

      retain_rule {
        count = 7
      }
    }
  }
}
```

The aforementioned Terraform example uses AWS Data Lifecycle Manager (DLM) to automate the creation of snapshots for EBS volumes. This configuration creates a lifecycle policy that targets

EBS volumes tagged with **Backup=true** and automatically creates daily snapshots, retaining the most recent 7 snapshots.

Multi-Cloud Backup with HashiCorp Vault and Terraform

HashiCorp Vault is a robust secrets management and data protection tool that provides encryption and access control for sensitive data. When it comes to backups, Vault not only encrypts data before it is stored in cloud environments but also centralizes secrets management to ensure uniform security across AWS, Azure, and GCP. Terraform can be used to provision and configure Vault along with its associated policies and backup scripts, thereby creating a cohesive and scalable multi-cloud backup strategy.

Vault encrypts backup data using its strong cryptographic mechanisms before the data is transmitted to and stored within cloud storage services. Terraform automates the deployment of Vault, defines policies, and orchestrates backup scripts to ensure consistency across different cloud providers. By doing so, it enables an integrated and automated approach where backup operations rely on predefined Vault policies to manage access and encryption uniformly. For example, when backing up Azure Blob Storage data, Vault policies can be applied to ensure that only authorized users or services have access to these encrypted backups, reducing the risk of data exposure.

- **Centralized secrets management:** Utilize a single Vault instance to manage secrets and encryption keys used for backups across multiple cloud providers, streamlining access control and reducing complexity.
- **Encryption-at-rest:** Ensure that all backups are encrypted by Vault before storage, thereby protecting data even if the underlying storage system is compromised.
- **Policy enforcement:** Implement strict Vault policies to govern backup access, ensuring that only authorized users can read or modify backup data.
- **Automated deployment:** Use Terraform to automatically provision, configure, and manage Vault and its policies, ensuring consistent backup processes across environments.
- **Audit logging:** Enable logging within Vault to maintain a detailed audit trail of who accessed or modified backup secrets, improving accountability and forensic capabilities.

```
provider "vault" {
  # Replace with your Vault address and token as appropriate
  address = "http://127.0.0.1:8200"
  token   = var.vault_token
}

# Create a Vault policy for managing Azure Blob backup secrets
resource "vault_policy" "azure_blob_backup_policy" {
  name   = "azure_blob_backup_policy"
  policy = <<EOT
path "secret/backup/azure/blob/*" {
  capabilities = ["create", "read", "update", "delete", "list"]
}
EOT
}

# Store a sample secret using the defined policy path
resource "vault_generic_endpoint" "azure_backup_secret" {
  path      = "secret/backup/azure/blob/my-secret"
  data_json = <<EOT
```

```
{
  "username": "admin",
  "password": "securepassword123"
}
EOT
}
```

This Terraform configuration sets up a Vault policy for managing Azure Blob backup secrets and stores a sample secret, ensuring secure and controlled access via HashiCorp Vault.

Enforcing Backup Retention Policies Across Providers

Backup retention policies specify the duration for which backup data is preserved before being automatically deleted. Enforcing these policies is critical for managing storage costs and ensuring compliance with regulatory requirements across various cloud providers such as AWS, Azure, and GCP.

Terraform scripts are used to define and enforce retention rules for different types of backups, such as snapshots, storage buckets, and database backups. These scripts leverage cloud-native lifecycle policies to automate the cleanup of outdated backups. This not only helps control storage expenses but also ensures that backup data is retained only as long as necessary, thus reducing the risk of retaining stale or non-compliant data.

- **Automated cleanup:** Lifecycle policies defined in Terraform automatically delete backups that exceed the retention period, reducing manual intervention and ensuring consistent policy enforcement.
- **Compliance and cost control:** By automating backup retention, organizations can avoid unnecessary storage costs and remain compliant with data retention regulations.

```
resource "google_storage_bucket" "backup_bucket" {
  name          = "backup-bucket-unique"
  location      = "US"
  force_destroy = true                  # Not recommended for prod

  retention_policy {
    retention_period = 2592000  # Retains backups for 30 days (in seconds)
  }
}
```

This Terraform snippet provisions a GCP Cloud Storage bucket with a retention policy that automatically deletes backups older than 30 days, ensuring cost control and compliance with backup retention requirements.

Data Replication and Cross-Region Backups

Multi-region backup strategies are critical for safeguarding data in today's dynamic cloud environments. When backups are replicated across multiple regions, organizations can ensure that their data remains protected even if an entire region experiences an outage. This approach not only enhances availability and disaster recovery capabilities but also helps organizations meet data retention policies and regulatory requirements.

Terraform plays a pivotal role in automating and standardizing backup workflows across various resources, such as storage volumes and databases. By defining backup and replication processes as code, Terraform ensures that these configurations are applied consistently across different cloud providers, including AWS, Azure, and GCP. This automation minimizes manual errors, reduces operational overhead, and provides a predictable means of managing backups.

For example, in AWS, Terraform can be used to configure cross-region replication for S3 buckets and manage EBS volume snapshots through AWS Backup, enabling secure and automated replication of critical data to secondary regions. In a similar fashion, Azure leverages Geo-Redundant Storage (GRS) to ensure that backups are maintained in multiple regions, while GCP employs dual-region buckets to replicate data and ensure high availability. These native cloud features, when provisioned and managed through Terraform, form the backbone of a resilient, multi-region backup strategy that ensures data integrity and rapid recovery in the event of failures.

```
# Primary Backup Vault in us-east-1
resource "aws_backup_vault" "primary" {
  name        = "primary-backup-vault"
  kms_key_arn = var.kms_key_arn
}

# Replica Backup Vault in us-west-2 (using provider alias for us-west-2)
provider "aws" {
  alias  = "west"
  region = "us-west-2"
}

resource "aws_backup_vault" "replica" {
  provider    = aws.west
  name        = "replica-backup-vault"
  kms_key_arn = var.kms_key_arn_replica
}

# AWS Backup Plan for EBS volumes
resource "aws_backup_plan" "ebs_backup_plan" {
  name = "ebs-backup-plan"

  rule {
    rule_name         = "daily-ebs-backup"
    target_vault_name = aws_backup_vault.primary.name
    schedule          = "cron(0 5 * * ? *)"  # Every day at 5 AM UTC
    lifecycle {
      delete_after = 7  # Retain backups for 7 days
    }
    copy_action {
      destination_vault_arn = aws_backup_vault.replica.arn

      lifecycle {
        delete_after = 30  # Retain copies in the replica vault for 30 days
      }
    }
  }
}

# AWS Backup Selection for EBS volumes tagged for backup
resource "aws_backup_selection" "ebs_backup_selection" {
  plan_id      = aws_backup_plan.ebs_backup_plan.id
  name         = "ebs-backup-selection"
  iam_role_arn = var.backup_role_arn

  selection_tag {
    key   = "Backup"
```

```
      value = "true"
      type  = "STRINGEQUALS"
    }
  }
```

This Terraform configuration establishes an AWS Backup plan for EBS volumes with a daily backup schedule and a 7-day retention period. It also adds a copy action to replicate the backup data to a different region, with a retention period of 30 days, thereby enabling cross-region backup capabilities.

Automating backup strategies across cloud providers using Terraform ensures data resilience, reduces operational overhead, and enhances security posture. By leveraging snapshots, HashiCorp Vault, retention policies, and cross-region replication, organizations can safeguard critical data against outages and disasters. This foundation of automated backups sets the stage for the subsequent sections on failover, resilience, and incident recovery.

Configuring Multi-Region Failover for Databases and Applications

Multi-region failover strategies ensure that cloud environments maintain high availability and resilience during outages. By leveraging Terraform to deploy redundant resources across multiple regions, organizations can minimize downtime, protect critical workloads, and ensure seamless failover. This section focuses on automating the deployment of failover architectures for databases and applications across AWS, Azure, and GCP.

Automating Database Replication and Failover

Database replication involves copying and synchronizing data from a primary database to one or more secondary (replica) databases, often deployed in different regions. This approach ensures that in the event of a primary database outage or failure, a replica can seamlessly take over, maintaining application availability and data integrity. Automating this process with Terraform minimizes manual intervention, ensures consistency across environments, and enhances disaster recovery strategies across cloud platforms such as AWS, Azure, and GCP.

Terraform is used to provision both primary and replica databases, configure replication settings, and define automated failover policies. For example, in Azure, Terraform can deploy an Azure SQL Database and set up geo-replication so that the database is automatically replicated to another region. If the primary instance becomes unavailable, the system can trigger a failover, where read or write operations are redirected to the secondary instance. This automated workflow not only reduces the risk of prolonged downtime but also ensures that data remains consistent and available, regardless of regional outages. The following are some features and best practices of database replication:

- **Automate replica creation:** Use Terraform to consistently deploy replica databases, ensuring that each backup instance follows the same configuration standards.
- **Monitor replication lag:** Implement robust monitoring to track replication lag and detect any inconsistencies between the primary and replica databases.
- **Failover testing:** Regularly test failover mechanisms to verify that transitions between primary and secondary systems occur seamlessly without impacting end-user experience.
- **Cross-region redundancy:** Deploy replicas in geographically distant regions to prevent correlated outages and maintain business continuity in the face of regional disruptions.

```
# Main Azure SQL Server
resource "azurerm_sql_server" "primary" {
  name                         = "primary-sqlserver"
  resource_group_name          = azurerm_resource_group.example.name
  location                     = azurerm_resource_group.example.location
  version                      = "12.0"
  administrator_login          = var.sql_admin
  administrator_login_password = var.sql_admin_password
}

# Primary Database
resource "azurerm_sql_database" "primary_db" {
  name                = "primary-database"
  resource_group_name = azurerm_resource_group.example.name
  location            = azurerm_sql_server.primary.location
  server_name         = azurerm_sql_server.primary.name
  edition             = "Standard"
  requested_service_objective_name = "S1"
}

# Secondary Azure SQL Server for Geo-Replication
resource "azurerm_sql_server" "secondary" {
  name                         = "secondary-sqlserver"
  resource_group_name          = azurerm_resource_group.example.name
  location                     = "West US"  # Different region for redundancy
  version                      = "12.0"
  administrator_login          = var.sql_admin
  administrator_login_password = var.sql_admin_password
}

# Secondary Database (Replica) - Created implicitly by geo-replication
resource "azurerm_sql_database_replication_link" "geo_replication" {
  name                  = "replication-link"
  resource_group_name   = azurerm_resource_group.example.name
  server_name           = azurerm_sql_server.primary.name
  database_name         = azurerm_sql_database.primary_db.name
  partner_server_name   = azurerm_sql_server.secondary.name
  partner_database_name = azurerm_sql_database.primary_db.name
}
```

This Terraform configuration provisions an Azure SQL Server and database in a primary region and sets up a replication link to a secondary SQL Server in a different region for geo-replication, enabling automated cross-region failover.

Deploying Global Load Balancers for Application Failover

Global load balancers are crucial for ensuring continuous application availability across multiple regions by distributing user traffic to various endpoints. By leveraging cloud-native load balancers, organizations can maintain service continuity during regional outages. Terraform automates the deployment of these load balancers across major providers such as AWS, Azure, and GCP, ensuring a consistent and scalable solution for global traffic distribution and failover.

Terraform provisions global load balancer resources and configures associated health checks to continuously monitor the status of application endpoints. In the event of a regional failure, the load balancer automatically reroutes traffic to healthy endpoints located in other regions. This dynamic traffic management ensures minimal downtime and helps maintain performance and user experience by directing traffic to the nearest available, healthy region. The following are some best practices for configuring global load balancers:

- **Deploy redundant endpoints:** Provision endpoints in multiple regions to eliminate single points of failure and ensure high availability.
- **Define health checks:** Implement robust health checks to continuously monitor the status of each endpoint. Quick detection of failures allows the load balancer to promptly redirect traffic to healthy resources.
- **Traffic routing:** Configure traffic policies to prioritize routing to the closest or least congested regions, thereby reducing latency and improving the overall user experience.

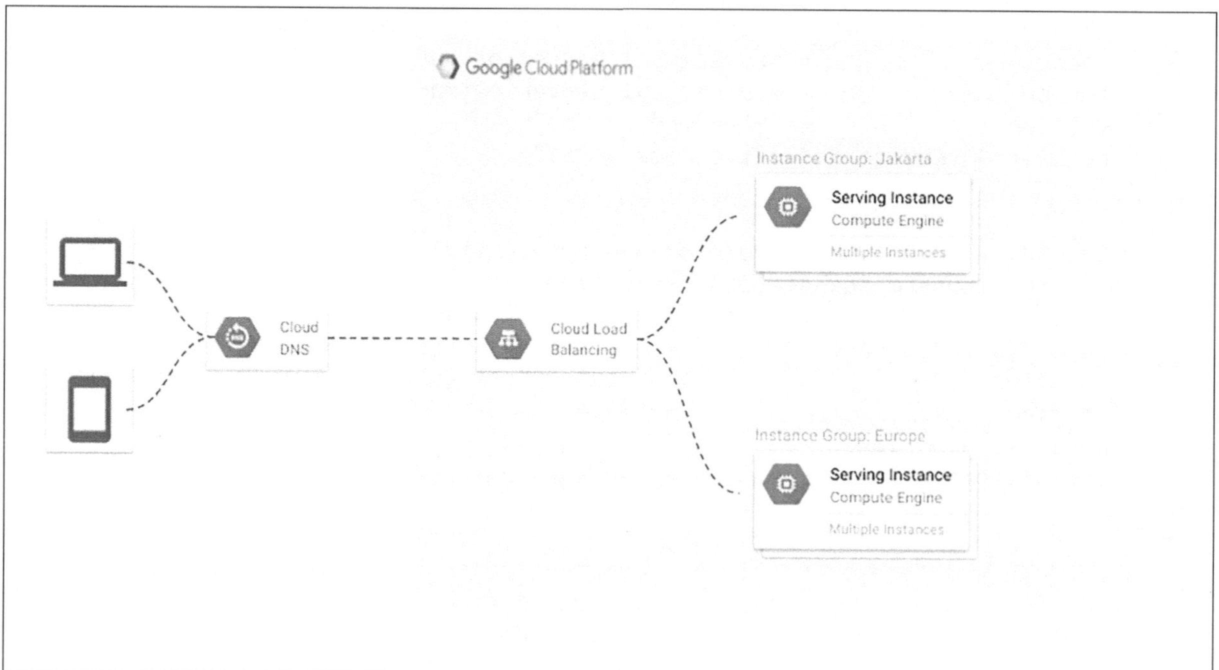

Figure 13.1: *GCP Load Balancer for application failover*

The following Terraform snippet provisions a global load balancer in GCP with a static external IP, backend service, URL map, target HTTPS proxy, and global forwarding rule to facilitate automatic traffic failover in case of regional outages. Additionally, monitoring and logging can be optionally defined to enhance observability and operational insights.

This Terraform code provisions a complete HTTPS global load balancer in GCP with a static external IP, backend service, health check, URL routing, target HTTPS proxy, and forwarding rule. It enables secure and resilient traffic distribution across backend instances, with optional observability via health checks.

```
# Allocate a global static IP for the load balancer
resource "google_compute_global_address" "lb_ip" {
  name         = "example-lb-ip"
  address_type = "EXTERNAL"
  ip_version   = "IPV4"
}

# Google vm health check
resource "google_compute_health_check" "example" {
  name = "example-health-check"
```

```
  http_health_check {
    port = 80
    request_path = "/healthz"
  }

  check_interval_sec  = 5
  timeout_sec         = 5
  healthy_threshold   = 2
  unhealthy_threshold = 2
}

# Create instance group in us-central1
resource "google_compute_instance_group" "us_central1_group" {
  name      = "us-central1-instance-group"
  zone      = "us-central1-a"
  instances = []  # Add instance self-links if required
  network = "default"
}

# Create instance group in europe-west1
resource "google_compute_instance_group" "europe_west1_group" {
  name      = "europe-west1-instance-group"
  zone      = "europe-west1-b"
  instances = []  # Add instance self-links if required
  network = "default"
}

# Create a backend service for the load balancer
resource "google_compute_backend_service" "backend" {
  name                  = "example-backend-service"
  load_balancing_scheme = "EXTERNAL"
  protocol              = "HTTP"

  # # Backend in us-central1
  backend {
    group = google_compute_instance_group.us_central1_group.self_link
  }

  # Backend in europe-west1
  backend {
    group = google_compute_instance_group.europe_west1_group.self_link
  }

  # Configure health checks (assumes a health check resource is defined else-
where)
  health_checks = [google_compute_health_check.example.self_link]
}

# Configure a URL map to route requests to the backend service
resource "google_compute_url_map" "url_map" {
  name            = "example-url-map"
  default_service = google_compute_backend_service.backend.self_link
}

# Create a target HTTPS proxy
resource "google_compute_target_https_proxy" "https_proxy" {
  name             = "example-https-proxy"
```

```
  url_map          = google_compute_url_map.url_map.self_link
  ssl_certificates = ["your-ssl-cert-self_link"]  # Replace with your SSL
certificate resource self-link
}

# Create a global forwarding rule to direct HTTPS traffic to the target proxy
resource "google_compute_global_forwarding_rule" "https_forwarding_rule" {
  name                  = "example-https-forwarding-rule"
  ip_address            = google_compute_global_address.lb_ip.address
  target                = google_compute_target_https_proxy.https_proxy.self_
link
  port_range            = "443"
  load_balancing_scheme = "EXTERNAL"
  ip_protocol           = "TCP"
}
```

Multi-Region DNS Failover with Terraform

Multi-region DNS failover is a strategy that ensures traffic is dynamically rerouted to healthy regions if an entire region becomes unavailable. This approach enhances application resiliency by guaranteeing high availability and minimizing downtime. By using Terraform, organizations can automate the configuration of DNS services (such as AWS Route 53, Azure Traffic Manager, and GCP Cloud DNS) to implement consistent failover policies across all cloud providers.

Terraform provisions DNS zones and records that include built-in health checks and failover routing policies. For example, in AWS, Terraform can configure Route 53 records that monitor both primary and secondary application endpoints. When the health check for the primary endpoint fails, the DNS service automatically routes traffic to a standby endpoint in another region. Similarly, Azure Traffic Manager and GCP Cloud DNS provide analogous failover capabilities, ensuring that any regional failure is quickly mitigated. The following are some best practices for DNS failover:

- **Deploy redundant Endpoints:** Provision primary and secondary endpoints across multiple regions to eliminate single points of failure.
- **Define Robust Health Checks:** Configure health checks to monitor endpoint availability continuously and trigger automatic failover when necessary.
- **Regular Testing:** Periodically test failover mechanisms to ensure that the system responds correctly during an outage.
- **Use Alias Records:** Leverage alias records for seamless integration and simplified management of traffic routing.

```
# Create a Route 53 Hosted Zone
resource "aws_route53_zone" "example" {
  name = "example.com"
}

# Configure the primary Route 53 record pointing to the primary ELB
resource "aws_route53_record" "primary" {
  zone_id = aws_route53_zone.example.zone_id
  name    = "example.com"
  type    = "A"

  alias {
    name                   = aws_elb.primary.dns_name
    zone_id                = aws_elb.primary.zone_id
    evaluate_target_health = true
  }
```

```
  failover_routing_policy {
    type = "PRIMARY"
  }
}

# Configure the secondary Route 53 record pointing to the secondary ELB
resource "aws_route53_record" "secondary" {
  zone_id = aws_route53_zone.example.zone_id
  name    = "example.com"
  type    = "A"

  alias {
    name                   = aws_elb.secondary.dns_name
    zone_id                = aws_elb.secondary.zone_id
    evaluate_target_health = true
  }

  failover_routing_policy {
    type = "SECONDARY"
  }
}

# Primary ELB configuration in the primary region
resource "aws_elb" "primary" {
  name = "primary-elb"
  subnets = [var.primary_subnet]
  # Additional required configuration...
}

# Secondary ELB configuration in the secondary region
provider "aws" {
  alias  = "secondary"
  region = var.secondary_region
}

resource "aws_elb" "secondary" {
  provider = aws.secondary
  name     = "secondary-elb"
  subnets  = [var.secondary_subnet]
  # Additional required configuration...
}
```

This Terraform configuration deploys an AWS Route 53 failover strategy with primary and secondary alias records pointing to ELBs in different regions, ensuring automatic traffic rerouting upon endpoint failure.

Multi-region failover strategies are essential for resilient cloud architectures. Terraform provides a unified approach to automate database replication, load balancing, DNS failover, and data synchronization across AWS, Azure, and GCP. By implementing these practices, organizations can enhance application uptime and protect against outages, reinforcing the foundations of cloud security and resilience.

Building Resilient Architectures with Autoscaling and Load Balancers

In cloud environments, resilience is essential for ensuring application uptime, performance, and scalability. Resilient architectures can dynamically adjust to traffic fluctuations, prevent single points of failure, and mitigate disruptions. This section explores how Terraform can automate the provisioning of autoscaling and load-balancing solutions across AWS, Azure, and GCP to create fault-tolerant infrastructures.

Autoscaling Workloads across Regions

Autoscaling is a mechanism that automatically adjusts the number of compute resources, such as virtual machines, based on traffic patterns and application demand. This ensures that applications maintain optimal performance during peak loads while scaling down during periods of low activity, thereby optimizing costs and resource utilization. Terraform automates the deployment of autoscaling configurations, ensuring that the same policies and resource definitions are applied consistently across AWS, Azure, and GCP. This results in enhanced availability, fault tolerance, and overall performance of the infrastructure.

Terraform provisions the components required for autoscaling, including instance templates, scaling policies, and monitoring triggers. For example, in AWS, you can configure Auto Scaling Groups and CloudWatch alarms. In Azure, Virtual Machine Scale Sets (VMSS), along with autoscaling settings, can be configured. Similarly, in GCP, this involves configuring Instance Group Managers with autoscaling policies. These components work together to dynamically add or remove instances based on predefined metrics, such as CPU utilization, memory utilization, network traffic, and so on, to ensure that applications are always served by an appropriately sized pool of resources. When autoscaling is combined with global load balancers, traffic is intelligently routed to the closest or healthiest region, providing continuous application availability even during regional disruptions. The following are some best practices for Autoscaling workloads:

- **Define thresholds properly:** Set realistic scaling thresholds based on historical data and performance metrics to prevent unnecessary scaling events.
- **Use multiple zones/regions:** Distribute workloads across various availability zones or regions to eliminate single points of failure and provide redundancy.
- **Combine with load balancers:** Integrate autoscaling with load balancers to evenly distribute incoming traffic across available instances and avoid bottlenecks.

```
# Create a Virtual Machine Scale Set in Azure
resource "azurerm_virtual_machine_scale_set" "example" {
  name                = "example-vmss"
  location            = azurerm_resource_group.example.location
  resource_group_name = azurerm_resource_group.example.name
  sku                 = "Standard_DS1_v2"
  instances           = 2
  upgrade_policy_mode = "Automatic"

  source_image_reference {
    publisher = "Canonical"
    offer     = "UbuntuServer"
    sku       = "18.04-LTS"
    version   = "latest"
  }

  os_profile {
```

```
    computer_name_prefix = "examplevm"
    admin_username       = "azureuser"
    admin_password       = var.admin_password
  }

  os_profile_linux_config {
    disable_password_authentication = false
  }

  network_profile {
    name    = "example-netprofile"
    primary = true

    ip_configuration {
      name                                   = "internal"
      subnet_id                              = var.subnet_id  # Must be defined elsewhere
      primary                                = true
      load_balancer_backend_address_pools_ids = var.lb_backend_ids  # Must be
defined if using LB
    }
  }
}

# Configure Autoscaling Settings for the VM Scale Set
resource "azurerm_monitor_autoscale_setting" "example" {
  name                = "example-autoscale"
  location            = azurerm_resource_group.example.location
  resource_group_name = azurerm_resource_group.example.name
  target_resource_id  = azurerm_virtual_machine_scale_set.example.id

  profile {
    name = "defaultProfile"

    capacity {
      minimum = "2"
      maximum = "10"
      default = "2"
    }

    rule {
      metric_trigger {
        metric_name        = "Percentage CPU"
        metric_resource_id = azurerm_virtual_machine_scale_set.example.id
        time_grain         = "PT1M"
        statistic          = "Average"
        time_window        = "PT5M"
        time_aggregation   = "Average"
        operator           = "GreaterThan"
        threshold          = 70
      }

      scale_action {
        direction = "Increase"
        type      = "ChangeCount"
        value     = "1"
        cooldown  = "PT5M"
      }
```

```
      }

      rule {
        metric_trigger {
          metric_name        = "Percentage CPU"
          metric_resource_id = azurerm_virtual_machine_scale_set.example.id
          time_grain         = "PT1M"
          statistic          = "Average"
          time_window        = "PT5M"
          time_aggregation   = "Average"
          operator           = "LessThan"
          threshold          = 30
        }

        scale_action {
          direction = "Decrease"
          type      = "ChangeCount"
          value     = "1"
          cooldown  = "PT5M"
        }
      }
    }
  }
```

This Terraform configuration deploys an Azure VM Scale Set with autoscaling settings that adjust the number of VMs based on CPU utilization, ensuring seamless scaling in response to workload demand.

Stateless Architecture Design for Application Resilience

Stateless architectures decouple application state from compute resources, enabling rapid recovery and simplified scaling. In these designs, session and persistent data such as user sessions, configuration settings, or transactional records are stored in external systems such as Redis, DynamoDB, or SQL databases rather than on the compute instances themselves. This separation applies across cloud providers (AWS, Azure, and GCP), where the compute layer operates without retaining any internal state. In doing so, individual compute nodes can be seamlessly replaced, scaled, or updated without impacting the continuity of data, resulting in a resilient system that minimizes downtime during outages or deployments.

Terraform provisions the necessary components for a stateless architecture by automating the deployment of compute resources (such as virtual machines, containers, or serverless functions), external state stores (such as databases or caches), and load balancers. The compute resources are configured to interact with these external data stores, where session information and persistent data are maintained. Load balancers distribute incoming traffic across available compute nodes, ensuring that if one node is replaced or fails, the loss of state does not impact the overall application. This approach is implemented consistently across cloud platforms. For instance, AWS might use Elastic Beanstalk with DynamoDB and ELB, Azure could leverage VM scale sets with Azure SQL or Redis Cache, and GCP might utilize managed instance groups with Cloud SQL and Cloud Load Balancing. Terraform makes these deployments repeatable and consistent by codifying the infrastructure in modules, enabling organizations to quickly spin up, replace, or scale resources while preserving data integrity. The following are some features and best practices for stateless architecture design:

- **Centralized state storage:** Store session and persistent state in external systems, ensuring that compute resources remain stateless.

- **Automated scalability:** Use Terraform to automate the provisioning of compute resources and load balancers, ensuring that applications automatically scale up or down based on demand.
- **Redundancy and resilience:** Deploy resources across multiple regions or availability zones to avoid single points of failure and guarantee high availability.
- **Consistent configuration:** Use Terraform modules to enforce standardized configurations across different cloud providers, maintaining uniform security and performance policies.
- **Regular testing:** Periodically simulate failover and recovery scenarios to ensure that the system can effectively handle resource replacements without data loss.

The following Terraform configuration demonstrates a stateless architecture design in Google Cloud Platform (GCP). It provisions a managed instance group for stateless compute, a Cloud SQL instance for external state storage, and integrates these components to ensure that any compute instance failure does not lead to data loss.

```
provider "google" {
  project = var.gcp_project
  region  = "us-central1"
}

# Create an Instance Template for stateless compute nodes
resource "google_compute_instance_template" "stateless_template" {
  name_prefix  = "stateless-instance"
  machine_type = "n1-standard-1"

  disks {
    boot        = true
    auto_delete = true
    initialize_params {
      image = "debian-cloud/debian-10"
    }
  }

  network_interfaces {
    network = "default"
    access_config {}
  }

  metadata_startup_script = <<-EOF
    #!/bin/bash
    echo "Starting stateless application"
    # Initialize application, which connects to an external DB (e.g. Cloud
SQL) for sessions.
  EOF
}

# Deploy a Managed Instance Group using the Instance Template
resource "google_compute_region_instance_group_manager" "stateless_group" {
  name               = "stateless-instance-group"
  region             = "us-central1"
  base_instance_name = "stateless-instance"
  instance_template  = google_compute_instance_template.stateless_template.
self_link
  target_size        = 2
}
```

```
# Provision a Cloud SQL instance for external state storage (e.g., for session
data)
resource "google_sql_database_instance" "stateful_db" {
  name             = "stateful-db"
  region           = "us-central1"
  database_version = "POSTGRES_13"

  settings {
    tier = "db-f1-micro"
    backup_configuration {
      enabled    = true
      start_time = "03:00"
    }
  }
}

# Create a database within the Cloud SQL instance
resource "google_sql_database" "sessions_db" {
  name      = "sessions"
  instance = google_sql_database_instance.stateful_db.name
  charset   = "utf8"
  collation = "utf8_general_ci"
}
```

Resilient architectures combining autoscaling, load balancing, and stateless design form the backbone of cloud-based disaster recovery strategies. By leveraging Terraform across AWS, Azure, and GCP, organizations can create infrastructures that respond dynamically to disruptions, ensuring consistent application availability and robust fault tolerance.

Conducting Disaster Recovery Drills and Testing Plans

Disaster Recovery (DR) drills are essential to validate the effectiveness of recovery plans and the resilience of cloud infrastructures. Terraform enables automated simulations, fault injections, and environment provisioning to test backup and failover processes. Regularly performing these drills helps identify weaknesses, refine workflows, and ensure cloud environments can withstand outages.

Simulating Outages with Terraform

Simulating outages involves deliberately triggering failures in cloud resources to test and validate an organization's disaster recovery and resilience strategies. By intentionally decommissioning virtual machines, disabling databases, or disrupting network components, teams can observe how well their infrastructure responds to failures and identify potential weaknesses before a real incident occurs. This practice is a proactive approach to ensuring that systems are robust and can quickly recover in the event of an actual outage, whether in AWS, GCP, or Azure environments.

Terraform is used to dynamically alter the state of cloud resources based on predefined variables or conditions, effectively simulating downtime or failures. For instance, by toggling a Boolean variable, Terraform can provision zero instances instead of the desired count, simulating an instance failure. These changes can target specific components such as Availability Zones, instance groups, or container services. The dynamic nature of Terraform's configuration allows for controlled testing of failover mechanisms, automated rollbacks, and the overall resilience of the deployed infrastructure. This enables organizations to continuously refine their disaster recovery procedures and ensure that even in the face of disruptive events, the system quickly reverts to a stable state. The following are some best practices for simulating outages:

- **Controlled failures:** Conduct outage simulations in non-production environments to avoid impacting live operations.
- **Fail fast, Learn fast:** Implement frequent, small-scale failure tests to quickly identify issues and optimize recovery processes without incurring significant risk.
- **Automate rollbacks:** Integrate automated rollback mechanisms using Terraform to ensure that resources are restored immediately after an outage simulation.
- **Document and analyze results:** Maintain thorough documentation of simulation outcomes to drive continuous improvement in resilience and recovery strategies.

```
variable "simulate_failure" {
  description = "Toggle to simulate an outage"
  default     = false
}

resource "aws_instance" "web" {
  count         = var.simulate_failure ? 0 : 1
  ami           = "ami-123456"
  instance_type = "t3.medium"

  tags = {
    Name = "WebServer"
  }
}
```

This Terraform snippet simulates an outage by dynamically setting the EC2 instance count to zero when the `simulate_failure` variable is enabled, facilitating controlled failure testing in AWS.

Automated Testing of Backup Restoration

Automated testing of backup restorations is a proactive strategy to ensure that backup data can be reliably recovered during an outage. By simulating backup restores in a controlled, temporary environment, organizations can verify that their backup processes are functional and that data remains intact. This approach is especially critical in multi-cloud environments across AWS, Azure, and GCP, as it provides confidence in disaster recovery procedures and helps meet regulatory requirements for data protection.

Terraform is used to deploy isolated test environments where backup restoration procedures are executed. For example, Terraform scripts can provision temporary compute or database resources that are restored from backups. This process mimics a real disaster recovery scenario, allowing you to validate that the restoration process works as expected without impacting production systems. Whether deploying in AWS, Azure, or GCP, Terraform automates every step from creating snapshots and backups to restoring them, ensuring that the backup lifecycle is consistent, repeatable, and auditable. The following are some best practices for testing and backup restoration:

- **Schedule routine restorations:** Automate frequent restore tests to ensure backups are valid and to catch any issues early.
- **Use isolated environments:** Restore backups in separate test or staging environments to avoid disruptions in production.
- **Version backups:** Maintain versioned backups to provide reliable restoration points at different times.

- **Integrate monitoring:** Continuously monitor restore operations to quickly identify and address any failures.

The following is an example Terraform configuration that demonstrates how to simulate a backup restoration for an Azure SQL database using the Point-In-Time Restore capability. This example assumes an existing primary SQL database and shows how to create a restored test.

```
# Testing backup restoration by creating a new database using Point-in-Time
Restore mode
resource "azurerm_sql_database" "restored_db" {
  name                = "restoreddatabase"
  resource_group_name = azurerm_sql_server.primary.resource_group_name
  location            = azurerm_sql_server.primary.location
  server_name         = azurerm_sql_server.primary.name

  # Restore from the primary database using the Point-In-Time Restore mode.
  # In an actual scenario, the restore_point_in_time should be set to a valid
backup timestamp.
  create_mode         = "PointInTimeRestore"
  source_database_id  = azurerm_sql_database.primary_db.id
  restore_point_in_time = "2023-01-01T00:00:00Z"  # Example timestamp; replace
with an actual restore point.
}
```

Monitoring and Reporting DR Drill Results

Monitoring and reporting Disaster Recovery (DR) drill results involves capturing and analyzing data from simulated recovery exercises to assess and improve your organization's resilience strategy. This process provides critical insights into the speed and efficacy of your DR procedures, enabling teams to identify areas for improvement, refine processes, and optimize future responses. Terraform automates the provisioning of logging and monitoring infrastructure, ensuring that the output from DR drills is systematically collected and reported. This centralized approach supports consistent data aggregation across multiple cloud providers such as AWS, Azure, and GCP. Thus, it enhances visibility into the performance of DR mechanisms.

Terraform scripts deploy a variety of cloud-native monitoring services that collect and centralize DR drill data. For example, in AWS, Terraform can set up CloudWatch Log Groups and CloudWatch Dashboards to capture metrics and logs during DR exercises. In Azure, Diagnostic Settings and Log Analytics work together to gather detailed drill data. And in GCP, Cloud Logging and Cloud Monitoring are configured to aggregate performance and event logs. This data is then processed through integrated dashboards and reporting tools to identify trends, measure recovery times, and detect weaknesses in the current DR setup. By automating these tasks, Terraform not only minimizes manual intervention but also ensures that comprehensive reporting and continuous improvement processes are seamlessly integrated into your DR strategy. The following are some features and best practices for monitoring and reporting disaster recovery drill results:

- **Automated logging:** Configure automated collection of DR drill metrics and event logs.
- **Centralized dashboards:** Use unified dashboards to aggregate and visualize data from multiple cloud providers.
- **Scheduled reporting:** Implement scheduled reports to consistently review DR performance and outcomes.
- **Post-drill analysis:** Integrate feedback loops to analyze results and refine disaster recovery procedures.
- **Continuous improvement:** Regularly update monitoring configurations to adapt to changes in the infrastructure and DR strategy.

Regular disaster recovery drills and simulations play a critical role in maintaining resilient cloud environments. Terraform's ability to automate outages, test restorations, and introduce chaos engineering enables cloud architects to proactively identify vulnerabilities and enhance system resilience. By integrating these practices across AWS, Azure, and GCP, organizations can ensure infrastructure stability and mitigate the risks of catastrophic failures.

Automating Recovery Plans and Configurations with Terraform

Effective disaster recovery hinges on rapid response, minimal downtime, and automated infrastructure restoration. By leveraging Terraform's capabilities, organizations can build automated recovery workflows that minimize manual intervention during incidents. Terraform allows cloud engineers to codify recovery plans, ensuring environments are consistently restored to their desired state across AWS, Azure, and GCP. This section explores strategies to automate and enforce recovery objectives, version DR plans, and roll back to stable configurations.

Building Infrastructure-as-Code Recovery Workflows

Infrastructure-as-Code recovery workflows enable organizations to automatically recreate their entire cloud environment using Terraform configurations and backup state files. In the event of an outage, these workflows allow for the rapid re-provisioning of virtual machines, databases, networks, and storage across AWS, Azure, and GCP, ensuring that critical infrastructure can be recovered reliably and consistently.

Terraform templates define all cloud resources, while state files capture the current environment configuration. In a disaster recovery scenario, Terraform can be re-executed to rebuild the environment based on these configurations. Terraform's automation capabilities ensure that resource dependencies are respected (using features such as **depends_on**), and the use of remote state storage (such as AWS S3, Azure Blob Storage, or GCP Cloud Storage buckets) guarantees that recovery is based on an accurate, up-to-date snapshot of your infrastructure. This automated process minimizes manual intervention and significantly reduces downtime while ensuring that all components are recreated in the correct order. The following are some features and best practices for IaC recovery workflows:

- **Automate resource dependencies:** Use **depends_on** to ensure resources are provisioned in the correct sequence.
- **Modular design:** Break the recovery workflow into reusable Terraform modules for scalability and easier maintenance.
- **Store configurations securely:** Use remote state backends to store and version your Terraform state files, ensuring you can reliably restore infrastructure.

```
# Provision a Virtual Private Cloud and Subnetwork
resource "google_compute_network" "vpc" {
  name = "recovery-vpc"
}

resource "google_compute_subnetwork" "subnet" {
  name          = "recovery-subnet"
  ip_cidr_range = "10.0.0.0/16"
  region        = "us-central1"
  network       = google_compute_network.vpc.id
}

# Deploy a Compute Engine instance as part of the recovery environment
resource "google_compute_instance" "app_instance" {
```

```
  name         = "recovery-instance"
  machine_type = "n1-standard-1"
  zone         = "us-central1-a"

  boot_disk {
    initialize_params {
      image = "debian-cloud/debian-10"
    }
  }

  network_interface {
    network    = google_compute_network.vpc.id
    subnetwork = google_compute_subnetwork.subnet.id
    access_config {}
  }
}

# Provision a Cloud SQL instance for database recovery
resource "google_sql_database_instance" "db_instance" {
  name             = "recovery-sql-instance"
  region           = "us-central1"
  database_version = "POSTGRES_13"

  settings {
    tier = "db-f1-micro"
    backup_configuration {
      enabled    = true
      start_time = "03:00"
    }
  }
}

# Create a database within the Cloud SQL instance
resource "google_sql_database" "db" {
  name      = "appdb"
  instance  = google_sql_database_instance.db_instance.name
  charset   = "utf8"
  collation = "utf8_general_ci"
}
```

This Terraform configuration provisions a complete recovery environment in GCP, including a VPC, managed compute instance, and Cloud SQL database, demonstrating how automated IaC workflows can rebuild infrastructure after an outage.

Automating RTO (Recovery Time Objective) and RPO (Recovery Point Objective) Policies

Recovery Time Objective (RTO) defines the maximum acceptable downtime after a disruption, while Recovery Point Objective (RPO) specifies the maximum period during which data loss is acceptable. Automating these objectives ensures that backup and recovery strategies are aligned with business continuity requirements. By leveraging Terraform, organizations can automate the scheduling of backups, configure replication strategies, and integrate failover mechanisms across AWS, Azure, and GCP. This automation not only enforces consistent backup intervals and retention policies but also supports rapid recovery by ensuring the infrastructure can be re-provisioned quickly in a different region or configuration.

Terraform is used to provision resources and orchestrate workflows that continuously back up data and replicate infrastructure across regions. For example, Terraform can automate the creation of snapshots for databases, schedule daily or incremental backups, and configure autoscaling groups and multi-availability zone deployments that facilitate automated failover. In the case of AWS RDS, Terraform can define parameters that determine the backup retention period (RPO) and enable multi-AZ deployments (to minimize RTO), ensuring that both backup frequency and infrastructure replication meet the organization's recovery objectives. Similar approaches can be applied in Azure and GCP using their native backup and replication services, ensuring a uniform strategy across multiple cloud providers. The following are some best practices of RTO and RPO:

- **Frequent backups for low RPO:** Automate daily snapshots and incremental backups to minimize data loss in case of an incident.
- **Failover and scale-out for low RTO:** Implement multi-region load balancers and auto-scaling groups, or multi-AZ configurations, to reduce recovery time during outages.
- **Monitor backup success:** Integrate monitoring and alerting mechanisms to continuously check the success of backup jobs and flag any failures.
- **Consistent configuration:** Use Terraform modules and templates to standardize backup and recovery settings across AWS, Azure, and GCP.
- **Regular testing:** Periodically test restoration procedures to ensure that both RTO and RPO targets are met consistently.

```
resource "aws_db_instance" "example" {
  allocated_storage          = 20
  storage_type               = "gp2"
  engine                     = "mysql"
  engine_version             = "8.0"
  instance_class             = "db.t3.medium"
  identifier               = "example-db"
  username                   = "admin"
  password                   = var.db_password
  db_subnet_group_name        = aws_db_subnet_group.example.name
  vpc_security_group_ids      = [aws_security_group.db.id]
  multi_az                   = true          # Enables automated failover (low RTO)
  backup_retention_period     = 7             # Backups retained for 7 days (low
RPO)
  preferred_backup_window     = "07:00-09:00"
  deletion_protection         = true          # Prevent accidental  deletion
}
```

This Terraform configuration deploys an AWS RDS instance configured for multi-AZ deployment with a daily backup schedule and a 7-day retention period, automating failover and ensuring low RTO and RPO for critical database workloads.

Instant Rollback and Disaster Recovery with Terraform

Rollback mechanisms enable cloud environments to quickly revert to a previously known good state by reapplying prior Terraform configurations and state files. This capability is crucial for mitigating deployment errors or outages, as it allows organizations to restore critical infrastructure rapidly across AWS, GCP, and Azure. By treating the Terraform state as a snapshot of the entire infrastructure, teams can recover from failures by leveraging historical state files, thereby minimizing downtime and ensuring business continuity.

Terraform state files (generally **`terraform.tfstate`**) store an exact representation of the deployed infrastructure. When an error or outage occurs, you can revert to an earlier, stable state by utilizing these versioned state files. For example, by executing commands such as **`terraform state`** show to inspect the current state and then running **terraform apply** with a backup state file, Terraform reinstates the environment to its last known good configuration. This automated process enables instant rollbacks, ensuring that any disruptive changes can be undone quickly, and services can continue to operate with minimal interruption. The following are some best practices:

- **Version state files:** Use version-controlled state files to track every change in your infrastructure, enabling precise rollbacks when needed.
- **Store state remotely:** Utilize remote backends (for example, AWS S3 with DynamoDB locking, Azure Blob Storage, or GCP Cloud Storage) to secure and manage state files, preventing local data loss.
- **Test rollbacks:** Regularly simulate rollback scenarios in test environments to verify that recovery workflows function smoothly during real incidents.
- **Automate snapshots:** Implement automated snapshot or backup strategies for critical resources, providing a solid fallback in case of infrastructure failure.

The following Terraform configuration provisions an Azure Virtual Machine. In an outage scenario, the **terraform state** command can be used to capture the current state, and then the environment can be rolled back by applying a previously backed-up state file:

```
resource "azurerm_virtual_machine" "example" {
  name                  = "example-vm"
  resource_group_name   = azurerm_resource_group.example.name
  location              = azurerm_resource_group.example.location
  vm_size               = "Standard_DS1_v2"
  network_interface_ids = [azurerm_network_interface.example.id]

  storage_os_disk {
    name              = "example-osdisk"
    caching           = "ReadWrite"
    create_option     = "FromImage"
    managed_disk_type = "Standard_LRS"
  }

  storage_image_reference {
    publisher = "Canonical"
    offer     = "UbuntuServer"
    sku       = "18.04-LTS"
    version   = "latest"
  }

  os_profile {
    computer_name  = "examplevm"
    admin_username = "azureuser"
    admin_password = var.admin_password  # Ensure this variable is defined
securely.
  }

  os_profile_linux_config {
    disable_password_authentication = false
  }
}
```

To perform a rollback, view the current state using the following command:

```
terraform state show azurerm_virtual_machine.example
```

If a failure is detected, restore the infrastructure by pulling a previous state file (for example, **`state-backup.tfstate`**) and applying it using the following command:

```
terraform apply state-backup.tfstate
```

Continuous DR Plan Updates and Versioning

Continuous DR plan updates ensure that your disaster recovery configurations evolve and align with the cloud infrastructure. This allows you to always be prepared for unforeseen outages. By versioning the Terraform code, organizations can roll back to previous configurations if needed while iterating and improving their DR strategies over time. This approach enables a proactive, continuously updated DR plan that is consistently aligned with evolving business needs and technological advancements.

Terraform code is managed in a version-controlled environment, such as Git, where every change is tracked and archived. Automated CI/CD pipelines can regularly deploy updated DR configurations, ensuring that recovery procedures, such as state file backup restoration and resource replication, remain current. For example, by storing Terraform state files in versioned storage (such as AWS S3, Azure Blob Storage, and GCP Cloud Storage buckets with versioning enabled), you can roll back to a previous version of your infrastructure configuration in the event of an outage, ensuring reliable disaster recovery with minimal downtime. The following are some best practices for disaster recovery:

- **Automate DR code updates:** Integrate DR workflows into CI/CD pipelines so that updates and new configurations are automatically applied and tested.
- **Tag versions:** Label Terraform modules and state files with version tags for easy tracking, auditability, and rollback.
- **Test new versions:** Regularly simulate outage scenarios using updated DR plans to verify that all components recover as expected.
- **Use remote and versioned state storage:** Store Terraform state files in remote backends with versioning enabled to safeguard against data loss and to maintain historical backups of your infrastructure.

```
# Create a GCP Storage Bucket with Versioning for Terraform State
resource "google_storage_bucket" "terraform_state" {
  name          = "my-terraform-state-bucket-unique"  # Bucket name must be
unique globally
  location      = "US"
  force_destroy = true

  versioning {
    enabled = true
  }

  lifecycle_rule {
    action {
      type = "Delete"
    }
    condition {
      age = 90  # Optional: delete older object versions after 90 days to
manage cost.
    }
  }
}
```

```
# Configure Terraform to use the versioned storage bucket as the remote backend
terraform {
  backend "gcs" {
    bucket = google_storage_bucket.terraform_state.name
    prefix = "terraform/state"
  }
}
```

This Terraform configuration creates a GCP Storage bucket with versioning enabled to serve as a remote backend for Terraform state files, ensuring continuous DR plan updates and enabling reliable rollbacks in disaster recovery scenarios.

Automating recovery plans with Terraform streamlines disaster response, ensuring cloud environments recover rapidly and consistently. By integrating Terraform with backup workflows, RTO/RPO policies, and versioning, organizations can achieve reliable DR outcomes across AWS, Azure, and GCP. This proactive approach reduces downtime, safeguards data, and enhances cloud resilience.

Conclusion

Disaster recovery is no longer a reactive process; it must be built into the DNA of modern, multi-cloud infrastructures. In this chapter, we explored how Terraform empowers organizations to build robust, automated, and scalable disaster recovery strategies that work seamlessly across AWS, Azure, and GCP. By leveraging provider-agnostic Terraform modules, engineers can schedule automated snapshots, enforce backup retention policies, and replicate critical data across regions. Combining these capabilities with HashiCorp Vault for secrets management further strengthens cross-cloud backup security and consistency, ensuring that no critical asset is left unprotected.

We also highlighted the importance of resilience through multi-region failover configurations, stateless architecture design, and autoscaling workloads that adapt to dynamic conditions. Using Terraform, disaster recovery drills can be simulated and validated with automated reporting, enabling teams to iteratively improve their recovery workflows. From defining RTO/RPO compliance policies to orchestrating full environment rollbacks, Terraform enables the creation of codified, repeatable recovery processes. As infrastructure complexity grows, the ability to automate and version DR plans ensures that recovery strategies evolve in lockstep with your cloud environment, reducing downtime, preserving data integrity, and enhancing organizational confidence during crises.

In the next chapter, we will explore advanced design patterns in Terraform, including the pros and cons of monorepo versus multi-repo approaches and writing dynamic, modular code. It also covers managing complex dependency graphs and optimizing configurations for scalability and maintainability.

Questions and Answers

1. **How can Terraform be used to create a provider-agnostic backup strategy across AWS, Azure, and GCP?**

   Terraform enables you to define infrastructure as code in a modular and reusable way, making it possible to implement backup strategies across different cloud providers with a consistent approach. By scheduling automated snapshots for services such as EBS, Azure Disks, and GCP Persistent Disks, and leveraging tools such as HashiCorp Vault for secure backup and secret storage, you can ensure uniform data protection regardless of the provider. This approach reduces complexity, avoids vendor lock-in, and increases operational resilience.

2. **What role does Terraform play in achieving multi-region failover and high availability for critical databases and applications?**

   Terraform can automate the provisioning of multi-region architectures by configuring database replication, setting up global load balancers (for example, AWS Global Accelerator, Azure Front Door), and managing DNS-based failover using services such as Route 53 or Azure Traffic Manager. This allows your infrastructure to quickly redirect traffic and continue operating during regional outages, maintaining service uptime and availability with minimal manual intervention.

3. **Why is stateless architecture important for disaster recovery, and how can Terraform help implement it?**

   Stateless applications can be scaled, destroyed, or rebuilt without affecting the application's state, which is stored separately (for example, in a managed database or object store). Using Terraform, you can design and deploy infrastructure that supports stateless patterns, enabling fast recovery and horizontal scaling. This design principle increases resiliency and simplifies failover and rollback strategies during outages or disasters.

4. **How can organizations simulate and validate their disaster recovery plans using Terraform?**

   Terraform can be used to script and simulate outage scenarios by selectively de-provisioning resources or failing over components in test environments. You can also use Terraform to spin up temporary environments to test backup restorations and validate that systems meet RTO and RPO requirements. These automated DR drills, combined with logging and reporting tools, ensure that your recovery plans are not only documented but also tested and continuously improved.

5. **What are some of the best practices for automating Disaster Recovery (DR) plans with Terraform?**

   Best practices include versioning all DR configurations using Git, creating reusable Terraform modules for recovery workflows, and defining explicit RTO/RPO objectives as part of your infrastructure code. Automating rollbacks using Terraform state files allows for rapid restoration to known-good states. Additionally, DR plans should be continuously updated alongside regular infrastructure changes, ensuring your recovery posture remains aligned with your live environment.

CHAPTER 14
Advanced Design Patterns in Terraform

Introduction

As Infrastructure-as-Code (IaC) adoption matures within organizations, the need for scalable, modular, and maintainable Terraform designs becomes paramount. In this chapter, we explore advanced Terraform design patterns that address the challenges of large-scale, multi-team cloud environments. We begin by comparing monorepo and multi-repo strategies, highlighting how different repository structures impact collaboration, version control, and risk containment. Readers will learn how to manage Terraform state, module versioning, and automation workflows in both centralized and decentralized codebases, including hybrid models tailored for enterprise use cases.

The chapter then dives deep into dynamic and modular Terraform coding practices, showcasing how to write reusable modules, leverage variables and dynamic blocks, and use outputs for seamless inter-module communication. We also examine how to manage complex dependency graphs using implicit and explicit dependencies, and how to decouple resources for faster parallel deployments. Lastly, we explore optimization techniques for large-scale deployments, including performance tuning and structuring Terraform projects for longevity and clarity. Whether you are working in a fast-moving startup or a highly regulated enterprise, these design patterns will help you build resilient, scalable, and efficient Terraform architectures.

Structure

In this chapter, we will cover the following topics:

- Comparing Monorepo and Multi-Repo Approaches for Terraform Projects
  - Monorepo Design for Large Terraform Projects
  - Multi-Repo Structure for Isolated Workloads
  - Versioning and State Management in Monorepo versus Multi-Repo
  - Hybrid Repo Approaches for Enterprise Workflows
- Writing Dynamic and Modular Terraform Code
  - Creating Reusable Terraform Modules
  - Leveraging Variables, Locals, and Dynamic Blocks
  - Templating with the Terraform Console and Functions
  - Managing Module Outputs for Inter-Module Communication
  - Configuring `terraform_remote_state` for Inter-Directory Communication
- Managing Complex Dependency Graphs Effectively
  - Using `depends_on` and Implicit Dependencies

- Understanding Terraform Graphs and Resource Dependencies
- Decoupling Resource Dependencies for Faster Deployments

- Optimizing Terraform Configurations for Scalability and Maintenance
  - Structuring Terraform Projects for Large-Scale Deployments
  - Performance Tuning Terraform Plan and Apply

Comparing Monorepo and Multi-Repo Approaches for Terraform Projects

Managing Terraform codebases effectively is critical for scaling infrastructure deployments in complex cloud environments. In this section, we explore the monorepo and multi-repo approaches, their benefits, challenges, and use cases. By understanding these design patterns, practitioners can choose the right repository structure for their projects.

Monorepo Design for Large Terraform Projects

A monorepo (monolithic repository) approach centralizes all Terraform configuration modules, environments, and shared components into a single Git repository. Rather than scattering code across multiple repos, teams store every `.tf` file, shared module, and environment-specific overlay (for example, dev, staging, prod) in one place. This design promotes consistency in coding standards, simplifies dependency management, and provides a single source of truth for infrastructure definitions across AWS, GCP, and Azure.

In a monorepo, Terraform configurations are organized into a clear directory hierarchy. At the top level, you might have a `modules/` directory containing reusable components (for example, network, IAM, databases, and so on). Beneath that, environment folders (`dev/`, `prod/`, and so on) contain their own `main.tf`, `variables.tf`, and `outputs.tf`, each referencing shared modules. Remote backends and workspace configurations are parameterized per environment, often via `backend.tf`. Changes are tracked centrally via Git, and CI/CD pipelines run validation, plan, and apply steps for each environment folder in isolation. This structure scales seamlessly across multiple cloud providers by simply adding provider-specific parameters or modules under the same repo umbrella. The following are some features and best practices of monorepo:

- **Code reusability:** Leverage shared modules for networking, compute, and security across all environments to avoid duplication.
- **Centralized collaboration:** All teams contribute to the same repo, improving visibility into changes and reducing `"configuration drift"`.
- **Consistency enforcement:** Apply repository-wide linting (for example, `terraform fmt`, `tflint`) and policy-as-code checks (Sentinel, OPA) to maintain standards.
- **Environment isolation:** Structure environment folders to encapsulate variables, backend settings, and provider credentials separately.
- **Robust CI/CD pipelines:** Implement automated workflows that detect changes in any path, run terraform validate and terraform plan, and fail fast on errors.

The following are some pros of monorepo:

- **Single source of truth:** All infrastructure code lives in one place, simplifying auditing and traceability.
- **Simplified dependency management:** Shared modules are centrally versioned, ensuring all environments use the same vetted code.

- **Easier refactoring:** Global changes (for example, updating a module) propagate across all environments in one commit.
- **Unified testing and validation:** A central pipeline can enforce checks across every environment and module.

The following are some cons of monorepo:

- **Repository size and complexity:** As projects grow, the monorepo can become large and harder to navigate.
- **Risk of unintended changes:** Developers may accidentally modify unrelated environments or modules.
- **Slower CI/CD feedback:** Comprehensive pipelines that scan the entire repo may increase build times.
- **Merge conflicts and coordination:** High collaboration can lead to more frequent conflicts, requiring careful branch management.

Multi-Repo Structure for Isolated Workloads

A multi-repo approach partitions Terraform code into separate repositories, often one per environment (for example, dev, staging, prod), application, or team rather than storing everything in a single monolithic repo. Each repo encapsulates the specific configurations, modules, and state for its scope. This division fosters isolation, clearer ownership boundaries, and targeted access controls, making it easier for large organizations to scale infrastructure development across multiple teams and projects.

In a multi-repo model, each repository contains its own **`main.tf`**, **`variables.tf`**, **`outputs.tf`**, and **`backend configuration`**. Shared modules can live in a dedicated **`"modules"`** repo, which other repos reference via Git tags or module registry URLs. To coordinate dependencies, such as a network created in one repo feeding into applications in another, Terraform outputs from one repo are stored in a remote state backend (for example, AWS S3 with DynamoDB locking, Azure Blob Storage, or GCP Cloud Storage). Consuming repos then use the **`terraform_remote_state`** data source to pull required values. Alternatively, data is directly injected into variables in **`terraform.tfvars`** files. CI/CD pipelines are configured per repository, triggering terraform plan and apply in isolation, ensuring that changes in one workload do not inadvertently impact others. The following are some features and best practices of multi-repo:

- **Isolation:** Keep each workload's state and configuration separate to minimize the impact of failures or misconfigurations in one area.
- **Scalability:** Allow teams to develop, review, and deploy changes independently, speeding up delivery cycles.
- **Granular access controls:** Grant repository-specific permissions, for example, AWS IAM roles or GCP service accounts, restricted to a single repo's resources for tighter security.
- **Explicit dependency management:** Use **`terraform_remote_state`** to fetch outputs from upstream repos, making dependencies transparent and versioned. Alternatively, pass data directly into the terraform.tfvars file.
- **Shared module registry:** Host reusable modules in a dedicated repo or Terraform Registry to avoid duplication and ensure consistent implementation of common patterns.

The following are some pros of multi-repo:

- **Enhanced isolation:** Problems in one repo cannot directly corrupt others, reducing blast radius.

- **Team autonomy:** Teams can manage their own lifecycle branches, pipelines, and releases without coordinating across the entire organization.
- **Simpler onboarding:** New teams can clone a single repo to get started on their workload without navigating a large codebase.
- **Security segmentation:** Apply stricter access controls per repo, limiting who can modify specific infrastructure.

The following are some cons of multi-repo:

- **Dependency complexity:** Managing cross-repo dependencies via remote state and module versioning requires careful coordination.
- **Code duplication risk:** Without diligent use of shared modules, common patterns may be reimplemented across repos.
- **Consistency enforcement:** Enforcing organization-wide policies and standards (for example, linting, compliance checks) across multiple repos can be challenging.
- **Operational overhead:** Maintaining multiple pipelines, state backends, and repository configurations adds administrative burden.

Versioning and State Management in Monorepo versus Multi-Repo

Terraform relies on state files to track resource mappings and module versioning to enforce consistent infrastructure patterns. In both monorepo and multi-repo models, you must carefully manage these state files and module versions to ensure reliable deployments across AWS, GCP, and Azure. Proper versioning prevents drift between environments and guarantees that teams can roll back or reproduce infrastructure at any point in time.

- **Monorepo:** A single repository holds all environments (for example, **`dev`**, **`staging`**, **`prod`**). Each environment has its own remote backend configuration, such as an S3 bucket with DynamoDB state locking (AWS), a GCS bucket with object versioning (GCP), or Azure Blob Storage with state locks so that each environment's state file is stored and versioned centrally. Module versions are referenced via tags or release branches, ensuring every environment uses the same vetted module code.
- **Multi-repo:** Each repository corresponds to a specific workload or environment. State files live in separate remote backends per repo (for example, distinct S3/GCS/Azure storage for each), isolating state changes and reducing the risk of accidental cross-environment updates. Shared modules are imported by explicit version references, so each repo can upgrade modules on its own schedule without impacting others.

The following are some features and best practices:

- **Versioned remote backends:** Enable object versioning on S3/GCS buckets or use Azure Blob versioning to retain historical state files and facilitate rollbacks.
- **State locking:** Use DynamoDB (AWS), Blob Storage leases or Azure Cosmos DB, or GCS generation-based locks to prevent concurrent apply operations from corrupting state.
- **Explicit module versioning:** Pin module sources (for example, **`?ref=v1.2.3`**) or registry versions to ensure predictable updates and simplify auditing.
- **State separation:** In monorepo, isolate state per environment folder; in multi-repo, isolate state per repository to reduce blast radius.
- **Automated state workflows:** Integrate CI/CD to validate state integrity and automatically back up state before every apply.

The following are some pros and cons:

- **Monorepo Pros:**
  - **Version consistency:** A single source for all environments ensures modules and providers are uniformly upgraded.
  - **Simplified governance:** A centralized state makes it easier to enforce policies and inspect history.
  - **Easier refactoring:** Global changes to modules propagate naturally across all environments.
- **Monorepo Cons:**
  - **Shared state risk:** A misconfigured backend can affect multiple environments at once.
  - **Operational complexity:** Large state repositories can become unwieldy, slowing CI/CD pipelines.
  - **Concurrent access challenges:** More teams working in the same repo may lead to lock contention.
- **Multi-Repo Pros:**
  - **State isolation:** Failures or misconfigurations in one repo cannot impact others, improving security.
  - **Team autonomy:** Teams control their own lifecycle upgrades, module versions, and backends without cross-team coordination.
  - **Scalability:** Independent repositories scale better as the organization grows, with smaller, focused codebases.
- **Multi-Repo Cons:**
  - **Dependency tracking:** Managing inter-repo dependencies via `terraform_remote_state` or module upgrades can be cumbersome.
  - **Consistency enforcement:** Ensuring all repos follow the same versioning standards and policies requires additional coordination.
  - **Duplication risk:** Without rigorous shared module practices, common patterns may be reimplemented, leading to drift.

Hybrid Repo Approaches for Enterprise Workflows

A hybrid repo model blends the advantages of monorepo and multi-repo structures. Core, organization-wide Terraform modules and shared infrastructure definitions live in a centralized repository, while teams maintain separate, smaller repositories for environment or application-specific configurations. This balance gives enterprises both consistency in shared assets and isolation where needed for rapid, independent development.

The hybrid approach typically involves one `"modules"` repo containing reusable components, networking, IAM roles, monitoring, and a set of per-team or per-environment repos that consume those modules. Each application or environment repo defines its own workspace, backend settings, and variable inputs, referencing the shared modules by versioned tags. Terraform state for shared resources may live in its own backend, while each application repo uses a distinct backend to keep state isolated. CI/CD pipelines then independently validate and apply changes in each repo, yet share a common set of approved building blocks. The following are some features and best practices of hybrid repo:

- **Flexibility:** Tailor the mix of mono-repo and multi-repo strategies based on team size, security boundaries, and compliance requirements.

- **Central module repository:** Store all shared modules in a single repo, versioned and audited, to enforce consistent patterns.
- **Isolated state backends:** Use separate remote backends per repo to prevent accidental state overlap while retaining central control over shared state.
- **Clear ownership:** Define which teams own which repos, shared modules versus application configs, so responsibilities and review processes are unambiguous.
- **Automated dependency updates:** Integrate Dependabot or similar tools to keep module references up to date across all application repos.
- **Unified testing framework:** Standardize on a common set of linting, validation, and compliance checks that run across every repository.

The following are some pros of hybrid repo:

- **Collaboration and consistency:** Shared modules ensure best practices and security controls are enforced, while feature teams move quickly in their own repos.
- **Scalable governance:** Centralized audits and versioning of modules reduce drift without constraining application-level agility.
- **Reduced blast radius:** Application or environment changes remain confined to their own repo and state backend, minimizing unintended side-effects.

The following are some cons of hybrid repo:

- **Initial setup complexity:** Establishing pipelines, remotes, and dependency workflows across multiple repos requires careful planning and investment.
- **Governance overhead:** Clear policies and communication channels are needed to manage module version updates and breaking changes.
- **Tooling coordination:** CI/CD, security scans, and dependency updates must be configured consistently across diverse repositories, which can be labour-intensive.

Choosing the right repository structure is essential for scaling Terraform projects. While monorepo designs foster collaboration and consistency, multi-repo setups offer isolation and scalability. Hybrid approaches provide a balance, making them suitable for enterprises with diverse teams and workloads. By understanding the trade-offs, organizations can implement repository structures that align with their operational and security goals.

Writing Dynamic and Modular Terraform Code

Dynamic and modular code in Terraform is the cornerstone of scalable and maintainable Infrastructure-as-Code (IaC). This section delves into strategies for creating reusable Terraform modules, leveraging dynamic constructs, and managing inter-module communication to streamline infrastructure provisioning across cloud providers.

Creating Reusable Terraform Modules

Reusable Terraform modules are self-contained bundles of Terraform configuration that encapsulate one or more infrastructure components such as VPCs, IAM policies, or databases into a consistent, versioned package. By abstracting common patterns into modules, teams eliminate duplication, enforce organization-wide standards, and accelerate onboarding by providing "plug-and-play" building blocks for AWS, GCP, and Azure resources.

A module lives in its own directory and typically includes:

- `main.tf`: This file contains resource definitions.

- **`variables.tf`**: This file is used to define input variables with descriptions and defaults.
- **`outputs.tf`**: This file exposes attributes for downstream consumption.
- **`providers.tf`**: Provider configuration specific to the module. Modules can be sourced from local paths (**`./modules/vpc`**), Git repositories (**`git::https://…?ref=v1.0.0`**), or the Terraform Registry (**`terraform-aws-modules/vpc/aws`**).
- **`locals.tf`:** This file defines reusable expressions and computed values within the module.
- **`data.tf`:** This file is used to define data sources that fetch read-only information from cloud providers or external systems

Once the module is defined, consumers invoke the module with a module block, passing in required variables. Terraform automatically fetches the module, validates inputs, and integrates its resources into the dependency graph.

The following are some features and best practices of modules:

- **Scalability:** Decompose large infrastructures into focused modules (for example, VPC, subnets, NAT).
- **Encapsulation:** Expose only necessary inputs and outputs, hiding internal resource details.
- **Version Control:** Tag releases and pin source references (**`?ref=v2.1.0`**) to guarantee predictable behavior.
- **Validation:** Use precondition/postcondition checks or module-level tests to enforce validation.
- **Documentation:** Include **`README.md`** with usage examples, variable descriptions, and output explanations.

The following reusable Terraform module provisions an AWS VPC with public and private subnets, an Internet Gateway, NAT Gateways in public subnets, and corresponding route tables and associations.

```
#modules/vpc/main.tf
resource "aws_vpc" "this" {
  cidr_block = var.cidr_block
  tags       = { Name = var.name }
}

resource "aws_subnet" "this" {
  for_each = var.subnet_specs

  vpc_id                  = aws_vpc.main.id
  cidr_block              = each.value.cidr
  availability_zone       = each.value.az
  map_public_ip_on_launch = each.value.type == "public" ? true : false

  tags = {
    Name = "${var.name}-${each.key}"
    Type = each.value.type
  }
}

resource "aws_internet_gateway" "gw" {
  vpc_id = aws_vpc.this.id
  tags   = { Name = "${var.name}-igw" }
}

resource "aws_eip" "nat" {
  count = length([for s in var.subnet_specs : s if s.name == "public"])
```

```
  vpc    = true
}

resource "aws_nat_gateway" "nat" {
  for_each      = { for s in var.subnet_specs : s.name => s if s.name
== "public" }
  allocation_id = aws_eip.nat[each.key].id
  subnet_id     = aws_subnet.this[each.key].id
  tags          = { Name = "${var.name}-nat-${each.key}" }
}

resource "aws_route_table" "public" {
  vpc_id = aws_vpc.this.id
  tags   = { Name = "${var.name}-public-rt" }

  route {
    cidr_block = "0.0.0.0/0"
    gateway_id = aws_internet_gateway.gw.id
  }
}

resource "aws_route_table" "private" {
  vpc_id = aws_vpc.this.id
  tags   = { Name = "${var.name}-private-rt" }

  route {
    cidr_block     = "0.0.0.0/0"
    nat_gateway_id = aws_nat_gateway.nat["public"].id
  }
}

resource "aws_route_table_association" "assoc" {
  for_each = aws_subnet.this

  subnet_id = each.value.id
  route_table_id = var.subnet_specs[each.key].type == "public"
    ? aws_route_table.public.id
    : aws_route_table.private.id
}

# modules/vpc/variables.tf
variable "name" {
    type = string
    description = "Name prefix for the VPC resources"
}

variable "cidr_block" {
    type = string
    description = "CIDR block for the VPC"
}

variable "subnet_specs" {
  type = map(object({
    az   = string
    cidr = string
    type = string  # "public" or "private"
  }))
```

```
  description = "Name, CIDR and type for subnet"
}

# modules/vpc/main.tf
output "vpc_id" {
  value = aws_vpc.this.id
}

// main.tf - usage in root module
module "network" {
  source       = "./modules/vpc"
  name         = "prod-vpc"
  cidr_block   = "10.0.0.0/16"
  subnet_specs = [
    { name = "public",  cidr = "10.0.1.0/24" },
    { name = "private", cidr = "10.0.2.0/24" }
  ]
}
```

Leveraging Variables, Locals, and Dynamic Blocks

Terraform's variables, locals, and dynamic blocks provide powerful mechanisms for writing DRY (Don't Repeat Yourself), parameterized, and adaptable infrastructure code. Variables allow end-users to supply configuration inputs, locals define reusable values or computed expressions within a module, and dynamic blocks enable the generation of nested resource blocks based on lists or maps, eliminating boilerplate and supporting complex, data-driven resource definitions across AWS, GCP, and Azure.

- **Variables:** Variables are declared using variable blocks (with optional type, default, and validation), and referenced as `var.<name>`. They enable modules to accept inputs such as project IDs, regions, or lists of settings.
- **Locals:** Locals are declared in a locals block and compute intermediate values, such as combined tags, derived names, or merged maps. Because locals are evaluated only once, they reduce repeated expressions and improve readability.
- **Dynamic Blocks:** Dynamic blocks use the dynamic keyword inside a resource to loop over complex data structures, emitting nested blocks conditionally or repeatedly. This is invaluable when a resource requires multiple similar sub-blocks, such as firewall rules or load balancer listeners whose count or content is driven by input variables.

The following are some salient features and best practices:

- **Variables:**
  - Define strict type constraints (for example, **`list(string)`**, **`object({…})`**) for early validation.
  - Provide sensible default values and clear descriptions to improve module usability.
- **Locals**
  - Encapsulate repeated logic (for example, constructing resource names or merging tag maps) to avoid duplication.
  - Use locals to simplify complex expressions and keep main.tf focused on resource definitions.
- **Dynamic Blocks**
  - Drive nested blocks (such as security rules, IAM bindings, disk attachments) from a single variable, reducing manual edits.

- Combine with **count** or **for_each** on resources for full data-driven provisioning.

```
// variables.tf
variable "project" {
  description = "GCP project ID"
  type        = string
}

variable "network" {
  description = "Name of the VPC network to attach the firewall"
  type        = string
}

variable "allowed_services" {
  description = "List of protocols and port ranges to allow"
  type = list(object({
    protocol = string
    ports    = list(number)
  }))
  default = [
    { protocol = "tcp"; ports = [80, 443] },
    { protocol = "icmp"; ports = [] } // empty ports list means all ICMP
  ]
}

// locals.tf
locals {
  firewall_name = "${var.project}-app-fw"
  common_tags   = {
    project     = var.project
    managed_by  = "terraform"
  }
}

// main.tf
resource "google_compute_firewall" "app_fw" {
  name    = local.firewall_name
  project = var.project
  network = var.network

  // Dynamically generate one allow block per service definition
  dynamic "allow" {
    for_each = var.allowed_services
    content {
      protocol = allow.value.protocol
      ports    = allow.value.ports
    }
  }

  // Apply common tags as labels
  labels = local.common_tags
}
```

This example shows a GCP firewall resource that uses input variables for project, network, and a list of allowed services. Locals to construct the firewall name and tags, and a dynamic block to emit multiple allow entries based on the provided protocol/port definitions.

Templating with the Terraform Console and Functions

Terraform's interactive console and its rich library of built-in functions let you prototype and generate dynamic infrastructure definitions on the fly. Whether you are targeting AWS, GCP, or Azure, these tools help you reduce manual coding, enforce DRY principles, and adapt configurations based on inputs or computed values. The Terraform console provides immediate feedback on expressions, while functions such as **`try()`**, **`cidrsubnet()`**, **`join()`**, and so on, enable powerful data transformations directly in your **`.tf`** files.

- **Terraform console:** Run terraform console in your workspace to evaluate interpolation syntax and function calls against your current configuration. You can experiment with **`variables (var.<name>)`**, **`locals (local.<name>)`**, and any function to see its output before embedding it in code.
- **Built-in functions:** Terraform includes many functions for string manipulation (**`replace()`**, **`join()`**), numeric operations (**`min()`**, **`ceil()`**), networking (**`cidrsubnet()`**), and data structures (**`lookup()`**, **`merge()`**, **`flatten()`**). These functions are resolved during plan/apply, letting you compute values such as subnet CIDRs or resource names dynamically. You can find details of all the functions on the Terraform documentation page.

The following are some key features and best practices:

- **Iterate in console:** Use the console to test complex loops and function outputs, for example, **`for i in range(2) : cidrsubnet("10.0.0.0/16", 8, i).`**
- **Safe lookups:** Wrap map access in **`lookup(my_map, key, default)`** or within **`try()`** to avoid unintentional errors.
- **Network CIDR generation:** Use **`cidrsubnet()`** to split larger networks into subnets without hand-calculating IP ranges.
- **String templating:** Combine **`join()`** and **`format()`** to build resource names or labels from lists and variables.
- **Heredoc blocks:** For multi-line user data or scripts, use **`<<EOF`** syntax and interpolate variables/functions inside.

```
variable "location" {
  type        = string
  description = "Azure region to deploy the network"
  default     = "eastus"
}

variable "vnet_cidr" {
  type        = string
  description = "CIDR block for the virtual network"
  default     = "10.0.0.0/16"
}

variable "subnet_count" {
  type        = number
  description = "Number of equal-sized subnets to create"
  default     = 3
}

locals {
  # Generate a list of subnet CIDRs by splitting the VNet CIDR
  subnet_cidrs = [
    for idx in range(var.subnet_count) :
    cidrsubnet(var.vnet_cidr, 8, idx)
  ]
```

```
  # Create human-readable subnet names
  subnet_names = [
    for idx, cidr in local.subnet_cidrs :
    join("-", ["subnet", format("%02d", idx + 1)])
  ]
}

resource "azurerm_virtual_network" "vnet" {
  name                = "templated-vnet"
  address_space       = [var.vnet_cidr]
  location            = var.location
  resource_group_name = azurerm_resource_group.rg.name
}

# Dynamically create one subnet per CIDR in local.subnet_cidrs
resource "azurerm_subnet" "subnets" {
  for_each             = zipmap(local.subnet_names, local.subnet_cidrs)
  name                 = each.key
  resource_group_name = azurerm_resource_group.rg.name
  virtual_network_name = azurerm_virtual_network.vnet.name
  address_prefixes     = [each.value]
}
```

This configuration uses Terraform's **`cidrsubnet()`** function to split a VNet CIDR into multiple subnets dynamically, combines **`format()`** and **`join()`** to generate subnet names, and leverages **`for_each`** to provision them in Azure.

Managing Module Outputs for Inter-Module Communication

Module outputs in Terraform let you expose specific resource attributes, such as IDs, IP addresses, or URLs from one module so they can be consumed by another. This mechanism enables you to compose complex, interconnected infrastructure stacks. For example, creating a VPC in one module and then passing its ID into another module that provisions compute instances within that VPC. Decoupling modules and using their outputs as inputs for downstream modules allows you to maintain clean separation of concerns and promote reusability across AWS, GCP, and Azure.

Within a module, you can declare `output` blocks that reference resource attributes you wish to share. In your root configuration (or another module), you instantiate the module with a **`module "<name>" {}`** block and then access its outputs via **`module.<name>.<output_name>`**.

The following are some features and best practices of inter-module communication:

- **Meaningful output names:** Choose clear, descriptive names (for example, **`vpc_id`**, **`subnet_ids`**) so consumers immediately understand each value's purpose.
- **Sensitive outputs:** Mark sensitive data (passwords, certificates) with **`sensitive = true`** to prevent exposure in logs or UIs.
- **Versioned modules:** Pin module source versions to guarantee output interfaces remain stable and backward-compatible.
- **Minimal surface area:** Only expose the values that are required by other module(s) to keep internal module details private.

```
#modules/vpc/main.tf
resource "aws_vpc" "this" {
  cidr_block = var.cidr_block
```

```
  tags = { Name = var.name }
}

resource "aws_subnet" "this" {
  vpc_id                  = var.vpc_id
  cidr_block              = var.subnet_cidr
  map_public_ip_on_launch = true
  tags = { Name = var.subnet_name }
}

output "vpc_id" {
  description = "The ID of the created VPC"
  value       = aws_vpc.this.id
}

output "subnet_id" {
  description = "The ID of the created subnet"
  value       = aws_subnet.this.id
}

#modules/ec2/main.tf
variable "subnet_id" {
  description = "The ID of the subnet to deploy instances into"
  type        = string
}

resource "aws_instance" "web" {
  ami           = var.ami_id
  instance_type = var.instance_type
  subnet_id     = var.subnet_id
  tags = { Name = "web-server" }
}

Main.tf
# Root configuration
module "network" {
  source     = "./modules/vpc"
  name       = "example-vpc"
  cidr_block = "10.0.0.0/16"
}

module "compute" {
  source          = "./modules/ec2"
  subnet_id          = module.network.subnet_id
  ami_id          = "ami-0abcdef1234567890"
  instance_type   = "t3.micro"
  subnet_cidr     = "10.0.1.0/24"
}
```

The root configuration calls a VPC module, exports its `subnet_id`, and passes that value into an EC2 module, which then provisions an instance within the specified subnet.

Configuring `terraform_remote_state` for Inter-Directory Communication

`terraform_remote_state` is a data source used to fetch output values from the state files of other Terraform configurations. In large or modularized infrastructures, especially in monorepo or multi-repo environments, different directories or modules may manage their own state files. terraform_remote_state enables inter-directory communication by allowing one configuration to consume outputs from another, creating **loose coupling** between separate parts of the infrastructure (for example, networking and compute).

Each Terraform configuration stores its state file in a remote backend such as GCS (Google Cloud Storage), AWS S3, or Azure Blob Storage. When using **`terraform_remote_state`**, you configure it with the same backend details (bucket/container name, path, region) to read the state file managed by another Terraform project. Terraform then accesses the outputs defined in that state file and makes them available in the current configuration, enabling modular and scalable architecture.

The following are some important features and best practices:

- **Loose coupling:** Use **`terraform_remote_state`** to share only the necessary outputs between modules, not entire configurations.
- **Backend consistency:** Ensure consistent backend configuration (for example, GCS bucket, Azure container, or S3 bucket) across projects.
- **Output naming:** Clearly define and document output variables in the source configuration for easy reference.
- **Versioning:** Use versioned state files or state locking to avoid unexpected changes.
- **Security:** Secure your remote backend with encryption and access controls to prevent unauthorized access.
- **Lifecycle management:** Treat the source of the remote state as a dependency–apply changes in the source before consuming updates.

This example demonstrates how to modularize infrastructure by managing a network in one Terraform directory (**`network/`**) and then referencing the network in another directory (**`compute/`**) using terraform_remote_state. This is common in large-scale environments where networking, compute, and services are managed separately.

```
#network/main.tf
terraform {
  backend "gcs" {
    bucket = "my-terraform-state-bucket"
    prefix = "envs/prod/network"
  }
}

variable "vpc_name" {
  default = "prod-vpc"
}

resource "google_compute_network" "vpc" {
  name                    = var.vpc_name
  auto_create_subnetworks = false
}

output "vpc_network_name" {
  description = "The name of the VPC network"
  value       = google_compute_network.vpc.name
}
```

Once this Terraform snippet is deployed, the state will be stored in GCS, and the network name will be available for consumption.

```
#compute/main.tf
terraform {
  backend "gcs" {
    bucket = "my-terraform-state-bucket"
    prefix = "envs/prod/compute"
  }
}

data "terraform_remote_state" "network" {
  backend = "gcs"
  config = {
    bucket = "my-terraform-state-bucket"
    prefix = "envs/prod/network"
  }
}

resource "google_compute_instance" "vm" {
  name         = "app-server"
  machine_type = "e2-medium"
  zone         = "us-central1-a"

  boot_disk {
    initialize_params {
      image = "debian-cloud/debian-11"
    }
  }

  network_interface {
    network = data.terraform_remote_state.network.outputs.vpc_network_name
    access_config {}
  }
}
```

The **google_compute_network** resource name created in the network directory is referenced in this directory using the **terraform_remote_state** data block from its state defined in the output block.

Dynamic and modular Terraform code is foundational for scalable and maintainable IaC. By leveraging reusable modules, parameterized variables, dynamic blocks, and effective inter-module communication, teams can streamline infrastructure provisioning while reducing errors. Best practices such as encapsulation, proper versioning, and secure output management ensure these patterns remain robust and adaptable to evolving cloud requirements. As infrastructure complexity grows, mastering these advanced techniques becomes indispensable for cloud security and operational efficiency.

Managing Complex Dependency Graphs Effectively

In Terraform projects, managing complex dependency graphs is essential to ensure smooth resource provisioning and avoid deployment failures. This section explores strategies to understand, optimize, and decouple resource dependencies, enabling efficient orchestration of infrastructure across multiple cloud providers.

Using depends_on and Implicit Dependencies

Terraform supports two types of dependencies between resources: implicit and explicit. These dependencies are vital to ensuring resources are created, updated, or destroyed in the correct order. Implicit dependencies are automatically determined by Terraform based on how resources are referenced in the configuration. However, when the relationship is not obvious through direct references such as outputs, names, or attributes, you can use **depends_on** to define an explicit dependency. This helps Terraform understand ordering that it would not infer by itself.

- **Implicit dependencies**: Whenever one resource refers to another (for example, using **azurerm_virtual_network.vnet.id** in a subnet), Terraform understands that the referenced resource must be created first. This inference is automatic and forms part of Terraform's dependency graph.
- **Explicit dependencies (depends_on)**: When a resource must depend on another but does not reference it directly (for example, a script or policy that depends on a network but does not use its ID), use **depends_on** to declare that relationship. This instructs Terraform to provision resources in the correct order, even if it cannot detect the dependency from the code alone.

The following are some features and best practices:

- **Implicit dependencies**: Prefer implicit references for simplicity, ensuring your resource relationships are intuitive and reducing unnecessary manual intervention.
- **Explicit dependencies**: Use **depends_on** for non-obvious or external dependencies that Terraform cannot infer automatically, such as custom provisioners or when using third-party modules.
- **Avoid overuse**: Excessive use of **depends_on** can clutter your configuration and reduce clarity. Rely on it only when necessary to enforce lifecycle order.

```
resource "azurerm_storage_container" "scripts" {
  name                  = "scripts"
  storage_account_name  = azurerm_storage_account.storage.name
  container_access_type = "private"
}

resource "azurerm_virtual_machine" "vm" {
  name                  = "example-vm"
  location              = azurerm_resource_group.rg.location
  resource_group_name   = azurerm_resource_group.rg.name
  network_interface_ids = [] # simplified for example
  vm_size               = "Standard_B1s"

  depends_on = [azurerm_storage_container.scripts]
}
```

This Terraform snippet in Azure uses depends_on to ensure that a virtual machine is provisioned only after a storage container used for scripts or extensions is fully created.

Understanding Terraform Graphs and Resource Dependencies

Terraform uses a Directed Acyclic Graph (DAG) internally to model the relationships and dependencies between resources in a configuration. This graph structure ensures that resources are provisioned, updated, or destroyed in a logical and safe sequence, based on how they depend on one another. This is essential for managing complex infrastructure across cloud providers such as AWS, GCP, and Azure, where services often rely on others (for example, a VM needing a network).

When you run terraform plan, Terraform parses the code and builds a dependency graph that maps out how each resource relies on the others. This graph helps Terraform decide what to do and in what order, ensuring correctness and avoiding race conditions.

- **Terraform graph generation**: Internally, Terraform analyzes input/output references, dependencies (both explicit and implicit), and resource lifecycles to generate the DAG.
- **Visualizing the graph**: You can use the command `terraform graph` to generate a DOT-format output, which can be visualized using tools such as Graphviz. This visual graph helps identify resource relationships and troubleshoot ordering issues.

For example, in AWS, a subnet must depend on a VPC, in GCP, a VM depends on the network and firewall, and in Azure, a virtual machine might depend on the NIC, which in turn depends on the virtual network.

The following are some salient features and best practices:

- **Identify cycles**: Avoid circular dependencies between resources. Terraform cannot resolve cycles and will fail to apply the configuration.
- **Minimize implicit dependencies**: While Terraform can infer dependencies (for example, using interpolation such as `resource_a.id`), it is better to define explicit dependencies using `depends_on` when the order is critical.
- **Simplify dependencies**: Use modules to encapsulate related infrastructure (for example, group VPC, subnets, and route tables into a network module) and reduce graph complexity.
- **Leverage Terraform's planning phase**: Regularly run terraform plan to verify that Terraform is interpreting dependencies correctly and no unexpected changes are introduced.
- **Use graphs for debugging**: Visual dependency graphs can help identify bottlenecks or incorrect assumptions in your infrastructure design.
- **Break down large graphs**: Separate large-scale infrastructure into smaller layers (for example, network, compute, storage), and manage their dependencies via `terraform_remote_state` or module outputs.

Decoupling Resource Dependencies for Faster Deployments

Decoupling resource dependencies refers to designing Terraform configurations in a way that minimizes unnecessary links between resources. By isolating resources that do not require direct interaction or data exchange, Terraform can deploy these components simultaneously rather than sequentially. This method leads to significantly faster deployments, especially in large, complex infrastructure setups across cloud platforms such as AWS, GCP, and Azure.

Terraform constructs an execution plan by creating a dependency graph of resources. If resources are not dependent on one another, either implicitly or explicitly, they can be created in parallel. By identifying and decoupling independent resources, you allow Terraform's built-in parallelism to handle those resources simultaneously. For example, an S3 bucket in AWS, a Google Cloud Storage bucket in GCP, and an Azure Blob container can be created in parallel if no interdependencies exist between them.

This strategy is particularly useful in modular designs or enterprise environments where resources are often grouped by function (networking, compute, storage) and can be independently managed. Terraform's execution engine then maximizes concurrency based on the structure of this dependency graph.

The following are some features and best practices:

- **Parallelism:** Use terraform apply **`-parallelism=N`** to control the number of concurrent operations during execution and take full advantage of decoupled resources.
- **Module independence:** Structure modules to be self-contained and avoid cross-module references unless absolutely necessary, allowing parallel provisioning across multiple modules.
- **Resource grouping:** Organize unrelated resources (for example, IAM roles, storage buckets, monitoring tools) into separate configurations or modules to minimize dependency chains and increase concurrency.

Managing complex dependency graphs is crucial for ensuring the reliability and efficiency of Terraform configurations. By understanding Terraform's DAG, leveraging explicit and implicit dependencies, and employing techniques such as workspaces, layers, and decoupling, you can tackle challenges posed by large-scale infrastructure projects. The practices outlined in this section not only optimize resource orchestration but also enhance scalability and maintainability, forming a solid foundation for advanced Terraform implementations.

Optimizing Terraform Configurations for Scalability and Maintenance

As infrastructure grows in complexity, ensuring that Terraform configurations are scalable and maintainable becomes critical. This section provides strategies for structuring projects, managing state, tuning performance, and enforcing code quality to handle increasing workloads while maintaining efficient workflows.

Structuring Terraform Projects for Large-Scale Deployments

Structuring a Terraform project for large-scale deployments involves organizing your codebase in a maintainable, scalable, and collaborative manner. As infrastructure complexity increases, especially when managing resources across cloud providers such as AWS, GCP, and Azure, a clear project structure becomes critical. It allows teams to operate independently, facilitates code reuse, reduces the risk of conflicts, and ensures that infrastructure changes are predictable and auditable.

Terraform relies on a directory and module structure that reflects the logical architecture of your infrastructure. At the top level, you typically organize by environment, such as **`dev/`**, **`staging/`**, and **`prod/`**, ensuring separation of concerns and minimizing risk between stages. Within each environment, resources are grouped into modules, such as networking, compute, or storage, each abstracting a particular component of infrastructure. These modules expose inputs and outputs to ensure loosely coupled yet integrated deployment logic. Environment-specific configuration files (for example, **`terraform.tfvars`**) allow tailored deployments using the same module logic. Additionally, Terraform workspaces or completely separate state backends are used to isolate environments further for safety and scalability.

The following are some features and best practices:

- **Hierarchical organization:** Create a multi-layered directory structure that reflects components such as **`networking/`**, **`compute/`**, **`security/`**, and **`apps/`** to isolate domains of infrastructure.
- **Avoid over-nesting:** Maintain a flat and intuitive layout. Deeply nested directories increase complexity and slow down navigation.

- **Use version control:** Pin module versions using Git tags or registries to avoid unintended changes and support consistent rollbacks or upgrades across environments.

Performance Tuning Terraform Plan and Apply

Performance tuning in Terraform focuses on reducing the time taken during the terraform plan and terraform apply phases, especially critical in large-scale deployments across AWS, GCP, and Azure. By optimizing how Terraform evaluates configurations, retrieves state, and provisions resources, teams can accelerate feedback loops and decrease deployment windows.

Terraform builds a dependency graph and then walks that graph to compute diffs (`plan`) and enact changes (`apply`). Tuning involves limiting the scope of what Terraform examines or modifies, increasing the number of concurrent API calls it makes, and ensuring the in-memory and remote state interactions are as frictionless as possible. Proper state synchronization and modular design reduce unnecessary work, while backend choice impacts the speed of state reads and writes.

The following are some features and best practices:

- **Selective targeting:** Use `-target` to scope operations to specific resources or modules, cutting down on graph evaluation and API calls.
- **Parallelism tuning:** Adjust `-parallelism=N` to match cloud provider rate limits and network bandwidth, provisioning independent resources concurrently.
- **State synchronization:** Regularly run `terraform refresh` or enable auto-refresh to keep the state in sync with live infrastructure, minimizing surprises during planning.
- **Modular design:** Break large configurations into small, focused modules that limit inter-resource dependencies and shrink the graph that Terraform must traverse.
- **Optimized backends:** Choose low-latency remote state backends (for example, regional S3/GCS buckets with versioning) and leverage state caching where supported to speed up state retrieval.

Optimizing Terraform configurations for scalability and maintenance is critical for managing growing infrastructure needs. By structuring projects effectively, implementing state file locking, tuning performance, and enforcing code standards, organizations can ensure their Terraform codebase remains robust and maintainable. These practices not only enhance collaboration and efficiency but also reduce the likelihood of errors, making them indispensable for managing modern cloud environments.

Conclusion

Mastering advanced design patterns in Terraform is essential for building scalable, maintainable, and secure infrastructure in modern cloud environments. Throughout this chapter, we explored how to structure Terraform repositories using monorepo, multi-repo, and hybrid approaches, each tailored to different organizational needs and development workflows. We examined techniques for managing Terraform state, module versioning, and collaboration in large teams, enabling infrastructure changes to be made safely and efficiently across cloud platforms.

We also delved into writing dynamic and modular code that simplifies infrastructure management and increases reusability. From managing complex dependency graphs to optimizing performance for large-scale deployments, these design patterns help engineers avoid common pitfalls and enhance deployment velocity. By applying these strategies, teams can confidently scale their Terraform usage across multiple environments while maintaining consistency, reliability, and operational excellence.

In the next chapter, we will dive deep into real-world case studies demonstrating Terraform's role in designing secure multi-cloud architectures, automating compliance, and integrating security into

CI/CD pipelines. It also highlights strategies for preventing data breaches and lessons learned from common pitfalls in Terraform projects.

Questions and Answers

1. **What are the key considerations when choosing between a monorepo and multi-repo strategy for Terraform projects?**

   A monorepo centralizes all infrastructure code in a single repository, promoting reusability and easier cross-team collaboration, especially in smaller or tightly integrated environments. However, it can lead to complex dependency management and larger blast radii. A multi-repo strategy provides isolation of workloads, better access control, and reduced risk during deployments, but may introduce challenges in coordinating changes across repositories and managing shared modules. A hybrid approach combines the best of both, especially for large enterprise setups.

2. **How do dynamic blocks and locals improve the flexibility and maintainability of Terraform code?**

   Dynamic blocks allow you to generate repeated nested blocks programmatically based on variables, reducing code duplication. Locals help abstract complex logic or expressions into simple, reusable labels. Together, they enhance readability, reduce redundancy, and make Terraform configurations more adaptable to change, especially in modular codebases.

3. **What role does `terraform_remote_state` play in inter-directory and inter-module communication?**

   The **`terraform_remote_state`** data source enables one Terraform configuration to access output values from another, facilitating loose coupling and reusability across environments or modules. It is especially useful in multi-repo or layered architecture setups, where different components of the infrastructure are managed independently but need to share critical data such as VPC IDs or IAM roles.

4. **How can dependency graphs be optimized to improve Terraform plan and apply performance?**

   By using a combination of explicit **`depends_on`**, implicit dependencies (via references), and decoupled resource organization, you can reduce unnecessary resource waits and enable parallelism. Visualizing dependency graphs helps identify bottlenecks, and isolating independent resources into separate modules or workspaces can accelerate apply times and minimize deployment impact.

5. **What are the best practices for structuring Terraform projects to support large-scale cloud deployments?**

   For scalability, it is recommended to organize projects by environment (for example, **`dev`**, **`staging`**, **`prod`**), separate reusable modules from environment-specific configurations, and maintain a clear directory structure. Implementing CI/CD automation, remote backends, consistent naming conventions, and module versioning ensures maintainability, scalability, and smoother collaboration across teams.

CHAPTER 15
Real-World Case Studies

Introduction

As organizations increasingly rely on cloud infrastructure to power mission-critical applications, the need for secure, scalable, and compliant Infrastructure-as-Code (IaC) becomes paramount. This chapter bridges theory with practical application by showcasing how enterprises have successfully implemented Terraform to automate, secure, and scale their cloud operations across various industries and use cases. From building resilient multi-cloud SaaS architectures to automating compliance in highly regulated environments, these examples provide concrete insights into how Terraform can address complex infrastructure and security challenges. Each section combines architectural patterns, automation strategies, and real-life enterprise implementations to demonstrate how Terraform enables operational excellence and robust security postures.

Readers will explore end-to-end use cases such as identity and access management across AWS, Azure, and GCP, secure CI/CD provisioning for global teams, and real-time threat mitigation using cloud-native tools. Industry case studies, featuring companies such as TeamSystem, Nedbank, State Farm, and LG Uplus illustrate how leading organizations leverage Terraform to drive digital transformation and enforce security at scale. The chapter concludes with a deep dive into lessons learned from real-world deployments, offering best practices for state management, dependency resolution, and long-term scalability. Thus, whether you are managing infrastructure for a startup or an enterprise, this chapter equips you with the practical knowledge to apply Terraform securely and effectively in complex, dynamic environments.

Structure

In this chapter, we will cover the following topics:

- Designing a Secure Multi-Cloud Architecture for SaaS Applications:
  - Requirements for a Multi-Cloud SaaS Platform
  - Implementing Identity and Access Management across Clouds
  - Configuring Secure Data Flows and Interconnectivity
  - Monitoring and Logging in Multi-Cloud Environments
  - TeamSystem's Strategic Transformation with Terraform for Scalable SaaS Infrastructure
- Automating Compliance in Financial and Regulated Industries:
  - Identifying Regulatory Requirements and Challenges
  - Creating Compliance-as-Code Templates
  - Continuous Monitoring and Auditing with Terraform
  - Automating Incident Response for Regulatory Violations
  - Transforming Digital Infrastructure in Financial Services: Nedbank's Journey with Terraform

- Integrating Security into CI/CD Pipelines for Global Operations:
  - Security Challenges in CI/CD for Global Teams
  - Provisioning Secure CI/CD Environments with Terraform
  - Embedding Security Scanning in Pipelines
  - Scaling CI/CD Security for Multi-Region Operations
  - Enhancing CI/CD Security and Efficiency: State Farm's Integration of Terraform Enterprise and GitOps
- Preventing Data Breaches with Robust Security Automation:
  - Protecting Sensitive Data with Encryption and Policies
  - Real-Time Threat Detection with Terraform-Orchestrated Tools
  - Implementing Automated Remediation Workflows
  - LG Uplus's Journey with Terraform for Strengthening Cloud Security with Automation
- Lessons Learned: Avoiding Common Pitfalls in Terraform Projects:
  - Handling State Management Challenges
  - Balancing Modularity and Complexity
  - Addressing Dependency Management Issues
  - Ensuring Long-Term Maintenance and Scalability

Designing a Secure Multi-Cloud Architecture for SaaS Applications

Multi-cloud architectures for SaaS platforms enable businesses to leverage the unique features of multiple cloud providers. However, this approach introduces challenges in security, compliance, and scalability that must be addressed to ensure robust and seamless operations. This section provides a comprehensive framework for building secure and scalable multi-cloud architectures using Terraform.

Requirements for a Multi-Cloud SaaS Platform

A multi-cloud SaaS platform that operates across AWS, GCP, and Azure must be designed to meet a range of technical and operational requirements, such as scalability, security, compliance, and interoperability. These platforms often serve global users, and need to deploy and manage resources consistently across multiple cloud environments. Terraform enables teams to define infrastructure as code, abstracting provider-specific configurations and ensuring uniform deployments across cloud providers. By using Terraform, organizations can automate infrastructure provisioning, enforce security standards, maintain compliance, and handle scaling requirements, regardless of the cloud vendor through reusable and modular code.

- **Scalability:** Use Terraform modules to declare autoscaling configurations that dynamically adjust compute resources in AWS (Auto Scaling Groups), GCP (Managed Instance Groups), and Azure (Virtual Machine Scale Sets) based on demand.
- **Security:** Terraform allows you to define cloud-specific network isolation mechanisms such as AWS VPCs, Azure Virtual Networks, and GCP VPCs, along with centralized IAM policies to control user and service permissions securely.
- **Compliance:** Terraform templates can be pre-configured to enforce compliance policies such as encryption, logging, and access controls, ensuring alignment with standards such as GDPR, HIPAA, and PCI DSS across all environments.

The following are some salient features and best practices:

- **Unified resource management:** Use a single centralized repository to manage multi-cloud infrastructure, ensuring consistency and traceability across AWS, GCP, and Azure from one source of truth.
- **Environment-specific configurations:** Separate configuration values for production, staging, and development using variables and workspaces to manage changes independently across environments without the risk of conflicts.
- **CI/CD integration:** Integrate Terraform into CI/CD workflows to automate provisioning, testing, and deployment steps for infrastructure updates, reducing manual errors, and improving delivery velocity.
- **Modular design:** Create cloud-agnostic and provider-specific modules to promote reuse and scalability across projects.
- **Secrets and credential management:** Integrate with tools such as AWS Secrets Manager, Azure Key Vault, or GCP Secret Manager to handle the sensitive data securely.
- **Consistent tagging and naming:** Define standard naming conventions in modules to ensure traceability, cost allocation, and compliance.

Implementing Identity and Access Management across Clouds

Identity and Access Management (IAM) is fundamental to securing any cloud environment, ensuring that only authorized users and services can access specific resources. In a multi-cloud SaaS or enterprise platform operating across AWS, GCP, and Azure, maintaining a unified and consistent IAM strategy helps reduce misconfigurations and enforces compliance. Also, it minimizes the risk of privilege escalation or data breaches. Terraform allows you to codify IAM rules and permissions, enforce role-based access policies, automate identity provisioning, and ensure that access rules are consistently applied across all cloud providers from a single source of truth.

- **AWS:** Use Terraform to declare IAM roles, policies, users, and groups that define access permissions to AWS resources such as EC2, S3, Lambda, and DynamoDB, ensuring that users and applications only have the necessary privileges.
- **GCP:** Manage IAM bindings and custom roles using Terraform to assign roles to users, service accounts, or groups with the principle of least privilege applied across services such as Compute Engine, Cloud Storage, BigQuery, and Pub/Sub.
- **Azure:** Leverage Terraform to configure role assignments and custom roles using Azure Role-Based Access Control (RBAC), defining granular access to resources such as Virtual Machines, Blob Storage, Key Vault, and Azure SQL by assigning roles to security principals such as users or managed identities.

The following are some salient features and best practices:

- **Role-Based Access Control (RBAC):** Use reusable Terraform modules to implement consistent RBAC policies across AWS IAM, GCP IAM, and Azure RBAC, ensuring that team roles such as Admin, Developer, and Viewer have standardized permissions in all environments.
- **Automated key rotation:** Configure automated rotation of secrets and credentials using Terraform-integrated tooling such as AWS Secrets Manager, Azure Key Vault, and GCP Secret Manager to reduce the risk of credential compromise.

- **Least privilege enforcement:** Design IAM roles and policies using the principle of least privilege by granting only the necessary permissions required for specific tasks, and continuously refine them based on audit feedback.
- **Environment isolation:** Use Terraform workspaces or separate configurations to define IAM policies independently for `dev`, `staging`, and `prod` environments, avoiding permission leaks or accidental over-provisioning across stages.
- **Identity federation and SSO integration:** Leverage Terraform to configure identity federation (for example, with SAML or OIDC) across cloud platforms, allowing centralized user authentication using external identity providers such as Okta, Azure AD, or Google Workspace.
- **Policy Validation Tools:** Integrate static analysis tools such as tfsec, checkov, or policy-as-code tools such as Open Policy Agent (OPA) into the Terraform pipeline to validate IAM policies before deployment.
- **Scoped service accounts:** For applications running across clouds, use Terraform to create tightly scoped service accounts with cross-platform API access (for example, AWS Lambda accessing Azure storage), while enforcing boundaries using explicit policies.

Configuring Secure Data Flows and Interconnectivity

In a multi-cloud SaaS platform, secure and efficient data transfer between services and environments is critical for performance, compliance, and security. With services often distributed across AWS, GCP, and Azure, configuring secure interconnectivity requires careful planning to avoid data leakage, latency, or misconfigurations. Terraform enables teams to codify and automate the provisioning of secure network paths, enforce encryption policies, and ensure private communication across cloud providers. This Infrastructure as Code (IaC) approach minimizes human error, ensures repeatability, and enables rapid deployment of network configurations across clouds in a secure and scalable manner.

- **AWS:** Use Terraform to provision secure inter-region and cross-account communication using Virtual Private Cloud (VPC) Peering, AWS Transit Gateway, and VPN connections, enabling private and encrypted data transfers across AWS environments and toward other clouds.
- **GCP:** Leverage Terraform to set up Shared VPCs, Cloud Interconnect, and Cloud VPNs for establishing secure connections between GCP projects, regions, and external cloud environments such as AWS or Azure, maintaining centralized network control and segmentation.
- **Azure:** Use Terraform to automate the configuration of Azure Virtual Network (VNet) Peering, VPN Gateways, and ExpressRoute to establish high-throughput, encrypted connections between Azure regions or to other cloud providers, avoiding the public internet for sensitive data.

The following are some important features and best practices:

- **Encryption in transit:** Ensure that all data transferred across and within clouds uses industry-standard encryption protocols such as TLS and IPsec by configuring VPN tunnels, and enforcing HTTPS endpoints using Terraform-managed security groups and firewall rules.
- **Private networking:** Isolate resources in private subnets, and use NAT gateways or cloud firewalls (for example, AWS NACLs, GCP Firewall Rules, Azure NSGs) to prevent unauthorized inbound traffic, while allowing outbound access for trusted endpoints.
- **Cross-cloud networking:** Use Terraform to automate creation of cross-cloud connections such as AWS Direct Connect, GCP Interconnect, and Azure ExpressRoute, enabling high-bandwidth, private, and secure data exchanges between clouds.

- **Zero trust principles:** Configure service-level policies and security groups to follow zero trust principles, ensuring each service communicates only with explicitly allowed destinations, even within private networks.
- **DNS and routing configuration:** Use Terraform to manage cloud-native DNS (for example, AWS Route 53, GCP Cloud DNS, Azure DNS) and route tables to control traffic flow securely between services and across clouds with minimal latency and maximum isolation.
- **Segmentation and firewalls:** Define logical network segments using Terraform and deploy next-generation firewalls (for example, Azure Firewall, AWS Network Firewall, GCP Cloud Armor) to inspect and control traffic between application tiers or cloud environments.
- **High availability and failover:** Configure HA-enabled VPN gateways and redundant interconnect links across clouds using Terraform to ensure continuous data flow during failures or maintenance.
- **Latency optimization:** Place services in geographically optimal regions and use Terraform to fine-tune route tables and load balancers (for example, AWS ALB/NLB, Azure Load Balancer, GCP Load Balancer) to reduce round-trip time between services across clouds.

Monitoring and Logging in Multi-Cloud Environments

In a multi-cloud SaaS environment, maintaining observability across distributed infrastructure is crucial to ensure performance, availability, security, and compliance. Monitoring helps detect performance degradation or failures, while logging enables detailed auditing and forensic analysis. Given the complexity of managing resources across AWS, GCP, and Azure, manual setup of monitoring and logging tools is error-prone and inconsistent. Terraform allows teams to codify the setup of these tools, ensuring standardized, repeatable, and scalable observability configurations. By automating this process, Terraform enables centralized visibility into health, usage patterns, anomalies, and incidents across all cloud platforms, reducing Mean Time to Detection (MTTD) and Mean Time to Resolution (MTTR).

- **AWS:** Use Terraform to provision and configure Amazon CloudWatch for resource-level metrics, dashboards, and alarms, and set up AWS CloudTrail for capturing detailed API activity logs for auditing and compliance purposes.
- **GCP:** Use Terraform to enable Cloud Monitoring for collecting metrics from Compute Engine, GKE, and other services, and set up Cloud Logging to ingest structured logs from all GCP resources into centralized log sinks and storage.
- **Azure:** Use Terraform to configure Azure Monitor for tracking metrics and health status of resources, and deploy Log Analytics workspaces to ingest and analyze diagnostic and activity logs from services such as VMs, databases, and applications.

The following are some salient features and best practices:

- **Centralized dashboards:** Use Terraform to integrate metrics and logs from AWS CloudWatch, GCP Cloud Monitoring, and Azure Monitor into unified dashboards using third-party observability tools such as Datadog, Splunk, or Grafana to get a single pane of glass view.
- **Alerting and notifications:** Automate the setup of threshold-based alerts using Terraform by configuring Amazon SNS for CloudWatch alarms, Pub/Sub for GCP Monitoring policies, and Action Groups for Azure Monitor alerts to notify teams via email, SMS, or chat platforms.
- **Retention policies:** Define log retention durations in Terraform for services such as AWS CloudTrail, GCP Logging sinks, and Azure Log Analytics to balance compliance requirements (for example, GDPR, HIPAA) with cost-effective data storage management.

- **Anomaly detection:** Integrate anomaly detection capabilities available in CloudWatch Anomaly Detection (AWS), Metrics Explorer (GCP), and Smart Detection in Azure Monitor using Terraform to proactively catch unusual behaviors in metrics data.
- **Metric export and correlation:** Configure Terraform to export key metrics and logs to external SIEM or APM tools for deeper analysis and correlation with application traces and user behavior to enhance root cause analysis and threat detection.
- **Log filtering and sampling:** Configure log ingestion rules using Terraform to include only relevant logs, for example, error-level or security-specific logs, to optimize performance and reduce noise and costs, especially in high-throughput environments.
- **Service-Level Objectives (SLOs):** Use Terraform to define monitoring configurations that align with business-defined SLOs, tracking metrics such as latency, availability, and error rates to ensure service reliability across cloud environments.

TeamSystem's Strategic Transformation with Terraform for Scalable SaaS Infrastructure

As TeamSystem expanded its digital solutions to over 1.4 million clients, it turned to Terraform to overcome infrastructure complexity, enforce governance, and accelerate cloud deployments across hundreds of AWS accounts.

Business Challenges

TeamSystem, a premier provider of digital solutions for businesses and professionals in finance and human resources, faced growing pressure to scale its cloud infrastructure efficiently, while maintaining governance and security. As their SaaS customer base expanded to serve over 1.4 million clients, the company had to manage hundreds of AWS accounts and a wide range of cloud services across various environments. Manual provisioning, lack of standardized practices, and inconsistent infrastructure policies created bottlenecks in deployment cycles, increased the risk of configuration errors, and hindered visibility into infrastructure changes. These challenges limited team autonomy, delayed feature rollouts, and made compliance more difficult to enforce at scale, all of which were critical to maintaining trust, and delivering consistent service quality in a regulated market.

Solution with Terraform

To address these operational complexities and accelerate cloud maturity, TeamSystem adopted Terraform and Terraform Cloud as the foundation of their Infrastructure as Code (IaC) strategy. They architected a modular, reusable set of Terraform modules to represent the core infrastructure components, enabling rapid and consistent provisioning across multiple AWS accounts and environments. Hence, by leveraging Terraform Cloud workspaces, TeamSystem isolated infrastructure deployments by team and application, while applying Sentinel policies to enforce compliance and security standards automatically. Integrating Terraform with version control systems such as Git and CI/CD pipelines allowed the team to introduce automation, peer-reviewed changes, and full auditability into their infrastructure lifecycle. This transition not only reduced complexity but also enabled decentralized teams to self-manage deployments with the confidence of central governance and policy enforcement in place.

Business Outcomes

The implementation of Terraform led to transformational outcomes across TeamSystem's engineering and operations teams. Deployment timelines improved significantly, with a 30% increase in speed, enabling the company to deliver features and updates more rapidly and efficiently. Standardizing infrastructure as code reduced manual tasks and human errors, resulting in more secure and reliable environments. Teams were empowered to take ownership of their own environments using a self-service model, improving productivity, while still adhering to company-wide standards. Moreover, Governance improved in both transparency and scalability, with security and compliance policies applied automatically across all deployments, ensuring that infrastructure met both internal and regulatory requirements. These improvements positioned TeamSystem to scale its SaaS offerings more confidently and securely in a highly competitive market.

Key Highlights

- Supports over 1.4 million SaaS customers across finance and HR industries with enterprise-grade reliability.
- Manages hundreds of AWS accounts efficiently through modular and reusable Terraform configurations.
- Enforces security and compliance policies automatically using Sentinel in Terraform Cloud.
- Achieved a 30% acceleration in deployment cycles, reducing time-to-market for critical updates and services.
- Adopted a workspace-based model in Terraform Cloud, enabling team-level autonomy without sacrificing control.
- Integrated Git-based version control and CI/CD pipelines for a fully automated and auditable infrastructure lifecycle.
- Reduced operational overhead and configuration drift through repeatable, consistent provisioning practices.
- Enhanced collaboration between development, operations, and security teams, aligning with DevSecOps best practices.

Designing a secure multi-cloud architecture for SaaS applications requires careful planning and execution. By leveraging Terraform, businesses can implement consistent security policies, configure secure inter-cloud communication, and monitor infrastructure performance. This approach not only enhances scalability and reliability but also minimizes security risks. The strategies and best practices outlined here provide a solid foundation for achieving secure and efficient multi-cloud operations.

Automating Compliance in Financial and Regulated Industries

Regulated industries such as finance and healthcare require strict adherence to standards such as GDPR, HIPAA, and PCI DSS to ensure data privacy, security, and operational transparency. Terraform simplifies achieving these compliance goals by allowing compliance-as-code automation, continuous monitoring, and rapid remediation workflows. This section explores how Terraform addresses these challenges effectively.

Identifying Regulatory Requirements and Challenges

Modern cloud-based infrastructure must comply with a growing set of regulatory frameworks such as GDPR, HIPAA, and PCI DSS, which impose rigorous standards for data security, privacy, access management, and auditability. Organizations operating in multiple jurisdictions or industries face the complex challenge of aligning their cloud infrastructure with these diverse compliance mandates. Terraform offers a scalable and automated way to codify and enforce these requirements within infrastructure provisioning processes. Thus, by embedding compliance as code, teams can reduce the risk of non-compliance, while accelerating delivery and maintaining consistency across AWS, GCP, and Azure environments.

The following are some widely used regulations:

- **GDPR:** Requires organizations to protect personal data through encryption, proper access control, data minimization, and explicit user consent mechanisms. Infrastructure must support data localization and rights, such as data erasure.
- **HIPAA:** Imposes stringent controls over Protected Health Information (PHI), requiring secure data transmission, access logging, and role-based access to infrastructure handling healthcare data.
- **PCI DSS:** Governs payment card data and mandates encrypted transmission, secure storage, strict access policies, and real-time monitoring for infrastructure components interacting with cardholder data.

The following are some challenges that you need to understand for regulations:

- **Mapping regulations to infrastructure:** Translating legal and regulatory text into actionable Terraform configurations can be complex, and may require collaboration between legal, security, and engineering teams.
- **Consistency across cloud providers:** Achieving compliance uniformly across AWS, GCP, and Azure is difficult due to differences in native services, IAM models, logging mechanisms, and encryption capabilities.
- **Dynamic compliance needs:** Regulations evolve, and Terraform configurations must be continuously updated to reflect the current compliance standards.

The following are some important features and best practices:

- **Conduct a gap analysis:** Perform a structured comparison between current infrastructure and regulatory requirements to identify missing controls and required changes.
- **Define compliance checklists in codes:** Create pre-deployment Policy-as-Code (for example, with Sentinel or OPA) to enforce encryption, tagging, access control, and logging standards.
- **Implement Role-Based Access Control (RBAC):** Use IAM roles (AWS), IAM policies (GCP), and Azure RBAC to restrict access to only authorized users based on least-privilege principles, all configurable with Terraform.
- **Enable logging and auditing:** Use Terraform to provision CloudTrail (AWS), Cloud Audit Logs (GCP), and Azure Monitor Logs to ensure that all access and changes are tracked for auditing purposes.
- **Use encryption everywhere:** Define encryption at rest and in transit using Terraform resources such as AWS KMS, GCP CMEK, or Azure Key Vault-backed disk encryption to comply with data protection laws.
- **Apply tagging for compliance scope:** Use Terraform to enforce consistent tagging (for example, `"compliance: HIPAA"`) for all resources, aiding visibility and automated compliance scanning.
- **Utilize environment-specific modules:** Create compliance-focused modules tailored for regulated environments (for example, HIPAA-compliant VPC, PCI-DSS secure database, and so on) for repeatable secure provisioning.
- **Integrate compliance dashboards:** Combine Terraform outputs with compliance monitoring tools (for example, AWS Security Hub, Azure Defender, and GCP Security Command Center) to track posture in real time.

Creating Compliance-as-Code Templates

Compliance-as-Code (CaC) is a proactive approach to embedding regulatory and security controls directly into your cloud infrastructure through Terraform templates. By codifying compliance requirements such as encryption, identity access management, and logging, you ensure repeatable, auditable, and consistent enforcement of policies across your environments. These templates reduce human errors, accelerate infrastructure provisioning, and ensure ongoing alignment with standards such as GDPR, HIPAA, PCI DSS, and SOC 2, regardless of whether you are operating in AWS, GCP, or Azure.

- **Encryption controls across providers:** Use Terraform modules to enforce encryption at rest and in transit by configuring platform-specific encryption settings such as AWS KMS, GCP CMEK, and Azure Disk Encryption.
- **Auditing and logging controls:** Provision Terraform code to enable cloud-native logging services such as AWS CloudTrail, GCP Audit Logs, and Azure Monitor for end-to-end audit visibility.
- **IAM and access controls:** Define Terraform-based policies and roles to implement least privilege access across cloud providers using IAM best practices.
- **Policy Enforcement with Sentinel or OPA:** Integrate policy-as-code engines such as Sentinel (Terraform Cloud) or Open Policy Agent to validate Terraform plans against compliance rules during CI/CD.
- **Environment Isolation and Segmentation:** Use Terraform modules and workspaces to define isolated configurations for dev, staging, and production environments with scoped permissions and guardrails.
- **Networking and Firewall Controls:** Configure secure network access using Terraform to manage AWS Security Groups, GCP VPC firewall rules, and Azure NSGs for defined ingress/egress rules.

The following are some salient features and best practices:

- **Create modular Terraform templates for common controls:** Break compliance areas (encryption, IAM, logging, and networking) into reusable modules that can be composed together depending on the use case or regulatory requirements.
- **Parameterize modules to support environment-specific variations:** Use variables to allow different settings per environment (for example, different retention periods, key rotation policies, and access scopes) while using the same underlying modules.
- **Regularly update templates to reflect new regulatory standards:** Stay informed on changes in laws such as GDPR or HIPAA, and revise your Terraform templates accordingly to maintain a compliance posture.
- **Maintain templates in version-controlled repositories**: Use Git to store and version compliance templates, enabling code reviews, audit trails, and rollback capabilities.
- **Use Terraform workspaces for multi-tenancy and isolation:** Leverage workspaces to isolate configurations and state for different customers or departments, while applying consistent compliance templates.
- **Generate compliance reports from Terraform outputs:** Output key compliance-related metadata (for example, encryption status, IAM assignments, and logging endpoints) from modules, and feed into compliance dashboards.

Continuous Monitoring and Auditing with Terraform

Continuous monitoring and auditing with Terraform involves integrating Infrastructure-as-Code

(IaC) workflows with security, compliance, and policy validation tools to ensure that infrastructure remains secure and compliant post-deployment. By leveraging tools such as Sentinel, TFSec, Checkov, and CI/CD systems, teams can proactively detect misconfigurations, enforce regulatory policies, and audit changes across cloud environments, AWS, GCP, and Azure, without manual intervention. This approach ensures consistent governance, auditability, and trust in the infrastructure state over time.

- **Policy-as-Code with Sentinel:** Use Sentinel to define policies that enforce security controls (for example, mandatory encryption or restricted IP CIDRs), which are evaluated before Terraform plans are applied.
- **Compliance tag enforcement:** Apply Sentinel or custom CI checks to reject resources lacking critical tags such as owner, environment, or `data_classification`, enhancing audit traceability.
- **Provider-agnostic misconfiguration detection**: Use TFSec or Checkov to run cloud-agnostic checks across AWS, GCP, and Azure, such as disabled logging, lack of IAM boundaries, or missing encryption.
- **Automated compliance checks in CI/CD pipelines:** Configure Jenkins, GitHub Actions, or GitLab CI pipelines to automatically run security and compliance validations before infrastructure is provisioned.
- **Real-Time alerts and notifications:** Connect Terraform Cloud or CI pipelines with alerting tools (for example, AWS SNS, Azure Monitor alerts, and GCP Pub/Sub) to notify teams when policy violations occur.

The following are some salient features and best practices:

- **Schedule periodic code scans:** Run recurring scans using TFSec, Checkov, or Terraform Cloud to detect drift or new vulnerabilities in infrastructure code.
- **Leverage workspaces for compliance separation:** Use Terraform workspaces to isolate compliance policies between dev, staging, and production environments for better governance control.
- **Generate compliance reports automatically:** Create Terraform-integrated pipelines that generate compliance reports (for example, CIS benchmarks, NIST 800-53 mapping) after each apply or scheduled run.
- **Centralize logs for compliance review**: Forward Terraform Cloud audit logs and CI/CD outputs to centralized log analytics tools (for example, ELK stack, Splunk) for streamlined review and compliance reporting.
- **Integrate with cloud-native tools**: Enhance coverage by integrating Terraform with AWS Config, Azure Policy, and GCP Organization Policy to catch non-IaC changes made via the console or APIs.

Automating Incident Response for Regulatory Violations

Automating incident response for regulatory violations involves using Terraform in conjunction with cloud-native services and external automation tools to detect, report, and remediate compliance breaches with minimal manual intervention. These violations might include unencrypted data storage, overly permissive network rules, or missing audit logs. By integrating Terraform with event-driven triggers, alerting systems, and remediation workflows, organizations operating in AWS, GCP, or Azure can ensure quick, consistent, and auditable enforcement of security policies. This approach reduces downtime, minimizes regulatory exposure, and enhances overall cloud posture management.

- **Event triggers using cloud-native monitoring tools:** Use Terraform to provision services such as AWS CloudWatch Events, GCP Cloud Monitoring, or Azure Event Grid that detect policy violations and initiate automated workflows (for example, triggering Lambda, Cloud Functions, or Logic Apps).

- **Real-time non-compliance alerts**: Deploy alerting infrastructure using Terraform that ties into SNS (AWS), Pub/Sub (GCP), or Azure Monitor to send notifications to email, Slack, or SIEM tools when regulatory rules are breached.
- **Automated remediation**: Configure CI/CD or automation platforms such as AWS Systems Manager, Azure Automation, or Google Cloud Run to apply corrective Terraform plans when violations are detected (for example, encrypting a storage bucket).
- **Tag-based enforcement and auto-correction**: Implement Terraform rules that auto-tag resources and use compliance engines (such as Azure Policy or AWS Config Rules) to auto-remediate misconfigured or untagged infrastructure.
- **Maintaining immutable logs of violations and responses**: Configure logging mechanisms (for example, AWS CloudTrail, GCP Audit Logs, Azure Activity Logs) using Terraform to capture violation incidents and remediation actions for future audit and forensic analysis.
- **Triggering external playbooks via webhooks**: Terraform can provision integrations with third-party incident management systems (for example, PagerDuty, ServiceNow, and Opsgenie) by triggering webhooks from alerting services when a policy breach occurs.

The following are some important features and best practices:

- **Define escalation policies based on severity levels:** Build tiered escalation strategies (for example, `email → Slack → on-call pager`) using alert thresholds defined in Terraform modules, ensuring that critical incidents are addressed promptly.
- **Separate remediation modules from core infrastructure:** Keep incident response automation in its own Terraform module to reduce coupling and risks when updating production infrastructure.
- **Simulate violations in staging environments:** Regularly test automated response workflows in a sandbox or test environment to ensure that they function as expected, before enabling them in production.
- **Audit every action taken by automation:** Ensure that all triggered events, responses, and outcomes are logged and traceable using cloud-native audit trails, and centralized logging solutions configured via Terraform.
- **Integrate remediation with approval workflows:** In sensitive environments, configure Terraform plans to require manual approval (for example, via GitHub pull requests or CI/CD gates) before execution, balancing automation with control.

Transforming Digital Infrastructure in Financial Services: Nedbank's Journey with Terraform

To accelerate its digital banking strategy, Nedbank adopted Terraform Cloud to replace legacy provisioning with self-service, automated infrastructure, cutting costs, boosting agility, and ensuring compliance across its multi-cloud environment.

Business Challenges

Nedbank, one of South Africa's leading banking institutions, faced significant pressure to modernize its infrastructure as part of a broader digital transformation strategy. With a cloud-first mandate initiated in 2019, the bank aimed to move all workloads to the cloud while embracing a DevOps culture. However, the traditional process of infrastructure provisioning was inefficient, as hardware procurement could take months, delaying project delivery and limiting agility. Moreover, the reliance on a central IT team to manage infrastructure for thousands of developers proved unsustainable. Nedbank needed a solution that enabled faster time to market, lowered operational costs, and ensured security compliance in a highly regulated financial environment.

Solution with Terraform

To overcome these challenges, Nedbank adopted HashiCorp Terraform Cloud, upgrading from their previous open-source IaC tools. This enterprise-grade solution enabled the development of a self-service ecosystem, where developers could provision infrastructure via a graphical user interface without needing deep Terraform expertise. Terraform Cloud's automation, security, and platform-agnostic architecture allowed seamless integration with Nedbank's multi-cloud environment comprising AWS, Azure, Kubernetes, and MongoDB. The implementation also enforced security and compliance through policy-as-code and audit trails. Additionally, HashiCorp Vault Enterprise was used for identity-based security automation and encryption, further strengthening the bank's compliance posture. This new model empowered developers, reduced IT bottlenecks, and fostered a culture of collaboration and continuous improvement.

Business Outcomes

Thus, by leveraging Terraform Cloud, Nedbank reduced infrastructure provisioning time from several months to just minutes. The bank achieved a 25% reduction in delivery costs, saving over approximately 1 million USD in two years. This transformation also improved the security posture and compliance by automating encryption and audit processes. Developers became more productive, and the central IT team was freed from repetitive infrastructure tasks. Most importantly, the bank gained a competitive edge as a first mover in digital banking innovations such as Rapid Payments, setting a benchmark for digital transformation in the financial services sector.

Key Highlights

- 25% reduction in delivery costs, saving over 1 million USD in two years.
- Infrastructure delivery accelerated by 99% – from months to minutes.
- Enhanced security and compliance via automated encryption and audit logging.
- Self-service provisioning for developers using a GUI, no deep IaC knowledge needed.
- Enabled multi-cloud workflows across AWS, Azure, Kubernetes, and MongoDB.
- Fostered DevOps culture, and cross-functional collaboration.
- Delivered more than 1,000 virtual machines per month via Terraform pipelines.
- Significantly reduced project delays, and time-to-market.

Automating compliance in financial and regulated industries is crucial for maintaining security and meeting legal obligations. Terraform provides a robust framework for translating complex regulatory requirements into actionable configurations, enabling continuous monitoring and rapid remediation. By leveraging compliance-as-code templates, policy-as-code, and automated workflows, organizations can enhance their security posture, reduce risks, and streamline compliance processes. This approach ultimately empowers teams to focus on innovation, while ensuring that compliance remains a top priority.

Integrating Security into CI/CD Pipelines for Global Operations

As organizations expand globally, their CI/CD pipelines face increased security challenges. Integrating robust security practices into these pipelines is essential to protect the sensitive data, ensure compliance, and maintain reliable deployments across regions. Terraform enables the automation of secure CI/CD infrastructure and processes, streamlining global operations, while embedding security at every stage.

Security Challenges in CI/CD for Global Teams

As organizations adopt CI/CD pipelines to streamline deployments, the introduction of globally distributed teams brings significant security complexities. Terraform, as an Infrastructure as Code (IaC) tool, plays a pivotal role in defining and enforcing security configurations within CI/CD workflows. However, when global teams operate across multiple time zones and cloud platforms (AWS, GCP, Azure), security risks such as misconfigurations, inconsistent compliance enforcement, and exposure of secrets increase dramatically. Without centralized security governance, these vulnerabilities can compromise sensitive infrastructure and data. Hence, Terraform offers capabilities to mitigate these challenges, but only when paired with security-conscious CI/CD practices.

- **Misconfigurations:** Globally distributed teams may unknowingly create insecure cloud resources such as open ports, weak firewall rules, or overly broad IAM policies. Terraform can define secure defaults, but inconsistent team practices can override them without governance.
- **Unsecured secrets:** Sensitive credentials (API keys, access tokens, database passwords) may be hardcoded in CI/CD pipelines or version-controlled Terraform files. This often happens when multiple teams lack access to a centralized secrets management system.
- **Compliance gaps:** Different regions may have different regulatory requirements (for example, GDPR in Europe, HIPAA in the U.S.), and CI/CD pipelines may not uniformly enforce policies across all geographies, leading to compliance violations.
- **Tool fragmentation:** Global teams may use varying CI/CD tools (for example, GitHub Actions, GitLab CI, Azure DevOps), creating difficulty in applying uniform security controls and policies.
- **Lack of visibility:** Without centralized logging or monitoring of Terraform executions in CI/CD pipelines, it is difficult to trace who deployed what and when, especially across time zones and teams.

The following are some salient features and best practices:

- **Enforce least privilege access:** Restrict CI/CD roles, and Terraform service accounts to have only the permissions needed for specific actions, minimizing blast radius in case of compromise.
- **Use secrets management solutions:** Integrate AWS Secrets Manager, GCP Secret Manager, or Azure Key Vault into Terraform and CI/CD pipelines to securely inject credentials at runtime, instead of hardcoding them.
- **Validate code with static analysis tools:** Integrate Checkov, TFSec, or Terrascan into CI/CD workflows to scan Terraform code for security risks, before deployment.
- **Centralized state management:** Use remote backends (for example, AWS S3 with DynamoDB locking, GCS with versioning, or Azure Blob Storage) to securely manage and version state files globally.
- **Periodic configuration reviews:** Regularly review CI/CD pipeline configurations, Terraform modules, and cloud IAM roles to ensure that no security drift has occurred over time.

Provisioning Secure CI/CD Environments with Terraform

Provisioning secure CI/CD (Continuous Integration/Continuous Deployment) environments is vital to ensure that the automation pipelines used for application and infrastructure deployments are not a weak link in your cloud security strategy. Terraform enables organizations to define and deploy these environments in a secure, repeatable, and auditable manner. Whether provisioning Jenkins on AWS, GitLab Runners in GCP, or Azure DevOps Agents in Azure, Terraform ensures consistent infrastructure security practices are embedded into the CI/CD setup from the beginning. This includes automated Role-Based Access Controls, encrypted storage, network isolation, and secure artifact management—all defined as codes.

- **Automating infrastructure setup:** Use Terraform to deploy CI/CD environments (for example, Jenkins on EC2, GitLab runners on GCP Compute Engine, or Azure Pipelines Agents), while embedding security best practices such as secure ports, limited access through security groups or NSGs, and isolated subnets.
- **Centralized role management:** Provision IAM roles and permissions using Terraform tailored specifically to CI/CD systems, ensuring pipelines can only access the minimum resources required for builds and deployments.
- **Network isolation:** Deploy CI/CD runners in private subnets or with restricted IP access to ensure that they are shielded from public exposure, and use NAT gateways or VPC peering where necessary to connect with dependent services.
- **Logging and monitoring:** Set up Terraform configurations to automatically enable logging for all CI/CD infrastructure components, for example, CloudWatch logs for AWS CodePipeline, Stackdriver for GCP, and Azure Monitor Logs for Azure DevOps environments.
- **Secrets integration:** Configure Terraform to integrate secrets managers (such as AWS Secrets Manager, Azure Key Vault, or GCP Secret Manager) with CI/CD tools for secure injection of secrets into build pipelines at runtime.
- **Resource quarantine and auto-healing:** Define automated health checks and scaling policies with Terraform to isolate failed CI/CD nodes, and restore healthy replacements.

The following are some important features and best practices:

- **Modular CI/CD infrastructure:** Use reusable Terraform modules for provisioning and maintaining CI/CD environments to maintain consistency, and reduce code duplication across teams and projects.
- **Resource tagging and auditing:** Enforce the tagging of all CI/CD resources (for example, environment, owner, project) using Terraform to support cost tracking, ownership, and auditability.
- **Isolated build agents:** Always provision build agents on separate instances from production infrastructure using Terraform to reduce the attack surface.
- **Immutable infrastructure:** Treat CI/CD infrastructure as immutable by using Terraform to destroy and recreate agents rather than modifying them in place, minimizing long-lived misconfigurations.

Embedding Security Scanning in Pipelines

Incorporating security scanning directly into CI/CD pipelines ensures that infrastructure code adheres to security and compliance best practices before deployment. Terraform configurations can be scanned using static analysis tools such as Checkov, TFSec, and dynamic scanners such as AWS Inspector to detect misconfigurations, insecure policies, and non-compliant resource definitions. By embedding these tools into automated workflows, teams can enforce "`shift-left`" security, catching issues early in the development lifecycle and reducing the risk of vulnerabilities reaching production environments.

- **Static code analysis:** Use tools such as Checkov, TFSec, or KICS to perform static code analysis on Terraform files, and detect common misconfigurations such as publicly exposed storage buckets, open security groups, and unencrypted databases.
- **Pipeline integration:** Embed security scanning tools as a step within CI/CD pipelines using GitHub Actions, GitLab CI, Jenkins, or Azure Pipelines to ensure that Terraform configurations are validated, before reaching production environments.
- **Policy-as-Code enforcement:** Integrate Policy-as-Code tools such as HashiCorp Sentinel or Open Policy Agent (OPA) to define and enforce security rules, such as prohibiting public-facing resources or enforcing mandatory tagging for traceability.
- **Runtime analysis with cloud-native tools:** Use AWS Inspector, Azure Defender, or GCP Security Command Center to complement static scans with runtime vulnerability detection and configuration drift analysis for deployed resources.
- **Artifact verification:** Validate container images or build artifacts during the CI/CD process using tools such as AWS CodePipeline, Google Cloud Build, or Azure DevOps integrated with Snyk or Trivy, ensuring that only secure components are deployed.

The following are some key features and best practices:

- **Automated alerts:** Configure pipelines to raise alerts or fail builds when critical or high-severity vulnerabilities are found, ensuring that security gates are enforced automatically.
- **Comprehensive coverage:** Run scans not only on Terraform code but also on Helm charts, Kubernetes manifests, and runtime infrastructure to ensure end-to-end security across the stack.
- **Scan pull requests and commits:** Trigger security scans on every pull request or commit to ensure that only compliant code gets merged into the main branches.
- **Contextual reporting:** Integrate scan outputs with centralized dashboards or SIEM tools (for example, Splunk, Azure Monitor, and GCP Logging) for correlation and monitoring over time.
- **Developer feedback loops:** Provide immediate feedback to developers with inline annotations or comments in code review tools such as GitHub or GitLab when issues are detected.

Scaling CI/CD Security for Multi-Region Operations

As organizations expand their cloud infrastructure across multiple regions, maintaining consistent CI/CD security becomes increasingly complex. Terraform provides a unified way to define, deploy, and manage CI/CD security practices at scale by abstracting region-specific variations into reusable infrastructure-as-code templates. This ensures that every pipeline, regardless of region, adheres to centralized security and compliance standards, improving visibility and reducing risks.

- **Multi-region infrastructure management:** Define Terraform modules with region-specific input variables to provision CI/CD pipelines, build agents, artifact stores, and infrastructure securely across AWS (for example, CodePipeline in `us-east-1` and `eu-west-1`), GCP (Cloud Build in multiple regions), or Azure DevOps (linked with regional agents).
- **Secure data transfers:** Use Terraform to provision encrypted storage and networking configurations (for example, enabling S3 server-side encryption and VPC peering for inter-region data flow), ensuring that CI/CD logs, artifacts, and secrets are securely transferred and stored across regions.

- **Immutable infrastructure for build environments**: Deploy immutable CI/CD environments (for example, Jenkins agents, build runners) using Terraform and autoscaling groups in each region, ensuring consistent security postures, and preventing drift.

The following are some salient features and best practices:

- **Use Terraform workspaces for managing multi-region deployments:** Workspaces help maintain isolated state files per region, enabling region-specific CI/CD infrastructure provisioning, and preventing cross-region interference or accidental overwrites.
- **Maintain a centralized repository of security configurations for global teams:** Store reusable Terraform modules in a shared version-controlled repository to promote consistency, collaboration, and reuse across global teams operating in different regions.
- **Automate the replication of security settings across regions:** Use Terraform to automate the replication of IAM policies, audit logs, pipeline configurations, and compliance settings, ensuring that each region follows uniform security practices.
- **Tag region-specific resources for better visibility and governance:** Apply consistent tagging strategies to CI/CD resources, based on region, environment, and purpose to enhance traceability and facilitate policy enforcement through automation.
- **Integrate multi-region logging and monitoring:** Deploy centralized logging agents (for example, CloudWatch Agent, Azure Monitor Agent, and GCP Ops Agent) using Terraform to send logs to a global SIEM system for unified analysis and alerting.
- **Apply CI/CD resource quotas and constraints per region:** Use Terraform to define and enforce quotas for CI/CD runners, build artifacts, and other pipeline components to prevent resource exhaustion or abuse in high-traffic regions.

Enhancing CI/CD Security and Efficiency: State Farm's Integration of Terraform Enterprise and GitOps

State Farm streamlined global infrastructure provisioning, and strengthened compliance by integrating Terraform Enterprise with GitLab-driven GitOps workflows, boosting deployment efficiency and developer autonomy.

Business Challenges

State Farm, a leading insurance provider with a vast operational footprint, faced significant challenges in modernizing its CI/CD pipelines to support global operations. With over 1,800 software developers and a diverse set of applications, the organization needed a solution that could ensure consistent infrastructure provisioning, maintain compliance across various environments, and streamline deployment processes. The existing systems lacked the agility and security controls necessary to support rapid development cycles, and enforce compliance uniformly, leading to inefficiencies and potential security vulnerabilities.

Solution with Terraform

To address these challenges, State Farm adopted Terraform Enterprise (TFE) in conjunction with a GitOps workflow utilizing GitLab. This integration allowed for Infrastructure as Code (IaC) practices to be embedded directly into the development lifecycle, promoting consistency and repeatability. By leveraging TFE's capabilities, State Farm could manage state files securely, enforce policies through Sentinel, and integrate with version control systems for automated deployments. The GitOps approach ensured that all changes were tracked, reviewed, and auditable, aligning with compliance requirements, and enhancing collaboration among development teams.

Business Outcomes

The implementation of Terraform Enterprise and GitOps significantly improved State Farm's CI/CD processes. Developers experienced increased autonomy and efficiency, as infrastructure changes could be managed through familiar Git workflows. The organization achieved greater consistency in deployments across multiple regions, reducing the risk of configuration drift, and enhancing security posture. Compliance enforcement became more streamlined, with policy-as-code ensuring that all deployments met regulatory standards. Overall, the integration led to faster delivery of applications, improved collaboration, and a more robust and secure infrastructure management strategy.

Key Highlights

- Transitioned to Terraform Enterprise for consistent and secure infrastructure provisioning across global operations.
- Implemented GitLab-based workflows to manage infrastructure changes, promoting transparency and collaboration.
- Utilized Sentinel for policy enforcement and secure state management, ensuring adherence to compliance requirements.
- Enabled developers to manage infrastructure changes through Git, reducing deployment times and increasing agility.
- Achieved uniform infrastructure configurations across various regions, minimizing configuration drift and enhancing reliability.

Integrating security into CI/CD pipelines is essential for organizations operating on a global scale. Terraform provides powerful tools to automate the provisioning of secure CI/CD environments, embed security scanning into pipelines, and scale security practices for multi-region operations. Thus, by addressing common challenges, embedding security at every stage, and maintaining region-specific configurations, Terraform enables organizations to balance agility with robust security, ensuring safe and reliable software delivery across the globe.

Preventing Data Breaches with Robust Security Automation

Data breaches pose significant risks to organizations, impacting reputation, financial stability, and customer trust. Terraform enables robust automation strategies to secure infrastructure, and prevent breaches. This section explores practical approaches to safeguard sensitive data, detect threats in real time, and implement automated remediation strategies. A case study demonstrates the effectiveness of these methods in addressing an insider threat.

Protecting Sensitive Data with Encryption and Policies

In today's cloud-native environments, safeguarding sensitive data is critical to prevent breaches, ensure compliance, and build customer trust. Sensitive data includes Personally Identifiable Information (PII), financial records, healthcare data, and intellectual property. Terraform enables organizations to automate the deployment of encryption settings, and access policies across AWS, Azure, and GCP, thereby minimizing human errors, and ensuring consistency. This automation allows for scalable, policy-driven protection mechanisms that are repeatable across multiple cloud environments.

- **Automated encryption:** Terraform can provision cloud storage resources such as AWS S3, GCP Cloud Storage, and Azure Blob Storage with encryption enabled by default, reducing the risk of misconfigured data storage. Organizations can define whether to use default encryption or integrate customer-managed keys from services such as AWS KMS, GCP Cloud KMS, or Azure Key Vault.

- **Access policies:** Fine-grained access control policies can be defined through Terraform to strictly govern who can access the sensitive data. This includes IAM policies, ACLs, and role-based permissions that are attached to storage buckets or databases.
- **Key rotation:** Terraform can be integrated with cloud-native key management services to automate encryption key rotation, ensuring compliance with regulations such as PCI DSS and HIPAA.
- **Audit logging:** Configure audit logging (for example, AWS CloudTrail, Azure Monitor, or GCP Audit Logs) using Terraform to track who accesses the encrypted data, helping identify anomalies or policy violations.
- **Environment-specific configurations:** Use Terraform workspaces or variable-driven modules to enforce different encryption, and access policies depending on the environment (for example, `dev`, `staging`, `production`, and so on).

The following are some salient features and best practices:

- **Use customer-managed keys for critical data to maintain full control over encryption:** Relying on your own KMS keys improves auditing capabilities, and gives tighter control over access and lifecycle management.
- **Regularly audit access policies to ensure compliance with least privilege principles:** Review and adjust IAM roles, service accounts, and ACLs to ensure that they grant only the permissions required.
- **Implement versioning and replication to safeguard against accidental data loss:** Enable versioning on storage resources, and replicate critical data across regions for added durability and disaster recovery.
- **Centralize key management using Terraform modules across providers:** Create standardized modules that enforce KMS or Key Vault provisioning, simplifying compliance and auditing.
- **Encrypt data both in transit and at rest:** Use Terraform to enforce HTTPS for data access, and configure automatic server-side encryption.
- **Restrict public access by default:** Prevent unintended exposure by explicitly blocking public access to cloud storage buckets during provisioning.

Real-Time Threat Detection with Terraform-Orchestrated Tools

Real-time threat detection is essential in modern cloud environments to identify suspicious behavior, and respond to potential security incidents before they escalate across AWS, GCP, and Azure, native threat detection services such as GuardDuty, Security Command Center (SCC), and Microsoft Defender for Cloud to analyze logs, monitor activity, and use threat intelligence to detect anomalous behavior. With Terraform, these tools can be deployed and configured automatically, ensuring consistent and scalable security postures across cloud providers. By integrating these services into Terraform workflows, organizations gain the ability to rapidly enable, manage, and audit threat detection across multi-cloud environments with Infrastructure as Code (IaC) principles.

- **Tool deployment:** Use Terraform to automate the provisioning and configuration of native threat detection services such as AWS GuardDuty, GCP SCC, and Azure Defender. This ensures that tools are deployed consistently, and enabled for all relevant accounts and projects.

- **Alerting mechanisms:** Configure Terraform to enable alerts via services such as AWS SNS, Azure Monitor Alerts, or GCP Pub/Sub. These alerts notify security teams when suspicious behavior, such as unusual login attempts or privilege escalations, is detected.
- **Multi-region and multi-account coverage:** Use Terraform modules to replicate threat detection services across regions and accounts or subscriptions, ensuring global coverage and unified policies.
- **Data classification integration:** Combine Terraform-managed threat detection with data classification tools to prioritize alerts, based on sensitivity (for example, detecting access to PII stored in S3 or GCS).

The following are some salient features and best practices:

- **Regularly update threat detection rules to address evolving threats:** Schedule Terraform jobs or integrate with CI/CD pipelines to refresh configuration as cloud providers release new managed rules or threat intelligence updates.
- **Integrate threat detection tools with SIEM platforms for centralized analysis:** Use Terraform to configure exports to third-party SIEM tools such as Splunk, Datadog, or native services such as Azure Sentinel or Chronicle.
- **Automate response mechanisms for high-severity alerts:** Connect detection tools with automated remediation workflows using Lambda (AWS), Azure Functions, or GCP Cloud Functions, all provisioned and managed via Terraform.
- **Tag critical resources for enhanced monitoring:** Ensure Terraform applies standardized tags or labels on sensitive resources so threat detection tools prioritize scanning and alerting on those assets.
- **Enable cross-cloud visibility through a unified dashboard:** Deploy Terraform-managed dashboards using tools such as Grafana or Elastic Stack to centralize alert visualization across providers.

Implementing Automated Remediation Workflows

Automated remediation workflows are necessary for quickly mitigating the impact of security incidents in cloud environments. By codifying these workflows with Terraform, organizations can automate responses to common threats such as misconfigurations, unauthorized access, or policy violations. Rather than relying on manual intervention, Terraform enables the provisioning of event-driven remediation pipelines that can take immediate action such as quarantining resources, revoking permissions, or applying patches when an issue is detected. This approach ensures rapid, repeatable, and consistent incident response across AWS, Azure, and GCP environments, reducing the risk of downtime and data loss.

- **Incident detection:** Integrate Terraform with cloud-native threat detection tools such as AWS GuardDuty, Azure Security Center, and GCP Security Command Center to trigger automated remediation workflows, when a suspicious activity is detected.
- **Remediation actions:** Use Terraform to define infrastructure that automatically performs actions such as revoking IAM credentials, terminating compromised virtual machines, or rolling back to previous safe configurations using snapshots or stored Terraform state.
- **Workflow automation:** Provision event-driven architectures using Terraform that link detection events to response functions, for example, AWS Lambda, Azure Functions, or Google Cloud Functions, to take immediate corrective action.
- **Centralized policy enforcement:** Enforce policies as code using OPA or Sentinel to validate infrastructure changes, and remediate non-compliant configurations automatically.

The following are some important features and best practices:

- **Simulate incidents to test and refine remediation workflows:** Conduct chaos engineering or scheduled drills using Terraform-simulated events to validate the effectiveness and reliability of automated workflows.
- **Ensure that workflows are auditable for compliance purposes:** Use Terraform logs and cloud-native logging services (for example, AWS CloudTrail, Azure Activity Logs, and GCP Audit Logs) to track remediation actions, and support regulatory reporting.
- **Implement approval gates for critical workflows:** Use Terraform with CI/CD tools such as GitLab or GitHub Actions to enforce manual approval steps before executing destructive remediation actions in production environments.
- **Design for modularity and reuse:** Create reusable Terraform modules for common remediation tasks (for example, disabling a user, deleting unsecured buckets) that can be triggered across different cloud environments.
- **Enforce least privilege execution:** Ensure that Terraform-provisioned remediation functions have just enough permissions to perform their tasks, without overexposing sensitive environments.

LG Uplus's Journey with Terraform for Strengthening Cloud Security with Automation

LG Uplus modernized its cloud infrastructure by adopting Terraform, embedding automated security controls and compliance policies to reduce risks, accelerate provisioning, and support secure growth across multi-cloud environments.

Business Challenges

LG Uplus, a major South Korean telecommunications provider, faced mounting pressure to modernize its infrastructure, while strengthening security and reducing human errors. With operations expanding rapidly and services becoming more cloud-native, manual security configurations and disparate tooling increased the risk of misconfigurations and delayed deployments. The organization needed a unified, consistent approach to managing cloud resources, and ensuring security compliance across teams as well as environments.

Solution with Terraform

To address these challenges, LG Uplus adopted HashiCorp Terraform as its Infrastructure as Code (IaC) platform, leveraging its automation capabilities to enforce consistent security and operational practices. Terraform was used to provision secure cloud environments across various platforms, including AWS and Azure, while also enabling modular, reusable templates. This ensured standardization, reduced configuration drift, and embedded security policies directly into the provisioning process. Additionally, Terraform Sentinel policies were used to enforce compliance controls, and prevent the deployment of misconfigured or non-compliant infrastructure.

Business Outcomes

By implementing Terraform, LG Uplus significantly improved the speed, reliability, and security of its cloud infrastructure provisioning. Teams were able to self-service infrastructure using pre-approved templates, reducing dependency on centralized IT, and minimizing human errors. Security automation with Terraform helped prevent data breaches by ensuring every deployed resource adhered to the organization's strict security posture. Ultimately, LG Uplus achieved faster delivery timelines, reduced costs, and strengthened regulatory compliance.

Key Highlights

- Embedded security controls using Terraform modules and Sentinel policies.
- Reduced provisioning times and manual effort across development teams.
- Enforced consistent policy checks, and audit trails using Terraform Cloud.
- Adopted a modular IaC approach to support future growth across multiple cloud platforms.
- Enabled self-service provisioning, while maintaining security and compliance.

Preventing data breaches requires a combination of proactive security measures, real-time threat detection, and automated remediation workflows. Terraform's automation capabilities enable organizations to enforce encryption, deploy robust security tools, and respond swiftly to incidents. The case study demonstrates how Terraform can effectively address real-world threats, underscoring its importance in modern cloud security strategies. By integrating these practices, organizations can minimize the risk of data breaches, and safeguard their critical assets.

Lessons Learned: Avoiding Common Pitfalls in Terraform Projects

Terraform projects can encounter various challenges, especially as infrastructure scales and complexity increases. This section highlights key lessons learned from real-world implementations, focusing on state management, modularity, dependency handling, and long-term scalability. Hence, by reflecting on these lessons, practitioners can mitigate risks, and enhance their Terraform practices.

Handling State Management Challenges

Terraform's state file plays a vital role in mapping configuration files to actual infrastructure deployed in cloud environments such as AWS, GCP, and Azure. It maintains a record of all managed resources, enabling Terraform to determine what changes need to be applied. However, in collaborative, large-scale, or multi-cloud projects, managing this state file can become complex and error-prone. Common challenges include race conditions during simultaneous operations, risk of state file corruption, and unauthorized access, if not properly secured. Terraform addresses these issues through remote backends and integrated locking as well as access control features.

- Terraform creates a `.tfstate` file that stores the current state of your infrastructure, and is used to detect infrastructure drift as well as plan changes accurately.
- By default, this file is stored locally, which works well for single-user setups but poses challenges for teams.
- Remote state backends such as AWS S3, GCP Cloud Storage, or Azure Blob Storage allow for centralized state management.
- Locking mechanisms (for example, AWS DynamoDB for S3 or built-in GCS locking) prevent concurrent operations that could corrupt the state.
- Terraform Cloud and Enterprise offer enhanced state management features, including secure sharing, versioning, and policy enforcement.

The following are some salient features and best practices:

- **Remote state storage:** Use remote backends such as AWS S3 (with optional encryption and access logging), GCP Cloud Storage, or Azure Blob Storage to centralize and secure state files across distributed teams.
- **State locking:** Implement locking mechanisms using DynamoDB with S3 backend, GCS-native locking, or Terraform Cloud to avoid conflicts from parallel operations by multiple users.

- **State versioning:** Enable versioning in your backend storage (for example, versioning for S3 buckets or GCS) to retain historical state data, allowing rollback and recovery in the event of corruption.
- **Access control:** Apply least-privilege IAM roles and policies to limit access to state files, ensuring that only trusted users or CI/CD pipelines can read or write the state.
- **State encryption:** Enable encryption at rest and in transit for state files using KMS (AWS), CMEK (GCP), or Azure-managed keys to protect sensitive data stored in the state.
- **Consistent backend configuration:** Store backend configuration securely and consistently across environments using Terraform CLI arguments or partial configuration files, avoiding hardcoding sensitive info.
- **Separate state per environment:** Use different state files or workspaces for dev, staging, and production to avoid cross-environment contamination, and simplify rollback strategies.
- **Terraform Cloud/Enterprise:** Adopt Terraform Cloud or Enterprise for robust remote state management, including secure state storage, team access controls, and integrated Sentinel policy enforcement.

Balancing Modularity and Complexity

Modularity in Terraform enables teams to break infrastructure configurations into reusable, manageable components. This is especially useful in multi-cloud deployments across AWS, GCP, and Azure, where standardized configurations can significantly reduce operational overhead. However, while modularization encourages best practices such as code reuse and separation of concerns, it also introduces complexity. Overly abstract or nested modules can obscure logic, make debugging more difficult, and reduce the readability of Terraform projects. The goal is to strike a balance creating modules that are clear, purposeful, and maintainable.

- Modules act as containers for multiple resources, such as VPCs, IAM policies, compute instances, or databases, allowing these configurations to be reused across different environments or services.
- Inputs and outputs define the module's interface, enabling the calling code to pass values in and retrieve computed values.
- Over-modularization, such as wrapping every small resource in its own module or deeply nesting modules, increases cognitive load and introduces debugging difficulties.
- Cloud providers offer different resource structures, so balancing provider-specific logic inside shared modules is crucial to avoid convoluted abstractions.

The following are some salient features and best practices:

- **Define clear boundaries:** Group logically related resources into modules (for example, a network module or a compute module) to promote reuse and maintainability, while avoiding overly abstract or catch-all modules.
- **Use Terraform registry:** Adopt well-maintained, community-supported modules from the Terraform Registry for standard infrastructure components such as AWS VPCs, Azure VNets, or GCP IAM bindings to align with the established patterns.
- **Limit nesting:** Avoid deeply nested modules unless absolutely necessary, as they can complicate variable passing, error tracing, and output debugging.
- **Document modules:** Include a `README.md` file within each module explaining the module's purpose, inputs, outputs, usage examples, and any limitations to make onboarding and maintenance easier.

- **Parameterize thoughtfully:** Expose only the necessary variables as inputs to avoid bloated modules, and improve the ease of use, while keeping the implementation behind the module opaque.
- **Version control your modules:** Use Git tags or release versions for modules to ensure predictable behavior during deployments, and reduce risk from upstream changes.
- **Enforce naming conventions:** Apply consistent naming for modules and resource identifiers across providers to ensure clarity and compatibility across multi-cloud environments.
- **Test independently:** Write unit or integration tests for individual modules using tools such as Terratest to validate logic in isolation, before full stack deployments.
- **Avoid cross-module hidden dependencies:** Ensure that dependencies between modules are passed explicitly via inputs and outputs to maintain clear and predictable execution flows.

Addressing Dependency Management Issues

In multi-cloud and complex Terraform configurations, managing dependencies between infrastructure resources becomes critical. AWS, GCP, and Azure resources often have interrelated requirements (for example, a subnet needing a VPC, or a VM requiring a storage account). Terraform relies on a dependency graph to determine the order in which resources should be created, modified, or destroyed. However, poorly defined relationships or over-complicated interdependencies can lead to issues such as cyclical dependencies, failed deployments, or delayed infrastructure changes. Addressing these dependency issues ensures faster, more reliable Terraform executions, and maintains consistency across cloud providers.

- Terraform builds a dependency graph, based on resource references, and creates resources in the order dictated by this graph.
- Implicit dependencies *are automatically* established when one resource references another (for example, referencing a resource ID).
- Explicit dependencies can be manually declared using the **`depends_on`** meta-argument to ensure correct sequencing when implicit relationships do not exist.
- Modules and remote states can introduce indirect dependencies that need careful coordination to avoid runtime errors or sequencing conflicts.

The following are some salient features and best practices:

- **Avoid cyclical dependencies**: Identify and refactor resource definitions or module structures that reference each other in a circular manner, as this causes Terraform to fail during graph construction.
- **Use `depends_on` wisely:** Declare **`depends_on`** only when Terraform cannot automatically determine the correct order, such as with third-party modules or when using provisioners.
- **Use data sources:** Incorporate **`data`** blocks to reference the existing infrastructure resources, without managing their lifecycle, reducing unnecessary resource dependencies.
- **Dependency outputs:** Use module `output` variables to explicitly pass identifiers or attributes required by other modules, maintaining modularity without hidden relationships.
- **Structure modules logically**: Group resources with natural dependencies (for example, **`subnet + route`** table) into the same module to simplify internal dependencies, and reduce external coupling.
- **Apply resource tags or labels:** Use tags/labels to categorize related resources, enabling better dependency tracking and operational auditing, especially in shared environments.
- **Validate with Terraform plan:** Always run *terraform plan* to visually inspect how Terraform intends to apply changes, helping to catch unintended dependency issues before execution.

Ensuring Long-Term Maintenance and Scalability

As cloud environments evolve and teams scale, maintaining Terraform codebases becomes increasingly complex. Infrastructure configurations must remain readable, reusable, and adaptable to future changes. So, whether you are managing environments on AWS, GCP, or Azure, designing Terraform for long-term maintenance and scalability means preparing for shifts in team structure, regulatory changes, service offerings, and business priorities. Terraform offers modular, declarative infrastructure-as-code practices that, when combined with good documentation, version control, and automated testing, enable organizations to scale their infrastructure without incurring technical debt.

- Terraform supports semantic versioning and modular design, which allows for incremental changes without breaking the entire infrastructure.
- By integrating Terraform with CI/CD systems, teams can validate, plan, and apply changes safely and automatically.
- Remote state management and backends such as AWS S3, GCP Cloud Storage, or Azure Blob ensure state consistency across teams and regions.
- Well-maintained modules and consistent tagging improve traceability, facilitate auditing, and help identify legacy components.

The following are some important features and best practices:

- **Version control:** Store all Terraform code in version control systems such as Git, use branching strategies such as GitFlow, and tag releases to track changes over time as well as support rollbacks.
- **Automate testing:** Integrate tools such as `terraform validate`, `terraform fmt`, and `terraform plan` into CI/CD pipelines to catch issues before deployment, and maintain code hygiene.
- **Refactor regularly:** Review and clean up unused variables, consolidate duplicated resources, and split large modules to improve maintainability as well as reduce complexity as infrastructure grows.
- **Use modules for reusability:** Break common patterns (for example, VPC creation, IAM policies, and VM provisioning) into modules that can be reused across projects and environments to promote consistency as well as reduce duplication.
- **Support multi-environment design:** Use Terraform workspaces or directory structures to manage dev, staging, and production configurations separately, while maintaining shared modules.
- **Apply organizational standards:** Create a standardized module library with predefined policies, controls, and naming conventions to enforce organizational compliance at scale.
- **Scale workflows with Terraform Cloud/Enterprise:** Leverage Terraform Cloud or Enterprise for policy enforcement, team collaboration, remote execution, and advanced access controls for large-scale operations.

The lessons learned from real-world Terraform implementations highlight the importance of effective state management, balanced modularity, dependency resolution, and long-term maintainability. By adopting best practices, organizations can mitigate common pitfalls, and ensure that their Terraform projects remain robust as well as scalable over time. This proactive approach enhances collaboration, reduces errors, and supports seamless infrastructure evolution.

Conclusion

The case studies and scenarios explored in this chapter underscore the transformative potential of Terraform in securing and scaling modern cloud environments. From architecting resilient multi-cloud SaaS platforms to embedding security into CI/CD pipelines, each section demonstrates how real-world organizations have leveraged Terraform to meet stringent security, compliance, and operational demands. These examples not only provide practical blueprints for implementing security automation at scale but also highlight how organizations such as TeamSystem, Nedbank, State Farm, and LG Uplus have achieved measurable improvements in security posture, operational efficiency, and regulatory alignment through infrastructure-as-code.

Beyond the technical implementations, this chapter emphasizes critical lessons learned, such as managing Terraform state files, maintaining a balance between modularity and complexity, and ensuring long-term project sustainability. These insights are invaluable for teams aiming to adopt Terraform in production or scale its use securely across diverse environments. So, by grounding best practices in real-world applications, this chapter equips readers with the knowledge to confidently architect, automate, and govern secure infrastructure using Terraform in even the most complex, regulated, and globally distributed cloud landscapes.

In the next chapter, we will emphasize treating security as a continuous process in Infrastructure as Code (IaC), and provide a comprehensive checklist for Terraform security automation. The chapter also explores the emerging trends in IaC, cloud security, and strategies for scaling Terraform in enterprise environments.

Questions and Answers

1. **How can Terraform help in unifying Identity and Access Management (IAM) across AWS, GCP, and Azure in a multi-cloud SaaS environment?**

   Terraform enables centralized IAM policy management through Infrastructure-as-Code modules that abstract provider-specific IAM constructs into reusable templates. By leveraging Terraform providers for AWS, GCP, and Azure, organizations can define consistent access control policies and roles, enforce least privilege principles, and integrate with identity federation mechanisms, ensuring secure and auditable user and service access across cloud platforms.

2. **What are the practical benefits of Compliance-as-Code in regulated industries such as finance and healthcare, and how does Terraform enable it?**

   Compliance-as-Code ensures that security and regulatory requirements (such as GDPR, HIPAA, and PCI DSS) are enforced programmatically through reusable Terraform modules. Terraform supports this by enabling consistent application of controls such as encryption, logging, tagging, and auditing across infrastructure. This minimizes manual errors, simplifies compliance audits, and allows for automated remediation when violations occur using tools such as Sentinel, TFSec, or external compliance frameworks integrated into the Terraform pipeline.

3. **How does Terraform help secure global CI/CD pipelines and prevent security drifts across regions?**

   Terraform automates the provisioning and configuration of CI/CD infrastructure (for example, Jenkins agents, GitLab runners, CodePipeline stages) with built-in security controls such as network restrictions, IAM roles, and secrets management. By codifying security scanning tools (for example, Checkov, TFSec) and embedding them into pipelines, Terraform ensures security policies are enforced continuously. For global teams, Terraform enables region-specific configurations through variables and workspaces, ensuring consistent and secure deployment practices across geographies.

4. **In the context of data breach prevention, how can Terraform orchestrate real-time threat detection and response?**

   Terraform automates the deployment of cloud-native threat detection tools—such as AWS GuardDuty, Azure Security Center, and GCP Security Command Center—across cloud environments. It can also define event-driven response mechanisms using Lambda functions, automation runbooks, or security orchestration workflows. For example, if a threat is detected, Terraform-defined workflows can isolate compromised resources or revoke access, enabling real-time remediation without manual intervention.

5. **What are the most common pitfalls teams face when managing Terraform at scale, and how can they be avoided?**

   Common pitfalls include poorly managed state files, overly complex module structures, dependency hell, and lack of long-term maintenance strategies. These can be mitigated by using remote backends with locking (for example, Terraform Cloud or S3 + DynamoDB), maintaining clear module boundaries, using **`depends_on`** judiciously, and documenting infrastructure decisions. Adopting version control, tagging, and standardized module registries helps teams scale Terraform, while reducing technical debt and onboarding friction.

Chapter 16
Best Practices and Future Trends

Introduction

As Infrastructure as Code (IaC) becomes the backbone of modern cloud infrastructure, treating security as a continuous, evolving practice is no longer optional, it is essential. This chapter focuses on operationalizing security throughout the Terraform lifecycle, from development and deployment to maintenance and scaling. We begin by examining how security can be embedded directly into the development process, and how organizations can automate the integration of security updates and policy changes within their Terraform modules. In today's dynamic threat landscape, where regulations and attack vectors evolve constantly, the ability to adapt IaC configurations proactively is critical. Thus, whether you are building new infrastructure or maintaining an existing environment, this section emphasizes the importance of treating security as a lifecycle concern, not a one-time task.

Beyond implementation strategies, this chapter provides a practical and actionable checklist for Terraform security automation, helping you verify compliance across areas such as state management, resource provisioning, and incident response. We then dive into emerging trends that are shaping the future of IaC and cloud security including the rise of policy-as-code, the integration of AI and ML for threat detection, and the increasing complexity of securing multi-cloud and hybrid environments. For organizations operating at scale, you will also learn best practices for structuring codebases, leveraging Terraform Enterprise, and managing compliance across global teams. We conclude with a forward-looking view of Terraform's evolution, including how it will intersect with next-generation cloud platforms, support zero-trust architectures, and be propelled by its vibrant open-source community. This chapter is your strategic guide to building not only secure, but future-ready Terraform practices.

Structure

In this chapter, we will cover the following topics:

- Treating Security as a Continuous Process in IaC
  - Embedding Security in the Development Lifecycle
  - Automating Security Updates in Terraform Modules
  - Adapting to Evolving Threats and Compliance Needs
- Comprehensive Checklist for Terraform Security Automation
  - State Management and Access Control
  - Secure Resource Provisioning
  - Monitoring and Incident Response Integration

- Exploring Emerging Trends in IaC and Cloud Security
  - The Rise of Policy-as-Code and Automation
  - AI and Machine Learning in Cloud Security
  - Multi-Cloud and Hybrid Cloud Security Innovations
- Scaling Terraform across Enterprise Environments
  - Structuring Terraform Codebases for Enterprise-Scale
  - Leveraging Terraform Enterprise for Centralized Management
  - Addressing Governance and Compliance at Scale
- Future Directions for Terraform and Cloud Security Automation
  - Integration of Terraform with Next-Gen Cloud Tools
  - Enhancing Terraform's Security Features
  - Adoption of Zero Trust Architectures
  - The Role of Community and Open Source in Terraform's Future

Treating Security as a Continuous Process in IaC

Security in Infrastructure as Code is not a one-time effort. It is a continuous process that integrates with every stage of the infrastructure lifecycle, from design to deployment and ongoing operation. This section delves into key strategies and best practices for embedding security as an ongoing focus in Terraform-based IaC workflows.

Embedding Security in the Development Lifecycle

Embedding security in the development lifecycle with Terraform involves integrating security validation, compliance enforcement, and vulnerability detection into each phase of infrastructure provisioning. Rather than treating security as a final check before deployment, this approach embeds automated controls and analysis directly into code authoring, versioning, and CI/CD workflows. This enables cloud teams working across AWS, GCP, and Azure to identify misconfigurations, and enforce policies as early as possible, minimizing the likelihood of exposing production environments to risk. It encourages a proactive rather than reactive security posture, particularly important in multi-cloud environments where configuration standards must remain consistent.

- **Early misconfiguration detection:** Developers use Terraform linters and static analysis tools such as Checkov, TFSec, Kics, and so on. in local development environments to catch misconfigurations such as unencrypted storage or overly permissive IAM roles, before pushing codes.
- **Pre-deployment policy enforcement:** Terraform Cloud and tools like HashiCorp Sentinel or Open Policy Agent (OPA) are integrated into the pipeline to prevent provisioning of insecure resources (for example, non-tagged resources, exposed public IPs) by enforcing Policy-as-Code, before changes are applied.
- **Cross-cloud security alignment:** Terraform modules and CI/CD pipelines enforce standardized security configurations across AWS (IAM, KMS, GuardDuty), Azure (RBAC, Defender, Key Vault), and GCP (IAM, CMEK, SCC), ensuring consistent posture in all regions and clouds.
- **Role separation and code review:** Access to modules is controlled via IAM roles, and all infrastructure changes must pass through pull requests with automated security checks and manual reviews.

Following are some salient features and best practices:

- **Shift-left security:** Begin enforcing security from the first line of Terraform code by integrating static analysis and policy enforcement tools directly into development environments and version control workflows.
- **Modular security standards:** Develop reusable Terraform modules with built-in security controls (for example, automatic encryption, least-privilege IAM policies) to enforce consistent practices across teams and services.
- **Policy-as-Code integration:** Define and manage security policies using Sentinel, OPA, or custom CI/CD scripts that validate every Terraform plan against internal and regulatory controls.
- **Environment-specific pipelines:** Separate CI/CD pipelines for dev, staging, and production environments, each with tiered security validations to prevent accidental exposure or configuration drift.
- **Secure artifact handling:** Use encrypted storage (for example, S3 with SSE, Azure Blob with customer-managed keys, or GCS with CMEK) to store Terraform state files, logs, and build artifacts. Enforce access through tight IAM controls.

Automating Security Updates in Terraform Modules

Automating security updates in Terraform modules refers to the practice of continuously integrating the latest security enhancements, patches, and configuration best practices into reusable Infrastructure as Code components. In multi-cloud environments such as AWS, GCP, and Azure, security practices and compliance requirements evolve regularly. Manual updates are error-prone, and can lead to inconsistent security baselines across teams and environments. By automating these updates, organizations ensure their infrastructure remains hardened, without delaying development workflows or increasing operational overhead.

- **Version control:** Use semantic versioning (for example, **`v1.2.3`**) in Terraform modules to track and manage security-related changes independently of feature updates, enabling safe rollbacks and updates across environments.
- **Dependency management:** Integrate tools such as **`Renovate`** or **`Dependabot`** to scan for outdated module versions in Terraform configuration files, and automatically raise pull requests with newer secure versions.
- **Centralized module registry:** Host internally-approved, secure Terraform modules in a centralized registry (for example, GitHub, Bitbucket, Terraform Cloud Private Module Registry), enabling consistent reuse across AWS, Azure, and GCP teams.
- **CI/CD integrated upgrades:** Implement CI/CD pipelines that validate and test updated module versions in staging environments using terraform plan and terraform validate, before they are merged and deployed.
- **Security patch subscription:** Subscribe to cloud provider security bulletins, and incorporate their recommended changes into Terraform modules proactively to stay ahead of emerging threats.

The following are some important features and best practices:

- **Version pinning with flexibility:** Use version constraints such as **`~> 1.2`** to safely adopt non-breaking security updates, while avoiding unintended upgrades that might introduce breaking changes.
- **Clear documentation and change logs:** Maintain a changelog (**`CHANGELOG.md`**), and update documentation (**`README.md`**) with each security patch or version bump so that teams can understand the intent and scope of updates.

- **Security feature flags:** Implement flags or variables in modules that allow toggling enhanced security features (for example, enabling VPC flow logs, encryption, and private endpoints) so that updates do not immediately impact sensitive environments.
- **Backwards compatibility testing:** Validate updated modules against previous configurations to ensure that environments using older parameters or structures are not broken by the latest changes.
- **Notify teams of critical changes:** Set up notification mechanisms using Slack, email, or GitHub Discussions to alert teams, when critical security updates are available or applied to modules.

Adapting to Evolving Threats and Compliance Needs

Adapting to evolving threats and compliance requirements means maintaining an agile infrastructure that can quickly respond to new vulnerabilities, policy mandates, or industry standards. In cloud environments such as AWS, GCP, and Azure, where security and compliance landscapes are continuously shifting, static configurations are insufficient. Terraform offers the ability to codify and version security and compliance controls, enabling rapid updates and consistent enforcement across multi-cloud environments. This adaptability is critical for staying secure and compliant in real time.

- **Threat intelligence:** Integrate external threat intelligence feeds and vendor advisories into security workflows to proactively identify infrastructure components needing updates (for example, newly discovered zero-days affecting cloud services or public images).
- **Policy updates:** Regularly review and update Terraform modules and Sentinel/OPA policies to reflect the latest compliance frameworks such as CIS Benchmarks, NIST, GDPR, HIPAA, and PCI DSS.
- **Infrastructure drift detection:** Incorporate tools such as AWS Config, Azure Policy, and GCP Config Validator with Terraform to detect and correct configuration drift that may violate security posture.
- **Dynamic resource configuration:** Implement feature toggles or variables in Terraform to dynamically enable or disable new compliance features (for example, mandatory TLS 1.2, enhanced logging, and encryption).

The following are some salient features and best practices:

- **Proactive monitoring:** Implement continuous monitoring using Terraform-provisioned tools such as AWS Config Rules, GCP SCC, and Azure Defender to detect misconfigurations and alert stakeholders immediately.
- **Agility:** Design reusable Terraform modules that support backward compatibility, allowing teams to quickly roll out updates to infrastructure, without breaking deployments.
- **Collaboration:** Encourage cross-functional collaboration between DevOps, compliance, and security teams to update Terraform policies in response to new business, regulatory, or threat changes.
- **Version control of policies:** Maintain policies and security modules in version-controlled repositories (for example, Git) with commit history to track the evolution of security and compliance practices.
- **Cross-cloud policy mapping:** Create unified Terraform policies that abstract security controls (for example, encryption, and IAM least privilege) across AWS IAM, Azure RBAC, and GCP IAM for consistent compliance.

Thus, treating security as a continuous process in IaC ensures that organizations can proactively address vulnerabilities, maintain compliance, and adapt to changing landscapes. By embedding security in the development lifecycle, automating validation and updates, and staying responsive to evolving threats, Terraform users can build secure, scalable, and resilient infrastructure. This approach not only enhances security but also instils a culture of proactive risk management in cloud operations.

Comprehensive Checklist for Terraform Security Automation

As Infrastructure as Code grows in adoption, securing Terraform projects becomes paramount. This section provides a comprehensive checklist to ensure robust security automation, covering state management, resource provisioning, secrets handling, and monitoring. These practices are essential for safeguarding cloud environments, and minimizing risks in Terraform-managed infrastructures.

State Management and Access Control

Terraform state files are the backbone of Infrastructure-as-Code operations, tracking every deployed resource and its current configuration. Because these files contain sensitive metadata including IPs, credentials, and resource identifiers, they pose a significant security risk if mishandled. They also ensure robust state management and access control that are necessary for maintaining consistency, security, and compliance across AWS, Azure, and GCP. This includes secure storage, encryption, access restrictions, and concurrency control.

- **Remote state storage:** Store Terraform state files in cloud-native secure storage services AWS S3 with encryption, GCP Cloud Storage with IAM controls, or Azure Blob Storage with container-level access to ensure centralized and resilient state management.
- **Encryption:** Enable server-side encryption (for example, SSE-S3, CMEK in GCP, and encryption with customer-managed keys in Azure) to protect state files, both at rest and in transit via secure HTTPS endpoints.
- **Locking mechanisms:** Prevent concurrent Terraform operations using locking mechanisms such as DynamoDB for AWS, Cloud Firestore for GCP, and Azure Cosmos DB or built-in state locking in Terraform Cloud to reduce the risk of state corruption during parallel execution.
- **Role-Based Access Control (RBAC):** Apply cloud-native IAM policies (AWS IAM, GCP IAM, Azure RBAC) to limit who can read, write, or delete state files, ensuring that only authorized teams have access to the critical infrastructure state data.
- **Versioning:** Enable versioning on state file storage (for example, S3 versioning, GCS object versioning, or Azure Blob snapshots) to roll back changes in case of accidental corruption or misconfigurations.
- **Audit trails:** Use native audit logging solutions AWS CloudTrail, GCP Cloud Audit Logs, Azure Monitor Logs to track access and changes to the state file, which is critical for security auditing and forensic investigations.
- **Separation of duties:** Enforce least privilege by separating roles (for example, read-only for audit teams, full access for DevOps) using fine-grained IAM configurations.
- **Terraform workspaces:** Leverage Terraform workspaces to maintain separate state files per environment (for example, dev, staging, prod), without needing distinct configurations or directories.
- **Automated backup and recovery:** Implement automated snapshots/versioning of state files to recover quickly from unintended changes or corruption.

Secure Resource Provisioning

Secure resource provisioning with Terraform refers to the process of deploying cloud infrastructure in a way that inherently enforces security best practices across all stages of the resource lifecycle. This includes ensuring that infrastructure resources such as virtual machines, databases, networking components, and storage are provisioned with security configurations that comply with industry standards and organizational policies. Across AWS, GCP, and Azure, Terraform enables security-by-default provisioning using codified templates, allowing teams to minimize risks related to misconfigurations, excessive permissions, and unsecured connectivity.

- **Pre-defined templates:** Use reusable Terraform modules that embed secure defaults such as enabling encryption, defining restrictive IAM policies, or using secure subnets so that all deployments adhere to baseline security standards automatically.
- **Network security:** Configure Terraform to provision virtual networks (VPCs in AWS/GCP or VNets in Azure) with security groups, firewall rules, NAT gateways, and private subnets that restrict unnecessary external access.
- **Secrets management integration:** Provision integrations with secrets managers (for example, AWS Secrets Manager, GCP Secret Manager, Azure Key Vault) so that sensitive credentials are not exposed in Terraform code or state.
- **Audit-ready infrastructure:** Define infrastructure in a way that is fully traceable and auditable by enforcing tagging, logging, and resource metadata in all Terraform configurations.
- **Encryption:** Protect sensitive data in state files using server-side encryption (for example, S3 with KMS in AWS, GCS with CMEK in GCP, or Azure Blob with customer-managed keys), and enforce encryption in transit via TLS.

The following are some salient features and best practices:

- **Encryption standards:** Enforce encryption-at-rest and in-transit using Terraform by enabling AWS KMS, GCP CMEK, or Azure Disk Encryption during provisioning to protect data integrity and confidentiality.
- **IAM best practices:** Assign minimal privileges to users, roles, or service accounts through fine-grained access control policies, avoiding overly broad permissions that could lead to privilege escalation.
- **Networking controls:** Configure all resources within private networks, restrict public IP assignments, and apply firewall rules to limit access to specific IP ranges and protocols.
- **Tagging and classification:** Implement tagging for ownership, environment, and sensitivity classification to support access governance and auditing across teams and environments.
- **Drift detection:** Monitor for configuration drift using Terraform's plan capabilities and external tools (for example, Terraform Cloud or custom scripts) to detect and remediate unauthorized changes.

Monitoring and Incident Response Integration

Monitoring and incident response integration with Terraform involves designing infrastructure that can detect, alert, and respond to security and operational issues in real time. As cloud-native applications grow in scale and complexity, it is essential that Terraform-provisioned infrastructure is monitored continuously and integrated with automated remediation workflows. This approach ensures minimal downtime, faster recovery, and proactive mitigation of threats across AWS, GCP, and Azure environments.

- **Monitoring tools:** Terraform provisions monitoring services such as AWS CloudWatch, GCP

Cloud Monitoring, and Azure Monitor to collect logs, metrics, and telemetry from cloud resources.

- **Incident triggers:** Configure alert rules based on defined thresholds (for example, CPU usage, unauthorized access, failed logins) to trigger incident workflows across regions or resource types.
- **Remediation scripts:** Combine Terraform with functions such as AWS Lambda, Azure Logic Apps, or GCP Cloud Functions to execute remediation scripts that automatically respond to incidents (for example, isolate VMs, revoke access, and restart services).
- **Alert routing:** Set up integrations with incident management platforms (for example, PagerDuty, Opsgenie, and ServiceNow) using Terraform to route alerts to appropriate response teams with full context.
- **Audit and logging integration:** Use Terraform to enable audit logs (for example, AWS CloudTrail, GCP Cloud Audit Logs, and Azure Activity Logs) as well as route them to centralized logging tools for threat analysis and compliance reporting.

The following are some vital features and best practices:

- **Real-time alerts:** Configure immediate alerting for critical events such as failed authentication attempts, elevated API call activity, or changes to IAM policies using Terraform-managed monitoring rules.
- **Incident playbooks:** Define reusable Terraform modules that create resources or workflows specifically for incident response scenarios (for example, launching a forensic environment, or enabling full packet capture).
- **Escalation policies:** Set up tiered notification systems where unacknowledged alerts escalate to higher-level responders using Terraform-managed notification channels.
- **Testing and simulation:** Regularly simulate incidents using Terraform-managed infrastructure (for example, disable a VM or misconfigure a firewall rule) to test response playbooks and improve team readiness.
- **Granular alert rules:** Avoid alert fatigue by defining specific metrics and thresholds that are tailored to each environment (for example, production vs. development), using Terraform variables and templates.

A comprehensive Terraform security checklist ensures that every aspect of infrastructure management is secure and compliant. From state management to secure resource provisioning, secrets handling, and incident response, these practices provide a strong foundation for mitigating risks in cloud environments. Thus, by following these guidelines, organizations can achieve a proactive and automated security posture, minimizing vulnerabilities, and ensuring resilience in the face of evolving threats.

Exploring Emerging Trends in IaC and Cloud Security

The dynamic landscape of cloud security and Infrastructure as Code introduces transformative trends that promise to redefine how organizations secure their environments. This section explores ground breaking advancements such as policy-as-code, AI-driven security tools, shift-left security, and multi-cloud innovations.

The Rise of Policy-as-Code and Automation

Policy-as-Code (PaC) refers to the practice of defining and enforcing governance, compliance, and security policies through machine-readable code. This approach automates validation during infrastructure provisioning, ensuring that all Terraform configurations adhere to organizational and regulatory standards before any changes are applied. Especially in multi-cloud environments (AWS, GCP, Azure), Policy-as-Code enables consistency, reduces manual reviews, and enhances control by embedding compliance checks early in the development lifecycle.

- **Policy engines:** Tools such as Open Policy Agent (OPA) and HashiCorp Sentinel interpret and enforce codified rules during terraform plan and apply, preventing non-compliant resources from being provisioned.
- **Integration:** Policies are embedded in CI/CD workflows using tools like Terraform Cloud, GitHub Actions, or Jenkins, where every pull request or pipeline execution is checked against the policy set.
- **Custom rules:** Teams can define custom policies tailored to business-specific needs such as disallowing unencrypted storage or ensuring all resources are tagged enforcing both technical and regulatory standards.
- **Cloud-specific enforcement:** Policies are mapped to cloud provider specifics, for example, rejecting public S3 buckets in AWS, enforcing private endpoint use in Azure, or requiring IAM role constraints in GCP.
- **Pre-commit and local testing:** Developers can test code against policies before they commit using local tools such as conftest or opa eval, improving efficiency and reducing noise in pipelines.

The following are some salient features and best practices:

- **Real-time feedback:** Integrate policy checks into pull request workflows to provide developers with immediate validation results, and actionable remediation guidance before merge.
- **Granular policy scope:** Write policies that apply selectively to environments or modules, enabling flexibility, without compromising on standards.
- **Fail-safe defaults:** Define deny-by-default behaviors in policies to prevent the deployment of any resource that does not explicitly meet the predefined requirements.
- **Policy testing and validation:** Use automated testing frameworks such as Rego unit tests for OPA or Sentinel mocks to validate policy behavior before rollout.
- **Visibility and reporting:** Generate reports from policy evaluation results to track violations, measure compliance over time, and satisfy audit requirements.

AI and Machine Learning in Cloud Security

AI and Machine Learning (ML) are playing a transformative role in enhancing cloud security by providing intelligent, automated insights throughout the infrastructure lifecycle. When integrated with Infrastructure as Code platforms like Terraform, AI/ML enables proactive detection of misconfigurations, predictive analysis of security flaws, and smart remediation guidance. These technologies help organizations maintain secure, compliant, and resilient cloud environments across providers such as AWS, GCP, and Azure by learning from patterns, behaviors, and threat intelligence.

- **Pattern detection:** AI platforms analyze historical infrastructure logs, Terraform plans, and runtime data to identify patterns that precede security incidents or misconfigurations.
- **Vulnerability prediction:** Machine learning models evaluate Terraform scripts and resource changes to predict future vulnerabilities, such as misconfigured IAM policies, open ports, or overly permissive network access.

- **Proactive suggestions:** AI-driven tools provide developers with real-time suggestions and secure configuration recommendations during Terraform code writing and validation stages.
- **Threat correlation:** AI systems correlate activity across regions, cloud services, and users to detect complex threat scenarios that span multiple environments.
- **Drift analysis:** ML models compare the desired state defined in Terraform to the current state of the infrastructure, and detect unauthorized changes or drift patterns indicative of compromise.
- **Adaptive policies:** AI-driven policy engines adjust enforcement rules over time based on environmental behavior, reducing false positives and improving precision in dynamic cloud environments.
- **Risk scoring:** AI assigns risk scores to infrastructure changes in Terraform plans, allowing teams to prioritize reviews, and automate approval workflows.

The following are some vital features and best practices:

- **Continuous learning:** Continuously train ML models with fresh infrastructure data, threat intelligence, and policy violations to maintain up-to-date accuracy and relevance.
- **Tool integration:** Integrate AI/ML engines into CI/CD pipelines, Terraform Cloud, and security scanners to deliver real-time insights, without disrupting development workflows.
- **Anomaly detection:** Use AI models to monitor runtime behaviors, such as traffic patterns or access logs, to detect outliers that may indicate credential misuse or lateral movement.
- **Multi-cloud visibility:** Deploy AI-based tools that unify data from AWS (for example, GuardDuty), Azure (for example, Defender for Cloud), and GCP (for example, Chronicle), enabling comprehensive threat detection and response.
- **Automated remediation:** Leverage AI to trigger Terraform workflows that automatically remediate detected vulnerabilities or revert insecure changes in stateful infrastructure.
- **Security awareness feedback:** Provide developers with contextual security feedback during pull requests or Terraform plan reviews to encourage secure coding practices.
- **Compliance mapping:** Map AI findings to regulatory frameworks (for example, PCI DSS and HIPAA) and automate Terraform checks for non-compliant configurations.

Multi-Cloud and Hybrid Cloud Security Innovations

As enterprises embrace multi-cloud and hybrid cloud strategies deploying workloads across AWS, Azure, GCP, and on-premises data centers the need for consistent, scalable, and secure infrastructure management has intensified. These environments introduce unique security challenges such as policy fragmentation, inconsistent identity management, and increased attack surface. Terraform helps address these complexities by enabling declarative, unified infrastructure provisioning and policy enforcement across providers. It empowers security and DevOps teams to build repeatable, secure, and compliant infrastructure patterns, regardless of where workloads reside.

- **Unified policy management:** Terraform, when paired with tools such as Sentinel or Open Policy Agent (OPA), enables centralized definition and enforcement of security policies across cloud providers ensuring that configurations like encryption, tagging, IAM roles, and firewalls follow a unified governance model.
- **Interoperability:** Terraform can provision hybrid connectivity solutions such as AWS Direct Connect, Azure ExpressRoute, or GCP Interconnect, ensuring secure and reliable communication between cloud and on-premises networks.
- **Dynamic adjustments:** By using provider-specific modules and conditional logic (for

example, `count`, `for_each`), Terraform can dynamically adjust infrastructure based on region, environment, or cloud provider-specific constraints ensuring security configurations are tailored, but still controlled centrally.

- **Consistent IAM controls:** Implement fine-grained, provider-specific identity and access management (IAM) policies using Terraform modules to align privilege management across AWS IAM, Azure RBAC, and GCP IAM consistently.
- **Cross-platform monitoring:** Terraform can deploy cloud-native monitoring tools (for example, AWS CloudWatch, GCP Operations, and Azure Monitor) and route logs to centralized SIEM platforms for unified threat detection.

The following are some salient features and best practices:

- **Cloud-native tools:** Use Terraform to provision and configure native security tools such as AWS GuardDuty, Azure Security Center, and GCP Security Command Center, ensuring full integration with provider services and automated threat detection.
- **Unified dashboards:** Build observability into Terraform configurations by deploying shared logging and monitoring agents, allowing aggregation of security events into centralized dashboards using tools such as Splunk, Datadog, or Elastic Stack.
- **Zero trust architectures:** Leverage Terraform to implement zero-trust principles such as identity-aware proxy configurations, encrypted service-to-service communication, and conditional access rules across environments.
- **Reusable security modules:** Build modular, reusable Terraform components for consistent provisioning of critical resources such as VPCs, VPNs, Key Management Systems (KMS), and IAM roles across providers.
- **Multi-cloud tagging and resource classification:** Apply consistent tagging strategies across providers using Terraform to support security auditing, cost tracking, and resource visibility.

Emerging trends in IaC and cloud security such as policy-as-code, AI-driven tools, shift-left security, and multi-cloud innovations, represent a significant leap forward in securing cloud environments. These advancements not only address current challenges but also set the stage for a future where security is an integral, automated, and dynamic component of IaC workflows. Organizations that adopt these trends early will be better equipped to navigate the evolving landscape of cloud security.

Scaling Terraform across Enterprise Environments

As organizations grow and adopt complex cloud architectures, managing Infrastructure as Code (IaC) at an enterprise scale becomes increasingly challenging. Terraform's flexibility and ecosystem make it a prime candidate for enterprise-wide IaC management. This section delves into the best practices and considerations for scaling Terraform effectively in large, distributed environments.

Structuring Terraform Codebases for Enterprise-Scale

Structuring Terraform codebases for enterprise-scale means organizing your Infrastructure-as-Code in a way that supports growth, maintainability, security, and collaboration across multiple teams and cloud environments (AWS, GCP, and Azure). In large organizations, infrastructure is managed by different teams across environments and regions, with hundreds or thousands of cloud resources. A scalable structure reduces complexity, prevents misconfigurations, and supports automation through CI/CD pipelines and policy-as-code tools. Terraform's modular approach allows enterprises to build reusable patterns, enabling consistent deployments, while maintaining flexibility and control.

- **Module-based architecture:** Break down infrastructure into smaller, reusable modules (for example, VPC, IAM, compute, and storage) that can be sourced locally or from private/public registries. This encourages DRY (Don't Repeat Yourself) principles, and enforces standards.
- **Environment segmentation:** Create separate folders or repositories for each environment (for example `dev/`, `staging/`, `prod/`) to isolate configurations and prevent unintentional cross-environment changes.
- **State file organization:** Use remote backends such as AWS S3 with DynamoDB locking, GCP Cloud Storage, or Azure Blob Storage to manage state centrally. Each environment and component should have its own state file to avoid conflicts, and enable parallel operations.
- **Workspace and directory strategy:** Adopt Terraform workspaces or a directory-based approach to manage parallel environments or tenants within the same codebase. This allows scalable and structured deployments across business units or regions.
- **CI/CD and automation integration:** Structure code to integrate seamlessly with automation tools. Use consistent pipeline configurations that validate (**`terraform validate`**), plan (**`terraform plan`**), and apply changes (**`terraform apply`**) across environments.

The following are some salient features and best practices:

- **Naming conventions:** Establish standardized naming for resources, modules, and outputs (for example, **`project-env-resource-type`**) to support traceability and minimize naming conflicts across providers.
- **Directory layouts:** Use a structured layout that separates reusable logic (**`modules/`**) from environment-specific configurations (**`environments/`**).

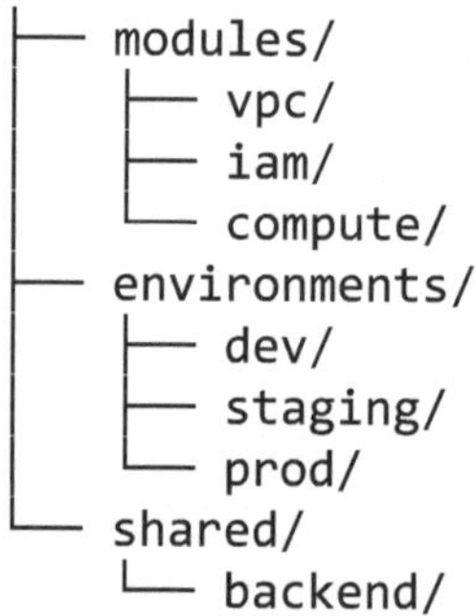

```
├── modules/
│   ├── vpc/
│   ├── iam/
│   └── compute/
├── environments/
│   ├── dev/
│   ├── staging/
│   └── prod/
└── shared/
    └── backend/
```

- **State isolation:** Store each module or environment's state in separate remote backends. This improves collaboration, prevents race conditions, and simplifies disaster recovery.
- **Code reviews:** Enforce peer reviews and automated checks via pull requests to catch security misconfigurations or architectural issues before merging.

Leveraging Terraform Enterprise for Centralized Management

Terraform Enterprise (TFE) is HashiCorp's commercial offering for organizations that need robust, scalable, and secure infrastructure-as-code management across cloud platforms such as AWS, GCP, and Azure. Unlike open-source Terraform, TFE introduces centralized controls such as policy-as-code enforcement, audit logging, team-based access control, cost estimation, and secure state management. It empowers teams to automate infrastructure with confidence, aligning infrastructure provisioning with enterprise governance, compliance, and security standards.

TFE is especially valuable in environments with multiple teams managing complex, multi-cloud deployments.

- **Workspaces:** Workspaces in Terraform Enterprise are used to separate Terraform state, variables, and configurations for different projects or environments (for example, `networking-dev`, and `compute-prod`). Each workspace is backed by a remote backend that provides isolation and concurrency control.
- **Policy enforcement:** Sentinel, the policy-as-code engine built into TFE, enables organizations to enforce mandatory governance rules, before any plan or apply operations are executed. These policies can include enforcing encryption, prohibiting open security groups, or ensuring cost limits.
- **Collaboration:** TFE supports Role-based Access Control (RBAC), enabling organizations to define fine-grained permissions (for example, `plan-only`, `plan-and-apply`, and `read-only`) per team or individual. Integration with version control and approval workflows enhances visibility and accountability.
- **Private module registry:** TFE hosts a private module registry where teams can publish, version, and reuse modules across the organization. This ensures consistency, and promotes the use of approved patterns.
- **Run triggers and workflows:** TFE supports chaining workspaces using run triggers. For example, when a networking workspace is updated, a downstream compute workspace can be triggered automatically, ensuring dependency-aware provisioning.

The following are some important features and best practices:

- **Governance:** Enforce enterprise-wide compliance by codifying organizational policies with Sentinel. Examples include mandatory resource tagging, restricting instance types, and prohibiting unmanaged external access.
- **Audit trails:** Enable detailed logging of all Terraform operations, including who ran a plan or applied changes. This is critical for regulatory compliance, and forensic investigations.
- **Scaling infrastructure:** Use organizations and teams to manage access and resource provisioning at scale. TFE supports thousands of concurrent users, and can be deployed in a highly available architecture.
- **Version control integration:** Connect workspaces to GitHub, GitLab, Bitbucket, or Azure DevOps to trigger Terraform runs based on code commits. This integrates IaC into GitOps workflows.
- **Cost estimation:** Enable cost estimation before resources are provisioned to provide financial visibility and enforce budgetary limits proactively.
- **Approval workflows:** Implement manual approval gates for specific workspaces to prevent unintended changes from being applied automatically, especially in production environments.
- **API and CLI access:** Leverage the TFE API and Terraform CLI to automate and script interactions with the platform for advanced scenarios such as workspace creation or policy application.
- **Single Sign-On (SSO) and authentication:** Integrate with enterprise identity providers using SAML or OAuth for centralized user authentication and provisioning.

Addressing Governance and Compliance at Scale

In modern cloud-native environments, governance and compliance are foundational pillars, especially for large enterprises operating across multiple cloud platforms such as AWS, GCP, and Azure. Addressing these requirements at scale involves enforcing policies, maintaining visibility into infrastructure changes, and ensuring alignment with regulatory frameworks such as GDPR, HIPAA, PCI, DSS, and others. Terraform facilitates this through policy-as-code, modular templates, and seamless integration with compliance tooling, enabling repeatable, and auditable infrastructure that satisfies both internal governance, and external regulatory mandates.

- **Policy enforcement:** Tools such as HashiCorp Sentinel, Open Policy Agent (OPA), and third-party platforms are integrated into CI/CD workflows to evaluate Terraform plans against compliance policies before deployment.
- **Region-specific configurations:** Terraform modules are parameterized with region-specific inputs to ensure that infrastructure adheres to jurisdictional compliance needs such as data residency in GDPR-compliant regions or HIPAA-encrypted storage in U.S. zones.
- **Continuous monitoring:** Cloud-native tools (for example, AWS Config, Azure Policy, GCP and SCC) can be provisioned with Terraform to track real-time compliance, and detect configuration drift or non-compliant changes.
- **Access and audit controls:** Terraform can configure centralized identity management and audit logging using IAM (AWS), Azure RBAC, and GCP IAM, enabling traceability and access governance at scale.
- **Automated reporting:** Terraform can provision monitoring tools and dashboards (for example, CloudWatch, Azure Monitor, and Stackdriver) that track policy compliance metrics, providing continuous visibility and auditability.

The following are some salient features and best practices:

- **Compliance automation:** Use Terraform to automate the provisioning of compliance enforcement tools such as AWS Config Rules, Azure Policy Definitions and Assignments, and GCP Organization Policies.
- **Documentation:** Maintain version-controlled documentation of all compliance rules, Terraform modules, and policy enforcement logic for audit readiness and cross-team visibility.
- **Module hardening:** Build secure, compliant-by-default modules that enforce encryption, tagging, logging, and network restrictions as part of resource creation.
- **Change approval gates:** Integrate change control approvals into CI/CD pipelines where policy violations or deviations require human review before applying infrastructure changes.
- **Version control of policies:** Store policy-as-code templates in Git repositories with branching strategies and pull request workflows to ensure traceability and peer reviews.
- **Security incident triage:** Configure Terraform to integrate with incident response tools (such as AWS Security Hub, Azure Security Center, or GCP SCC) for compliance violations that may require remediation.

Scaling Terraform across enterprise environments requires strategic planning and adherence to best practices. By structuring codebases effectively, leveraging Terraform Enterprise, optimizing CI/CD pipelines, and addressing governance at scale, organizations can manage infrastructure efficiently and securely. These strategies empower enterprises to adopt Terraform as a cornerstone of their IaC strategy, while ensuring compliance and scalability in distributed, multi-cloud environments.

Future Directions for Terraform and Cloud Security Automation

As technology evolves, Terraform and cloud security automation are poised to play pivotal roles in shaping the next generation of cloud infrastructure management. This section provides a forward-looking perspective on emerging trends and innovations, examining how Terraform and cloud security will adapt to meet the challenges of tomorrow.

Integration of Terraform with Next-Gen Cloud Tools

As cloud platforms evolve, the need to integrate Terraform with next-generation tools becomes essential for building intelligent, scalable, and secure infrastructure. These tools include AI-driven services, automated DevOps platforms, low-code/no-code orchestration engines, and advanced observability frameworks. Terraform's extensible provider ecosystem allows seamless integration with such tools, enabling organizations to transition toward predictive infrastructure, automated incident response, and real-time resource optimization across AWS, GCP, and Azure. This integration enhances operational efficiency, reduces manual overhead, and positions Terraform as a strategic layer in modern cloud-native workflows.

- **Evolving cloud services:** Terraform supports integrations with modern services such as AWS Proton (for automated infrastructure provisioning), GCP Autopilot (for managed Kubernetes), and Azure OpenAI (for embedding intelligent capabilities). These integrations allow infrastructure to adapt dynamically to application needs and development velocity.
- **AI-driven platforms:** By integrating Terraform with tools such as AWS SageMaker, GCP Vertex AI, and Azure Machine Learning, teams can provision scalable ML infrastructure as code. AI can also be used to detect misconfigurations or suggest improvements in Terraform plans via machine learning pipelines or rule-based engines.
- **Real-time decision making:** Terraform plans can be augmented with external decision systems or AIOps platforms that provide real-time recommendations based on usage trends, cost forecasts, or security posture. This enables intelligent application of configurations based on contextual inputs.
- **Custom providers and API integrations:** Terraform's plugin architecture allows the development of custom providers to interface with any API-based next-gen tool, including observability platforms, ITSM systems (like ServiceNow), or compliance scanners, ensuring that Terraform remains interoperable across evolving ecosystems.

The following are some important features and best practices:

- **Predictive automation:** Integrate Terraform with AI/ML systems to enable predictive scaling, cost estimation, anomaly detection, or capacity planning minimizing waste and downtime, while aligning infrastructure with demand.
- **Seamless API integration:** Extend Terraform's capabilities through direct REST API calls using external data sources or the http provider to interact with SaaS and AI-powered platforms for dynamic plan generation.
- **Use provider specific optimizations:** Leverage platform native features exposed by Terraform providers such as AutoML recommendations in GCP or inference endpoint monitoring in AWS to enhance resource provisioning and governance.
- **Event-driven provisioning:** Connect Terraform workflows with event-driven systems such as AWS EventBridge, GCP Eventarc, or Azure Event Grid to trigger that Terraform runs based on real-time cloud events, enabling responsive infrastructure changes.
- **AI-powered Policy-as-Code:** Integrate with AI based policy systems to analyze historical Terraform usage, and automatically generate policy rules for security, performance, or cost optimization using Sentinel or OPA.
- **Feedback loop integration:** Use observability platforms Datadog, Prometheus, or Azure Monitor to feed metrics and logs into Terraform decision logic via dynamic providers or automation scripts, closing the loop between operations and infrastructure.

Enhancing Terraform's Security Features

As infrastructure threats become more dynamic, and compliance requirements more stringent, Terraform is evolving to embed security deeper into its core functionalities. The future of Terraform security is centered around the *expansion of policy-as-code*, automation of *threat detection* and remediation, and improved cross-cloud policy governance. With support from tools such as Sentinel, Open Policy Agent (OPA), and a growing ecosystem of security-integrated modules, Terraform is poised to provide more native capabilities for enforcing, auditing, and adapting security at every stage of infrastructure provisioning across AWS, GCP, and Azure. These advancements will enable organizations to implement Infrastructure-as-Code securely and compliantly at scale.

- **Policy-as-Code evolution:** Terraform is increasingly aligning with sophisticated policy-as-code frameworks such as Sentinel and OPA. These tools are expanding in capabilities to support more contextual, dynamic, and condition-based policy enforcement. For example, policies can block untagged resources or enforce encryption settings, based on deployment region or environment context.
- **Threat mitigation:** Future integrations are expected to include built-in vulnerability scanning and threat intelligence integrations. This means Terraform runs could automatically halt if misconfigured resources are detected, or if a resource violates real-time security rules.
- **Secure defaults and smart modules:** Security-conscious Terraform modules will become more common, embedding the least-privilege IAM, encryption, and logging settings by default. These modules help teams deploy secure infrastructure, without reinventing security logic repeatedly.
- **Context aware policies:** Next-gen Terraform security features may include contextual awareness allowing different rules based on environment (for example, stricter policies in production than in development), resource type, or cloud provider specifics.

The following are some key features and best practices:

- **Dynamic policies:** Adopt policies that can change behavior based on runtime context, for example, enforcing different access controls or backup settings, depending on the resource's environment tag or region.
- **Cross-cloud consistency:** Create reusable security modules or policy libraries that abstract cloud-specific implementations but enforce uniform security posture across AWS, GCP and Azure.
- **Security telemetry integration:** Feed security telemetry (for example, failed policy checks, and compliance drift reports) into monitoring and SIEM platforms such as Azure Monitor, Google Cloud Operations, or AWS Security Hub for centralized visibility.
- **Terraform registry controls:** Use signed and verified Terraform modules from trusted sources. Enforce internal policies restricting module sources to approved registries.
- **Encrypted plan artifacts:** As plan files contain sensitive information, use tooling to encrypt `.tfplan` files before storing or transferring across systems.
- **Least privilege Terraform runners:** Ensure that Terraform agents or runners are provisioned with minimum necessary permissions to prevent misuse or escalation in the event of compromise.

Adoption of Zero Trust Architectures

Zero Trust Architecture (ZTA) is a security model that assumes no entity internal or external is inherently trustworthy. It enforces strict identity verification, least-privilege access, and continuous validation of trustworthiness. Terraform plays a pivotal role in implementing Zero Trust in cloud environments by codifying identity-centric security, automating network segmentation, and integrating with cloud-native monitoring tools. With Terraform, organizations can standardize and enforce Zero Trust principles across AWS, GCP, and Azure, ensuring scalable and consistent security.

- **Identity centric security:** Terraform provisions cloud-native IAM roles, service principals, and policies across AWS (IAM roles/policies), GCP (IAM bindings), and Azure (RBAC assignments), ensuring that each service and user has only the permissions they need.
- **Micro segmentation:** Using Terraform, you can define private subnets, route tables, and security groups or firewall rules to isolate workloads, reducing the attack surface, and limiting lateral movement.
- **Continuous verification:** Terraform integrates with security tools such as AWS GuardDuty, Azure Security Center, and GCP Security Command Center to ensure that the deployed infrastructure is continuously monitored and verified against defined policies.
- **Access logging and auditing:** Terraform enables provisioning of logging services (for example, AWS CloudTrail, GCP Audit Logs, and Azure Activity Logs) to track all identities, and access activities as part of a Zero Trust posture.
- **Just-in-Time (JIT) access controls:** Terraform can help configure JIT access mechanisms such as temporary IAM role assumptions in AWS which grant access only when necessary, and revoke it automatically.

The following are some salient features and best practices:

- **Network isolation:** Use Terraform to deploy isolated network segments using private subnets, VPCs (AWS), VNets (Azure), or Shared VPCs (GCP), along with restrictive firewall or security group rules.
- **Monitoring and response:** Automate integration of threat detection tools such as AWS GuardDuty, GCP Security Command Center, and Azure Security Center to enable real-time anomaly detection and automated response workflows.
- **Identity federation and conditional access:** Provision identity federation policies using Terraform to enforce MFA, IP restrictions, and device trust settings, particularly in Azure AD and AWS IAM Identity Center.
- **Immutable infrastructure:** Design infrastructure with immutability in mind. Terraform helps enforce resource recreation over in-place modifications, ensuring that any tampered instance is replaced, rather than patched.
- **Logging and telemetry integration:** Set up centralized logging systems with Terraform to forward logs to SIEM platforms, enabling comprehensive auditing and forensics.
- **Secrets isolation:** Integrate Terraform with secrets managers (AWS Secrets Manager, Azure Key Vault, and GCP Secret Manager) to prevent hardcoded credentials, and enforce encrypted secret access.
- **Application aware access:** Provision fine-grained access rules tied to application-level identities such as Azure Managed Identities, GCP Service Accounts, and AWS IAM Roles for Service Accounts (IRSA) in EKS.

The Role of Community and Open Source in Terraform's Future

The Terraform community and open-source ecosystem play a foundational role in its continued evolution. Community-driven collaboration has fostered an expansive library of providers, reusable modules, and integrations that significantly accelerate infrastructure-as-code adoption across AWS,

GCP, and Azure. As Terraform progresses, its future will remain tightly coupled with the growth of its open-source base, which supports rapid innovation, cross-industry best practices, and a shared repository of knowledge.

- **Community contributions:** Contributors from around the world enhance Terraform's functionality by building providers, writing modules, developing plugins, and fixing issues through public GitHub repositories.
- **Collaboration:** Companies and individuals share feedback, contribute pull requests, and engage in design discussions, improving Terraform's flexibility and real-world applicability.
- **Knowledge sharing:** Through blogs, YouTube tutorials, and community forums such as HashiCorp Discuss, and events like HashiConf, practitioners share their expertise and solutions to common challenges.
- **Third-party integrations:** Open-source projects provide integrations for security scanning, CI/CD tools, testing frameworks, and cloud services that enrich Terraform workflows.

The following are some key features and best practices:

- **Open-source providers:** Use community-maintained providers from the Terraform Registry to extend functionality beyond officially supported cloud services, including niche APIs or specialized platforms.
- **Shared modules:** Adopt peer-reviewed modules from the Terraform Registry or GitHub to implement proven patterns, reduce duplication, and align with the industry best practices.
- **Knowledge resources:** Participate in Terraform-focused communities such as GitHub discussions, Reddit, and HashiCorp Community forums to stay updated on new features, bugs, and innovations.
- **Continuous contribution:** Contribute back by submitting bug reports, improving documentation, or publishing useful modules, reinforcing a virtuous cycle of knowledge and quality.
- **Security reviews:** When using third-party modules or providers, perform code reviews to ensure security standards are met before integrating them into production systems.
- **Event participation:** Attend and present at events such as HashiConf, AWS reinvent, or GCP Next to learn from others, and influence the Terraform roadmap through shared use cases.
- **Open governance and feedback:** Engage with the RFC (Request for Comments) process for Terraform's core tooling and providers to shape the future direction of the ecosystem.

The future of Terraform and cloud security automation is deeply intertwined with technological advancements and community contributions. By integrating with next-gen tools, enhancing security features, supporting zero-trust architectures, and leveraging the power of the open-source community, Terraform will remain a cornerstone of Infrastructure as Code for years to come. Organizations adopting these forward-thinking approaches will be well-positioned to harness the full potential of Terraform in securing and automating their cloud environments.

Conclusion

As Terraform continues to evolve as a foundational tool in the cloud security landscape, adopting best practices and staying aligned with future trends is no longer a luxury, It is a necessity. By treating security as a continuous process embedded in every phase of the IaC lifecycle, organizations can proactively defend against modern threats, enforce compliance, and reduce operational risk. Automating security updates, integrating monitoring and incident response, and validating state and access controls are critical steps toward achieving a resilient and secure Terraform ecosystem. The practical checklists and strategies shared in this chapter offer readers a robust framework to evaluate and enhance their Terraform implementations from both technical and operational standpoints.

Looking ahead, the rapid advancements in policy-as-code, artificial intelligence, and zero trust architecture signal a paradigm shift in how cloud security will be managed at scale. Enterprises must prepare to adapt Terraform for more complex multi-cloud environments, leveraging tools such as Terraform Enterprise for centralized governance and compliance. At the same time, the open-source community will play a vital role in shaping the future of Terraform through innovation and collaboration. As the cloud ecosystem becomes more dynamic, forward-thinking organizations that embrace automation, community-driven practices, and emerging technologies will be best positioned to secure their infrastructure, and their future with Terraform.

Questions and Answers

1. **Why is it essential to treat security as a continuous process in Infrastructure as Code (IaC), and how can Terraform practitioners embed it effectively into the development lifecycle?**

   Security in IaC must be ongoing and adaptive because cloud environments evolve rapidly, and are constantly exposed to new threats. Embedding security into the development lifecycle means integrating security checks from the earliest stages of code development, using automated scans, policy enforcement, and compliance validations. Regularly updating Terraform modules to include the latest security practices, and dynamically modifying configurations in response to new threats or compliance requirements ensures that infrastructure remains secure over time.

2. **What are the core elements of a robust Terraform security automation checklist, and how can teams operationalize them?**

   A strong security automation checklist includes secure state management with encrypted remote backends and controlled access, role-based access control for sensitive operations, and secure provisioning of cloud resources with proper encryption, IAM policies, and network boundaries. Additionally, integrating Terraform with monitoring and incident response systems helps detect and respond to issues proactively. These elements can be operationalized by embedding them into CI/CD workflows, using reusable secure modules, and conducting regular audits.

3. **How are emerging trends like policy-as-code and AI transforming the cloud security landscape for Terraform users?**

   Policy-as-code enables teams to define and enforce security rules directly in code, making compliance and governance scalable and repeatable. Tools such as OPA and Sentinel allow for granular control over what configurations are permitted. Meanwhile, AI and Machine Learning (ML) are enhancing cloud security by detecting misconfigurations, predicting potential vulnerabilities, and offering intelligent remediation suggestions, helping teams stay ahead of threats in increasingly complex infrastructure environments.

4. **What strategies can enterprises adopt to scale Terraform securely across multiple teams and environments?**

   To scale Terraform securely, enterprises should structure codebases using modular design patterns, manage state effectively across environments, and separate responsibilities using workspaces or directories. Utilizing centralized platforms such as Terraform Enterprise helps enforce policies, track changes, and support collaboration across teams. It is also critical to implement governance frameworks and compliance checks that align with regional and industry standards to maintain security and auditability at scale.

5. **What future directions should security-conscious Terraform users be aware of, and how can they prepare?**

   The future of Terraform in cloud security is shaped by growing integration with AI-powered tools, enhancements to native security features, and increasing adoption of zero trust architectures. Terraform is also expected to play a greater role in orchestrating secure deployments across multi-cloud and hybrid environments. To prepare, practitioners should stay engaged with the open-source community, contribute to shared modules and policies, and continuously learn about new security trends and automation techniques.

Index

A

C

G

H

I

K

M

T

V

W

Y

Z